APPROACHES TO MATERIAL CULTURE RESEARCH FOR HISTORICAL ARCHAEOLOGISTS

2nd Edition

I0528671

Compiled by David R. Brauner

A Reader from

Historical Archaeology

Published by
THE SOCIETY FOR HISTORICAL ARCHAEOLOGY

Ronald L. Michael, editor

Anthropology Section
California University of Pennsylvania
California, Pennsylvania 15419

2000

Cover art by Toby White and Jeremy Harrison

Composition by
TransVisions
Uniontown, Pennsylvania

Contents

Assemblage and Meaning

Preface

David R. Brauner
Department of Anthropology
Oregon State University
Corvallis, OR 97331-6403

The journal, *Historical Archaeology* published by The Society for Historical Archaeology (SHA) has been the flagship publication of North American historical archaeologists for 33 years. In 1991, George Miller, Olive Jones, Lester Ross, and Teresita Majewski, selected 19 articles from the journal and compiled them into a reader entitled *Approaches to Material Culture Research for Historical Archaeologists*. The compilers, working from an underlying theme focused on material culture research by historical archaeologists, distributed a list of 125 SHA journal articles conforming to this theme to SHA members involved with teaching historical archaeology classes. The potential respondents were asked to select 12 articles, from the list, they would find most useful in the classroom. The most frequently recommended articles were subsequently organized into the text which a generation of historical archaeology students have "lovingly" referred to as "the purple reader."

Although the reader was conceptually designed for a broad audience within the historical archaeology community, classroom sales have sustained the publication of this book for almost a decade. The typical limited shelf life of a college text has been far surpassed by the reader simply because there is nothing like it available elsewhere.

The discipline of historical archaeology has matured during the 1990s. The number of colleges and universities adding historical archaeology to their curriculums or expanding existing undergraduate and graduate programs over the past decade is significant. "Word of mouth" is no longer an adequate means of keeping current on the number of academic programs in historical archaeology. A directory of programs published in each October issue of the *Newsletter* of The Society for Historical Archaeology over the past few years is a testament to the phenomenal growth of the discipline. Changes in the federal regulations governing the management of cultural resources--those which recognize the unique skills and academic backgrounds needed to manage our historical archaeological heritage--are partially responsible for the increased academic attention paid to the discipline and are almost entirely responsible for private sector employment opportunities. By almost any measure the last decade of the 20th century has seen significant growth and maturation in historical archaeology.

Material culture research, which is central to what we do as historical archaeologists, has not kept pace with other areas of growth within the discipline. "While the amount of material culture research being published has increased substantially, the literature is scattered and sometimes difficult to find for students and other researchers. Compilations of articles published on material culture to date contain few articles written from an historical-archaeological perspective" (Miller et al. 1991:1-2). These words written almost a decade ago still ring true. The 1990s have seen a proliferation of material culture books written by collectors for collectors which augmented an astounding number of titles that predate 1990. Although many of these books are little more than laundry lists and price guides, the majority of the collectors books, newsletters, and journals do contain valuable historical, technological, typological, and chronological information. The growing body of material culture books, articles, and traditional site reports written by historical archaeologists will always rely on the work of serious and dedicated collectors. Conversely, serious researchers and collectors are discovering the growing body of literature produced by the archaeological community and incorporating this work into their own monographs.

Material culture books, whether authored by collectors or archaeologists, are usually incorporated into an historical materials analysis class in bibliographic format as reference works available as the analytical needs require. Hands-on experience with this literature is limited. Two or three of these reference books may be used as texts but the student's funds and class project time are finite.

As copyright laws are more strictly enforced, gathering widely-scattered journal articles, book excerpts, and contract report chapters to create a makeshift reader for a materials analysis class is getting prohibitive. Gathering all the original documents to put on reserve in a library is also difficult and there is strong student resistance to this access format.

The internet is rapidly improving access to traditionally hard-to-find information as more collectors and archaeologists are going on-line with their data. Material culture researchers can no longer ignore the electronic media. Internet research has become an integral part of classroom training. Although the print media still surpasses the electronic media for material culture data, in the not-too-distant-future the reverse will be true. Modern college students do use the internet.

What students still need in a materials analysis class is a published reader that can serve as a backbone for lecture material, classroom discussions, and a touchstone for supplementary reading assignments. Miller and compilers recognized this need in 1991 and filled a critical void experienced by those of us teaching historical archaeology courses. A few of my colleagues and I found the reader more useful in a materials analysis course although some of the articles crossed over into method and theory courses.

Since the Miller et al. (1991) reader was published, nine volumes of *Historical Archaeology* have been issued. With the passage of time, articles in the reader have been supplanted by newer information published in the SHA journal or in other sources. Users of the reader have been loyal over the years but have been looking for a more up-to-date text for their classes. None have been forthcoming. The SHA, recognizing the need for an updated reader, asked me to revise the reader since I was one of those loyal customers and had made a few comments about recommended revisions. Since the primary usage of the reader has been as a classroom text, the instructions were to approach the next reader from the perspective of its usefulness in the classroom as a supplement to a materials analysis course.

Rather than follow the original model used to compile articles for the 1991 reader, a student user group was put together. The group was composed of 12 graduate and undergraduate students who were enrolled in a material analysis class. All of the students had archaeological field experience ranging from one summer to four years. Four students had extensive laboratory experience. Ten students were anthropology majors and two were historic preservation majors. All but two students had worked on historical archaeology sites.

The students were divided into two-person task groups, organizing reading assignments into the initial subject breaks in the Miller et al. (1991) reader. Also added as subject areas were ethnicity, gender, method and theory, settlement pattern, historic landscapes, zooarchaeology, botany, and curation. Each task group identified articles, from *Historical Archaeology* beginning with volume 1, that fit their assigned areas. We met as a group to compare notes and solidify the placement of articles in the agreed-upon categories. We met once or twice a week over a 12-week period. Each task group ranked their respective readings and discussed the articles with the larger group. Articles that were ranked high by the smaller task groups were subsequently read by the entire group and ranked again for possible inclusion in the new reader. Reading evaluation data from previous student course reviews was also interjected when appropriate. Usually the student review group was like-minded with their predecessors. The students were assessing the articles based on their perception of readability, applicability, and durability of the article's informational content as applied to material analysis.

Midway through the review process it became apparent that one reader could be assembled with a gender, status, and ethnicity theme. These articles were set aside and we refocused on material analysis. The special issues of the journal were also eliminated from consideration since they were already thematically organized. If one wants to use the thematic volumes in the classroom they need no modification. Method and theory was eliminated due to the paucity of articles found in the journal. By the end of the 12-week review period a working table of contents containing 39 articles was assembled. The proposed table of contents included topical sections on plants and animals, historic landscapes, and curation. Subsection headings of glass, ceramic, metal and stone, and analysis of assemblages were retained from the original reader for organizational purposes. The working table of contents needed to be winnowed down to about 20 articles for the final publication.

A list of names of instructors who had used the original reader in their classes was provided by the society. Of these individuals, 34 were mailed the working table of contents. Feedback was solicited concerning deletions, additions, and general comments about the proposed reader. Ten responses were received. Five articles were suggested as additions to the reader and some well thought out comments for deletions were noted. Hard decisions still had to be made, however, to get the reader down to a manageable size. Any shortcomings in the final selection process are mine alone.

The sections on plants, animals, and historic landscapes were deleted with the thought that these articles could serve as the basis for another reader. The curation section was also removed. Several synthetic articles were eliminated in favor of focused material analysis articles. The underlying motivation for article selection stems from my long held belief that the importance of artifact description and analysis is downplayed in modern archaeology.

The lack of understanding of historical material culture among practicing field archaeologists is appalling. Functional and chronological errors made by an archaeologist in the early stages of artifact description and analysis negate all subsequent analysis and conclusions generated from these data. The majority of articles in this reader are designed to offer the student of historical material culture fundamental information about morphology, technology, chronology, and function of objects commonly found in archaeological contexts.

An important lesson that must be woven into a materials analysis class is that determining an artifacts function is not always as straight forward at it may seem. The physical and cultural context of an object recovered from an archaeological site must be taken into account before a meaningful functional determination can be made. A mustard jar is easy to identify and its primary function clearly understood. If, however, the mustard jar were recovered above a domestic dog burial, the function of the jar in the context of the site may have been as a container for flowers which served to mark the grave of a beloved family pet. The jar, which is commonly associated with food consumption, should, as a result of its physical context, be associated with mortuary behavior.

The final section of the reader includes four articles that discuss the meaning of artifacts in the context of physical location, associated artifact assemblage, and cultural association. Parker Potter's article is very appealing in that he discusses a variety of issues dealing with context and meaning generated from a critique of Adams and Boling's article included in the ceramics section. David Burley's article on the *Hivernant* Metis is cited by Potter as an example of the direction we must explore to draw valid interpretations of the meaning of artifacts in the context of cultural associations. These three articles represent the closest approximation of an issue related dialogue found in *Historical Archaeology*. As such, they provide an excellent departure point for a discussion of context and meaning in a classroom setting.

Reference

MILLER, GEORGE L., OLIVE R. JONES, LESTER A. ROSS, AND TERESITA MAJEWSKI (COMPILERS)

1991 *Approaches to Material Culture Research for Historical Archaeologists*. The Society for Historical Archaeology, California, PA.

Approaches to Material Culture Research for Historical Archaeologists

COMPILED BY GEORGE L. MILLER
DEPARTMENT OF ARCHAEOLOGICAL RESEARCH
COLONIAL WILLIAMSBURG FOUNDATION
WILLIAMSBURG, VIRGINIA 23185

OLIVE R. JONES
CANADIAN PARKS SERVICE
1600 LIVERPOOL COURT
OTTAWA, ONTARIO K1A 0H3

LESTER A. ROSS
56489 EL DORADO DRIVE
YUCCA VALLEY, CALIFORNIA 92284

TERESITA MAJEWSKI
DEPARTMENT OF ANTHROPOLOGY
UNIVERSITY OF ARIZONA
TUCSON, ARIZONA 85721

Introduction

> "Incompatible data are useless data."
> (Leontief 1971:6)

The field of material culture research has expanded at a phenomenal rate over the last quarter of a century. Scholars from the traditional disciplines of archaeology, anthropology, history, art history, folklore, American studies, geography, and sociology have examined in detail the roles played by manufactured goods in the industrialized world. Approaches to the subject have ranged from simple antiquarian descriptive studies to complex Marxist interpretations of how material culture has reflected dominance and resistance in the class struggle. Structuralism, functionalism, symbolic anthropology, and a variety of other orientations have been and are being used to provide a framework for understanding material culture. This rich diversity of approaches is chronicled in essays by Thomas Schlereth (1982:1–75, 1985:1–34) that describe the evolution of the field of material culture research. To some extent, the study of material culture has encouraged the breakdown of established academic disciplinary lines of inquiry, which is leading to an enriched body of literature on the relationship between people and the goods associated with them.

Material culture research has always been an important part of historical archaeology. The "study of things" was an area of contention in the 1960s and 1970s during the developmental phase of the field, with heated discussions ensuing as practitioners of the "new," or "processual," archaeology attempted to set the agenda in terms of "pattern recognition" and the construction of "cultural laws" to explain the archaeological record. Material culture was reduced to artifact counts as whole sites were lumped into single assemblages as part of "quantification" (e.g., South 1977a, 1977b). Those who did not embrace the new archaeology were characterized as "humanistic," "particularistic," or even worse, "antiquarian" in their approaches and methods.

One of the impacts of labeling scholars such as Ivor Noël Hume and Iain Walker as particularistic archaeologists was to cast a shadow over anyone working on chronologies, typologies, a single group of artifacts, or in-depth studies of production technology. In many areas, research on artifact chronology has not advanced beyond what was provided in Noël Hume's (1969) classic reference *A Guide to Artifacts of Colonial America*. Consequently, and to the detriment of historical archaeology, archaeologists' ability to date contexts or "tell time" has not improved much beyond where it was when Noël Hume's book first appeared in 1969. Other shortcomings of the new archaeology are detailed in Paul Courbin's (1988) recently translated *What Is Archaeology?* (cf. Patrik 1985; Shanks and Tilley 1987; Gibbon 1989). As the new archaeology becomes old, there has been a renewed interest in material culture research that is reflected in the increasing numbers and variety of articles appearing in the journal *Historical Archaeology* and elsewhere.

While the amount of material culture research being published has increased substantially, the literature is scattered and sometimes difficult to find for students and other researchers. Compilations of articles published on material culture to date contain few articles written from an historical-archaeological perspective (e.g., Schlereth 1982, 1985; Bronner 1985). Robert Schuyler's (1978) *Historical Archaeology: A Guide to Substantive and Theoretical Contributions* and Mary Beaudry's (1988) *Documentary Archaeology in the New World* both contain articles on material culture. However, there has not been a reader which pulls together the disparate approaches and types of studies being done by researchers working with historical archaeological materials. To fill this need, the Society for Historical Archaeology has compiled this reader from articles previously published in the journal *Historical Archaeology*. No one reader could satisfy everyone, and this volume clearly does not begin to cover the full range of potential subjects involved. However, by using the reference sections in these articles and in this Introduction, one can quickly gain access to much of the literature on the subjects covered. An additional source for the material culture research field is the bibliography edited by Ames and Ward (1989).

Organizing the Reader

This volume draws together a selection of 19 articles, published in *Historical Archaeology* between 1967 and 1990, that have as an underlying theme the use of an historical-archaeological perspective in material culture research. To aid in the selection of articles to be reprinted, a listing of 125 articles was sent to over 90 people teaching historical archaeology, who were asked to choose the 12 articles they would find most useful. The choices of the 44 individuals who responded formed the basis for selection of the articles included here, which represent a sampling of the diverse approaches to material culture research taken by historical archaeologists. The volume is not encyclopedic, nor does it aim to embrace one philosophical approach at the expense of others.

For organizational purposes, the articles appearing in the reader are grouped by *material of manufacture* and by *analysis and description of assemblages* (see Contents). Within each grouping, articles are arranged chronologically by the time period of the materials described and/or analyzed. Artifacts have traditionally been studied by material and by date of manufacture, but this fact should not prejudice the reader as to the usefulness of the articles for other kinds of research. Articles are reprinted in their entirety, with the exception of Kenmotsu (1990) and Miller (1980), where the appendixes were not reprinted due to space constraints. The index values presented in Miller (1980) have recently been superseded by those in Miller (1991). Several typographical errors in the original publications also have been corrected. Complete citations for the original articles may be found in the References section at the end of this Introduction.

Organizing the Approaches

Material analysis and classification provide descriptive data needed for subsequent interpretation. Issues relating to material analysis, classification, and interpretive, behavioral studies are discussed below.

Material Analysis

Where to begin? The archaeologist begins with the site and the excavated objects, which often come from mixed temporal and cultural deposits. Before the assemblage from a site can provide meaningful insights into the past, however, it often is necessary to isolate artifacts recovered from tightly dated and functionally specific contexts. The key archaeological question of dating is omnipresent. These "focused" materials can represent a specific event, activity, cultural group, or temporal period.

Archaeologists generally focus attention on a site's inhabitants, studying those who used and discarded the materials recovered. Artifacts recovered from Postcolumbian sites, however, also reveal aspects of a broader cultural context, including information on technology, manufacture, commerce, recycling, ethnic preference, and site formation processes (Busch [1987], Jones [1971],

Orser [1989], and Staski [1984], this volume). Types of investigations are generally determined by the content and context of assemblages, and secondarily on such mundane considerations as the competence of investigators, levels of funding, and length of time allocated for research. Focused assemblages will support multiple studies, but reality dictates that only a few studies can ever be completed.

Studies of the life cycle of an artifact also fall within the domain of material culture research. Studies might focus on the procurement of raw materials used to manufacture finished products; the technology of manufacture; trade, use, reuse, discard, and eventual destruction of cultural material; and its social, cultural, economic, and historical interpretation. Knowing where the materials under study fit within the life cycles of particular artifact classes improves the ability to marry research questions with the appropriate data.

The life cycle of cultural material begins with the procurement and conversion of raw material; continues to the manufacture and assembly of preforms and finished products; proceeds to use, repair, and reuse; seemingly ends through discard and catastrophe; only to resurface for identification, description, and classification as archaeological evidence. Studies generally focus on specific stages in the life cycle, but occasionally others may examine the life cycle itself (e.g., Jones 1981). Each artifact has a unique, built-in message as to what it was and how it was used. Ross's ([1985], this volume) article on casks recovered from a sunken 16th-century Basque whaling vessel and Holt's (1991) study of faunal remains clearly illustrate the usefulness of analyzing the life cycle of an artifact. Understanding where one is in the life cycle of a particular artifact group is essential to any material culture study.

Classification

As can be seen from the above discussion, there are myriad questions that can be asked of artifacts. However, the way in which they are classified sets limits on the information that can be obtained. The organization of materials will vary depending on the research questions being addressed; *there is no one "right" way to classify an artifact.* It is important, however, that criteria used for classification are well defined and readily recognizable by other researchers. Misidentification negates subsequent interpretations and renders comparative studies almost impossible.

One of the problems that historical archaeologists have to contend with is classifications developed by collectors. Terms such as "Gaudy Dutch," "case" bottles, "kaolin" pipes, and others have crept into archaeological literature and are loosely used with minimal recognition that such terms are ambiguous and often incorrect. In other cases, such as with creamware and pearlware, type definitions do not reflect changes made over time. Creamware of the 1760s is different from the creamware of the 1780s and very different than creamware of the 1830s. Wedgwood's pearlware of the 1780s differs greatly from pearlware made by the same company in the 1860s. It is important to recognize that typologies established for chronological purposes may or may not coincide with types recognized by the manufacturers or consumers of material goods. On the other hand, typologies based on functional categories have minimal use as temporal markers.

Classifications included in this reader which depend to some extent on technological attributes are those on tin cans (Busch 1981), glass trade beads (Sprague 1985), gunflints (Kenmotsu 1990), and wooden casks (Ross 1985). Other important references on identification and classification, not cited in the above works, include studies on ceramics (Watkins 1950; Goggin 1960, 1968; Watkins 1960; Lister and Lister 1978; Turnbaugh 1983, 1985; Majewski and O'Brien 1987; Walthall 1991), clay pipes (Walker 1977), glass (Jones 1986; Jones and Sullivan 1989), bricks (Gurke 1987), and marbles (Carskadden and Gartley 1990). These works address specific classes of cultural material, focusing on their importance for historical-archaeological research.

It is important to realize that various classes of artifacts have different research potentials related to their *intrinsic* and *extrinsic* characteristics. Intrinsic

TABLE 1
INTRINSIC CHARACTERISTICS

Characteristic	Ceramic Tableware	Iron Tools
Durability or length of use life	A few years	Can last generations
Potential for repair	Limited	Generally very high
Ability to be recycled	Almost nil	Generally very great
Stability in the ground	Very great	Subject to oxidation
Ability to be reconstructed	Very high	Very limited
Range of functional types represented	Very few	Very many

TABLE 2
EXTRINSIC CHARACTERISTICS

Characteristic	Ceramic Tableware	Iron Tools
Use value after breakage	Nil	Moderate (scrap iron)
Rate of change due to fashion	Very high	Almost none
Rate of change due to technological innovations	High	Low
Price spread for different types of the same object	Very great	Minimal
Ability to convey social status	Fairly high	Low
Percentage that becomes part of the archaeological record	Very high	Fairly low
Usefulness for dating	Very great	Very limited

qualities pertain to the essential nature of the material, i.e., an artifact's inherent characteristics, attributes that are not culturally imposed. Conversely, extrinsic characteristics are imposed by an artifact's maker or user; they are culturally dictated. Consider the difference between the intrinsic and extrinsic characteristics of ceramic tableware and iron tools as outlined in Tables 1 and 2.

Of the 125 articles related to material culture research published in *Historical Archaeology* as of 1990, the five most commonly researched topics were ceramics (36 articles, 28.8%), glass (15 articles, 12.0%), clay pipes (10 articles, 8.0%), gunflints (7 articles, 5.6%), and beads (5 articles, 4.0%). These percentages illustrate a very important point, that not all archaeological materials have been studied equally. The choice of what to study has been based on a number of factors, many of them related to an artifact's intrinsic and extrinsic characteristics. How easily can the object or material be dated? Does the material of manufacture survive well in the ground? Are the artifacts studied representative of primary or de facto refuse (Schiffer 1987)? Was the artifact reused or recycled (Light 1991)? What are the questions shaping the research being conducted with the artifacts? What is studied also tends to reflect work already done in the field. For example, ceramic studies lead to more ceramic studies, proposed bead classifications lead to refinements in bead classification, dating clay pipes by measuring bore diameters leads to refinements in the technique, and so

on. Because there are fewer readily available sources to aid in their identification and interpretation, objects made of wood and metal tend to receive less attention. As a result, the activities that they represent also receive less attention.

Historical archaeologists are well aware that studies of excavated cultural material cannot rely solely on archaeological data for the analysis of the artifacts. As important as these materials are, one's understanding of them is greatly expanded through historical accounts documenting the manufacture and use of material goods (Beaudry 1988). As Garry Wheeler Stone (1988), Beaudry et al. (1983), and Miller (1980) have noted, classification often can be best served by employing ''emic'' historical categories. Miller's ([1980], this volume) article demonstrates the interpretive value of using ''emic'' historical classifications, as well as the need to change the criteria as the ''emic'' classification changes. In the 17th and 18th centuries, potters, merchants, and users classified ceramics by ware types. However, as creamware and pearlware began to dominate the market in the late 18th century, the manufacturers, merchants, and users began to classify and price ceramics by decoration rather than ware type. Accordingly, archaeologists once accustomed to classifying by ware type are now classifying 19th-

century ceramics by decoration (Adams and Boling [1989], this volume; Spencer-Wood 1987).

Behavioral Studies

Comprehending past human behavior, perceiv-
ing patterns of culture, and recognizing temporal
changes through the analysis of material culture
are complementary to material analysis and classification in historical archaeology. James Deetz and
others, such as Henry Glassie and Mark Leone,
prefer to view artifacts as cultural rather than material phenomena and propose a "mentalist" approach to the interpretation of material culture
(e.g., Glassie 1975; Deetz 1977; Leone 1977). As
one scholar notes:

> It is a fine pastime to mull over the uses of old artifacts, but
> the theorist of use would learn most quickly and efficiently
> in situations involving live people. If we choose to begin
> with the artifact, then our first goal should be the attempt to
> face the thing, not as a usable entity or a mere object, but as
> a sign, as the result of an intention. However it was used,
> the artifact was the largely unconscious realization and ma-
> terialization of a mental dynamic (Glassie 1977:27).

For the archaeologist studying the remains of
Euroamericans, the questions asked are typically
those engendered by large, politically and economically complex societies. The artifacts and the society that produced them are global in scope, but
the underlying cultural norms of the European-
based societies have been powerful and long-lived,
surviving over great distances, several centuries,
and contact with completely different ideologies.

Behavioral analysis is most often driven by the
functions of objects, i.e., their use in cultural settings such as eating, drinking, transporting goods,
and making a living. Functional categories often
cross material lines. Objects are seen as parts of
functioning assemblages, which are generally
more comprehensive and meaningful groupings of
artifacts than historical archaeologists are able to
reconstruct using just the archaeological record
(Horn [1988], Martin [1989], this volume; Mc-
Cracken 1988:118–129). Studies of objects, particularly by curators, collectors, and art historians,
are often limited to a single material culture cate-

gory. For example, scholars studying pewter tableware rarely consider ceramic or glass tableware of
the same time period. This is especially true when
the objects under study are unprovenienced items
in museum collections or from the antique market. Historical archaeologists, however, generally
work with provenienced artifacts that are part of an
assemblage, which allows for the placement of artifacts into temporal and functional categories
(Sprague 1980). Articles in the reader, for example, analyze assemblages from St. Mary's City,
Maryland (King and Miller [1987]); Fort Pentagoet, Maine (Faulkner [1986a]); and St. Augustine, Florida (Deagan [1978]).

As with the life cycle of objects, behavioral research begins with investigations into the processes and products of the technology employed to
manufacture goods. Behavioral technology studies
often focus on manufacturing sites, such as
the armorer's workshop discussed in Faulkner's
([1986a], this volume) article, or a pottery site
(e.g., Kelso and Chappell 1974), a glass factory
site (e.g., Noël Hume 1976), a blacksmith shop
(e.g., Light and Unglik 1987), or a fishery (e.g.,
Faulkner 1985, 1986b). Studies of specific industries are not confined to individual sites, but may
cover an entire regional enterprise, such as western
silver mining (Hardesty 1988), or the reconstruction of an ethnic and temporal process, such as
Spanish Basque coopering (e.g., Ross [1985], this
volume) or Canadian pottery manufacturing (Ross
1982).

Site reports by historical archaeologists often
lack clear discussions of the diagnostic marks on
objects resulting from different types of manufacturing techniques. This is compounded by the fact
that discussions of industrial processes are often
published in industrial archaeological journals,
which tends to reinforce a belief that industrial
archaeology and historical archaeology are minimally related fields. Fortunately, articles such as
those by Jones ([1971], this volume), Kenmotsu
([1990], this volume), Miller and Sullivan ([1984],
this volume), Busch (1981), and Light (1991),
which focus on close examinations of technological information left on artifacts, have helped to
close this gap. Combined with site contextual and

temporal information studies such as theirs, these can facilitate the understanding of technological advancements in the Historic period in the Americas.

"Use"-oriented studies of material culture have included use-wear analysis of ceramic vessels (Griffiths 1978), the recycling of glass bottles (Busch [1987], this volume), recycling of Spanish pottery (Lister and Lister 1981), and the reuse of clay pipe stems (Huey 1974). Almost all forms of material goods eventually become refuse. The study of refuse-disposal patterns can result in the recognition of culturally meaningful patterns of behavior (Pogue 1988). Disposal of goods also reflects the "improvement" of manufactures and results in the creation of temporally sensitive assemblages useful for other archaeological investigations.

Behavioral studies of material culture traditionally have relied heavily on previous work on the classification of materials, as discussed above, and partially on studies of temporal variability. Analyses of temporal variability may focus on regional or international variations (e.g., Harrington 1954; Binford 1961; South 1972; Bonath 1978; Roenke 1978), may contribute to revisions of earlier classification systems (e.g., James 1988), or may address intrasite and intersite variability (King and Miller [1987], Turnbaugh and Turnbaugh [1977], this volume; King 1984). Studies of intrasite variability also contribute to an understanding of site function (e.g., King 1988) and human behavior (e.g., Turnbaugh et al. 1979).

Attempts to identify similarities and differences in the material culture of archaeological assemblages and attribute them to cultural patterns were advanced during the 1970s by Stanley South (1977a, 1977b, 1978). Patterns of culture were attributed to sites having similar artifact assemblages, but as Orser's ([1989], this volume) article illustrates, patterns for complex sites can be difficult to define and may mask complexities of human behavior associated with these sites (e.g., Tordoff 1979). Cultural patterning can also be addressed at more mundane levels, such as the recognition of patterns for the use and discard of specific goods such as Staski's ([1984], this volume)

article on the relationship of ethnic drinking patterns that may be reflected in the glass bottles from such groups. This more specific application of pattern analysis contributes to investigations of behavioral and economic issues.

Material culture research on economic conditions has focused primarily on consumer behavior and the relative status of site inhabitants in relation to their ability to obtain and purchase manufactured commodities (Spencer-Wood 1987). Horn's ([1988], this volume) article illustrates the value of combining historical and archaeological methods to address relative living standards for populations at varying distances from major commercial markets. One of the earliest works to view cultural material within its larger mercantile domain is William Adams's ([1976], this volume) analysis of the network for goods supplied to the rural agricultural settlement of Silcott, Washington. Adams's study illustrates the degree to which an isolated community is tied to broader economic and cultural spheres of influence. Other studies by Miller and Hurry (1983) and Riordan and Adams (1985) evaluate the degree to which site assemblages reflect access to national markets. Related to such investigations of economic access are studies of the social status of site inhabitants (Adams and Boling [1989], this volume; O'Brien and Majewski 1989; Yentsch 1990), and the ethnicity of inhabitants as illustrated by studies of Asian-American sites in western North America (Olsen 1978; Lister and Lister 1989; Wegars 1992).

Concluding Remarks

It is the hope of the compilers that this collection of articles will provide a wealth of information and a perspective on the diverse approaches applied by historical archaeologists to material culture research. The volume will be used in varying contexts for different purposes, but hopefully the overarching message will be that material culture—in all of its guises—is the "stuff" of archaeology. Finally, it is a tribute to colleagues whose articles make up this reader that there is such a wide range of innovative approaches to the subject of material culture research in historical archaeology.

REFERENCES

ADAMS, WILLIAM H.
1976 Trade Networks and Interaction Spheres—A View from Silcott. *Historical Archaeology* 10:99–112.

ADAMS, WILLIAM HAMPTON, AND SARAH JANE BOLING
1989 Status and Ceramics for Planters and Slaves on Three Georgia Coastal Plantations. *Historical Archaeology* 23(1):69–96.

AMES, KENNETH L., AND GERALD W. R. WARD (EDITORS)
1989 *Decorative Arts and Household Furnishings in America 1650–1920: An Annotated Bibliography.* Henry Francis du Pont Winterthur Museum, Winterthur, Delaware.

BEAUDRY, MARY C. (EDITOR)
1988 *Documentary Archaeology in the New World.* Cambridge University Press, Cambridge.

BEAUDRY, MARY C., JANET LONG, HENRY M. MILLER, FRASER D. NEIMAN, AND GARRY W. STONE
1983 A Vessel Typology for Early Chesapeake Ceramics: The Potomac Typological System. *Historical Archaeology* 17(1):18–43.

BINFORD, LEWIS R.
1961 A New Method of Calculating Dates from Kaolin Pipe Stem Samples. *Southeastern Archaeological Conference Newsletter* 9(1):19–21.

BONATH, SHAWN
1978 An Evaluation of the Mean Ceramic Date Formula as Applied to South's Majolica Model. *Historical Archaeology* 12:82–92.

BRONNER, SIMON J. (EDITOR)
1985 *American Material Culture and Folklife: A Prologue and Dialogue.* University of Michigan Research Press, Ann Arbor, Michigan.

BUSCH, JANE
1981 An Introduction to the Tin Can. *Historical Archaeology* 15(1):95–104.
1987 Second Time Around: A Look at Bottle Reuse. *Historical Archaeology* 21(1):67–80.

CARSKADDEN, JEFF, AND RICHARD GARTLEY
1990 A Preliminary Seriation of 19th-Century Decorated Porcelain Marbles. *Historical Archaeology* 24(2):55–69.

COURBIN, PAUL
1988 *What Is Archaeology? An Essay on the Nature of Archaeological Research,* translated by Paul Bahn. University of Chicago Press, Chicago.

DEAGAN, KATHLEEN
1978 The Material Assemblage of 16th Century Spanish Florida. *Historical Archaeology* 12:25–50.

DEETZ, JAMES
1977 *In Small Things Forgotten, The Archaeology of Early American Life.* Doubleday, Anchor Books, New York.

FAULKNER, ALARIC
1985 Archaeology of the Cod Fishery: Damariscove Island. *Historical Archaeology* 19(2):57–86.
1986a Maintenance and Fabrication at Fort Pentagoet 1635–1654: Products of an Acadian Armorer's Workshop. *Historical Archaeology* 20(1):63–94.
1986b Followup Notes on the 17th Century Cod Fishery at Damariscove Island, Maine. *Historical Archaeology* 20(2):86–88.

GIBBON, GUY E.
1989 *Explanation in Archaeology.* Basil Blackwell, Oxford.

GLASSIE, HENRY
1975 *Folk Housing in Middle Virginia.* University of Tennessee Press, Knoxville.
1977 Archaeology and Folklore: Common Anxieties, Common Hopes. In Historical Archaeology and the Importance of Material Things, edited by Leland Ferguson. *Special Publication Series* No. 2:23–35. Society for Historical Archaeology, California, Pennsylvania.

GOGGIN, JOHN M.
1960 The Spanish Olive Jar: An Introductory Study. *Publications in Anthropology* No. 62. Yale University, New Haven, Connecticut.
1968 Spanish Majolica in the New World: Types of the Sixteenth to Eighteenth Centuries. *Publications in Anthropology* No. 72. Yale University, New Haven, Connecticut.

GRIFFITHS, DOROTHY M.
1978 Use-Marks on Historic Ceramics: A Preliminary Study. *Historical Archaeology* 12:68–81.

GURKE, KARL
1987 *Bricks and Brickmaking: A Handbook for Historical Archaeology.* University of Idaho Press, Moscow.

HARDESTY, DONALD J.
1988 The Archaeology of Mining and Miners: A View from the Silver State. *Special Publication Series* No. 6. Society for Historical Archaeology, California, Pennsylvania.

HARRINGTON, J. C.
1954 Dating Stem Fragments of Seventeenth and Eighteenth Century Clay Tobacco Pipes. *Quarterly Bulletin of the Archaeological Society of Virginia* 9(1):9–13.

HOLT, CHERYL A.
1991 Plants, Humans, and Culture: An Edible Model of Consuming Behavior. *Historical Archaeology* 25(2): 46–61.

HORN, JAMES P. P.
1988 "The Bare Necessities:" Standards of Living in England and the Chesapeake, 1650–1700. *Historical Archaeology* 22(2):74–91.

HUEY, PAUL R.
1974 Reworked Pipe Stems: A 17th Century Phenomenon from the Site of Fort Orange, Albany, New York. *Historical Archaeology* 8:105–111.

JAMES, STEPHEN R., JR.
1988 A Reassessment of the Chronological and Typological Framework of the Spanish Olive Jar. *Historical Archaeology* 22(1):43–66.

JONES, OLIVE R.
1971 Glass Bottle Push-Ups and Pontil Marks. *Historical Archaeology* 5:62–73.
1981 Essence of Peppermint, A History of the Medicine and Its Bottle. *Historical Archaeology* 15(2):1–57.
1986 *Cylindrical English Wine and Beer Bottles, 1735–1850.* Studies in Archaeology, Architecture, and History. Environment Canada-Parks, Ottawa.

JONES, OLIVE, AND CATHERINE SULLIVAN
1989 *The Parks Canada Glass Glossary for the Description of Containers, Tableware, Flat Glass, and Closures.* Revised edition. Canadian Parks Service, Ottawa.

KELSO, WILLIAM M., AND EDWARD A. CHAPPELL
1974 Excavation of a Seventeenth Century Pottery Kiln at Glebe Harbor, Westmoreland County, Virginia. *Historical Archaeology* 8:53–63.

KENMOTSU, NANCY
1990 Gunflints: A Study. *Historical Archaeology* 24(2): 92–125.

KING, JULIA A.
1984 Ceramic Variability in 17th Century St. Augustine, Florida. *Historical Archaeology* 18(2):75–82.
1988 A Comparative Midden Analysis of a Household and Inn in St. Mary's City, Maryland. *Historical Archaeology* 22(2):17–39.

KING, JULIA A., AND HENRY MILLER
1987 The View from the Midden: An Analysis of Midden Distributions and Composition at the van Sweringen Site, St. Mary's City, Maryland. *Historical Archaeology* 21(2):37–59.

LEONE, MARK P.
1977 The New Mormon Temple in Washington, D.C. In Historical Archaeology and the Importance of Mate-

rial Things, edited by Leland Ferguson. *Special Publication Series* No. 2:43–61. Society for Historical Archaeology, California, Pennsylvania.

LEONTIEF, WASSILY
1971 Theoretical Assumptions in Nonobserved Facts. *American Economic Review* 61(1):1–7.

LIGHT, JOHN D.
1991 Recycled Files. *Research Bulletin* No. 285. Environment Canada, Parks Service, Ottawa.

LIGHT, JOHN D., AND HENRY UNGLIK
1987 *A Frontier Fur Trade Blacksmith Shop, 1796–1812.* National Historic Parks and Sites, Ottawa.

LISTER, FLORENCE C., AND ROBERT H. LISTER
1978 The First Mexican Maiolicas: Imported and Locally Produced. *Historical Archaeology* 12:1–24.
1981 The Recycled Pots and Potsherds of Spain. *Historical Archaeology* 15(1):66–78.
1989 The Chinese of Early Tucson: Historic Archaeology from the Tucson Urban Renewal Project. *Anthropological Papers* No. 52. University of Arizona, Tucson.

MAJEWSKI, TERESITA, AND MICHAEL J. O'BRIEN
1987 The Use and Misuse of Nineteenth-Century English and American Ceramics in Archaeological Analysis. In *Advances in Archaeological Method and Theory*, Vol. 11, edited by Michael B. Shiffer, pp. 97–209. Academic Press, Orlando.

MARTIN, ANN SMART
1989 The Role of Pewter as Missing Artifact: Consumer Attitudes Toward Tablewares in Late 18th Century Virginia. *Historical Archaeology* 23(2):1–27.

McCRACKEN, GRANT
1988 *Culture and Consumption: New Approaches to the Symbolic Character of Consumer Goods and Activities.* Indiana University Press, Bloomington.

MILLER, GEORGE L.
1980 Classification and Economic Scaling of 19th Century Ceramics. *Historical Archaeology* 14:1–40.
1991 A Revised Set of CC Index Values for Classification and Economic Scaling of English Ceramics from 1787 to 1880. *Historical Archaeology* 25(1):1–25.

MILLER, GEORGE L., AND SILAS D. HURRY
1983 Ceramic Supply in an Economically Isolated Frontier Community: Portage County of the Ohio Western Reserve. *Historical Archaeology* 17(2):80–92.

MILLER, GEORGE L., AND CATHERINE SULLIVAN
1984 Machine-Made Glass Containers and the End of Production for Mouth-Blown Bottles. *Historical Archaeology* 18(2):83–96.

NOËL HUME, IVOR
1969 *A Guide to Artifacts of Colonial America.* Alfred A. Knopf, New York.

1976   Archaeological Investigations on the Site of John Frederick Amelung's New Bremen Glassmanufactory, 1962–1963. *Journal of Glass Studies* 18:138–214. Corning, New York.

O'BRIEN, MICHAEL J., AND TERESITA MAJEWSKI
1989   Wealth and Status in the Upper South Socioeconomic System of Northeastern Missouri. *Historical Archaeology* 23(2):60–95.

OLSEN, JOHN W.
1978   A Study of Chinese Ceramics Excavated in Tucson. *Kiva* 44:1–50.

ORSER, CHARLES E.
1989   On Plantations and Patterns. *Historical Archaeology* 23(2):28–40.

PATRIK, LINDA E.
1985   Is There an Archaeological Record? In *Advances in Archaeological Method and Theory*, Vol. 8, edited by Michael B. Schiffer, pp. 27–62. Academic Press, Orlando.

POGUE, DENNIS J.
1988   Spatial Analysis of the King's Reach Plantation Homelot, ca. 1690–1715. *Historical Archaeology* 22(2):40–56.

RIORDAN, TIMOTHY B., AND WILLIAM HAMPTON ADAMS
1985   Commodity Flows and National Market Access. *Historical Archaeology* 19(2):5–18.

ROENKE, KARL G.
1978   Flat Glass: Its Use as a Dating Tool for Nineteenth-Century Archaeological Sites in the Pacific Northwest and Elsewhere. *Northwest Anthropological Research Notes Memoir* No. 4. University of Idaho, Moscow.

ROSS, LESTER A.
1982   The Archaeology of Canadian Potteries: An Evaluation of Production Technology. *National Museum of Man Material History Bulletin* 16:3–20. Ottawa.
1985   16th-Century Spanish Basque Coopering. *Historical Archaeology* 19(1):1–31.

SCHIFFER, MICHAEL B.
1987   *Formation Processes of the Archaeological Record*. University of New Mexico Press, Albuquerque

SCHLERETH, THOMAS J.
1982   *Material Culture Studies in America*. American Association for State and Local History, Nashville, Tennessee.

SCHLERETH, THOMAS J. (EDITOR)
1985   *Material Culture: A Research Guide*. University Press of Kansas, Lawrence.

SCHUYLER, ROBERT L. (EDITOR)
1978   *Historical Archaeology: A Guide to Substantive and Theoretical Contributions*. Baywood, Farmingdale, New York.

SHANKS, MICHAEL, AND CHRISTOPHER TILLEY
1987   *Social Theory and Archaeology*. Cambridge University Press, Cambridge.

SOUTH, STANLEY A.
1972   Evolution and Horizon as Revealed in Ceramic Analysis in Historical Archaeology. *Conference on Historic Site Archaeology Papers, 1971* 6:71–116.
1977a   *Method and Theory in Historical Archeology*. Academic Press, New York.
1978   Pattern Recognition in Historical Archaeology. *American Antiquity* 43:223–230.

SOUTH, STANLEY A. (EDITOR)
1977b   *Research Strategies in Historical Archeology*. Academic Press, New York.

SPENCER-WOOD, SUZANNE M. (EDITOR)
1987   *Consumer Choice in Historical Archaeology*. Plenum Press, New York.

SPRAGUE, RODERICK
1980   A Functional Classification for Artifacts from 19th and 20th Century Sites. *North American Archaeologist* 2:251–261.
1985   Glass Trade Beads: A Progress Report. *Historical Archaeology* 19(2):87–105.

STASKI, EDWARD
1984   Just What Can a 19th Century Bottle Tell Us? *Historical Archaeology* 18(1):38–51.

STONE, GARRY WHEELER
1988   Artifacts Are Not Enough. In *Documentary Archaeology*, edited by Mary C. Beaudry, pp. 68–77. Cambridge University Press, Cambridge.

TORDOFF, JEFFREY P.
1979   Some Observations on the Quantitative Relationship between Stanley South's Artifact Patterns and "Primary De Facto" Refuse. *Historical Archaeology* 13:38–47.

TURNBAUGH, SARAH PEABODY
1983   17th and 18th Century Lead-Glazed Redwares in the Massachusetts Bay Colony. *Historical Archaeology* 17(1):3–17.
1985   *Domestic Pottery of the Northeastern United States, 1625–1850*. Academic Press, Orlando.

TURNBAUGH, WILLIAM, AND SARAH PEABODY TURNBAUGH
1977   Alternative Applications of the Mean Ceramic Date Concept for Interpreting Human Behavior. *Historical Archaeology* 11:90–104.

TURNBAUGH, WILLIAM A., SARAH PEABODY TURNBAUGH, AND ALBERT P. DAVIS, JR.
1979   Life Aboard *HMS Orpheus*. *Archaeology* 32(3):43–49.

WALKER, IAIN C.
1977   Clay Tobacco Pipes, With Particular Reference to the Bristol Industry. *History and Archaeology* No. 11. Parks Canada, Ottawa.

WALTHALL, JOHN A.
1991   Faience in French Colonial Illinois. *Historical Archaeology* 25(1):80–105.

WATKINS, C. MALCOLM
1960   North Devon Pottery and Its Export to America in the Seventeenth Century. *National Museum Bulletin 225, Contributions from the Museum of History and Technology.* Paper 13:17–59. Smithsonian Institution, Washington, D.C.

WATKINS, LURA WOODSIDE
1950   *Early New England Potters and Their Wares.* Harvard University Press, Cambridge.

WEGARS, PRISCILLA (EDITOR)
1992   *Hidden Heritage: Historical Archaeology of the Overseas Chinese.* Baywood, Farmingdale, New York, in press.

YENTSCH, ANNE
1990   Minimum Vessel Lists as Evidence of Change in Folk and Courtly Traditions of Food Use. *Historical Archaeology* 24(3):24–53.

MARY C. BEAUDRY
JANET LONG
HENRY M. MILLER
FRASER D. NEIMAN
GARRY WHEELER STONE

A Vessel Typology for Early Chesapeake Ceramics: The Potomac Typological System

ABSTRACT

A tentative scheme for classifying vessel shapes excavated in the Chesapeake region of Maryland and Virginia is presented. The result, dubbed "The Potomac Typological System" (POTS), links gradations of forms of vessels commonly excavated on Tidewater sites to terms used in inventories and other documents of the period. Although many of the colonial terms also belong to the modern lexicon, their connotations and referents were not always identical in the past. The aim is not to produce a standardized, all-purpose typology but rather a preliminary foundation for comparisons enabling the exploration of what sorts of functional variability exist within and between assemblages. The important role of data from documentary sources in the interpretation of excavated ceramic material is also discussed.

Introduction

This paper is the result of a general dissatisfaction with the way in which archaeologists working on colonial Chesapeake sites (including the authors) have typically analyzed their excavated ceramics. Historical archaeologists spend considerable time excavating, sorting and gluing together pots. Yet there is very little to show for it, save the contents of exhibit cases. While architectural data from a number of sites excavated in the Chesapeake are beginning to increase the understanding of the effects in daily life of demographic and economic instability (Carson et al. 1981) and of changing social relations between planters, their laborers and their neighbors (Neiman 1980; Upton 1979), it is impossible to cite any similarly systematic contributions based on ceramic analysis.

The failure to impart much analytical utility to ceramics is the product of a number of factors. Some of these infect the discipline of archaeology as a whole. The lack of general archaeological theory and the failure to be imaginative make convincing attempts to connect the things dug up with other areas of past experience very rare (Leone 1978). Others are related to the often unhappy way ceramic data are cast once the pots are out of the ground. Categories are employed which, despite frequent assertions of an interest in past behavior, poorly reflect functional variation. The variety of such schemes in use makes comparisons between assemblages excavated by different archaeologists impossible. Finally, there is the failure to make good use of the documentary record with which we are blessed (or cursed).

Antidotes for the fear and trembling engendered by the call to make interesting connections and to manufacture fascinating hypotheses are hard to come by—so too are remedies for archaeology's theoretical deficiencies. However, it may be useful to offer some suggestions about the categories used in the interpretation of excavated ceramics in the light of documentary evidence and about the use of the documentary record in archaeological research focusing on ceramics.

The immediate goal is to begin to systematize the chaos in the categories used to describe excavated ceramic vessels and the assemblages they comprise, in a way that will make the cultural dynamics behind them more accessible. The Potomac Typological System (POTS) is the result. It is a first attempt whose ultimate purpose will have been served if it provokes historical archaeologists to begin to think seriously and critically about the analytical utility of the pottery typologies they currently employ.

Vessel Typologies in Historical Archaeology

Discussions of typology have long had a central place in the archaeological literature. The importance of the topic is understandable for archaeology pivots upon the initial ordering of data. The disagreement that runs through the literature concerns how one brings about order. Does it exist in recoverable form in the data, or is it imposed by the investigator (Brew 1946; Spaulding 1953; Hill and Evans 1972; Doran and Hodson 1975)? Since these stump–infested fields have been plowed before, an extended discussion of the issues will not be undertaken here. However, let the cards be laid on the table at the outset. The authors sympathize with the second position: that all classifications are arbitrary. People impose categories, and hence order, upon objects to facilitate communication; this is as true of the archaeologist as much as it is of the people he or she studies.

The theoretical underpinnings of this view, which has found acceptance in a host of fields from physics to literary criticism, runs something as follows. Despite our everyday notions, our world does not consist of independently existing objects whose nature is immediately known to the observer. In fact, this sort of immediate knowledge is impossible since any object, from a white saltglaze mug to a suspension bridge, presents the observer with a potentially infinite array of sensory data. If persons are to make sense of this bewildering variety of experience, they must pick and choose, recognizing certain features as significant and disregarding others. Perception is a creative process. People of different groups construct reality in characteristically different ways. Thus, the "true" nature of the world is not to be found in the world itself but in the relationships which one chooses to perceive among the objects in it. An object is a mug and not a cup only because the observer

chooses to recognize a rather limited number of features which make it so.

Obviously, from the researcher's point of view, there is no single best or true classificatory scheme for ceramics or for anything else for that matter. It is equally obvious that different classifications can and must coexist peacefully if we are to make the most of our data. Any system will have limitations which can only be remedied by the complementary use of other systems. For example, there has long been a working recognition of the fact that technological and stylistic attributes are best suited to the definition of units of temporal significance. *Termini post quem*, marker types, and the Mean Ceramic Date are all dating tools whose efficacy turns on the chronological significance of ceramic technology and decorative style. But if pots are to be used for more than dating sites and the features on them, some attention needs to be paid to function. Given the primitive state of research in this area, what is needed is a scheme which will allow the systematic description and comparison of assemblages and which, by attending function in even a crude way, will allow a preliminary appreciation of just what sort of functional variation exists between assemblages in time and space. Since direct evidence for past use of ceramic vessels (e.g., knife marks on a plate) is spotty, the criteria used to assess functional variation must be indirect. They must trade on the physical and traditional cultural constraints on possible use. There are of course several ways in which such a measurement device might be constructed.

Archaeologists working on the colonial Chesapeake have long used shape to describe their ceramic finds. All of these workers have written about cups, mugs, pitchers, bowls and who knows what else. By giving these items names, some sense is made of them (Tyler 1969:6). The names are of course English, and, more important, the categories which they represent are those unconsciously employed in our own day-to-day transactions, often supplemented by notions inherited from late 19th and 20th century antiquarians and collectors. By naming objects from the past, they are made comprehensible in behavioral terms. They silently slip into our own familiar world so subtly that one feels little need for theoretical or methodological reflection. Problems can be expected.

The most glaring problem is consistency. The pages of even scholarly works on the pottery of a particular period show vessels that are given the same name even though they have significantly different shapes. Even worse, two identical vessels illustrated on different pages may be given different names. If individual authors have a hard time being consistent, there would appear to be little hope for a group of feisty archaeologists. One person's plate is another's charger and another's dish. If nothing else, this situation is embarrassing.

Complacency in the face of this situation may be a product of the way in which most archaeologists have until recently reported excavated ceramics. Either a few particularly complete or spectacular pieces are chosen for illustration, in which case the names given the vessels are unimportant since the vessels themselves are there on the page for public inspection, or sherd counts by ware are presented for each excavated context, in which case the question of shape is otiose. Occasionally the two approaches are combined.

The interpretive possibilities of data cast in either of these two forms are rather limited. It is difficult to imagine why one vessel which has by chance survived the passage of time relatively intact should possess more behavioral significance than one represented by only a few sherds. The relevance of sherd counts to the explication of past behavior is equally obscure. One needs to remember the obvious: the people whom archaeologists study worked with, ate from and drank from whole vessels, not the sherds the vessels

would eventually become. If archaeologists are interested, at the very least, in the systematic description of the way in which these folks lived, they need to consider every vessel represented in the archaeological record as well as some that are not.

When the desirability of a systematic morphological description of the entire ceramic assemblage from a given period at a given site is recognized, inconsistency in the classification and naming of vessels ceases to be simply embarrassing and becomes intolerable. On a practical level, since one cannot illustrate every vessel from a relatively complex site, some naming (and/or verbal description) becomes unavoidable. Under such circumstances, unless there is some standardization in vessel nomenclature, inter–assemblage comparison is impossible. The need for explicitness to facilitate functional interpretation is one of the primary motivations behind this paper.

The analytical morass attendant on such inconsistency has not gone unnoticed, and attempts have been made to rid the field of the problem. One solution has been to discard traditional names entirely in favor of two categories which at least have the virtue of being unambiguous: flatwares and hollowwares. This is the Stoke–on–Trent approach (Celoria and Kelly 1973). In justifying this solution, its authors plead ignorance and understandable dissatisfaction with the fact that in recent numbers of *Post Medieval Archaeology*, "a bewildering variety of vessels have been called dishes" (Celoria and Kelly 1973:16). The authors also suggest that the flat/hollow dichotomy is legitimate by virtue of its use by 17th century Staffordshire potters. Despite this historical validity, the wholesale acceptance of this two–term typology would send the baby out with the bath water. While the two terms may have served the potter's primarily technological concerns well, distinguishing those vessels which were usually press-molded from those which were thrown ("reckoned by their different breadths . . . or their contents [volume]'') and stacked or nested for firing and storage, by themselves they scarcely can be considered useful tools in the functional explication of an assemblage. In a behavioral context, cups and butter pots, both hollowwares, have little in common.

A second sort of remedy is to attempt to give everyday and antiquarian terms, along with the fuzzy notions behind them, a degree of precision. Many people, for example, have called any two–handled vessel, roughly square in profile, with pint or more capacity, a posset pot. The name of course implies a very specific use, and the term was used in the 17th century. Unfortunately, it did not then apply to the wide class of vessels often described as such today (see below). Small mistakes of this sort will inevitably distort the reading of individual excavated vessels, not to mention the interpretation of entire ceramic assemblages, especially when comparisons with documentary evidence are made.

Both the above approaches meet one criterion for typological adequacy. They allow the unambiguous assignment of new objects to their categories. In addition, the Stoke–on–Trent solution is adequate insofar as it accounts for the entire range of variability in the objects under study, and the second approach could be elaborated without much difficulty to the same end (and in fact has been by many). However, adequacy is not the sole basis on which a typology should be evaluated (Binford 1972:247). While any adequate typology allows the systematic description of similarities and differences between assemblages, not all are equally well equipped to make possible insights into the significance of this variability in the context in which the objects themselves were used.

POTS is one attempt to circumvent these problems. The distinctions made by colonial Virginians and Marylanders who named and described their neighbor's possessions in probate inventories were used as clues to where breaks of possible functional significance occur along the continuum of formal variation. The characterizations of contemporary terms which POTS offers were arrived at by considering variation in adjectives applied to the terms in a sample of Virginia and Maryland inventories and descriptions (verbal and pictorial) of the terms' referents in other contemporary sources. The categories used by inventory takers appear to have been based largely on three dimensions of formal variation: shape, size and ware. Since the categories resulting from the intersection of these dimensions successfully mediated people's everyday interactions (behavior) with the objects denoted, they can serve as a reasonable basis for the construction of a functionally sensitive typology. Descriptions of the categories which comprise POTS provide a glossary for terms encountered in inventories, making more accurate comparisons between excavated and inventoried ceramic assemblages possible.

The Use of Documents in Ceramic Analysis

In putting POTS together, documentary sources have served as texts. In these sources, the manner in which their authors categorized a small part of the material world (which happens to be ubiquitous on archaeological sites) could be approximated. The application of POTS to an excavated assemblage, or any other sort of explication of archaeological material from an historic period site, should also proceed with the documents in mind. Here, however, the archaeologist will be on more familiar ground, using the historical record, initially at least, as a source of data about the artifactual contents of the past. Doing history with objects is considerably easier and the results certainly more complete if the historical record is used to fill in the holes in the archaeological records and *vice versa*. Of more far–reaching importance however is the fact that, by using documents, one can ask more interesting questions about the things one excavates. These objects, in turn, can be expected to suggest more interesting questions about the documents. Documents do not provide archaeologists with a "telephone to Glory." However, ignoring the documents is at one's own peril. This point can be illustrated through several cautionary tales. Two widely held propositions, derived from archaeological sources, about the cultural significance of ceramics in 17th century Anglo–America suffer quite devastating defects which are the inevitable result of the failure to take full advantage of the historical record.

The attempt to define socioeconomic status through ceramic assemblages is a genre which has gained considerable popularity in recent years, as historical archaeologists have struggled with the challenge to impart some anthropological or social-historical significance to their work. While explicit written statements on this topic (and many others) are rare in the study area, the proposition that in the 17th century Chesapeake there was a strong correlation between the numbers and kinds of ceramics an individual possessed and his wealth appears to have some currency. Confronted with two ceramic assemblages from a pair of sites whose occupants are known through the historical record to have been of considerably different means, it is quite easy for one to attribute any quantitative or qualitative differences which he or she is able to define in the pottery to differences in the wealth of his owners, consider no other factors, and leave the matter at that.

This sort of analysis has been the bread and butter of prehistoric archaeologists for years. Whereas historical archaeologists are here treating assemblage variability as an index to wealth, prehistorians have traditionally treated it as an index to the presence of different tribes or cultural groups. In both cases percentage and/or empirical frequencies, calculated for a variety of artifact classes, are used as a measure of distance, cultural in one case and economic in the other, between the occupants of a number of sites. As Lewis Binford (1968, 1972), among others, has pointed out, this kind of approach severely limits the interpretive possibilities of the archaeological record and its potential to inform us about the past. The problem is that in both cases it is simply assumed that the contents of the archaeological record and its determinants are unidimensional. It would be surprising indeed to discover that any set of phenomena for which human beings were responsible was attributed to the operation of a single variable.

Theory aside, this particular projection of our own ethnocentric notion that the rich will invariably possess lots of pretty pots has another shortcoming. A cursory examination of the inventories indicates that it simply does not fit the 17th century Chesapeake. Ceramics were optional for many of the early Chesapeake's wealthiest men. A case in point is Capt. John Lee, a Westmoreland County, Virginia, gentleman whose estate was probated in 1674. Lee was a quorum justice, the brother of a member of the Governor's Council, and with an estate valuation in excess of 200,000 lbs of tobacco and 24 laborers, the wealthiest decedent appraised in the county during the 17th century. Yet Lee's collection of ceramics was exceedingly limited. The six quarts of oil and an equal amount of honey which the appraisers found "In Capt. Lee's Chamber" may have been kept in a couple of earthen jars. Lee's kitchen contained the three chamber pots, two old close stool pans, two porringers and a chafing dish. But all these items, save the chafing dish, may well have been pewter, given their relatively high valuations. The chamber pots were worth 15 lbs of tobacco each, and the two close stool pans and porringers were valued at 40 lbs for the lot, this at a time when butter pots, typically one of the most common ceramic forms, were worth only 7 lbs each (*Westmoreland County, Virginia, Deeds, Patents and Accounts 1665–1677*: 180). But even if one assumes in the face of this evidence that all these objects were ceramic,

Lee's assemblage was modest indeed in terms of quantity as well as quality. Lee's inventory is characteristically detailed, containing specific entries for items as trifling as "a small parcell of twine." In addition, there are no non-specific entries like "a parcell of lumber," or "small things forgotten" for that matter, which might conceal ceramics. Nor was Lee married, so there are no pots hiding in an uninventoried widow's portion.

In Westmoreland County, Virginia, Lee was by no means unique. Mr. Robert Jadwin, who died in the same year with a hefty estate valued at 46,749 lbs of tobacco, had no ceramics at all (*Westmoreland County, Virginia, Deeds, Patents and Accounts 1665–1677*: 188). In fact, of the 19 pre–1677 Westmoreland County, Virginia, inventories valued at over 20,000 lbs of tobacco, ceramics are not mentioned in seven. Of the remaining 12, seven contain only coarse earthen and/or dairy–related forms. Typical of these for example is the inventory of Mr. Richard Sturman (d.1669), valued at 55, 015 lbs. Sturman's only ceramic possessions were "milke trays potts & panns" (*Westmoreland County, Virginia, Deeds, Patents and Accounts 1665–1677*: 54). Another example, slightly lower down the economic scale, is Mr. Daniel Hutt (d.1674), worth 20,820 lbs. whose inventory contained the following uninspiring ceramic entries: "crakd earthenware & a prcell of nales in it" and "In the Milke-house . . . a prcell old lumber" (*Westmoreland County, Virginia, Deeds, Patents and Accounts 1665–1677*: 194).

What one might consider fine ceramics appear with certainty in only three of the remaining inventories: Robert Nurses's "prcell painted earthen ware" (1672), Nathaniel Pope's "2 juggs" (1660), and John Roasier's "earthen porringer" (1661) (*Westmoreland County, Virginia, Deeds, Patents and Accounts 1665–1677*: 198; *Westmoreland County, Virginia, Deeds, and Wills 1660–1661*: 42; *Westmoreland County, Virginia, Deeds, Wills and Patents 1653–1659*: 8).

In Charles County, Maryland, settled like Westmoreland County, Virginia, in the 1650s, from 1658 to 1684 only 36% of the inventories of middling and wealthy planters list any ceramics (Walsh 1979: Table 2A).

On a practical level, these examples from the documents mean that a meager ceramic assemblage from a 17th century Chesapeake site does not guarantee that its occupants were of meager means. This is not meant to imply that the appearance of vast quantities of porcelain and delft, for example, on a site suggests nothing about the wealth of its occupants. Quite obviously it does. But once one realizes that ceramics were not *de rigeur* among the rich in the early Chesapeake, the interesting question is not whether rich people could afford more pottery than the poor, something anyone might have deduced without touching a trowel, but why some individuals chose to buy lots of fancy pots while many of their peers did not.

The second example is drawn from the work of James Deetz (1972, 1977). In attempting to develop a model for changing patterns of ceramic use in 17th and 18th century Anglo–America, Deetz noticed a dearth of nearly all but dairy–related wares on pre–1660 sites around Plymouth, Massachusetts. Drawing on Anderson's (1971) work on Tudor and Stuart English foodways he concluded, correctly, that eating and drinking vessels were generally not ceramic. Specifically, Deetz suggested that shared wooden trenchers and shared pewter and/or leather drinking vessels comprised the typical dining assemblage in early 17th century Anglo–America. Deetz outlined two phenomena visible in the archaeological data after ca. 1660. The first was a general scarcity of ceramic plates, the second a gradual increase in the absolute numbers of ceramic drinking vessels. He concluded that wooden trenchers continued to be the norm for food consumption, that ceramic plates served primarily as decorative items in lieu of costly pewter and that since trenchers do not survive in the ground, the increase in the number of drinking vessels might be taken as indicative of a general trend toward more individualized consumption of both liquids and solids.

While much of Deetz's (1972) article relies on documentary evidence and the companion piece by Marley Brown (1972) is based solely on inventories, both suffer a preoccupation with excavated ceramics. Apparently when the inventory data were assembled for comparison with information from the ground, only entries for ceramics were systematically collected, a procedure not uncommon in the field. As one of the present authors (Stone 1977:57) has pointed out elsewhere, because archaeologists excavate ceramics they wish also to "excavate" them from inventories. In the process, they often ignore the other forms listed there which comprised the larger context in which the ceramics had meaning.

Deetz's model was of course designed specifically for early New England. It may not be appropriate to attack it with data from the Chesapeake. Nevertheless, its applicability to all of Anglo–America is at least implicit throughout Deetz (1977). The criticisms offered below, however, can be supported with data from New England as well.

The claim that trenchers were standard eating vessels is difficult to support, once one looks beyond the ceramic entries in the inventories. In the earliest Potomac inventories, those taken in frontier St. Mary's County, Maryland, 1638–1650, wooden trenchers and dishes (other than Indian bowls used as utility vessels) were important only in newly established households—the households of recent immigrants or recently freed servants. In well-established households, even of tenants, pewter predominated (*Archives of Maryland* 1887; Stone 1977: 60).

On the Virginia side of the river, the same pattern prevailed. In Westmoreland County, Virginia, in 14 extant inventories taken during the decade following the county's incorporation in 1653, four contained *only* wooden eating vessels. Dishes and trays are mentioned

specifically. In the rest, eating vessels were of pewter: saucers, plates, dishes, among other forms. In 31 inventories taken between 1668 and 1677 in the county, again only four listed eating vessels of wood, to the exclusion of other materials. And again all the rest contained pewter saucers, plates, or dishes.

The number of eating vessels, either in pewter or wood, was considerable. In the earlier Westmoreland County, Virginia, sample, Nathaniel Pope, with an estate worth ca. £380, owned nine saucers, 12 plates, and 36 dishes, all of pewter. At the other end of the economic scale, George Poper, worth a paltry 1035 lbs of tobacco (ca. £5) had three pewter saucers and three pewter plates (*Westmoreland County, Virginia, Deeds, Wills and Patents 1653–1659*: 72). The pattern was the same in the later sample. Capt. John Ashton, with the second largest estate in the group, worth 94,000 lbs of tobacco (ca. £470) owned 51 pewter plates, two pewter dishes, and "40 pewter dishes basons and pye plates" (*Westmoreland County, Virginia, Deeds, Patents and Accounts 1665–1677*: 321–22). Francis Lewis, worth only 1,395 lbs of tobacco, the second poorest member of the sample, had three pewter plates and two pewter dishes. Men who owned smaller amounts of pewter typically supplemented their collection of eating vessels with wooden ones. Richard Sampson, a middling planter whose estate was not valued, had only three pewter dishes, but he also owned nine trenchers. Even the few planters who owned only wooden vessels owned them in quantities which suggest, given the small size of their households, that they were not shared. Henry Alday, for example, with an estate worth 5,840 lbs of tobacco (ca. £29), had seven wooden trays, and Thomas Baron, whose estate valued at 394 lbs of tobacco (ca. £2) made him the poorest individual in the sample, had four wooden dishes (*Westmoreland County, Virginia, Deeds, Patents and Accounts 1665–1677*: 72; *Westmoreland County, Virginia, Deeds, Wills and Patents 1653–1659*: 88). These examples could be extended, *ad nauseam*, from the St. Mary's County, Maryland, inventories.

Clearly, then, the great majority of the 17th century Virginians and Marylanders were eating from pewter plates and not wooden trenchers, and eating vessels in either material were not being shared at the table in all save perhaps the poorest households.

This apparently had been the case in the most economically advanced areas of England since the late 16th century. In 1587, William Harrison, commenting on the effects of the price revolution, included in his famous three things "marvelously altered in England within . . . sound remembrance" the appearance of quantities of pewter in the households of "inferior artificers and many farmers." The ordinary farmer had recently changed his "treen platters into pewter," providing himself with a "fair garnish of pewter for his cupboard" (Harrison 1968:200–01). According to Harrison, a "garnish" was comprised of 12 platters, 12 dishes and 12 saucers (Harrison 1968:367). Without doubt, the pewter vessels which proliferated in the houses of English yeomen were flatwares. It should not be surprising then to find Chesapeake planters following a pattern set by their ancestors in the previous century. Obviously the quantities of pewter plates in Chesapeake households make Deetz's suggestion that ceramic plates were commonly displayed in lieu of pewter ones questionable.

If pewter eating vessels were numerous in the 17th century Chesapeake, pewter drinking vessels were not. While the number of pieces of pewter a planter possessed was to some extent correlated with the size of his estate and household, the number of drinking vessels remained consistently small across the economic continuum. In Westmoreland County, Virginia, Nathaniel Pope had only four pewter drinking pots, and John Hiller, a planter of far more modest means (9, 529 lbs of tobacco, ca. £48), owned two drinking pots and three cups (*Westmoreland County,*

Virginia, Deeds and Wills 1660–1661: 16). Of the remaining six estates inventoried in the county between 1654 and 1661 in which pewter vessels were listed entirely by shape, none contained more than three pewter drinking vessels, although three of the individuals involved were more than twice as wealthy as Hiller. The pattern which emerges from the extant Westmoreland County, Virginia, inventories taken between 1668 and 1677 is similar. Capt. John Ashton, second wealthiest member of the group, had no pewter drinking vessels at all. Two middling planters had six each, and the remaining members of the sample owned three or less. Unless similar forms were present in ceramic or, in the wealthiest households, silver, the inevitable conclusion is that drinking vessels were being shared, if not with laborers, at least with neighbors when they came visiting.

It would seem that the increase in absolute numbers of ceramic drinking vessels noted by Deetz in the archaeological record toward the end of the 17th century might be taken to represent a trend toward more individualized consumption of beverages. But in social and religious ceremony, shared drinking vessels continued to be used as symbols of intimacy until the mid-19th century (Stone 1977:61–62).

Developing the Potomac Typological System

The method behind the construction of POTS was unabashedly democratic. The authors have attempted to assign excavated forms to common categories and names derived from a number of documentary sources, most importantly probate inventories taken in Maryland (St. Mary's County) and Virginia (Westmoreland and York counties) during the 17th and early 18th centuries. It appears that Englishmen in the Chesapeake took vessels from a wide variety of European potting traditions and applied relatively standardized uses and names to them. The functional significance of shape differences unique to a particular regional English folk culture may not have survived long on the Chesapeake frontier, where consumers could be less discriminating and where their needs were considerably altered. Similarly, some taxonomic distinctions with only regional distribution at home proved of little relevance to life in the Chesapeake, where they were discarded in favor of those which did.

In general, the process was akin to that by which Virginians and Marylanders developed a distinctive vernacular architecture by drawing on a variety of English forms to combine and alter them according to local requirements. The general impression is that, as with architecture, the ways in which Chesapeake planters and New England farmers categorized their food vessels differed considerably in some domains. While there seems to have been significant variation between communities with different subsistence orientations in New England (Yentsch 1977), such regional differences do not seem to have been characteristic of the Chesapeake (Beaudry 1980).

While many of the categories derived from the documents are fairly straightforward, some do require discussion.

Dish appears to have been used both as a specific and a generic term. Randle Holme, an English artist who between 1640 and 1680 attempted to record and illustrate all of the symbols employed in English heraldry, provided a valuable source of information about 17th century objects and their uses. Holme (1905:4) listed the following terms under "the several names of a dish":

A platter if large.
A dish, which [is] of a lesser sort.
A midleing dish
A Broth dish, deeper bottomed than flesh dishes.
A Bason, is almost half round in the concave. . . .
A sallet dish
A trencher plate or plate
A saucer

Holme's specification that a basin is "almost half round in the concave" suggests that the term denoted a vessel different from the others. Elsewhere he pictures a vessel, round in plan, and labels it "a dish, a platter, a saucer, a trencher plate." Leaving basins aside then, one can map "the several names of a dish" in a tree diagram in which the lower levels are related to the higher levels by inclusion:

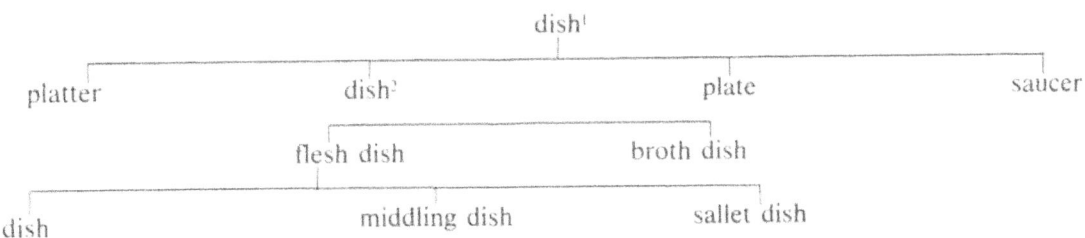

The arrangement of the terms in Holme's (1905) list is not accidental. They are given in order of decreasing size, a relation which obtains between the terms in the second row of the tree, from left to right. Depth was not a factor in distinguishing between terms at this level: *dish²* subsumes both *flesh dish* and *broth dish*. William Harrison looked at the matter in a similar fashion, noting in 1587 that "dishes and platters in my time begin to be made deep like basins" (Harrison 1968:367).

If the terms *platter, dish², plate,* and *saucer* denote vessels differing primarily in size (diameter), where do the breaks come? The anonymous author of *The Complete Appraiser* (1770:42–43), published in the mid-18th century, provides a partial answer in a table detailing prescribed weights and diameters for pewter plates and dishes. Plates run from 7 ¾ in to 9 ¾ in. Dishes range from 10 ¾ in all the way up to 28 in (Montgomery 1973:135). Criteria similar to these were apparently in use in the 17th century Chesapeake. Corduroy Ironmonger's 1675 inventory, taken in Westmoreland County, Virginia, listed dishes weighing 5.4 lbs each and plates weighing 1.5 lbs each (*Westmoreland County, Virginia, Deeds, Patents and Accounts 1665–1677*: 243). The figures fit comfortably with *The Compleat Appraiser*'s listing of the smallest dish at 1 lb, 12 oz. One can infer that saucers, as the smallest members of the dish family, were of something less than ca. 7 in diameter and that platters were the largest members of the group. *Platter* may have had other referents as well. There is some evidence that it was on some occasions synonymous with *oval dish*. Holme makes the equation twice, noting that John the Baptist's head was served up to King Herod on an oval dish "although some call it a platter" (Carson 1970:44, 296; Holme 1905:4). It would seem then that platters were *dishes* which were either very large, or oval, or both. As the distinction between *platter* and *dish* was even then unclear, *platter* has been excluded from the POTS typology. All flat vessels greater in diameter than 10 in are defined as *dishes*.

As indicated, Holme (1905) made a distinction, echoed by Harrison (1968), between *flesh dishes* and *broth dishes*. However, the distinction does not appear in the authors' inventory sample until the early 18th century when it applies to plates. In 1756, William Wallet advertised in the *Maryland Gazette* that he would recast "either flat or soup dishes or flat or soup plates" (Montgomery 1973:135). Surviving pewter pieces from the period suggest that soup dishes and plates ranged in height between 1 in and 2 in. Rather than offer absolute criteria for soup dishes and plates versus flat dishes and plates, it is suggested that the distinction in an excavated ceramic assemblage be based on the objects in it. If the excavated material exhibits a continuum of depths relative to diameters, the distinction might best be ignored. However, if the distribution of shapes exhibits a break, the

distinction may reflect functional differences and therefore be of utility.

Holme gives two functions for basins. He implies a food function by classifying basins as members of the dish family, and in this he was paralleled by many estate appraisers who grouped or found pewter basins with pewter dishes and plates. Holme also illustrates a barber's basin and a "stand . . . used for to set a Bason on whilest washing . . ." (Holme 1688:432, 438; 1905:18, 18a). Both food basins and a great (wash) basin on a stand are listed in Robert Slye's inventory (see Appendix). While some basins may have been used for both dining and washing, archaeologists should try to determine the functions of the vessels that they recover from the find contexts of the sherds. At the Clifts site in Westmoreland County, Virginia, one of the authors excavated sherds of decorated basins matching plate fragments from early 18th century contexts (Neiman 1980). At Rosewell, Noël Hume found undecorated wash basin fragments in a ca. 1763–1762 pit (Noël Hume 1962:203–07). In the Rosewell report, Noël Hume rightly grouped the wash basins with the chamber pots, while in the author's report on the Clifts site, the basins will be counted as dining vessels.

Apart from the problems presented by *platter* and *basin*, the sources used above describe a relatively straightforward typology for categorizing flat dining vessels. It is a comfortable typology as much of it remains in use today. But readers of 17th century documents should be aware that alternate taxonomies were in use during that century. Some appraisers recorded many dishes and few plates. Others listed "platters great & small" to the exclusion of both dishes and plates (*Archives of Maryland* 1887:93).

Drinking vessels presented fewer problems. *Pot* is the most troublesome form as well as the most common. Fortunately Holme illustrates one pot shape—a pitcher-like form (Carson 1970:14, 68, 196; Holme 1688:167).

The name also seems to have been applied to bulbous and squat cylindrical drinking vessels as probate and potters' inventories do not provide alternate designations. "Drinking bowl" seems to have been applied to metal vessels only. Except in silver, *cup* was restricted to small containers. "Pint cup" appears rarely in Chesapeake inventories, while (in pewter) drinking pots routinely appear in pint, quart, and pottle (2 qt) sizes.

The procedure of naming by plebiscite bypassed most of the problems of describing food preparation vessels. Thus, all large pans are typed as *milk pans*, although some were used as wash basins and cooking pans. All dairy pots will be considered as *butter pots* until someone defines—in Chesapeake terms—the difference in form between a butter pot and a cream pot. While excavated dairy pots vary in shape, the most important variable seems to be place of manufacture. Thus, most North Devon pots have constricted shoulders (Watkins 1960:45), while Flintshire pots are generally more cylindrical (Noël Hume 1976:135). In a similar fashion, a 17th century definition of *pipkin* has evaded these authors; it is assumed that the term encompassed most of the cooking pots excavated on Chesapeake sites. No other term identifiable as an earthen cooking pot appears in the inventories, and most excavated specimens are of one general shape.

Commonly used categories for summarizing excavated vessels have been too general. More gradations are needed to distinguish between shared and individual drinking vessels, and dining vessel groups oriented toward hominy and pottage versus boiled, baked, or roasted foods. The recommended categories are illustrated below. These are simplified groupings. It is realized, for example, that bottles were storage as well as serving vessels and that jugs of less that a pottle could be used for serving. In English America as well as in England, some families undoubtedly used pitchers as jugs and drinking pots as well as utility vessels. However, without some simplification, summary would be impossible, and these categories represent the best fit achievable between the multifarious uses suggested by the documents and employable archaeological categories (Table 1).

The logical conclusion of an article such as this would witness the application of POTS to several excavated assemblages. Presumably, this would demonstrate the virtues of the typology by comparing ceramic assemblages from successive periods at the same site and from the same period at different sites. At the present time, however, such comparisons cannot be undertaken. Analyses of the excavated materials from St. John's and the Clifts Plantation sites are still underway, although they both will be used as test cases for POTS, along with materials from sites on the James River. This typology is presented in its tentative form as a means of informing colleagues in historical archaeology of the direction this research is taking and in hopes of eliciting comments, suggestions and shared information from others concerned with the problems of ceramic typologies and functional interpretations based on archaeological assemblages from historical sites.

Chesapeake Ceramic Forms and Definitions

Ceramic forms discussed previously and listed in Table 1 are illustrated and defined below. Groupings are determined primarily on the basis of vessel shape and only secondarily by vessel function. These groupings are not necessarily those used in the course of ceramic analysis, and infrequently excavated forms are neither illustrated nor defined. Some of these forms are mentioned in the accompanying probate inventories, however (Appendix).

TABLE 1
A SUGGESTED FUNCTIONAL DIVISION OF VESSEL FORMS FROM 17TH CENTURY SITES

FOOD PROCESSING
(Cooking and Darying)
    Pipkin
    Pudding Pan
    Bowl
    Milk Pan
    Collander

FOOD AND DRINK STORAGE

    Storage Pot
    Jar
    Bottle

BEVERAGE CONSUMPTION

Individual   Communal or Individual   Serving

(1 pt or less)   (More than 1 pt)
Cup   Mug   Pitcher
Mug   Jug   Ewer
Jug   Drinking Pot   Punch Bowl
Footed Bowls   Flask   Large Jug
                                        Sillabub Pot

FOOD CONSUMPTION

Stews/Pottages/Soups   Solid Food Consumption and Serving
    Porringers   Caudle Pots
    Soup Plates   Basins
    Small Bowls   Plates
                                        Dishes
                                        Saucers
                                        Salts

HEALTH/HYGIENE   OTHER
Galley Pots- Large   Chafing Dish
          - Small   Candlesticks
Chamber Pots   Betty Lamp
Basins- Plain
      - Barber's

Hollow Vessels for Liquids—1/8 size

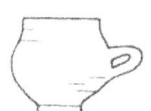

CUP. A small, handled drinking vessel of less than a pint in capacity. In form, cups are closely related to drinking pots.

DRINKING POT. A one or multi–handled vessel, usually bulbous, but sometimes cylindrical in form, ranging in capacity from 1 pt to 2 qts or more. Cylindrical drinking pots are distinguished from mugs by being wider than tall and/or having two or more handles.

MUG. A single–handled, straight–sided drinking vessel, taller than wide, ranging from 1 gill (¼ pt) to 2 qts (or more).

JUG. A handled vessel of bulbous form with a cylindrical neck rising from a pronounced shoulder, with or without a gutter. In size, jugs range from small drinking vessels to large serving vessels. Jugs occur generally in refined earthenwares and stonewares.

PITCHER. A handled vessel with bulbous body, having a flaring neck with a gutter. In America, used primarily in the kitchen and dairy. Pitchers occur in coarse earthenwares.

EWER. A handled, bulbous-bodied serving vessel, similar in shape to a jug, but with a narrower, elongated neck with a gutter or spout. Ewers occur in refined earthenwares or stonewares.

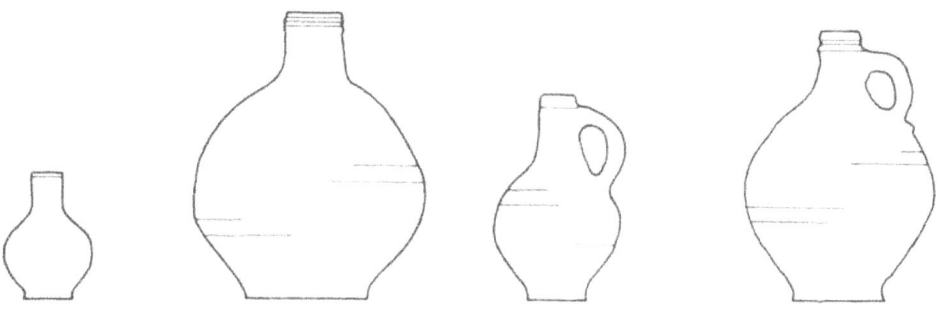

BOTTLE. A bulbous-bodied storage and serving vessel with a neck narrower than a jug or ewer, with or without a handle.

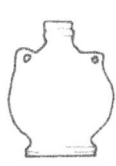   

FLASK/COSTREL. A bulbous-bodied vessel with a very narrow neck, similar in form to a bottle, but having two ears or strap handles rising from the shoulder. A drink container carried by travelers and field workers.

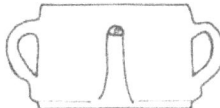

SILLABUB POT. A pot with a spout, two handles, and sometimes a cover, for drinking and serving sillabub, posset, and wassail.

Hollow Vessels for Liquids and Semi-solid Foods—1/8 size

CAUDLE CUP/POT. A two-handled, covered cup, for making and serving fermented gruel. The appearance of the term caudle pot suggests that it occurs in sizes larger than that illustrated.

PORRINGER. A vessel usually hemispherical in shape and shallower in relation to its diameter than a cup or a pot. Porringers have at least one and sometimes two handles, either horizontal or vertical. Used for eating porridge, pottage (stew), soup, etc.

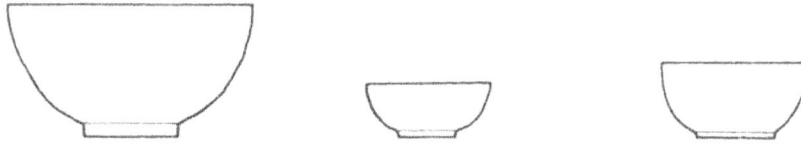

PUNCH BOWL. A hemispherical vessel with a plain rim. Punch bowls occur in refined earthenwares, stonewares, and porcelain. They range in capacity from ½ pt to several gallons. The smallest sizes were used by individuals for drinking punch and perhaps eating semi-solid foods. The larger sizes were used for making and serving punch.

BOWL. An open vessel with convex sides terminating in either a plain or everted rim or brim. Bowls have no footrings and occur only in coarse earthenwares. Bowls were used primarily in the kitchen and dairy.

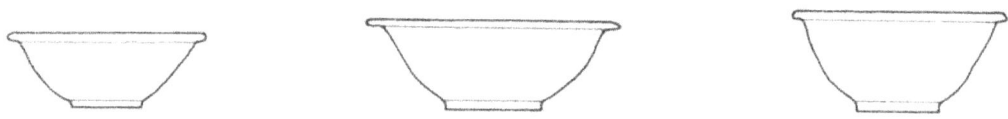

BASIN. An open vessel with convex sides, of greater width than depth, having a brim or everted lip. Basins occur with or without footrings but only in refined earthenwares and porcelain. These forms were used for washing, shaving and for dining.

Flat Vessels for Food—1/8 size

DISH. A serving vessel larger than 10 in either in diameter or in length, with or without a footring. Dishes were made in shallow and deep forms.

PLATE. An eating vessel from 7 in to 10 in in diameter, with or without a footring. Plates were made in shallow and deep (i.e., soup) forms.

SAUCER. A vessel less than 7 in in diameter, with or without a footring. Saucers were used for serving condiments (hence: sauce--r) and perhaps as small plates.

Miscellaneous Dining Forms—1/8 size

SALT. A pedestaled serving vessel in refined earthenware or stoneware with or without supports at the rim.

CHAFING DISH. A coarse earthenware vessel on a pedestal with supports around the rim. Chafing dishes held coals used to warm food at the table.

Cooking Vessels—1/8 size

PIPKIN. An earthen cooking pot. Two varieties of pipkins have been excavated in the Chesapeake. The handled pipkin (above left) is a small, bulbous cooking pot, frequently with a rod handle. The pot/flesh pot (above right) is a cooking vessel with two ears and three legs. While the form is a metal one, it was occasionally copied in coarse earthenwares.

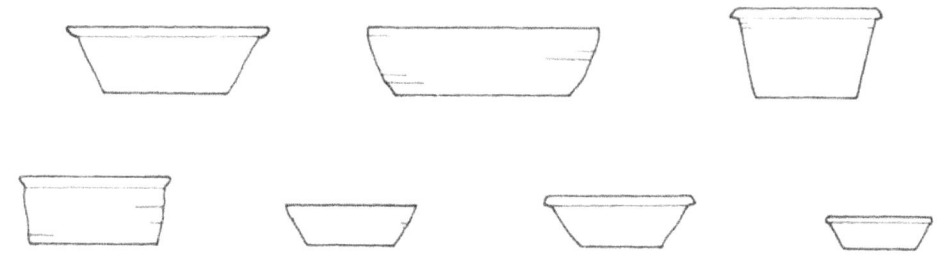

PAN/PUDDING, PASTRY, PATTY, ETC. A coarse earthenware cooking vessel, roughly in the shape of an inverted, truncated cone, less than 10 in in diameter

Dairy and Kitchen Vessels—1/8 size

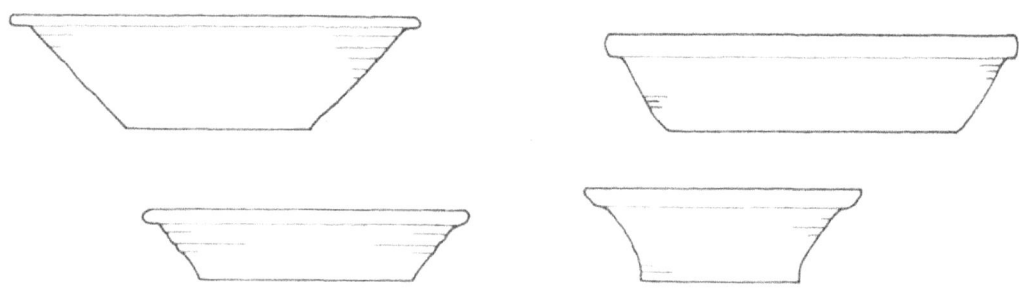

MILK PAN. A vessel roughly in the shape of an inverted, truncated cone, 10 in or more in diameter. Used for cooling milk, as a wash basin and probably for cooking

COLANDER. A pan–like, handled utensil with a perforated bottom. Colanders were used for making cheese, washing vegetables, etc.

POT/BUTTER POT. A large, cylindrical or slightly convex-sided vessel, taller than wide, used for souring cream or storing butter, fat (lard), etc.

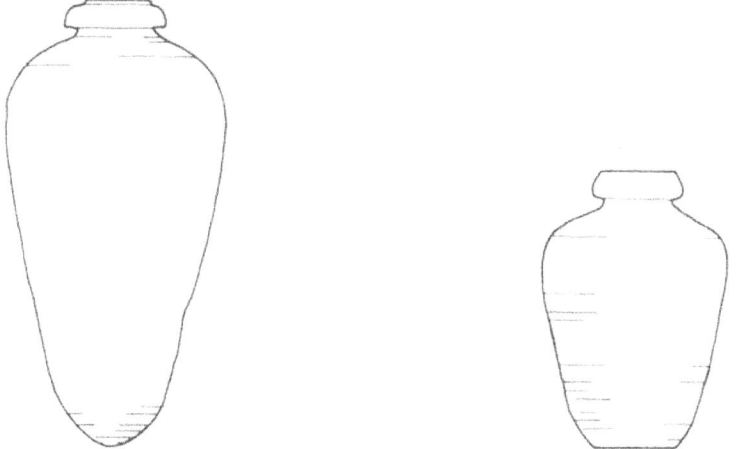

JAR. A large vessel, taller than wide, with pronounced shoulders and constricted neck, bearing a heavy, rounded lip Jars were used for storing water, oil, beer, etc.

Hygiene-related Forms—1/8 size

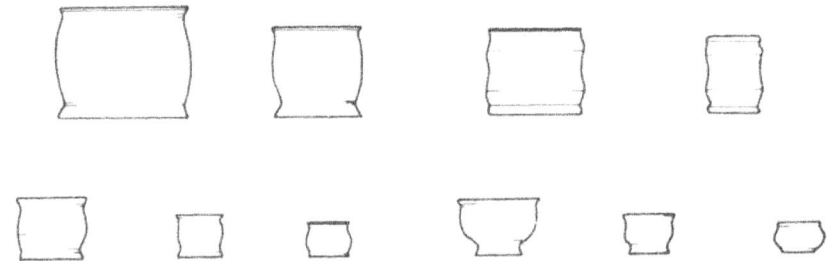

GALLEY POT. A cylindrical tin–glazed vessel with slightly flared rim and base. Large and small sizes may be distinguished. Used for drugs, ointments, cosmetics and, occasionally, condiments.

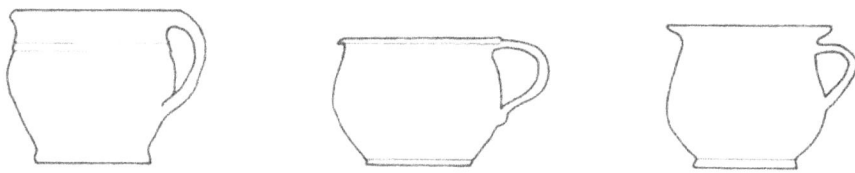

CHAMBER POT. A handled vessel with convex sides and a sturdy flared rim or brim. The eventual repository of the contents of all of the above.

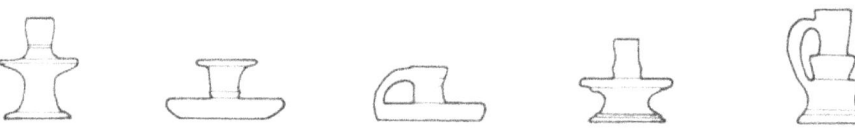

CANDLESTICK. A lighting device consisting of a hollow tube, a foot and/or a drip tray.

ACKNOWLEDGMENTS

The authors would like to thank the following people for taking time to comment on this manuscript: John Austin, Norman Barka, Barbara Carson, James Deetz, William Kelso, Ivor and Audrey Noël Hume, Alain and Merry Outlaw, and C. Malcolm Watkins. All of the drawings in the text are by Janet Long. An earlier version of this manuscript was presented at the Jamestown Conference on Archaeology, Jamestown, Virginia, April 1979

REFERENCES

ANDERSON, JAY
1971 *A Solid Sufficiency. An Ethnography of Yeoman Foodways in Stuart England*. Ph.D. dissertation, University of Pennsylvania, University Microfilms, Ann Arbor.

ANONYMOUS
1770 *The Compleat Appraiser* (fourth edition). London.

ARCHIVES OF MARYLAND
1887 *Archives of Maryland*. Judicial and Testamentary Business of the Provincial Court, 1637–1650 (Vol. 4). Edited by William Hand Browne. Maryland Historical Society, Baltimore.

BEAUDRY, MARY C.
1980 *"Or What Else You Please to Call It": Folk Semantic Domains in Early Virginia Probate Inventories*. Ph.D. dissertation, Brown University. University Microfilms, Ann Arbor.

BINFORD, LEWIS R.
1968 Archaeological Perspectives. In *New Perspectives in Archeology*, edited by Sally R. Binford and Lewis R. Binford, pp. 5–32. Aldine Publishing Company, Chicago.
1972 Model Building-Paradigms, and the Current State of Paleolithic Research. In *An Archaeological Perspective*, edited by Lewis R. Binford, pp. 244–294. Seminar Press, New York.

BREW, JOHN OTIS
1946 Archaeology of Alkali Ridge: Southeastern Utah. *Papers of the Peabody Museum of American Archaeology and Ethnology* 21. Harvard University, Cambridge, Massachusetts.

BROWN, MARLEY R. III
1972 Ceramics from Plymouth, 1621–1800: The Documentary Record. In *Ceramics in America*, edited by Ian M. G. Quimby, pp. 41–74. University of Virginia Press, Charlottesville.

CARSON, BARBARA G.
1970 Illustrations and Extracts from the Text of Randle Holme's *The Academy of Armory*. Ms. on file, Plimoth Plantation, Plymouth, Massachusetts.

CARSON, CARY, NORMAN F. BARKA, WILLIAM M. KELSO, GARRY W. STONE AND DELL UPTON
1981 Impermanent Architecture in the Southern Colonies. *Winterthur Portfolio* 16(2/3):135–196.

CELORIA, F. S. C. AND J. H. KELLY
1973 A Post Medieval Pottery Site with a Kiln Base Found Off Albion Square, Hanley, Stoke-on-Trent, Staffordshire, England SJ 885 474. *City of Stoke-on-Trent Museum Archaeological Society Report* 4.

DEETZ, JAMES
1972 Ceramics from Plymouth, 1635–1835: The Archaeological Evidence. In *Ceramics in America*, edited by Ian M. G. Quimby, pp. 15–40. University of Virginia Press, Charlottesville.
1977 *In Small Things Forgotten: The Archaeology of Early American Life*. Anchor Books, Garden City, New York.

DORAN, J. E. AND F. R. HODSON
1975 *Mathematics and Computers in Archaeology*. Harvard University Press, Cambridge, Massachusetts.

HARRISON, WILLIAM
1968 *The Description of England*. Edited by George Edden. The Folger Shakespeare Library. Cornell University Press, Ithaca, New York.

HILL, H. N. AND R. K. EVANS
1972 A Model for Classification and Typology. In *Models in Archaeology*, edited by David L. Clarke, pp. 231–274. Methuen and Company, London.

HOLME, RANDLE
1688 *The Academy of Armory*. Chester, England.
1905 *The Academy of Armory, Part 2*. Edited by I. H. Jeayes. Printed for the Roxburghe Club, London.

LEONE, MARK P.
1978 *Archaeology's Relationship to the Present and the Past*. Paper Delivered to the American Anthropological Association Symposium, "The Archaeology of US." Los Angeles, California, November, 1978.

MARYLAND PROVINCIAL RECORDS (St. Mary's County)
Testamentary Proceedings 5. Hall of Records, Annapolis.
Testamentary Proceedings 6. Hall of Records, Annapolis.

MONTGOMERY, CHARLES F.
1973 *A History of American Pewter*. Weathervane Books, New York.

NEIMAN FRASER D.
1980 The "Manner House" before Stratford (Discovering the Clifts Plantation). Robert E. Lee Memorial Association, Stratford, Virginia.

NOEL HUME, IVOR
1962 Excavations at Rosewell, Gloucester County, Virginia, United States National Museum Bulletin 225. The Smithsonian Institution, Washington, D.C.
1977 Early English Delftware from London and Virginia. Colonial Williamsburg Occasional Papers in Archaeology 2. Colonial Williamsburg Foundation, Williamsburg.

SPAULDING, ALBERT C.
1953 Statistical Techniques for the Discovery of Artifact Types. American Antiquity 18:305–313.

STONE, GARRY WHEELER
1977 Artifacts Are Not Enough. The Conference on Historic Site Archaeology Papers 1976 11:43–63.

TYLER, STEPHEN A.
1969 Cognitive Anthropology. Holt, Rinehart and Winston, Inc., New York.

UPTON, DELL
1979 Early Vernacular Architecture in Southeastern Virginia. Ph.D. Dissertation, Brown University. University Microfilms, Ann Arbor.

WALSH, LORENA
1979 A Culture of "Rude Sufficiency": Life Styles on Maryland's Lower Western Shore Between 1658 and 1720. Paper Delivered to the Society for Historical Archaeology, January 1979.

WATKINS, C. MALCOLM
1960 North Devon Pottery and Its Export to America in the Seventeenth Century. Contributions from the Museum of History and Technology, Paper 13. Smithsonian Institution, Washington, D.C.

WESTMORELAND COUNTY, VIRGINIA
Deeds, Wills and Patents 1653–1659. Westmoreland County Courthouse.
Deeds and Wills 1660–1661. Westmoreland County Courthouse.
Deeds, Patents and Accounts 1665–1677. Westmoreland County Courthouse.

YENTSCH, ANNE E.
1977 Farming, Fishing, Trading, and Whaling: Subsistence Patterns Revealed by Probate Inventories for Eighteenth Century Cape Cod Towns. Paper Delivered to the Society for Historical Archaeology, January 1977.

MARY C. BEAUDRY,
ARCHAEOLOGICAL STUDIES PROGRAM,
BOSTON UNIVERSITY,
232 BAY STATE ROAD, BOSTON, MASSACHUSETTS, 02215

JANET LONG,
DEPARTMENT OF ANTHROPOLOGY,
UNIVERSITY OF WASHINGTON,
SEATTLE, WA, 98195

HENRY M. MILLER,
ST. MARY'S CITY COMMISSION,
ST. MARY'S CITY, MD, 20686

FRASER D. NEIMAN,
DEPARTMENT OF ANTHROPOLOGY,
YALE UNIVERSITY,
NEW HAVEN, CT, 06520

GARY WHEELER STONE,
ST. MARY'S CITY COMMISSION,
ST. MARY'S CITY, MD, 20686

Appendix: Probate Inventories

The following inventories were selected to provide a sample of the vessel types found in 17th century Chesapeake households. Examples have been taken from various wealth groups in the society including slave or servant quarters (in Slye and Lee inventories), poor and middling planters and extremely wealthly planter-merchants. Vessels and other food–related items have been extracted from the inventories, edited and the spelling modernized. Of particular interest in these examples in the variability in ceramic frequencies and the often minor portion of the total assemblage they comprise. Iron, pewter, tin, leather, and wooden wares are more common than ceramics. This low frequency of ceramic forms is apparently not related to their being overlooked because of low value, since many seemingly inconsequential items, such as remnant of cloth or a "staple for the spring lock," are noted.

The first inventory represents a small planter of limited means. When Francis Lewis died, he left his orphans five barrels of corn and eight cattle.

Inventory of the estate of Francis Lewis (*Westmoreland County, Virginia, Deeds and Wills 1665–1677*: f. 241, 1677):

2 pewter dishes, 3 plates, 2 porringers, 3 spoons
2 iron pots, 1 frying pan
1 candlestick
5 earthen pans, 2 trays, 3 earthen pots, 1 pan

Thomas Thomas was a planter of modest means with an estate valued at 7,140 lbs of tobacco. He owned no servants. He left his heirs 12 cattle and a simple collection of household possessions which included no ceramics.

An Inventory of the Chattles and Goods belonging to the estate of Thomas Thomas (*Maryland Provincial Records, Testamentary Proceedings* 5: f. 126–127, 12 August 1671):

4 iron pots, 1 iron kettle
4 new pewter dishes
Half a dozen of plates

10 pewter porringers
2 old pewter dishes, two old basins, 20 pewter spoons
1 pewter chamber pot
2 old frying pans
9 wooden trays, 2 platters

Robert Cole, a St. Mary's County planter, inventoried his own estate prior to his departure for England in 1662. He left his family with movable goods valued at over 28,887 lbs of tobacco. They included four indentured servants and numerous cattle and hogs. Cole was a successful planter of better than average wealth.

An Inventory of the estate of Robert Cole (*Maryland Provincial Records, Testamentary Proceedings* 6: f. 121–124, 25 April 1662):

5 iron pots, 2 small iron kettles, 2 skillets
1 copper kettle of 18 gallons, 2 frying pans
15 milk trays, 5 cedar tubs for the dairy, 1 cedar cheese tub, 1 oaken milk tub, 1 oaken milk tub
1 great round bowl, 5 pails
2 dozen trenchers, 18 spoons
1 collander of tin, 3 tin drip pans, 1 tin funnel, 5 tin candlesticks
2 wyar candlesticks, 1 pewter bottle, 1 pepper box of tin, 1 pepper grinder
1 straining dish, 1 chafing dish, 1 tin skimmer, 2 wooden platters
2 lifting trays, 1 gridiron, 1 iron ladle
5 pewter platters, 1 pewter basin, 4 pewter porringers, 2 small pewter dishes
5 wooden spoons, 3 wooden ladles
2 pewter pint pots, 1 pewter quart pot, 1 tin quart pot
1 salt box, 2 great butter pots, 5 smaller earthen:
1 earthen frying pan, 1 three legged cream pot of earthen
3 large stone jugs
1 iron bound case with six bottles with pewter screws
1 earthen pitcher, 1 earthen jug, 2 gallons of sweet oil
1 butter tub, 2 cases of quart bottles
5 speckled Dutch pots to drink in, 9 other like pieces but they are butter pots, dishes and porringers
Some gunpowder in a bottle left for use, 2 round glass bottles
10 quarts of rum in bottles
2 tin pudding pans

The inventory of Nathaniel Pope represents the estate of a wealthy Potomac planter with his total value approximately 76,000 lbs of tobacco. Pope owned 15 servants, 40 cattle, 40 swine and extensive lands.

A true and perfect inventory of the personal estate of Mr. Nathaniel Pope (*Westmoreland County, Virginia, Deeds and Wills 1660–1661*: f. 8, 14 May 1660):

3 dozen knives
1 silver bowl and 12 silver spoons
1 dram cup
1 two quart pot and 1 three pint pot
36 dishes and a basin of pewter
12 plates and 9 saucers
3 candlesticks, 12 spoons and 2 quart pots
1 knife and 2 frying pans
6 old chamber pots, 2 salts
4 iron pots, a skillet
3 great kettles and 2 small ones
2 jugs
6 porringers
2 wooden bowles
1 stew pan
1 frying pan
2 trays, a bowl and 1 iron pot

At his death, Captain John Lee was the richest man in Westmoreland County. His estate, appraised at more than 200,000 lbs of tobacco, included 13 indentured servants, 15 slaves, 88 cattle, 32 sheep, and eight horses. Lee was a merchant–planter with a well-stocked store. His servants and slaves grew tobacco on several plantations, tanned hides, and made shoes. He owned few or no ceramic vessels.

An Inventory of the estate of Captain John Lee (*Westmoreland County, Virginia, Deeds, Patents and Accounts 1665–1677*: f. 180, 2 March 1673/4):

In the Hall Chamber
2 frying pans

In the Parlor
Silver Plate valued at 4000 lbs. tobacco

In Capt. Lee's Chamber
6 qts honey
6 qts oil

In the Kitchen
1 frying pan
1 iron pot
115 lbs of pewter
1 gallon flagon
3 old chamber pots
2 close stool pans and 2 porringers
1 chafing dish and a skillet
2 brass kettles
4 brass candlesticks

In the loft over the store
Some empty bottles

In the English Quarter
2 pots

At the New Plantation
2 iron pots
1 frying pan

Robert Slye probably was even wealthier than Lee. (The goods listed in Slye's inventory were not appraised.) A merchant, Slye had extensive contacts in England, the West Indies, and New England. In addition to merchandise and several plantations, Slye owned 11 indentured servants, 14 slaves, 43 horses, 23 sheep, 83 cattle, 124 hogs, and three bee hives. Slye's inventory includes one of the largest and most detailed listings of vessels to survive from the 17th century Chesapeake.

An Inventory of the Goods, Chattles and Debts belonging to the Estate of Mr. Robert Slye of St. Mary's County, Merchant (*Maryland Provincial Records, Testamentary Proceedings 5*: f. 152–190, 19 December 1671):

In the Kitchen
3 great brass kettles
2 smaller kettles
4 iron pots
4 brass skillets
1 stew pan
1 frying pan
1 brass chafing dish
1 iron chafing dish
1 small brass skillet
1 iron kettle
4 pewter dishes
3 pewter basins
12 pewter plates
1 pewter porringer
12 alchemy spoons
3 iron bound pails
4 wooden trays
3 wooden bowls
5 old earthen pans
1 latten pudding pan

In the Dairy
12 great pewter dishes
7 small pewter dishes
2 pewter basins
1 pewter collander
12 pewter plates
9 pewter porringers

9   pewter saucers
2   small pewter salts
1   pewter flagon
1   pewter tankard
1   great pewter basin
2   latten collanders
1   latten watering pot for a garden
2   latten pudding pans
2   latten sauce pans
1   latten fish place
1   latten pie plate
1   latten covering plate
2   great milking pails
3   small milking pails
5   kimmels
13 milk trays
1   butter bowl
2   cheese tubs
1   wooden pail
16 earthen milk pans
4   large earthen dishes
4   small earthen dishes
6   white earthen porringers
8   large gallypots
1   earthen chamber pot
25 earthen butter pots
1   cream pot
5   small earthen jugs
4   small earthen flower pots
11 quart glass bottles
1   latten pepper box
2   earthen pitchers

In the Beer Room
4   empty jars
7   small earthen jugs
1   earthen chamber pot

In the Beer Room Loft
2   iron candlesticks
1   great copper kettle
1   frying pan
8   earthen butter pots
5   earthen honey pots
2   earthen drinking cups

In the Hall
1   iron bound case of bottles
1   pewter salt
1   white earthen salt
1   great earthen basin
1   basin stand
1   white earthen sillabub pot
1   case with 6 knives

In the Hall Chamber
2   pewter chamber pots

In the Parlor
1   silver flagon

1   silver bowl
1   silver caudle cup
1   large silver tumbler
1   silver salt
1   silver porringer
1   silver sack sup
2   silver dram cups
22 silver spoons
1   pewter flagon
1   pewter cup
1   pewter quart pot
1   pewter wine pot
1   latten broad candlestick
2   great stone jugs
2   small stone jugs

In the Parlor Closet
1   small box full of vials with chemical biles
13 small earthen painted dishes
1   earthen chamber pot
4   small earthen jugs
8   gallypots
6   beer glasses
6   wine glasses
2   great glass bottles
4   quart glass bottles
2   horn cups
4   vials with chemical biles
6   earthen pots

In the Parlor Chamber
1   pewter chamber pot

In the New House Hall Chamber
23 earthen butter pots
22 earthen milk pans
1   earthen pitcher

"In the Said Hall remaining of a Cargo received last voyage by the Constant Friendship. Captain Benjamin Cooper, Comander from London"
9   dozen and 4 alchemy spoons
3   latten stew pans
39 latten sauce pans
1   latten pail
17 latten funnels
3   latten collanders
10 latten pudding pans
8   latten pottle pots
9   latten quart pots
4   latten pint pots

In the Store
12 latten saucepans
2   iron bound cases and bottles
1   pewter gallon pot
1   latten pottle pot
1   latten quart pot
1   latten pint pot
1   latten funnel

30   gross of tobacco pipes
431 earthen porringers
10   butter pots
31   milk pans
3   small jugs
4   small painted dishes
3   iron chafing dishes

In the Tobacco House store
6   iron pots
9   stone jugs

In Clanse the Negro's Quarters
1   iron bottle
1   iron pot
1   frying pan

In Dockey the Negro's Quarter
1   old brass kettle
1   brass skillet

In Tony the Negro's Quarter
1   great iron pot
1   brass skillet

At Lapworth Plantation
3   iron pots
1   old brass kettle, 1 frying pan
4   latten pudding pans
1   latten pail
1   latten quart pot
1   latten sauce pan
1   milk pan
2   butter pots
8   alchemy spoons
a iron bound pail

LYNNE SUSSMAN

Changes in Pearlware Dinnerware, 1780–1830

ABSTRACT

Information concerning changes in style and execution of pearlware has been neglected in modern published sources on ceramic history. This paper attempts to put together changes in decoration and manufacturing methods in pearlware dinnerware from 1780–1830. Datable archaeological contexts for Fort Beauséjour, a military site in New Brunswick, Canada, provided the data.

In 1779, Josiah Wedgwood introduced a new earthenware that he called pearl white. It is a tribute to his business acumen that he successfully introduced a product that did not personally appeal to him. His cynical but accurate assessment of the buying public indicated that a change from "creamcolor" was due. In a letter to Thomas Bentley on 6 August 1779 he states:

> . . . You know what Lady Dartmouth told us, that she and her friends were tired of creamcolor, and so would be of Angels if they were shewn for sale in every chandlers shop through the town. The pearl white must be considered as a *change* rather than an *improvement*, and I must have something ready to succeed it when the public eye is palled (Finer and Savage 1965: 237).

Pearlware, as it is now called, was created by the simple expediency of covering a creamware fabric with a blue-tinged glaze. Although Wedgwood and other manufacturers claimed to have used a whiter, harder fabric, comparisons have failed to reveal any differences in either density or color between creamware and the early pearlware fabrics. The effect of the blue-tinged glaze, especially in combination with blue painted decoration, was, however, to give the appearance of a seemingly whiter fabric.

As with most of Wedgwood's inventions and innovations, his new ware was not pat- ented. For this reason, and because its production required no major changes in manufacturing methods, pearlware was being manufactured by many British factories soon after its introduction. Contemporary references to pearlware are remarkably sparse, considering the 50 years' popularity that this ware enjoyed. It seems to have been consistently referred to by the popular types of decoration used on it, such as blue- or green-edged, blue painted and blue printed (Cruickshank 1929: 150). Several manufacturers, notably Spode and Davenport, called it "White ware," thereby causing some confusion for ceramic historians studying 19th century white earthenware (Shaw 1968: 215).

Unfortunately, pearlware is similarly neglected in modern published sources on ceramic history and in museum collections. Most of the information concerning changes in style and execution is derived from archaeological specimens. Since very little pearlware was marked, it is necessary to rely upon datable archaeological contexts. Most of the conclusions outlined in this paper concerning changes in decorative and manufacturing methods are based on the analysis of the large quantities of pearlware retrieved in excavation of Fort Beauséjour, a military site in New Brunswick, Canada (Sussman 1975).

Fort Beauséjour, built by the French in 1751, was captured in 1755 by the English who changed the name to Fort Cumberland and who continued to occupy it until 1768. After a temporary abandonment, it was reoccupied by the British between 1776 and 1793. The fort was again abandoned, then reoccupied from 1812 to 1833 (Nadon 1968). As pearlware was in common use from shortly after 1780 until about 1830, the break in occupation between 1793 and 1812 facilitated the sorting of this ware into 18th and 19th century types. The following observations are primarily a comparison of the characteristics of the early (pre-1793) pearlware and the later pearlware deposited after 1812.

Eighteenth century pearlware, in general, is characterized by a light, cream-white fabric covered with a thin, soft, blue- or blue/green-tinged glaze. The walls of the objects tend to be thinly potted and the edges especially at the foot ring, are sharply defined. The 19th century pearlware is heavier and whiter with a harder, more brilliant glaze that may vary from deeply blue-tinged to almost colorless. The walls are thicker and the edges softer and more rounded. These 19th century traits are more noticeable after about 1810.

Decoration

By far the most common decoration on excavated 18th century pearlware is the molded shell edge pattern with blue or green underglaze painting (Figures 1–4). Shell edge appears as early as 1775 on creamware (Meteyard 1963: 330) and was probably one of the first patterns used to decorate pearlware. It continued to be manufactured in great quantities during the 19th century although the occurrence of green painting diminishes towards the end of the pearlware period.

The molded relief on early shell edge dinnerware is most frequently an intricate ruffle that is presumably intended to represent naturalistic shell rims (Figure 1). Another frequently occurring early version of the shell edge pattern consists of a series of closely spaced im-

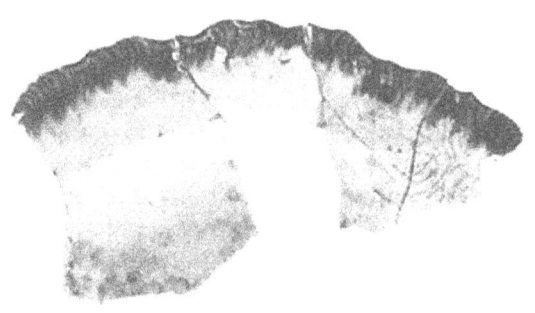

FIGURE 1. Eighteenth century pearlware, shell-edge decoration

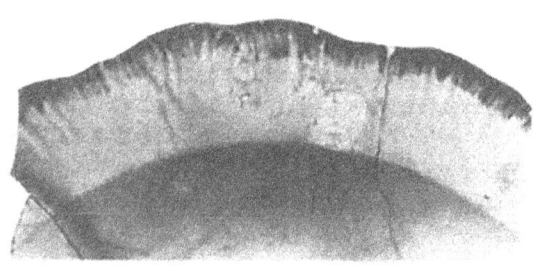

FIGURE 3. Eighteenth century pearlware, shell-edge decoration

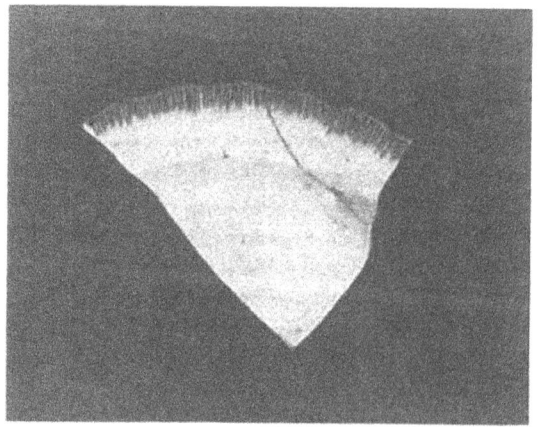

FIGURE 2. Eighteenth century pearlware, shell-edge decoration

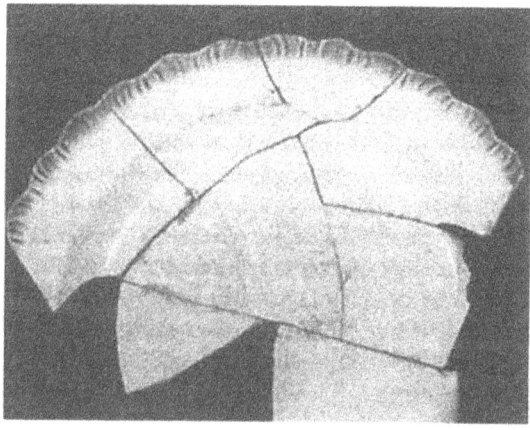

FIGURE 4. Late 18th or early 19th century pearlware, shellware decoration

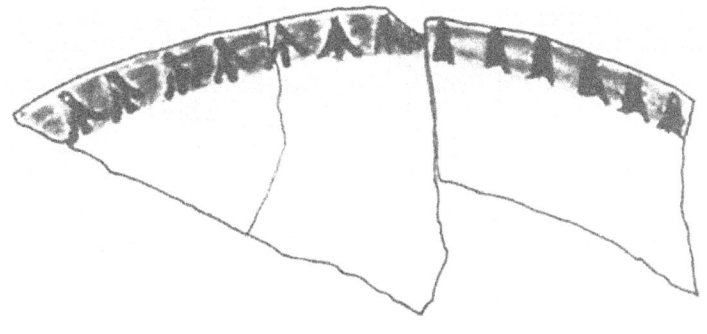

FIGURE 5. Nineteenth century pearlware, shell-edge decoration

pressed vertical lines (Figure 2). The introduction of this simple, highly stylized version undoubtedly post-dates that of the more elaborate shell edge. No examples have as yet been found on creamware. However, its presence on 18th century pearlware contradicts a commonly held belief in the gradual "decadence" or stylization of the shell edge pattern throughout the 19th century. The most elaborate and naturalistic versions of this pattern do eventually disappear in the 19th century, but simple, stylized versions were apparently manufactured at the same time as the intricate versions and at an earlier date than has been heretofore acknowledged.

A group of shell-edge variations that has been found only on 19th century pearlware and white earthenware is the "chicken foot (Figure 5)" regularly spaced clusters of two or three curved lines.

Many variations employing irregularly spaced impressed curved lines and evenly spaced curved lines appear on both 18th and 19th century pearlware (Figures 4 and 6). A

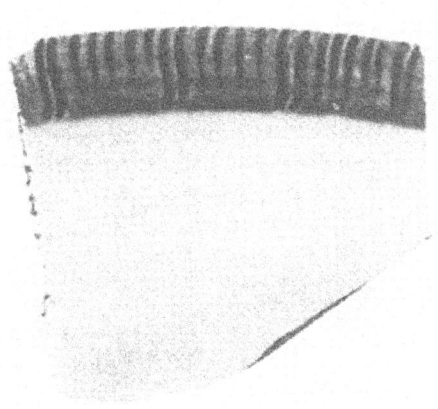

FIGURE 6. Nineteenth century pearlware, shell-edge decoration.

study of edge-decoration motifs is currently being carried out by George Miller of Canadian National Historic Parks and Sites Branch in Ottawa. It is hoped that this study will enable him to trace the development of several ubiquitous motifs such as the 'peacock feather'' or ''bud'' that are associated with these curved line shell edge variations (Figure 3).

The degree of sharpness of the molded relief was not helpful in dating the shell edge dinnerware. Many objects had obviously been made from worn molds, and the molded designs of some are discernible only by touch. Differences in the manner of painting were likewise unhelpful for dating. Simple banding, fine feathery painting, and combinations of both were found on both 18th and 19th century pearlware. Although cobalt was used as the coloring agent throughout the entire pearlware period, the blue on 18th century pearlware is a dark rather grey-toned color with a Munsell reading of 5PB3/6-3/10, whereas the blue or pearlware after about 1820 is a brighter purple-toned color with a Munsell reading of 7.5PB3/8-3/10. The green painted shell edge occurs in various shades ranging from blue-toned to yellow-toned, but the shade differences do not appear to be chronologically significant.

A considerable number of edge-decorated patterns other than shell edge occur in much smaller quantities on dinnerware. The molded relief consists of floral, leaf, scroll, or geometric motifs and the painting, almost always in blue, is applied underglaze in a band along the rim (Figure 7). These patterns have been found only on 19th century pearlware and on white earthenware. The only non-shell edge dinnerware pattern found on excavated examples of early pearlware is a simple pattern of narrow banding in underglaze blue (Figure 8). Banded decoration of this type was popular in brown or red on creamware during the late 18th and early 19th centuries. The same pattern in underglaze brown was found at Fort Beauséjour on a Davenport creamware dinner service dated 1793–1810.

During the 19th century, blue underglaze transfer printing became the favored method for decoratng pearlware. As this subject has been quite thoroughly covered in the published literature, only a few observations based on the material retrieved from Canadian archaeological sites will be mentioned. Although blue underglaze prints had been used as decoration on earthenware since 1780 (Meteyard 1963: 330), very little pearlware has been found on Canadian sites that can definitely be dated to the 18th century. The blue color used for prints, like that used for painting edge-decoraton, changed from a grey-toned blue on pearlware made before about 1820 to a brighter royal blue. No excavated examples were found on pearlware printed in any color other than blue.

The decorative methods and patterns used on pearlware can be divided roughly into two groups, those used for dinner services, that is, a set of plates and matching serving pieces,

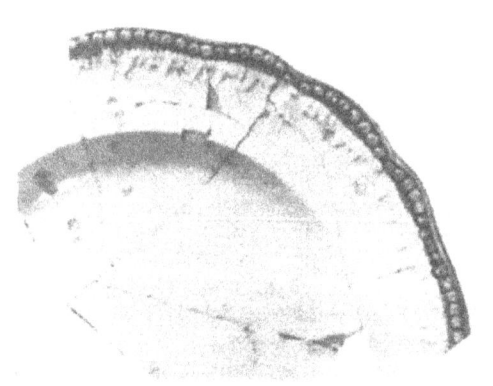

FIGURE 7. Nineteenth century pearlware, edge decoration.

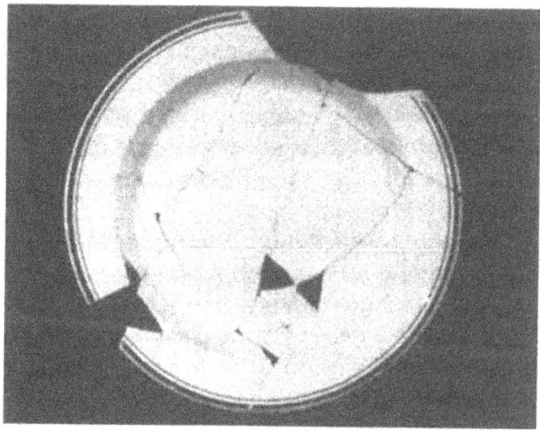

FIGURE 8. Late 18th or early 19th century pearlware, banded decoration.

and those found only on plates. Since one serving piece such as a covered dish costs as much as a dozen plates and a large dinner service could include as many as 20 serving pieces, the acquisition of a dinner service involved considerably more expense than the acquisition of a set of plates. A dinner service including such articles as sauce boats, condiment containers, and salad bowls implies, moreover, a diet and style of dining that requires some expense to maintain. Some indication of the status of a pattern can thus be determined by its occurrence or non-occurrence on elaborate serving pieces. The shell edge pattern on early pearlware is found on a great variety of serving pieces while toward the end of the pearlware period the occurrence of shell edge serving pieces other than platters is quite rare. The other 19th century edge-decorated patterns, even though they are more elaborate than the shell edge, fare no better. They have been found only as decoration on plates. Late pearlware serving pieces are almost always decorated with blue transfer-print. Edge-decoration in general suffered a fall in status during the 19th century probably due to the widespread acceptance of transfer printing.

Differences in size and shape in the following discussion will apply primarily to plates as they are the only dinnerware objects found in great quantity on archaeological sites. Dinnerware serving pieces such as tureens, sauce boats, covered serving dishes, bakers, etc. have been found in too few quantities for us to be able to determine chronological changes in their size and shape.

Size

In general the early pearlware plates are ½ inch smaller in diameter than those made after about 1820. The usual size for creamware and early pearlware dinner plates is 9½ inches, whereas the usual size for later pearlware and white earthenware dinner plates is 10 inches.

Plates

Dinnerware shapes in pearlware initially exhibited many of the same features as those of its predecessor, creamware. The following traits are characteristic of 18th and early 19th century pearlware. Brims are totally flat or flat with an upturned rim (Figures 9–11). They are narrow by modern standards (not over 1¼ inches wide on dinner plates) with a sharply defined brink or brim edge (cf. Figures 9 and 14). Bases are flat, countersunk, or are given a very small round foot ring (Figures 9–11).

Nineteenth century pearlware shapes, especially after 1810, exhibited many of the same traits as were found on white earthenware. The following traits have been found only on 19th century pearlware. Brims are highly concave or S-shaped with rounded brinks (Figures 13–14). Foot rings are (in cross section) truncated wedges or double low ridges (Figures 12, 15–16). Traits characteristic of the 18th century ware did not suddenly disappear in the 19th century; often 19th century pearlware objects were a mixture of old

FIGURE 9 Pearlware plates with 18th century traits.

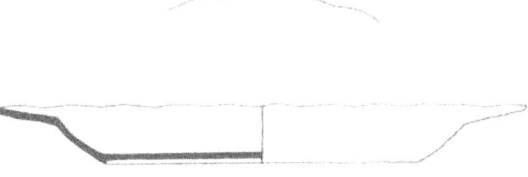

FIGURE 10 Pearlware plates with 18th century traits.

FIGURE 11. Pearlware plates with 18th century traits.

FIGURE 12. Pearlware plates with 19th century traits.

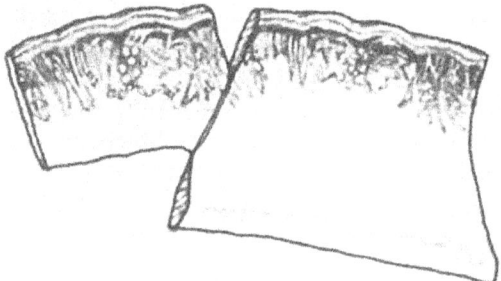

FIGURE 13. Pearlware plates with 19th century traits.

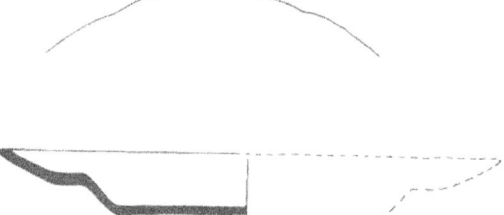

FIGURE 14. Pearlware plates with 19th century traits.

FIGURE 15. Pearlware plates with 19th century traits.

FIGURE 16. Pearlware plates with 19th century traits.

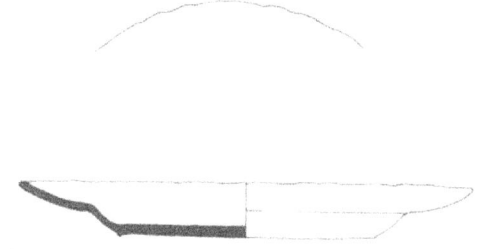

FIGURE 17. Pearlware plates with 19th century traits.

and new traits (Figures 14, 16–17). For this reason, 19th century pearlware seems more varied in shape than 18th century pearlware and creamware.

During the 18th century, plates were trimmed with a hand-held knife after being jiggered. This procedure made it possible to carve the rim in the irregular fashion associated with the ruffled shell-edge pattern. The rim treatment most frequently found on pearlware plates is a series of regular scallops. Even on the scalloped rims hand-trimming can be identified. The upper edge of the rim tends to be sharply defined while the carved lower edge will be rounded or bevelled. The trimming is often on several planes, a phenomenon that occurs when the cutting angle alters and is only possible using hand-held tools.

During the 19th century, the hand-trimming step was eliminated by improving the jiggering process so that forming and trimming were performed simultaneously. The mechanical trimming can be recognized by the sharper edge along the bottom of the rim and the rounded molded edge along the top. A raised line resembling a mold line can sometimes be seen along the edge of the rim. All mechanical trimming is, of course, on a single plane. The differences between mechanical and hand-trimming techniques apply only to circular objects. Non-circular objects such as platters and serving dishes were press-molded, then hand-trimmed.

Plain rims were used throughout the entire pearlware period, but because they were the preferred rim type on transfer-pearlware, they are more common in the 19th century. Rims with indentations at alternately short and long intervals (Figures 7 and 17) have been found only on 19th century pearlware after about 1810. This type of rim was later very popular on transfer-printed white earthenware.

No ware type changed so drastically in the course of its production as did pearlware. During the 50 years that this ware was manufactured, almost every trait underwent change including fabric, glaze, decorative method, decorative color, shape and size. It is one of the very few ceramics to form a link between two distinct ware types. At the time of its introduction it was identical to creamware in all traits except glaze color. By the time the blue-tinged glaze was abandoned, pearlware was indistinguishable from white earthenware. Pearlware is thus a unique phenomenon, a formally introduced and marketed ceramic that quickly sank into anonymity and yet one that succeeded in permanently changing the accepted standards of appearance for 19th and 20th century tableware.

REFERENCES

ANONYMOUS

1783   Price List Agreement for British Manufacturers of "Queen's Earthenware." Newcastle, England.

1833   Price List Agreement for Staffordshire Potteries. W. Rowley, Hanley, England.

CRUIKSHANK, E. A.

1929   A Country Merchant in Upper Canada, 1800–1812. *Ontario Historical Society Papers and Records* 35: 150.

FINER, ANN AND GEORGE SAVAGE (EDITORS)

1965   *The Selected Letters of Josiah Wedgwood.* Cory, Adams and Mckay, London.

METEYARD, ELIZA

1963   *The Wedgwood Handbook.* Timothy Trace, Peckskill, (Reprint of 1875 edition).

NADON, PIERRE

1968   Fort Beauséjour (1755–1833), a Technical Study. Manuscript on file, National Historic Parks and Sites Branch, Parks Canada, Ottawa.

SHAW, SIMEON

1968   *History of the Staffordshire Potteries.* Beatrice C. Weinstock, Great Neck. (Reprint of 1829 edition).

SUSSMAN, LYNNE

1975   Pearlware from Fort Beauséjour, N.B. Manuscript on file, National Historic Parks and Sites Branch, Ottawa.

LYNNE SUSSMAN
PARKS CANADA
OTTAWA, ONTARIO
CANADA K1A OH4

LYNNE SUSSMAN

British Military Tableware, 1760-1830

ABSTRACT

The fine stoneware and earthenware table articles found on British-Canadian military sites were, for the most part, associated with the officers' mess. Although each regimental mess acquired its furnishings independently, the conformity of military taste and custom and the exigencies of supply to garrisons far from manufacturing or retail sources has resulted in a certain homogeneity in the tableware used by the military at any one time.

It has been possible, using the large samples from Fort Beauséjour, New Brunswick, as well as evidence from other military sites, to select tea and dinner services that were used for regimental messes during the period 1760-1830. Since the replacement of one service by another naturally did not occur at a specified time shared by all regiments, a series of four dates, 20 years apart (1760, 1780, 1800, and 1820) have been selected as milestones. Seventeen different patterns are described and illustrated.

Only one example of identifiable military ceramics has been retrieved from excavations of military sites in Canada—a dinner service inscribed with the insignia of the 13th Regiment of Foot (Figure 1). The thousands of other ceramic objects found at these sites are indistinguishable in ware type, function, or decoration from those found in civilian settlements. This is not surprising when it is realized how these ceramics were manufactured and marketed and for what purposes they were made. Almost all the ceramics found on British military sites in Canada were made in the 18th and 19th centuries. During this period most British ceramics were manufactured by mass production. Unless a special order was requested of the factory, as was the case in the single example of inscribed military dinnerware, the merchandise produced in large quantities by the factories was the ceramics most readily available to all buyers. British ceramics, because of widespread marketing, were available at a relatively reasonable price to a wide range of Canadian buyers. Finally, it must be remembered that most ceramic objects were, and still are, made for use in eating, drinking, and elimination, universal activities that occur on any occupied site regardless of its function.

Because the individual ceramic objects from military sites did not differ greatly from those found at other types of sites, it was initially assumed that there were no identifiable differences. However, when a highly organized institution such as the British army is faced with the problem of supplying and maintaining thousands of men, it will, in the interest of efficiency, try to acquire large quantities of material from relatively few sources. The objects it supplies can be expected to exhibit a lesser degree of variability than the same types of objects bought individually. Larger numbers of identical or similar-appearing ceramic objects can, therefore, be expected to

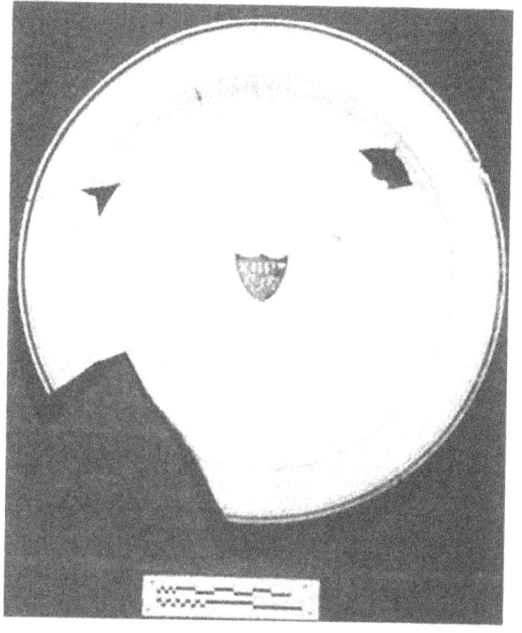

FIGURE 1 Creamware plate with brownish-red banded decoration and transfer-printed insignia (overglaze) of the 13th regiment of foot

occur in military contexts than on civilian settlements.

The analysis of the ceramics from Fort Beauséjour, a large military site in New Brunswick, confirmed beyond expectation the phenomenon of low variability (Sussman 1974, 1975). Extremely large numbers of tableware objects bore identical or very similar versions of the same patterns; e.g., the Blue Willow, royal rim, and blue shell-edge patterns are each represented by over 100 objects. On the basis of sheer quantity, it was evident that these objects were part of institutional rather than personal table services.

It was first assumed that the army supplied this tableware to the enlisted men; however, the dinnerware found was all of comparable status and cost. Moreover, during certain periods of the occupation of the site, only one pattern was found. This would mean either that the enlisted men were supplied with the same type of dinner services as those used by the officers, or that one of the two groups did not use ceramic dinnerware. Furthermore, acquaintance with British military procedure and custom revealed the unlikelihood of the rank-and-file soldier being supplied such eating and drinking utensils. By all accounts, the enlisted British soldier enjoyed a standard of living incomprehensible to us in its lack of comforts (Carol Whitfield 1977, pers. comm.). Between 1800 and 1860, the daily rations consisted of brown bread and coffee or tea for breakfast, and bread and soup (made of boiled beef and potatoes or other vegetables) for dinner (Public Archives of Canada, MG29F46, T. Wiley Papers, 1828, p. 181). The wage of an enlisted soldier from 1797 to 1891 was about one shilling per day (De Watteville 1954: 82), over half of which was deducted towards "Messing and Washing" (Public Archives of Canada, RG8, Vol. 34 General Order 422, 1824, p. 74). It seemed highly improbable that men provided with the barest essentials in food and wages would have been supplied with the nicety of china tableware.

Documentary evidence of what actually was supplied (or should have been supplied) to the men was found in the Barrack Regulations for 1794. The regulations list the following equipment to be supplied to the barracks:

For every 12 men
  1 water bucket
  1 candle stick
  1 tin can for beer
  1 large earthen pan for meat
  2 drinking horns
  1 wooden urinal [this was a wooden bucket used both
    as a urinal and wash basin]
  1 broom
  2 iron pots
  2 wooden lids
  2 iron pot hooks
  2 iron trivets
  2 wooden ladles
  1 iron flesh fork
  1 frying pan
  2 large bowls or platters
  2 small bowls or porringers
  12 trenchers [flat wooden plates, usually in the shape of
    a square with a round depression]
  12 spoons (England, Public Record Office, WO47/2366,
    Barracks Regulations, 1795, p. 1045).

Examples of the earthen pans for meat and the large bowls or platters have been retrieved from excavations at Fort Beauséjour. They are coarse earthenware vessels, characteristically of red fabric with black lead glaze on the interior surface (Schurman 1977). British ceramic porringers or small bowls have not been found, and presumably these vessels were made of tin or other non-ceramic material. In addition to their barracks utensils, the men would have been supplied with field kits which included a tin plate and tin cup (Public Archives of Canada, Picture Division, Powell Scrap Book, Vol. 1, 1863, p. 73).

Prior to 1794, the British army did not always supply the actual eating and drinking utensils, at least not to regiments posted in North America. An allowance was made for each man, and this money was presumably used collectively to purchase utensils in quantity at large centers such as Boston or Halifax. A ledger, datable to sometime between 1763 and 1768, quotes an allowance as "9-½d (pence) . . . for Bowls, Platters and

Spoons." (University of Michigan). It is possible that these bowls and platters were coarse earthenware, but considering their absence in archaeological contexts, it is more likely that they were made of wood or metal. British army policy was evidently to supply enlisted men with cheap, probably unbreakable, eating and drinking utensils.

The fine earthenware and stoneware table articles found in abundance at Fort Beauséjour and other military sites must therefore have been used by the officers. Military policy regarding officers, however, was to supply nothing in the way of cooking or eating utensils. The ledger, quoted previously, identifies the furniture supplied for officers' rooms, but no mention is made of utensils or an allowance for utensils. An officer in the British army was expected to maintain himself, in a style appropriate to an officer and gentleman, at his own expense. Although a rigid social hierarchy ensured the relationship between "officer" and "gentleman," military financial policy ensured that only a man of means could comfortably afford to be an officer. The cost of his commission alone ranged officially from £ 400 for ensign to £ 6,700 for lieutenant-colonel, and unofficially, considerably more (Dupin 1822:89).

The officer's mess somewhat alleviated the financial strain of this situation. Each officer was charged dues, graduated according to rank, for maintenance of the regimental mess. Most mess furnishings, including the tableware, were purchased collectively by the officers. It was customary for the colonel to set the tone for the regiment and although the wishes and financial states of the other officers were taken into consideration, the colonel's choice of mess furnishings was generally accepted.

It was common military procedure for the colonel to commission an agent in London to supply his regiment (Carol Whitfield 1977, pers. comm.) It is not known whether these agents were given precise descriptions and specifications or whether they exercised their own discretion in their choice of ceramic tableware. The excavated examples of military ceramics indicate the predominant choice of very popular patterns for regimental tableware. The tableware could thus be ordered using a brief, easily recognized description, or even its commercial name. Documentary evidence as to how and where the regimental agent purchased the ordered tableware has not been found. During the late 18th and early 19th centuries in England, there were two principal means of purchasing ceramics in large quantities.

It was possible to order large quantities of ceramics directly from the factory, and there is archaeological and documentary evidence that the military did this in a number of cases. A creamware dinner service found at Fort Lennox, Québec, bears the transfer printed insignia of the 13th Regiment of Foot (Figure 1). This service would have been specially commissioned by the officers of the regiment. It is, however, the only example of inscribed military ceramics found on Canadian sites and the only unquestionable example of tableware ordered directly from the manufacturer. Elizabeth Collard describes a set of tableware ordered from Wedgwood in 1791 by the 7th Regiment of Fusiliers (Collard 1967: 106); however, the Royal Fusiliers were commanded by H. R. H. Prince Edward, later father of Queen Victoria, and his regiment probably maintained a higher standard of luxury than was expected in ordinary regiments of the line.

Although there are probably many more instances of regiments ordering their tableware from factories, in general the type of tableware found at Canadian military sites suggests the second method of acquisition—the London wholesale warehouse. During the late 18th and early 19th centuries, these warehouses sold huge quantities of ceramics from numerous factories even when the warehouses were owned and operated by one particular factory (Whiter 1970: 15-16). A mess table service purchased at a warehouse would likely be made up of the wares from several factories; the military favored popular patterns such as Blue Willow which were produced by most English manufacturers. Most of the regimental services represented by archaeological specimens from Canadian sites are made up of similar but not identical pieces. The differences in molded decoration, printed decoration, and shape are such as could only result from different manufacturing equipment, namely molds and engraved copper plates. Master molds and engraved copper plates were expensive to produce as they required skilled labor. Except in the case of shell-edge wares, it was not usual for a factory to have, at any given time, several versions of the same shape or pattern. The similar pieces, threfore, represent for the most part merchandise produced by different factories, and the table services made up of these pieces conform in this respect to the type of services available at wholesale warehouses. In selling the common popular types of merchandise, the warehouses were, of course, concerned more with selling quantity than quality. Much of their merchandise consisted of "seconds," usable but imperfect objects that were bought and sold at lower prices than the selected "first" line of production (Griffiths 1979). A large proportion of the regimental ceramics retrieved in excavation has smeared transfer prints and painted decoration, pinholes, indistinct molded relief resulting from the use of worn molds, and other unobtrusive flaws characteristic of "seconds." The regimental ceramics conform in this respect also with the type of merchandise available from wholesale warehouses.

The merchandise offered for sale by the factories and the wholesale warehouses changed in ware type and decoration as fashion changed and as technological innovations were introduced. These changes are naturally reflected in the various mess services used by the regiments. It is impossible to set precise dates for the changes from one type of regimental tableware to another, as each of the 124 regiments purchased replacement table services independently and at different times according to need. In order to describe the various regimental table services that have been identified without over emphasizing their possible date ranges, a series of four dates 20 years apart (1760, 1780, 1800, and 1820) have been selected as milestones. The ceramics described and illustrated for each date have been recovered for the most part from Fort Beauséjour.

Fort Beauséjour was constructed by the French in 1751 and captured by the British in 1755. The British, who renamed it Fort Cumberland, occupied the site with two brief abandonments until 1833. All of the tableware described below occurred in institutional services on other British military sites as well as Fort Beauséjour. All information concerning commonness of patterns is based, however, on the sample from Fort Beauséjour, since the ceramics from the other military sites have not yet been examined in detail.

1760

In 1760 the ware type most commonly in use for regimental tableware was salt-glazed stoneware. The pattern found most frequently on regimental dinner services is the basket pattern and its variations (Gusset 1971) (Figures 2 and 3). The barley-grain (Figure 4) and the gadrooned-edge (Figure 5) are two patterns that have also been identified as institutional although they occur less frequently than the basket pattern. The decorative method used for these three patterns is molded relief. Regimental teaware of salt-glazed stoneware was usually plain in appearance. The only decorated institutional pattern found in white salt-glazed stoneware is a scratch-blue floral pattern and its variations (Figure 6). One institutional dinner service made of cream colored earthenware and dated to 1760-1770 was found at Fort Beauséjour (Dorothy Griffiths 1977, pers. comm.). It is decorated with the molded feather-edge pattern (Figure 7), later very popular on creamware.

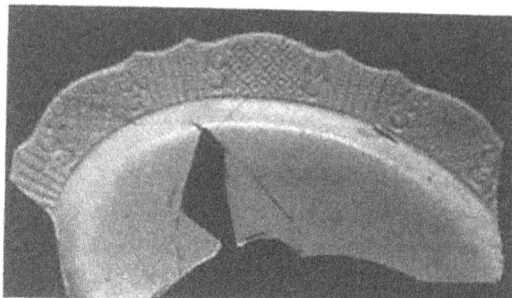

FIGURE 2. Salt-glaze stoneware platter with molded relief decoration using basketry motifs.

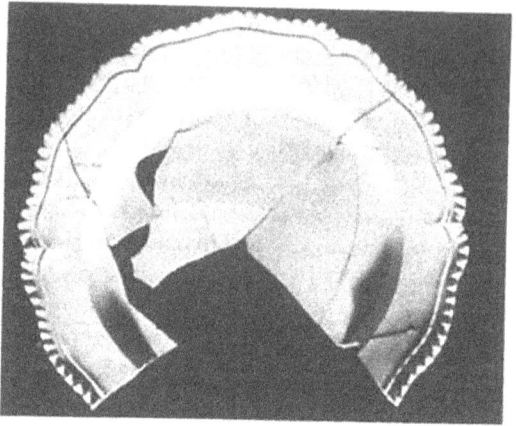

FIGURE 5. Salt-glaze stoneware plate with molded relief "gadrooned" edge

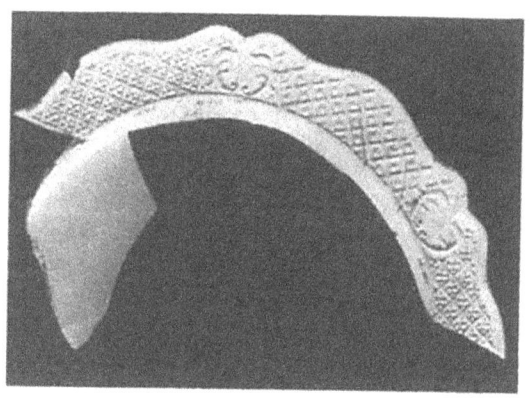

FIGURE 3 Salt-glaze stoneware platter with molded relief decoration using basketry motifs

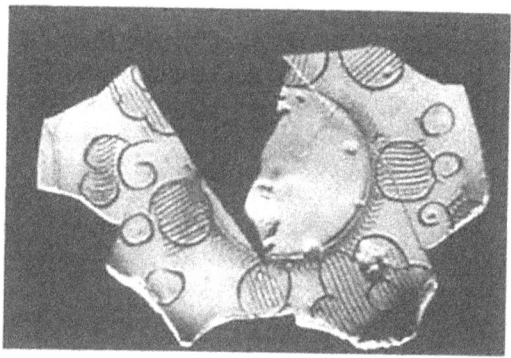

FIGURE 6. Salt-glaze stoneware saucer with scratch-blue decoration using floral motifs.

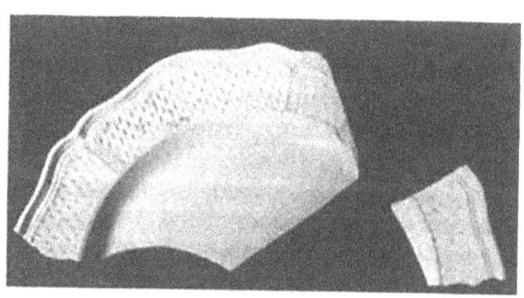

FIGURE 4 Salt-glaze stoneware plate with molded relief decoration using the barley motif.

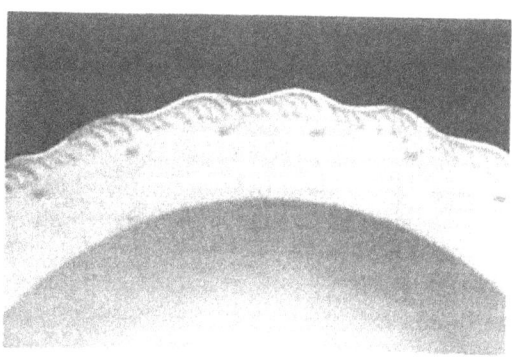

FIGURE 7 Cream-colored earthenware plate with molded relief feather-edge decoration

1780

By 1780, creamware, introduced by Josiah Wedgwood 20 years previously, had replaced salt-glazed stoneware as the most common ware for regimental table services. Indeed, between 1770 and 1780 nothing but creamware was available in large quantity from the manufacturers. The most frequently occurring regimental patterns at this date were Royal Rim (Figure 8) and plain, the latter being produced with either a flat or concave brim (Dorothy Griffiths 1977, pers. comm.). The feather-edge was also an institutional pattern, but it was most popular on creamware between 1760 and 1770. Regimental teaware made of creamware, like that made of salt-glazed stoneware, was usually undecorated.

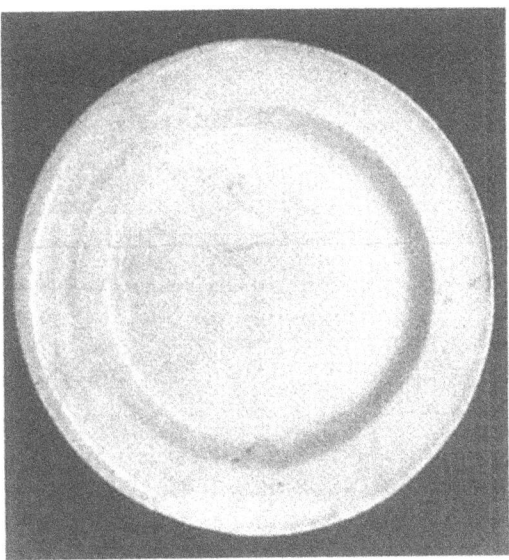

FIGURE 9. Creamware plate, plain.

1800

By 1800, pearlware, introduced by Wedgwood in 1780, had become as popular as, if not more popular than, creamware for regimental services. By far the most frequently occurring dinnerware pattern on pearlware is the molded shell-edge pattern with blue or green underglaze painting at the rim (Sussman 1975). Only one other institutional dinnerware pattern has been identified in the pearlware from Fort Beauséjour. Its decoration consists of simple

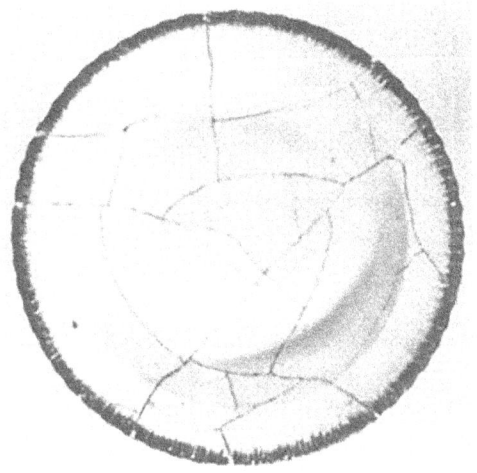

FIGURE 10. Pearlware plate in shell-edge pattern.

narrow banding painted underglaze in blue (Figure 11).

Only one pearlware pattern or group of patterns can be associated definitely with regimental teaware. This pattern is made up of variations of several similar appearing chinoiserie patterns painted underglaze in blue (Figures 12 and 13). Several patterns painted

FIGURE 8. Creamware plate in royal rim pattern

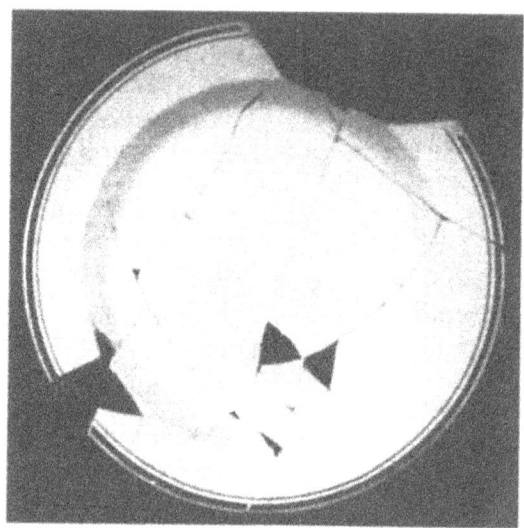

FIGURE 11. Pearlware plate with blue underglaze banded decoration.

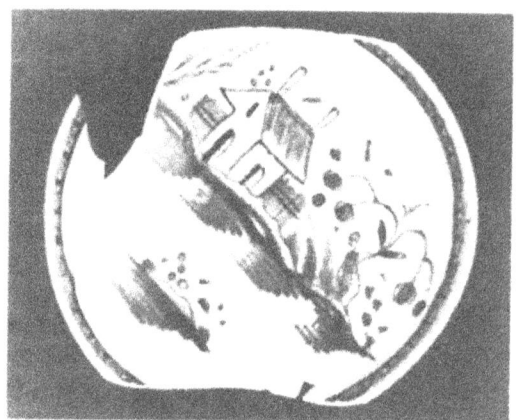

FIGURE 12. Pearlware saucer with blue underglaze painted decoration; version of the chinoiserie "house" pattern.

edge dinnerware is obviously an unexceptional combination. The polychrome-painted patterns that are possibly institutional all include rather large areas of blue, and they too might have been combined with the blue shell-edge pieces. The green shell-edge dinnerware, however, was either combined with other, as yet unidentified patterns, or the colors blue and green were considered complimentary in tableware of this date.

On creamware of this date (1800), the most frequently occurring regimental dinnerware patterns are, as they were in 1780, Royal Rim and plain. The other institutional dinnerware patterns on creamware are the same as those described above on pearlware—blue or green shell-edge and narrow banding. However, the banding on creamware is brown or brownish-red, painted either overglaze or underglaze, whereas on pearlware the banding is underglaze blue. Creamware regimental tea services are, as they were in 1780, undecorated.

1820

In 1820, creamware, pearlware, and white earthenware, the three major ware types of

in polychrome "underglaze" colors were represented by 10 or more objects, but this is not quite a large enough number to eliminate the possibility of ownership by individual officers. Since teaware and dinnerware would have been used together at breakfast, and possibly at other meals, the appearance of the combined patterns would be expected to produce a pleasing or at least acceptable effect. Blue-painted chinoiserie teaware with blue shell-

FIGURE 13. Pearlware saucer with blue underglaze painted decoration; version of the chinoiserie "house" pattern.

the late 18th and 19th centuries, are all used for mess tableware. Creamware is the least frequently occurring ware type, and it is noticeably paler in color than the creamware made in the 18th century. At Fort Beauséjour, only dinnerware services were found in creamware of this period. The dinnerware patterns are the same Royal Rim, narrow banding, and plain patterns introduced in the 18th century.

For pearlware and white earthenware, at this date, the ware type is less important than the decoration. Blue and green shell-edge dinnerware is found in both pearlware and white earthenware although the percentage of green-edge decoration has diminished since 1800. The most common regimental pattern found at Fort Beauséjour from this period is the famous transfer printed Blue Willow pattern (Figure 13). This pattern also occurs on both pearlware and white earthenware. The most frequently occurring pattern on teaware is the Broseley, a chinoiserie pattern designed in 1782 as the teaware equivalent to the dinnerware pattern, Blue Willow (Figure 14) (Sussman 1974). The most popular transfer printed pattern is also widely known under the name Temple. Several blue-and-polychrome-painted patterns found at Fort Beauséjour may also be institutional, but they occur on

too few objects to eliminate the possibility of private ownership (Figures 15 and 16).

After about 1740, with the development of mass production in ceramics, the accepted mode in Britain of table setting became the matching service. The dinner service consisted of a set of matching plates and serving pieces. A large dinner service included as many as 20 serving pieces: covered dishes, open dishes, platters in several sizes, salad bowls, condiment containers, sauce tureens, sauceboats, soup tureens, and salts. The typical tea service, in a different but complimentary pattern, included matching cups or tea

FIGURE 15. White earthenware saucer in the Broseley pattern.

FIGURE 14. White earthenware plate in the Willow pattern.

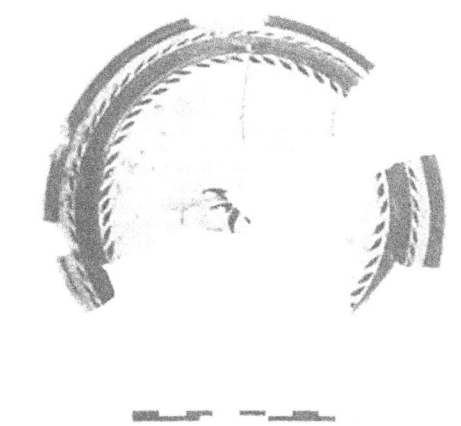

FIGURE 16. Pearlware saucer with underglaze polychrome painted decoration. This pattern may have been used in a mess tea service during the 1780—1800 period.

bowls and saucers, teapot, cream pitcher, sugar container, and slop bowl. All of these dinnerware and teaware articles have been found in association with regimental services. It is evident by the specialized functions and the diversity of the serving pieces alone that the officers maintained rather elaborate and formal dining tables. That this custom took place in primitive isolated posts and during times of frequent troop movement indicates the importance to the officers of maintaining their customary civilized lifestyle regardless of the inconvenience and expense of transporting large quantities of fragile tableware.

On the other hand, the ceramics chosen by the officers for their regimental services falls consistently into a "middle" class when compared with the range of ceramics available at that time and the objects bought by the officers as personal possessions. All the regimental tableware found is made of fine earthenware or fine stoneware, ceramic groups that are much more expensive than

FIGURE 17. Pearlware cup with blue painted decoration. This pattern may have been used in a mess tea service during the 1800—1820 period.

coarse earthenware but much less expensive than porcelain or bone china. Even the previously mentioned service ordered by the Royal Fusiliers, H. R. H. Prince Edward's regiment, was made of creamware (Collard 1967:106). The methods of decoration employed on the military tableware are generally either the least expensive, that is, plain, or are methods that lend themselves to mass production and require little skilled labor, e.g., molded relief, banding, and 19th century transfer printing. Even the blue-painted chinoiserie on pearlware tea services is characteristically crudely executed in comparison with the enamel painting and underglaze polychrome-painting found on privately owned teaware. In addition, the decoration is found in patterns manufactured in such large quantities that the pattern itself is less expensive than others produced in the same manner (Anonymous 1814). It has already been mentioned that the regimental services include many pieces that are unobtrusively flawed and would be purchased at lower prices than selected perfect objects.

This does not mean that cheap, crude tableware, as long as it matched, was considered good enough for the officers' mess. Fine stoneware and fine earthenware were not cheap, and they certainly were not crude. It is evident, however, that the most expensive wares, i.e., porcelain and bone china, and the most expensive decorative methods—enamel painting, gilding, and bat-printing—were not chosen for regimental tableware used in Fort Beauséjour.

There may be several reasons for the types of ceramics being used for regimental services. In the main, these reasons relate to the problems of supplying regiments far from manufacturing sources, rather than the table-setting standards of the officers. The ceramics required for regimental services would be ordered in large quantities, and only wares and patterns that were produced in large quantity could be bought without difficulty. Moreover, troop movements would result in a high

FIGURE 18. Whiteware saucer with polychrome painted decoration in chrome-based colors. These patterns may have been used in mess tea services after 1820.

1975; Gusset 1971; Dorothy Griffiths 1977, pers. comm.). Tea and coffee articles constitute the major portion of the personal tableware with slightly smaller quantities of beverageware (tankards, punch bowls, and pitchers) and a very small quantity of dinnerware making up the remaining portion. Although these objects represent a wide range of wares and decoration, in general they would have been more expensive than the institutional tableware and some of them, such as the enamelled and gilded porcelain, would have been very costly indeed.

Considering that each regiment chose its tableware independently, the military ceramics retrieved in excavation is surprisingly homogeneous in both quality and, within given time periods, in appearance. The reasons for this homogeneity are again probably related to the problems of supplying large amounts of breakable tableware to far-flung regiments. Only a relatively small number of patterns and wares were produced in the quantities suitable for their use in regimental services. The institutional ceramics described and illustrated on the previous pages are, without exception, among the most profusely

rate of breakage, and replacements could more easily be found for a table service of common pattern and ware. If the ceramics were ordered through an agent in London, it would be easier to specify commonly recognized terms such as Queensware, Blue Edge, or Blue Willow, than to describe the decorative motifs of little known patterns. Two further advantages of a common pattern are its resistance to rapid changes in fashion and the unlikelihood of it offending the officers' taste. Not surprisingly, the most popular wares and patterns, produced in the greatest quantity, were not the most expensive. For this reason, a regimental service chosen for ease of supply and replacement would probably be made of a less expensive material or would be decorated in a less expensive fashion than tableware purchased by the officers as personal possessions.

About a quarter of the ceramics retrieved from Fort Beauséjour belonged personally to the officers stationed there (Sussman 1974,

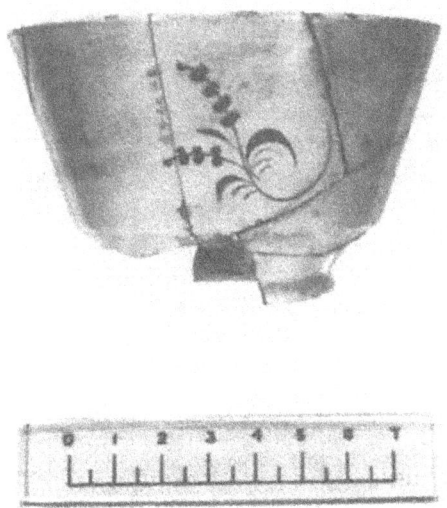

FIGURE 19. Whiteware cup with polychrome painted decoration in chrome-based colors. These patterns may have been used in mess tea services after 1820.

manufactured ceramics of their period. If the officers of a regiment decided to choose a practical set of mess dishes that were easily acquired and easily replaced, they would likely choose one of these common ceramic types. Given the small selection of ceramic types and the large number of British regiments, choices would probably be duplicated by several regiments. Each pattern illustrated in this article was found on at least two, and in some cases on as many as 10, separate regimental table services in Parks Canada archaeological collections.

Fort Beauséjour was a relatively unimportant post, occupied by detachments from ordinary regiments of the line. Prestigious regiments, such as the cavalry or the royal regiments, were never stationed there nor was it used as a regimental headquarters. Because of this, it is dangerous to generalize on military custom using only the military ceramics found at Fort Beauséjour. It is not known if the ceramic types found at Fort Beauséjour represent the kinds of tableware used by more prestigious regiments. It is not known whether the officers' tableware was part of larger services from headquarters messes in Halifax or whether the officers were provided with less costly or out-of-date alternatives. Nor is it known if the lifestyle of officers at Fort Beauséjour was the same as that enjoyed by officers of the same rank and regiment at different postings.

Neither is it suggested that the military ceramic types found at Fort Beauséjour are unique to that site. All of the ceramic types described in this article have been found at other military sites in Canada. The ceramics from these sites, however, have not yet been analyzed beyond ware identification and dating. Only the most obvious examples of institutional tableware have been identified. When the ceramics used by several different types of regiments in a variety of situations have been identified, it will be possible to pursue lines of research on military behaviour and custom. If there are no discernible differences in the ceramics used by regiments of different function and status, and under different conditions, military homogeneity would be an interesting phenomenon to examine. If noticeable differences are found, the reasons for this heterogeneity should be explored.

Fortunately, there is no dearth of excavated military sites in Canada. Several sites such as the Fortress of Louisbourg, Halifax Citadel, Fort George, Fort Lennox, and Fort Chambly were occupied by a variety of regiments including cavalry and royal regiments (Stewart 1962). They also served as headquarters for a number of regiments (Stewart 1962). Others, such as the fort at Coteau-du-Lac and Fort Wellington were less important but were close to civilian settlement. Posts such as Fort Gaspareaux, Fort St. Joseph, and Castle Hill were similar to Fort Beauséjour in their function and isolation. Considering that so many military sites have been excavated and that the research programs and the staff to interpret these sites are already in existence, there should be little problem in accumulating enough data for several interpretive and thematic studies on military material culture, and on military behaviour and custom.

REFERENCES

ANONYMOUS.
1814 Staffordshire Potteries. Prices Current of Earthenware, Tregortha, Burslem, Staffordshire.

COLLARD, ELIZABETH
1967 Nineteenth Century Pottery and Porcelain in Canada. McGill University Press, Montreal.

DE WATTEVILLE, H
1954 The British Soldier: His Daily Life from Tudor to Modern Times. J. M. Dent & Sons, London.

DUPIN, CHARLES
1822 View of the History and Actual State of the Military Force of Great Britain by Charles Dupin . . . Translated with Notes by An Officer. . . J. Murray, London. Vol. 1.

ENGLAND. PUBLIC RECORD OFFICE.
1795 Barracks Regulations. W047/2366.

GRIFFITHS, DOROTHY
1979 "Wedgwood—Marked Ceramics and Canadian National Historic Sites." *Canadian Collector* 14(2).

GUSSET, GERARD
1971 *Inventaire des grès blancs fins à glacure saline.* Manuscript Report Series No. 43. Parks Canada, Ottawa.

PUBLIC ARCHIVES OF CANADA.
MANUSCRIPT DIVISION.

1824 MG29, F46, Lieutenant Colonel T. Wiley Papers.
1828 R68, Vol. 34, General Order No. 422, Horse Guards, 24th December, 1824.

PUBLIC ARCHIVES OF CANADA.
PICTURE DIVISION.
1863 C-11482, Powell Scrap Book, Vol. 1, Field Kit.

SCHURMAN, MICHAEL
1977 "Coarse Earthenware from Fort Beauséjour". Typescript on file National Historic Parks and Sites Branch, Parks Canada, Ottawa.

STEWART, C. H.
1962 "The Service of British Regiments in Canada and North America," Manuscript on file. Department of National Defense, Ottawa.

SUSSMAN, LYNNE
1974 "Transfer-printed Ceramics from Fort Beauséjour (Cumberland)." Typescript on file, National Historic Parks and Sites Branch, Parks Canada, Ottawa.

SUSSMAN, LYNNE
1975 "Pearlware from Fort Beauséjour (Cumberland)." Typescript on file, National Historic Parks and Sites Branch, Parks Canada, Ottawa.

UNIVERSITY OF MICHIGAN.
1763 Letter Books of General Thomas Gage. William L. Clement Library. Ledger datable to some time between 1763 and 1768.

WHITER, LEONARD
1970 *Spode: A History of the Family, Factory and Wares from 1733 to 1833.* Barrie & Jenkins, London.

LYNNE SUSSMAN
PARKS CANADA
1600 LIVERPOOL COURT
OTTAWA, ONTARIO K1A 0H4

PATRICIA M. SAMFORD

Response to a Market: Dating English Underglaze Transfer-Printed Wares

ABSTRACT

At the end of the 18th century, the Staffordshire pottery industry began transfer printing designs on refined earthenwares. Gaining immediate acceptance from both the British and American markets, printed earthenwares remained immensely popular until the mid-19th century. Hundreds of printed patterns were produced, and these patterns formed distinctive decorative styles based on central motifs and borders. Using characteristics of datable, marked vessels as a database, this study establishes a chronology for dating printed earthenwares based on decorative styles and color.

Introduction

Ceramics are one of the primary dating tools used by archaeologists working on 18th- and 19th-century North American sites. Over the last several decades, research combining primary documents, such as potters' invoices, trade catalogs, and store accounts, with archaeological data has created a greater understanding of the variety of ceramics available to American consumers during these periods. Information on characteristics such as body composition, glaze type, and decorative attributes is often available in potters' records, allowing accurate date ranges to be assigned. Often, identifying and dating ceramics using evidence from documents is critical, since the majority of individual ceramic vessels were not marked by their manufacturers. While greater effort has gone into developing dating schemes and discovering the social functions of colonial-period ceramics, a growing body of research on 19th-century wares has also developed. In addition to creating classification and dating tools for post-colonial ceramics (Price 1979; Majewski and O'Brien 1987), work has focused on the availability and marketing of ceramics in North America (Miller and Hurry 1983; Miller 1984), household expenditure patterns (Miller 1980), and the effects of ethnicity, gender, and economic class on ceramic purchasing patterns (Baker 1978; Felton and Schulz 1983; Wall 1994).

This paper develops a dating scheme for one particular type of English pottery produced primarily from the late 18th to the mid-19th centuries. The technique of transfer printing designs under the glaze on ceramics, which revolutionized the Staffordshire ceramic industry, enabled complex decoration to be applied quickly and relatively inexpensively. It also allowed uniformity of design between vessels, something not possible with painted decorations. Thousands of designs were manufactured in a variety of colors and styles, with the Staffordshire potters producing patterns they hoped would be in demand by consumers both in England and abroad. While some patterns, such as Blue Willow, Asiatic Pheasants, and Canova, were extremely popular and manufactured by a number of potteries, the production span of most patterns was short-lived and limited to one potter. These designs reflected the larger social and decorative trends taking place within England and North America.

This study uses marked vessels to establish the chronological ranges for the major decorative styles on printed wares. Information from these dated vessels documents a series of styles that began at a point in time, rose to a level of popularity, and declined in frequency as other styles became more popular. Chronological information on motifs, used in conjunction with data on print color, vessel form, and manufacturing innovations, can assist archaeologists in refining date ranges for archaeological assemblages that contain printed wares. Such a dating tool is valuable because of the problems encountered in dating many 19th-century assemblages, where the majority of the ceramic assemblage is generally undecorated or minimally decorated white earthenware and white granite. Since printed wares were popular for almost a hundred years, they are common on late 18th- and 19th-century archaeological sites. Because the intent is to create a dating tool for archaeologists, the focus of this study is underglaze printed patterns on commonly available vessels forms. Data were not gathered on vessels decorated with overglaze printing, which are rarely found in 19th-century archaeological contexts and are less common overall.

This paper begins with a discussion of the various printing processes which have been used on pottery and a brief historical overview of printing on English ceramics. This section is followed by an explanation of the study methods and the composition of the database. Results of the study follow and are divided into sections on identifying and dating central motifs, border patterns, ink colors, and printing techniques. Discussed separately are ceramics decorated using flown colors.

Before discussing dating, it is important for the reader to understand the technical processes involved in printing on ceramics. Some technological advances in the printing process and materials used resulted in discernible evidence which can be used to help date printed wares. These advances and how to recognize their use on printed wares are discussed.

The Transfer Printing Process

Transfer printing, which involved the transferring of a design engraved into a copper plate via tissue paper or a glue bat to a ceramic vessel, was first used beginning in the 1750s (Coysh and Henrywood 1982:8). There were two primary types of printing on ceramics: prints applied over the final glaze and prints applied onto bisque-fired earthenware prior to glazing. Early efforts in printing were on vessels which had already received a final glazing. Printing over the glaze was known by three names: bat printing, cold printing, and overglaze printing (Copeland 1980:26–27; Majewski and O'Brien 1987:141).

Overglaze printing was used as a decorative technique on tin-glazed earthenware tiles in the 1750s, as well as on porcelain and, slightly later, on creamware (Holdway 1986:24–25). It soon thereafter began to be used as a means of decorating earthenware vessels and was generally restricted to high-status items such as tea wares or large jugs printed to order in Liverpool. Most of these earlier earthenwares were printed over the glaze in black on creamware bodies and were probably done using a technique known as bat printing. Developed in the third quarter of the 18th century, this technique used the transfer, in oil, of the engraved design to a thin sheet, or bat, of glue (des Fontaines 1966:102; Drakard and Holdway 1983:11). This glue bat was placed, oiled side down, on the glazed pottery surface, leaving the design in oil (Halfpenny 1994a:46). Powdered enamels were then dusted onto the oil. The design was fixed into place by firing the pottery in a low-temperature kiln. The powdered enamel colors most suitable for bat printing were black, red, chocolate-brown, and purple (Holdway 1986:22). Because the design was placed over the lead glaze, which slightly blurred the ink in underglaze printing, bat printing allowed a great level of detail.

As a technique for decorating ceramics, bat printing was firmly established by 1805 and stayed popular for several decades (Halfpenny 1994a:57). Bat printing was suitable for irregularly shaped vessels, because the flexible glue bat could be easily fitted along convex surfaces where tissue paper designs would have to be folded. This technique was most effective with small vessels like mugs or teapots, since it was difficult to work with large glue bats (Halfpenny 1994a:46). The process was also unsuitable for transferring continuous border patterns (Drakard and Holdway 1983:11). Bat printing was also known as cold printing, since the engraved copper plates used in this technique were not heated before being charged with oil (Majewski and O'Brien 1987:141).

The development of a printing process for ceramics using the transfer of an inked design by paper allowed a wider range of vessel forms to be decorated. Underglaze, or hot process, printing on earthenwares did not begin in England until Thomas Turner's first attempts around 1780 (Coysh 1970), but was quickly adopted by other Staffordshire potters. Spode was printing under the glaze on earthenwares by 1784 (Drakard and Holdway 1983). The process of printing on ceramics allowed standardization of decoration, permitting complex designs to be created quickly and in larger quantities. Using this technique, a design was first engraved onto a copper plate (Coysh and Henrywood 1982:8). After the plate was heated to help thin and spread the ink, it was then inked with a thick mixture of boiled linseed oil, powdered flint, and metallic oxide or some other coloring agent. Ink color was determined by the metallic oxide: cobalt produced a blue color; manganese and cobalt, shades of purple, brown, and red; and chromium oxide, maroon (Williams 1975:131–132). Black was produced by adding manganese and cobalt to brown tints made with iron, chromium, and zinc, and greens were made using chromium oxide (Majewski and O'Brien 1987:139–140). Excess ink was removed from the copper plate, leaving the color only in the engraved areas of the design. A dampened tissue paper, which was placed over the copper plate and the inked design, was then transferred by passing the plate and paper through the rollers of a press (Coysh and Stefano 1981:12). After being lifted from the copper plate, this tissue paper was cut apart if necessary, and pressed, inked side down, onto the porous ware (biscuit fired, but still unglazed), which absorbed the ink (des Fontaines 1966:102). The ceramic item was then fired at a low temperature to burn off the linseed oil and set the coloring agent. Next the vessel was dipped in liquid glaze and refired in a glost oven (des Fontaines 1966:102).

Although the process of transfer printing involved a series of steps, all but the initial carving of the design on a copper plate could be accomplished by minimally skilled labor. These plates, done by expert engravers, would have to be made to fit each vessel form and size desired in the pattern, but, as the engraved plates could be used repeatedly, the most substantial cost in this form of decoration was up front. While some manufacturers retained full-time engravers on staff, many of the smaller potteries purchased their engraved plates from independent workshops (Coysh and Stefano 1981:15; Halfpenny 1994b:61). Popular designs were frequently sold to more than one manufacturer, with small changes often made (Gurujal 1988:16). Additionally, some potters sold or traded their used

copper plates to other potteries (Halfpenny 1994b:65). Copper plates engraved for transfer onto ceramics had to be engraved more deeply than those used for book illustrations, since the heat of the glost oven lightened the colors of the ink and the biscuit ware absorbed more ink than paper (des Fontaines 1966:101; Coysh 1970:7). The more deeply the plate was engraved, the darker the color of the resulting print.

In the late 18th century and the early years of the following century, a limited number of factories were producing printed wares; consequently, printed wares were expensive relative to other decorated and undecorated English ceramics. George Miller's (1980) research on the economic scaling of 19th-century ceramics has shown that printed wares were three to five times the cost of undecorated cream-colored earthenwares (CC) in the 1790s. By the mid-19th century, however, the relative price of printed wares had dropped to within one to two times the cost of undecorated wares. While at first only the members of the upper economic classes could afford to purchase printed wares, by 1842, a group of New York pottery dealers considered that Staffordshire wares were now so inexpensive that they were within reach of the poorest (Ewins 1990:8).

Despite the fact that the technique of transfer printing under the glaze had been possible for over two decades, it was not until after the War of 1812 that printed wares began to appear in great numbers in America, as indicated by New York invoices for pottery (Miller 1994:38). This increase in consumption of printed wares following the War of 1812 was probably the result of a major fall in ceramic prices (Miller et al. 1994:234–238). Large fortunes were being amassed in the growing cities of the northern Atlantic coast, and the westward expansion also created new markets for the products of Staffordshire (Tracy 1963:19, 23). After the opening of the American market in the years following the war, Staffordshire potters found a willing market in the American consumer, and pottery in hundreds of patterns made the journey across the Atlantic Ocean to grace the tables of the New Republic. Almost 43% of the plates and soup plates ordered by New York merchants between 1838 and 1840 were printed (Miller 1994:34). Printed wares remained popular until around the mid-19th century, when they gave way to undecorated or minimally decorated white earthenwares and ironstones for a time. Printed wares in certain colors, such as flow mulberry, continued to remain popular into the 1860s, and, beginning around 1870, printed wares enjoyed a revival which lasted until the use of decals became popular in the early 1900s (Majweski and O'Brien 1986:145, 147).

Methods

The date ranges for printed earthenwares given in this study were derived using a process related to seriation, a technique particularly valuable on sites where pottery and other sensitive cultural traits are common. Using changes in stylistic attributes of pottery and other material culture has figured prominently in archaeological literature (Petrie 1972[1904]; Spier 1917; Kroeber and Strong 1924; Dethlefsen and Deetz 1966; Marquardt 1978). Seriation involves ordering units based on similarity. Basic to its theoretical focus is the assumption that a given attribute originates at a specific time, becomes gradually and increasingly common, and is slowly replaced by a different attribute (Clarke 1968:205). Seriation assumes that the popularity of an attribute or trait is transient in nature; experiencing one peak in frequency of occurrence. Arrangement of these attributes over time produces an overlapping effect. For example, as one attribute wanes in frequency, the frequency of another may be increasing. By using this technique to analyze decorative attributes on marked and datable examples of ceramics, it is possible to see changes in stylistic motifs over time. Once these different motifs can be assigned a date range of production, it is then possible to date unmarked fragments from archaeological contexts.

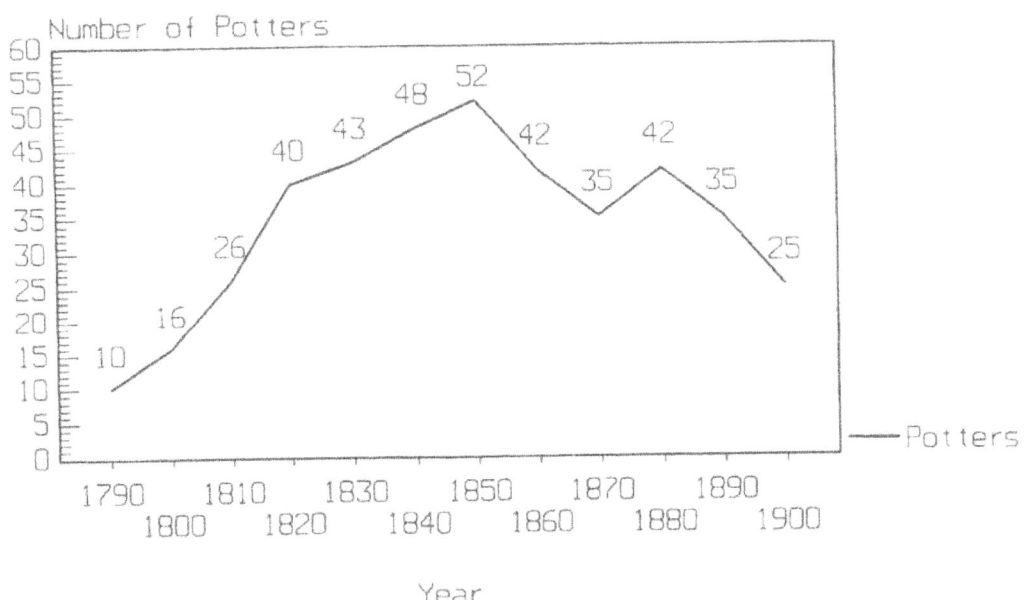

FIGURE 1. The number of potters producing printed wares increased dramatically in the first decades of the 19th century, peaked at mid-century, and enjoyed a brief resurgence in the 1880s.

The study sample included 3,250 pottery vessels made by 176 different British pottery firms. The majority of these potteries were located in Staffordshire, the leading world supplier of decorative and utilitarian ceramics at that time (Tracy 1963:108). Several Scottish firms were also included in the sample. The greatest number of firms producing printed wares as at least one of their products occurred between 1835 and 1855, with a high of 52 of the sampled potteries in business in 1845 (Figure 1).

Information on decorative motifs and other attributes was cataloged into a Paradox database that allowed sorting by various categories. In order to qualify for inclusion in the database, each vessel had to meet several prerequisites. Each had to be marked in a way that would allow it to be positively attributed to a specific maker. Most contained printed or impressed manufacturers' marks, as shown in Geoffrey Godden's (1964) *Encyclopaedia of British Pottery and Porcelain Marks*. Some vessels contained no maker's mark, but did have printed or impressed registry marks, which allowed the manufacturer to be identified by using registry records. To be included in the database, the use-span of the mark, as defined in Godden (1964), or the total operation span of the potter's firm had to date to less than 40 years, in order to maintain greater temporal control. This meant that several important firms, including William Adams and Sons, Ltd. (1769–present) and Josiah Wedgwood (1759–present) could not be included in the sample.

Data for this study were gleaned from a number of primary and secondary sources. These sources are listed below, and the manner in which the data were gathered for each is given.

Primary documents consisted of potters' invoices for wares that were shipped to the United States in the first half of the 19th century. These documents usually contained information about vessel form, size, decoration, color, and pattern name. Published photographs or actual vessels in these patterns by the same manufacturers were located in order to gather the information on decorative attributes, such as central

and border motifs, as well as vessel shape, molded motifs, and the like. Primary documents used in this study were contained within the Joseph Downs Collection of Manuscripts and Ephemera at the Henry Francis DuPont Winterthur Museum, and in the U.S. Customs House Papers (1790–1869) for the Port of Philadelphia, held at the University of Delaware and available on microfilm at Winterthur. The sources used at Winterthur included the Printed Bills Collection (Box 3, Pottery and Glassware Folder) and the Gallimore Collection in the Joseph Downs Collection (71x166.1–.68). Additionally, information on printed pottery as discussed by Ann Eatwell and Alex Werner (1991) was used.

Collections of marked, printed ceramics were examined at the Colonial Williamsburg Foundation Department of Collections and Department of Archaeological Research, at the Smithsonian Museum of American History, and at the Henry Francis DuPont Winterthur Museum. Several sizeable private collections of printed earthenwares were also cataloged, including those of George L. Miller, Ann Smart Martin, and Robert Hunter.

The following secondary sources were used for data gathering. These sources contained photographs of the patterns cataloged, as well as information on makers and marks. In some instances, color and size information was also available. These sources included Robert Copeland (1980), A. W. Coysh (1970, 1972), A. W. Coysh and R. K. Henrywood (1982, 1989), David Drakard and Paul Holdway (1983), Ellouise Baker Larsen (1975[1950]), Sam Laidacker (1938, 1951), Veneita Mason (1982), Silber and Fleming's 1882 trade catalogue (in Bosomworth 1991), and Petra Williams (1971, 1973, 1978). Several archaeological publications and reports were also used where there was a body of information about marked printed earthenwares. These works were David L. Felton and Peter D. Schulz (1983) and Lynne Sussman (1979).

Several minor problems were encountered in using the secondary sources. In the printed sources, every pictured pattern with a known manufacturing range of less than 40 years was recorded. In instances where photographs were not clear enough to adequately identify the pattern type, no information was recorded. Additionally, the research interests of the scholars who have published on printed wares have introduced some potential biases. There has been great interest in blue printed wares and patterns depicting American buildings, landscapes, and historical events. Consequently, many of the published sources concentrate on these limited categories (Camehl 1948[1916]; Larsen 1975[1950]; Fennelly 1967; Copeland 1982; Coysh and Henrywood 1982, 1989). Other sources are more comprehensive in terms of a representative sample (Laidacker 1938, 1951; Williams 1971, 1973, 1978).

In addition to makers' mark data, information was collected on central design motifs, border (or marley) decorations, ink color, vessel shape, measurements, and additional decorative attributes. Many of these decorative attributes,

such as engraving techniques, were in fact closely linked to technological innovations in the ceramic industry. For those vessels recovered from archaeological excavations, data were also collected on the context from which each was recovered.

To arrive at the date ranges presented in the results section of this report, the beginning and end production dates for each vessel within a category were listed. The sum of all beginning production dates in each category was totaled and divided by the number of examples to arrive at a mean beginning date. The same was done with the end production dates, thus providing a date span for a period of peak production. In general, the results revealed a peak production range of between 15 and 20 years for each design or decorative category. Also shown in each table are the inclusive ranges of production for each type or category, based on the earliest beginning and latest ending dates for marks. In cases where a specific pattern was listed in more than one vessel form by the same potter, the

TABLE 1
DATE RANGES FOR CENTRAL DESIGNS ON PRINTED WARES

Design	N	Mean Beginning and End Production Dates		Range of Production
Chinese	22	1797	1814	1783–1834
British Views	401	1813	1839	1793–1868
Chinoiserie	33	1816	1836	1783–1873
Pastoral	88	1819	1836	1781–1859
Exotic Views	214	1820	1842	1793–1868
American Historical	49	1826	1842	1785–1880
American Views	192	1826	1838	1793–1862
Floral				
Sheet Patterns	7	1826	1842	1795–1867
Central Floral	56	1833	1849	1784–1869
Classical	104	1827	1847	1793–1868
Romantic	376	1831	1851	1793–1870
Gothic	20	1841	1852	1818–1890
Japanese	44	1882	1888	1864–1907
No Central	11	1868	1878	1845–1920

Note. Mean beginning and end dates for all the tables in this paper reflect the period of highest production for these wares, while range of production is based on the earliest beginning date and latest end date of the manufacturers making them.

pattern was only counted once in order to avoid weighting the data. For example, the pattern Marble by John Ridgway (ca. 1830–1855) was listed 30 times in the database, once for each vessel form in which it was available. In calculating dates for central or border motifs, however, this pattern was only listed once.

Results

Analysis did show that significant dating differences occurred in many of the decorative attributes on printed earthenwares. The results discussed below are divided into central motifs, border designs, print color, and other decorative techniques.

Central Motifs on Printed Earthenwares

Staffordshire printed wares can be seen as commercial and industrial art that reflected social and decorative trends of the time (Krannert Art Museum 1988:4). A series of revivals influenced design and the decorative arts in England and Europe in the 18th and 19th centuries. These revivals of classical, romantic, and gothic tastes were just as important in American design as they were in England. Even after the two wars that pitted the United States against England, Americans continued to look to England, as well as France, for guidance in fashion and refined taste (Cooper 1993:11). In general, upper-class Americans, who traveled and read more extensively than did their middle-class counterparts, were the first purveyors of fashionable decorative arts and home furnishings in America. The presence of fashionable items in the home, particularly those displaying exotic scenes of faraway lands, conveyed messages about one's place in the world and one's knowledge of culture, history, and travel. Interestingly, many of the design motifs and stylistic trends of the 19th century were influenced by the findings of archaeological excavations of English medieval churches and monuments and on classical-period sites. In many ways, the industrial environment and development of technologies that allowed transfer printing as a means of decorating ceram-

ics were the phenomena being reacted against in many of the design motifs seen on these printed wares; this is especially true of the romantic patterns.

Central design motifs have been divided into 13 different categories, corresponding to decorative trends evident in the 19th century and based on examining printed vessels. Analysis showed distinct temporal differences in the periods of peak production for most of these stylistic motifs. Table 1 lists the categories used and the period of peak production for each of these central motifs. A discussion of each type follows.

Chinese and Chinoiserie

The western fascination with things Chinese had long preceded the advent of underglaze printing on earthenwares. Trade with the East had introduced the West to tea, spices, fine silks, embroidery, lacquered items, and porcelain (Jarry 1981). For decades, consumers desirous of owning expensive Chinese porcelains, but unable to afford them, contented themselves with painted renditions of Chinese-style designs on less costly ceramics, in particular tin-glazed earthenwares. Later in the 18th century, English import duties on porcelain went through a series of increases,

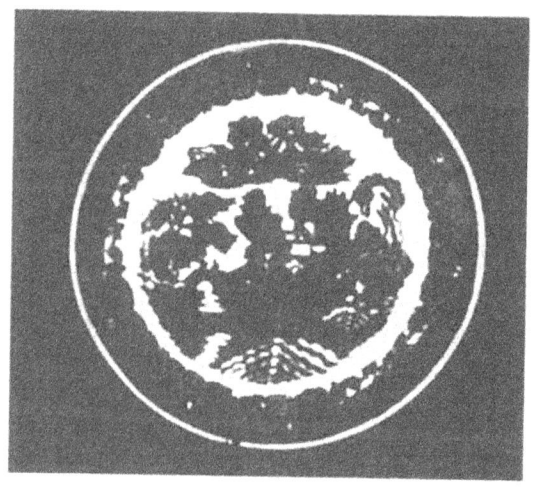

FIGURE 2. Early printed patterns were primarily based directly on Chinese porcelains, like the Broseley pattern shown here on bone china, maker unknown. (Photo by P. Samford, courtesy of George L. Miller.)

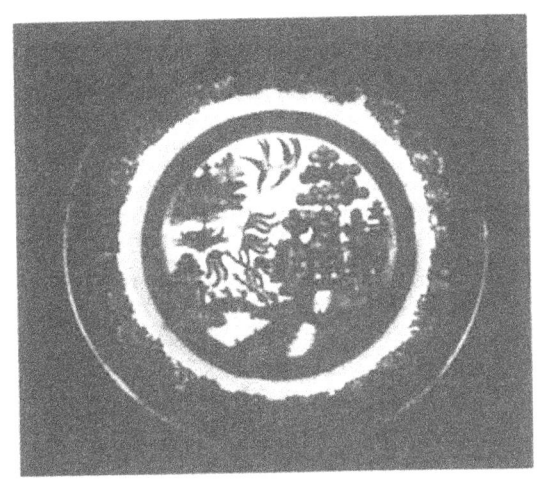

FIGURE 3. Blue Willow was the most commonly produced pattern, popular with both English and North American potters. This example was manufactured by the Buffalo Pottery Company (1916–present) of New York. (Photo by P. Samford, courtesy of George L. Miller.)

reaching 109 percent by 1799 (Copeland 1982:7), and even those who had been able to drink their tea or serve dinner guests from porcelain found it increasingly difficult to obtain replacements and additions to their services. With the advent of printed underglaze designs in blue on white-bodied earthenwares, production of the complex landscapes and geometric borders common on Chinese porcelains became more cost efficient. Additionally, the whiteness of the newly developed pearlware body and glaze were well-suited to the traditionally blue Chinese motifs. In fact, the Staffordshire potters called Wedgwood's new "Pearl white" bodied ware "China glaze" in imitation of Chinese porcelain (Miller 1987). The combination of Chinese style designs and vessel forms with the China glaze was aimed at filling a niche previously occupied by Chinese porcelain. Copies of original Chinese designs, such as Broseley, Buffalo, and Mandarin, printed on English earthenware provided a sufficient, albeit poorer quality, substitute for Chinese porcelain.

For the purposes of this study, Chinese-style printed wares have been divided into two categories—those based directly on Chinese designs and those based on interpretations of Chinese patterns. The earliest printed earthenware designs were copied directly from Chinese porcelain motifs, such as the Buffalo and Broseley patterns (Figure 2). Perhaps the most enduring of the Chinese-style patterns was Blue Willow (Figure 3). Based on the Mandarin pattern, it was first introduced around 1790 by Josiah Spode (Copeland 1980:33). The Blue Willow pattern has been made by numerous potters since its introduction, and at times its name was synonymous with that of printed wares. The peak ranges of production of marked Chinese designs fall between 1797 and 1814, but these wares were the dominant types from the introduction of underglaze printing in Staffordshire in 1784 until 1814. As time passed, elements such as figures in western dress and western architectural features began to appear (Impey 1977:11; Coysh and Henrywood 1982:9). The term "chinoiserie" is used here to designate all styles based on European interpretations of oriental designs (Impey 1977:10). Chinoiserie designs were most commonly produced between 1816 and 1836.

Because this was a period of experimentation with the new method of underglaze printing on earthenwares, late 18th- and early 19th-century Chinese-style and chinoiserie printed earthenwares designs generally appear two dimensional and in one shade of blue (Coysh and Henrywood 1982:9). Common decorative motifs found on printed Chinese-style and chinoiserie earthenwares include pagodas, temples, weeping willow trees, cherry blossoms, orange trees, figures in eastern dress, junks and sampans, and

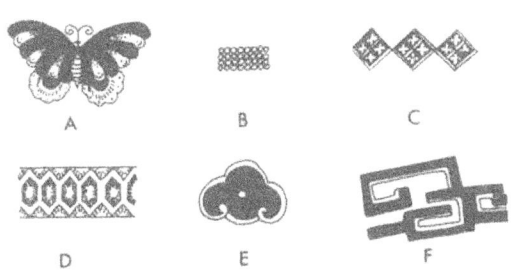

FIGURE 4. These motifs are among those commonly found on Chinese and chinoiserie-style printed wares: a, butterfly, b, fish roe; c, lozenges, d, honeycomb, e, Joo-I, and f, key motif (after Copeland 1980)

FIGURE 5. New York from Heights Near Brooklyn (James and Ralph Clews, 1818–1834) is a typical American view. The combined use of line and stipple engraving give it a soft, watercolor-like appearance (Larsen Collection, Smithsonian Institution)

chinoiserie persisted throughout the 19th century, disenchantment with the exoticism of this style occurred in mid-century (Jacobson 1993:178). The opening of Japan to the west in the latter part of the 19th century and the subsequent interest in Japanese design sparked a revival of interest in chinoiserie (Jacobson 1993:202).

British Views

Between ca. 1815 and 1840, potters produced a number of designs depicting English cities, colleges, estates, and country homes. In the early 19th century, as the British empire expanded, patriotism increased, and the Napoleonic Wars made travel in Europe and other parts of the world more dangerous, numerous books were published portraying the beauty of Great Britain and its buildings. These prints were the primary sources for British views produced on pottery (Coysh and Stefano 1981:7). Enoch Wood and Sons (1818–1846) produced a series of over 50 known views based on the prints of John

Chippendale-style fencework. The marleys or rim designs on chinoiserie-style earthenwares are often densely printed geometric designs with butterflies, key motifs, honeycombing, and latticing (Figure 4). Although the penchant for

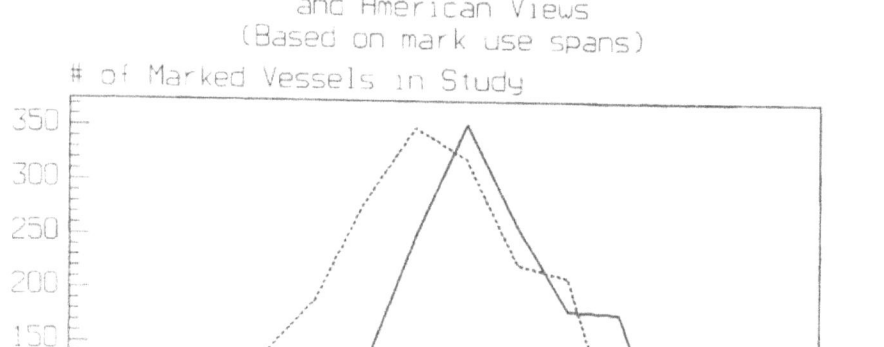

FIGURE 6. Graph illustrating how the production of American views skyrocketed after the end of the War of 1812 and the Embargo of 1807

TABLE 2
DATE RANGES FOR AMERICAN VIEWS

Color	N	Mean Beginning and End Production Dates		Range of Production
Dark Blue	65	1822	1836	1810–1850
Black	31	1826	1839	1810–1854
Brown	21	1830	1840	1818–1854
Light Blue	23	1830	1845	1818–1854
Reds/Purples	52	1828	1838	1818–1854

Preston Neale, published in a book entitled *Views of the Seats of Noblemen and Gentlemen in England, Wales, Scotland, and Ireland* (1818–1829). Other series of British views on earthenwares include "Metropolitan Scenery" by Goodwins and Harris (1831–1838), and "Picturesque Scenery" and the "Select Views" series by Ralph Hall (1822–1849).

Often a different design was engraved for each vessel form in a set; in the Grapevine Border series, over 50 different designs were used by Enoch Wood and Sons on one of their dinner services (Laidacker 1951:93). In many instances, the engravings or aquatints were not copied exactly; studies have shown that elements were added or subtracted from the published sources in order to create a better fit with the shape of the ceramic vessel intended for decoration (Maguire 1988:4). Despite this artistic license, the passage of the Copyright Act of 1842, which made it illegal to copy book illustrations, dealt a fatal blow to the British views category (Coysh and Henrywood 1982:11). This category peaks in production popularity around 1823, with mean beginning and end dates of 1813 and 1839.

American Views

Similar to British views were those depicting American scenes. By the second decade of the 19th century, many of the Staffordshire potteries were encountering financial difficulties brought about in large part by the effects of the Napoleonic Wars, the Embargo of 1807, and the War of 1812. As a result of these events, there had been little direct trade between Britain and the United States between 1808 and 1815, and ceramic manufacturers were understandably anxious to reestablish North American trade ties after the close of the War of 1812. Staffordshire potters found a willing and ready market for their products with the flourishing population and rising middle class of the early 19th-century United States.

Many Staffordshire potters appealed specifically to the American market by creating series of views depicting American landmarks, such as churches, hotels and resorts, government build-

FIGURE 7. The Monopteros pattern (John Rogers and Son, ca. 1814–1836) is an example of an exotic view with a border that is a continuation of the main scene. (Photo by P. Samford; courtesy of George L. Miller.)

FIGURE 8. The Monopteros pattern in Figure 7 was based on this print taken from Thomas Daniell's *Oriental Scenery.*

ings and homes, city vistas, and natural wonders (Figure 5). The production of these wares began in 1815, almost immediately after the reestablishment of trade with the United States, and showed a rapid increase in production, peaking in 1831 (Figure 6). As with British views on ceramics, published prints were used as the primary source materials. In some cases, the potters sent engravers or artists to America to document the latest architecture and monuments. In 1818, for example, William Wall sent English potter Andrew Stevenson sketches of some of America's most important buildings (Gurujal 1988:16). Engraver William Birch moved from England to Philadelphia in 1794, where he published *Views of Philadelphia and Country Seats*

in the United States (Bloom 1988:36). Ellouise Larsen's research has turned up almost 800 American scenic and historical views (Larsen 1975[1950]). The sheer quantity of American views recorded to date suggests that they were popular, but, like the British views category, their production was essentially brought to an end by the 1842 Copyright Act. Analysis shows that the production of British and American views, although already on the decline, does taper off considerably after 1842 and ceases completely by the mid-1850s.

Distinguishing between British and American views, particularly at the sherd level, may be difficult. In general, both British and American views show a high degree of skill and detail in engraving, with the finished vessels displaying an almost watercolor-like appearance. While it does appear that many of the American views produced and exported to the United States—and disproportionately recorded in this survey due to the attention they have been given by scholars and collectors—were printed in dark blue, they were also available in other colors, such as light blue, brown, black, purple, and pink. In general, the copper plates produced for these other colors do not appear to have been engraved with the

FIGURE 9. The Palestine pattern (William Adams, 1769–present) is an example of a composite exotic view (Photo by P. Samford; courtesy of George L. Miller.)

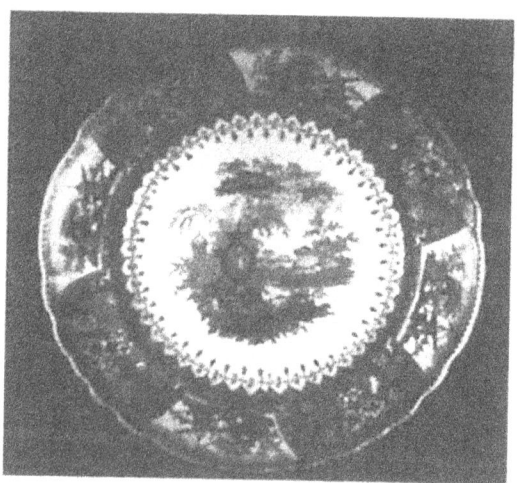

FIGURE 10. Patterns with classical motifs, such as Canova (Thomas Mayer, ca. 1826–1838), contain columned temples, urns, and draped figures (Photo by P. Samford, courtesy of George L. Miller.)

attention to detail and tonal gradations evident in the slightly earlier dark blue American views. Table 2 illustrates date ranges for various print colors on American views.

A smaller, but nonetheless important, category of American ceramics created by the Staffordshire potteries specifically for the American market included designs featuring military battles, heroes, and special events. One of the more popular subjects of these historical views was General Lafayette's triumphant return visit to the United States in 1824 (Larsen 1975[1950]:57). These patterns are generally well documented in secondary literature and can be dated fairly easily, but data suggest that the majority of American historical views were produced between 1826 and 1838.

Exotic Views

In the early 19th century, the expanding British colonization of India and other foreign countries sparked a great deal of interest in places outside Great Britain (Bloom 1988:33). For the wealthy, travel to exotic places was not difficult, and "The Grand Tour" of Europe was standard for young men (Coysh and Henrywood 1989:8). But for most Victorians, the cost of travel was prohibitive and the desire to learn about and experience foreign lands had to be satisfied through published travel diaries and books of engravings. As with American and British views, the Staffordshire potters took advantage of published illustrations of cities, monuments, and landscapes in places like India, the Middle East, and even the Arctic to provide them with subjects for their wares. For example, the Monopteros pattern (Figure 7) by John Rogers and Son (1815–1842) was based on a print entitled "Remains of an Ancient Building near Firoz Shah's Cotilla, Delhi" (Figure 8) taken from Thomas Daniell's *Oriental Scenery* (Coysh and Henrywood 1982:157). Additionally, some Staffordshire potters sent engravers to Italy, Greece, and India to produce drawings for pottery design (Bloom 1988:32).

The exotic views category encompasses all designs that contain motifs of foreign architecture, ruins, and nonnative animals such as elephants or tigers. These scenes could either be based on published engravings of actual places, as was common before 1842, or could be more fanciful, romantic interpretations of exotic places. An example of a composite interpretation of an exotic view is the pattern entitled Palestine (Figure 9) by William Adams and Sons Ltd. (1769–present). The exotic buildings shown are well in the background, and the focus of the view is on the tent and eastern-garbed figures in the foreground. The scene portrayed is romanticized and lacks the distinct architectural detail present on views of actual foreign locales. The mean beginning and end dates for the production of exotic views were 1820 and 1842.

Classical

Archaeological excavations at the ancient cities of Herculaneum, Pompeii, and similar sites were one of the driving factors behind the Greek Revival style of the late 18th and early 19th centuries (Cooper 1993:10). Archaeological reports were used as source material by architects

FIGURE 11. The Messina pattern, by Edward Challinor (1853–1862), shows figures and water in the foreground and buildings typical of Romantic patterns in the background. (Photo by P. Samford, courtesy of George L. Miller.)

and designers, and the purity of line and form of ancient Greece and Rome began to replace the excesses of the baroque and rococo styles (Tracy 1963:12). Classical motifs were particularly embraced by Americans, with the use of these motifs in architecture and art perceived as a way for the new nation to join the ranks of great past civilizations (Bushman 1993:16). Appearing in America by the first decade of the 19th century, the classical style was dominant during the emergence of the new middle class, whose desire for fashionable objects helped spread the influence of classical motifs in the decorative arts (Cooper 1993:11; Bushman 1993:14). The taste for classical furnishings had begun to wane by the 1840s, and was replaced in popularity by Gothic Revival themes (Cooper 1993:12).

Since classical motifs permeated every aspect of the decorative arts, Staffordshire potters were not immune to the economic opportunities afforded by using these motifs. Many of their designs from this time period feature classical elements such as columned temples, urns, draped figures, and acanthus leaves. Prints of Greek and Roman ruins were often the inspiration for these designs (Bloom 1988:33). A well-known example of a classical motif is the Canova pattern (Figure 10). Antonio Canova (1757–1822), an Italian neoclassical sculptor, was popular in England. Legend has it that his heart was placed in a neoclassical urn after his death, and the Canova pattern prominently features just such an urn (Williams and Weber 1986:59; Coysh and Henrywood 1989:46). Classically-inspired motifs on English earthenwares enjoyed a brief period of popularity between 1827 and 1847.

Romantic

The 19th-century Romantic movement in England and Europe influenced music, art, literature, and even social and political thought (Meijer 1959:38). Stressing emotion and intuition over tradition and reason, the Romantic movement arose in opposition to the classical revival and in response to the increasing industrialization sweeping through England. Humans were seen as subordinate to the all-powerful but

FIGURE 12. The Girl at the Well (John Heath, 1809–1823) is representative of pastoral patterns (Photo by P. Samford.)

benign forces of nature. One of the manifestations of this movement was evident in garden design. The formal, geometric gardens of the 17th and early 18th centuries began to be replaced by expansive parklands whose relaxed style evoked wilderness.

Given the interest in nature, it is perhaps not surprising that much of the decorative art associated with the Romantic movement contains depictions of the landscape. Landscape painting continued as a means of expression, and nature was a favorite subject for the newly developing field of photography (Millard 1977; Vaughan 1978). Certain picturesque elements were predominant in romantic imagery: mountains, waterfalls, trees, cottages, and castles evoked images that excited the Victorian imagination. Philosopher Friedrich von Schelling wrote in 1796 on viewing Heidelburg Castle, "The castle hovers above the town and dominates it completely, increasing the romanticism of this moment" (quoted in Sandkuhle 1970:66).

Ceramics printed with Romantic-style motifs typically follow a formula: they were generally bucolic scenes containing several elements (Coysh and Henrywood 1982:11). In the background were generally one or more stylized buildings, whose fanciful nature or lack of distinguishing architectural detail indicated that they were not depictions of actual buildings. In the mid-ground was usually a water source such as a river or lake, and the foreground contained small human figures or animals, generally placed there to provide a sense of scale. Nature in the form of trees, mountains, or wooded valleys completed the Romantic formula (Figure 11). Research has suggested that elements from different sources were combined in some Romantic views (Bloom 1988:34). Many of the names given to Romantic patterns bear little or no resemblance to the subject portrayed on the vessel, but were chosen instead to help boost sales (Coysh and Henrywood 1989:8). For example, the pattern Scinde began production after this part of India was annexed in 1845 (Coysh and Henrywood 1982:11). Camden, a geometric pattern produced by Ridgway, was inspired by Sir Charles Pratt, the first Earl of Camden. With a number of towns in the United States and several in Australia named Camden, Ridgway may have been banking on export sales for this pattern (Coysh and Henrywood 1989:46). Many patterns were named after European cities and

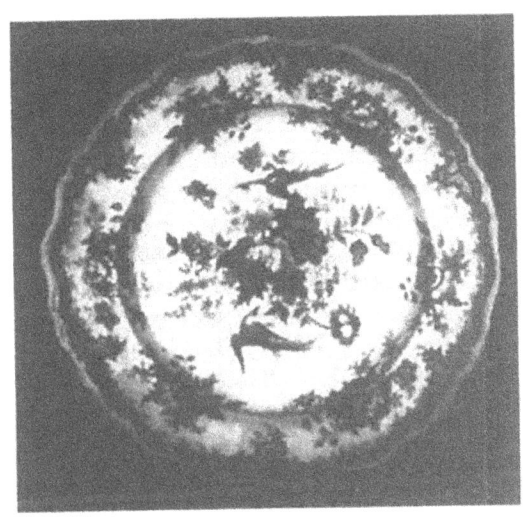

FIGURE 14 Asiatic Pheasants (Ralph Hall and Company 1822–1849) was one of the most commonly produced floral patterns. Its border consists of a discontinuous repeating floral motif. (Photo by P. Samford; courtesy of George L. Miller.)

towns, like the Roselle—registered in 1848 by John Meir and Son—and the Geneva—Joseph Heath, 1845–1853—patterns (Coysh and Henrywood 1989:8). Romantic views, although remaining popular throughout the 19th century, were at their peak of highest production ca. 1831 to 1851.

Pastoral

Closely related to Romantic views were those which have been given the designation of pastoral. These views depicted generally rural-based scenes containing detailed views of farm animals, such as cows or horses, or persons engaged in working pursuits, such as milking cows, chopping wood, or drawing water from a well (Figure 12). In the pastoral category, the focus of the view was on the activities of the figures portrayed prominently and in detail in the foreground. Pastoral views were at their peak of production between 1819 and 1836.

Gothic Revival

The Gothic Revival style, an offshoot of the Romantic period, began as a literary movement

FIGURE 13 The pattern Gothic Ruins by Davenport (ca. 1793–1887) is typical of Gothic motifs (Photo by P. Samford.)

and gained popularity through the works of authors like Sir Walter Scott. Using the Middle Ages as inspiration, the Gothic Revival drew upon the design motifs depicted in medieval illuminated manuscripts and in archaeological publications that described Gothic medieval monuments (Vaughan 1978:127). In many ways a reaction against the severity and formality of classicism, the Gothic style reinterpreted many of the themes and motifs that had been predominant in the Middle Ages and stressed irregularity, drama, melancholy, and unity with nature. The year 1820 is given as the beginning of the Gothic Revival in England, and it flourished throughout the middle of the 19th century in England and America (Addison 1938:60; Howe and Warren 1976:5). The Gothic style influenced home and garden design—country homes with turrets, towers, and crenelated walls began to spring up in Britain and the United States, naturalistic garden landscaping became common, and gardens and estates were embellished with picturesque ruins. For example, Prospect Hill, an estate in Norwalk, Connecticut, was converted from a Greek Revival style to a Gothic style during the late 1840s (Howe and Warren 1977:91).

The Gothic Revival style enjoyed its greatest popularity in Britain, where it influenced design

FIGURE 16. The asymmetry of the Melbourne pattern by Gildea and Walker (1881-1885) is typical of Japanese-influenced motifs of the late 19th century. (Photo by P. Samford, courtesy of George L. Miller.)

between around 1820 and 1870 (Addison 1938:60, 94). It particularly appealed to the British, since they felt that this style, with its overtones of castles and medieval churches, was more in keeping with British national character than that of the classical style (Germann 1972:182). In mid-19th century Britain, many public and private buildings, especially churches, were constructed in the Gothic style. The publication of numerous design books, such as Pugin and Willson (1895[1821]) and Alexander Jackson Davis (1980[1838]), helped familiarize people with the Gothic style. Although the Gothic Revival began as a primarily literary movement, it permeated every aspect of the decorative arts, with Gothic motifs finding their way onto pottery, bottles, wallpaper, bird houses, and the like (Howe and Warren 1976:9). In the United States, the Gothic Revival style was at its most popular in the mid-19th century, from about 1840 to the outbreak of the Civil War (Davies 1976:5). Additionally, the Great Exposition of 1851 brought added exposure of the Gothic Revival style with the medieval exhibit held in the Crystal Palace (Addison 1938:85).

Given its popularity, it was inevitable that Gothic designs would find their way into the

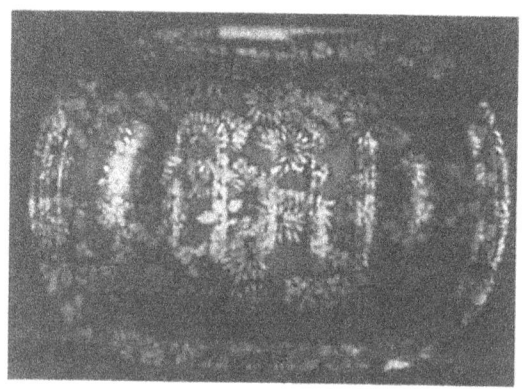

FIGURE 15. This 20th-century soapdish by an unknown maker displays a floral sheet pattern. On this example, the tissue paper used to transfer the inked design is still in place and is peeling away along the upper edge of the vessel. (Photo by George L. Miller.)

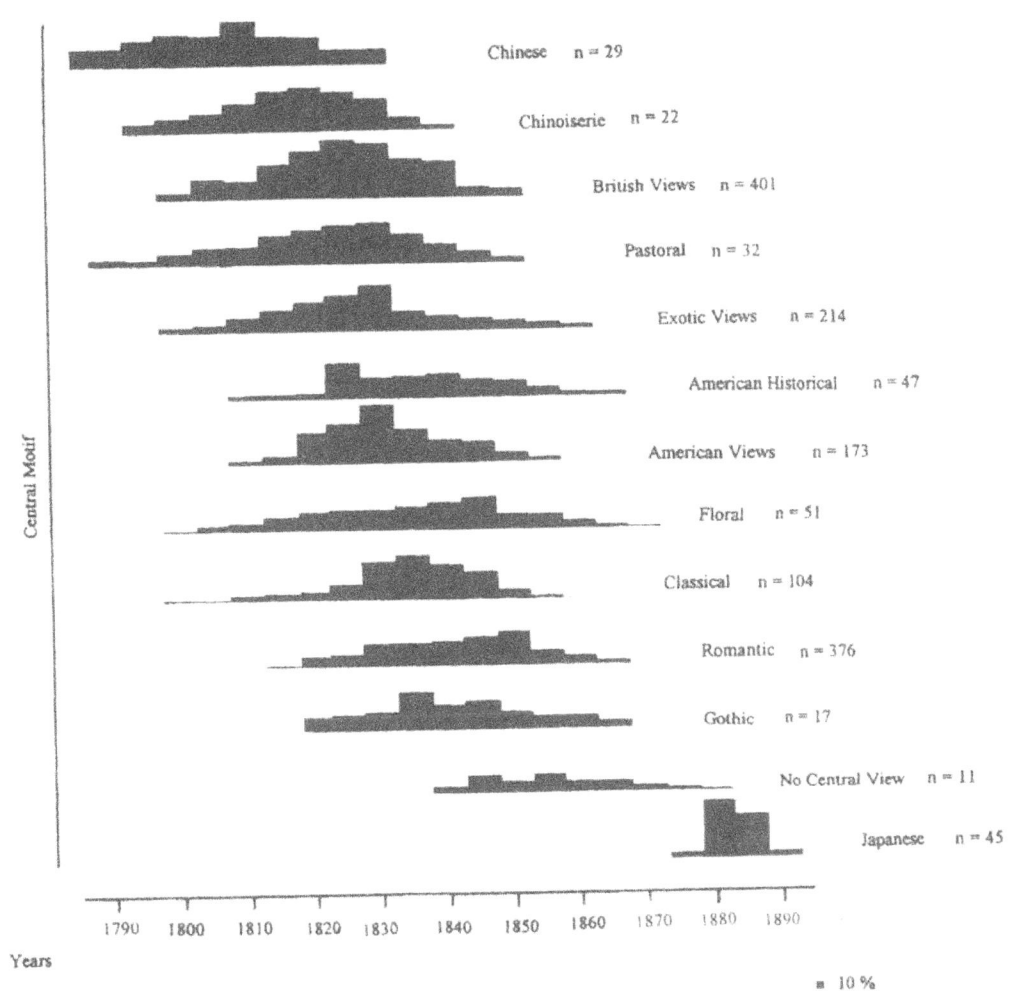

FIGURE 17 This graph illustrates the overlapping periods of production for central designs on printed wares. Bars represent percentage of total patterns produced during five-year intervals. (Illustration by Jane Eastman.)

engravings of the Staffordshire potters. From the mid-1830s through ca. 1860, Davenport of Longport (ca. 1793–1887) printed a series entitled "Scott's Illustrations," based on the novels of Sir Walter Scott. Another Gothic pattern, Fonthill Abbey, was inspired by the country estate of the same name, built between 1796 and 1799 for author William Beckford (Addison 1938:50). Structural flaws caused the house to collapse in 1825, and it subsequently and rather appropriately became the subject for a Gothic-style dinner service produced by James and

Ralph Clews between 1818 and 1834 (Coysh and Henrywood 1982:144). This pattern was also produced by Enoch Wood (1818–1846) and Ralph Stevenson (ca. 1810–1832).

Gothic Revival patterns on Staffordshire earthenwares are characterized by depictions of church and other building ruins, structures with architectural details such as arches, turrets, towers, bastions, and crenelated walls (Figure 13). Gothic designs were most commonly produced on pottery after the more composite Romantic views began to decline in production, with peak

TABLE 3
CHARACTERISTIC MOTIFS ON CENTRAL DESIGNS

Central Designs	Motifs
Chinese/Chinoiserie	1. Pagodas/temples 2. Willow trees 3. Junks/sampans 4. Orange trees 5. Figures in eastern garb 6. Chippendale fencing
American and British Views	1. Building or landscape feature displayed prominently with attention to specific detail.
American Historical	1. Detailed scenes of military battles, or special events, such as treaty signings, and war ships. 2. State seals or coats of arms bearing U.S. state names.
Exotic Views	1. Animals not indigenous to America or the British Isles, such as camels, tigers, and elephants. 2. Exotic architecture, such as mosques, minarets, etc. 3. Figures in foreign garb.
Romantic	1. Small figures in foreground, strolling, fishing, etc. 2. Water source such as river or pond in mid-ground. 3. Fanciful building in background. 4. Gazebos or pavilions in foreground
Classical	1. Urns 2. Acanthus leaves 3. Columned temples 4. Figures in classical garb 5. Greek key elements
Floral	1. Central Floral—group of flowers located in center of plate or vessel, usually surrounded by unengraved (white) area. 2. Sheet Floral—a small repeating pattern, usually of flowers, across the entire surface of the vessel.
Pastoral	1. Rural-based scenes with focus on animals or people working.
Gothic	1. Architectural ruins. 2. Buildings with turrets, arches, towers, or battlements.
Japanese	1. Prunus branches 2. Fans 3. Asymmetrical designs, often on ivory-dyed ceramic body 4. Birds/plants 5. In-filled half circles

TABLE 4
DATE RANGES FOR
MARLEY DESIGNS ON PRINTED WARES

Marley Type	N	Mean Beginning and End Production Dates		Range of Production
Continuation				
Main Scene	38	1815	1837	1784–1903
Continuous				
Repeating:				
Floral	858	1820	1836	1784–1856
Geometric	105	1818	1829	1784–1864
Other	164	1825	1848	1784–1910
Linear	44	1842	1858	1820–1891
Noncontinuous				
Repeating:				
Floral	121	1829	1843	1799–1894
Vignettes:				
Floral	49	1832	1848	1802–1889
Scene	132	1832	1847	1790–1889
Object	27	1838	1849	1809–1889

years of manufacture between 1841 and 1852. Central Gothic designs are often accompanied by border motifs that contain scrolled or arched designs against a background of concentric circles or lines, as shown in Figure 19.

Floral

Floral motifs were popular transfer-print subjects for potters throughout the course of the 19th century. Temporal differences were apparent, however. The most prevalent floral designs had a central floral motif, generally accented with a floral printed marley or border (Figure 14). The peak years of production for central floral patterns were 1833–1849. Another type of floral pattern is that with an overall repeating design, known as a sheet pattern (Figure 15). These were most commonly produced between 1826 and 1842.

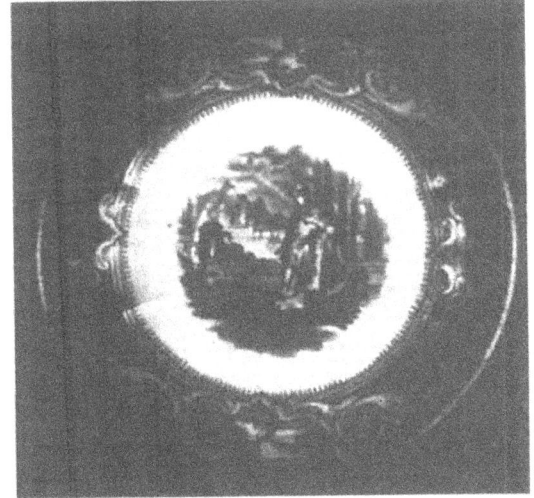

FIGURE 18. This unmarked classical pattern with a vignette border, was imported to the United States by the Davenport Brothers of New York. (Photo by P. Samford; courtesy of George L. Miller.)

Japanese Aesthetic

The opening of trade with Japan to the west in the mid-19th century sparked the popularity of Japanese-style designs in British decorative arts that occurred in the 1870s and 1880s (Pickford 1983:153). Intrigued by the perceived romanticism and exoticism of Japan, westerners began purchasing Japanese prints, fabrics, and lacquer (Meech 1989:19). British manufacturers, inspired by the exhibits displayed at the 1862 International Exhibition, saw the monetary potential of "Japonisme" or the "taste for things Japanese" and began to produce a number of household and decorative items in this style (Sato and Watanabe 1991:14, 127). Japanese-inspired designs formed one component of the aesthetic movement, where decorative emphasis was on asymmetry and imagery that combined birds and butterflies with exotic flowering plants (Bosomworth 1991:8). Many of the Japanese-inspired earthenwares are printed in brown, black, red, or green on ivory-dyed ceramic bodies. Common design motifs on Japanese aesthetic vessels are fans, half circles filled with decorative patterns, prunus blossoms, bamboo, birds, and butterflies in asymmetrical collage-like effects (Figure 16).

Summary

In summary, the data from marked vessels support temporal patterning of central designs on printed wares. Each of the central motifs exhibited a peak range of production that generally spanned about 20 years. Designs based on Chinese porcelains were the earliest motifs to appear on Staffordshire earthenwares, followed by anglicized variations of these designs. Blue printing on a white background, in imitation of Chinese porcelain, was standard for these early Chinese-influenced patterns. As technological advances occurred that allowed greater detail in engraving and a wider range of colors to be produced, potters began to broaden the range of designs. These motifs can be readily related to major decorative trends occurring in England and the United States during the 19th century (Table 3). Scenes depicting places in North America and

FIGURE 19. The Venus pattern, by Podmore, Walker, and Company (1834–1859), has a border with a continuous repeating linear pattern. (Photograph by P. Samford; collection of the author.)

Britain were also among the earliest designs used by the potteries; these gave way to fanciful Romantic, Pastoral, and Gothic scenes after the Copyright Act of 1842 made it illegal to use published prints as sources for the engravers. Classical designs enjoyed a brief span of popularity coinciding with the Greek Revival in the United States. Japanese-inspired designs were popular after Japan was opened to the West toward the end of the 19th century. Figure 17 illustrates the overlapping periods of production for each of the different central motifs. The graph for each motif type shows what percentage of the total number of patterns, in the study sample, were in production at different times. For example, of the 214 different exotic views patterns in production between 1793 and 1868, a total of 133, or 67 percent, of the patterns were being produced in 1830. Some of the graphs show short, sharp peaks of production for motifs, such as Japanese-inspired designs, while others show slower, longer periods of production.

Borders on Printed Wares

Another key to dating printed wares lies within the border, or marley, designs that served as a frame around the central decorative element on many vessel forms. Inspiration for border design appears to have been drawn from many sources, including lace and wallpaper (Coysh 1970:7; Postlewait 1988:21). While some borders were distinctive to one particular manufacturer, popular patterns were often imitated, and potter attribution based on border style can be dangerous (Postlewait 1988:20). Marley designs, however, do fall into several easily characterizable categories with distinct production periods (Table 4).

Continuation of Main Scene

These rather uncommon transfer-print treatments are found on plates, dishes, and other flat vessel forms and are distinct in that there is no separate border motif (Figure 7). The central design continues to the rim of the flatware vessel, although the border area is often "framed" with a tree or other vegetation which is part of the main design. This treatment appears to have been restricted to British, American, and exotic views. Enoch Wood and Sons used this treatment in their Italian Scenery series, as did James

and Ralph Clews in their Foliage and Scroll Border series. This border treatment is most common on vessels produced between 1815 and 1837, corresponding well with the dates for these American, British, and exotic views.

Geometric

Geometric borders are those whose primary elements consist of unbroken, repeating patterns of lozenges, honeycombs, butterflies, Joo-1, and key motifs (Figures 3, 4). These designs are found most typically in conjunction with Chinese and chinoiserie central motifs and have a peak range of production between 1818 and 1829.

Floral

Floral borders fall most readily into two types: those with continuous repeating motifs whose patterns run unbroken around the marley (Figure 5), and those whose floral motifs are broken by unprinted white areas or areas with a light or airy background pattern (Figure 14). The marleys with noncontinuous floral motifs were most commonly produced between 1829 and

TABLE 5
DATE RANGES FOR COLOR ON PRINTED WARES

Color	N	Mean Beginning and End Production Dates		Range of Production
Dark blue	122	1819	1835	1802–1846
Medium blue	120	1817	1834	1784–1859
Black	49	1825	1838	1785–1864
Brown	69	1829	1843	1818–1869
Light blue	89	1833	1848	1818–1867
Green	21	1830	1846	1818–1859
Red	20	1829	1842	1818–1880
Purple	56	1827	1838	1814–1867
Lavender	13	1830	1846	1818–1871
Mulberry	29	1837	1852	1818–1870
Pink	52	1827	1842	1784–1864
Two color printing	18	1831	1846	1818–1866
Brown on ivory body	24	1881	1888	1873–1895
Black on ivory body	26	1883	1889	1879–1890

1843. Those with boldly printed, unbroken floral borders date somewhat earlier, with peak production occurring between 1820 and 1836.

Vignettes or Reserves

In the 1830s and 1840s, marley designs incorporating small oval or oblong cartouches enclosing a variety of designs became popular (Figure 18). These vignettes, usually found in conjunction with floral elements, were often printed on white granite bodies (Teresita Majewski 1996, pers. comm.). Floral vignettes were most often produced between 1832 and 1848. Vignettes containing objects such as musical instruments or statuary were common between 1838 and 1849, and those with scenes or landscapes had a peak production range of 1832 to 1847.

Linear

During the later decades of printed ware popularity, a border treatment that has been designated as a continuous repeating linear element was common. With a period of peak production ranging from 1842 to 1858, this border treatment consisted of closely spaced concentric lines running around the rim of the marley. These concentric lines served as a background for discontinuous floral or scroll marley motifs (Figure 19).

Summary

In summary, while there are not as many distinct marley motifs as there are central design motifs, several recognizable themes occur which show temporal patterning. Specific types of marley decoration appear to be related to central motif: Chinese and chinoiserie central motifs usually have geometric repeating borders; continuous floral motifs are typical of American, British, and exotic views, as is the less common treatment where there is no distinct border. Later central motifs, such as Romantic, pastoral, Gothic, and floral, are usually characterized by

FIGURE 20. This plate, depicting the pattern Ulysses Weeps at the Song of Demodocus, by Joseph Clementson (1839–1864) is an example of a negative pattern. It is part of the Classical Antiquities Series, and was registered on 13 March 1849 (Photo by P. Samford; courtesy of George L. Miller.)

noncontinuous floral marleys, or those with floral and vignette elements.

Colors on Printed Wares

Underglaze printed vessels produced at the end of the 18th century and into the first several decades of the following century were primarily blue in color. At that time, cobalt was the only coloring agent that could withstand the high heat of the glost oven without excessive blurring (Coysh 1970:7). Blue was undoubtedly the most popular color for printed decoration on English earthenwares; in addition to the dark blue typical of the early period of transfer wares, a variety of lighter shades was also common.

As technology improved and glazes became clearer, other colors began to be developed successfully for underglaze printing. Various combinations of metallic oxides produced different colors; for example, a mixture of manganese, copper, and cobalt produced a black printed transfer (Williams 1975:131). Simeon Shaw wrote:

Very recently several of the most eminent Manufacturers have introduced a method of ornamenting Table and Dessert Services, similarly to Tea Services, by the Black Printers using red, brown and green colours, for beautiful designs of flowers and landscapes; on Pottery greatly improved in quality, and shapes formed with additional taste and elegance. This pottery has a rich and delicate appearance, and owing to the Blue Printed having become so common, the other is now obtaining a decided preference in most genteel circles (Shaw 1900[1829]:234–235).

Consumers could purchase matching dinner, tea, or toilet sets in an assortment of colors. In August of 1833, Philadelphia merchants S. & T. Tams purchased from potters Job and John Jackson table, tea, and toiletwares of the pattern "Clyde Scenery" in purple, pink, brown, and blue (U.S. Customs House Papers 1790–1869). The following year, the same pottery firm shipped "Clyde Scenery" printed in green to the United States (Downs Collection Bill of Lading).

Black appears to have been among the first successful colors other than blue, but was followed by various shades of brown, purple, green, red, and lavender. The color brown was used in printing prior to 1829, but it became more common in the 1830s (Miller 1984:44). The peak periods of production for green, red, and brown wares confirmed the mean beginning date of

1829 (Table 5). Red was one of the more difficult colors to produce successfully (Williams 1975:133). For the purposes of this analysis, dark red or maroon printed vessels have been included with the "red" category, while a distinction was made between purple wares and those more of a mulberry, or brownish purple, color. Appendix A lists the Munsell color values used for each color designation in this study (Munsell 1929).

Printing in two or more colors was introduced around 1840 (Honey 1952:622–623). Generally, the central design of a vessel would be depicted in one color, and the border in a contrasting color. The production of these vessels could involve two different copper plates, one for each ink color, or a single copper plate where different colored oils were applied to different parts of the engraved design (Halfpenny 1994c:69–70). When multicolored prints were first produced, multiple firings, one for each color, were required (Majewski and O'Brien 1987:143). By 1848, however, blue, red, and yellow could be fixed in a single firing. Four years later potters could also fix brown and green colors at the same time (Hughes and Hughes 1968:54). The most commonly appearing color combination in the study's database was red and green.

Some printed wares display a type of polychrome decoration known as clobbering, consisting of colored enamels—pinks, greens, yellows, reds—hand-applied as highlights over the final lead glazing (Coysh and Henrywood 1982:87). Clobbering is generally restricted to small areas along the rim or marley of the vessel and is a technique quite distinct from one practiced somewhat later in the century of printing a design with larger areas intended to be filled with enamels. Clobbering used as a decorative technique most commonly appears on vessels manufactured after 1840.

Other Printing Techniques

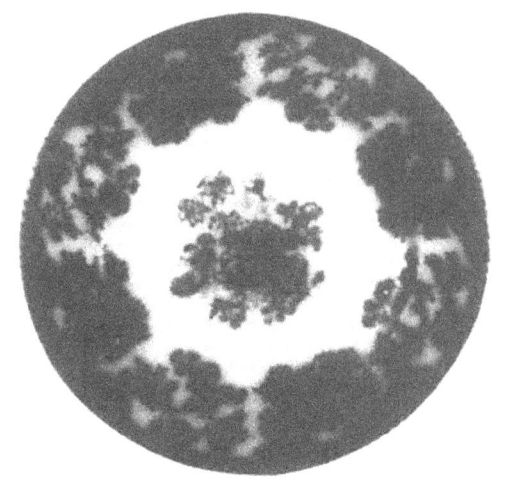

FIGURE 21. Persian Rose, a flow pattern by W. Baker and Company (1839–1932), shows the soft blurring typical of the flow process. (Photo by George L. Miller.)

Engraving technology, field dots, negative printing, and flown colors are other technologies, addressed briefly below.

TABLE 6
DATE RANGES FOR ENGRAVING ELEMENTS ON PRINTED WARES

Technique	N	Mean Beginning and End Production Dates		Range of Production
Line Engraving	13	1797	1812	1785–1833
Field Dots	34	1816	1841	1790–1853
Negative Print	13	1821	1840	1802–1864

Engraving Technology

Improvements in the materials used in the engraving process changed the look of printed wares in the first decade of the 19th century. During the first several decades of printing as a decorative technique, the tissue paper used for transferring the inked design to the bisque-fired vessel was coarse and thick. Due to poor paper quality, engraving of the copper plates had to be rendered in thick lines to enable the paper to absorb the ink and resulted in finished wares (Figure 3) with little or no tonal value (Whiter 1970:142). After the 1803 invention of the Fourdrinier paper machine, capable of producing finer quality tissue, artists employed by the potteries enjoyed more freedom in engraving techniques. Line engraving could be combined with stippling to allow fine tone gradations in color and three-dimensional shading of the entire surface (Figure 5). The use of combined line and stipple engraving began around 1807, with ceramic vessels showing a mastery of the technique by the end of the first decade of the century (Coysh and Henrywood 1982:9). Vessels in the study sample with simple line engraving showed a peak production range between 1797 and 1812 (Table 6). The use of line and stipple

TABLE 7
DATE RANGES FOR FLOWN COLORS ON PRINTED WARES

Type	N	Mean Beginning and End Production Dates		Range of Production
Flow Blue				
Chinoiserie landscape	38	1841	1854	1828–1867
Romantic	15	1849	1863	1830–1920
Chinoiserie floral	10	1839	1856	1834–1887
Central floral	17	1890	1904	1862–1929
No central design	18	1891	1908	1878–1920
Flow Mulberry	25	1840	1858	1828–1867

combination engraving continued throughout the remainder of the period of printed ware popularity.

Field Dots

With this decorative element, the marley design is printed on a background, or field, of small white dots against the colored ground. Of the examples used in this study, 88 percent (30 out of 34) were on vessels with British or American views as their central motif. The use of field dots was typical of the firms of Enoch Wood and Sons (1818–1846), Ralph Stevenson (1810–1832), and Andrew Stevenson (1816–1830).

Negative Print

This category includes vessels which have been printed "in reverse" to typical vessels. For example, the background of the vessel will be blue and the design elements will appear in white (Figure 20). This treatment appears to have been uncommon, and the sample size from this study was quite small (N = 13). The period of peak production for these vessels was 1821 to 1840.

Flow Blue and Other Flown Wares

In the early 1830s, a new process for decorating ceramics was introduced by the Staffordshire potters (Williams 1984). It was not until the 1840s, however, that flown decorated wares were available in any quantity in the U.S. market (Collard 1967:118; Miller 1991:9) Believed to produce a softer visual effect than the mechanical look of the standard underglaze printing technique, flown colors on earthenwares were achieved by placing a cup with a volatizing solution, such as lime or chloride of ammonia, in the saggars during the glaze firing of traditionally printed wares. These chemicals caused the printed color to flow outside the original pattern lines and produce a soft, halo-like effect (Williams 1984). While a misty or cloudy effect was produced in lighter colored pieces, designs in some of the more heavily printed or darker flown pieces were almost completely obscured from view.

The popularity of flown wares was enormous and long-lived, with production continuing from the early 19th century well into the 20th century. There seem to have been two periods of popularity for flow blue ceramics, one period falling in the mid-19th century (1840s and 1850s) and the other at the end of the same century (ca. 1890–1904). Several distinctive stylistic motifs occur within each of these periods (Table 7). Earlier patterns tended to have chinoiserie themes, with landscapes most common between 1841 and 1854. Chinoiserie florals—peonies, chrysanthemums, lotus blossoms, and butterflies were typical elements—were at their peak range of production between 1839 and 1856. Designs with a romantic theme were popular slightly later, and were more typically produced between 1849 and 1863. At the end of the 19th century, floral designs predominated (Figure 21). They consisted of either small central non-chinoiserie flowers with a corresponding floral marley, or vessels decorated only with a border and no central motif. The period of highest popularity for these later central floral patterns fell between 1875 and 1886. Vessels with no central motif, but with a marley design in flown colors, were most popular between 1891 and 1908. The marley designs on flow decorated vessels of all types were generally discontinuous repeating floral patterns.

Although blue was by far the most popular color for flown decorated wares, vessels were printed in mulberry (also called puce), brown, black, and green (Collard 1967:118). Blue remained a popular color throughout the period of flow production, while the manufacture of mulberry-colored vessels was much more temporally restricted. The period of heaviest production of mulberry-printed flow vessels fell between 1841 and 1858. Not enough data were collected on other flow colors to establish date ranges. The use of gold gilt as a decorative element on flown wares began in the 1860s (Mason 1982:9).

Conclusions

In a segment of *Eliza Cook's Journal*, entitled "The New Crockery Shop," Cook addressed the role of printed ceramics in the middle-class household:

> Poussins may arise; Claudes may paint their glorious landscapes; Raphaels their divine countenances; but pictures such as these are not always accessible; and even when accessible, not always intelligible to mental faculties, wholly or partially uneducated. But a well-shaped jug, or cup with a hanging bunch of flowers, or pastoral landscapes on them, in these our days of cheap and cheapening art, in relation to domestic life, can go every where; and the germ of many a great intelligence will be fostered, by thus placing the true foundation of progressive art in ALL the forms which minister to the conveniences of every-day life. The vital impulse necessary to artistic love and artistic excellence may be given to the child by the figure on his dinner-plate. . . .Neat tea services have likewise led to many a well scrubbed table, a cleaner hearth, a cheerfuller fireside. . . .and such sound comforts as lead men and women from the gin shops (Cook 1849:37–38).

While certainly not all purchasers of printed wares would have endowed their crockery with the significance that Eliza Cook did, the proliferation of motifs and individual patterns on printed earthenwares attests to their popularity. Not immune to the desires of consumers, Staffordshire potters tried a variety of decorative techniques to attract new markets and stimulate purchases of their wares. The design motifs that they chose to use reflected the larger decorative trends of the day, and, as this study illustrates, their manufacture dates closely paralleled them. As seen earlier in Simeon Shaw's 1829 quotation, new colors were developed because blue printed wares had become so commonplace they no longer attracted a genteel clientele. As the market among the wealthy for printed wares became saturated toward the end of the first quarter of the 19th century, the potters, desirous of appealing to the middle classes, cut the cost of printed wares by decreasing the size and amount of detail in the engravings. The soft, watercolor-like effect typical of American, British, and early exotic views gave way to smaller and more two-dimensional prints. By the end of

the 1850s, production of printed wares was tapering off as molded white granite and other minimally decorated wares were becoming more popular. The introduction of decals as a means of decorating ceramics beginning in the late 19th century may have also played a role in the decline of printed decoration (Majewski and O'Brien 1987:147; Majewski 1996, pers. comm.). Underglaze printing did continue, but by the end of the 19th century, the most common printed designs in the study sample were floral or geometric border designs surrounding an undecorated central area.

Researchers using this dating tool should keep in mind that the dates provided in this paper are dates of peak production for specific motifs, colors, or engraving techniques. Ceramics found in archaeological contexts will have a use-span which will need to be considered during analysis. Future research could address the question of how production date ranges correlate with date ranges for use of ceramic items.

Additional studies on printed wares could include linking vessel form with design motifs and other decorative attributes to see if a time lag exists between the appearance of motif types on teawares, and other costly, high-status vessel forms, and those of humbler ceramics, such as chamberpots, basins, and ewers. Additionally, larger sample sizes for some categories used in this study, particularly print colors, could help confirm or refine the date ranges shown here. In addition, dates from this study, used in conjunction with archaeological data on well-documented sites could help determine whether motif and color preferences exist regionally or socioeconomically. Work in Texas (Pollan et. al. 1996), Alaska (Jackson 1991), California (Felton and Schulz 1983), and the Pacific Northwest (Chapman 1993) would be good comparisons for sites excavated east of the Mississippi.

Using the results of this study, it is possible to look at central design motifs and other decorative and technological details on printed wares and date them with greater accuracy than previously possible. Although archaeologists may not find a large enough portion of a vessel to determine the central motif, the elements listed in

Table 4 are useful for picking out likely elements in these motifs. Fortunately, marley designs and vessel color are much easier to assign based on small sherds. Using the dating tools given here, either singly or in combination, should provide another means by which late 18th- and 19th-century sites can be dated.

ACKNOWLEDGMENTS

I would like to thank the reviewers, who, to my great delight, decided to waive their anonymity when sending their comments. They were Meta Janowitz, Teresita Majewski, and George L. Miller. Their careful editing and greater knowledge of English ceramics caught my mistakes and helped me flesh out the paper in more than one area. Any errors, however, are entirely my responsibility. I also would like to acknowledge the generous support of the Henry Francis DuPont Winterthur Museum, for providing me with a research fellowship that allowed me time to gather additional data and write up the results of this research. The staff of the museum was supportive in every way. I would like in particular to thank Ann Smart Martin, Patricia Elliott, Amanda Lange, Eleanor Thompson, Mary Elise Haug, Iris Snyder, Gail Stanislaw, Mary Alice Cicerale, Bert and Ellen Denker, and Kate Hutchins. I would also like to thank the staff of the Smithsonian Museum of American History, who allowed me the opportunity to use the catalog files of the Larsen collection; and the departments of Collections and Archaeological Research at the Colonial Williamsburg Foundation for access to their collections of printed earthenwares. George L. Miller, Ann Smart Martin, and Robert Hunter shared their private collections for cataloging; I am also in their debt. Thanks go as well to Jane Eastman, Vincas P. Steponaitis, and Amy Earls. R. P. Stephen Davis, Patrick Livingood, and Tom Maher, all of the Research Laboratories of Anthropology at the University of North Carolina, and David Muraca at the Colonial Williamsburg Foundation, fielded computer questions for me. Last, but far from least, I am grateful to George L. Miller, who was the driving force behind this project in all of its phases. His inspiration, support, and, at times, less than gentle pushing have ensured that the results of this research are available.

REFERENCES

ADDISON, AGNES
    1938 *Romanticism and the Gothic Revival.* Richard R. Smith, NY.

BAKER, VERNON G.
    1978 Historical Archaeology at Black Lucy's Garden, Andover, Massachussetts: Ceramics from the Site of a Nineteenth-Century Afro-American. *Papers of the Robert S. Peabody Foundation for Archaeology,* Vol. 8. Phillips Academy, Andover, MA.

BLOOM, LINDA S.
    1988 Exotic Scenes. In *At Home and Abroad in Staffordshire,* pp. 32–34. University of Illinois, Champaign.

BOSOMWORTH, DOROTHY
    1991 *The Victorian Catalogue of Household Goods.* Portland House, NY.

BUSHMAN, RICHARD
    1993 Popular Culture and Popular Taste in Classical America. Introduction. *Classical Taste in America 1800–1840,* by Wendy A. Cooper, pp. 14–23. Abbeville Press, NY.

CAMEHL, ADA WALKER
    1948 *The Blue-China Book: Early American Scenes and History Pictured in the Pottery of the Time.* Reprint of 1916 edition. Tudor, NY.

CHAPMAN, JUDITH SAUNDERS
    1993 French Prairie Ceramics: The Harriet D. Munnick Archaeological Collection, ca. 1820–1860: A Catalog and Northwest Comparative Guide. *Anthropology Northwest 8.* Department of Anthropology, Oregon State University, Corvallis.

CLARKE, DAVID
    1968 *Analytical Archaeology.* Methuen, London

COLLARD, ELIZABETH
    1967 *Nineteenth-Century Pottery and Porcelain in Canada.* McGill University Press, Montreal, PQ.

COOK, ELIZA
    1849 The New Crockery Shop. *Eliza Cook's Journal,* pp. 20–25, 36–38. John Owen Clarke, London.

COOPER, WENDY A.
    1993 *Classical Taste in America, 1800–1840.* Abbeville Press, NY.

COPELAND, ROBERT
    1980 *Spode's Willow Pattern and Other Designs After the Chinese.* Rizzoli, NY.
    1982 *Blue and White Transfer Printed Pottery.* C.I. Thomas and Sons, Haverfordwest.

COYSH, A. WILLIAM
    1970 *Blue and White Transfer Ware, 1780–1840.* Charles

E. Tuttle, Rutland, VT.

1972   *Blue-Printed Earthenware, 1800–1850.* Charles E. Tuttle, Rutland, VT.

COYSH, A. WILLIAM, AND RICHARD K. HENRYWOOD

1982   *A Dictionary of Blue and White Printed Pottery, 1780–1880,* Vol. 1. Baron, Suffolk.

1989   *The Dictionary of Blue and White Printed Pottery, 1780–1880,* Vol. 2. Antique Collectors Club, Woodbridge, Suffolk.

COYSH, A. WILLIAM, AND FRANK STEFANO, JR.

1981   *Collecting Ceramic Landscapes; British and American Landscapes on Printed Pottery.* Lund Humphries, London.

DANIELL, THOMAS

1816   *Oriental Scenery: 150 Years of the Architecture, Antiques, and Landscape Scenery of Hindoostan.* Published by the author, London.

DAVIES, JANE B.

1976   Introduction. *The Gothic Revival Style in America, 1830–1870,* by Katherine S. Howe and David Warren, pp. 1–9. Museum of Fine Arts, Houston, TX.

DAVIS, ALEXANDER JACKSON

1980   *Rural Residence.* Reprint of 1838 edition. Da Capo Press, NY.

DES FONTAINES, UNA

1966   Ceramic Transfer-Printing Techniques, 1750–1850. *The Eleventh Wedgwood International Seminar,* pp. 100–103. Henry Ford Museum, Dearborn, MI.

DETHLEFSEN, EDWIN, AND JAMES DEETZ

1966   Death's Heads, Cherubs, and Willow Trees: Experimental Archaeology in Colonial Cemeteries. *American Antiquity* 31(4):502–510.

DRAKARD, DAVID, AND PAUL HOLDWAY

1983   *Spode Printed Ware.* Longman, NY.

EATWELL, ANN, AND ALEX WERNER

1991   A London Staffordshire Warehouse—1794–1825. *Journal of the Northern Ceramic Society* 8:91–124.

EWINS, NEIL M. D.

1990   *Staffordshire Ceramic Trade with North America, ca. 1780–1880.* Unpublished B.A. thesis, Staffordshire Polytechnic, Stoke.

FELTON, DAVID L., AND PETER D. SCHULZ

1983   The Diaz Collection: Material Culture and Social Change in Mid-Nineteenth-Century Monterey.

California Archaeological Reports 23. California Department of Parks and Recreation, Sacramento.

FENNELLY, CATHERINE

1967   *Something Blue: Some American Views on Staffordshire.* The Meriden Gravure, Meriden, CT.

GERMANN, GEORG

1972   *Gothic Revival in Europe and Britain: Sources, Influences, and Ideas,* translated by Gerald Onn. Lund Humphries, London.

GODDEN, GEOFFREY

1963   *British Pottery and Porcelain, 1780–1850.* Baker, London.

1964   *Encyclopaedia of British Pottery and Porcelain Marks.* Crown, NY.

GURUJAL, L. CHAVONNE HOYLE

1988   The Historical Development of the Staffordshire Transfer Ware Process. In *At Home and Abroad in Staffordshire,* pp. 12–17. University of Illinois, Champaign.

HALFPENNY, PAT A.

1994a Bat Printing on 19th-Century Porcelain. In *Penny Plain, Twopence Coloured; Transfer Printing on English Ceramics, 1750–1850,* edited by Pat A. Halfpenny, pp. 45–58. Stoke-on-Trent City Museum and Art Gallery, Stoke.

1994b Underglaze Blue Printed Ware. In *Penny Plain, Twopence Coloured; Transfer Printing on English Ceramics, 1750–1850,* edited by Pat A. Halfpenny, pp. 61–68. Stoke-on-Trent City Museum and Art Gallery, Stoke.

1994c Colour and Multi-Colour Transfer-printed Pottery. In *Penny Plain, Twopence Coloured; Transfer Printing on English Ceramics, 1750–1850,* edited by Pat A. Halfpenny, pp. 69–74. Stoke-on-Trent City Museum and Art Gallery, Stoke.

HOLDWAY, PAUL

1986   Techniques of Transfer Printing on Cream Coloured Earthenware. In *Creamware and Pearlware,* edited by Terence A. Lockett and Pat A. Halfpenny, pp. 20–23. Print George Street Press, Stoke-on-Trent.

HONEY, W. B.

1952   *European Ceramic Art from the End of the Middle Ages to about 1815.* Faber and Faber, London.

HOWE, KATHERINE, AND DAVID B. WARREN

1976   *The Gothic Revival Style in America, 1830–1870.* Museum of Fine Arts, Houston, TX.

HUGHES, BERNARD, AND THERLE HUGHES
    1968 *English Porcelain and Bone China, 1743–1850*.
        Frederick A. Praeger, NY.

IMPEY, OLIVER
    1977 *Chinoiserie: The Impact of Oriental Styles on Western
        Art and Decoration*. Charles Scribner's Sons, NY.

JACKSON, LOUISE M.
    1991 *Nineteenth-Century British Ceramics: A Key to
        Cultural Dynamics in Southwestern Alaska (Russian
        America)*. Ph.D. dissertation, Department of
        Anthropology, University of California, Los Angeles.
        University Microfilms International, Ann Arbor, MI.

JACOBSON, DAWN
    1993 *Chinoiserie*. Phaidon Press, London.

JARRY, MADELEINE
    1981 *Chinoiserie: Chinese Influence on European
        Decorative Arts, 17th and 18th Centuries*. Vendome
        Press, NY.

KRANNERT ART MUSEUM
    1988 *At Home and Abroad in Staffordshire*. Exhibit catalog.
        Krannert Art Museum, University of Illinois,
        Champaign.

KROEBER, ALFRED L., AND WILLIAM STRONG
    1924 The Uhle Pottery Collections from Ica. *University of
        California Publications in American Archaeology
        and Ethnology* 21(3):95–133.

LAIDACKER, SAM
    1938 *The Standard Catalogue of Anglo-American China
        from 1810 to 1850*. Sam Laidacker, Scranton, PA.
    1951 *Anglo-American China, Part 2*. Sam Laidacker,
        Bristol, PA.

LARSEN, ELLOUISE BAKER
    1975 *American Historical Views on Staffordshire China*.
        Reprint of 1950 edition. Doubleday, NY.

MAGUIRE, EUNICE D.
    1988 What's in a Name? In *At Home and Abroad in
        Staffordshire*, pp. 2–10. Krannert Art Museum,
        University of Illinois, Champaign.

MAJEWSKI, TERESITA, AND MICHAEL J. O'BRIEN
    1987 The Use and Misuse of Nineteenth-Century English
        and American Ceramics in Archaeological Analysis.
        Advances in Archaeological Method and Theory
        11:97–207. Michael B. Schiffer, editor. Serial
        Publication Series. Academic Press, NY.

MARQUARDT, WILLIAM H.
    1978 Advances in Archaeological Seriation. *Advances in
        Archaeological Method and Theory* 1:257–314.

        Michael B. Schiffer, editor. Serial Publication Series.
        Academic Press, NY.

MASON, VENEITA
    1982 *Popular Patterns of Flow Blue China with Prices*.
        Wallace-Homestead, Des Moines, IA.

MEECH, JULIA
    1989 Japonisme at the Turn of the Century. In *Perspectives
        on Japonisme: The Japanese Influence on America*,
        edited by Phillip D. Cate, pp. 18–28. Rutgers University
        Press, New Brunswick, NJ.

MEIJER, E. R.
    1959 On the Romantics and Their Times. In *The Romantic
        Movement: Fifth Exhibition to Celebrate the Tenth
        Anniversary of the Council of Europe*, pp. 38–43. Arts
        Council of Great Britain. Shenval Press, London.

MILLARD, CHARLES
    1977 Images of Nature: A Photo-Essay. In *Nature and the
        Victorian Imagination*, edited by U. C. Knoepflmacher
        and G. B. Tennyson, pp. 3–26. University of California
        Press, Berkeley.

MILLER, GEORGE L.
    1980 Classification and Economic Scaling of 19th-Century
        Ceramics. *Historical Archaeology* 14:1–40.
    1984 George M. Coates, Pottery Merchant of Philadelphia,
        1817–1831. *Winterthur Portfolio* 19(1):37–92.
    1987 Origins of Josiah Wedgwood's "Pearlware." *Northeast
        Historical Archaeology* 16:83–95.
    1991 A Revised Set of CC Index Values for Classification
        and Economic Scaling of English Ceramics from
        1787 to 1880. *Historical Archaeology* 25(1):1–25.
    1994 New York Earthenware Dealers and the Country
        Trade in the Nineteenth Century. Manuscript on file,
        University of Delaware Center for Archaeological
        Research, Newark.

MILLER, GEORGE L., AND SILAS D. HURRY
    1983 Ceramic Supply in an Economically Isolated Frontier
        Community: Portage County of the Ohio Western
        Reserve, 1800–1825. *Historical Archaeology*
        17(2):80–92.

MILLER, GEORGE L., ANN SMART MARTIN, AND NANCY S.
DICKINSON
    1994 Changing Consumption Patterns: English Ceramics
        and the American Market from 1770 to 1840. In
        Everyday Life in the Early Republic, edited by
        Catherine E. Hutchins, pp. 219–248. Winterthur
        Museum, Winterthur, DE.

MUNSELL COLOR COMPANY
    1929 *Munsell Book of Color*. Baltimore, MD.

PETRIE, WILLIAM M. F.
  1972 *Methods and Aims in Archaeology.* Reprint of 1904 edition. Benjamin Blom, NY.

PICKFORD, IAN
  1983 *Silver Flatware: English, Irish, and Scottish, 1660–1980.* Baron, Woodbridge. Suffolk.

POLLAN, SANDRA D., W. SUE GROSS, AMY C. EARLS, JOHNNEY T. POLLAN, JR., AND JAMES L. SMITH
  1996 *Nineteenth-Century Transfer-Printed Ceramics from the Townsite of Old Velasco (41BO125), Brazoria County, Texas: An Illustrated Catalogue.* Prewitt and Associates, Austin, TX.

POSTLEWAIT, DEBORAH S.
  1988 Borders on Transfer Ware. In *At Home and Abroad in Staffordshire*, pp. 20–22. Krannert Art Museum, University of Illinois, Champaign.

PRICE, CYNTHIA
  1979 Nineteenth-Century Ceramics in the Eastern Ozark Border Region. *Southwest Missouri State University Center for Archaeological Research Monograph Series* 1. Center for Archaeological Research, Springfield, MO.

PUGIN, A. W., AND E. J. WILLSON
  1895 *Specimens of Gothic Architecture.* Reprint of 1821 edition. John Grant, Edinburgh.

SANDKUHLE, H. J.
  1970 *F. W. J. Schelling.* Stuttgart.

SATA, TOMOKO, AND TOSHIO WATANABE
  1991 The Aesthetic Dialogue Examined. In *Japan and Britain: An Aesthetic Dialogue, 1850–1930*, edited by Tomoko Sato and Toshio Watanabe, pp. 14–17. Lund Humphries, London.

SHAW, SIMEON
  1900 *History of the Staffordshire Potteries.* Hanley. Reprint of 1829 edition. Scott and Greenwood, London.

SPIER, LESLIE
  1917 An Outline for a Chronology of Zuni Ruins. *Anthropological Papers of the American Museum of Natural History* 18 (part 3). American Museum of Natural History, NY.

SUSSMAN, LYNNE
  1979 Spode/Copeland Transfer-Printed Patterns Found at 20 Hudson's Bay Company Sites: Canadian Historic Sites. *Occasional Papers in Archaeology and History* 22. Parks, Canada, Ottawa, ON.

TRACY, BERRY
  1963 *Classical America, 1815–1845.* Baker, Newark, NJ.

U.S. CUSTOMS HOUSE PAPERS
  1790–1869   *United States Customs House Papers, Philadelphia, Pennsylvania.* University of Delaware, Newark. Microfilm.

VAUGHAN, WILLIAM
  1978 *Romantic Art.* Oxford University Press, NY.

WALL, DIANA DIZEREGA
  1994 *The Archaeology of Gender: Separating the Spheres in Urban America.* Plenum Press, NY.

WHITER, LEONARD
  1970 *Spode: A History of the Family, Factory and Wares from 1733 to 1833.* Barrie and Jenkins, London.

WILLIAMS, PETRA
  1971 *Flow Blue China: An Aid to Identification.* Fountain House East, Jeffersontown, KY.
  1973 *Flow Blue China II.* Fountain House East, Jeffersontown, KY.
  1975 *Flow Blue China and Mulberry Ware.* Fountain House East, Jeffersontown, KY.
  1978 *Staffordshire Romantic Transfer Patterns: Cup Plates and Early Victorian China.* Fountain House East, Jeffersontown, KY.

WILLIAMS, PETRA, AND MARGUERITE R. WEBER
  1986 *Staffordshire II: Romantic Transfer Patterns: Cup Plates and Early Victorian China.* Fountain House East, Jeffersontown, KY.

WILLIAMS, SUSAN R.
  1984 Flow-Blue. *Antiques* 126(4):923–931.

PATRICIA M. SAMFORD
RESEARCH LABORATORIES OF ANTHROPOLOGY
UNIVERSITY OF NORTH CAROLINA
CHAPEL HILL, NC 27599-3120

APPENDIX A
MUNSELL COLOR DESIGNATIONS

Dark Blue			**Red**		
7.5 PB 2.5/10	7.5 PB 2.5/8	5 PB 3/8	10RP 3/10	10RP 4/12	
2.5 PB 3/7	7.5 PB 2/6				
			Maroon		
Medium Blue			7.5RP 3/6	7.5RP 3/8	2.5R 3/10
7.5 PB 3.5/12	2.5 PB 4/10		5R 2/8		
Light Blue			**Mulberry**		
7.5B 7/6	7.5B 9/4	2.5PB 8/6	5RP 3/4	5RP 2/4	5RP 2/6
2.5PB 7/8			5RP 2/8	2.5R 2/6	2.5R 2/4
Purple			**Brown**		
7.5P 5/8	7.5P 5/10	7.5P 4/6	2.5Y 4/4	2.5Y 3/4	2.5Y 3/2
5RP 3/6	7.5RP 2/2	10R 3/4	7.5YR 3/6	7.5YR 3/4	7.5YR 3/2
			7.5YR 2/4		
Lavender					
7.5P 7/8	7.5P 7/6	7.5P 6/8	**Green**		
7.5P 6/10			2.5BG 3/6	2.5BG 3/8	2.5BG 4/8
			2.5BG 4/6	2.5BG 3/4	5BG 4/8
Pink			10GY 3/6	10GY 4/8	7.5GY 3/6
5RP 6/8	5RP 7/8	5RP 6/10			
10RP 6/6					

GEORGE L. MILLER

A Revised Set of CC Index Values for Classification and Economic Scaling of English Ceramics from 1787 to 1880

ABSTRACT

This paper presents an updated and expanded set of CC index values for plates, teas, and bowls for the period 1787 to 1880. It is meant to replace the index values in the article "Classification and Economic Scaling of 19th-Century Ceramics" (Miller 1980). In addition to expanding the range of years covered, it adds values for dishes and for Irish size teas, as well as correcting a misconception about the stability of the price of CC ware during the first half of the 19th century. A better understanding of the discount rates has made it necessary to recalculate the index values for the post-1844 period. This paper also presents extensive chronological and descriptive information on the common types of ceramics that were imported from the 1780s to the 1880s.

Introduction

During the second half of the 18th century, a revolution took place in the English ceramic industry in Staffordshire. Developing technology, transportation, introduction of new raw materials, glazes, and marketing culminated in the Staffordshire industry becoming one of the dominant suppliers of ceramics to a world market (Miller et al. 1989). One of the major products of that revolution was creamware, which was introduced in the early 1760s and went on to become the dominant ceramic ware used during the rest of the century.

By the late 1790s, however, the demand for creamware was declining, and it had become the cheapest refined ware available. From that time on, creamware was referred to as "CC ware" in potters' and merchants' records. CC ware remained the cheapest type available from the late 1780s through the 19th century. While it consistently remained the cheapest ceramic, its appearance changed over that period. By the 1830s, CC ware was considerably lighter in color and would be classed as a whiteware by most archaeologists.

Because CC ware remained the cheapest type available for over a century, it makes an excellent bench mark to gauge the cost of other wares in terms of its price. A set of index values based on the cost of CC ware was published in *Historical Archaeology* in 1980 (Miller 1980). Over the last decade, those index values have been widely used to examine and compare expenditure patterns represented in archaeological assemblages. The CC index values presented here are the results of research made possible by a recent fellowship and two grants and are intended to supersede those prices provided in the earlier 1980 article.

CC Index Values: An Update

One of the basic assumptions of the 1980 article was that the cost of CC ware was relatively stable from 1796 to around 1860. That assumption was based on the prices of 16 dozen CC vessels from the Staffordshire Potters' price fixing lists of 1796, 1814, 1833, and 1846 (1796, 1846 reprinted in Mountford 1975:11–14; 1814 reprinted in Miller 1984; Staffordshire Potters 1833), and from the 1855 price list of the Fife Pottery (Miller 1980:23). Because the prices of these vessels in the above lists remained somewhat stable, it was assumed that CC index values from various years could be used to compare expenditure patterns from different time periods.

Research funded by the National Endowment for the Humanities (NEH) located Staffordshire potters' price fixing agreements from 22 different years between 1770 and 1885, and individual potters' price lists for an additional eight years during that period (Miller 1988:Appendix D). In addition to these price fixing lists, 167 potters' invoices with discount information for the period 1809 to 1875 have been located (Miller 1988: Appendix B).

This new information provides a clearer picture of the price structure for English ceramics and the relationship between the *list* prices in the price fixing lists and the *net* prices being charged by the

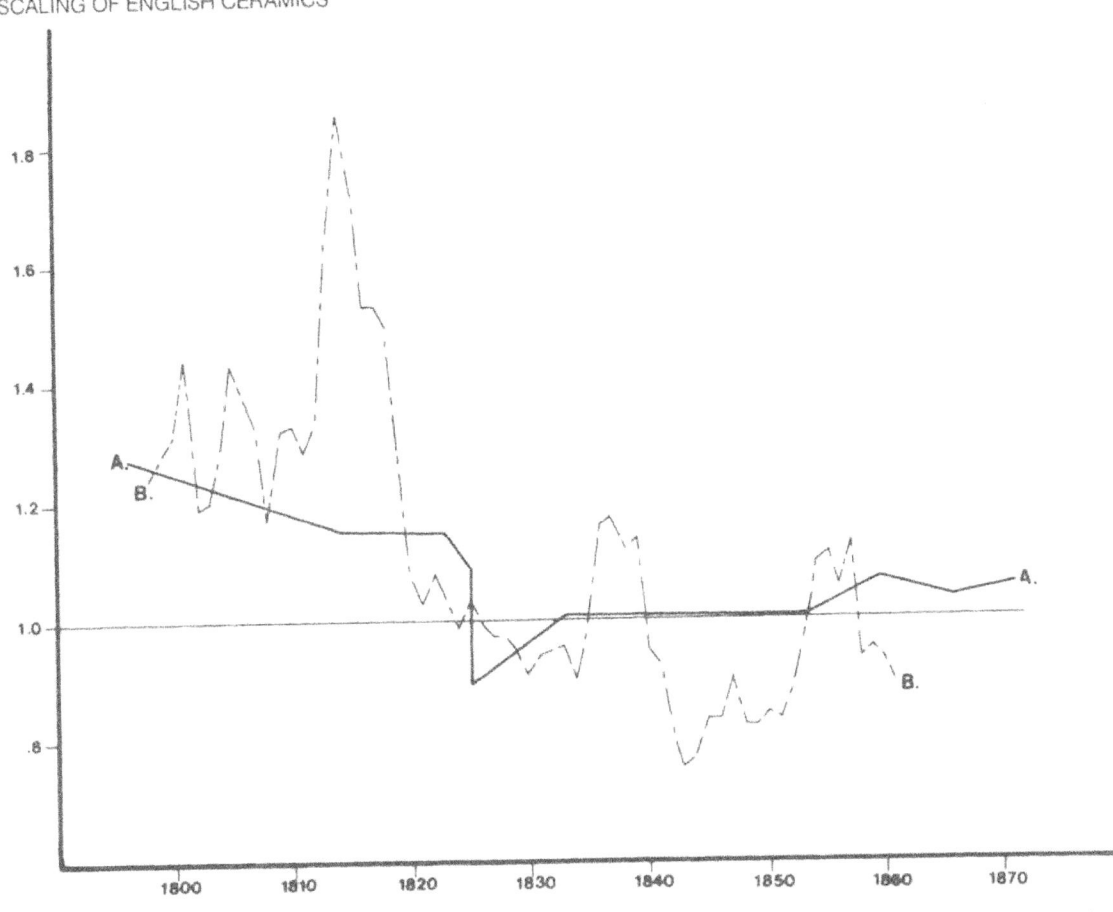

FIGURE 1. Comparison of Ceramic *List* Prices with the New York All Commodities Index of Wholesale Prices, both indexed to the period 1824 to 1842. A. = *list* prices for 48 dozen vessels, one-third creamware, shell edge, and printed wares for 1796, 1814, 1816, 1817, 1818, 1823, 1825, 1833, 1846, 1853, 1859, 1866, and 1871. B. = New York All Commodities Index of Wholesale Prices (Cole 1969: 135–136; Miller et al. 1989).

Staffordshire potters. Using these data, the list prices of 48 dozen vessels (one-third CC, edged, and printed wares) were extracted from 14 potters' price fixing lists and catalogues from 1796 to 1871 (Miller 1988:Appendix A). These *list* prices were then indexed to the period 1824 to 1842 and plotted against the New York All Commodities Index of Wholesale Prices (Cole 1969:135–136). Figure 1 illustrates the results of that price comparison. The graph suggests that prices of the common Staffordshire wares were relatively stable from 1796 to 1871.

That stability, however, is an illusion. Using the discount information from 122 potters' invoices from 25 different years, the Staffordshire average *net* prices per year were calculated for the period 1809 to 1848 (Miller 1988:Appendix C). These prices were also indexed to the period 1824 to 1842 and plotted against the New York All Commodities Index. Figure 2 presents that data. From this graph it can be seen that English ceramic prices dropped significantly from 1809 to 1848.

Clearly the prices of all wares, including CC, were dropping. CC ware remained the cheapest

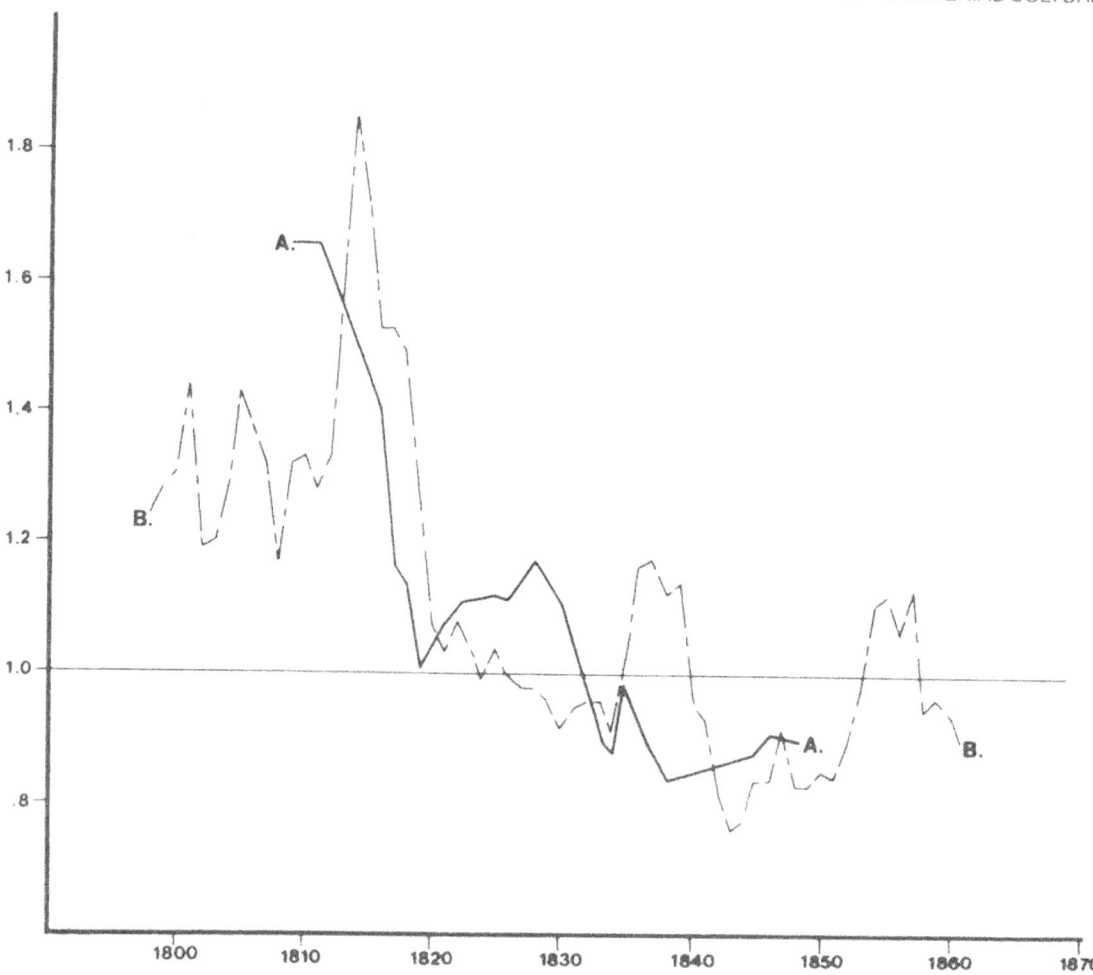

FIGURE 2   Comparison of Ceramic *Net* (wholesale) Prices with the New York All Commodities Index of Wholesale Prices, both indexed to the period 1824 to 1842. A = *list* prices for 48 dozen vessels, one-third creamware, shell edge, and printed wares for 25 different years between 1809 and 1848. B = New York All Commodities Index of Wholesale Prices (Cole 1969. 135–136. Miller et al. 1989)

refined earthenware throughout the entire period; however, it was dropping in price just like the other wares. This means that CC index values from one period should not be compared to those from another period without taking into consideration the declining prices and changing tariff rates. From the discount information gathered so far, indices within the following four periods appear to be comparable:

1780–1814 Period of the traditional discount, which was 5 percent for breakage plus 5 percent for cash payment, for a total discount of 10 percent. There was a 5 percent tariff on imported earthenware from 1789 until 1816.

1816–1830 The discount from the invoices for this period averages 28.8 percent. In addition, the tariff on earthenware had been raised to 20 percent in 1816.

1832–1842 The discount from the invoices for this period averages 39.5 percent. The tariff on earthenware continued at 20 percent until 1842.

1844–1859 The discount rate is more volatile during this period; however, the average rate of discount is 39.8 percent which is close to the previous period. The tariff rate went up to 30 percent in 1842 and remained at that rate until the Civil War.

For the periods after 1860, the quality of the information is not sufficient to set up periods or provide average discount rates. During the Civil War, the tariff rates went up and the exchange rate on the dollar dropped because of the large volume of greenback currency issued to finance the War. Assemblages from the Civil War period probably should not be compared to other time periods, and those from after the War probably should not be compared to earlier periods without taking into consideration differences in tariff and discount rates. A summary of the rates of discount and United States tariff rates on ceramics is covered more fully in appendices given in Miller (1988).

Around 1844, a change took place in the way that wares were discounted. Prior to that time, a single rate of discount was applied to all the wares on an invoice. After 1844, printed wares began to be discounted at a different rate than the other wares. As a result, the index values provided in Miller (1980) for printed wares from the post-1844 period had to be corrected. Table 1 provides a comparison of the old and new values for printed wares for 1846.

The index values for edged, painted, and dipt—or dipped—wares remained the same as those published in 1980.

The set of 1980 index values was created from a variety of sources, including potters' price fixing lists, invoices, jobbers' bills, and account books. Until now, there has not been a sufficient amount of data to build a set of index values based solely on potters' price records. Funding provided by NEH remedied this problem (Miller 1988). All of the index values presented here are based on prices from English potters' documents, such as their price fixing lists, catalogues, and invoices.

This paper presents four times as many CC index values as were available in 1980. The earlier article had values for 24 different years, while the current index values cover 38 years and also extend over a longer time period. In addition, index values are provided for new decorative types and vessel forms. Along with the above data is an expanded description of the basic decorative types and information on their periods of popularity. Further information on the technology of decoration can be found in Majewski and O'Brien (1987).

The Use of CC Index Values

Using CC index values is quite simple. Once the minimal vessel count has been completed, the plates, cups, and bowls are grouped by their decorative type. Then the user selects a year from the indexes in the appendices that follow. In dealing with sites that have been occupied for a long period of time, one should attempt to break down the site assemblages into meaningful time units such as periods of occupation for different families or generations of a family. Generating average CC index values for lumped assemblages representing over 20 years of occupation seems to be a meaningless exercise.

Once one has established the assemblage or assemblages to be compared, the index value for each vessel type is multiplied times the number of

TABLE 1
CORRECTED INDEX VALUES

	1980	Corrected
Plates		
10 inch	2.63	2.11
8 inch	2.57	2.42
7 inch	2.50	2.37
Teas		
unhandled	2.45	2.27
handled	3.00	2.77
Bowls	2.80	2.58

vessels of that type. The results for each vessel type are summed and divided by the total number of vessels, which yields the average CC index value for the assemblage. This analysis is done for plates, cups, and bowls which provides three sets of index values for each archaeological assemblage under consideration. For a more detailed explanation of how the index values were derived and are used in the study of expenditure patterns see Miller (1980:11–12).

The most common expenditure pattern that has emerged from the study of archaeological assemblages has been for the highest average index value to be from the teas and the lowest to be from the bowls. The resulting index values can be compared with ceramic index values from other sites. A recent article lists ceramic index values for 44 archaeological assemblages (Adams and Boling 1989).

In the current study, the term "white granite" has replaced "white ironstone." This term was adopted for two reasons. First, it is the most common name used for white ironstone in the potters' documents. Second, "white granite" avoids the confusion between the highly decorated stone chinas, such as Mason's 1813 "Patent Ironstone," with the plain white and molded wares from the second half of the 19th century.

Descriptions of Common Decorative Types

The following descriptions of the types of decoration used on English ceramics are to be used in conjunction with the appendices of CC index values. They cover the most common types of ceramic tea, table, and toilet wares found on North American sites occupied from the 1790s to the 1880s and provide some new chronological information. Guidance to an extensive literature on English ceramics can be found in Miller and Martin (1989).

CC Ware

CC is the potters' term for cream colored or creamware. When the term CC was used by itself,

it referred to undecorated creamware. Almost all underglaze decorated, refined earthenwares from the 1780s on were either pearlware or whiteware. Those wares, however, were consistently referenced in potters' and merchants' records by their type of decoration rather than by ware type.

Early creamware has a deep yellow tint. In 1775, the Staffordshire potters gained the right to use kaolin clays from Cornwall (Miller 1987:88), resulting in a lighter colored creamware which became common after that date. By 1830, an even lighter colored CC ware had evolved. The resulting product is what most archaeologists call whiteware. Some have attempted to attribute this change to the development of a leadless glaze around 1820; however, lead glazes continued to be the dominant type throughout the 19th century (Binns 1907:83).

Before the War of 1812, CC ware was common in most forms of tea, table, kitchen, and toilet wares (Miller et al. 1989:17). CC ware remains in the potters' price fixing lists and continues to show up in invoices of wares imported to America into at least the 1890s. However, from the 1830s on, it was more commonly found in utilitarian forms such as bowls, mugs, and chamber pots, which were less involved in status display.

Because CC ware is the base for measuring the cost of the other types, its index value is always one. Therefore, it is not listed in the tables of index values. Index values are given for CC teas, however, because the addition of handles or fluting can create CC teas with an index value greater than one.

Shell Edge Decorated Wares

"Edged" is the most common potters' term for what was called "shell edge" in Wedgwood's 1775 pattern book and in Leeds' pattern book of 1783 (Mankowitz 1966:59; Towner 1965:57–61). The 1783 Staffordshire potters' price fixing list, reprinted in Mountford (1975:9), enumerates a full range of tableware vessels available in shell edge that are listed as "edged in blue," indicating that shell edge was an item of considerable production by that date. Overglaze painted, shell-edged creamware was first produced in the 1770s (Mankowitz 1966:59). Underglaze painted shell edge was most commonly available on pearl or white wares with blue or green edges. By around 1840, green shell edge had become rare, while blue shell edge remained a commonly available type listed in potters' and merchants' invoices into the 1860s. After that date, shell edge is not commonly found in archaeological assemblages, although production continued into the 1890s and possibly later (Miller 1989).

Edged wares are generally limited to flat wares, sauce boats, tureens, and butter boats, which as a general class are known as tablewares. From the index values presented in this study, it can be seen that edged wares were the cheapest decorated tableware available for most of the 19th century.

Sponge Decorated Wares

Spatter and sponge decorated wares are two closely related types under this classification. Spattered wares have the color powdered on, whereas sponged wares have their color applied with a sponge. Powdered decoration, which has been labeled "spatter" by collectors, has a long tradition, dating back to the delft wares from the 17th century (Shlasko 1989:39). Spattered decoration occurs on "China glaze," i.e., early pearlware from the late 1770s (Ferguson 1975:6). Most of the pre-1830s wares with this type of decoration are spattered (or powdered), and they often are found with simple painted birds which collectors have called peafowl (Godden 1966:160). These painted wares continued into the mid-19th century with the broader sponged decoration.

Sponged wares without painting are not common before the introduction into the Staffordshire potteries of cut sponges with simple patterns in the late 1840s (Turner 1923:149). Most of the early examples are tea wares. After the introduction of the cut sponge, this type of decoration became more common on table, tea, and toilet wares. CC price index values for sponged wares are only available for the period from 1848 to 1871. In the

1855 Fife pottery list, sponged wares were the same price as edged wares. For their period, sponged wares are usually the cheapest vessels available with decoration (Finlayson 1972:118).

Dipped Wares

Dipped—or dipt—wares cover various types of decoration that were produced by the application of a colored clay slip. Potters' terms for these types include: variegated, mocha, moco, common cable, chainband, banded, blue banded, French gray, brick, and checkered (Mountford 1975:20; Miller 1987:91). Collectors have added to this list terms such as annular, finger-painted, finger-trailed, tree, wave, worm, and cat's eye. The most common terms used in the potters' price lists, invoices, and account books are dipt, dipped, colored, mocha, and banded.

Dipped wares were slip decorated on the green ware before it was bisque fired. Most underglaze decoration was applied to bisque fired wares. Colors of dipped wares are generally muted earth tones such as tan, rust, brown, olive drab, ocher yellow, and gray. An exception is blue-banded ware which became the most common type of dipped ware after the 1840s.

These wares occupied a grouping by themselves that was commonly referred to as "Mugs and Jugs Ware." Dipped decoration was generally limited to bowls, mugs, jugs (the English term for pitchers), chamber pots, mustard pots, castors, or shakers. Dipped teas and teapots exist, but they are rare. Dipped wares were the cheapest holloware available with decoration. These wares were not finger-painted.

The term mocha should only be used to describe those dipped wares with the dendritic pattern (Evans 1970[1846]:31). Mocha was most popular from the period 1795 to 1835 on American sites; however, mocha mugs continued to be produced in England for tavern use until the 1930s. Mocha was also developed on yellowware and was common throughout the second half of the 19th century. Index values for yellowware have not yet been worked out.

With the exception of simple banded types,

dipped wares are not common after the 1840s. Blue-banded wares continued to be produced well into the 20th century.

Underglaze and Enamelled Lined Wares

Underglaze-lined and enamelled-upon-glaze-lined wares are types listed on Staffordshire potters' price fixing lists from 1814 to 1833. They have a simple line painted around the rim and the inner edge of the marley that can be either on or under the glaze. The Wedgwood catalog for 1774 lists green double lines, brown double lines, and blue lines as decorative types (Mankowitz 1966: 57; Finer and Savage 1965:116–118). These early versions of lined types would have been enamelled on the glaze.

Underglaze-lined and enamelled-upon-glaze wares are different from the other decorative types in that they often occur on creamware with brown lines. Most other types of underglaze decoration were on pearl or white wares. Lined wares were almost always limited to tableware and are rare in teaware. Creamware and pearlware plates with one or two lines around the rim and marley are common on British military sites that have been excavated by Parks Canada from the period of the War of 1812.

Band-and-Line Wares

Band-and-line wares became common during the last quarter of the 19th century and are usually associated with hotel wares. The band-and-line type is underglaze painted with the two lines usually right next to each other at the vessel's rim. Green was the most common color. Green band-and-line hotel wares remained a common institutional ware into the late 1950s when they began to be replaced by paper plates. One still occasionally finds these wares being used in small non-chain restaurants such as "Hank's Place" in Chadds Ford, Pennsylvania, as recently as December 1989. Band-and-line wares were available in tea and table wares.

Painted and Enamelled Wares

Enamelled means painted on top of the glaze. It is not necessary to refer to such wares as enamel painted wares. This type of decoration is most commonly associated with creamware and porcelain. However, it is also found on white salt-glazed stoneware, pearlware, whiteware, and the stone chinas. Because enamel painting was done after the pottery had been produced, the enameler did not have to be associated with the pottery that produced the ware and often worked independently (Prime 1929:128; Gottesman 1965:127).

Because enamel painting is fired at a lower temperature, a wider range of colors is available than is the case for underglaze colors which had to withstand the high temperature of the glazing oven. In addition to a greater color range, enamel painting produces a sharper image because the colors were not melted into the glaze. Underglaze painting has a slight blurring of the line due to the acidity of the glaze. The main disadvantage of enamelled decoration is that it was subject to being worn away by use. Enamelled wares were more expensive than underglaze painted wares because overglaze painting was added after the pottery was produced and required an additional firing.

By the late 1760s, a series of enamelled border patterns was being developed by Wedgwood (Mankowitz 1966:59–66). These patterns were copied and augmented by other potters. Many of those designs were later used as underglaze painted patterns. Enamelling was the most common type of decoration on creamware and did not begin to be superseded by underglaze painting until late in the 1780s (Miller 1987:90).

The term painted refers to underglaze decoration. Production of underglaze painted cream and pearl wares became more common after 1772, when the technology for the refining of cobalt for blue paints was introduced into Staffordshire (Shaw 1968[1829]:211). Staffordshire did not have much of a tradition of painting or enamelling prior to the development of creamware. The rapid rise of the popularity of creamware slowed the growth of the porcelain industry and destroyed the delft ware industry in England during the last quarter of the 18th century. Blue painters from both of these industries began to migrate to Staffordshire looking for employment in the late 1760s (Finer and Savage 1965:90).

Unlike the enamelers, the blue painters had to work within the factory structure because the painting was done prior to glazing. Widespread use of blue painting existed by 1775 when the potters developed "China Glaze" ware, which was a direct copy of Chinese porcelain in an earthenware. It contained kaolin clays from Cornwall and had a blue tinted glaze in imitation of Chinese porcelain. In addition to these elements, the wares were painted in a Chinese style to take the place of Chinese porcelain which was being eliminated from the English market by a tariff that by 1799 had reached over 100 percent (Haggar 1972:185). This ware was named "pearl white" by Josiah Wedgwood in 1779, and today it is generally known as pearlware (Miller 1987).

Blue painted wares in a Chinese style were the dominant painted ware from ca.1775 to around the War of 1812. The demand for wares painted in a Chinese style was somewhat stemmed by the introduction of underglaze transfer printing, introduced in Staffordshire around 1784. According to Shaw (1968[1829]:215), the "Blue Painters experienced such a diminution of employment and remuneration, that they employed every artifice to prevent" the development of underglaze printing. The blue painters working for Josiah Wedgwood were able to extract a promise from him not to produce blue printed ware (Shaw 1968[1829]: 123).

Around 1795, various other high temperature colors began to be introduced for underglaze painting (Noël Hume 1982:129). The new colors were brown, mustard yellow, and olive green. These colors remained common through the 1820s and are most commonly painted in floral motifs on tea wares.

In the 1820s, blue painted tea wares with floral motifs became popular, and on many sites they are more common than polychrome painted tea wares. Around the 1830s, a new color grouping came into use which included red, black, and some lighter shades of blue and green. These may be related to

the introduction of chrome colors. It is at this time that painting again became more common on plates as well as teas. From the 1840s on, it is common to have painted wares in which part of the motif has been done with a cut sponge.

A series of style changes occurred in the floral painting, such as sprig painted wares, which became common after the late 1840s. Large painted floral polychrome motifs come back into popularity during the 1870s, and these often are found on table and tea ware. Flow-painted wares in blue and purple also appear from the 1840s through the 1870s and possibly later.

Gaudy Dutch and peasant painted ware are two 20th-century collectors' terms that have been applied to painted wares, but have no historical timedepth (Anne Wolfe 1989, pers. comm.; Laidacker 1938:82). There is no evidence of these terms having been used by the potters or merchants selling these wares. It would be better to refer to these wares simply as painted.

"Willow Ware"

Willow is a pattern rather than a ware. The term "willow ware" had close to universal usage in the potters' records. By 1814, willow had been set aside as the cheapest available transfer printed pattern in the potters' price fixing lists. It appears to remain in that position throughout the 19th century. Willow ware was made by many potters in England and other countries. Its production was, for the most part, limited to tableware until the second half of the 19th century, when tea wares begin to appear in the willow pattern.

Willow, according to many accounts, was the earliest underglaze printed pattern developed in Staffordshire. It is a composite of two or more Chinese porcelain patterns. A good history of the pattern can be found in Copeland's book on Spode's Willow Pattern. The pattern became standardized around 1790 and has been in production ever since (Copeland 1980:33–44). Shaw (1968[1829]:216) refers to an "Old Willow" with a "dagger boarder," which is probably the first underglaze transfer printed pattern developed in Staffordshire.

Brosley is another pattern that was copied from Chinese porcelain. Like willow, it was a generic pattern that was made by many potters. Brosley was almost always limited to tea wares (Shaw 1968[1829]:212–216).

Printed Wares

"Printed" is the most commonly used term in the potters' and merchant's records to refer to transfer printed wares. The first patent application for transfer printing was made in 1751 (Williams-Wood 1981:53). Large-scale printing of ceramics, however, did not begin until after Saddler and Green's patent for the process was taken out in 1756 in Liverpool (Williams-Wood 1981:103). All of this early printing was on top of the glaze.

Printing under the glaze was first used around 1760 on English porcelain, which was over 20 years before its first use on Staffordshire earthenware (Watney 1964: 52–53). Underglaze blue printing was introduced around 1783 into Staffordshire (Shaw 1968[1829]:214). Like the blue painted wares, the early blue printed earthenwares were also done in Chinese patterns which remained popular until around the War of 1812.

Early blue printed wares were line engraved and have cruder and heavier designs with minimal shading. Early in the 19th century, the engravers began to use stipples—small dots in the engraving—as a shading device which gave greater perspective to the prints. The earliest dated piece with stipple engraving is from 1807 (Coysh and Henrywood 1982:9). Around 1810, prints of English and foreign landscapes began to become more common on Staffordshire wares, as did American scenes following the War of 1812. These patterns began to be replaced by romantic views by the 1830s (Samford 1985).

Color is another area that can be helpful chronologically. Around 1818 there was an American craze for very dark blue printed wares (Stachiw 1988). The Staffordshire potters accommodated it by producing a series of dark blue prints, many of which were negative patterns—that is, the subjects of the views were left white while the background

was filled with blue. Dark blue patterns were popular through the 1820s, which was also a period of popularity for blue painted floral patterns. Brown printed pearlwares were being imported into the American market as early as 1809 (Smith 1809).

Simeon Shaw's 1829 account stated that "very recently several . . . Manufacturers . . ." had introduced red, green, and brown transfer printed patterns (Shaw 1968[1829]:234–235). Potters' invoices from 1829 into the 1840s list quantities of red, green, brown, and purple printed wares. The printed wares from this period, however, are on white wares with minimal traces of blue in the glaze.

The last major change in printed wares came with the introduction of flowing colors in the 1840s. The earliest known advertisement for this ware in North America occurs in the *Montreal Gazette* for April 10, 1844, where it is described as "the new . . . FLOWING STONEWARE" (Collard 1967:118).

Transfer printed wares declined in popularity in the 1850s and were replaced by white granite ware (Miller 1990). The demand for printed wares picked up again in the early 1870s (Warburton 1931:155–156). Many patterns in a Japanese style were introduced in that period, and these were commonly printed in brown on an ivory tinted body. Kamm illustrates six different Japanese style patterns registered between 1877 and 1882 (Kamm 1970:75,76,87,91–93).

Stone Chinas

One of the most confusing terms used to describe the 19th-century ceramics is ironstone. The term ironstone comes from "Mason's Patent Ironstone China," patented in 1813 (Godden 1980:102). Several potters produced early stone chinas including: William Turner's Stone China, patented 1800 (Hillier 1965:22); John Davenport's Stone China, produced ca.1805–1820 (Godden 1980:221); Josiah Spode's Stone China, introduced ca.1814 (Godden 1980:248–249); and Hicks & Meigh, ca.1804–1822, also an early producer of stone china (Godden 1980:227).

These stone chinas were vitrified or semi-vitrified heavy, dense wares. Most of those produced prior to the 1830s were heavily decorated, commonly combining painting or enamelling with printing. Stone chinas were mostly copies of Chinese porcelains. Decoration for the early period was usually in a Chinese style, and the glaze was almost always tinted blue with cobalt as were the china glazed and pearl wares of that period.

There is strong evidence that the stone chinas were produced by potters such as Spode, Davenport, and Turner (Copeland 1980:97) to take the place of Chinese porcelain which the British East India Company stopped importing in 1791 (Godden 1980:22–25). In 1799, a customs duty of over 100 percent was placed on the importation of Chinese porcelain in England (Godden 1980:29). Miles Mason was a London Chinaman, a merchant who dealt in Chinese porcelain imported by the British East India Company. When the source of that porcelain was closed off, Mason purchased a pottery in Staffordshire and began trying to make porcelain (Godden 1980:17–32). That attempt was not as successful as a subsequent product, Mason's "Patent Ironstone China."

White Granite Wares

"White granite" and ironstone are the most common names applied to a group of hard white wares which were often vitrified or semi-vitrified. These wares evolved out of Mason's Ironstone and the stone chinas, discussed above, and are still evolving today. White granite has been selected as the term for their classification because it avoids the confusion of these plain white wares with the highly decorated stone chinas or early ironstone.

Invoices for earthenware shipped to Philadelphia show that white granite was being imported in the United States by the 1840s. Terms used in these documents include "White Glaze" (Ridgway 1844, 1846) and "White Granite" (Heath 1848). After the 1850s, the term white granite, or "W.G.," becomes very common in invoices for wares sent to America. From the invoices and price lists examined for this study, it is clear that white granite became the dominant type in use from the 1850s until the end of the 19th century.

Gold-Banded Earthenware

Gold gilding on porcelain was perfected at Meissen ca.1723 (Hunt 1979:118). The early process involved grinding the gold by hand in mediums like honey, then applying the gilding on top of the glaze. In addition, the gold had to be burnished after firing. Because gilding was expensive, its use was mostly associated with porcelain and finely enamelled earthenware. The process was to change in the 19th century with the development of "liquid bright gold" in Germany in 1836 (Hunt 1979:124). In this process, the gold was dissolved by acids and mixed with chemicals which produced a gold that could be fired with enamel colors and would come out of the muffle kiln bright and shiny without having to be burnished (Hunt 1979: 124).

Wenger Company, a pottery supply company, introduced liquid gold gilding into the Staffordshire potteries by 1870 (Wenger 1893). After that date, bright gilding began to be more commonly found on cheap earthenwares such as the gold-banded plates listed in Appendix A. Use of cheap gilding increased on common wares by the late 19th century and continues today.

Basalt Ware

Basalt is Wedgwood's name for what other potters called "Egyptian Black." It is a dense, fine-grained stoneware that has been dyed black with cobalt and manganese (Savage and Newman 1976: 44–45). These wares were usually unglazed; however, there is a glazed variety which was referred to as "Shining Black" (Shaw 1968[1829]:209).

Basalts are most commonly found in teapots, creamers, sugars, and bowls for tea slops. They were also used for decorative wares such as vases and busts, but these rarely show up in archaeological collections. The CC index values for basalt wares presented in this paper are from bowls associated with teawares in the Staffordshire potters' price fixing lists.

Black-dyed stonewares were produced as early as the 1690s by the Elers brothers in Staffordshire (Shaw 1968[1829]:118). Wedgwood perfected his version of Egyptian Black in 1768, which he renamed Basalt (Savage and Newman 1976:44). The other potters continued to call it Egyptian Black, which is the name used in the Staffordshire price fixing lists of 1795, 1796, 1814, and 1846 (in Mountford 1975:9–14; Miller 1984:42–43).

English Porcelains

Beginning in the 1740s, various soft paste porcelains were developed in England. These were attempts to discover the secret of how to produce Chinese porcelain, which was a hard paste made with kaolin and petuntse. Different soft paste formulas were developed. Then, in 1768, William Cookworthy produced the first English true hard paste porcelain using kaolin and petuntse from Cornwall (Watney 1964:116–119). However, the growth of the English porcelain industry was checked by the success of Josiah Wedgwood's creamware.

Most of the porcelain types developed in the 18th century were replaced by bone china which was introduced by Josiah Spode around 1794 (Savage and Newman 1976:51). Bone china became the dominant type produced in England by the early 19th century and holds that position today. Even the Worcester porcelain factory, which had a very successful soapstone porcelain, made the switch to bone china in the 1830s (Sandon 1978:189). Bone china had a couple of advantages over hard paste porcelain, including a lower firing temperature which means it can be decorated with a wider color range. In addition, it is a very translucent white porcelain. One of its disadvantages for consumers is that it will stain if the glaze is crazed.

English porcelains are relatively rare in invoices of wares sent to America and in American archaeological assemblages prior to the second half of the 19th century. Therefore, this section of CC index values is very limited, and the descriptions from the invoices are minimal. The porcelains indexed here are most likely bone china which was the dominant type for the period.

Discussion

The following appendices provide an expanded and updated set of index values for platters, plates, twifflers, muffins, London size teas, Irish size teas, and bowls. They are meant to replace the previously published index values (Miller 1980). The tables are organized chronologically by vessel form. The forms and their size ranges are described at the beginning of each appendix.

Appendix A: Flatware

The late 18th- and 19th-century Staffordshire potters' price fixing lists consistently use the following terms to describe the most common types of flatware:

Dish	10–20-inch platters (commonly oval or oblong-hexagonal in shape)
Table plate	10-inch plates
Supper plate	9-inch plates
Twifflers	8-inch plates
Muffins	3–7-inch plates

All of the above vessels are generally larger than their stated sizes. One of the ways in which the potters got around the price fixing agreements was to provide their customers with slightly larger sized vessels for the cost of smaller ones. For example, a potter might sell 9.75-inch plates as "Suppers" which, by the price list for 1796 (in Mountford 1975:11), should only have been 9 inches in diameter.

CC INDEX VALUES FOR SHELL EDGE WARES

	Dishes			Plates	Twifflers		Muffins	
	14	12	10	10–9	8	7	6	5
1787	1.5	2.0	2.0	1.67	2.0	2.11		
1793				1.35				
1796	1.67	1.5	1.5	1.33	1.28	1.33	1.41	
1802	1.6	1.58	1.67	1.38	1.23	1.4		
1804	1.5	1.25	1.25	1.33	1.5	1.51	1.49	
1814	1.64	1.57	1.2	1.33	1.28	1.33	1.41	1.24
1816	1.64	1.57	1.2	1.43	1.32	1.28	1.33	1.41
1821	1.64	1.57	1.2	1.33	1.28	1.33	1.49	1.24
1823	1.64	1.43	1.2	1.33	1.28	1.4	1.41	1.49
1825	1.64	1.57	1.2	1.33	1.28	1.33	1.41	1.5
1833	1.64	1.57	1.64	1.33	1.43	1.33	1.4	1.5
1836				1.33	1.25	1.38	1.45	1.25
1838	1.64	1.57	1.2	1.33	1.29	1.33	1.4	1.25
1846	1.64	1.57	1.2	1.14	1.13	1.14	1.17	1.2
1848		1.57	1.2	1.33	1.28	1.33	1.41	
1853	1.64	1.57	1.2	1.12	1.11	1.13	1.16	1.2
1859	1.13	1.05	1.09	1.09	1.05	1.06	1.07	1.09
1866	1.13	1.1	1.08	1.12	1.11	1.13	1.15	1.2
1869	1.13	1.1	1.08	1.14	1.11	1.13	1.15	1.2
1870	1.1	1.08	1.13	1.07	1.08	1.1	1.09	1.12
1871	1.13	1.1	1.08	1.08	1.11	1.12	1.25	1.3
1874				1.09	1.10	1.11	1.14	1.18
1880				1.09	1.1	1.12	1.14	1.18

UNDERGLAZE LINED WARES

	Dishes			Plates	Twifflers		Muffins	
	14	12	10	10–9	8	7	6	5
1814	2.18	2.0	1.6	1.67	1.71	1.68	1.81	2.0
1816	2.18	2.0	1.6	1.43	1.5	1.43	1.5	1.6
1823	2.18	2.0	1.6	1.67	1.71	1.8	1.81	1.99
1825	1.82	1.71	1.4	1.5	1.5	1.5	1.61	1.75
1833	2.18	2.0	1.6	1.67	1.71	1.67	1.8	2.0

BAND-AND-LINE WARES

	Dishes			Plates	Twifflers		Muffins	
	14	12	10	10–9	8	7	6	5
1873	1.27	1.43	1.2	1.2	1.29	1.22	1.32	1.2
1886	1.22	1.33	1.13	1.13	1.17	1.2	1.25	1.18

ENAMELLED-UPON-GLAZE LINED WARES

	Dishes			Plates	Twifflers		Muffins	
	14	12	10	10–9	8	7	6	5
1814	2.73	2.68	2.4	2.33	2.35	2.5	2.41	1.99
1816	2.6	2.67	2.86	2.22	2.0	1.83	1.69	1.5

PAINTED WARES

	Dishes			Plates	Twifflers		Muffins	
	14	12	10	10–9	8	7	6	5
1787				1.5	1.67			
1822							2.1	2.25
1838				2.17	2.36	2.25	2.1	2.25
1853	2.73	3.0	2.4	1.68	1.67	1.63	1.62	1.8
1854							1.56	1.5
1859	1.88	2.0	2.18	1.64	1.58	1.53	1.5	1.64
1866	1.88	2.1	2.0	1.75	1.67	1.62	1.62	1.8
1869	1.88	2.1	2.0	1.71	1.67	1.62	1.62	1.8
1871	1.88	2.1	2.0	1.57	1.5	1.45	1.5	1.64

ENAMELLED WARES

	Dishes			Plates	Twifflers		Muffins	
	14	12	10	10–9	8	7	6	5
1804	3.0	3.0	3.0	3.67	4.0	3.61	2.99	
1814	5.45	6.0	4.8	4.67	5.13	5.0	4.82	5.22
1833	3.27	3.57	3.0	2.33	2.57	2.5	2.7	2.62

SPONGED WARES

	Dishes			Plates	Twifflers		Muffins	
	14	12	10	10–9	8	7	6	5
1855	1.22	1.33	1.25	1.2	1.25	1.2	1.25	1.33
1871					1.5	1.45		1.5

CHILDREN'S ABC AND MOTTO PLATES—PAINTED

	Dishes			Plates	Twifflers		Muffins	
	14	12	10	10–9	8	7	6	5
1845						1.71	1.67	1.8
1868							1.16	1.3
1874								1.74

CHILDREN'S ABC AND MOTTO PLATES—PRINTED AND COLORED

	Dishes			Plates	Twifflers		Muffins	
	14	12	10	10–9	8	7	6	5
1871							6.94	8.12

WILLOW WARE

	Dishes			Plates	Twifflers		Muffins	
	14	12	10	10–9	8	7	6	5
1793				4.0	5.0			
1814	3.82	4.29	3.6	2.67	3.0	3.0	3.01	2.99
1823	3.82	4.29	3.6	2.67	3.0	3.0	3.01	2.99
1825	3.82	4.29	3.6	3.00	3.21	3.25	3.49	3.37
1836				2.5	2.44	2.77	2.73	
1854	1.4	1.38	1.5	1.62	1.5	1.5	1.33	1.38
1855	1.44	1.5	1.5	1.6	1.5	1.8	1.5	1.67
1870	1.25	1.32	1.38	1.52	1.33	1.4	1.22	1.25

PRINTED WARES

| | Dishes | | | Plates | Twifflers | | Muffins | |
	14	12	10	10–9	8	7	8	5
1796	6.0	5.25	7.5	4.33	3.93	4.0	4.22	
1814	5.45	6.0	4.8	3.33	3.42	3.5	3.61	3.73
1816	5.45	5.14	4.8	2.86	3.0	3.0	3.0	3.01
1823	5.45	6.0	4.8	3.33	3.41	3.5	3.61	3.73
1825	4.91	5.14	4.0	3.00	3.21	3.25	3.49	3.37
1833	3.82	4.29	3.6	2.67	3.0	3.0	3.0	3.0
1836				3.0	2.81	3.0	3.0	
1838	3.82	4.29	3.6	2.67	3.0	3.0	3.0	3.0
1844				2.11	2.44			
1845	3.82	4.29	3.6	2.67	3.0	3.0	3.0	3.0
1846	3.52	3.96	3.32	2.11	2.42	2.37	2.31	2.22
1848	3.47	3.9	3.27	2.42	2.72	2.73	2.74	2.72
1854	2.2	2.46	2.3	1.86	1.75	1.8	1.67	1.62
1855	2.22	2.67	2.25	1.6	1.5	1.8	1.5	1.67

DARK BLUE PRINTED WARES

| | Dishes | | | Plates | Twifflers | | Muffins | |
	14	12	10	10–9	8	7	8	5
1846	3.82	4.29	3.6	2.29	2.63	2.57	2.5	2.4

FLOW PRINTED WARES

| | Dishes | | | Plates | Twifflers | | Muffins | |
	14	12	10	10–9	8	7	6	5
1846	4.41	4.95	4.15	2.64	3.03	2.97	2.88	2.77
1848	4.14	4.64	3.9		3.25	3.25		3.25
1855	3.11	3.33	2.75	2.4	2.5	2.4	2.25	2.5

DECORATED STONE CHINA WARES

| | Dishes | | | Plates | Twifflers | | Muffins | |
	14	12	10	10–9	8	7	6	5
1833		"JAPAN PATTERN"		3.33	3.43	3.5		

WHITE GRANITE WARES

| | Dishes | | | Plates | Twifflers | | Muffins | |
	14	12	10	10–9	8	7	6	5
1846	3.23	3.63	3.05	1.93	2.22	2.18	2.12	2.03
1858	3.27	3.63	3.09		2.0	1.93	1.98	
1868						1.93	2.06	2.06
1871	2.25	2.57	2.57		2.07	2.0	2.09	2.20
1874	1.93	2.2	2.21		1.66	1.59	1.73	1.81
1880	1.84	2.11	2.11		1.57	1.53	1.67	1.73

GOLD-BANDED EARTHENWARE

| | Dishes | | | Plates | Twifflers | | Muffins | |
	14	12	10	10–9	8	7	6	5
1871		3.57	3.57		2.98	2.9	3.06	3.24

ENGLISH PORCELAINS

		Dishes		Plates	Twifflers		Muffins	
	14	12	10	10–9	8	7	6	5
1836	White						7.14	
1838	Enamelled						7.0	
1871	White					4.0	3.92	3.4
1871	Gold-Banded							5.06
1871	Sprig							5.54

Appendix B: Teas, London Size

Teas, the potters' terms for cups and saucers, are more complex than tablewares because of available options, different shapes, and the size system. Two sizes were commonly referred to in the price fixing lists and potters' invoices. "London" size was the most common and the smaller of the two. "Irish," the larger size, was sometimes referred to as "Breakfast" size. The great majority of the cups recovered from American sites are of the London size. In addition to London and Irish size teas, there were also bowls and saucers which are a size larger than Irish size. These are rarely reported in archaeological assemblages, perhaps because they have not been recognized. Evidence of this combination would be confirmed by a matching bowl and saucer.

The term London size is further complicated by the fact that the most common cup shape for the period from 1810 to 1840 has been labeled "London Shape," which is the name that the Spode factory gave to this shape. London shape cups look like an inverted truncated cone with a steeply angled shoulder just above a high standing foot ring. Other potters appear to have called this shape "Grecian," which is what an illustration of this shape is labeled in the Wedgwood catalogue of 1880 (des Fontaines 1971:28). London or Grecian shape occurs in all sizes of cups as well as bowls.

Some of the options that were available with teas included handles, color-lined rims, fluted shapes, and scalloped rims. These options all involved an additional cost which, on the potters' price fixing lists, commonly added a shilling per dozen to the teas. This resulted in a greater range of prices for teas for most of the period under consideration. For example, taking all of the combinations of these options in the 1796 price fixing list, there were 18 options which are listed below:

TEAS

	Unhandled			Handled		
		Fluted			Fluted	
	Simple	or edged	& edged	Simple	or edged	& edged
CC	1.0	1.8	2.6	1.8	2.6	3.4
Painted	1.8	2.6	3.4	2.6	3.4	4.2
Printed	3.4	4.2	5.0	4.2	5.0	5.8

One can see that a set of handled, fluted or edged CC teas would cost as much as a simple printed set of teas. However, edged, fluted, and handled teas are not very common in American archaeological assemblages.

The following descriptions apply to the forms indexed in the appendices.

Handled   The great majority of cups were unhandled until the second half of the 19th century. A New York merchant writing to his Liverpool agents in 1816 stated that "Handled cups & saucers will Never never sell in our Market there can not be a worse article" (Ogden 1816). The above range of index values provides a possible clue as to why handled cups may have remained unpopular. For the price of CC teas with handles, one could have painted teas without handles. A set of fluted painted teas with handles could have cost more than a set of simple printed teas. In other words, the consumer may have chosen to have a more highly decorated set of teas without handles rather than a simpler handled set for the same amount of money.

Brown Edged Brown Edged or "Topped" teas have an enamelled or painted brown line on the top of the rim of the cups and saucers, in imitation of the brown iron rim line on Chinese porcelain. Edged teas are listed in the Staffordshire potters' price fixing lists for 1795, 1796, 1808, and 1825 (1795, 1796 in Mountford 1975:9–11; Staffordshire Potters 1808, 1825). Occasionally the rim was lined with blue. Lined teas seem to have been most popular from the 1790s to around the War of 1812.

Fluted These teas have molded fluting, usually spiraled, up the outside surface of the cups and on the inside surface of the saucers. Fluted teas are listed in the Staffordshire potters' price fixing lists for 1796, 1808, 1814, 1846, 1853, and 1859 (1796, 1846 in Mountford 1975; 1814 in Miller 1984; Staffordshire Potters 1808, 1853, 1859). They seem to be most popular from the 1790s to the 1820s.

Scalloped Scalloped teas appear to be a good time marker, as they appeared for a short period from the mid-1820s through the 1830s (Staffordshire Potters 1825). These teas have a slight rim scallop.

Extra Thick These teas were hotel wares meant for use in institutions such as hotels, restaurants, hospitals, and schools.

Pressed Most teas were wheel thrown until the Jolly came into use in the potteries after 1863 (Lamb 1977:6). The Jolly was an automatic throwing device that used a plaster mold to shape the cups with the aid of a template mounted on the wheel to form the inside profile of the cup. Teas could be pressed, a slower process than throwing. In 1859, pressed teas were the same price as fluted teas (Staffordshire Potters 1859:2). These are listed as "pressed shapes" and appear to refer to eight-, 10-, and 12-sided teas which make their appearance in the 1850s.

CC TEAS—LONDON SIZE

	Unhandled			Handled		
	Simple	Fluted or Edged	Fluted & Edged	Simple	Fluted or Edged	Fluted & Edged
1796	1.0	1.8	2.6	1.8	2.6	3.4
		Fluted			Fluted	
1804	1.0			1.28		
1814	1.0	1.67		1.67	2.33	
18.16	1.0	1.5		1.5	2.0	
1823	1.0	1.67		1.67	2.33	
		Scalloped			Scalloped	
1825	1.0		1.17	1.67		1.83
1833	1.0			1.57		
1836	1.0			1.67		
1838	1.0			1.67		
1845	1.0			1.67		
1846	1.0			1.55		

CC TEAS—LONDON SIZE (continued)

	Unhandled			Handled		
	Simple	Fluted or Edged	Fluted & Edged	Simple	Fluted or Edged	Fluted & Edged
1848	1.0			1.67		
1853	1.0			1.55		
		Fluted or Pressed	Extra Thick		Fluted or Pressed	Extra Thick
1859	1.0	1.63	2.0	1.5	2.13	2.5
1866	1.0		2.0	1.5		2.5
1871	1.0		1.92	1.38		2.31

PAINTED TEAS—LONDON SIZE

	Unhandled			Handled		
	Simple	Fluted or Edged	Fluted & Edged	Simple	Fluted or Edged	Fluted & Edged
1787	2.5					
1796	1.8	2.6	3.4	2.6	3.4	4.2
		Fluted			Fluted	
1802	1.6					
1804	1.71			2.14		
1814	1.5	2.17		2.17	2.83	
1816	1.25	1.75		1.75	2.25	
1823	1.5	2.17		2.17	2.83	
			Scalloped			Scalloped
1825	1.5		1.67	2.17		2.33
1833	1.43			2.0		
1836	1.5					
1838	1.5					
1845	1.5					
1846	1.23			1.77		
1848	1.5					
1853	1.23			1.77		
		Fluted or Pressed	Extra Thick		Fluted or Pressed	Extra Thick
1859	1.13	2.0	2.13	1.63	2.5	2.63
1866	1.17		2.17	1.67		2.67
1868	1.16					
1869	1.17					
1871	1.15		2.08	1.54		2.46

ENAMELLED TEAS—LONDON SIZE

	Unhandled		Handled	
	Simple	Fluted or Edged	Simple	Fluted or Edged
1814	3.0	3.67	3.67	4.33
1823	3.0	3.67	3.67	4.33
1833	2.0		2.57	

DIPT TEAS—LONDON SIZE

	Unhandled		Handled	
	Simple	Scalloped	Simple	Scalloped
1825	1.5	1.67	2.17	2.33

SPONGED TEAS—LONDON SIZE

	Unhandled	Handled
	Simple	Simple
1848	1.5	2.17
1858	1.5	2.17
1871	1.16	

BAND-AND-LINE TEAS—LONDON SIZE

	Unhandled	Handled
	Simple	Simple
1873	1.22	1.45
1886		1.18

PRINTED TEAS—LONDON SIZE

	Unhandled			Handled		
	Simple	Fluted or Edged	Fluted & Edged	Simple	Fluted or Edged	Fluted & Edged
1795	4.09	5.18	6.27	5.18	6.27	7.36
1796	3.4	4.2	5.0	4.2	5.0	5.8
		Fluted			Fluted	
1799	5.36	5.95				
1804	3.42	4.29	5.14			
1814	3.0	3.67		3.67	4.33	
1816	2.25	2.75		2.75	3.25	
1823	3.0	3.67		3.67	4.33	
			Scalloped			Scalloped
1825	3.0		3.17	3.67		3.83
1833	2.57			3.14		
1836	3.0					
1838	3.0					
1845	3.0			4.0		
1846	2.27	2.52		2.77	3.02	
1848	2.89					

DARK BLUE PRINTED TEAS—LONDON SIZE

	Unhandled		Handled	
	Simple	Fluted	Simple	Fluted
1834	3.0			
1846	2.45	3.15	2.73	3.27

FLOW PRINTED TEAS—LONDON SIZE

	Unhandled		Handled	
	Simple	Fluted	Simple	Fluted
1846	2.83	3.15	3.46	3.78
1848		3.25		

WHITE GRANITE TEAS—LONDON SIZE

	Unhandled		Handled	
	Simple	Fluted	Simple	Fluted
1846	2.08	2.31	2.54	2.77
1868	2.15			
1871	2.04		2.45	
1874	1.71		2.05	
1875	2.0		2.75	
1880	1.69		1.95	

ENGLISH PORCELAIN TEAS—LONDON SIZE

	Unhandled	Handled	
1823		14.5	Gilded
1835	4.44		Decorated
1836	3.70	4.20	Decorated
1871	2.20	3.01	White

Appendix C: Teas, Irish Size

Irish size teas have been discussed above. Their index values are given here.

CC TEAS—IRISH SIZE

	Unhandled			Handled		
	Simple	Fluted or Edged	Fluted & Edged	Simple	Fluted or Edged	Fluted & Edged
1796	1.0	1.67	2.6	1.67	2.33	3.4
		Fluted			Fluted	
1814	1.0	1.5		1.5	2.0	
1816	1.0	1.4		1.4	1.8	
1823	1.0	1.5		1.5	2.0	
			Scalloped		Scalloped	
1825	1.0		1.13	1.5		1.65
1833	1.0			1.5		
1846	1.0			1.43		
1853	1.0			1.43		
		Fluted or Pressed	Extra Thick		Fluted or Pressed	Extra Thick
1859	1.0	1.42	1.67	1.33	1.75	2.0
1866	1.0		1.73	1.36		2.09
1871	1.0		1.73	1.36		2.09

PAINTED TEAS—IRISH SIZE

	Unhandled			Handled		
	Simple	Fluted or Edged	Fluted & Edged	Simple	Fluted or Edged	Fluted & Edged
1787	2.4					
1796	1.83	2.5	3.17	2.5	3.17	3.83
		Fluted			Fluted	
1814	1.38	1.88		1.88	2.38	
1816	1.2	1.6		1.6	2.0	
1823	1.38	1.88		1.88	2.38	
			Scalloped			Scalloped
1825	1.38		1.5	1.88	2.0	
1833	1.5			2.0		
1846	1.18			1.61		
1853	1.29			1.71		
		Fluted or Pressed	Extra Thick		Fluted or Pressed	Extra Thick
1859	1.17	1.67	1.83	1.5	2.0	2.17
1866	1.27		2.0	1.64		2.36
1869	1.27					
1871	1.27		2.0	1.64		2.36

ENAMELLED TEAS—IRISH SIZE

	Unhandled		Handled	
	Simple	Fluted	Simple	Fluted
1814	3.0	3.67	3.67	4.33
1823	3.0	3.67	3.67	4.33
1833	2.25		2.75	

BAND-AND-LINE TEAS—IRISH SIZE

	Unhandled	Handled
1886		1.07

PRINTED TEAS—IRISH SIZE

	Unhandled			Handled		
	Simple	Fluted or Edged	Fluted & Edged	Simple	Fluted or Edged	Fluted & Edged
1795	4.07	4.93	5.79	4.93	5.79	6.64
1796	3.5	4.17	4.83	4.17	4.83	5.5
		Fluted			Fluted	
1814	2.75	3.25		3.25	3.75	
1816	2.2	2.6		2.6	3.0	
1823	2.75	3.25		3.25	3.75	
			Scalloped			Scalloped
1825	2.75		2.88	3.25		3.38
1833	2.75			3.25		
1846	2.18	2.37		2.57	2.77	

DARK BLUE PRINTED TEAS—IRISH SIZE

	Unhandled	Handled
1846	2.36	2.79

FLOW PRINTED TEAS—IRISH SIZE

	Unhandled		Handled	
	Simple	Fluted	Simple	Fluted
1846	2.72	2.97	3.21	3.46

WHITE GRANITE TEAS—IRISH SIZE

	Unhandled		Handled	
	Simple	Fluted	Simple	Fluted
1846	1.99	2.18	2.36	2.54

Appendix D: Bowls

Bowls' sizes were ranked by the potters' dozen. The potters' dozen began as a unit of pay for throwers and other workers. After a vessel was thrown, it was placed on a 6-ft. drying board. A board full of wares of a single size counted as a dozen. Thus, a dozen bowls could range from four one-gallon punch bowls to 30 half pint bowls (Copeland 1983). The former would be called 4s while the latter would be called 30s. Bowls were available in the following sizes: 3s, 4s, 6s, 12s, 18s, 24s, 30s, 36s, 42s, and 48s. The potters attempted to stabilize the capacities assigned to these various sizes, but they got larger as various potters attempted to get around the price fixing lists by selling bigger bowls under smaller potters' dozen sizes. A 1796 potters' agreement (in Mountford 1975:11) set the following sizes:

BOWLS AND WASH BASINS

Size	Maximum volume
3s	6 pints
4s	4 pints
6s	3 pints
12s	1 1/2 pints
24s	3/4 pints
30s	1/2 pints

Sometimes the size number was impressed in the bottom of hollowares. The following summary, for example, gives prices per dozen bowls from the 1814 Staffordshire potters' price fixing list, reprinted in Miller (1984:42–43), and the cost per individual bowl:

COST, IN PENCE, FOR BOWLS

	Price per potters' dozen	Individual bowl prices			
		6s	12s	24s	30s
CC	30d	5.0@	2.5@	1.25@	1.0@
Dipt	36d	6.0	3.0	1.5	1.2
Painted	48d	8.0	4.0	2.0	1.6
Printed	84d	14.0	7.0	3.5	2.8

Thus, a potters' dozen of bowls purchased in 1814 could range from 6 to 30 bowls depending on the size ordered. The price per potters' dozen would be the same with adjustments made for the size by varying the quantity of bowls included, rather than by changing the price for each size category.

CC INDEX VALUES FOR BOWLS

	Dipt	Painted	Sponged	Enamelled	Flow Painted	Printed	Dark Blue	Flow Printed	White Granite	Basalt	"White China" Porcelain
1787		3.75 (sortable)									
1795						4.32 (Sortable)					
1799	1.6	2.0									
1802		2.33									
1804		2.0				3.14					
1814	1.2	1.6				2.8				6.0	
1821	1.2	1.6				2.8					
1822	1.2	1.6		2.8		2.8					
1823	1.2	1.6				2.8				6.0	
1825	1.2	1.6				2.6					
1832	1.2	1.6									
1833	1.2	1.6		2.4		2.8					
1836	1.2	1.8				3.0					
1838	1.2					2.8					
1842	1.22					3.0					
1846	1.2	1.6				2.58	2.8	3.25	2.37	6.0	
1848	1.2					2.91		3.03			
1853		1.64									
1854	1.14					2.0		2.29			
1855			1.11			2.0		2.4			
1858									2.49		
1859	1.08	1.38									
1866	1.17	1.5									
1868									2.29		
1869	1.17	1.17									
1870	1.13	1.38		3.5	1.5	2.0			2.25	2.25	
1871	1.16	1.5							2.42		2.54
1873	1.11	1.33			1.67						
1874									2.46		
1877	1.08	1.33									
1880									2.34		
1886	1.08										

ACKNOWLEDGMENTS

The generation of this expanded set of index values was made possible by funding from a fellowship and two grants. I would like to thank the Winterthur Museum for awarding me a NEH/Winterthur Fellowship in 1979. I would also like to thank Pat and Barbara Garrow of Garrow and Associates for a grant in 1985 to work on the 1814 Staffordshire potters' price list. In 1986, Ann Smart Martin, Nancy Dickinson, and I received a two-year grant from the National Endowment for the Humanities for our project "English Ceramics in America, 1760–1860: Marketing, Prices, and Availability" (NEH Grant RO-21158-86) Working as a team, we were able to cover a very broad range of documents from many areas. I also thank my boss, Marley Brown, for his support during this project I would like to thank Colonial Williamsburg for providing the matching funds for this project.

I would like to thank the following institutions for generous access to their archives and records: in

England, Josiah Wedgwood and Sons; Keele University Library; the Stoke-on-Trent City Museum and Art Gallery; the Spode Company Archives; the Minton Company; the Horace Barks Reference Library in Hanley; and the Stafford County Record Office; on this side of the Atlantic, Winterthur Museum; New York Historical Society; Massachusetts Historical Society; Maryland Historical Society; Virginia State Archives; Smithsonian Institution; Colonial Williamsburg Foundation Library; National Archives, Washington, D.C.; Canadian National Archives, Ottawa; Hagley Museum, Wilmington; Pennsylvania Historical Society; Kress Library of Business and Economics of Harvard University; and University of Delaware Library.

My research in England was greatly facilitated by Robert Copeland and Helen Dent. Others in England to whom I owe special thanks include: Martin Phillips, Pat Halfpenny, Gaye Blake Roberts, Una and John des Fontaines, Eileen and Rodney Hampson, David Barker, David Furniss, Christine Fyfe, Margaret Morris, John Smith, Arnold Mountford, and Terry Lockett. On this side of the Atlantic, I thank Susan Myers, Reggie Blaszczyk, Lynne Sussman, Elizabeth Collard, Arlene Palmer Schwind, Mary Beaudry, Georgeanna Greer, Barbara Teller, Rob Hunter, Silas Hurry, Henry Miller, Kate Hutchins, Neville Thompson, Rich McKinstry, Beatrice Taylor, Karen Stuart, Bill Adams, Steve Pendery, Myron Stachiw, Ellen Shlasko, Sarah Peabody Turnbaugh, Suzanne Spencer-Wood, and John L. Seidel.

Many people were more than generous with help in the form of suggestions, sending copies of price lists, invoices, and other records. Because this research has been going on for over a decade, it is difficult to remember everyone who provided help and information. I apologize to anyone I may have left off the list of acknowledgments.

REFERENCES

ADAMS, WILLIAM H., AND SARAH JANE BOLING
1989 Status and Ceramics for Planters and Slaves on Three Georgia Coastal Plantations. *Historical Archaeology* 23(1):69–96.

BINNS, CHARLES F.
1907 *The Manual of Practical Potting*. Scott, Greenwood and Son, London.

COLE, ARTHUR H.
1969 *Wholesale Commodity Prices in the United States, 1700–1861*. Johnson Reprint Corporation, New York.

COLLARD, ELIZABETH
1967 *Nineteenth-Century Pottery and Porcelain in Canada*. McGill University Press, Montreal.

COPELAND, ROBERT
1980 *Spode's Willow Pattern and Other Designs after the Chinese*. Rizzoli International Publications, Inc., New York.
1983 Pottery Trade Sizes. Ms., on file with the author.

COYSH, A. W., AND R. K. HENRYWOOD
1982 *The Dictionary of Blue and White Printed Pottery, 1780–1880*. Antique Collectors' Club, Woodbridge, England.

EVANS, WILLIAM
1970 Art and History of the Potting Business. Compiled from the Most Practical Sources, for the Especial Use of Working Potters. Reprint of 1846 edition. *Journal of Ceramic History* 3:21–43.

FERGUSON, LELAND G.
1975 Analysis of Ceramic Materials from Fort Watson, December 1780–April 1781. *Conference on Historic Site Archaeology Papers, 1973* 8:2–28.

FINER, ANN, AND GEORGE SAVAGE (EDITORS)
1965 *The Selected Letters of Josiah Wedgwood*. Cory, Adams and Mackay Ltd., London.

FINLAYSON, R. W.
1972 *Portneuf Pottery*. Longman Canada Limited, Don Mills, Ontario.

DES FONTAINES, JOHN K.
1971 *The Wedgwood 1880 Illustrated Catalogue of Shapes*. The Wedgwood Society, London.

GODDEN, GEOFFREY A.
1966 *An Illustrated Encyclopedia of British Pottery and Porcelain*. Crown Publishers, New York.
1980 *Godden's Guide to Mason's China and the Ironstone Wares*. The Antique Collectors' Club Ltd., Woodbridge, England.

GOTTESMAN, RITA S. (COMPILER)
1965 *The Arts and Crafts in New York, 1800–1804: Advertisements and News Items from New York City Newspapers*. New York Historical Society, New York.

HAGGAR, REGINALD
1972 Miles Mason. *English Ceramic Circle* 2:183–199.

HEATH, JOSEPH
1848 Invoice for Earthenware Sold by Joseph Heath, Manufacturer of Earthenware, Tunstall, to P. A. Rovendt of Philadelphia, 12/9/1848. Customs House Collection, University of Delaware Library, Newark.

HILLIER, BEVIS
1965 *Master Potters of the Industrial Revolution: The Turners of Lane End*. Cory, Adams and Mackay Ltd., London.

HUNT, L. B.
1979 Gold in the Pottery Industry. *Gold Bulletin* 13(3): 116–127.

KAMM, MINNIE WATSON
1970 *Old China*. Kamm Publications, Grosse Pointe, Michigan.

LAIDACKER, SAM (EDITOR)
1938 *The Standard Catalogue of Anglo-American China from 1810 to 1850*. Sam Laidacker, Scranton, Pennsylvania.

LAMB, ANDREW
1977 The Press and Labour's Response to Pottery-making Machinery in the North Staffordshire Pottery Industry. *Journal of Ceramic History* 9:1–8.

MAJEWSKI, TERESITA, AND MICHAEL J. O'BRIEN
1987 The Use and Misuse of Nineteenth-Century English and American Ceramics in Archaeological Analysis. *Advances in Archaeological Method and Theory* 11: 97–209. Academic Press, New York.

MANKOWITZ, WOLF
1966 *Wedgwood*. Spring Books, London.

MILLER, GEORGE L.
1980 Classification and Economic Scaling of 19th-Century Ceramics. *Historical Archaeology* 14:1–40.
1984 George M. Coates, Pottery Merchant of Philadelphia, 1817–1831. *Winterthur Portfolio* 19:42–43.
1987 Origins of Josiah Wedgwood's Pearlware. *Northeast Historical Archaeology* 16:80–92.
1988 Prices and Index Values for English Ceramics from 1787 to 1860. Ms., on file with the author.
1989 *A Chronology of English Shell Edged Pearl and White Wares*. George L. Miller, Williamsburg, Virginia.
1990 The 'Market Basket' of Ceramics Available in Country Stores from 1790 to 1860. Paper Presented at the Annual Meeting of the Society for Historical Archaeology Conference on Historical and Underwater Archaeology, Tucson, Arizona.

MILLER, GEORGE L., AND ANN SMART MARTIN
1989 English Ceramics in America. In *Decorative Arts and Household Furnishings Used in America, 1650–1920: An Annotated Bibliography*, edited by Kenneth L. Ames and Gerald W. R. Ward, pp. 201–219. University Press of Virginia, Charlottesville.

MILLER, GEORGE L., ANN SMART MARTIN, AND NANCY S. DICKINSON
1989 Changing Consumption Patterns: English Ceramics and the American Market from 1770 to 1840. In *Everyday Life in the Early Republic 1789–1828*, edited by Catherine E. Hutchins. Twenty-ninth Winterthur Conference, Wilmington, Delaware, in press.

MOUNTFORD, ARNOLD R.
1975 Documents Relating to English Ceramics of the 18th and 19th Centuries. *Journal of Ceramic History* 8: 3–41.

NOËL HUME, IVOR
1982 *A Guide to the Artifacts of Colonial America*. Alfred A. Knopf, New York.

OGDEN, JONATHAN
1816 Letter to Bolton and Ogden in Liverpool, 9/12/1816. Letterbook of Jonathan Ogden. Ferguson, Day and Successor Company papers, New York Historical Society, New York.

PRIME, ALFRED COXE (COMPILER)
1929 *The Arts and Crafts in Philadelphia, Maryland, and South Carolina, 1721–1785*. The Walpole Society, Philadelphia.

RIDGWAY, JOHN
1844 Invoice for Earthenware Sold by John Ridgway & Company, Manufacturer of Earthenware, Cauldon Place, to J. Y. Rushton of Philadelphia, 12/28/1844. Collection of Business Americana, National Museum of American History, Smithsonian Institution, Washington, D.C.
1846 Invoice for Earthenware Sold by John Ridgway & Company, Manufacturer of Earthenware, Cauldon Place, to Adam Southern of Philadelphia, 10/31/1846. Collection of Business Americana, National Museum of American History, Smithsonian Institution, Washington, D.C.

SAMFORD, PATRICIA M.
1985 Response to a Market: English Transfer Printed Wares in North America. Paper Presented at the 18th Annual Meeting of the Society for Historical Archaeology, Boston.

SANDON, HENRY
1978 *Flight and Barr Worcester Porcelain: 1783–1840*. Antique Collectors' Club, Woodbridge, England.

SAVAGE, GEORGE, AND HAROLD NEWMAN
1976 *An Illustrated Dictionary of Ceramics*. Van Nostrand Reinhold Company, New York.

SHAW, SIMEON
1968 *History of the Staffordshire Potteries and the Rise and Progress of the Manufacture of Pottery and Porcelain*. Reprint of 1829 edition. Beatrice C. Weinstock, Great Neck, New York.

SHLASKO, ELLEN
1989 Delftware Chronology: A New Approach to Dating English Tin-Glazed Ceramics. Unpublished M.A. thesis, Department of Anthropology, College of William and Mary, Williamsburg, Virginia.

SMITH, MATTHEW
1809 Letter to Jonathan Wyld of Liverpool from the Baltimore Earthenware Dealer Matthew Smith, 12/20/1809. *Matthew Smith Letterbook, 1803–1812* 1: M3621-1. Maryland Historical Society, Baltimore.

STACHIW, MYRON O.
   1988 Research notes on the Letter and Order Books of Ho-
         race Collamore, a Boston Earthenware Dealer, 1814–
         1818. Ms., on file with the author.

STAFFORDSHIRE POTTERS
   1808 A List of Prices, Settled, and Finally Agreed to by the
         Manufacturers, as the Lowest Prices, of the Following
         Articles, Below which None of Them Are to Sell after
         1st of March, 1808. *Enoch Wood Scrapbook* 1. Stoke-
         on-Trent City Museum and Art Gallery, Hanley, Staf-
         fordshire.
   1825 Staffordshire Potteries, Price Current of Earthenware,
         July 1, 1825. Ferguson, Day and Successor Company
         papers. New York Historical Society, New York.
   1833 Staffordshire Potteries. General Meeting of Manufac-
         turers, Held at the Swan Inn, Hanley, October 21,
         1833; Mr. Ralph Stevenson in the Chair. Ferguson,
         Day and Successor Company papers. New York His-
         torical Society, New York.
   1846a At a Meeting of Manufacturers Engaged in the Amer-
         ican Trade, Held Pursuant to Notice, At the Trentham
         Inn, on Monday, January 26th, 1846. John Ridgway,
         Esq., in the Chair. Foxwell Collection of Broadsides
         and Circulares, Item 24954. Kress Library of Busi-
         ness and Economics. Baker Library. Harvard Univer-
         sity, Cambridge, Massachusetts.
   1853 Prices Current of Earthenware, 1853. Wedgwood Ar-
         chives. Keele University Library, Keele Stafford-
         shire.
   1859 Prices Current of Earthenware, 1859. Wedgwood Ar-
         chives. Keele University Library, Keele, Stafford-
         shire.

TOWNER, DONALD
   1965 *The Leeds Pottery.* Taplinger Publishing Co., New
         York.

TURNER, WILLIAM
   1923 *William Adams, An Old English Potter.* Chapman and
         Hall Ltd., London.

WARBURTON, W. H.
   1931 *The History of Trade Union Organization in the North
         Staffordshire Potteries.* George Allen & Unwin, Ltd.,
         London.

WATNEY, BERNARD
   1964 *English Blue and White Porcelain of the 18th Cen-
         tury.* Thomas Yoseloff, New York.

WENGER, A.
   1893 *Liquid Gold of the Highest Standard, for Earthen-
         ware, China, and Glass; Introduced by Me to the
         English Potters, Since 1870.* A. Wenger, Hanley,
         Staffordshire. One-page circular, on file with the au-
         thor.

WILLIAMS-WOOD, CYRIL
   1981 *English Transfer-Printed Pottery and Porcelain: A
         History of Over-Glaze Printing.* Faber and Faber,
         London.

GEORGE L. MILLER
DEPARTMENT OF ARCHAEOLOGICAL RESEARCH
COLONIAL WILLIAMSBURG FOUNDATION
WILLIAMSBURG, VIRGINIA 23187

WILLIAM HAMPTON ADAMS
SARAH JANE BOLING

Status and Ceramics for Planters and Slaves on Three Georgia Coastal Plantations

ABSTRACT

Previous work on Georgia plantations has provided useful data about life on the large plantations on barrier islands. More recent work on small to mid-sized plantations reveals that slaves' acquisition of ceramics may reflect more of their own decisions on what was purchased and what was used. Coarser ware frequencies indicate food preparation and storage in the slave quarters. Porcelain was often found in greater numbers in the slave quarters than in the plantation bighouse kitchen. Like earlier research, slaves at Kings Bay were found to have relatively more small bowls, but surprisingly they had relatively more plates as well. Comparison of slaves and planters using CC Index revealed that for several vessel forms the slaves had more expensive ceramics than their masters. This suggests that the slaves themselves viewed ceramics as status indicators and purchased them accordingly.

Introduction

The plantation is basically an agricultural factory using capital to manage labor to grow a product for the world market. Inherent in plantations is the creation of separate social and economic classes. While the degree of separation varied greatly through time and space, the presence of this dichotomy was inherent in the system. This article examines status as revealed by material culture on three plantations on the Georgia coast, and compares those plantations to ones elsewhere on that coast. The discussion centers upon the following research questions for different status groups (slave vs. planter; tenant vs. planter; small planter vs. middle planter; slaves of small planter vs. slaves of middle planter). The following analyses were run on these status groups for comparative purposes:

— Do these status groups differ in the ceramic wares used?
— Do these status groups differ in the ceramic vessel forms used?
— Do these status groups differ in the value of the ceramic tableware used?

These data were obtained from three nearly adjacent plantations on the mainland portion of the Georgia coast, in the southern-most county, Camden County. The plantations examined here were: Kings Bay Plantation (9CAM172; 1791-ca. 1850); Cherry Point Plantation (9CAM182, 1801–1806; 9CAM183, 1791–1823), and Harmony Hall Plantation (9CAM194; 1793-ca. 1832) (Figure 1).

While this article primarily focuses upon economic status, as revealed by goods produced for the mass market, economic status was related to social status in the antebellum South. The two are different, but interrelated. Furthermore, this is an etic analysis, from the perspective of a American society as a whole, and with an emphasis on manufactured items. This is not an emic analysis of social status within slave society where status was defined in ways which were not likely to leave traces in the archaeological record. Status among slaves was based upon occupations, as well as the ability to control the supernatural and fool their masters. Much slave material culture was made by them of perishable materials, so if one is to investigate relative status it is through the mass-produced materials bought by them or furnished to them.

Status in the Antebellum South

In the antebellum South, one's parents' statuses determined whether one was ascribed the status of being free or slave. While clearly linked to race, it was much more arbitrary than commonly believed for some planters were black or Native American (Adkins 1980; Olmsted 1856:636; Woodson 1968: 3–4). Status for slaves in the antebellum South was largely a legal condition, rather than one of race or skin color. However, their occupation and

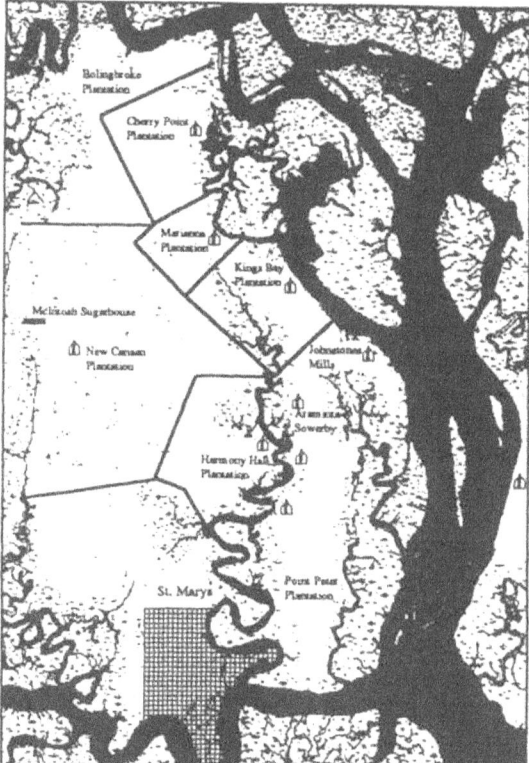

FIGURE 1. Plantations at Kings Bay, Georgia

the status of their owners played an even greater role in their daily lives.

Slaves of planters with a higher status regarded their own status as being higher than that of slaves owned by poorer planters. "They seemed to think that the greatness of their masters was transferable to themselves. It was considered bad enough to be a slave; but to be a poor man's slave was deemed a disgrace indeed" (Rawick 1972:3). Many slaves considered their economic status to be superior to that of poor whites; as David Hundley (1860:256) has remarked these were the "Poor White Trash, a name said to have originated with the slaves, who look upon themselves as much better off than all 'pó white folks' whatever." The slaves' social status on each plantation also depended upon their occupation. Field slaves had a lower social status than house slaves as viewed by the planter and

their fellow slaves alike (Frazier 1930:209; Hundley 1860:351–52; Kelso 1984:26; Orser 1987:126–28), because their acculturation was influenced through interacting with the planter's family and guests.

Slaves on task system plantations had a potentially different economic status than the slaves on gang system plantations because they provided more of their own subsistence needs and participated within the region's market economy selling their own produce and handcrafts; plantations with task systems permitted slaves to garden and raise chickens, eggs, and pigs, as well as making baskets, canoes, and other handcrafts for sale (Adams 1987:11–13; Adams et al. 1987:228–34; Morgan 1982, 1983). Such slaves were very much akin to peasants working on their landlord's manor or hacienda. Because of this participation, most of the material culture slaves possessed on a task system plantation were made by them or purchased using their own funds. Of course, on any plantation the slaves made much of what they possessed. One may hypothesize that the task labor plantation slaves could have had a higher amount of material goods through their own individual initiative.

Achieved status is that position in society obtained by an individual through his or her own achievements in life, like elected positions, and sometimes wealth and power or the lack of such. Status is relational; an individual's status is determined by reference to someone else's status. Each person has many different statuses, depending upon the circumstances of the moment and the people present (see Orser 1987:124–26 for discussion of this). One can be a father in one's own household, and a son in one's parents' household, wealthier than a beggar, and poorer than a merchant. The planters' relative economic status can be measured by the number of slaves owned, or acreage controlled. The planters' relative social status can be inferred by levels of interaction with their fellow planters and townspeople, as well as from the material culture indicating such interaction.

Three main classification schemes have been developed for the relative status of free whites in the South (Figure 2). David R. Hundley's (1860)

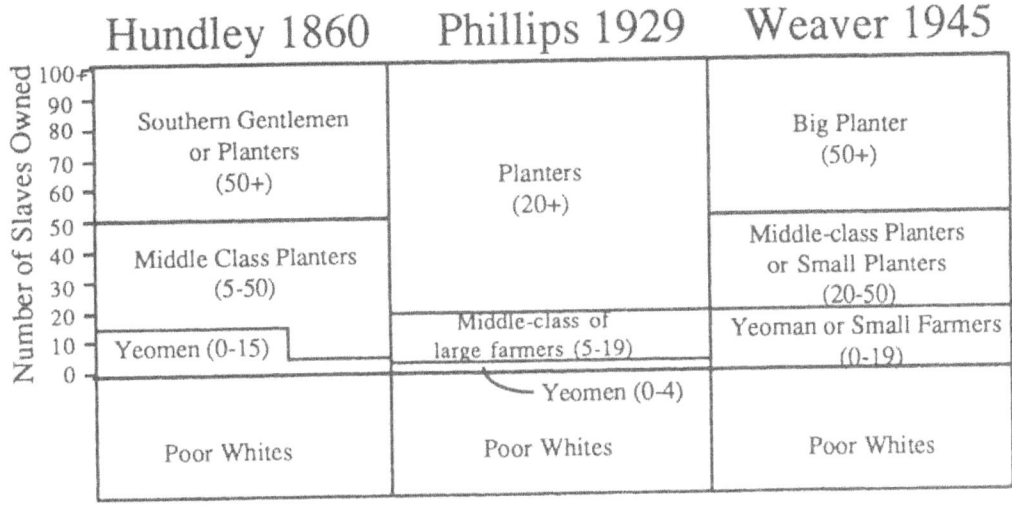

FIGURE 2. Comparison of social status of free whites on the basis of number of slaves owned.

classification centered upon slave ownership, with three classes of slave owners and a fourth class, Poor Whites, who owned no slaves. Ulrich B. Phillips (1929:339) thought a minimum of 20 slaves was needed to define a plantation, whereas owners of 5–19 slaves formed ''a middle-class of large farmers and comfortable townsmen.'' Phillips admired Hundley's work and differs from it only by not distinguishing between middle class and upper class planters. Herbert Weaver (1945) objected to the above classifications because those were based solely upon slave ownership and did not take into consideration landownership. The problem in classifying slaveowners as planters, without considering their land as well, is that the two were not necessarily the same. ''Quite frequently men without land owned large numbers of slaves whom they hired out to plantation owners; others were found to own extensive tracts of improved land but no slaves. The former were obviously not planters and the latter were probably middle-class farmers'' (Weaver 1945:37).

Does Weaver's classification add anything to what Hundley or Phillips had done, or does it merely complicate it by adding a second variable? Weaver still based the definition of each class on the number of slaves owned. His Big Planter is the

same, in terms of slaves, as Hundley's Southern Gentleman or Planter. He uses Phillips' dividing line of owning 20 slaves to distinguish planter from yeoman farmers. While he did not label these groups as upper, middle, and lower class, the distinction is implicit in his designating one group as middle-class planters. How does one classify a person with 150 slaves and only 100 acres who rented out his slaves or put them to work in a mill, or one with 5000 acres but only 10 slaves, using Weaver's classification? The economic control which can be brought to bear, not ownership, provides the relative economic status or worth. For example, at Waverly Plantation in Mississippi, George H. Young, owned 916 hectares (324 improved hectares) and 117 slaves in 1850, 1368 hectares (594 tillable) and 137 slaves in 1860, or ratios of 10.0 and 11.6 acres per slave (Adkins 1980:85–87). Young would be classified as a big planter on the basis of acreage and slave ownership, but he also rented other plantations and controlled twice as much land. Land control is as important as landownership as a socio-economic variable. Furthermore, to use acreage owned as the only criterion is misleading. How much of that land is forest or swamp? How much is in pasture or fields? While a census provides information on

TABLE 1
SLAVEHOLDERS IN THE UNITED STATES, 1850 (FROM DEBOW 1854:95)

	1	2–4	5–9	10–19	20–49	50–99	100–199	200–299	300–499	500–999	1000 +	Total
Alabama	5204	7737	6572	5067	3524	957	216	16	2	—	—	29,295
Arkansas	1383	1951	1365	788	382	109	19	2	—	—	—	5,999
Columbia, D of	760	539	136	39	2	1	—	—	—	—	—	1,477
Delaware	320	352	117	20	—	—	—	—	—	—	—	809
Florida	699	991	759	588	349	104	29	—	1	—	—	3,520
Georgia	6554	11716	7701	6490	5056	764	147	22	4	2	—	38,456
Kentucky	9244	13284	9579	5022	1198	53	5	—	—	—	—	38,385
Louisiana	4797	6072	4327	2652	1774	728	274	36	6	4	—	20,670
Maryland	4825	5331	3327	1822	655	72	7	—	1	—	—	16,040
Mississippi	3640	6228	5143	4015	2964	910	189	18	8	1	—	23,116
Missouri	5762	6878	4370	1810	345	19	—	1	—	—	—	19,185
North Carolina	1204	9668	8129	5898	2828	485	76	12	3	—	—	28,303
South Carolina	3492	6164	6311	4955	3200	990	382	69	29	2	2	25,596
Tennessee	7616	10582	8314	4852	2202	276	19	2	1	—	—	33,864
Texas	1935	2640	1585	1121	374	82	9	1	—	—	—	7,747
Virginia	11385	15550	13030	9456	4880	646	107	8	1	—	—	55,063
U.S. TOTAL	68,820	105,683	80,765	54,595	29,733	6,196	1,479	187	56	9	2	347,525
U.S.%	19.80	30.41	23.24	15.71	8.56	1.78	0.42	0.05	0.02	<0.01	<0.01	100.0
Georgia %	17.04	30.47	20.03	16.87	13.15	1.99	0.38	0.06	0.01	<0.01	0.00	100.0

improved acreage, often this information is not available for a particular archaeological site.

While the above classifications can be used for mid-19th century plantations, using them for earlier plantations is riskier because the slave population was increasing during the 18th and early 19th centuries. And, of course, it is entirely useless after Emancipation, even though plantations continued to the present day. What is not clear from the literature is whether this increase meant more people could be slaveholders with time or if the increase was relative. Would a slaveholder with 30 slaves in 1780 be the equivalent of a slaveholder of 50 slaves in 1860? Furthermore, applying this classification to an individual plantation has problems, for a plantation may change classes through time with growth or from difficulties. Like most discussions of plantations, these classifications are ahistorical. Does a big planter who sells or emancipates his slaves lose status as a big planter?

Federal census-takers collected information on slaveholding within specific categories of slaveowners (Table 1; Figure 3). Whether these were emic categories or bureaucratic ones, they surely would have affected classification systems of later historians. The 1850 U.S. Census of Population summarized by DeBow (1854:95) revealed that Georgia slaveholders were in very similar proportions to the U.S. average, with 47.51% owning one to four slaves, 36.90% owning 5–19 slaves, 13.15% owning 20–49 slaves, and only 2.44% owning more than 50 slaves (Table 1; Figure 3). Thus, 84.41% of the *slaveholders* in Georgia in 1850 would be classified as small planters, 13.15% middle planters, and 2.44% large planters. Using these large planters to characterize plantation life is as valid as using millionaires to portray American life.

Figures for the county north of Kings Bay, Glynn County, during the 1820–1860 period also reveal that large and middle planters comprised only a small portion of the total population and of the slaveholders. Small planters comprised roughly 60–80% of the slaveholders, while slaveholders themselves were less than 15% of the white population (Otto 1979). The latter figure is somewhat misleading, however, for it does not show slave-

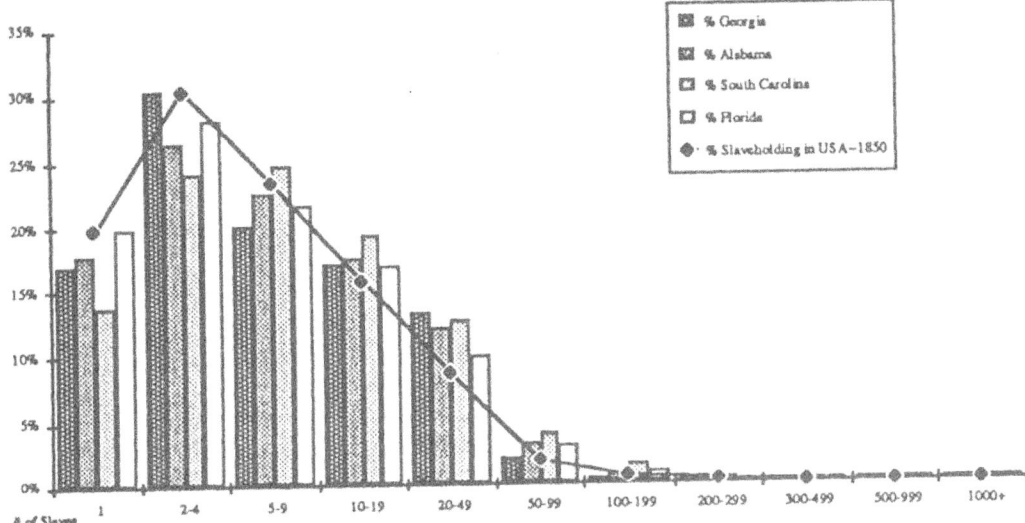

FIGURE 3. Slaveownership in the South, 1850.

holding by household, which would be a much higher percentage. In 1860, only a small number of free Southerners were involved directly with slavery, for most were small farmers or city dwellers who could not afford the expense of providing for slaves (Stampp 1956:29–30). For every plantation, there were many more small farms with no slaves at all.

Using the numbers of slaves owned as the determining factor in assigning status presents other problems. Knowing the total number of slaves on a plantation is not as useful as knowing the demography of that population. A plantation with about 50 slaves in a normal distribution of ages and sexes provides fewer full hands than one with about 30 young male slaves; in terms of economic output of the labor, the latter plantation would provide much more production for the short term. Yet to use the above classifications of Hundley and Weaver, one would be a big planter, while the latter plantation would be of a middle class planter. Furthermore, the labor system used determines the slave population to a great extent. For example, if two adjacent plantations having identical acreage cultivated and identical crops planted, were to use the different labor systems,

gang labor and task labor, the number of slaves required would differ. The plantation with task labor would have relatively more slaves, since each one would produce less than they would in a gang system; the planter can afford to have more slaves because he is providing proportionately less in weekly rations and the slaves are using their free time in gardening, raising meat, and hunting (Adams 1987:11–13; Morgan 1982, 1983; Reitz, Gibbs, and Rathbun 1985:165–166, 183–184). So if one uses the numbers of slaves owned by a planter as a status criterion, one should adjust for the labor system used.

More meaningful classifications need to be developed using other criteria. Clearly, a planter with more than 50 slaves was wealthy, even if his capital was invested only in slaves. Such individuals were upper class, economically (and probably socially as well). But based upon the investigation of one plantation with about 28 slaves—the Kings Bay Plantation—the Thomas King family would also have to regarded as upper class during the 1791–1819 period. The planter, Thomas King, served as an officer in the local militia, owned a town house as well as a plantation bighouse, and entertained at parties friends who were coming from Savannah and St. Augustine. He poured drinks from matched sets of decanters into gold inlaid goblets and decorated tumblers. His prominence would have been known outside the county, probably for much of the Georgia coast, since his parties were mentioned even in the Savannah paper.

By contrast, John King and son James King, who owned Cherry Point Plantation (1791–1823), had only eight slaves and, while locally prominent, were on a different economic and social level as Thomas King (not a relative). John and James King were small planters, while Thomas King was a middle planter, if we use slave ownership as the quantitative unit of measurement. If indeed Thomas King was wealthier, would this be revealed in the ceramic assemblages from these two planter's kitchens? Using the CC Index (Miller 1980) to compare these assemblages should (and does) reveal significant differences, as will be examined later here.

Status and Ware

Much of what we know about the planters' more mundane lives comes from archaeology and from studying probate inventories. Few descriptions of kitchens can be gleaned from historical sources, although what few do exist would offend most modern ideas of cleanliness. Fanny Kemble described her kitchen at Cannon's Point in 1838 as ''a mere wooden outhouse, with no floor but bare earth'' (Kemble 1863:26). Each kitchen at Kings Bay was dirt floored also and contained hundreds of broken ceramic vessels inside them and in the middens just outside.

Small plantations may have provided food storage and preparation in the planter's kitchens, whereas this was less feasible when one was feeding 28 slaves as Thomas King was faced with doing at the Kings Bay Plantation. Since coarse wares, tablewares, and food bone were all found at the small plantations' slave quarters we know some food preparation was done at the quarters.

Utilitarian vessels for storage and processing foods were made from coarse stoneware, coarse

redware, and yelloware. The higher frequency of coarser wares at the slave sites was evidence that food storage and processing was undertaken at the slave quarters. Refined stonewares included Westerwald from Germany and white saltglazed tableware from England. But few such vessels were found at Kings Bay, and those can be considered heirlooms. Coarser wares (yelloware, coarse redware, coarse stoneware) were used primarily for food storage and preparation.

The ceramic assemblage at the tenant site (the John King Site, 9CAM182, occupied by Woodford Mabry, 1801–1806), yielded only 7.3% of these coarser wares by vessel count (Tables 2 and 3); this may be a function of the short occupation which did not permit sufficient time to break enough vessels, or it may reflect less storage and food preparation at that site. Small planters at Harmony Hall Plantation and at Cherry Point Plantation had 8.4% coarser wares in their kitchen middens, compared to 6.4% at the middle planter's kitchen and yard at Kings Bay Plantation. Lumping planters together, the average for coarse wares was 7.6%, compared to the slave average of 15.7% (Table 3; Figure 4). The slave and planter site areas on small plantations were nearly identical in the amount of coarse wares, with 8.5% for slaves and 8.4% for planters. On the middle-sized plantation, the slaves' assemblage contained 22.8% coarse wares, compared with 6.4% of the planter's assemblage. Taken as a whole, the importance of coarse wares was essentially the same on all sites, except the Kings Bay Plantation slave quarters. This may reflect a different provisioning system on the middle-sized plantation, with the slaves there being responsible for their own food storage and preparation.

Porcelain was not a commonly recovered ware from the Kings Bay sites, as would be expected due to its cost. No porcelain was found at the John King Site (the tenant house), while the other sites had less than 7% of their ceramic assemblage in porcelain. Harmony Hall kitchen (9CAM194A) had the highest frequency of porcelain, 6.2%, while the slave quarters there (9CAM194B) had the next highest at 4.2%, followed by the Kings Bay Plantation slave quarters (9CAM172B),

TABLE 2
VESSELS BY WARE FOR SITES AT KINGS BAY

Site	John King Sawyer 182		James King Planter 183a		James King Planter 183c		Harmony Hall Planter 194a		Kings Bay Planter 172a		James King Slave 183 d		Harmony Hall Slave 194b		Kings Bay Slave 172b	
	N	%	N	%	N	%	N	%	N	%	N	%	N	%	N	%
Yelloware	0	0.0	4	3.7	3	1.3	3	1.6	5	1.4	1	2.9	0	0.0	13	8.5
Redware, coarse	0	0.0	3	2.8	6	2.6	4	2.1	6	1.7	2	5.9	2	1.7	12	7.8
Stoneware, coarse	3	7.3	1	0.9	14	6.0	6	3.1	11	3.0	3	8.8	5	4.2	10	6.5
Other earthenwares	0	0.0	0	0.0	0	0.0	1	0.5	1	0.3	0	0.0	0	0.0	0	0.0
Redware, refined	0	0.0	4	3.7	3	1.3	3	1.6	4	1.1	1	2.9	1	0.8	3	2.0
Stoneware, refined	0	0.0	3	2.8	3	1.3	2	1.0	1	0.3	0	0.0	0	0.0	0	0.0
Porcelain	0	0.0	2	1.8	2	0.9	12	6.2	9	2.5	0	0.0	5	4.2	6	3.9
Delft/Majolica	0	0.0	0	0.0	0	0.0	0	0.0	2	0.6	0	0.0	2	1.7	1	0.7
Creamware	18	43.9	26	23.9	33	14.0	37	19.3	62	17.1	6	17.6	7	5.9	31	20.3
Pearlware	20	48.8	66	60.6	171	72.8	124	64.6	259	71.6	21	61.8	97	81.5	77	50.3
Whiteware	0	0.0	0	0.0	0	0.0	0	0.0	2	0.6	0	0.0	0	0.0	0	0.0
Total	41	100.0	109	100.2	235	100.2	192	100.0	362	100.2	34	99.9	119	100.0	153	100.0

TABLE 3
VESSELS BY WARE AND STATUS AT KINGS BAY

	Sawyer		Small Planter		Middle Planter		Slave of Small Planter		Slave of Middle Planter		Kings Bay Planters		Kings Bay Slaves	
	N	%	N	%	N	%	N	%	N	%	N	%	N	%
Yelloware	0	0.0	10	1.9	5	1.4	1	0.7	13	8.5	15	1.7	14	4.6
Redware, coarse	0	0.0	13	2.4	6	1.7	4	2.6	12	7.8	19	2.1	16	5.2
Stoneware, coarse	3	7.3	21	3.9	11	3.0	8	5.2	10	6.5	32	3.6	18	5.9
Other earthenwares	0	0.0	1	0.2	1	0.3	0	0.0	0	0.0	2	0.2	0	0.0
Redware, refined	0	0.0	10	1.9	4	1.1	1	0.7	3	2.0	14	1.6	4	1.3
Stoneware, refined	0	0.0	8	1.5	1	0.3	1	0.7	0	0.0	9	1.0	1	0.3
Porcelain	0	0.0	16	3.0	9	2.5	5	3.3	6	3.9	25	2.8	11	3.6
Delft/Majolica	0	0.0	0	0.0	2	0.6	2	1.3	1	0.7	2	0.2	3	1.0
Creamware	18	43.9	96	17.9	62	17.1	13	8.5	31	20.3	158	17.6	44	14.4
Pearlware	20	48.8	361	67.4	259	71.6	118	77.1	77	50.3	620	69.0	195	63.7
Whiteware	0	0.0	0	0.0	2	0.6	0	0.0	0	0.0	2	0.2	0	0.0
Total	41	100.0	536	100.1	362	100.2	153	100.1	153	100.0	898	100.0	306	100.0

which at 3.9% was higher than the planter's kitchen at 2.5%. For porcelain, the planters do not differ significantly in their ceramic assemblages (3.0% vs. 2.5% for small vs. middle; Table 3). Slaves on the two small plantations had 3.3% of their ceramics as porcelain, compared to 3.9% for slaves on the middle plantation. The slaves' porcelain average was 3.6%, compared to the planter average of 2.8%. Due to porcelain's being more expensive, we would not expect it to be found frequently on slave sites, much less in higher quantities than at their masters'. Otto found at Cannon's Point, that porcelain was 1.1% on the slave site, 2.8% at the overseer's, and 1.4% at the planter's kitchen (Otto 1984:90). Perhaps the mistress of that bighouse simply wiped out or rinsed the tea service and that this resulted in less breakage of it there. Porcelains were most often found in tea service.

Pearlware gradually supplanted creamware as the vessel of choice for the table, so much so that by the early 1800s creamware was the cheapest tableware available (Miller 1980). The Kings Bay sites can be seriated (ordered) on the basis of the relative frequency of creamware and pearlware, with later sites having more pearlware. For example, the 1801–1806 John King Site had 48.8% pearlware, while the longer occupied and later sites like Harmony Hall had 64.6%. While the range of creamware:pearlware ratios is consider-

able between some of these sites, it is not part of this analysis. The ratio is thought to be mostly influenced by time, and we are considering distinct marks of status. On the basis of ware types, we found little meaningful difference between small and middle planter assemblages, or between their slaves' assemblages. Slave sites tended to have a few more coarse ware vessels than did the planters (or fewer refined wares for the table).

Status and Vessel Form

Vessel form has been suggested as indicating status on plantations (Otto 1977, 1984). If vessels were used for the purpose each was made, then the more vessel forms in a site, the greater the complexity of the meals partaken there. Researchers have observed that slave sites yielded a disproportionate amount of bowls and have inferred this has resulted from the cooking methods employed by the slave, particularly using *pot-au-feu*. The interpretation for Cannon's Point Plantation was that slaves ate from bowls, while at the planter's house people ate from plates, reflecting different methods of cooking there, stewing and roasting (Otto 1977:98, 1984:167). Others also found that slaves used bowls more (Booth 1971:33).

At Kings Bay, small bowls at the planters' kitchens ranged from 7.9% to 22.4% of the ce-

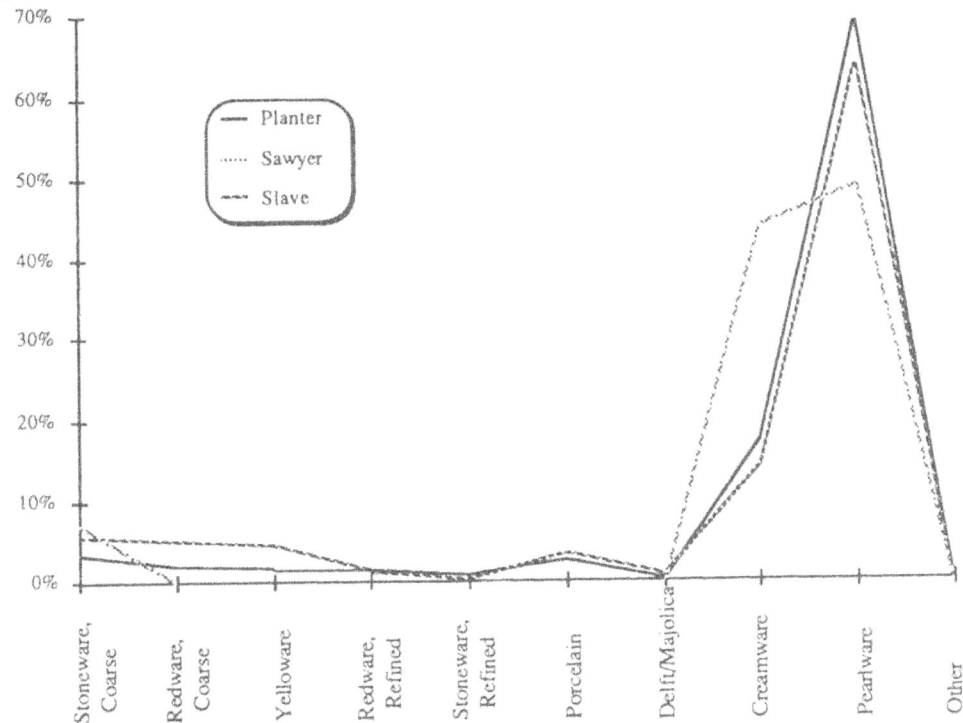

FIGURE 4 Vessels by ware for planters, sawyer, and slaves at Kings Bay

ramic assemblage, while at the slave quarters there the small bowls ranged from 15.4% to 32.2%, consistently more than for the planters' kitchen (Table 4; Figures 5–8). If small bowls and large bowls are combined, the planters' kitchens totals ranged from 15.8% to 28.5%, while those at the slave quarters ranged from 24.1% to 35.8%. When we compare bowl frequency for planter and slave on the same plantation, the slave always has relatively more small bowls and fewer large bowls than the planter, but the range for slaves on one plantation overlaps that for planters on other plantations. Plates ranged from 23.2% to 37.6% at the planters' kitchens and from 24.8% to 40.4% at the slave quarters. Plates were more frequent at the Harmony Hall Plantation Slave Cabin and the Kings Bay Plantation Slave Quarters, compared to their planters. But for the Cherry Point Plantation, the slaves' plate frequency is less than that of the planter.

Oral histories of ex-slaves collected in the 1930s

indicated wooden implements and tableware were common in many areas of the South (Cade 1935: 300–301). Conversely, planters likely used pewter plates as well as ceramic ones (even though few pewter vessels were found in the Kings Bay sites). These are biases for which there can be no control. While it is true slave sites at Kings Bay did have relatively more small bowls (20.5% vs. 13.2%), they also had relatively more plates (31.2% vs. 30.7%) than the planters (Tables 4–6). The reason for this is that slaves had relatively few vessels other than plates and bowls, while the planter's assemblage contained a fuller complement of tableware vessels like cups, platters, teapots, and miscellaneous vessels. With the sites at Kings Bay we can now see that the variation between slave sites is much the same as the variation between planter sites, and that some slaves had higher frequencies of plates than the planters did.

Research suggests the tea ceremony in British-

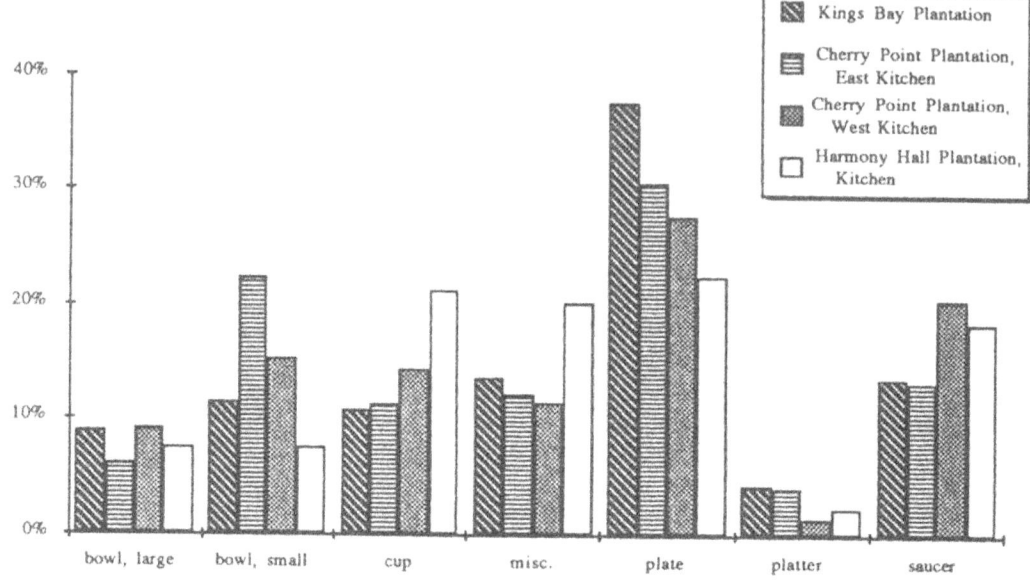

FIGURE 5. Vessel forms for the planters at Kings Bay.

American society had important status implications on a plantation, even though elsewhere after
the Revolution its importance as a status indicator
becomes less distinct (Roth 1961). On a plantation, however, the tea ceremony (not just tea
drinking) should have been restricted to the planters and their guests; it would seem unlikely that
slaves partook of it and hence the presence of tea
service, especially porcelain, might have valid
usage in defining status of site occupants. However, some archaeologists believe household servants may have become acculturated to the tea
ceremony and acquired tea service for their personal use (K. Lewis 1985:58; Otto 1977:106,
1984:166). But we do not know whether the
presence of tea pots and tea cups at a slave site
implies the tea ceremony, or other uses. Otto noted
that while the slaves and the overseer had teawares, these were not matched sets like the planter
used (Otto 1984:166). Some of the slave sites at
Kings Bay had more porcelain vessels for tea
service than did the planter's assemblage. At
Kings Bay, porcelain was not a common ware,
only 1.8%, 0.9%, 6.2%, 2.5% at the four planter's

kitchens, and 0.0%, 4.2%, and 3.9% at the slave
quarters (Table 2). This porcelain was almost
always teaware, but matching vessels were found
only at planter kitchens. At Kings Bay Plantation,
the slave quarters had more porcelain than the
planter's kitchen, not at all what would be expected on the basis of cost, for porcelain was more
expensive than earthenwares (Miller 1980).

Comparing the Kings Bay vessels to other plantations on the Georgia coast is difficult because the
level of analysis between reports differs considerably. Sue Mullins Moore in a study of status on the
coastal plantation (Moore 1985:153) lumped all
vessels into either holloware or flatware without
defining either category or noting whether the data
included pitchers, chamberpots, and other vessels
associated with an assortment of activities in the
bedroom, kitchen, dairy, and elsewhere. John S.
Otto (1984) lumped cups, mugs, and other vessels
into teaware, but did not explicitly define the
category for Cannon's Point. Singleton (1980) did
not distinguish between cups and bowls in her
analysis of the material from Butler Island. Given
the lack of any detailed analysis by previous

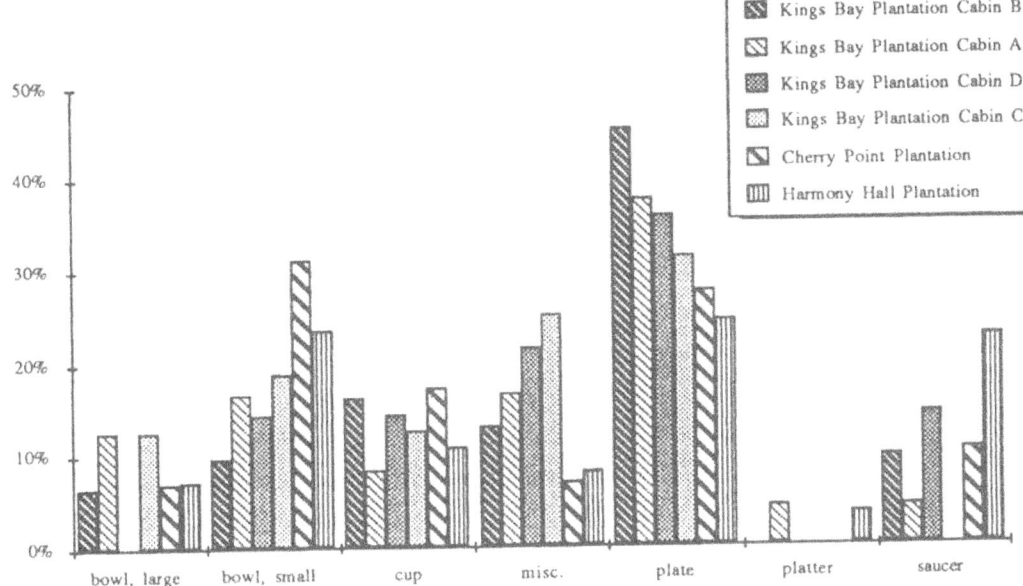

FIGURE 6. Vessel forms for the slaves at Kings Bay.

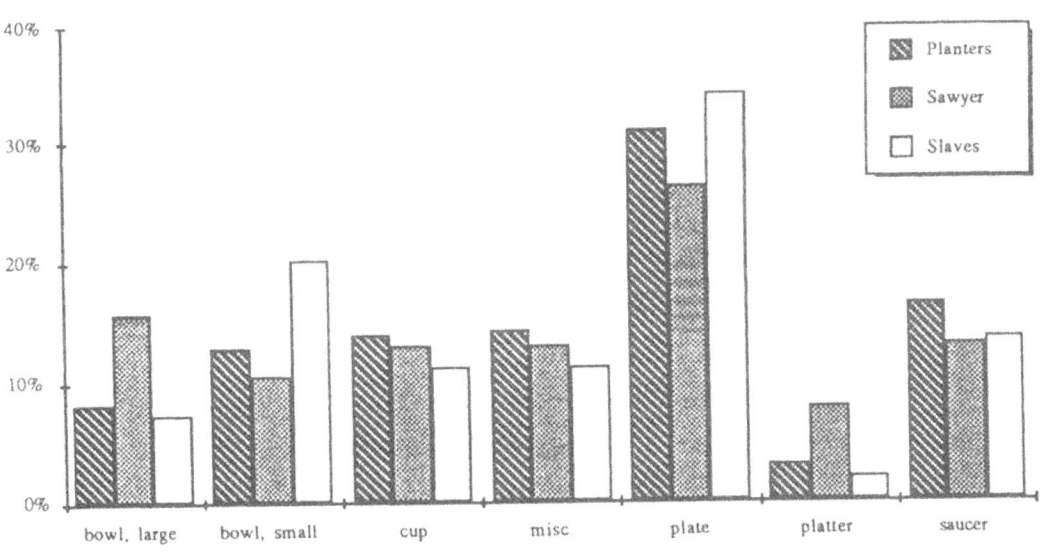

FIGURE 7. Vessel forms, comparing the planters, sawyer, and slaves at Kings Bay.

researchers, we can only compare using the simplistic dichotomy of flatware versus holloware.

For the following discussion, cups, teapots, miscellaneous vessels, and bowls will be subsumed into holloware, while saucers, plates, and platters will be lumped together as flatware. As one can easily see, functional groupings like vessels for serving food or liquids, for eating, for

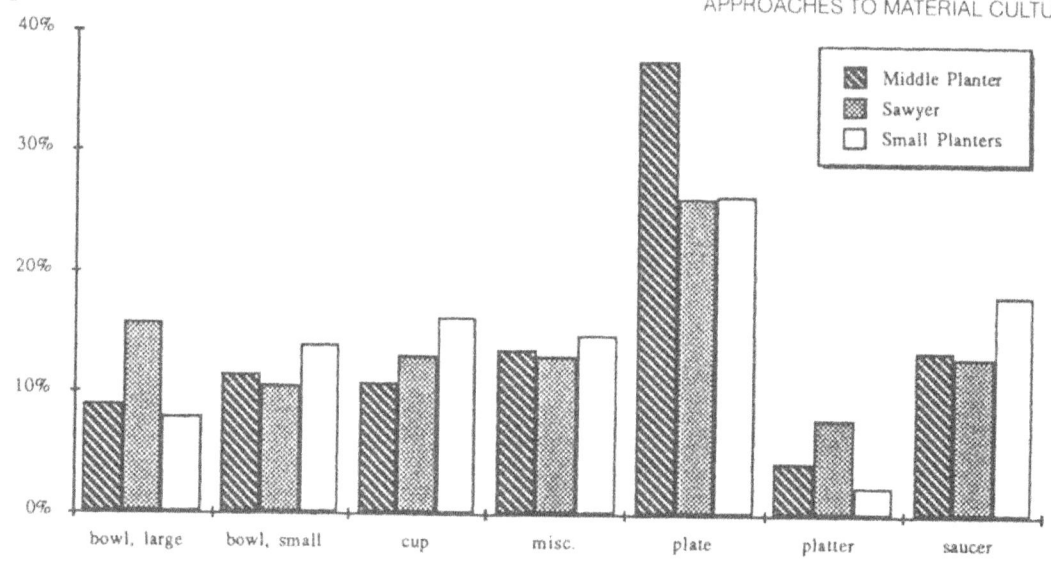

FIGURE 8. Vessel forms, comparing the middle planter, sawyer, and small planters at Kings Bay.

drinking, for storage, cross-cut these two arbitrary shapes of flat and hollow.

By ranking these sites on the frequency of flatwares in the tableware asemblage we derived three groupings. The group with the highest frequency of flatwares—roughly 55%—are planters' kitchens from the large planter at Cannon's Point Plantation, and the middle planters at Sinclair Plantation and at Kings Bay Plantation (Table 4). The second group, 45.1%–51.4% flatware, includes two slave cabins, the James King Site kitchens (Cherry Point Plantation), the overseer at the Cannon's Point Plantation, and the planter at Harmony Hall Plantation. The third group, 19.0%–39.3% flatware, includes the Pike's Bluff planter's assemblage and five slave cabin assemblages. Thus, we may conclude that this analysis, as simple as it is, does provide useful information regarding relative status.

Slaves had higher quantities of holloware, mostly bowls, while planters had more flatware. This generality simply confirms what Otto (1975) found at Cannon's Point more than a decade ago, but with a greater range of data we now see the situation is much more complicated. Indeed, some slave sites were found to have a higher flatware frequency than some planter sites had. Thus, while there is a strong linear correlation between vessel form and status, with lower status sites having more holloware, too many sites show exceptions to this trend for it to be any more than suggestive. In addition to this kind of analysis we must therefore turn to other methods to determine relative status.

Status and the CC Index

One way to analyze relative economic status is by assigning each vessel an index value, with plain creamware (CC, or cream colored ware) having an index of 1.0. The CC Index values were derived from potters' price fixing lists assembled by George Miller (1980); thus, vessels with a higher index were more expensive than ones with lower indices. Because the initial settlement of the Kings Bay sites began about 1791, the authors chose to use the 1796 price list whenever possible, or the next closest one when certain categories were not available. The price list chosen should be the one nearest to the date when the ceramics are assumed to have been purchased.

TABLE 4

PERCENTAGE OF CERTAIN VESSEL FORMS IN THE CERAMIC TABLEWARE ASSEMBLAGE FOR KINGS BAY SITES COMPARED TO OTHER PLANTATIONS ON THE GEORGIA COAST

Site	Area	Cup	Teapot	Misc.	Plate	Saucer	Platter	Large Bowl	Small Bowl
Kings Bay Plantation	Kitchen	10.5	1.0	12.7	37.6	13.1	4.2	9.2	11.6
James King Plantation	Kitchen, East	11.2	1.0	11.2	30.6	13.2	4.1	6.1	22.4
James King Plantation	Kitchen, West	14.5	3.4	7.2	28.0	20.7	1.4	9.2	15.5
Harmony Hall Plantation	Kitchen	22.6	4.2	12.1	23.2	19.5	2.4	7.9	7.9
John King	House	13.2	—	13.2	26.3	13.2	7.9	15.8	10.5
Kings Bay Plantation	Slave Cabins	10.6	0.9	16.4	40.4	6.7	1.0	8.7	15.4
Harmony Hall Plantation	Slave Cabin	11.0	1.8	4.6	24.8	22.9	3.7	7.3	23.8
James King Plantation	Slave Cabin	17.9	—	7.1	28.6	10.7	—	3.6	32.2

		FLATWARE		TEAWARE		MISC.		BOWLS	
Cannon's Point Plantation[1]	Planter's Kitchen	55.3		34.0		5.7		4.9	
Cannon's Point Plantation[1]	Overseer	46.7		35.0		2.5		15.8	
Cannon's Point Plantation[1]	Slave Cabin	36.4		24.3		5.6		32.7	

		FLATWARE	HOLLOWARE
Sinclair[3]	Planter	55.9	44.1
Cannon's Point Plantation[1]	Planter's Kitchen	55.3	44.7
Kings Bay Plantation	Planter's Yard and Kitchen	54.9	45.1
Harmony Hall Plantation	Slave Cabin	51.4	48.6
James King Plantation	Planter's West Kitchen	50.1	49.9
Kings Bay Plantation	Slave Cabins	48.1	51.9
James King Plantation	Planter's East Kitchen	47.9	52.1
John King	House	47.4	52.6
Cannon's Point Plantation[1]	Overseer	46.7	53.3
Harmony Hall Plantation	Planter's Kitchen	45.1	54.9
James King Plantation	Slave Cabin	39.3	60.7
Cannon's Point Plantation[1]	Slave Cabin	36.4	63.6
Pikes Bluff[3]	Planter	35.2	64.8
Sinclair[4]	Slave Cabin	28.6	71.4
Butler Island[2]	Slave Cabin	26.1	73.9
Jones[3]	Slave Cabin	19.0	81.0

[1] calculated from Otto 1984:180 and Table 3.14; Teaware was not defined by Otto, but presumably included teapots, cups, creamers, and saucers. Flatware was defined (Otto 1984:69) as plate, platter, soup plate. The figures here differ from those calculated by Moore (1985:153) for the Cannon's Point assemblages apparently because Moore used Otto's 1975 dissertation.
[2] from Singleton 1980: Table 8; cups and bowls were not distinguished
[3] from Moore 1985:153

The inhabitants of these sites bought their dishes between 1770 and 1834 (median date ranges from 1795 to 1820); it is impossible to tell what year, or at what price, any given vessel was purchased. Likewise, one cannot take into account birthday presents, inheritance, shipping delays, or estate sales. The authors used the price list from the earliest year a decorative type was mentioned in the lists, as long as it was between 1796 and 1834, to evaluate the whole range of decorative types. Porcelain and sponged wares appeared on the price lists so late that the former was left out of the calculations and the latter treated as dipped. All edgeware and transferprinted vessel prices were taken from the 1796 price lists, even when some patterns had not been manufactured until a later date, to avoid confusing the issue. Each tally of indices is made up of scores for different years. Analysis used 1.33 as CC Index for edged large serving bowls.

Ceramics were divided into gross types based on form as shown above: plates, platters, cups, saucers, small and large ($\geq 6''$) bowls, teapots, chamberwares and other ceramic forms (Table 7). Over-

TABLE 5
TABLEWARE VESSEL FORMS FOR THE PLANTATIONS AT KINGS BAY.

vessel	CHERRY POINT PLANTATION				HARMONY HALL PLANTATION		KINGS BAY PLANTATION	
	WOODFORD MABRY 182	PLANTER KITCHEN 183a	PLANTER KITCHEN 183c	SLAVE CABIN 183d	PLANTER KITCHEN 194a	SLAVE CABIN 194b	PLANTER KITCHEN 172a	SLAVE CABIN 172b
bowl, large	6	6	19	1	13	8	28	9
bowl, small	4	22	32	9	13	26	36	17
cup	5	11	30	5	37	13	35	13
plate	10	30	58	8	40	26	111	45
platter	3	4	3	0	4	5	12	1
saucer	5	13	43	2	32	25	44	9
miscellaneous	5	12	24	3	26	8	40	20
Tableware Totals	38	98	209	28	165	111	306	114

TABLE 6
PLATE INDEX FOR TABLEWARE VESSEL FORMS FOR THE PLANTATIONS AT KINGS BAY.

vessel	CHERRY POINT PLANTATION				HARMONY HALL PLANTATION		KINGS BAY PLANTATION	
	WOODFORD MABRY 182	PLANTER KITCHEN 183a	PLANTER KITCHEN 183c	SLAVE CABIN 183d	PLANTER KITCHEN 194a	SLAVE CABIN 194b	PLANTER KITCHEN 172a	SLAVE CABIN 172b
bowl, large	.60	.20	.33	.12	.32	.31	.25	.20
bowl, small	.40	.73	.55	1.12	.32	1.00	.32	.38
cup	.50	.37	.52	.62	.92	.50	.32	.29
plate	1.00	1.00	1.00	1.00	1.00	1.00	1.00	1.00
platter	.30	.13	.05	.00	.10	.19	.11	.02
saucer	.50	.43	.74	.25	.80	.96	.11	.02
miscellaneous	.50	.40	.41	.38	.65	.31	.36	.44

glaze polychrome and plain blue painted pearlware received the same value, although overglaze painted wares may not have been in the potters' lists. Willow cups and saucers were classified with other blue transferprinted wares, porcelain was omitted, and blue or green scalloped edging on any vessel not plate or platter was classified as painted.

The results are quite surprising and indicate that while this method is useful, its application on slave sites must be done with caution. First, each plantation kitchen will be compared with its slave site. At the James King Site, the slaves had more expensive cups, the saucers and plates were of similar cost, but small and large bowls were considerably less expensive than the planter's assemblage (Figure 9). At Harmony Hall Plantation, the CC Index shows that the slaves' small bowls were considerably less expensive, while the plates and platters were more expensive, and the cups and saucers considerably more expensive, than those of the planter there. Large bowls were about the same cost, for the ceramics *discarded at their site*. For the Kings Bay Plantation, the slaves also had somewhat less expensive small bowls, but at least one cabin had more expensive bowls than did the planter; otherwise the slaves had less expensive ceramics.

Comparison between slave sites at Kings Bay reveals that cups and saucers form one subset of the ceramic assemblage as do large and small bowls, because when the assemblage is ordered on the basis of cup CC Index values, the bowl values are inversely proportional. In other words, slave sites with expensive cups and saucers have inex-

TABLE 7

CC INDEX FOR VARIOUS SITES ARRANGED BY INDEX YEAR AND MEAN

SITE	AREA	LOCATION	DATE	INDEX	STATUS	N	CUPS	PLATES	BOWLS	MEAN	SOURCE
Diaz	Privy	Monterey, CA	ca 1842-ca 1858	1846	merchant	74	3.59	1.92	1.68	2.69	c
Walker Tavern	—	Detroit, MI	ca 1834-ca 1850	1846	tavern	35	2.31	2.44	2.32	2.37	b
Moses Tabbs	Context #1	St. Marys, MD	1800-1840	1846	tenant farmer	16	1.44	1.46	1.29	1.42	b
Green Mansion	—	Windsor, VT	1814-1870	1833	merchant	94	3.04	1.83	1.59	2.29	d
Black Lucy's Garden	—	Andover, MA	1815-1845	1833	freed slave	58	1.68	1.61	1.24	1.53	c
Cannon's Point	Kitchen	St. Simons, GA	1820s-1850s	1824	big planter	166	2.50	2.79	1.22	2.61	d
Franklin Glass	House	Portage Co., OH	1824-1832	1824	glass worker	94	2.15	1.86	1.54	1.90	b
Franklin Glass	Factory	Portage Co., OH	1824-1832	1824	laborers	62	2.11	1.47	1.37	1.67	e
Skunk Hollow	B	NJ	—	1824	black laborer	64	1.53	1.51	1.18	1.43	e
Moses Tabbs	Context #2	St. Marys, MD	1840-1860	1824	tenant farmer	41	1.50	1.43	1.20	1.44	b
Jonathan Hale Cabin	—	Summit Co., OH	1810-ca 1830	1824	farmer	45	1.45	1.23	1.36	1.34	b
Kings Bay Plantation	Kitchen	Camden Co., GA	1791-ca 1840	1814	middle planter	274	1.94	1.87	1.60	1.81	f
Harmony Hall	Slave Cabin	Camden Co., GA	ca 1793-ca 1832	1814	slave	98	2.10	1.88	1.36	1.72	f
Cannon's Point	Slave Cabin	St. Simons, GA	1820s-1850s	1814	slave	80	1.71	2.07	1.27	1.68	c
Kings Bay	Planter average	Camden Co., GA	1791-1850	1814	planter	672	1.78	1.67	1.63	1.68	a
Kings Bay	Slave Average	Camden Co., GA	1791-1832	1814	slaves	208	1.95	1.62	1.61	1.66	f
Kings Bay Plantation	Slave Cabin C	Camden Co., GA	1791-ca 1815	1814	slave	11	2.25	1.13	1.45	1.64	f
James King	West Kitchen	Camden Co., GA	1806-ca 1823	1814	small planter	184	1.72	1.55	1.71	1.62	f
Harmony Hall	Kitchen	Camden Co., GA	ca 1793-ca 1832	1814	small planter	129	1.69	1.53	1.56	1.60	f
James King	Slave Cabin	Camden Co., GA	1791-ca 1823	1814	slave	26	2.30	1.53	1.36	1.59	f
Kings Bay Plantation	Slave Cabin Avg.	Camden Co., GA	1791-ca 1815	1814	slave	93	1.71	1.37	1.84	1.55	f
James King	East Kitchen	Camden Co., GA	1791-ca 1806	1814	small planter	83	1.72	1.42	1.62	1.53	f
Kings Bay Plantation	Slave Cabin A	Camden Co., GA	1791-ca 1815	1814	slave	34	1.33	1.44	1.57	1.47	f
Kings Bay Plantation	Slave Cabin B	Camden Co., GA	1791-ca 1815	1814	slave	24	2.00	1.44	1.28	1.47	f
John Hamlin	House	Warren Co., NJ	1810-1856	1814	wealthy farmer	18	1.50	1.31	1.86	1.45	a
175 Water St.	Fea. 43	New York, NY	1795-1820	1814	merchants	58	1.80	1.19	1.29	1.33	a
175 Water St.	Fea. 49	New York, NY	1795-1820	1814	merchants	44	1.46	1.00	1.28	1.26	f

John Richardson	Privy Cistern	Wilmington, DE	1810–ca. 1816?	1802	wealthy	21	3.40	1.93	2.53	2.31	a
Kings Bay Plantation	Kitchen	Camden Co., GA	1791–ca 1840	1796	middle planter	274	2.22	2.08	1.81	2.03	f
Harmony Hall	Kitchen	Camden Co., GA	ca 1793–ca 1832	1796	slave	—	2.30	2.11	1.60	1.95	f
Kings Bay	Planter average	Camden Co., GA	1791–1850	1796	planter	672	2.06	1.84	1.90	1.89	a
Kings Bay	Slave average	Camden Co., GA	1791–1832	1796	slaves	208	2.23	1.77	1.93	1.88	f
James King	West Kitchen	Camden Co., GA	ca. 1806–ca. 1823	1796	small planter	184	2.02	1.69	2.03	1.84	f
Harmony Hall	Kitchen	Camden Co., GA	ca 1793–ca. 1832	1796	small planter	129	1.94	1.68	1.77	1.77	f
James King	East Kitchen	Camden Co., GA	1791–ca 1806	1796	small planter	83	2.02	1.52	2.00	1.74	f
James King	Slave Cabin	Camden Co., GA	1791–ca 1823	1796	slave	26	2.60	1.61	1.43	1.74	f
Kings Bay Plantation	Slave Cabin C	Camden Co., GA	1791–ca 1815	1796	slave	11	2.60	1.13	2.00	1.71	f
Thomas Hamlin	—	Warren Co., NJ	ca 1790–1810	1796	farmer	74	1.67	1.19	2.14	1.68	a
Telco	Test Cut AX	New York, NY	ca. 1810	—	elite	33	1.65	2.02	1.39	1.68	a
Kings Bay Plantation	Slave Cabin A	Camden Co., GA	1791–ca 1815	1796	slave	37	1.53	1.51	2.02	1.68	f
Kings Bay Plantation	Slave Cabin Avg	Camden Co., GA	1791–ca 1815	1796	slave	93	2.00	1.46	1.89	1.66	f
John King	House	Camden Co., GA	ca 1801–ca 1806	1796	sawyer	32	2.10	1.37	1.85	1.64	f
Kings Bay Plantation	Slave Cabin B	Camden Co., GA	1791–ca 1815	1796	slave	24	2.33	1.54	1.57	1.64	f
Kings Bay Plantation	Slave Cabin D	Camden Co., GA	1791–ca 1815	1796	slave	11	1.80	1.37	1.76	1.52	f
Barclays	Fea 48	New York, NY	ca 1800	1796	several occupants	60	1.53	1.48	1.25	1.39	a

Sources: a Morin et al. 1986:6.43–45, Morin and Klein n d.
b Miller 1980
c Felton and Schulz 1983:76–81
d Spencer-Wood and Heberling 1984
e Geismar 1982
f Adams and Boling 1987

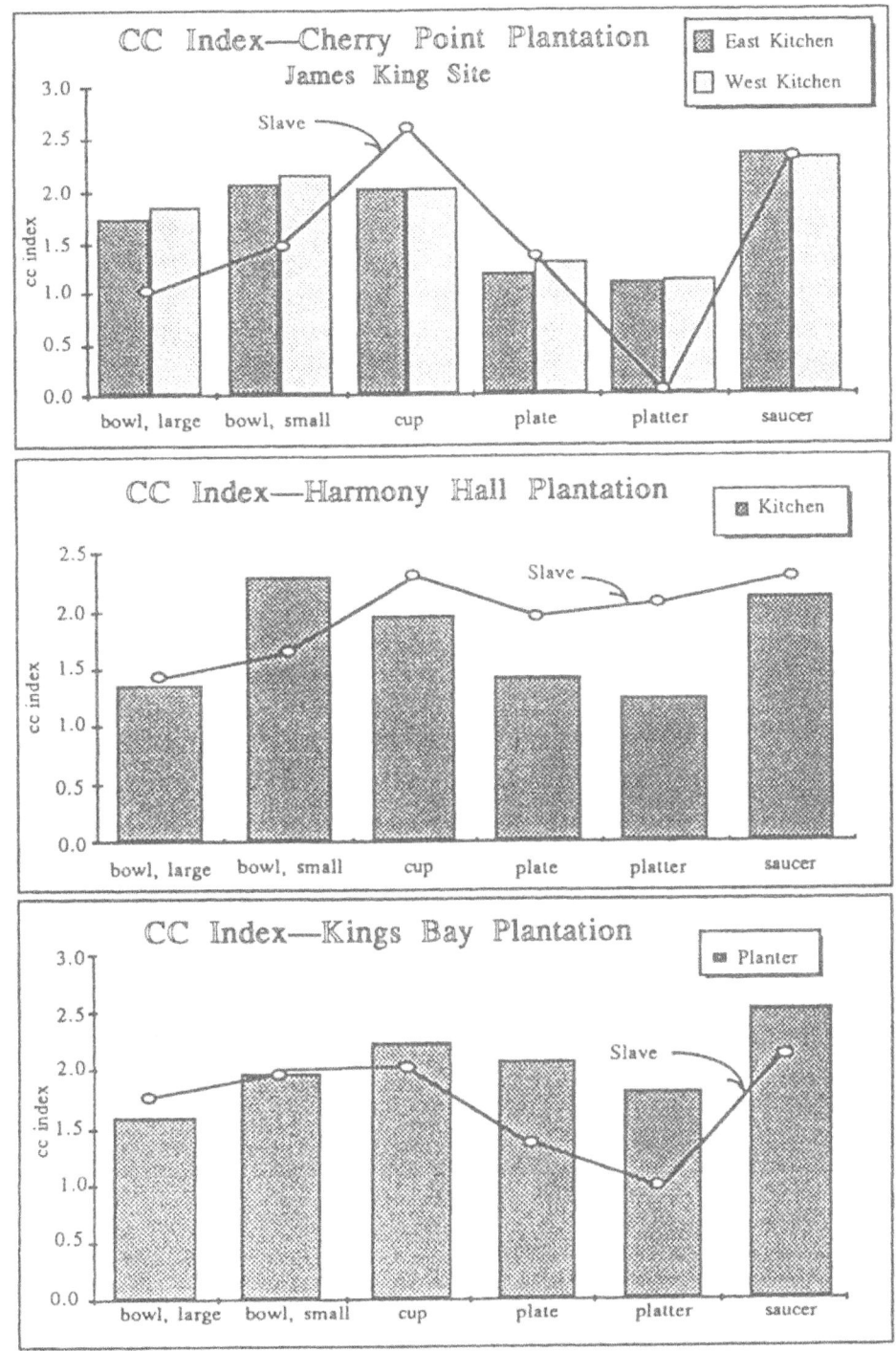

FIGURE 9. CC index for the planters and slaves on different plantations at Kings Bay.

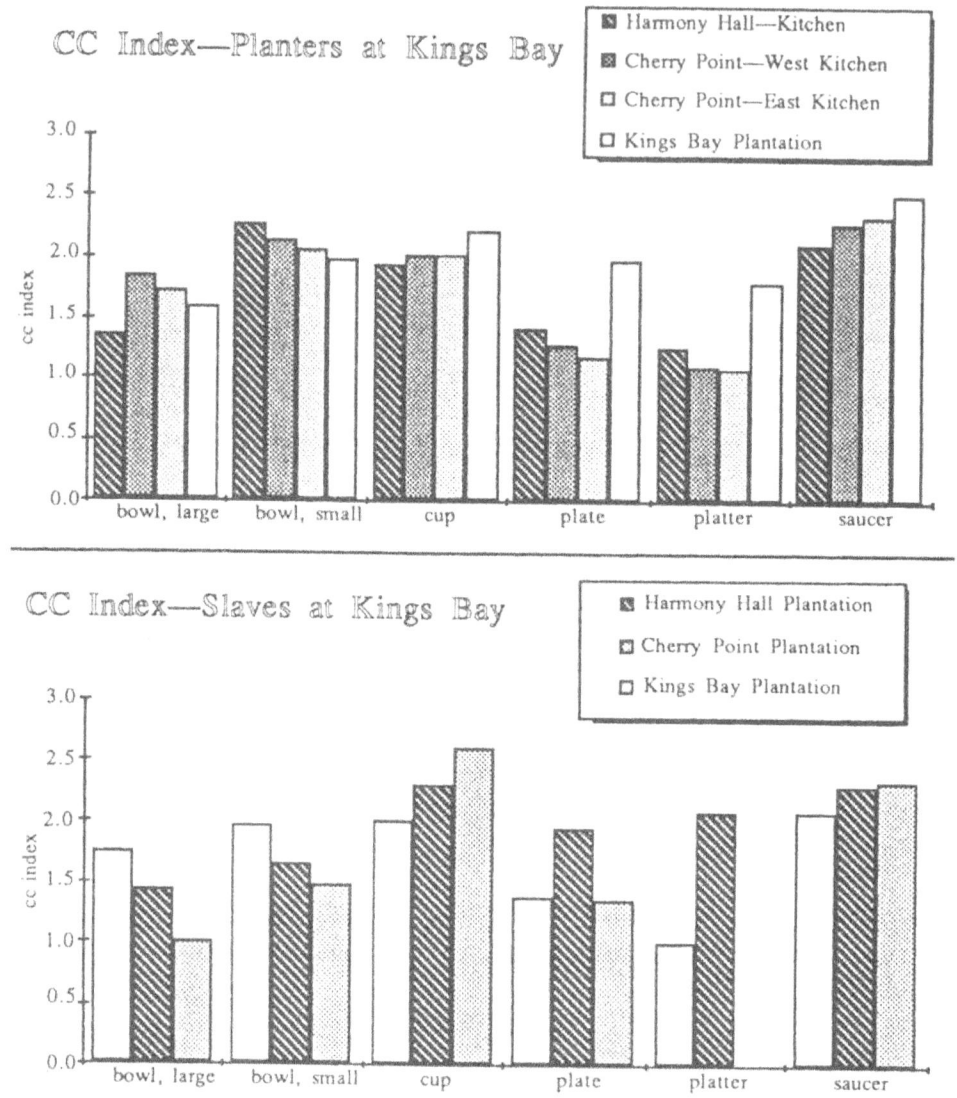

FIGURE 10 CC index for planters and for slaves at Kings Bay

pensive bowls, while sites with inexpensive cups and saucers have more expensive bowls (Figure 10). The same is true in the planter households, but the differences are not as impressive. Since these are not dependent values, except in terms of capital expended on a given amount of ceramic vessels, this observation has some meaning. Why would planters and slaves alike have good tea service and cheap bowls or conversely cheaper tea service and more expensive bowls?

One would expect that the two kitchens at the James King Site (the east one is slightly earlier than the other) would have similar CC Index values, since they represent the same household.

Indeed, the two assemblages have very similar CC Indices, with the later kitchen having a slightly higher (1.84 vs. 1.74) value. If other evidence were available to support it, one would suggest a slightly higher economic status for James King, than for his parents (who built the first kitchen). Unfortunately, such supportive data do not exist for this site.

If the two kitchens at the James King Site are combined with the planter assemblage from the Harmony Hall Plantation to represent the small planter at Kings Bay, one can compare that with the CC Index for a middle planter, Thomas King at Kings Bay Plantation, a free white sawyer at the John King Site (Woodford Mabry), and their slaves. One would assume that order (based upon posited wealth) would be revealed in the ceramic assemblages of each. For the whites, this was true, but this was not the case if the slaves were included (Figure 11). The one middle planter had more expensive plates and saucers, the small planter had the most expensive small bowls and large bowls, and the slaves had the most expensive cups and platters. In every ceramic vessel form except bowls, the slave had more expensive vessels than the small planter and the sawyer. The middle planter generally had better ceramics than his neighboring small planters, bowls being the only exception. But this was tempered somewhat by the slaves having some even better ceramic vessels.

Grouping the planters together, to compare with the sawyer and slaves, yields essentially the same observations. Planter and renter had nearly the same price large bowls and cups, but in every other vessel the sawyer renter, Woodford Mabry at the John King Site, had much less expensive items (Figure 11). But the slaves had more expensive small bowls, cups, and platters. With the exception of large bowls, the slaves had more expensive ceramics than the white renter. (The identification of Woodford Mabry as white is based upon the paucity of free blacks in the county in 1800 and the fact that he rented the land from John King. He does not show up in the 1800 or 1810 censuses.)

The Thomas King ceramics do stand out for all but cups, large bowls, and small bowls. Thomas and Mary King's plates and platters were nearly half again as expensive as those of the other planters, but their cups and saucers were only somewhat more expensive. If glassware could be considered on a similar scale the entire dinner table of Thomas and Mary King would stand high over those of the smaller landowners, who had nothing near the splendor represented by gold-painted goblets, other fine stemware, and decanters. Likewise if porcelain tablewares could be calculated in the Thomas King and Harmony Hall tea equipages, well supplied with porcelain, would rise in apparent status. If miscellaneous tableware (teapots, vases, soup tureens) could be measured the small planters would cluster more closely, and Thomas King would again come out far above them.

Since this discussion treats ceramics as indicators of household finances, platters and serving dishes, which are nonessential, even luxury items, must be taken into account somehow. For convenience in this analysis, platters were given the index value of a 10″ plate of the same decorative category. However, a platter's price varied as much with size as it did with decoration. The price lists used have little chance of providing a ranking between archaeological assemblages, in which two or three broken rim fragments were classified as "platter," because the size of a platter must be known before its price can be attached, and determining if an oval platter was 10″ or 11″ from a small sherd is impossible. Also, the price difference between the two is comparatively large (Miller 1980:23–25). However, it hardly seems reasonable to exclude platters from this analysis, since they were such valuable items. A large creamware platter was more of of a luxury item than a transferprinted dinner plate—half again as expensive, and not as generally useful.

Therefore, a system of ranking sites by the value of serving dishes in the assemblage was necessary. In this case the results fit well with the other ceramic price patterns. Estimations, based on the dimensions of the few measurable platters, and how rim and base fragments of the others compared to them, were made of the size of each platter found on a site. Serving dishes of types listed on the Staffordshire Potters' price list for 1796, used by Miller, were counted from each site.

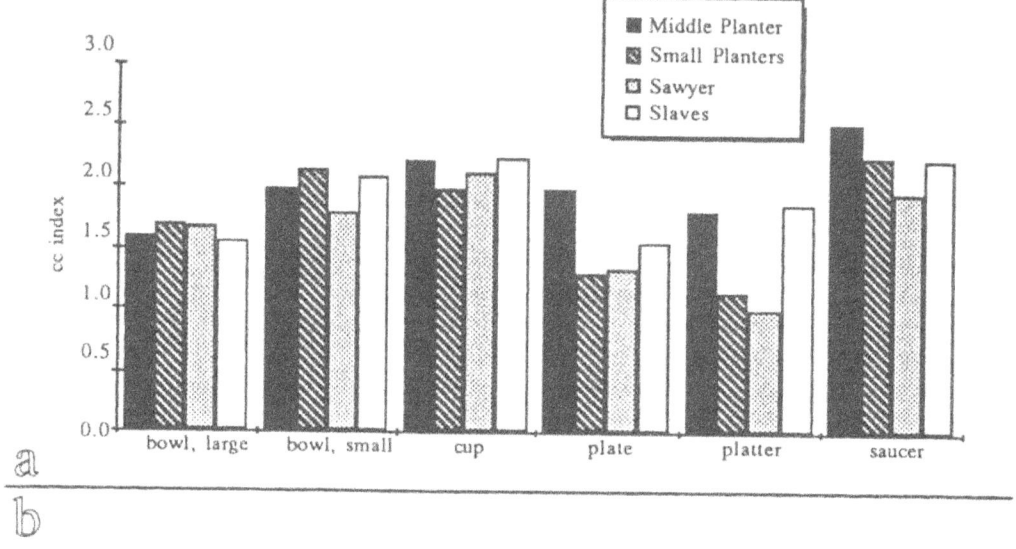

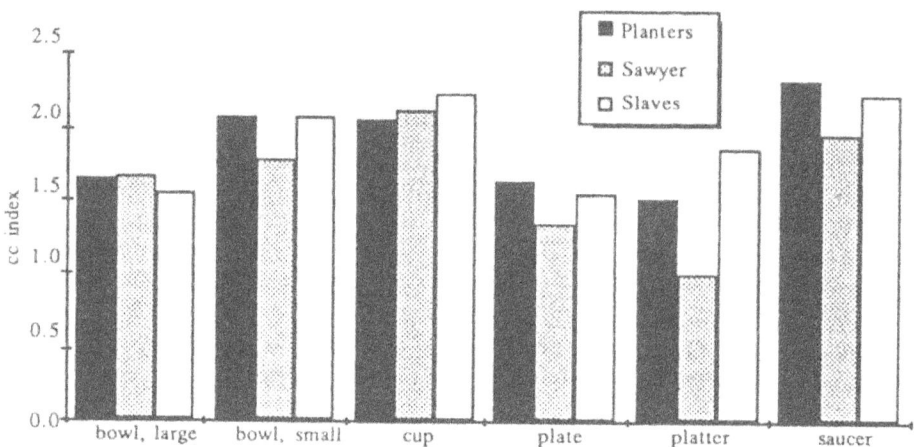

FIGURE 11. CC index by economic status at Kings Bay.

The price in English pence per dozen for each vessel was determined, and various weighting systems were tested to find one which made sense for Kings Bay.

The system which proved most useful for ranking sites by average value of platters also was least meaningful, in that it did not correct for the sample size (which in most cases was one to three vessels). That index gave a 12″ creamware platter, which seemed to be a good generic vessel, a value of 1.00 (in real terms, 48 pence/dozen). When all platters from all sites were run through this equation, the results were: Harmony Hall Slave, 3.75; Kings Bay Plantation Kitchen, 2.40; James King West Kitchen, 1.75; Harmony Hall Kitchen, 1.44; James King East Kitchen, 1.00; Woodford Mabry, 0.75, Kings Bay Plantation Slave, 0.62 (dividing the total 2.50 by the four cabins), and James King Slave 0.00, for there were no platters there.

This order, with one exception, is in keeping

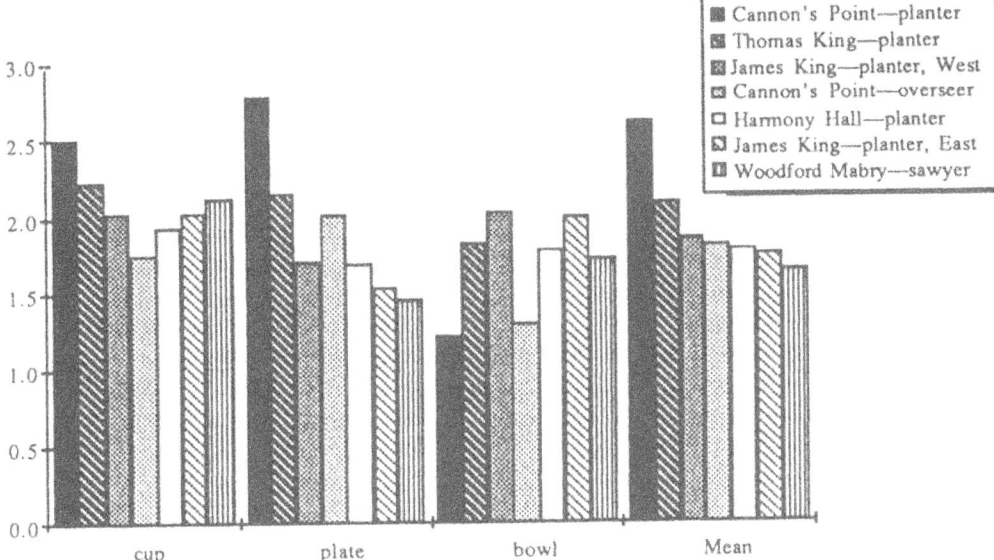

FIGURE 12. CC index for planters, overseer, and sawyer on the Georgia coast.

with the expected economic ranking of the occupants. The middle planter is first, the small planters next and close together, the sawyer close below them and the slaves, last; the Harmony Hall slave site does not fit into any appropriate pattern. One other approach which proved equally interesting was to add up the raw prices of all the platters and serving dishes for which prices were available, and rank the sites by this sum. In this case, the costliness of the Kings Bay Plantation ceramics was even more marked, and the anomalous Harmony Hall slave site became much more nearly equal to the small planter sites. It seemed to be the most vivid measure of conspicuous consumption possible.

The Harmony Hall Plantation slave quarters cannot, in fact, be compared well to any other site examined here in terms of average ceramic value, and another approach will be necessary to describe it. Its expensive platters distorted comparison of slaves and planters, in which a 40% lead in cost of platters appears in the slave column. Only one platter was recovered among the five other slave cabins excavated around the bay, and it was of the

most inexpensive variety. Plates, which are important in tableware in Kings Bay area slave quarters, come out the same in both social classes. Leaving aside platters as an unmanageable form to sample, one can see some of the cruder trends already mentioned reestablished as general. Specifically, cups and saucers are higher in average price among the slaves, large bowls are very close, and small bowls inexpensive, at a price between dipped and painted. The next detail to consider is, of course, how many of the different-priced wares each domestic site possessed.

Comparison of the Kings Bay sites with those at Cannon's Point Plantation reveals that the large planter there had far more expensive ceramics (Figure 12). One explanation for the high index values there may be that a later price list should have been used to calculate it—the 1814 and 1824 price lists were used, instead of the 1833 list (Spencer-Wood and Heberling 1984). While the Cannon's Point Plantation dates from 1791 to 1860 (and later), re-examination of the ceramics from those sites revealed no creamware and no other ceramics with dates definitely earlier than about

1830. The entire assemblage is much later than that from Kings Bay.

Following Cannon's Point Plantation in value, the Thomas King assemblage from Kings Bay Plantation was next, followed by the James King West Kitchen, the Cannon's Point Plantation Overseer, and the other sites at Kings Bay. Clearly, using the mean CC Index, the sites can be ordered in what we would surmise is a reasonable approximation of wealth, except that the Cannon's Point Plantation overseer should, it would seem, have been closer to the values for Woodford Mabry, the sawyer on Cherry Point Plantation. What this suggests is that the relative economic status of an overseer on a large plantation is roughly equal to that of a small planter. That overseer, though, had the lowest value of cups, perhaps suggesting that his household did not have a public position to maintain through entertaining guests on the premises.

Comparison of the Kings Bay sites with others outside the Southeast provides a way of ranking these sites (Figures 13, 14; Table 7). Selection of these sites was based upon the available published data (Felton and Schulz 1983:76–81; Geismar 1982; Morin et al. 1986:43–45; Morin and Klein n.d.; Miller 1980; Spencer-Wood and Heberling 1984). These were divided into three groups, those with a mean over 2.0, with a mean of between 1.5 and 2.0, and those with a mean below 1.5. Each of the individuals in the high grouping is known to have been a wealthy individual, upper class would not be an unreasonable label for these people (Table 5). The individuals with a mean less than 1.5 could be labelled lower class, for they are small farmers, tenant farmers, and tenement dwellers. The middle group, 1.5–2.0 is not necessarily what would be called middle class, and should not be labelled such. It is most interesting that each of the slave sites analyzed falls into this group, along with the small planters, factory worker, plantation overseer, and so forth.

A number of sites have been identified as having been occupied by blacks exclusively, for example, Black Lucy's Garden (Baker 1980) and Skunk Hollow (Geismar 1982). Comparing those sites to Cannon's Point and to the Kings Bay site averages revealed that in every vessel category, the slaves

had more expensive ceramics than the free blacks (Figure 15a). However, when the sites at Kings Bay are compared individually with the free black sites, the free black was found to have more expensive plates than half of the Kings Bay slave sites (Figure 15b). The general implication of this, bearing further investigation with a much larger sample of sites, is that free blacks may have had less disposable income, less access to expensive cast-offs, or chose to use their income in a different manner.

Using crude measures of income-disposal to determine status is a difficult process. Even when the subjects are still alive and willing to respond to questionnaires on what their, and their neighbor's, dishes mean to them, evaluating the household's status is even more complicated. For this reason, information about the Kings Bay inhabitants' dishes, beyond relative market price, is included here. Clear differences existed among the decorative quality of dishes on the various sites. By this we mean that a coherent taste, or devotion to ornament, of the family which had purchased the dishes emerged from the ceramic assemblages. The Harmony Hall planter household had a wide selection of fruit decorated early polychrome vessels, plenty of which represented partial sets. The household also owned a small selection of restrained blue transferprinted teawares and a miscellaneous collection of lathe decorated dipped bowls, plain creamware, and edged plates. The two James King kitchens were furnished with a heterogeneity of small-patterned printed, early polychrome painted, blue painted, overglaze painted, saltglazed, and creamwares. The Kings Bay Plantation kitchen had several sets of elaborate, large-pattern printed dishes, in tea and table sets, more variety in edged plates and dipped bowls than any other site, and a minimal assortment of unmatched painted dishes. Woodford Mabry set plain tablewares. The slaves had plain ceramics, like their masters did also, along with a few expensive decorated ones.

Conclusions

While the plantation bighouse has been studied in numerous circumstances as part of architectural

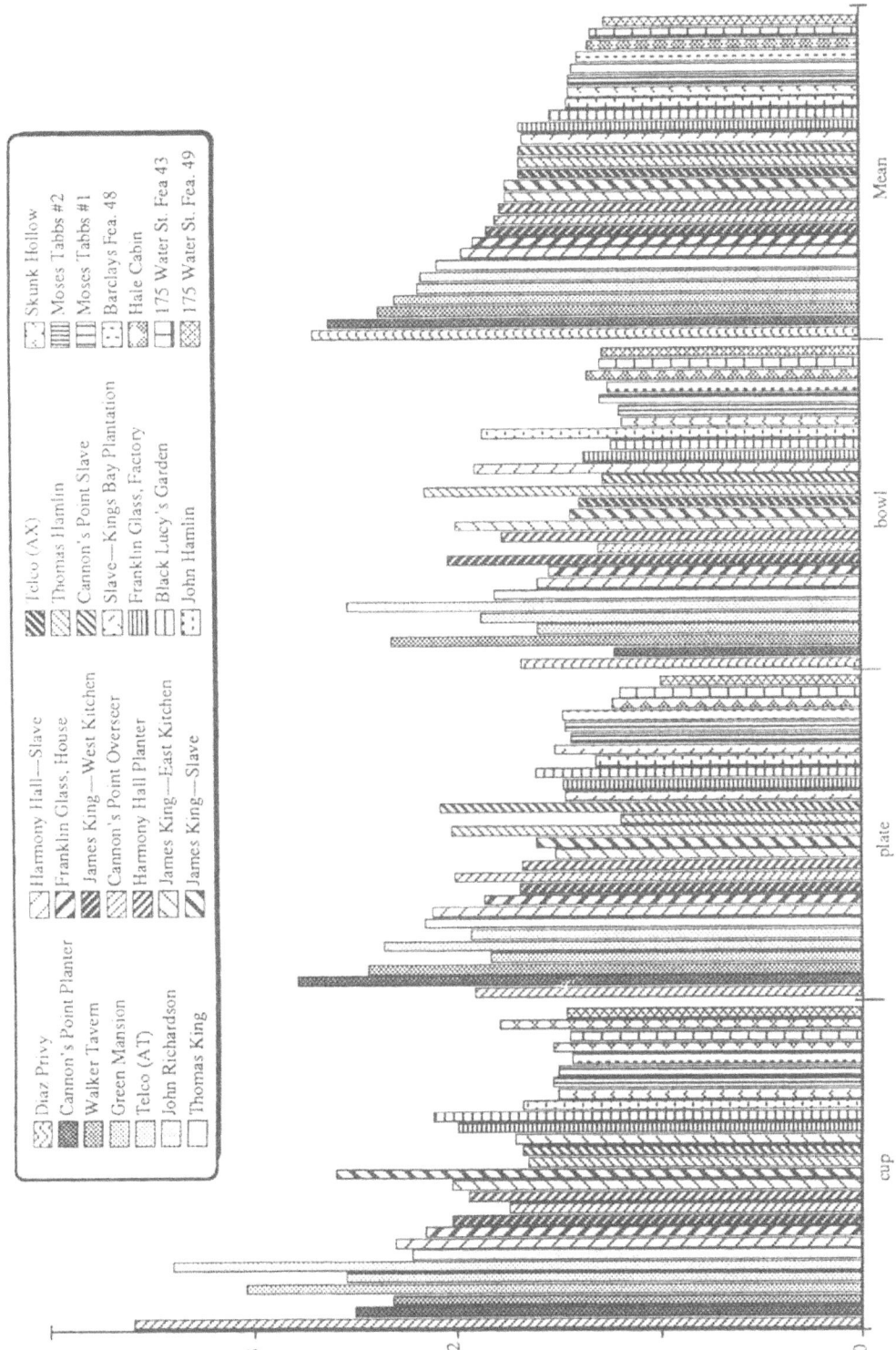

FIGURE 13. CC index for selected sites

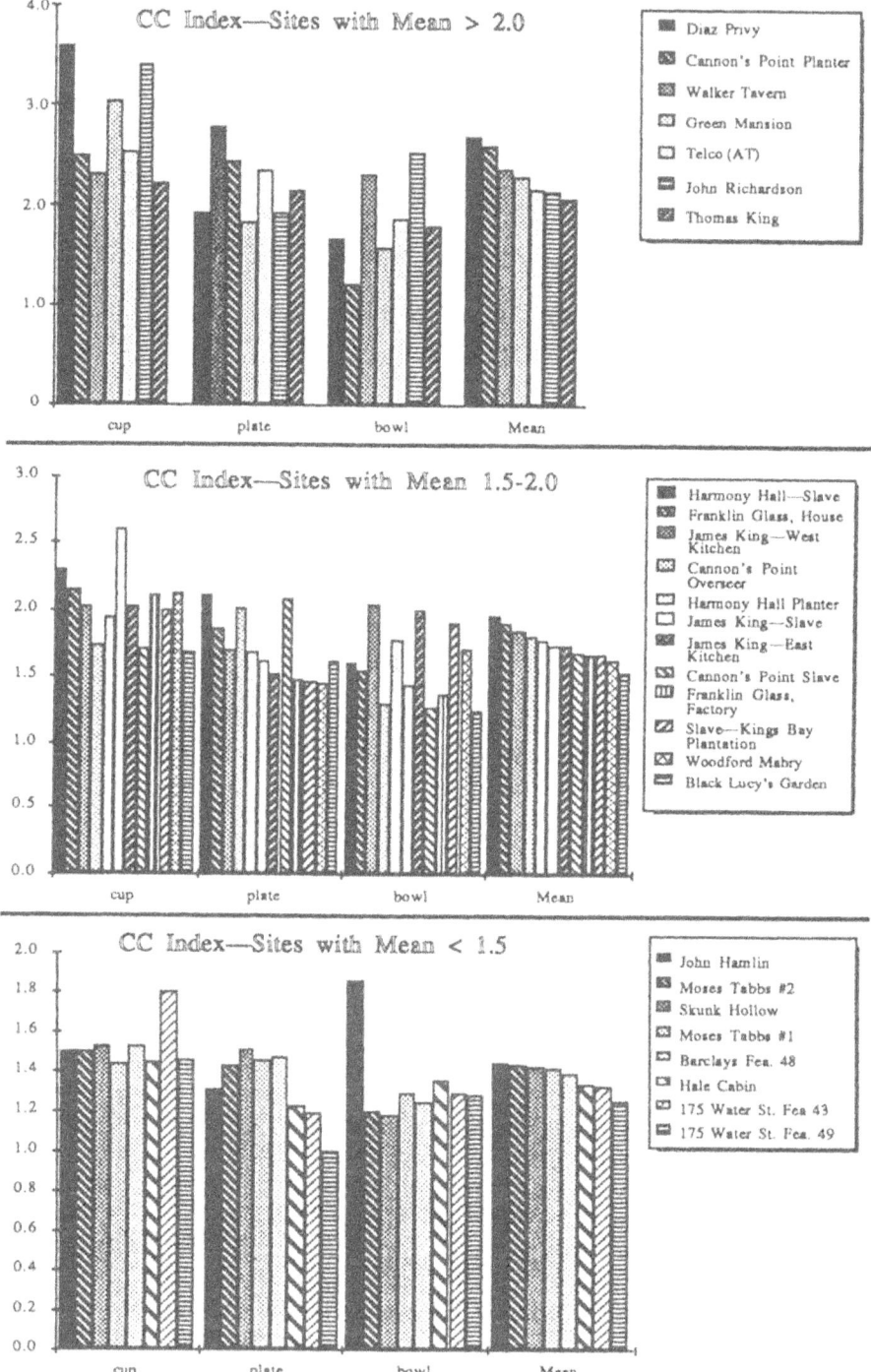

FIGURE 14 CC Index, comparing sites by mean range.

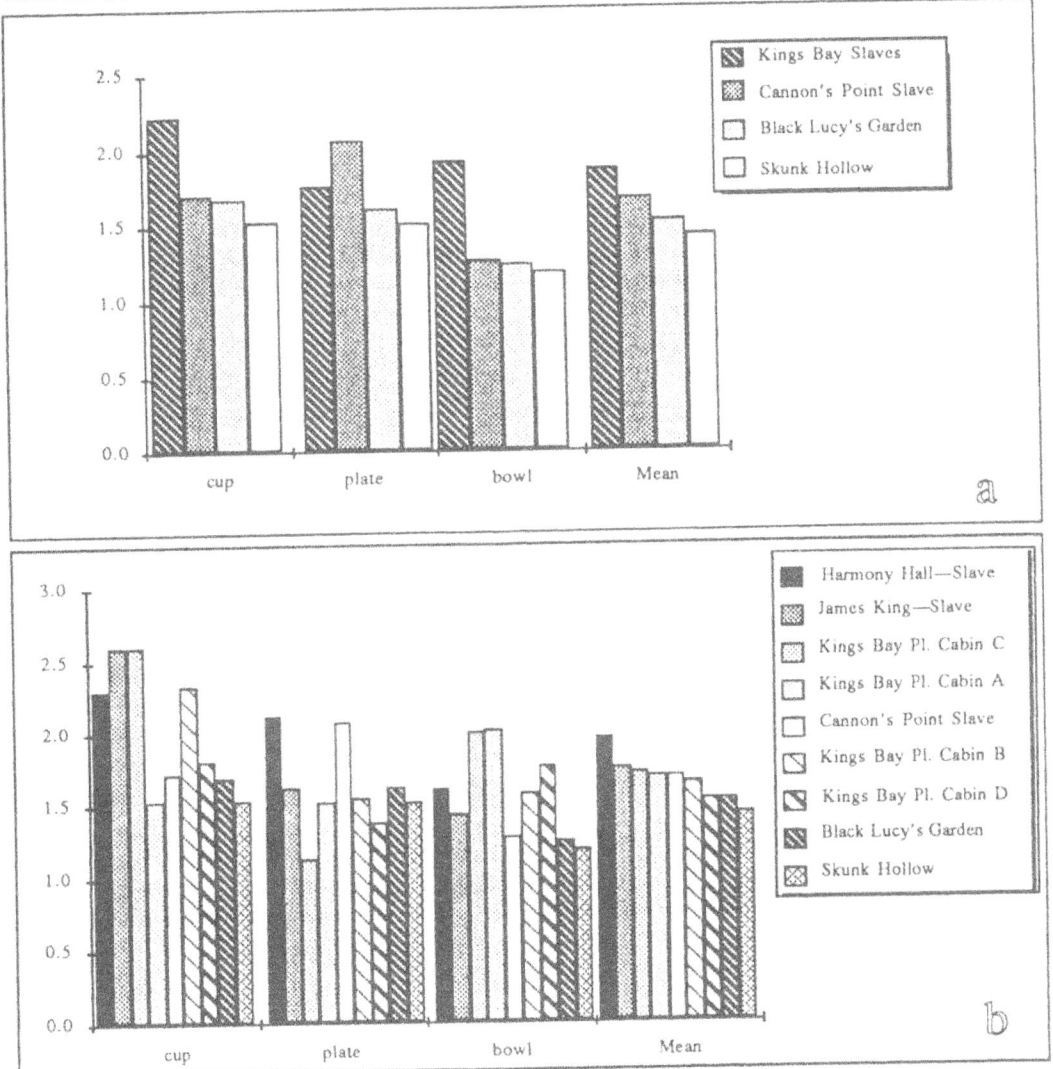

FIGURE 15 CC Index for sites with black occupants.

reconstruction, less work has been done on the material culture of the planter class. Otto found that the planter's wife at Cannon's Point set her table primarily with transferprinted plates, in sharp contrast to the banded bowls of the slave cabins (1984:151). Charles Orser (n.d.) in a re-analysis of the published data on Cannon's Point artifacts, found that ceramics were among the least sensitive indicators of status. William Kelso argued that it is

in other material culture that we should be looking for status indicators. "As for other artifact patterns, matched sets of ceramics, monogrammed wine bottles, book clasps, jewelry, and coats of arms are indisputably all items that indicate wealth and high status far more strongly than whatever one can tentatively conjecture from masses of numbers of mugs or cups or bowls that happened to have been broken and thrown away" (Kelso

1984:205–206). The work at the various planta-tions at Kings Bay suggested that the wealthier planter had a greater variety of vessel forms for ceramics and glassware, rather than simply more expensive ones.

Status can be inferred from the artifacts, when we have sufficient sample size and a regional data base for comparison. Comparison by ceramic wares, for instance, revealed that slaves tended to have more coarse wares, that planters had more refined wares, or both possibilities together. Com-parison by vessel form showed that while slaves did have many bowls, they also had many plates.

Using the CC Index was useful, because it showed that when one examines a larger variety of sites and distinguishes their ceramic assemblages by vessels, slaves might have more expensive vessels than their masters had for certain forms, and the slaves on these plantations had more expensive ceramics than many of the Northern white farmers and businessmen had on their table. Ceramics provide a good indicator of status, when approached as done here, but other indicators are also important, like the frequency of French gun-flints, durable architecture, and reliance on differ-ent food species (Adams et al. 1987).

One important question not answered by this analysis was where the slaves acquired their ce-ramics and other material culture. The underlying assumption of nearly all previous research was that of a paternalistic system of the planter providing the ceramics and other material goods used by the slave. Whether these consisted of hand-me-downs from the planter's family or items purchased spe-cifically for the slaves is an important distinction, but another alternative must be considered. The plantations at Kings Bay used the task system, which meant the slaves had the opportunity to earn outside income. The slaves may have purchased their own ceramics with money they themselves earned. Few, if any, of the ceramics from the slave quarters of the three plantations were hand-me-downs, for the matches between the planter and slave assemblages were in the commonest types of dishes and those assemblages showed no evidence of any substantial time lag. This means the ceram-ics were purchased and were used immediately:

perhaps the planter bought the ceramics solely for the slaves' usage, or the slaves bought them. Quite possibly the planter bought expensive transferprin-ted dishes for his slaves, even when plain cream-ware or pearlware would have sufficed. The slave assemblages ranged from 7.81% to 19.33% trans-ferprinted wares, compared to 10.94% to 24.31% for the planter assemblages, with the means being 13.17% for slaves' vessels and 17.61% for the planters' vessels. Conversely, is it likely that the slaves would spend their income on more expen-sive items? Perhaps not, if one wishes to continue the paternalistic viewpoint of so many historians and historical archaeologists. But if one wishes to recognize that the slaves developed their own culture and some participated freely within the Southern market economy, archaeologists should reassess the evidence collected previously.

In the future, it is hoped that researchers will not eliminate slave data just because it does not fit their preconceived notion of slave access to mate-rial culture. Yet current studies of market access only tend to perpetuate this misunderstanding (e.g., Orser 1987:127; Spencer-Wood and Heber-ling 1987:70, 80). On gang labor system planta-tions most of the material culture was provided to the slave by the planter or made by slaves on the plantation, but on task labor system plantations the slave had the opportunity to participate directly within the market system. The degree of this participation has not been investigated adequately, but if the work of Morgan (1982, 1983) and the CC Index analysis here is any indication, that market participation was considerable. Indeed, on such plantations slaves may be better understood within the context of being peasants or serfs, regarding their economic status. Their legal status was still as chattel slave, of course, but their economic free-doms were much greater than most people realize.

ACKNOWLEDGMENTS

Archaeological research was conducted at Kings Bay with a contract (N00025-79C-0013) between the U.S. Navy and the University of Florida; the senior author served as Principal Investigator. We would like to thank Stephen Alexandrowicz, Susan Alexandrowicz, George L. Miller, and Timothy B. Riordan for their assistance in the ceramic analysis. This article was adapted from Chapters 12 and 13 of the site report (Boling and Adams 1987; Adams and Boling 1987). We would like to thank the anonymous reviewers of *Historical Archaeology* for their comments and suggestions.

REFERENCES

ADAMS, WILLIAM HAMPTON
1987 Plantation Archaeology: An Overview. *In* Historical Archaeology of Plantations at Kings Bay, Camden County, Georgia, edited by W.H. Adams, pp. 9–22. *Reports of Investigations* 5. Department of Anthropology, University of Florida, Gainesville.

ADAMS, WILLIAM HAMPTON, WILLIAM R. ADAMS, CAROLYN ROCK, AND JANIS KEARNEY-WILLIAMS
1987 Foodways on the Plantations at Kings Bay: Hunting, Fishing, and Raising Food. *In* Historical Archaeology of Plantations at Kings Bay, Camden County, Georgia, edited by W.H. Adams, pp. 225–76. *Reports of Investigations* 5. Department of Anthropology, University of Florida, Gainesville.

ADAMS, WILLIAM HAMPTON AND SARAH JANE BOLING
1987 Material Culture and Status on the Plantations at Kings Bay. *In* Historical Archaeology of Plantations at Kings Bay, Camden County, Georgia, edited by W. H. Adams, pp. 293–310. *Reports of Investigations* 5. Department of Anthropology, University of Florida, Gainesville.

ADKINS, HOWARD G.
1980 The Antebellum Waverly Community. *Waverly Plantation: Ethnoarchaeology of a Tenant Farming Community*, edited by W.H. Adams, pp. 75–100. National Technical Information Service, Washington, D.C.

BAKER, VERNON G.
1980 Archaeological Visibility of Afro-American Culture: An Example from Black Lucy's Garden, Andover, Massachusetts. *Archaeological Perspectives on Ethnicity in America*, edited by Robert L. Schuyler, pp. 29–37. Baywood, Farmingdale, New York.

BOLING, SARAH JANE, AND WILLIAM HAMPTON ADAMS
1987 Foodways on the Plantations at Kings Bay: Putting Food on the Table. *In* Historical Archaeology of Plantations at Kings Bay, Camden County, Georgia, edited by W.H. Adams, pp. 277–92. *Reports of Investigations* 5. Department of Anthropology, University of Florida, Gainesville.

BOOTH, SALLY S.
1971 *Hung, Strung, and Potted: A History of Eating in Colonial America*. Potter, New York.

CADE, J. B.
1935 Out of the Mouths of Ex-Slaves. *Journal of Negro History* 20:294–337.

DEBOW, J.D.B.
1854 *Statistical View of the United States*. Beverley Tucker, Washington, D.C.

FELTON, DAVID L. AND PETER D. SCHULZ
1983 The Diaz Collection: Material Culture and Social Change in Mid-Nineteenth-Century Monterey. *California Archeological Reports 23*. Cultural Resource Management Unit, Resource Protection Division, California Department of Parks and Recreation.

FRAZIER, E. FRANKLIN
1930 The Negro Slave Family. *Journal of Negro History* 15(1):198–259.

GEISMAR, JOAN H.
1982 *The Archaeology of Social Disintegration in Skunk Hollow, A Nineteenth Century Rural Black Community*. Academic Press, New York.

HUNDLEY, DAVID ROBINSON
1860 *Social Relations in Our Southern States*. Henry B. Price, New York. [reprinted 1973, Arno Press]

KELSO, WILLIAM M.
1984 *Kingsmill Plantations, 1619–1800: Archaeology of Country Life in Colonial Virginia*. Academic Press, New York.

KEMBLE, FRANCIS ANNE
1863 *Journal of a Residence on a Georgian Plantation in 1838–1839*. Longman, Green, Longman, Roberts, & Green, London.

LEWIS, KENNETH E.
1985 Plantation Layout and Function in the South Carolina Lowcountry. *The Archaeology of Slavery and Plantation Life*, edited by Theresa Singleton, pp. 35–65. Academic Press, New York.

MILLER, GEORGE L.
1980 Classification and Economic Scaling of 19th Century Ceramics. *Historical Archaeology* 14:1–41.

MOORE, SUE MULLINS
1985 Social and Economic Status on the Coastal Plantation: An Archaeological Perspective. *The Archaeology of Slavery and Plantation Life*, edited by Theresa Singleton, pp. 141–60. Academic Press, New York.

MORGAN, PHILIP D.
1982 Work and Culture: The Task System and the World of Low Country Blacks, 1700 to 1880. *William and Mary Quarterly* 39(Series 3):563–99.
1983 The Ownership of Property by Slaves in the Mid-19th Century Low Country. *Journal of Southern History* 49(3):399–434.

MORIN, EDWARD M., TERRY H. KLEIN, AMY FRIED-
LANDER, MALLORY GORDON, AND META JANOWITZ
1986 *Hamlin Site (28WA532) Archaeological Data Recovery I-78, (103) Section Four Pohatcong Township,
Borough of Alpha, Warren County, New Jersey.*
Report prepared by Louis Berger & Associates, East
Orange, New Jersey, for the Federal Highway Administration and the New Jersey Department of Transportation.

MORIN, EDWARD M., AND TERRY H. KLEIN
n.d. The Hamlin Site, 1780 to 1856: A Study of Rural
Consumer Behavior. *Pennsylvania Archaeologist.* In
press.

OLMSTED, FREDERICK LAW
1856 *Journey in the Seaboard Slave States: With Remarks
on Their Economy.* Dix and Edwards, New York.

ORSER, CHARLES E., JR.
n.d. Archaeology and Antebellum Plantation Society in the
American South. Ms.
1987 Plantation Status and Consumer Choice: A Materialist
Framework for Historical Archaeology. *Consumer
Choice in Historical Archaeology,* edited by S.
Spencer-Wood, pp. 121–37. Plenum, New York.

OTTO, JOHN SOLOMON
1975 *Status Differences and the Archaeological Record: A
Comparison of Planter, Overseer, and Slave Sites
from Cannon's Point Plantation (1794–1861), St.
Simons Island, Georgia.* PhD dissertation, Department of Anthropology, University of Florida. University Microfilms, Ann Arbor.
1977 Artifacts and Status Differences—A Comparison of
Ceramics from Planter, Overseer, and Slave Sites on
an Antebellum Plantation. *Research Strategies in
Historical Archaeology,* edited by Stanley South, pp.
91–118. Academic, New York.
1979 Slavery in a Coastal Community—Glynn County
(1790–1861). *Georgia Historical Quarterly* 64(2):
461–68.
1984 *Cannon's Point Plantation, 1794–1860: Living Conditions and Status Patterns in the Old South.* Academic Press, New York.

PHILLIPS, ULRICH BONNELL
1929 *Life and Labor in the Old South.* Little, Brown,
Boston.

RAWICK, GEORGE P.
1972 The American Slave: A Composite Autobiography.
(Vol. 1. From Sundown to Sunup: The Making of the

Black Community.) *Contributions in Afro-American
and African Studies* 11. Greenwood Press, Westport,
Connecticut.

REITZ, ELIZABETH J., TYSON GIBBS, AND TED A.
RATHBUN
1985 Archaeological Evidence for Subsistence on Coastal
Plantations. *The Archaeology of Slavery and Planta-
tion Life,* edited by Theresa Singleton, pp. 163–91.
Academic Press, New York.

ROTH, RODRIS
1961 Tea Drinking in Eighteenth Century America: Its
Etiquette and Equipage. *United States National Museum Bulletin 225.* Washington, D.C.

SINGLETON, THERESA A.
1980 The Archaeology of Afro-American Slavery in
Coastal Georgia: A Regional Perspective of Slave
Household and Community Patterns. Unpublished
Ph.D. dissertation, Department of Anthropology,
University of Florida, Gainesville.

SPENCER-WOOD, SUZANNE M. AND SCOTT D. HEBER-
LING
1984 Ceramics and Socio-Economic Status of the Green
Family, Windsor, Vermont. *Northeast Historical Archaeology* 13:33–52.
1987 Consumer Choices in White Ceramics: A Comparison
of Eleven Early Nineteenth-Century Sites. *Consumer
Choice in Historical Archaeology,* edited by S.
Spencer-Wood, pp. 55–84. Plenum, New York.

STAMPP, KENNETH
1956 *The Peculiar Institution.* Vintage, New York.

WEAVER, HERBERT
1945 *Mississippi Farmers, 1850–1860.* Peter Smith, Gloucester, Massachusetts.

WOODSON, CARTER G. (EDITOR)
1968 *Free Negro Owners of Slaves in the United States in
1830, Together with Absentee Ownership of Slaves in
the United States in 1830* (reprint of 1924 ed.).
Negroe Universities Press, New York.

WILLIAM HAMPTON ADAMS
DEPARTMENT OF ANTHROPOLOGY
OREGON STATE UNIVERSITY
CORVALLIS, OREGON 97331

SARAH JANE BOLING
LIBRARY AND INFORMATION SCIENCE
SIMMONS COLLEGE
BOSTON, MASSACHUSETTS 02115

JOHN R. WHITE

Bottle Nomenclature: A Glossary of Landmark Terminology for the Archaeologist

ABSTRACT

Recognizing the lack of uniformity in the literature with regard to bottle nomenclature, an attempt is made to provide some degree of consistency. The problem does not lie entirely with the terminology currently being used but rather with a lack of a precise definition of that terminology. Although not exhaustive, the glossary should be of assistance to the average archaeologist.

Introduction

Some efforts more than others take their rise out of necessity. So it is with the following—a respectfully complete, though somewhat short of exhaustive, glossary of bottle nomenclature.

Recent work carried out at two historic archaeological sites in Northeastern Ohio, the Eaton (Hopewell) Furnace (33MH9) and the Austin Log House complex (33MH11) led to the recovery of hundreds of bottles and bottle fragments of various ages dating from the present back to the 1840's. When the time came to describe these ubiquitous artifacts, the writer found himself in a quandary of fair proportions, being totally unprepared for the abundance of terms being used to define and describe just the landmarks on glass bottles and jars. The examination of texts and treatises on bottles and bottlemaking soon led to the inevitable conclusion that: 1) authors often have their own idiosyncratic terms for some landmarks; 2) some terms are used in different ways (some slightly different, some grossly different) by different authors; 3) terms in common usage by the layman are often (if not usually) too imprecise (or even incorrect) for use in descriptive reports, and 4) somehow, some degree of uniformity had to be brought to the material. Answers to letters written to numerous experts reinforced this need.

The problem does not lie in the terminology used in describing types of containers or types of materials. There are, fortunately, a number of experts who can tell the archaeologists new to the field almost everything they need to know about shapes, uses, dates, material, styles, makers, and methods of bottle or glassmaking. Unfortunately for most archaeologists—and again this is especially true of the investigator newly arrived in the field of historic sites archaeology—the question they need most answered is that for which the answer is least available—the correct term to use in describing the bits and pieces of the artifact itself. In short, there is a need for a lexicon of bottle nomenclature.

It is true that at the back of some (but certainly not most) longer articles and texts there is a glossary of terms. But a perusal of these glossaries leaves the reader with the distinct impression that while the more unusual terms or those being applied in a unique way are defined, the more casual (and what end up being most vague) terms are the ones which most often are left undefined. Terms such as base, neck, lip, bead, collar, etc. are assumed to be part of the reader's vocabulary and are ignored. it seems that these "easy" words are by far the most difficult to grasp, the most elusive. Their elusiveness lies in their generality, their universality, their ultimate simplicity.

It is the goal of this paper to contain some of this elusiveness. Some of the definitions given herein can be found elsewhere in other forms, some stated in ways which the reader might perhaps find preferable to those here listed. However, most readers will find this lexicon more complete than most, at least in the area of bottle landmarks. As stated at the outset, this endeavor arose out of need; it is not exhaustive, especially to the bottle expert, but it should help the average archaeologist.

GLOSSARY

Applied lip: A lip applied to the neck after the bottle has been formed. It might be straight (Figure 1a), flaring (Figure 1b), or contracting (Figure 1c) or just a ring of glass trailed around the opening. Many forms exist.

Bail: That part of a toggle device which is connected to the lever wire and passes over the lid holding it in place on the bottle or jar. Also called *yoke.* (Figure 3).

Basal diameter: The diameter across the base of round or polygonal bottles.

Base: The surface of the bottle on which it rests when in an upright position; the bottom (Figure 3).

Bead: A raised ridge of glass having a convex section which encircles the neck of a bottle. The term itself can be applied to any such circle or molding; also a modifier indicating its specific location e.g. closure bead (Figure 1d), collar bead, (or beaded collar) (Figure 1e), etc.

Beaded seal: A bottle that makes its seal or point of maximum contact on a beaded ridge which encircles the bottle neck (Figure 1f).

Bernadin disc: A metal (usually tin) disc placed over wired cork stoppers to prevent them from being cut deeply by the taut wire. These discs were often made with scalloped edges to prevent slippage (Figure 1g).

Black glass: The name given to a thick, dark olive green glass. Often a container for porter or ale.

Blob top: The name given to the thick, rounded lip usually applied to the neck of bottles containing carbonated liquids (Figure 1h).

Bottle glass green: The natural aquamarine color of bottle glass resulting from the presence of iron oxides in the sand.

Bottom plate: The shallow depression in the bottom of machine-made bottles and jars designed to allow for stability and to serve as a nest for the closure of another bottle when stacking containers.

Bull's eye: The small, thick, translucent concentration of glass occurring on pieces of crown glass. It is the point at which the pontil was attached during rotation.

Bust-off and grind lip: Found on wide-mouthed bottles, it consists of a lip which was broken or sheared from the blowpipe and subsequently ground to a satin smoothness (Figure 1i).

Buttons: Small knobs or protruberances on the neck of bottles around which the lever wire of a toggle device was wrapped (Figure 1j).

Chip marks: See *whittle marks.*

Closure: A device, such as a cork, cap, stopper, etc., used to seal a bottle.

Closure Sidewall: The portion of the closure between the rolled edge and the top of the skirt (Figure 1k).

Closure skirt: The vertical part of a closure which fits to the outside of the bottle finish. It includes the *closure sidewall, curl* or *rolled edge,* and/or *flange* (Figure 1k).

Codd ball stopper: See *Codd stopper.*

Codd "face": The appearance of a "face" given to Codd stopper bottles by virtue of the addition of a pair of indentations in the bottle below the neck. These indentations served to catch the marble before it could reseal the bottle.

Codd stopper: (After Hiram Codd) A closure consisting of a glass marble held by pressure against a ring of cork or rubber which rested in a groove which encircled the inside top of the neck. The seal was broken by pressing down on the marble and sending it down into the bottles' contents (Figure 1l). Also *Codd ball stopper.*

Coil: See *continuous thread.*

Cold mold marks: See *whittle marks.*

Collar: A band, bead, or ring of glass applied to and encircling the finish of a bottle. It may sit immediately adjacent to the lip or some distance below it (Figure 2i).

Continuous thread (C.T.): A continuous spiral projecting glass ridge encircling the finish of

FIGURE 1. Illustrations of bottle landmarks and nomenclature

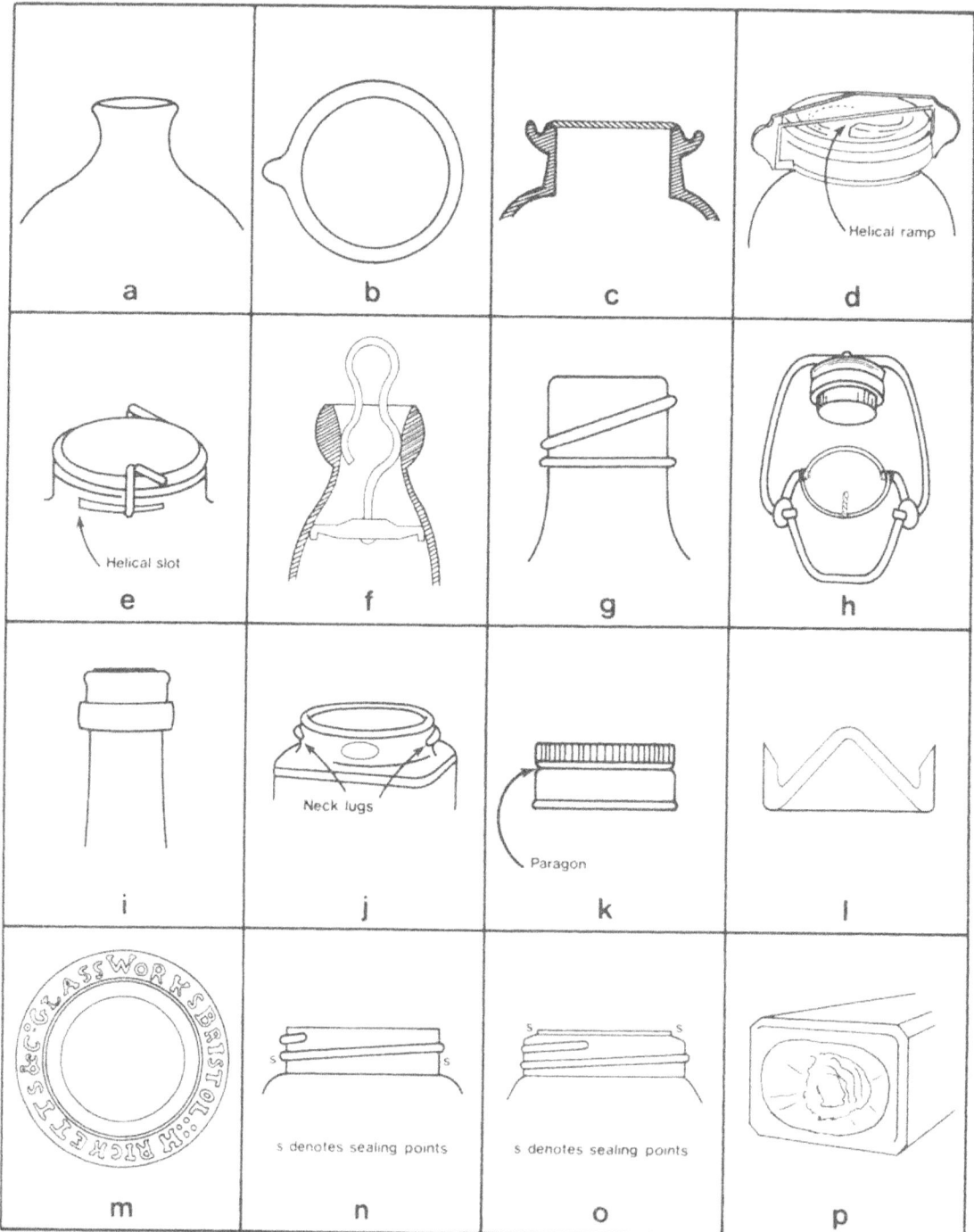

FIGURE 2. Illustrations of bottle landmarks and nonmenclature.

a bottle intended to mesh with the thread of a screw-type closure. Also called *helix* or *coil* (Figure 1m).

Cover groove: In Lightning-type closures it is a groove of varying lengths which sits atop the closure and receives the yoke or bail. It keeps the closure from slipping (Figure 3).

Crown cap: A metal closure usually faced with cork which has its edges crimped over the rounded lip of a bottle (Figure 1n).

Curl: See *rolled edge.*

Cut glass: Glass decorated by incising the surface with iron or stone wheels.

Date line: The vertical mold seam or mold line on a bottle. Called such because it can often be used to approximate the date of manufacture. Also called *seam* or *seam line* (Figure 3).

Dimple: The small depression or hole on the bottle neck into which the lever wire of a toggle device is hooked (Figure 1o).

Dish base: A concavity in the base of a bottle which is somewhat shallower than a push-up or kick.

Embossed lettering or embossing: The raised letters, figures, trademarks, etc. on a bottle.

Filamented ring: A ring on the base of early machine-made bottles formed when a gob of glass was severed after being drawn into the mold.

Finish: The neck formation i.e., that part of the bottle between the shoulder and the top. Often used to designate specifically the upper portion of the neck to which the closure is affixed (Figure 3).

Flange (closure): That part of the closure that protrudes from the bottom of the sidewall and eventually becomes the rolled edge or curl (Figure 1p).

Flared lip: A lip that spreads outward so as to create an opening whose diameter is wider at the top than at any other point on the neck (Figure 2a).

Flashing: The method where a decorative effect is achieved by dipping white or clear glass in a batch of colored glass to coat it. Also called *plating.*

Flat base: A base which is as flat as production will allow.

Flint glass: A heavy, leaded glass of high quality with high refractive power, and great luster used in the choicest cut glassware.

Frosted: The sand-blasted or satiny appearance given to glass as a result of exposure to the abrasive nature of the elements.

Gasket: A liner applied between the sealing surface of the bottle lip and the closure to provide the ultimate seal (Figure 1n).

Gilding: The method wherein glass is decorated by painting brown gold oxide on it then refiring it.

Goose pimples: See *whittle marks.*

Graphite pontil: See *bare-iron pontil mark,* under *pontil scar.*

Greatest diameter: See *maximum diameter.*

Green glass: The relatively coarse glass used chiefly for utilitarian bottles. It is a silicate of lime and soda and is greenish in tint from the iron impurities in the sand.

Griffen gasket: A rubber ring gasket used on canning jars having a thumb tab or projection which allows graspability (Figure 2b).

Ground pontil: The smooth and often slightly concave circle which remains after the rough pontil scar has been ground off. Also called *polished pontil.*

Grooved-ring: A groove encircling the mouth of some early bottles into which a closure having a male counterpart was nestled and sealed (Figure 2c).

Helical ramp: A circular ramp on the outside top of glass lids which was designed to receive a neck yoke and was employed in tightening the seal by a rotating action (Figure 2d).

Helical slot: Slots or grooves in the bottle finish which were designed to receive a closure

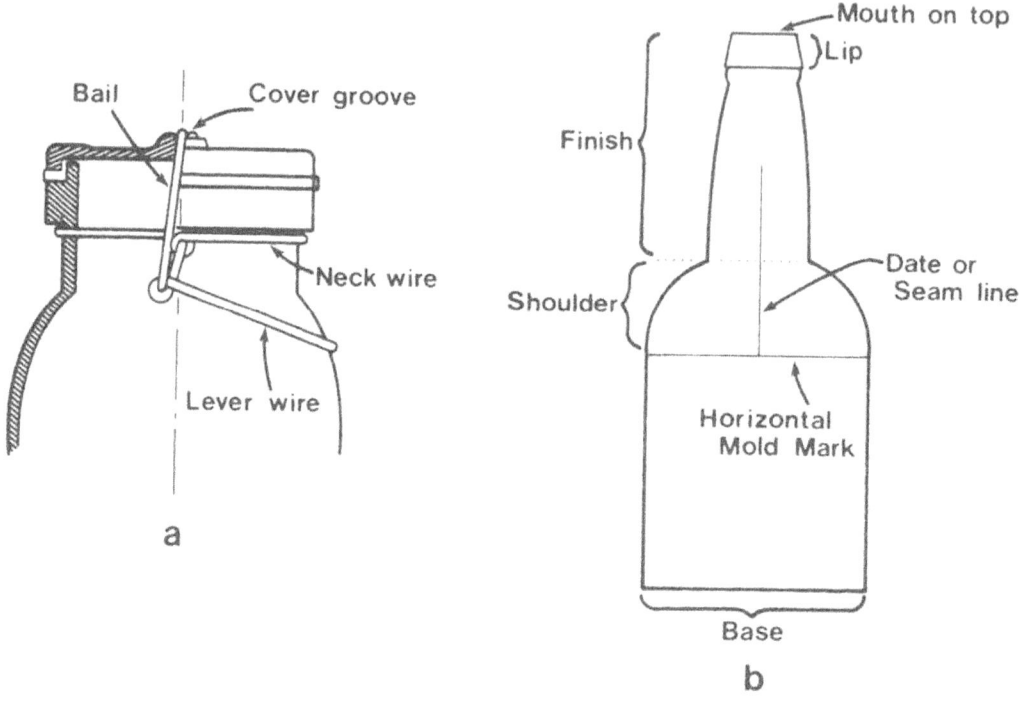

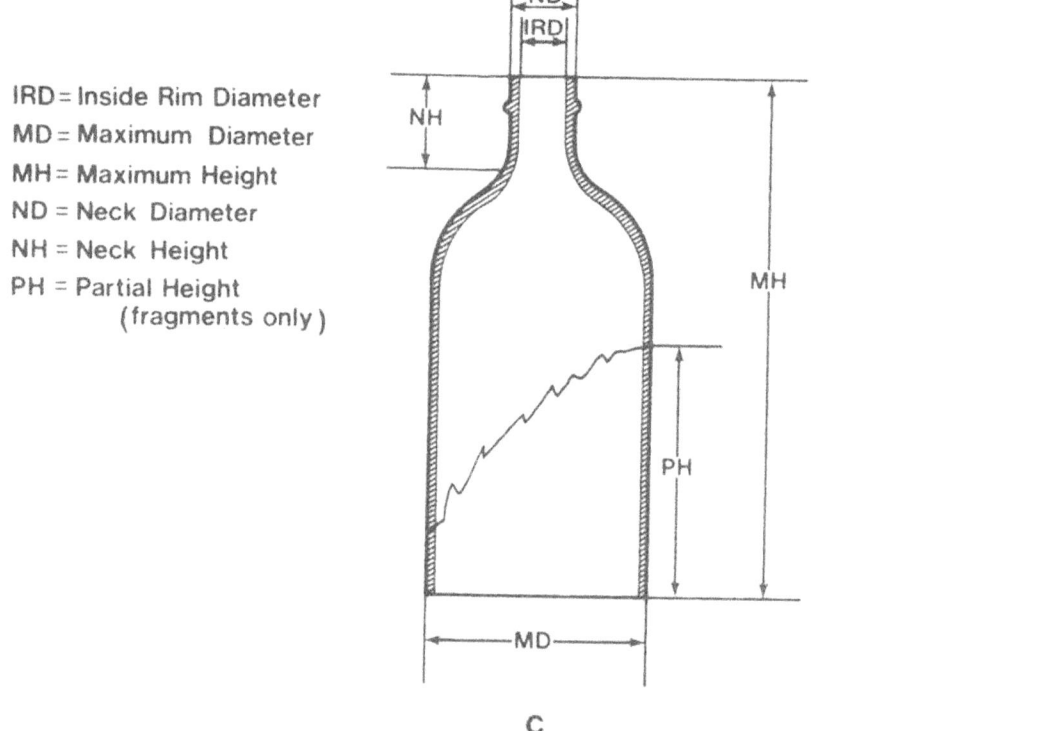

FIGURE 3. Illustrations of landmarks and nomenclature. a, lever closure; b, bottle anatomy; c, points of measurement.

with a corresponding lug or other such projection (Figure 2e).

Helix: See *continuous thread*.

Horizontal mold marks: Mold marks which encircle the bottle (Figure 3).

Hutchinson stopper: An internal stopper composed of a stiff wire with a loop at one end and a rubber disc on the other. The disc served as a seal between the liquid and the neck and was dislodged by pushing downward on the exposed wire loop (Figure 2f).

Improved pontil: See *bare-iron pontil mark* under *pontil scar*.

Infolded lip: The lip is folded into the opening creating a smooth exterior surface and a slight interior ledge. This inner ledge can be detected by rotating a finger around the inside of the neck.

Inside rim diameter: The diameter immediately inside the mouth of the bottle (Figure 3).

Interrupted thread (I.T.): Threads on the bottle that are not continuous throughout the circumference of the finish but are gapped to receive a cap with lugs (Figure 2g).

Kick or *kick-up:* See *Push-up*.

Knurl: Series of vertical indentations around the top of a closure skirt which allow for gripping during application and removal (Figure 1k, p).

Lady's leg: Collector's term for bottles with long curving necks.

Laid-on ring: Ranging from crude to refined, this consisted of a glass ring or bead trailed around and/or slightly below the opening and fused to the bottle. It was added to strengthen the opening or neck (Figure 2i)

Lever: A closure device, the movement of which, applies pressure to hold a lid against the sealing surface of the bottle (Figure 3).

Lever wire: That part of a toggle device which is raised or lowered to loosen or tighten a seal (Figure 3).

Lightning stopper: An external stopper, usually made of porcelain, with a rubber ring encircling it as a sealant and held in place on the bottle by a bent wire attached to the stopper and anchored to the outside of the neck just below the rolled lip (Figure 2h).

Lip: The edge or margin of glass immediately surrounding the bottle opening (Figure 3).

Lipping tool marks: See *swirling*.

Looping: Decoration made up of colored loopings or beads of glass of one or more colors added to a bottle body of a different color.

Maximum diameter: The maximum diameter in circular or polygonal bottles measured at any point. Also *greatest diameter*. (Figure 3).

Maximum height: The distance measured from the base of the bottle to the maximum height i.e., the top of the lip (Figure 3). Also called *total height*.

Membrane: The liner or secondary closure which adheres to the lip of a bottle or jar and is a separate unit from the lid. It usually is made from paper and must be peeled off or torn through to get to the product.

Metal: A glassmaker's term for glass either in the molten or finished state.

Mold line: Raised lines or ridges left on the body of a piece of mold-made glass. The marks are created when the hot glass is forced out the interstices between parts of the mold (Figure 3).

Mouth: See *top*.

Neck: See *finish*.

Neck diameter: The diameter measured at the point of junction of the shoulder and the neck (Figure 3).

Neck height: Distance measured from the junction of the shoulder and neck to the top of the lip (Figure 3).

Neck lugs: Projections or spurs on the bottle neck which act to engage the closure. Interrupted thread projections are often referred to as neck lugs (Figure 2j).

Neck swirls: See *swirling*.

Neck wire: In Lightning-type closures, it is the part of the wire holding device which articulates directly with the bottle neck (Figure 3).

Opalescence: Trait due to moisture on the glass surface leaching out or dissolving the soda within the glass and depositing it on the surface of the bottle. Opalescence may take the form of nacreous discoloration or whitish, scale-like patina.

Open pontil mark: See *blowpipe pontil* under *pontil marks.*

Overlay: A method of decorating glass by applying several layers of glass, usually of different colors, then cutting through one or more layers to provide a contrast of hues.

Panel: Square or rectangular insets on one or more sides of rectangular bottles on which are raised letters or figures giving content information, manufacturer, etc.

Paragon: The depression encircling the outside top of continuous thread bottle caps (just below the knurl) designed to give them rigidity (Figure 2k).

Partial height: The distance measured from the base to the maximum height extant short of total height. Used to denote fragment sizes only (Figure 3).

Plate glass: A refined silicate of lime and soda rolled into sheets and used in the better windows and mirrors.

Plating: See *flashing.*

Point of seal: See *sealing surface.*

Pointed base: A bottle base which rather than being round is more plummet-or torpedo-shaped. Also called *torpedo base.*

Polished pontil: See *ground pontil.*

Pontil scar or mark: The irregular scar left on the base of the finished bottle after removal of the pontil (Figure 2p). Pontil marks may be of various types, including a.) *glass-tipped pontil marks* are comparatively small (usually < 30 mm) and characterized by an excess of glass left on the base or by a scar caused by the removal of small bits of glass from the base; b.) *sand pontil marks* are

larger than the glass-tipped ones and consist of a thin line of glass chips encircling the push-up and enclosing a pebbled surface caused by the grains of sand, some sand may be embedded in the base; c.) *blowpipe pontil marks* are distinct ring-shaped marks with the same diameter as the neck; as with the sand pontil, scar glass may be left on or torn out of the base; as the only area of contact is the ring of glass, any markings, etc. remain as undisturbed on the inside as they do outside; also called *tubular pontil scars;* and *open pontil marks;* and d.) *bare iron pontil marks* are circular marks covered with a reddish or black ferric oxide deposit; the push-up associated with this scar is often distorted; also called *improved pontil* or *graphite pontil.*

Prunts: Blobs of glass added as decoration to bottles and glassware and molded into various shapes such as leaves, seals, etc.

Push-up: The characteristic wherein the base of the bottle is pushed up into the body of the bottle forming a more or less deep basal concavity; also called *kick, kick-up* (Figure 2l).

Quilting: Wavy lines or ribbons of glass swirled or cross-notched on the outside of a still-hot blown flask as decoration. Also called *trailing.*

Quatrefoil: The impression left in the top of the push-up by a pontil-like rod having its end divided into quadrants.

Ribbing: Protruding ridges on bottles and other glass objects produced either by the use of molds or by tooling.

Rickett's ring: A lettered ring encircling the push-up on the underside of a bottle base usually bearing such information as the address of the manufacturer or the volume of the bottle (Figure 2m).

Rigaree: Parallel lines of ribbons added as decoration to the sides of bottles and glassware.

Rolled edge: The turned in (or out) portion of

the open end of the closure skirt, usually to form a tubular structure. Also called *curl* or *wire* (Figure 1k).

Round base: A bottle base which is completely round having no flat surface at all. This bottle cannot stand on its own.

Screw band: A screw-cap, generally used with canning jars, with a cut-out center. It is used to hold down a sealing disc.

Screw thread, inside: Where the screw threads for holding the closure are on the inside of the neck.

Screw thread, outside: Where the screw threads are on the outside of the bottle neck. They receive screw-on caps rather than stoppers.

Sealing surface: The surface of the bottle or jar on which the closure makes maximum or sealing contact. Also called *point of seal.*

Seam or seam line: See *date line.*

Sheared top: A bottle top that has been cut off by shears while still in a soft state. It may be fire-polished or not.

Shoulder: The part of the bottle between the base of the neck and the point on the bottle at which the sides turn inward toward the neck (Figure 3).

Shoulder seal: A bottle that makes its seal or point of maximum contact on the apex of the shoulder (Figure 2n).

Sick glass: Glass whose surface has been corroded by long exposure to moisture.

Snap case mark: Barely noticeable and shallow indentations in the sides of a bottle caused by the snap case grasping the hot, pliable glass.

Spot crown: A cork lined crown cap having a smaller disc of aluminum or other material centrally located on the cork liner. These spots prevented the imparting of an off-taste to the bottle contents.

Stopper: A closure which fits inside the neck of a bottle rather than atop or outside e.g. a cork, bung, plug, etc.

Straps: Flat, wide ridges (or "straps") of glass running vertically up both sides of bottles which are narrower fore and aft than they are left to right. The straps usually measure between ¼ and ½ inch in width and up to ⅛" thick depending on the bottle size.

Sun coloring: Glass turned either amethyst or amber by the action of the sun on manganese oxide and selenium contained therein.

Swirling: The vague marks encircling the neck of bottles which have had lips applied by the rotation of a lipping tool. Also called *lipping tool marks.*

Tears: Bubbles of air imprisoned in the glass.

Toggle: A bottle locking and sealing device consisting of at least two elements, usually wires or bails, which present three fulcrums or centers of force. The familiar lightning closure is one type of toggle (Figure 3).

Top: The part of the bottle incorporating the lip and the opening the lip surrounds. Also called *mouth* (Figure 3).

Top seal: A bottle that makes its seal or point of maximum contact on the top (Figure 2o).

Torpedo base: See *pointed base.*

Total height: See *maximum height.*

Trailing: See *quilting.*

Tubular pontil scar: See *blowpipe pontil scar* under *pontil scar.*

Vertical mold marks: Mold marks which run in the direction of the bottle's length.

Whittle marks: Rough marks of a stippled or wavy nature on the surface of a hand blown bottle. Actually a misnomer as these marks result from blowing the bottle in a mold which has not been properly warmed. Also called *chip marks* or *cold mold marks.*

Window glass: A relatively crude silicate of lime and soda made into window panes.

Wire: See *rolled edge.*

Wired cork stopper: Cork stoppers which are wired into place on the bottle neck. Modern champagne bottles are usually corked in such a manner (Figure 1g).

Yoke: See *bail.*

REFERENCES

The following articles and books, though not specifically cited, were valuable sources of insight in the compilation of this glossary.

ADAMS, JOHN P.
1969   *Bottle Collecting in New England.* New Hampshire Publishing Co. Somersworth, New Hampshire.

BAUMAN, RICHARD
1968   "Glass and Glasswares." In *Handbook for Historical Archaeology, Part 1,* edited by John Cotter, pp. 30–36.

BROSE, DAVID
1967   "The Custer Road Dump Site: An Exercise in Victorian Archaeology." *The Michigan Archaeologist* 13(2):37–128.

COHEN, HAL L.
1975   *Official Guide to Bottles Old and New.* House of Collectibles, Florence, Alabama.

FERRARS, PAT AND BOB FERRARS
1966   *A Bottle Collector's Book.* Western Printing and Publishing Company, Sparks, Nevada.

FREEMAN, LARRY
1964   *Grand Old American Bottles.* Century House, Watkins Glen.

HUNT, CHARLES
1959   "Dating of Mining Camps with Tin Cans and Bottles." *Geotimes* 3(1):8–10, 34.

JONES, OLIVE
1971   "Glass Bottle Push-ups and Pontil Marks." *Historical Archaeology,* 5:63–73.

KENDRICK, GRACE
1971   *The Antique Bottle Collector.* Pyramid, New York.

LIEF, ALFRED
1965   *A Close-up of Closures.* Glass Container Manufacturers Institute, New York.

LORRAIN, DESSAMAE
1968   "An Archaeologist's Guide to Nineteenth Century American Glass." *Historical Archaeology* 2:35–44.

NEWMAN, T. SNELL
1970   "A Dating Key for Post-Eighteenth Century Bottles." *Historical Archaeology* 4:70–75.

NOEL HUME, IVOR
1970   *A Guide to Artifacts of Colonial America.* Alfred Knopf, New York.

TIBBITS, JOHN C.
1967   *John Doe, Bottle Collector.* Heirloom Press, Santa Cruz.

TOULOUSE, JULIAN
1969   "A Primer on Mold Seams." *Western Collector* 7, (11), Pt. 1:526-535; (12), Pt. 2:578-87.
1971   *Bottlemakers and Their Marks.* Thomas Nelson, Inc., New York.

WILSON, REX
1961   "A Classification System for 19th Century Bottles." *Arizoniana,* 11(4):2–6.

JOHN R. WHITE
PROFESSOR
DEPARTMENT OF SOCIOLOGY AND
ANTHROPOLOGY
YOUNGSTOWN STATE UNIVERSITY
YOUNGSTOWN, OHIO 44555.

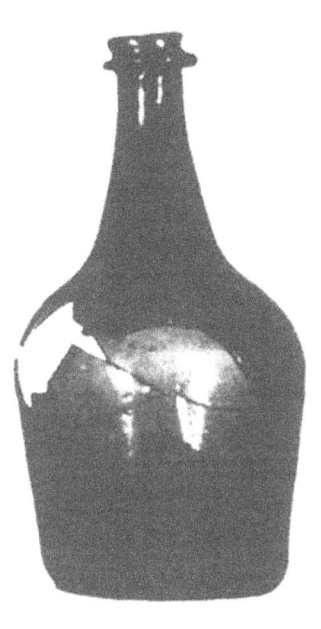

GLASS BOTTLE
PUSH-UPS
AND
PONTIL MARKS

OLIVE JONES

INTRODUCTION

Originally this study started as an attempt to explain the varied markings on bottle bases found in the National Historic Sites Service collection. These markings appeared to have been left on the glass by glassmakers during the formation of the base and while holding the bottle on the pontil. In the process of identifying the marks, some relationships between the marks and certain types of bottles and their country and date of manufacture became apparent.

Because most modern authors, with the exception of Dr. Julian Toulouse, have not discussed in detail the question of base formations and empontilling techniques, I have had to concentrate on bottles excavated by the Canadian National Historic Sites Service. I have also looked at some local private collections and the "wine" bottles in the Bristol City Museum and the Guildhall Museum in London. In general, these collections corroborated some of the conclusions in this paper.

The National Historic Sites Service collection has a built-in bias because very few of our excavated sites predate the 1720s and from that date to 1760, the predominant trading influence was French. After 1760, when New France passed into British control, the trading emphasis shifted to Great Britain. This means that there are few English bottles in the collection from before 1760, and after that date, very few French bottles. Because of this situation, the attempt to assign the different tools and techniques to specific countries and dates should be regarded by the reader as a question and a challenge, rather than as an immutable fact.

Although there are many variations in technique, a bottle is made in the following basic manner (Figure 1). A sufficient amount of glass is gathered on the end of a blowpipe. The glass is given a preliminary shape, called a parison, by marvering (turning) on a flat stone or metal slab and by preliminary insufflation. The parison is then usually inserted in a mould which may form only the body or almost the whole bottle. After the partially formed bottle is removed from the mould, if the base has not already been mould-formed, the base is pushed up. A tool, such as a pontil or a sabot, then holds the bottle at the base while the blowpipe is detached from the bottle. Extra glass is added at the mouth and then the glassmaker forms the finish (Figure 9). The completed bottle is carried to the annealing oven where it is slowly cooled to remove the stresses in the glass.

The two stages of the bottle-making process that are discussed in this paper are the formation of the base and the techniques used to hold the bottle while the finish is being made.

FIGURE 1. *Interior of a 19th century French bottle factory (Peligot 1877:299).*

PUSH-UPS

One of the familiar aspects of bottles is the base that has been pushed up into the body cavity. This formation is called a "push-up" (Toulouse: personal communication; Moody 1963:303) or "kick". Several explanations have been given for its presence:

1) Because glassmakers had difficulty making a bottle base flat enough for a bottle to stand upright without wobbling, they partially solved the problem by indenting the base.

2) A push-up helped to produce a stronger bottle. Part of the reason was that the glassmaker, while the bottle was being made, often rested the bottle on its base which allowed the glass to flow towards the basal area (Bontemps 1868:510). In pushing up the base, the glass was redistributed and thinned. If glass is too heavily concentrated in one place the annealing process is less effective and stresses are set up in the bottle which make it weaker. It is also possible that the push-up is structurally useful in helping the bottle withstand great internal pressure from contents such as sparkling wines.

3) Many authors suggest that push-ups were made deliberately deep, particular-ly in dark green glass bottles, so the bottles looked much larger than they actually were.

4) Many people also believe that the push-up assists in the sedimentation of wines (Mendelsohn 1965:51).

The practice of making a deep push-up probably continued long after its need was over because of conservatism on the part of the glassmakers and the consumers.

The push-up seems to have been formed by a variety of tools. In Diderot's *Encyclopédie* (1967:109), the base was formed by a mollette, *"morceau de fer plat, d'environ un pié de longueur"* (Figure 2). As forming the push-up could cause distortion in the body of the bottle, it was rolled again on the marver. Although there were no really distinguishing marks left by this process, bases which were formed in this way probably resemble those in Figure 3. This type of base is found on the familiar French "flower pot" wine bottles (Noël Hume 1970:71; Diderot 1772: Pl. V, VI) which have been excavated on many sites in Canada that were occupied by the French. The bases are normally very regular, with symmetrical, rounded conical profiles and a small pontil mark, usually between 25 mm. and 35 mm. in diameter, in the top of the push-up.

FIGURE 2. *The glassmaker forming the bottle base with the mollette and then remarvering the bottle to restore its symmetry (Diderot 1772: Pl. V).*

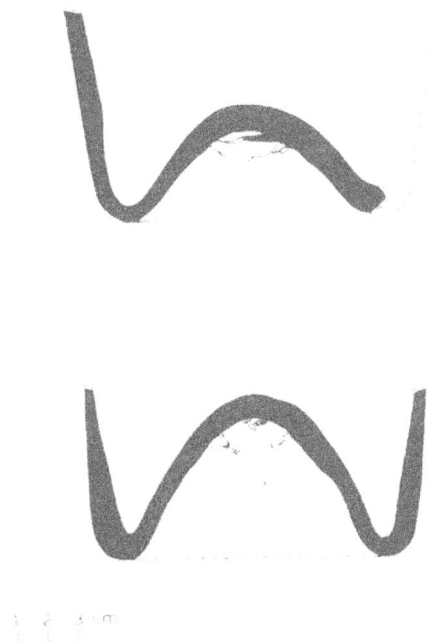

FIGURE 3. *Two bases, probably formed by a mollette, showing the regular, rounded conical profile and the pontil mark in the tip of the push-up.*

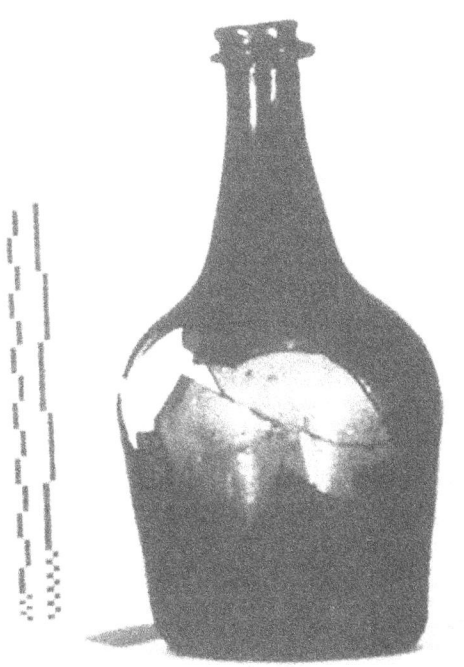

FIGURE 4. *An 18th-century French "flower pot" wine bottle excavated from a site dating from 1732 to 1745.*

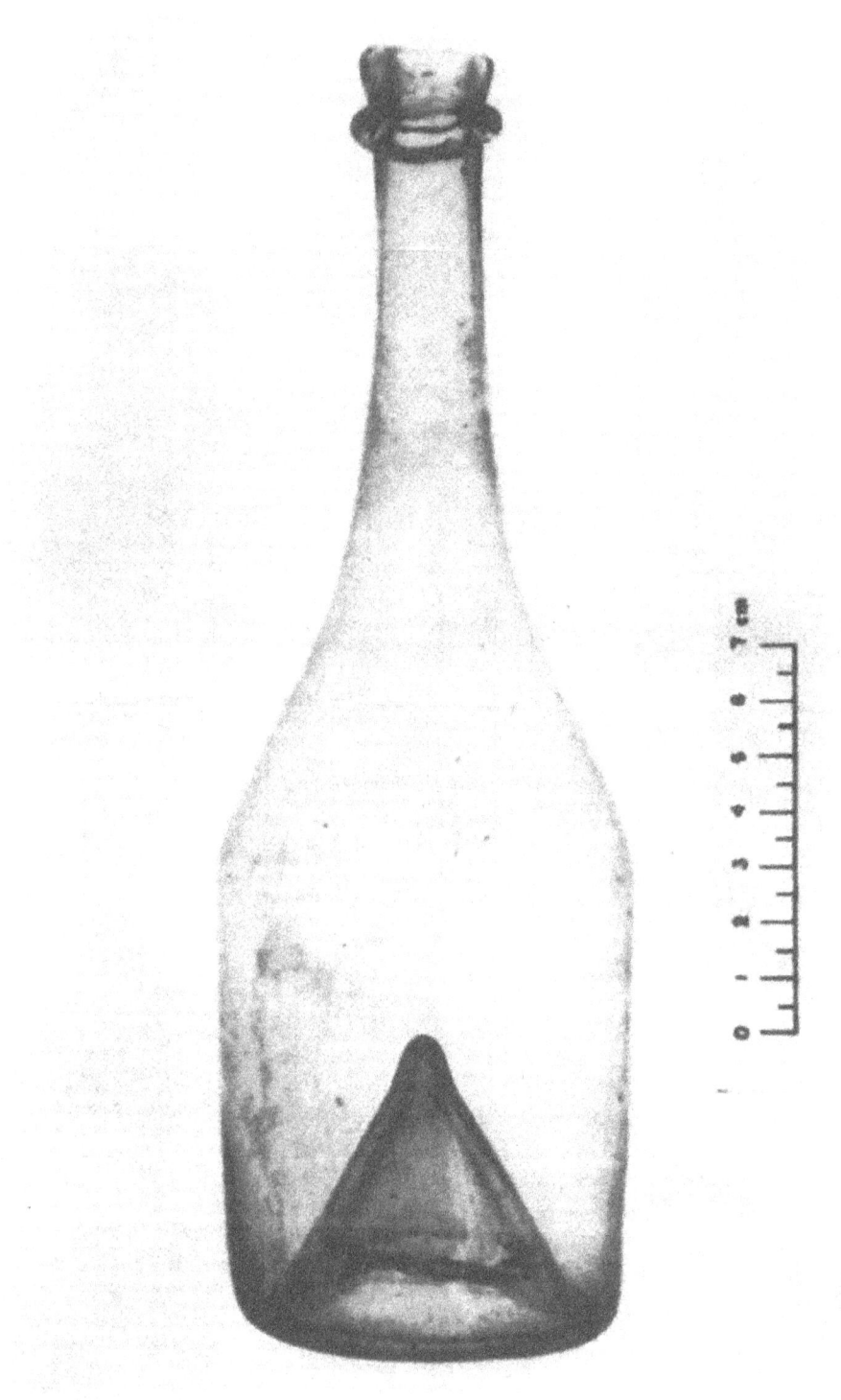

FIGURE 5. A bottle showing how the base has been indented by a sharply pointed rod and the position of the pontil mark partway down the push-up.

Another tool used to form the push-up appears to have been a thin, sharply pointed rod of wood or metal. As shown in Figure 5, the tip of the push-up often has a distinct, sharp point, visible on both the exterior and interior surfaces. The pontil mark is visible about two-thirds of the way down from the tip. On some small bottles, the push-up was so narrow that the pontil had to be applied on the resting surface. These sharply pointed push-ups appear primarily on medicine bottles and vials, occasionally on small rectangular bottles with chamfered corners and on olive oil bottles. Push-ups formed in this way are never found on the "wine" bottles. The use of this tool appears to have become less common during the 19th century as it was replaced by moulding techniques.

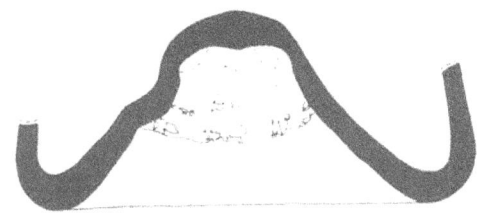

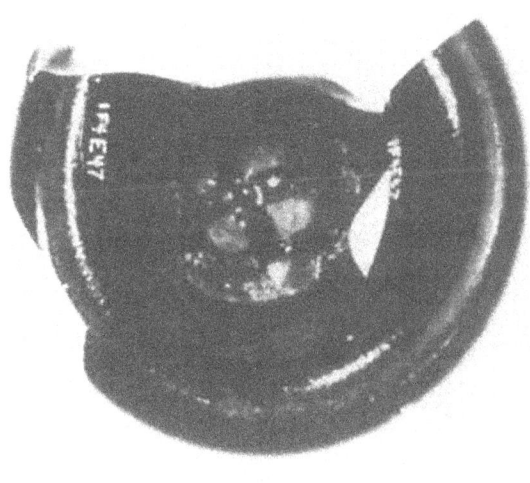

FIGURE 6. *The basal view of a bottle showing the quatrefoil impression in the tip of the push-up. The pontil mark can be seen as rough chips of glass.*

A third type of tool used to form push-ups appears to have been a circular iron rod, like a pontil, with the working end split into quadrants. The Canadiana Gallery of the Royal Ontario Museum, Toronto, has such a rod about 34 in. long with a working end about 7/8 in. in diameter. The separated quadrants left a quatrefoil impression in the top of the push-up. On some kicks the mark can barely be felt and on others, as in Figure 6, it is unmistakeable, even to the extent of distorting the profile. Occasionally iron oxide deposits from the iron tool are found in the impres-

FIGURE 7. *The same base as Figure 6 showing the relationship of the quatrefoil impression and the pontil mark. Note the distortion in the profile.*

sion (Toulouse 1968:140, 141). From above, on the interior surface, the push-up top often looks roughly square. In 75 examples from one Canadian site, the diameters of the impressions ranged from 16 mm. to 51 mm. In addition to the quatrefoil impressions, there is invariably a pontil mark consisting of an area of rough glass which encircles the push-up towards the resting surface. The pontil mark diameters range from 38 mm. to 64 mm. Figure 7 illustrates a base in which the push-up profile was distorted both by the forming tool and by the application of the pontil. Although split iron rods are still used today as pontil rods, the presence of both a distinct pontil mark and the quatrefoil impression on the same base suggests that the quatrefoil mark is logically explained if the split rod was used to indent the base.

The quatrefoil marks have been appearing almost exclusively in dark green glass "wine" bottles manufactured in the English shapes, such as Noël Hume's types 12, 15, 21, 22 (Noël Hume 1961:100-101). The earliest bases in the National Historic Sites Service collection with these marks date from the 1720s and they continue throughout the 18th and into the 19th century. Generally speaking, as the diameters of the bottles decreased towards the end of the 18th century, the quatrefoil marks also became smaller.

A fourth way of forming the push-up was by using a specially designed mould part which fit into the bottle mould. An example of this method was developed by the H. Ricketts Company of Bristol in 1821. The patent included a lettered ring which could be placed close to the circumference of the base and "according to the thickness or

FIGURE 8. *The base of a bottle formed in the Ricketts mould showing the marks left by the device.*

thinness of the said ring is the body of the mould shortened or increased, and the various sizes of bottles produced'' (Ricketts 1821: 3). On the ring could be cut such information as the address of the manufacturer or the volume of the bottle.

As the Ricketts "three-piece" mould formed only the base, body and shoulder, the neck and finish were completed in a separate operation by hand. After a bottle was withdrawn from the mould, therefore, a pontil was attached to the base while the neck was finished. The base in Figure 8 illustrates the different markings left by the manufacturing process. The speckled area is the pontil mark and the raised ridge inside the lettering is the edge of the removable lettered plate. There is also a raised mould line on the resting surface which is not visible in the draw-

ing. Incidentally, these bottles negate a popularly held belief (Kendrick 1968:138) that basal lettering and pontil marks cannot be found on the same bottle.

Originally the Ricketts mould was "An Improvement in the Art or Method of Making or Manufacturing Glass Bottles, such as are used for Wine, Porter, Beer, or Cyder;" (Ricketts 1821:1) in other words, it was used to make the dark green glass "wine" bottle. Later in the 19th century and even in the early 20th century, however, this mould type was used for bottles holding other products, including solids. The Ricketts mould was used very widely. The French writers De Fontonelle and Malepyre (1854:272) recommended the Ricketts mould because it made bottles of exact capacity and was easy to use, saving of both time and fuel. As well as in France, the Ricketts type of mould appears to have been used in the United States by several companies (McKearin 1970:106-7).

In Figure 12,*d* is another example of a base formed in what appears to be a special multipiece conical tool which may have been part of the mould or which may have been used separately. This type of base has distinctive characteristics. A distinct mould line is visible as a slight projection at the base of the body. A rounded ridge is visible on the push-up close to the resting surface. A small but distinct impression is located in the tip of the push-up. This mark is usually dome-shaped, as in Figure 12,*d*, but may be slightly square or pointed and will sometimes have an iron oxide deposit caused by being formed by a hot bare iron tool. All these marks have obviously been made deliberately but why this somewhat complicated arrangement was chosen is not known. In addition, the glass distribution is often very uneven and, if a pontil mark is present, it is usually large and consists of many sharp bits of embedded glass or sand. These bases, found mainly on dark green glass "wine" bottles, were probably manufactured during the second and third quarters of the 19th century. Their country of origin is not known.

Obviously the above discussion does not include all of the tools or moulds that have been used to form bases. For example, Bontempts (1868:509) mentions that the glassmakers used the handle of the battledore (see McKearin and McKearin: 1948, xv) or "*un crochet special*", and Peligot (1877:301) writes, "*il comprime le fond plat de la bouteille avec un crochet en fer.*" The bases made with these tools may or may not be

FIGURE 9. *The bottle is being held on the pontil while additional glass is added to the neck (Diderot 1772: Pl. VI).*

identifiable. Toulouse, in his article on mould seams, mentions other types of moulds used to form bases (Toulouse 1969:526-35, 578-87).

PONTIL MARKS

The pontil is a long iron rod used to hold a glass article during the finishing process after it is detached from the blowpipe (Mc-Kearin and McKearin 1948: xvi). In Figure 9, from the Diderot *Encyclopédie*, the bottle is empontilled while the bottlemaker adds additional glass to the neck to form the finish. When the pontil is detached from the bottle, usually by a sharp tap on the rod, there is a scar left in the base which is called a pontil mark. Figure 10 illustrates four empontilling techniques: (a) the plain glass-tipped pontil; (b) the sand glass-tipped pontil; (c) the blow-pipe as pontil, and (d) the bare iron pontil. Each of these processes leaves a characteristic pontil mark.

The plain glass-tipped pontil (Fig. 10.*a*), hereafter called a "glass-tipped" pontil, con-

sists of a solid iron bar with a slightly wid-ened end which is dipped in molten glass. The glass on the pontil rod adheres to the glass of the base. The mark left by the glass-tipped pontil is comparatively small, usually no larger than 30 mm., although this will vary according to the size of the vessel being held. Usually there is evidence within the pontil mark that the whole area has been in contact with other glass, either because there is excess glass left when the pontil is de-tached (Figure 11) or because bits of glass are torn out of the base. This empontilling tech-nique was commonly used on tableware, medi-cine and toiletry bottles, and on flasks. The small glass-tipped pontil mark in the centre of the push-up is not found after the 1720s on dark green glass "wine" bottles manufactured in the English tradition (see Noël Hume 1961:100-101, Types 12-16, 19-22). Some of the French "flower pot" wine bottles discussed in the push-up section do appear to have been empontilled in this way (Figure 3). The technique is still used for objects manufac-tured by hand.

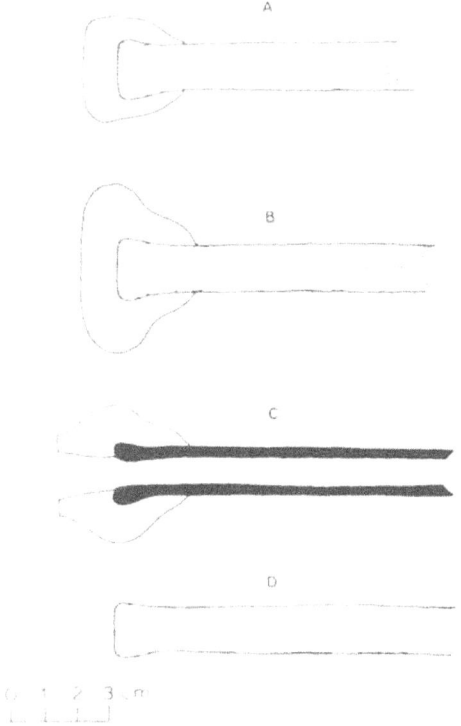

FIGURE 10. *Four empontilling techniques: a) the glass-tipped pontil; b) the sand pontil; c) the blowpipe as pontil; d) the bare iron pontil.*

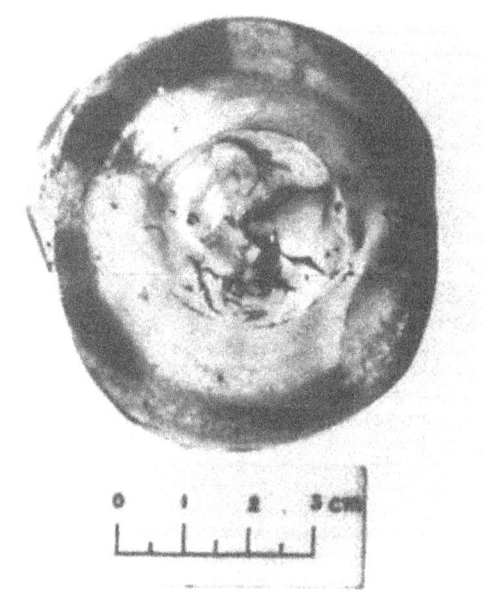

FIGURE 11. *Tumbler base showing excess glass left on the base after removal of the pontil.*

The sand glass-tipped pontil (Figure 10,*b*), hereafter called a "sand" pontil, consists of a gather of glass on the pontil which has been shaped to conform to the basal profile and then dipped in sand (Toulouse: personal communication; Larsen, Riismøller and Schlüter 1963:397). The sand prevents the glass on the pontil from adhering too closely to the bottle.

The sand pontil mark is larger than the glass-tipped one, although again the size varies according to the size of the bottle. It consists of a thin line of glass chips encircling the push-up and enclosing a pebbled surface caused by the grains of sand (Figure 12). Some of the sand may also be embedded in the base (Toulouse: personal communication). Toulouse also points out that this type of pontil will conform to the shape of the already formed base without distorting it.

Sand pontil marks are very common on English dark green glass "wine" bottles, octagonal bottles and occasionally case bottles. The four "wine" bottle bases in Figure 12 have sand pontil marks (Toulouse: personal communication). In the upper two, dating from the 18th century, the pontil has been applied closer to the top of the push-up, which is usually hemispherical or dome-shaped. In 128 examples from one Canadian site, the diameters of the sand pontil mark ranged from 40 mm. to 71 mm., but 86 per cent were between 50 mm. and 64 mm. Sometimes one can feel a quatrefoil mark in addition to the pontil mark, but more often there is a pinch mark or wrinkle in the centre of the push-up which may be indicative of the tool used to form the push-up. In the lower pair (Figure 12, *c,d*), dating from the late 18th and 19th centuries, the sand pontil mark is less distinctive. Almost the entire basal surface is disturbed and is frequently roughened by embedded grains of sand or glass chips. The pontil mark usually begins close to the resting surface. In 76 examples from the same site, the pontil mark diameter ranged from 46 mm. to 71 mm., but 80 per cent were between 50 mm. and 60 mm. Sand pontils are still used on glass manufactured by hand (Toulouse: personal communication).

The third type of empontilling technique (Figure 10,*c*), probably no longer in use, consisted of using the glass left on the blow-pipe after the bottle had been snapped off. In other words, the blowpipe itself was used as a pontil. The bottle was laid on a V-shaped structure (Figure 13) while the glass-

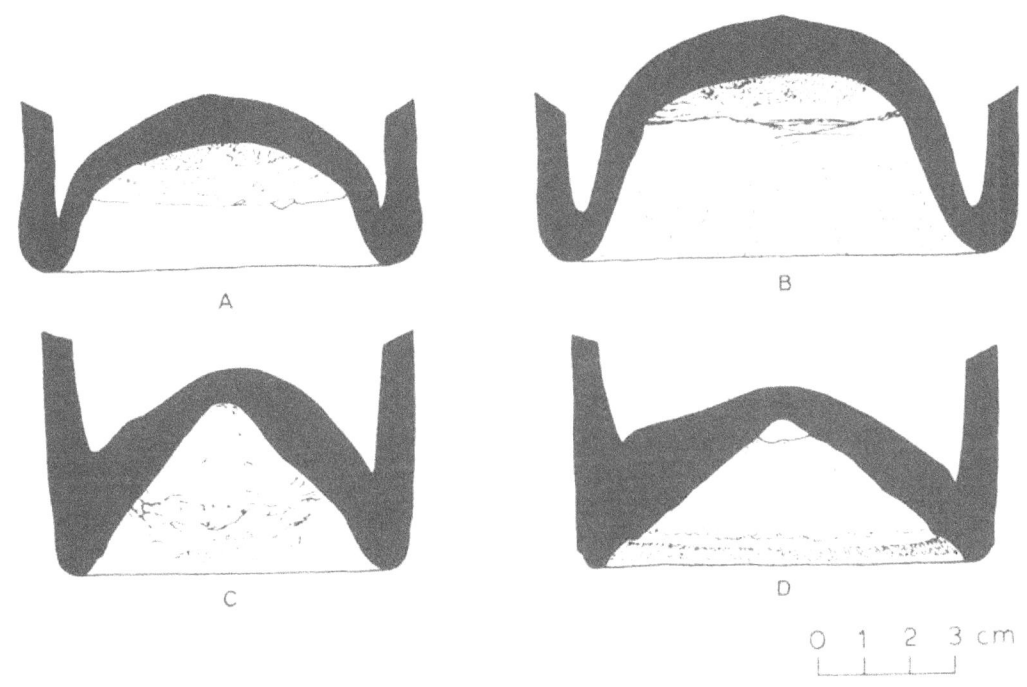

FIGURE 12. *"Wine" bottle bases with sand pontil marks: a) and b) 18th century, c) late 18th, early 19th century, d) 19th century.*

FIGURE 13. *Bottle lying in a V-shaped structure while the blowpipe is attached to the base (Diderot 1772: Pl. V).*

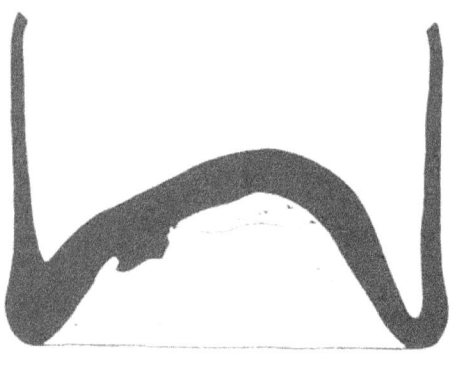

FIGURE 15.   *"Wine" bottle base showing distortion which may have been caused by using a bare iron pontil.*

FIGURE 14.   *Base of a case bottle showing the ring-shaped mark characteristic of the blowpipe used as a pontil. The embossed moulded cross is as undisturbed inside the ring as outside.*

maker applied the blowpipe with its excess glass to the base of the bottle. The pontil mark is a distinct ring-shaped mark about the same diameter as the neck (Toulouse 1968:139). When the blowpipe was removed from the base it either tore glass out with it or left extra glass behind. As the only area of contact is the ring of glass, any mould lines, embossed markings, and distinctive surface textures remain as undisturbed inside the ring as they do outside (Figure 14) (Toulouse 1968:139).

These ring-shaped marks are found on case bottles, champagne bottles, flasks, medicine bottles and other small vials, but they are not found after 1720 on the dark green glass "wine" bottles manufactured in the English tradition illustrated by Noël Hume (1961:100-101). This empontilling technique, described by Diderot (1772: Pl. V), was used for the French "flower pot" wine bottles, although the distinctive ring shape is not always obvious. Bottles of this type have appeared on a Canadian site occupied by the French be-

tween 1732 and 1745. The French writers Peligot (1877:300) and Bontemps (1868:509) described this technique, but whether this was straight copying from Diderot or whether the practise was still common has not been determined. Certainly it was still being used in the United States in the 19th century (McKearin 1970:89-91).

The fourth empontilling technique (Figure 10,*d*), probably discontinued, consisted of using a bare iron pontil with a suitably shaped end, usually a shallow arch, which was heated red hot and applied directly to the base of the bottle (Toulouse 1968:140). The pontil mark is a distinct circular mark covered with a reddish or black deposit which, when tested, indicated the presence of ferric oxide and occasionally ferrous oxide (Toulouse 1968:141). Toulouse (personal communication) also suggests that the bare iron pontil tended to distort the push-up more than any of the glass-tipped pontils (Figure 15). Some of the marks that I have seen on bottles in local collections are unmistakeable, but others in the National Historic Sites Service collection have iron oxide deposits spread unevenly over the pontil mark area (Figure 15). The deposit could be explained in a number of ways. Possibly a bare iron pontil was used to hold the bottle; the push-up may have been formed by a bare iron tool, or the bottle may have been buried next to an iron object.

The distinct form has been found in American flasks, fruit jars and carbonated beverage bottles dating from about 1845 to 1870 (Tou-

FIGURE 16. *Moulded lettering in the centre of the base, a position formerly occupied by the pontil mark.*

louse 1968:141-2). The indistinct marks in the National Historic Sites Service collection occur in 18th- and early 19th-century dark green glass bottle bases. Obviously further investigations will have to be carried out on this technique.

The pontil was gradually replaced by other tools, such as the sabot (Figure 1) and the snap case (Kendrick 1968:128), which held the bottle around the body and did not leave disfiguring scars in the base. These tools were introduced sometime between the late 1840s and the 1850s (Bontemps 1868:511; Larsen, Riismøller, and Schülter 1963:389; McKearin 1970:107; Scoville 1948:17), and by the 1870's had superceded the pontil for holding bottles during the finishing process (Toulouse 1968: 204). With the disappearance of the pontil mark, the glassmakers began to use the centre of the base for moulded lettering and numbers (Figure 16).

CONCLUSIONS

Several relationships became obvious during the course of this study. Different empontilling techniques and methods of form-

ing push-ups were used for different types of bottles. Possibly these differences can be related to the size of the bottle.

A regular, rounded, cone-shaped push-up, probably made with a mollette, as described by Diderot, in combination with a small pontil mark, either from a glass-tipped pontil or from a blowpipe used as a pontil, occurs on 18th-century French wine bottles. I have seen the same combination on 18th-century European spa water bottles and suspect that the Belgian wine bottles illustrated in Chambon (1955: Pl. T, facing p. 113) were formed in a similar way. The combination, therefore, should probably be regarded as Continental rather than strictly French in origin.

The glass-tipped pontil or the blowpipe as a pontil appear to have been favoured by the French, and possibly the Continental glassmakers, for holding all bottles, even those of larger capacity (about 26 oz.). The English, however, favoured these two methods for their smaller bottles and used the larger sand pontil for bottles of larger capacity (about 26 oz.).

A separate mould part designed specifically to form the push-up appears to have been first introduced in England in the 1820s for the dark green glass "wine" bottles. Afterwards, however, this technique was used in many countries for most types of bottles.

The bare iron pontil appears to have been used in the 19th century. Iron oxide deposits on the bases of earlier bottles may be from the use of this type of pontil or from a tool used to form the push-up.

Obviously there are a great many questions left unanswered by the above study. The relationships between different bottle types, techniques, country and period of manufacture are very complex. Often the different types of marks are difficult or impossible to identify, and available literature on glass has, with few exceptions, not covered this aspect in detail.

In combination with other criteria such as body shape, size, and finish formation, the formation of the push-up and the empontilling techniques can be used as additional evidence in determining bottle types made during the 18th and 19th centuries.

ACKNOWLEDGEMENTS

My appreciation and thanks are extended to Dr. Julian Toulouse, retired glass Consulting Engineer, for his inestimable help and comments in the preparation of this article. I would also like to thank the National Historic Sites Service for permission to publish the information relating to the archaeological collections made by the Service. The photographs were done by Georges Lupien and the drawings by Mrs. Jane Moussette, both of the National Historic Sites Service.

REFERENCES

BONTEMPS, GEORGES
1868 *Guide du verrier, traité historique et practique de la fabrication des verres, cristaux, vitraux.* Librairie du dictionnaire des arts et manufactures, Paris.

DIDEROT AND D'ALEMBERT
1967 *Encyclopédie, ou dictionnaire raisonné des sciences, des arts, et des métiers.* Facsimile reprint of 1765 ed. of Vol. 17, text. Friedrich Fromann Verlag (Gunther Holzboog), Stuttgart.

1772 "Vetterie en bouteilles chauffée en charbon de terre." *Recueil de Planches sur les sciences, les arts libéraux et les arts méchaniques, avec leur explication.* Vol. 10. Briasson, Paris.

CHAMBON, RAYMOND
1955 *L'Histoire de la verrerie en Belgique du IIme siécle à nos jours.* Editions de la Librairie Encyclopédique, Bruxelles.

DE FONTONELLE, JULIA, AND F. MALEPEYRE
1854 *Nouveau manuel complet de verrier et du fabricant de glaces, cristaux, pierres précieuses factices, verres colorés, yeux artificiels, etc.* Vol. I. La librairie encyclopédique de Roret, Paris.

KENDRICK, GRACE
1968 *The Mouth-Blown Bottle.* Grace Kendrick, Fallon, Nevada.

LARSEN, ALFRED, P. RIISMØLLER, AND M. SCHLÜTER
1963 *Dansk Glas 1825-1925.* Nyt Nordisk Forlag Arnold Busck, Copenhagen.

McKEARIN, GEORGE, AND HELEN McKEARIN
1948 *American Glass.* Crown Publishers, New York.

McKEARIN, HELEN
1970 *Bottles, Flasks and Dr. Dyott.* Crown Publishers, New York.

MENDELSOHN, OSCAR A.
1965 *The Dictionary of Drink and Drinking.* Macmillan, Toronto.

MOODY, B. E.
1963 *Packaging in Glass.* Hutchinson and Co., London.

NOËL HUME, IVOR
1961 "The Glass Wine Bottle in Colonial Virginia." *Journal of Glass Studies,* Vol. 3, pp. 91-119. The Corning Museum of Glass, Corning, New York.

1970 *A Guide to Artifacts of Colonial America.* Alfred A. Knopf, New York.

PELIGOT, E.
1877 *Le verre: son histoire, sa fabrication.* G. Masson, Paris.

RICKETTS, H.
1821 *Ricketts' Specification: An Improvement in the Art or Method of Making or Manufacturing Glass Bottles, such as are Used for Wine, Porter, Beer, or Cyder.* British Patent, No. 4623.

SCOVILLE, WARREN C.
1948 *Revolution in Glassmaking: Entrepreneurship and Technological Change in the American Industry.* Harvard University Press, Cambridge, Mass.

TOULOUSE, JULIAN
1968 "Empontilling—A History." *The Glass Industry,* Pt. I (March), pp. 137-42; Pt. II (April), pp. 204-5. New York.

1969 "A Primer on Mold Seams." *The Western Collector,* Pt. 1, Vol. 7, No. 11, pp. 526-35; Pt. 2, Vol. 7, No. 12, pp. 578-87. San Francisco.

GEORGE L. MILLER
CATHERINE SULLIVAN

Machine-Made Glass Containers and the End of Production for Mouth-Blown Bottles.[1]

ABSTRACT

Between 1880 and 1920 a major revolution in the production of glass containers transformed the glass industry and launched an ancient craft into a modern "mechanized engineering activity" (Meigh 1960:25). The number of patents for and improvements of semi-automatic and automatic bottle blowing machines in this period is very confusing. This discussion is an attempt to outline these developments with an emphasis on their chronology and impact on bottle and jar production. Although this discussion is limited to containers, it should be borne in mind that similar mechanization was occurring in other branches of the glass industry.

Introduction

During the late 19th century, improvements in the finish portion of glass containers in combination with the development of convenient, reliable closures, helped increase the demand for glass commercial containers. Two very important closures were the crown top for bottles and the Phoenix cap for jars, both patented in 1892 (Lief 1965:17–20). During this same period, automatic canning and bottling machinery was being developed, along with better knowledge of sterilization and a wider availability of refrigeration (Hampe & Wittenberg 1964:115–21). All of these developments were part of a broad change in food consumption patterns and emerging brand-name products.

Statistics illustrating the impact of these developments on glass container demand and production for Canada and England are very limited; however, in the United States, container produc-

[1]This article is reprinted by permission of Park Canada, Ottawa, Ontario k1A1G2, from *Research Bulletin* Number 171.

tion increased 50 per cent between 1899 and 1904, that is, before the development of the fully automatic machine (Barnett 1926:70). From 1897 to 1905 the number of hand bottle-blowers in the United States increased from 6000 to 9000, which matches the 50 per cent increase in glass container production (Barnett 1926:71). By 1919 the amount of glass containers produced was 180 per cent higher than the number produced in 1904 (Barnett 1926:70, 89). The increasing market for glass containers helped provide the capital necessary for mechanization and the drive for its success.

All glass-blowing machines (semi-automatic and automatic) that have been successfully taken into production, have involved three separate molding steps. These involve a ring mold which shapes the finish, a parison or part-size mold to give initial shape to the hot glass, and a blow or full-size mold to form the container's final shape, size and any embossed letters or designs it might have. Machine production follows these steps:

1. A gob of molten glass enters the ring and parison mold and is forced by air pressure, suction, or a plunger to take the shape of the full-sized finish mold and that of the part-sized parison mold. The role of the parison mold is to distribute the glass into the shape needed for blowing the full-sized container.
2. With the finish ring mold still attached, the parison mold is removed. In some cases, the body of the parison is allowed to elongate.
3. The full-sized or blow mold is joined to the ring mold around the parison and the bottle is blown to full size by air pressure.

While both semi-automatic and automatic machines went through the above steps, there was a fundamental difference recognized by the glass industry. Semi-automatic machines were supplied with gobs of molten glass and operated by semi-skilled laborers. Fully automatic machines, on the other hand, gathered glass directly from the furnace and all processes in molding and blowing were independent of human labor. Semi-automatics were limited in their production capacity by the speed with which the worker could feed glass to the machine and run the machine through the molding sequence. Limited production capacity and the cost of labor led to the elimination of

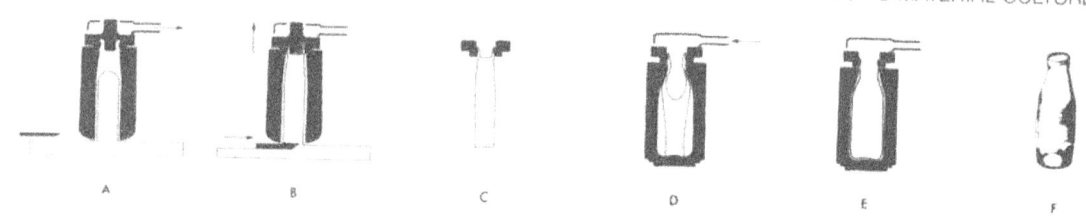

FIGURE 1   The Owens suction-and-blow process (*Drawing by S. Epps*). A. Gob sucked up into blank mold. B. Neck formed and gob sheared off at base. C. Blank (parison) shape with ring mold still attached. D. Blank shape transferred to full size mold. E. Final shape blown; F. Finished bottle

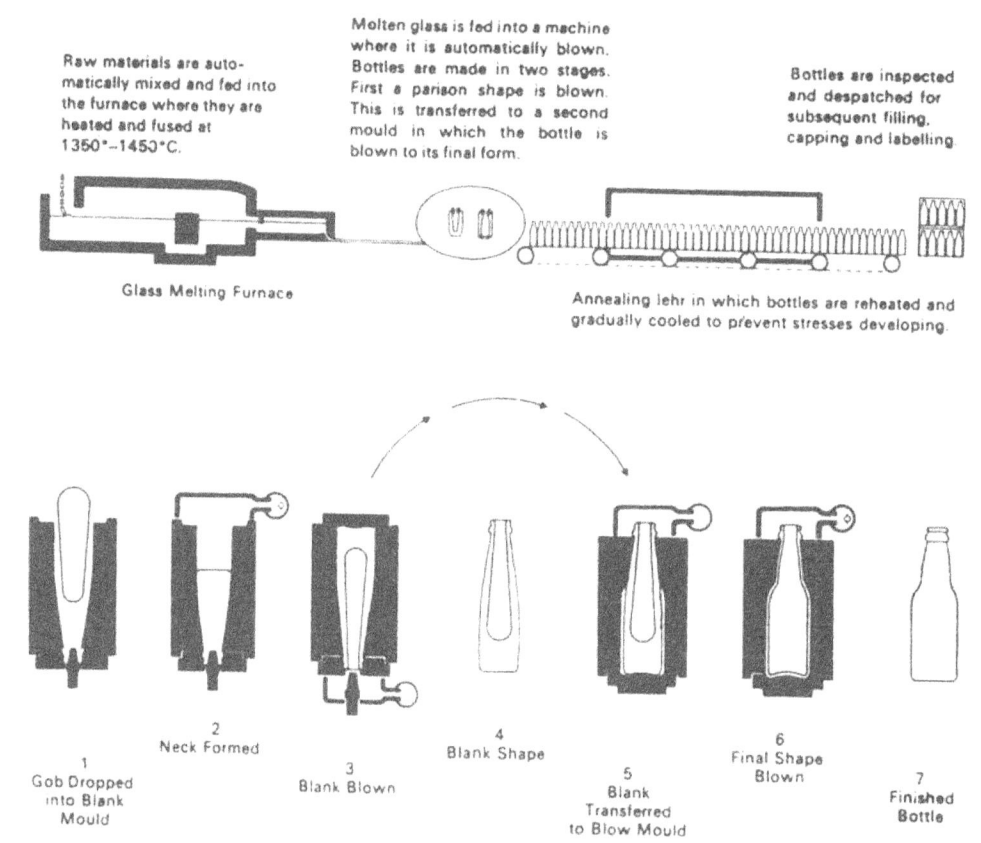

FIGURE 2   Blow-and-blow process (Published with permission of *Glass Manufacturers Federation 1973:25*)

semi-automatic machines in favor of the more productive automatic bottle-blowing machines.

In the hand-blowing process, the glass blower gathered a gob of molten glass on the blow pipe, shaped it and then blew it into shape with or with-

out molds. After the vessel was fully blown, the bottle was disconnected from the blowpipe and then the neck was shaped. Because the mouth of the container was the last part completed, it became known as the finish. A major development

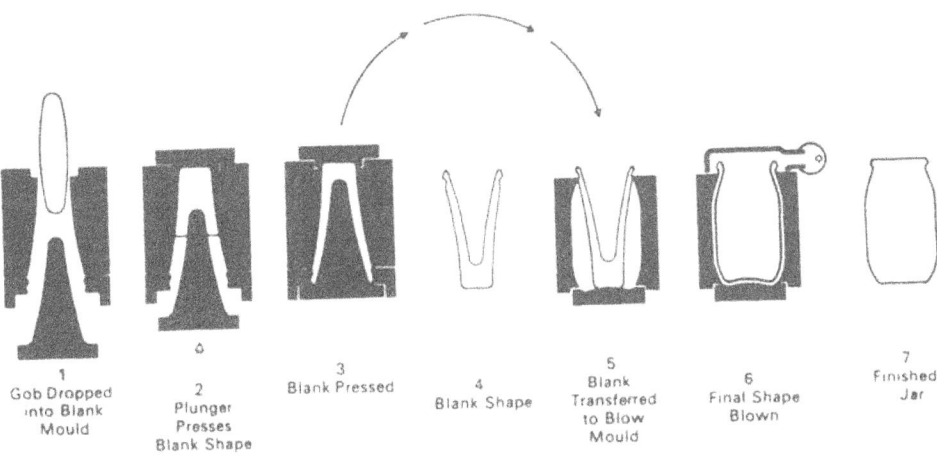

1
Gob Dropped
into Blank
Mould

2
Plunger
Presses
Blank Shape

3
Blank Pressed

4
Blank Shape

5
Blank
Transferred
to Blow
Mould

6
Final Shape
Blown

7
Finished
Jar

FIGURE 3 Press-and-blow process (*Glass Manufacturers Federation* 1973:25)

towards machine-made glass bottles was the recognition that the finish had to be the first part formed rather than the last. It is the finish that provides the momentary connection of the glass to the machine for blowing of the container. Two American patents, Gillender's in 1865 and Atterbury's in 1873, both described molding processes where the finish was formed as the first part of machine blowing; however, neither of these patents seems to have come into production (Barnett 1926:67).

Two semi-automatic blowing machines were developed in the 1880s—one, by Philip Arbogast, patented in 1881 in the United States, and the other, by Howard Ashley, patented in 1886 in England (Meigh 1960:26–27). Use of machines was limited by strong glass blowers' unions in their respective countries. Arbogast's machine established the principle of using a parison and a blow mold in a press-and-blow method which formed wide-mouthed containers. Use of his machine did not enter large scale production until 1893 when it was used in a non-union shop to make vaseline jars, and, later, fruit and other jars as well (Meigh 1960:27). The Ashley machine used a blow-and-blow process with a parison and full-sized mold to produce small-mouthed containers (Meigh 1960:28). Its successful application to mass production of containers did not take place until 1899 (Meigh 1960:27).

After the development of these prototypes, several other machines were developed in quick succession. These have been well described by Edward Meigh (1960) in "The development of the automatic glass bottle machine: a story of some pioneers." The 1890s was a period of revolution in glass technology; however, the new technology did not begin to cut down on the number of hand glass blowers until after 1905, because expanding demands for glass containers accommodated both the new technology and the old (Barnett 1926:71). This situation could not last forever.

In 1903 Michael Owens of the Libbey Glass Works in Toledo, Ohio, patented his fully automatic glass-blowing machine. He had been making a series of improvements towards machine-blown bottles since 1898 (Meigh 1960:29–31). The machine Owens developed was a major advance over the semi-automatic machines, and in 1903 The Owens Bottle Machine Company was organized with a capital of $3,000,000 to license rights to the machine to various glass companies for production of specific types of bottles (Walbridge 1920:67–68). By 1909 three other companies had taken up licences to use the machine and had put 46 machines into production (Scoville 1948:105, 115). Their success with the machine and further improvements by Owens increased the number of glass companies taking out licences. In the two years from September 1909 to September 1911, the number of Owens machines in production doubled from 51 to 103.

Between 1903 and 1923, Owens designed a series of 12 automatic bottle-blowing machines which increased productivity and expanded the types of containers that could be produced from three-ounce bottles to carboys (Meigh 1960:33). By 1917 half of the production of glass containers in the United States was done on Owens machines (Barnett 1926:88).

The spread of the Owens Bottle Machine to other countries was fairly rapid. In 1906 a licence from the Owens Company was issued to the Canadian Glass Manufacturing Company for a glass works in Hamilton, Ontario (King 1965:90). By 1914 there were 60 Owens machines in Europe (Barker 1968:317).

During the period when the Owens machine was being developed, semi-automatic machines were being improved and automatic feeding devices were being invented. These devices, such as the Brooke's continuous stream-feeding device and the Peiler Paddle Gob Feeder, transformed semi-automatics into automatic glass bottle-blowing machines (Meigh 1960:35–40). They were much simpler than Owens machines and much less costly to build and operate. The feeding devices took a small amount of glass to the machines, whereas the Owens device took the whole machine to the glass. Owens machines could weigh up to 120 tons and were raised and lowered by counterweights to suck up the molten glass (Walbridge 1920:93). Each arm of the Owens machine was dipped into a revolving circular tank furnace to suck glass up into the mold. Each mold-filling required the whole machine to move up and down (Figure 1). Some Owens machines had up to 15 arms and could produce 350 gross pint bottles in 24 hours, production equal to the output of 50 glass workers (Meigh 1960:33).

While the Owens machine was highly successful in large production runs, it was of limited use for short runs due to the necessity of shutting down the whole machine to change a mold on any one arm. As well, the larger the Owens machine, that is the greater the number of arms, the larger the revolving tank needed, which meant that fuel costs were higher for the more complex machines (Meigh 1960:34).

Rapid adoption of machines for manufacturing glass containers was a matter of economics. Semi-automatic and automatic glass bottle-blowing machines worked in two ways to lower the cost of glass container production. First, mechanization greatly increased the productivity of the workers making glass containers, and second, it eliminated the need for highly-skilled craftsmen. Prior to the development of bottle-blowing machines, glass blowers were very well paid, for their skills were essential to produce bottles and jars. Minimal skill was needed to operate semi-automatic machines, and the fully automatic machines almost completely replaced laborers.

In terms of productivity, the machines greatly increased output of containers per man-hour. Boris Stern's 1927 study of *Productivity of Labor in the Glass Industry* established that semi-automatic machines were between 42 and 171 per cent more productive per man-hour than hand production methods and that fully automatic machines were between 642 and 3806 per cent more productive than hand manufacture (1927:8). These ranges relate to the size of containers being produced and differences in the capacity of the various types of bottle-blowing machines.

The same study indicates that the labor cost per gross of bottles produced on the semi-automatics were from 23 to 52 per cent cheaper than hand-blown bottles. Labor costs per gross of bottles produced on fully automatic machines were between 90 and 97 per cent lower than hand-blown bottles (Stern 1927:8). Lower labor costs were of course offset by the capitalization necessary to acquire the machines.

Development of the Semi-Automatics into Automatic Bottle-Blowing Machines

Semi-automatic bottle-blowing machines which began development before the Owens machine had their significance eclipsed by the speed and efficiency of the Owens machine. The step needed to make the semi-automatic fully automatic was the development of automatic feeding devices. One of the earliest such devices to be successfully developed was the Brooke's stream feeder, patented in 1903 (Scoville 1948:182–83). Between 1911 and 1915 the Graham Glass Company adapted the stream feeder to their semi-automatic machine. When it became apparent that the Graham Glass Company had developed a workable automatic glass-blowing machine, the Owens company bought them out. However, attempts to further the production of this machine met with limited success (Scoville 1948:182–83). Brooke's feeder used a gravity flow of glass in a stream from the glass furnace. The flow was husbanded in a cup until the desired quantity was collected and it was then dumped into the mold. Cooling of the glass in the cup caused it to be stringy and often entrapped air blisters. These defects did not stop Hazel-Atlas from using a stream feeder to produce pressed jar lids (Meigh 1960:36).

The Hartford-Fairmont Feeding Devices

An engineering firm in Hartford, Connecticut, and a glass company in Fairmont, West Virginia, were incorporated in 1914 to develop an automatic feeding device to be used with semi-automatic bottle-blowing machines (Meigh 1960:36–37). The engineer who developed the feeding device was Karl E. Peiler, with an engineering background from the Massachusetts Institute of Technology rather than from the glass industry. The first successful feeder he developed used a fire clay paddle to push a gob of molten glass from the furnace onto a metal chute kept moist to create a cushion of stream for the gob to ride on into the mold (Meigh 1960:37–38). In 1915 this device was put into use for the production of milk bottles and Hartford-Fairmont began marketing it to other glass manufacturers.

The gob feeder was limited to the production of wide-mouth glass containers. To overcome this limitation, Peiler created an improved gob feeder, a Paddle-needle Feeder that came into production in 1918 (Meigh 1960:38). It had a lip on the tank furnace with a hole at its base, through which a plunger needle fed the glass. Success of Peiler's feeding devices led to their wide usage. In fact, the Owens Company entered into an agreement with Hartford-Fairmont and became a major lessee of gob feeders in 1924 (Meigh 1960:39). By 1925, in the United States, the gob feeders working with various glass bottle- and jar-blowing machines were producing approximately 8,500,000 gross of glass containers as compared to roughly 12,500,000 gross by the Owens machine (Scoville 1948:185).

Use of the gob feeders with bottle-blowing machines involved mechanical alignment of parison and blow molds, usually by means of one or two rotating tables. This complexity was simplified by the I.S. or Individual Section Machine developed by Henry Ingle of the Hartford Empire Company in 1925 (Meigh 1972:62). Instead of moving molds to the feeding device, the I.S. feeder had a bank of parison and blow molds in a straight line on a fixed-bed plate. Gobs of hot glass were delivered to each mold in sequence and any one section of the machine could be shut down to change the molds without stopping production in the other sections (Meigh 1972:62–64). This was a great advantage over other automatic machines and by 1960 there were 1250 I.S. machines in production (Meigh 1960:47).

Because the various machines with gob feeders were less expensive than the Owens machine and more versatile for small orders, they began to supersede the Owens machine during the 1920s. Sometime between 1927 and 1930, the number of glass containers produced on gob feeder machines surpassed the amount produced on the Owens machines (Meigh 1972:57). By 1947, in the United States, it is estimated that only 30 per cent of production was on the Owens machine while the gob feeders produced 67 per cent of the glass containers (Phillips 1947:188–89). Meigh estimates that over 90 per cent of world production of glass containers by the early 1970s was produced on gob feeder machinery (Meigh 1972:58). Whether any Owens machines are still in production today is not clear from the literature. In Canada the Owens machine stopped being used at Dominion Glass Company in about 1945.

Impact of the Machine-made Glass Container

The impact of automatic machine production of glass containers was extensive and rapid. Hand production of bottles and jars declined rapidly from the second decade of the 20th century. For archaeologists, two immediate questions come to mind: when did hand production stop, and what characteristics might be used to identify bottles from the various machines that came into production? Much broader than these questions is the impact of cheap glass containers on society.

The period of overlap for hand and machine production is fairly long. Types of bottles being blown by hand were continually being reduced as semi-automatic, automatic, and feeding device machines were developed. Barnett's *Chapters on Machinery and Labor* (1926) estimates the number of hand glass bottle-blowers working in the United States during the period when bottle-blowing machinery was being developed:

Year	No. of Blowers	Page Ref.
1896	6229	83
1897	6000	70
1905	9000	71
1917	2000	90
1924	1000	86

Declines in the number of bottle blowers were occurring at a time when glass container production was rapidly increasing. Once again, Barnett provides the statistics on container production used below:

Year	No. of Gross Produced	Page Ref.
1899	7,777,000	70
1904	11,942,000	89
1909	12,313,000	89
1914	19,288,000	89
1917	24,000,000 est	89
1919	22,289,000	89
1924	18,000,000 est	85

The drop in production reflected in the figures for 1919 and 1924 was caused by prohibition which began in 1919 in the United States. Rising glass

container production from the beginning of the 20th century was of course related to increased use of semi-automatic and later fully automatic bottle-blowing machines: in 1900 there were 80 semi-automatic machines producing wide-mouthed glass containers; by 1904 when Owens machines came into production there were 200 semi-automatics in production and the number increased to a high of 459 in 1916 (Barnett 1926:69, 92). After that, the Owens machine and gob feeding devices adapted to existing machines cut into bottle production by semi-automatics. By 1924 there were only 72 semi-automatics in production (Barnett 1926:111). Impact of the automatics is reflected in a 1927 government study by Boris Stern, *Productivity of Labor in the Glass Industry,* which states that:

> In 1926, out of 25 bottle plants inspected only one plant was found using the semi-automatic to a large extent. In another plant the semi-automatic was found standing by the furnace but dismantled and ready to be displaced by an automatic. In still another plant a semi-automatic machine had recently been consigned to the scrap heap (Stern 1927:35).

Adoption of Owens machines was retarded by the leasing system used by the Owens Company. In the 1905–06 period there were only eight Owens machines in production. By 1916–17 there were 200 in production (Barnett 1926:88). It was shortly after this period that the gob-feeding devices and the Individual Section Machine began making inroads on the market serviced by Owens machines. As mentioned earlier, by 1917 the Owens machine was producing half of the glass containers made in the United States. The other half was produced by 2000 hand blowers and 2000 operators of semi-automatic machines. According to Barnett, the 12,000,000 bottles produced by glass blowers and semi-automatic machine operators in 1917 was equal to the 12,000,000 bottles produced by 9000 glass blowers and 1000 semi-automatic machine operators in 1905 (Barnett 1926:88–89). Stated as mathematical equations, these figures come out as follows:

1905

9000 blowers' production + 1000 machine workers' production = 12,000,000 gross

1917
2000 blowers' production + 2000 machine workers' production = 12,000,000 gross

Assuming that productivity for blowers remained the same and solving the above equations gives the following results:

Hand-blown   Semi-automatic
1905 7,714,000 gross + 3,286,000 gross = 12,000,000 gross
1917 1,500,000 gross + 10,500,000 gross = 12,000,000 gross

Total 1917 production
1,500,000 gross by hand blown methods
10,500,000 gross by semi-automatics
12,000,000 gross by Owens machines

These figures are rather rough, but they suggest that hand-blown containers made up between 5 and 10 per cent of all the bottles and jars produced in the United States in 1917.

One of the myths about the Owens bottle-blowing machine is that it greatly lowered the cost of glass containers and thus expanded the demand for them. In reality, the price of bottles made on Owens machines fell only about 15 per cent from 1905 to 1914 (Barnett 1926:130). Thus, the cost of production was a marginal consideration in expanding the use of glass containers. More important was that machines could produce highly standardized, reliable finishes and sizes that could be used on the automatic machines that filled the containers. These developments combined to meet and change consumer demands for products put up in glass containers.

The types of bottles produced on the Owens machine were limited to those for which there was a fairly large demand. Stern's 1927 report sums up the machine-made bottle market as follows:

The principle advantage of the machine lies in mass production. The high cost of making the necessary number of molds and the time required in adjusting the machine and changing molds make it uneconomical for large machines to work on orders less than 1,000 gross of bottles. Even for the smaller six-arm machines the order has to be at least 250 gross to make production economical. Hence the smaller orders, especially those below 100 gross, necessarily go to the hand plants. Among bottles of this kind the principle place is occupied by perfumery and toilet ware, individually shaped bottles being used as a means of identifying and advertising their contents.

As a competitive factor in the bottle branch of the glass industry hand production is absolutely non existent. At best it fills the gaps left by the machine and must therefore be considered as supplementary to the machine rather than competitive (1927:55).

Some idea of just how costly the molds for the Owens machine were is given in B. E. Moody's *Packaging in Glass:*

A 'single' mould, i.e., the equipment required for one head on a machine, consists of at least nine separate parts. . . . and a complete set for a six-head machine could cost well over £1000. It is clearly vital that the bottle maker should be able to obtain a long working life from the moulds; a single mould may be capable of producing something like a million bottles before it has to be scrapped (1963:21).

The minimum number for an economical run of glass containers appears to have increased between 1927 and 1963 when Moody wrote his book. He states that:

We have seen above that it is not an economic proposition to run a bottle machine for short periods, and generally a run of about three days would be regarded as an absolute minimum. The output from a modern bottle machine might be in the region of 100 to 1200 gross per day, depending on the size of the bottle and size of machine, so the minimum number of bottles which can be made economically in a run is of the order of 1,000 gross (1963:20).

The economics of machine production changed the characteristics of bottles. Prior to machine domination of glass container production, the industry produced a wide variety of bottles and jars for small companies such as local breweries and soft drink bottlers. Through the use of plate molds, glass manufacturers made distinctive bottles for small pharmacies and medicine companies. These small-run orders were not compatible with machine production. Barnett summarizes the situation in 1926.

Many articles put up in glass containers have a small market and the orders of the makers of these articles are for only a small number of bottles. The Owens machine is an instrument of large scale production, and the manufacturers who were using the older methods of manufacture—hand and semi-automatic—were able, therefore, to hold the orders for small lots of special bottles. This advantage has been less

important in recent years, as the small user of glass containers, in order to secure cheaper bottles, has become willing to
use standard sizes and to rely on the label for his distinctive
mark (1926:91).

Hand-blown tradition for commercial containers
was still going on in 1934 for "small orders and
oddly-shaped bottles" (Jerome 1934:106).

World War II further consolidated the standardization of glass containers when the American
federal government, with the glass manufacturers,
reduced the number of types and varieties of bottles to maximize production.

Prior to the war, there were many odd shapes and sizes of
bottles. War standardization, and elimination of small sizes,
provided an increased output with the same production
machinery. Janssen stated in 1946 that a return to the prewar
pattern would cut output by 20% in grossage, or 40% in
gallonage (Holscher 1953:375).

Hand-blowing of commercial containers in the
United States probably was close to non-existent
by World War II, and in the period between the
World Wars it was limited to odd shaped containers, perfumery, toiletware and carboys.

Machine-made Glass Containers in England

Information for countries other than the United
States is not as easy to locate. In England, according to Angus-Butterworth, mechanization of the
glass industry was fairly complete by 1924
(Angus-Butterworth 1948:177–78). Mechanical
production of glass containers in England began
with the use of the Ashley semi-automatic machine
in Castleford in 1887. Further modifications produced several models, one of which, the Plank
machine, had 20 units in commercial operation by
1889. A semi-automatic jar machine was in production in the early 1890s, and before the end of
the 19th century, three factories had put bottle
machines into operation and a further three or four
had used jar machines (Turner 1938:251–52).

Shortly after the Owens automatic bottle-
blowing machine was developed in the United
States, the Owens Company attempted to lease
rights to it in Europe. Not finding a buyer, they

formed the Owens European Bottle Machine Company and built a factory at Manchester, England,
which was in production by 1907 (Meigh
1960:34). Successful demonstration of the
machine's capabilities in the mass production of
cheap glass containers convinced the European
manufacturers to speedily form a cartel, the *Eu-
ropaischer Verband der Flaschen-fabriken Gesell-
schaft* (E.V.), to purchase the European rights to
the Owens machine for 12 million gold marks
(Meigh 1960:34). The English part of the cartel
was the British Association of Glass Bottle Manufacturers Ltd.

The E.V. cartel was interested in minimizing the
impact of the Owens machine on glass production
and union resistance to it. Therefore, they set goals
of 10 per cent of glass container production for the
first year with an increase of 5 per cent for the
following two years of each country's production
(Barker 1968:317). If they had continued to increase at the rate of 5 per cent a year, then 100 per
cent automation would have occurred around
1925. Angus-Butterworth suggests that by 1924
the English glass container industry was under
"fairly complete mechanization" (1948:177–78).
Supporting this is Meigh's statement that the English glass container industry was fully automated
by the early 1920s (1960:34). However, Meigh,
writing in 1934, indicates that a small number of
hand-blown bottles was being produced in England
for "special bottles and those used in small
quantities" (1934:123–24).

One of the English companies that continued
hand production on a large scale was Beatson,
Clark & Company Ltd., a large manufacturer of
druggists' ware. Their production in 1929 was 98
per cent mouth-blown and 2 per cent semi-
automatic, with an output of 1100 gross per week
(Beatson, Clark & Co. Ltd. 1952:40). While this
seems like a large production, it would be less than
one per cent of the British glass container production which was over eight million gross in 1928
(Meigh 1960:43). In 1929 Beatson, Clark and Co.
began building a glass works capable of fully automatic production and by 1949, 80 per cent of their
production was fully automatic, 19 per cent semi-
automatic and less than 1 per cent mouth-blown

(Beatson, Clark & Co. Ltd. 1952:30–40). As in the United States, it was the pharmaceutical and cosmetic bottles that were the last types to be mouth-blown.

Machine-made Glass Containers in Germany

For the rest of Europe, the history of the transition to machine-made glass is much more sketchy. Germany had the largest glass container production in Europe prior to the introduction of the Owens machine and was the major shareholder in the E.V. cartel formed in 1907 to purchase European rights to the Owens machine (Barker 1968:317). Before the Owens machine came on the scene, a very successful device known as the Schiller Semi-Automatic, a press-and-blow machine, was in 1906 put into commercial use in Germany. Between 1906 and 1932, it is claimed, 1150 Schiller Semi-Automatic bottle-making machines were installed throughout Europe, 223 of them in Germany itself (Turner 1938:257).

The first Owens fully-automatic bottle-blowing machine was installed in Germany in 1907, the year the E.V. cartel was formed (Turner 1938:58). As mentioned earlier, the E.V. cartel attempted to minimize the impact of the Owens machine by limiting its production to 10 per cent of the glass containers for the year of introduction with 5 per cent increases for the following two years. If this schedule were followed by Germany, then roughly 40 per cent of German bottle production by 1914 would have been made on fully-automatic machines. In 1914, half of the 60 Owens machines authorized by the E.V. cartel were in Germany (Barker 1968:317), a higher proportion than the original agreed-upon distribution of machines based on pre-machine production for each country in the cartel. This suggests that Germany may have been ahead of England in the proportion of Owens machine-made bottles being produced. What happened to the German glass industry during World War I is not clear, and it is difficult to say when mouth-blown bottle production ended in Germany.

Machine-made Glass Containers in France

Prior to the introduction of Owens machines into Europe, the French production of glass containers almost equalled English production, making France the third largest European producer of such wares (Barker 1968:317). Like manufacturers in the United States, England, and Germany, the French had developed a successful semi-automatic bottle machine. Claude Boucher began developing his machine in 1894 and was successful by 1897 (Turner 1938:253). According to Henrivaux, the Boucher bottle machine was used in countries other than France, and he estimates world-wide production by this machine to have been in excess of 200,000 bottles in 1909 (Henrivaux 1909:395). Unfortunately, figures are not given for French production of machine-made vs. hand-made glass containers.

French glass manufacturers joined the E.V. cartel in 1907 and then withdrew from the agreement (Barker 1968:317). How long they remained outside the cartel is not clear; however, the first Owens machine was installed in France in 1910, following installations in England, Germany, Holland, Austria, and Sweden (Turner 1938:258). How fast the French industry converted to mechanized bottle production is not clear from the literature consulted.

Machine-made Glass Containers in Canada

Information on the transition of the Canadian glass industry from a craft to an automated industrial activity is very limited. For example, the available literature provides little information on the introduction of semi-automatic bottle machines into the Canadian market and no quantitative information on their output. The dramatic technological developments in the United States probably entered Canada much faster than England, due to physical proximity, the constant flow of information carried by glass workers moving between Canada and the U.S., and contact between the unions involved in setting wages in both countries.

For example, one of the early manufacturers of semi-automatic machines was Frank O'Neill (of Toledo, Ohio) who had one of his jar-lid power presses operating in Ontario by around 1901 (Scoville 1948:333 n42). Newspapers from Wallaceburg, Ontario, for 24 September, 1903, report fruit jar-making machines at the Sydenham Glass Works but unfortunately do not mention the type of machine being used (Stevens 1967:29). Among the types of semi-automatic machines documented in use in Canada are the O'Neill, Teeple-Johnson, Olean, and Lynch machines (Stevens 1967:20, 21, 54, 55, 88, 90, 91; King 1965:89; Meigh 1960:40). The relationship of Frank O'Neill with the Canadian glass manufacturers appears to have been fairly significant. After selling his United States interests in the O'Neill Machine Company in Toledo in 1912, he set up the O'Neill European Machine Company factory in Montreal (Meigh 1960:40). How much impact the semi-automatic machines had on hand-blown production of glass containers and how rapidly they spread in Canada is not documented in the literature.

Information on the introduction of the Owens machine to Canada is better documented, due to the leasing structure set up by the Owens Company, and, no doubt, also because of the great costs involved. Rights to the Owens automatic machine for Canada were secured before the European rights were leased. In 1906, for $104,900, the Canadian Glass Manufacturing Company purchased exclusive Canadian container rights on the Owens bottle machine (Scoville 1948:141, Table 14). This company was established specifically to lease Owens machines to operating glass plants in Canada. One of the prime movers in the company was George A. Grier who had acquired control of the Diamond Glass Company and changed its name to Diamond Flint Glass Company (King 1965:90). The first Owens machines in Canada were set up in the Hamilton Glass Works in 1906 (Stevens 1967:9–10).

Control of container rights for the Owens machines was instrumental in the amalgamation of Diamond Flint Glass, Sydenham Glass Company, and the Canadian Glass Company into the Domin-ion Glass Company in 1913 (King 1965:90). This was the dominant Canadian glass company until the founding of Consumers Glass Company in 1917 (Stevens 1967:54–55). By that time the feed-and-flow devices discussed earlier were being adapted to semi-automatics, such as the O'Neill, Hartford, and Lynch machines, which made them competitive with the Owens machine, and they were a great deal cheaper (Meigh 1960:39).

How long it took bottle-blowing machines to replace bottle blowers in Canada is not well documented. Because the Dominion Glass Company had a practical monopoly on glass production in Canada, it was not a case of hand factories competing against mechanized factories. When Dominion Glass built its new glassworks in Redcliff, Alberta, in 1913, the company combined production on the Owens machine with hand-blown shops. In 1915 the Redcliff operation had an Owens ten-arm machine, a lamp chimney machine, and three bottle shops in operation (Stevens 1967:69). The bottle shops would have produced orders that were too small for production on the Owens machine. Most likely these included such types as pharmaceutical bottles, cosmetic wares and probably demijohns. By the mid-1920s the amount of glassware being hand-blown in Canada was very small, as was the case in the United States and England. Gerald Stevens describes the declining role of glass blowers at the Redcliff plant in the 1930s:

> Mechanization was to take its toll. A jurisdictional issue arose in 1937 and the last of the glass blowers declared a lengthy strike. Eventually, they returned to work, "but things were never the same. Their time had run out and they and their skills and songs are gone." (Stevens 1967:69–70).

According to E. G. Davis, manager of the Dominion Glass Works plant at Wallaceburg, Ontario, there were no glass blowers employed in Canadian glass factories in 1959 and the last hand-blowing operation at the Wallaceburg works was in about 1942 (Stevens 1967:91).

The Owens machine in Canada began being replaced by the Individual Section Machine in the 1940s (King 1965:91).

Discussion and Chronological Summary

For the purposes of archaeology, the machine-made bottle provides an excellent, readily-identifiable time marker. Because all semi-automatic and automatic bottle-blowing machines work on the principle of forming the finish first as an attachment to the blowing machine, and the use of a parison mold followed by a full-size mold, identification of the differences between bottles made on the various machines is limited. The major exception to this is the Owens scar.

Characteristics of Machine-made Bottle Manufacture

1. A large number of mold seams, particularly related to the finish.
2. Finish seams:—horizontal mold seam encircling the neck-finish junction. This seam must appear with other machine-made characteristics: an 1860 patent for hand-blown bottles features this seam (Toulouse 1969:584).—1 or 2 horizontal mold seams around the top of the finish or lip caused by a neck-shaping plug and a collar to guide it. On beer and beverage bottles these seams have sometimes been fire-polished off, so other evidence must be sought.—continuous vertical mold seams up the side of the body and over the finish (Figures 4 and 6).
3. Body seams:—wandering vertical "ghost" mold seams on the body of the container, left by the parison mold halves, which join the full-sized mold seams at the finish. A "ghost" seam is certain proof of machine manufacture (Toulouse 1969:585) (Figure 5).
4. Base:—either cup or post bottom mold seams can appear on machine-made bottles and should not be confused with the mouth-blown versions.
   —Owens scar, a distinctive, circular mark with "feathery" edges, caused by the shears that cut off the gob of glass in the suction

FIGURE 4 a & b. Two bottles showing typical machine-produced mold seams, including on b a "ghost" seam from the parison mold on the body (*Photo by R. Chan. Drawing by D. Kappler*)

machines. An Owens scar is usually off-center and may sometimes even extend onto the heel. It dates from 1904 until at least 1969 (Toulouse 1969:582) (Figure 8).
   —valve mark. A non-symmetrical indented groove on the base, found on wide-mouthed containers and milk bottles. 1930s into 1950s (Toulouse 1969:583) (Figure 7).
   —"ghost" seam from the base part of the parison mold.

The main difference between semi-automatic and automatic machines was the degree of mechanization and thus the rate of production, not the appearance of the container. Bottles produced by either method should look the same and have similar "typical" seams and evidence of manufacture.

Roughly speaking, the chronology of mechanization for production of glass containers is as follows:

FIGURE 5. Close-up view of a wandering "ghost" mold seam on the body of a container (*Photo by R. Chan*)

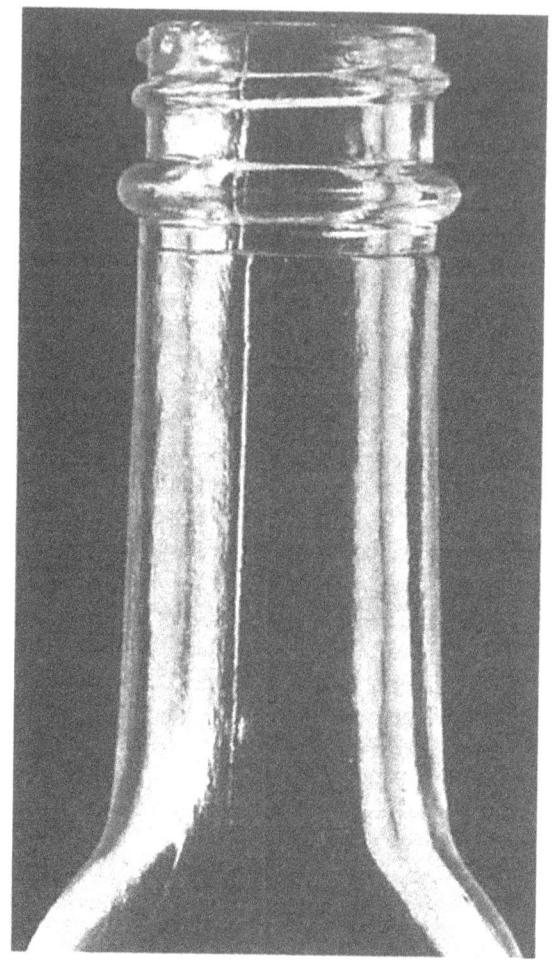

FIGURE 6. Close-up view of a container finish, showing the large number of seams left by the mold parts (*Photo by R. Chan*)

A. Semi-automatic machines for wide-mouthed containers: commercial production begins 1893, peak ca. 1917, end ca. 1926.

B. Semi-automatic machines for production of narrow-mouthed containers: commercial production begins 1889, peak ca. 1917, end ca. 1926.

C. Fully-automatic production on the Owens machine for narrow- and wide-mouth containers: commercial production begins 1904; by 1917 they were producing half of the bottles in the United States; began being replaced by feeders in the 1920s; end of production around the late 1940s or early 1950s.

D. Semi-automatic made automatic by flow-and-feed devices: introduced in 1917, continued to grow in importance and offered an inexpensive alternative to the Owens machine.

E. The Individual Section Machine: developed in 1925; by the 1940s this had become the machine most commonly used in producing bottles.

Hand-blown bottles, as discussed earlier, lasted into the 1930s but only for small run types such as pharmaceutical bottles, cosmetic wares and demijohns. Their quantities would be very small in any post-1920 archaeological assemblage.

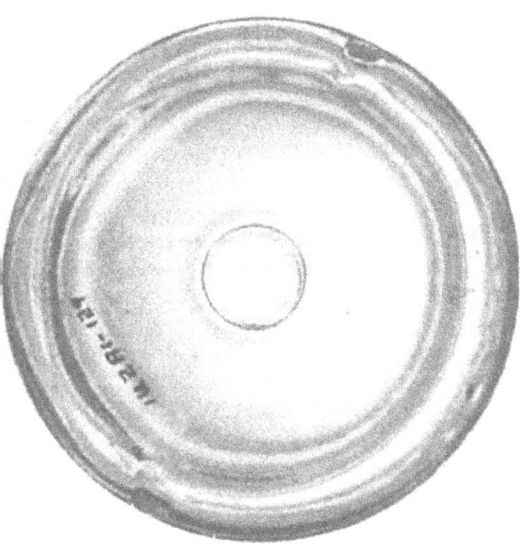

FIGURE 7. Owens suction scar caused by shearing the glass when the mold is full. The shears leave a cooled glass surface, creating a scar from the cutting action: *a* also shows the base and heel mold seams from the parison mold (*Drawing by D. Kappler, Photo by R. Chan*)

REFERENCES

ARGUS-BUTTERWORTH, L. M.
   1948 *The Manufacture of Glass.* Pitman Publishing Corporation, New York.

BARKER, T. C.
   1968 The Glass Industry. In *The Development of British Industry and Foreign Competition: 1874–1914, Studies in Industrial Enterprise*, edited by Derek H. Aldocroft, pp. 307–25. University of Toronto Press, Toronto.

BARNETT, GEORGE E.
   1926 *Chapters on Machinery and Labor.* Harvard University Press, Cambridge.

BEATSON, CLARK & CO. LTD.
   1952 *The Glass Works Rotherham: 1751–1951.* Beatson, Clark & Co. Ltd., Rotherham, England.

THE GLASS MANUFACTURERS FEDERATION
   1973 *Making Glass.* Glass Manufacturers Federation, London.

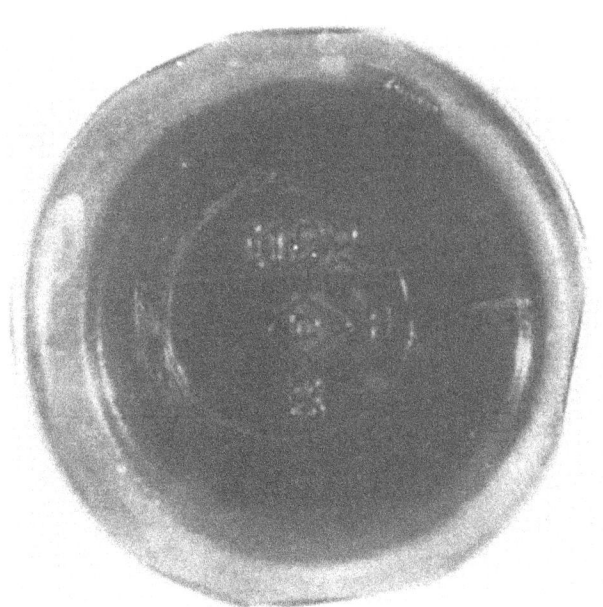

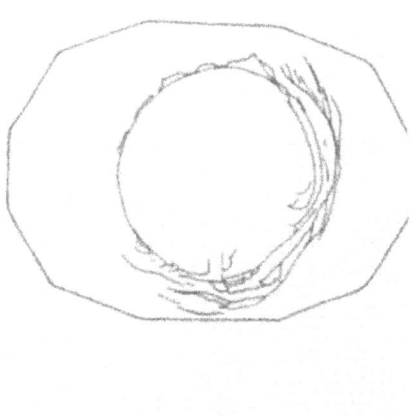

FIGURE 8. Valve mark on a bottle base. Toulouse (1969:583) says that this mark is caused by a valve that ejects the parison out of the mold so that it can be transferred to the blow mold for completion (*Photo by R. Chan*)

HAMPE, EDWARD C., JR., AND MERLE WITTENBERG
1964 *The Lifeline of America: Development of the Food Industry.* McGraw-Hill Book Company, New York.

HENRIVAUX, JULES
1909 Fabrication mecanique des bouteilles. *La Nature* 37:392–95.

HOLSCHER, H. H.
1953 Feeding and Forming. In *Handbook of Glass Manufacture: A Book of Reference for the Plant Executive, Technologist and Engineer,* compiled and edited by Fay V. Tooley, pp. 299–388. Ogden Publishing Co., New York.

JEROME, HARRY
1934 *Mechanization in Industry.* National Bureau of Economic Research, New York.

KING, THOMAS B.
1965 History of the Canadian Glass Industry. *Journal of the Canadian Ceramic Society* 34:86–91.
1977 19th century Bottle Moulds. *Glasfax 10th Anniversary Seminar, June 11, 1977,* pp. 53–59. Montreal.

LIEF, ALFRED
1965 *A Close-up of Closures: History and Progress.* Glass Containers Manufacturers Institute, New York.

MEIGH, EDWARD
1934 Notes on the Design of Glass Bottles. *Journal of the Society of Glass Technology* 18:122–127.
1960 The Development of the Automatic Glass Bottle Machine: A Story of Some Pioneers. *Glass Technology* 1:25–50.
1972 *The Story of the Glass Bottle.* C. E. Ramsden & Co. Ltd., Stoke-on-Trent, England.

MOODY, E. B.
1963 *Packaging in Glass.* Hutchinson, London.

PHILLIPS, C. J.
1947 *Glass the Miracle Maker: Its History, Technology and Applications.* Pitman Publishing, New York.

SCOVILLE, WARREN C.
1948 *Revolution in Glassmaking: Enterpreneurship and Technological Change in the American Industry 1880–1920.* Harvard University Press, Cambridge.

STERN, BORIS
1927 *Productivity of Labor in the Glass Industry.* Bulletin of the United States Bureau of Labor Statistics No. 441. Government Printing Office, Washington, D.C.

STEVENS, GERALD
1961 *Early Canadian Glass.* McGraw-Hill, Ryerson, Toronto.
1967 *Canadian Glass: c. 1825–1925.* Ryerson Press, Toronto.

TOOLEY, FAY V. (COMPILER AND EDITOR)
1953 *Handbook of Glass Manufacture: A Book of References for the Plant Executive, Technologist and Engineer.* Ogden Publishing Co., New York.

TOULOUSE, JULIAN HARRISON
1967 When did hand bottle blowing stop? *The Western Collector* 5 (8):41–45.
1969 A Primer on Mold Seams. *The Western Collector* 7 (12):578–587.

TURNER, W. E. S.
1938 The early Development of Bottle Making Machines in Europe. *Journal of the Society of Glass Technology.* 22:250–58.

WALBRIDGE, WILLIAM S.
1920 *American Bottles Old & New: A Story of the Industry in the United States.* The Owens Bottle Company, Toledo.

GEORGE L. MILLER
SENIOR LABORATORY ANALYST
OFFICE OF EXCAVATION AND CONSERVATION
COLONIAL WILLIAMSBURG FOUNDATION
WILLIAMSBURG, VIRGINIA 23185

CATHERINE SULLIVAN
1600 LIVERPOOL COURT
PARKS CANADA
OTTAWA, ONTARIO K1A 1G2

JANE BUSCH

Second Time Around: A Look at Bottle Reuse

ABSTRACT

Until recently, glass bottles were generally used more than one time. This study investigates customs of bottle reuse in the United States during the 18th and 19th centuries, with particular attention to the secondhand bottle business and returnable bottle systems. Effects of bottle-manufacturing machinery and reasons for the decline of bottle reuse are discussed. The implications of reuse for the analysis of bottles from archaeological sites are considered.

Introduction

Bottles are seductive. Bottle shapes and markings often indicate function and provenience, inviting archaeologists to guess the tastes, wealth, connections, and habits of the people who used the bottles. Nevertheless, archaeologists know that empty bottles were often reused for different purposes. Consider an empty soda pop bottle, embossed with a Philadelphia address, found at a house site in rural Pennsylvania. The occupant of the house might have received the bottle filled with homemade catsup from a relative in New York city. Reuse must be considered whenever bottles are found, and it complicates analysis.

The following account traces the history of bottle reuse in the United States from the 18th century, when bottles were relatively scarce and valuable, through the development of complicated collection systems during the 19th century, to the decline of bottle reuse following World War I. It is possible to see the extent, and the limits, of bottle reuse, and some patterns for specific bottle types and different geographic areas. This information should help to interpret bottles from archaeological sites. Furthermore, the history of bottle reuse is part of the history of trash disposal, a basic concern in all archaeology.

Reuse in the Eighteenth Century

Bulk packaging in ceramic and wooden containers was the norm during the 18th century. Glass bottles were relatively expensive, and the demand was greater than the supply. Most bottles were imported, a costly process. American glassworks produced some bottles, but they were hampered by shortages of capital and skilled labor and by inadequate transportation. In 1800 only eight glassworks are known to have been operating in the United States (McKearin and Wilson 1978:7, 28–68, 229).

New and old bottles were more than containers for other goods; they had trade value and property value. Brewers, snuff manufacturers, druggists, and other entrepreneurs who needed bottles to market their products gave cash or goods for new and old bottles (McKearin and Wilson 1978:229, 260, 262, 289). Peter Barbour offered money or snuff for bottles in the *Boston Gazette* in 1756 (Dow 1927:280–81). Jonathan Nash advertised ''a good price'' for quart bottles for his New York brewery in 1769 (Baron 1962:61). In 1779, Harmon & Lewis of Philadelphia offered ''the highest price for empty claret bottles'' (McKearin and Wilson 1978:223). Merchants attempted to conserve their supply of bottles by offering lower prices when bottles were returned. In May 1774, a New York brewer offered a dozen bottles of beer for 10 shillings, or 7 shillings if the bottles were returned (Baron 1962:62). A dealer in Hartford, Connecticut, in 1797 reduced his price for a dozen bottles of porter from 16 shillings, 2 pence, to 12 shillings when the bottles were returned (McKearin and Wilson 1978:230). In another approach to the shortage, customers provided their own bottles, as seen in this 1766 advertisement from the *Virginia Gazette:* ''Any person who sends bottles and corks may have them carefully fitted and corked with beer and porter at 6s. or with ale at 4 s. the dozen'' (Baron 1962:62). Sam Hudson sold cider in the same manner in Philadelphia during the Revolutionary War, when bottles became even scarcer (McKearin and Wilson 1978:230).

Seals were applied to wine and liquor bottles to

identify them as private property. Wine merchants used bottles with seals bearing their initials to designate ownership and to insure return of the bottles for refilling. Among affluent gentlemen, who could afford to custom order bottles from England, sealed bottles were fashionable for private use (McKearin and Wilson 1978:204). The chattel value of bottles is also evident in household inventories, which frequently list empty bottles. The estate left by Samuel Ruggles in 1716 included a small case with eight bottles among the hall furnishings. The 1763 inventory of the estate of Robert Oliver listed a case with small bottles in the setting parlour, and a case with two bottles in the dining room. Inventories list bottles in cellars, garrets, back rooms, and out of doors, often in large quantities: one-half gross (72) in the 1737 estate of Jacob Williams, one gross (144) in the 1732 estate of William Tailor. In the 1771 inventory of the estate of James Foster, $1\frac{1}{2}$ gross (216) quart-size bottles were valued at 48 shillings. By comparison, two brass kettles were valued at 40 shillings in the same estate (Cummings 1964).

Archaeological excavations have shown that bottles could be kept for decades before they were discarded. Wine bottles excavated from the John Custis house well in Williamsburg were at least 20 years old when they were deposited (Noël Hume 1974:188). A trash pit at Rosewell mansion in Virginia was filled sometime between 1763 and 1772, but most of the bottles (from a total of more than 350) were manufactured between 1725 and 1750 (Noël Hume 1962:172). At Wormslow plantation in Georgia, wine bottles manufactured between 1735 and 1760 were found in trash pits with artifacts post-dating 1770 (Kelso 1979:95).

The Growth of Supply and Demand

After the War of 1812 the supply of bottles more closely approached the demand. Bottle imports from England resumed at the end of the war. At the same time, the domestic glass industry was encouraged by protective tariffs, a greater supply of capital and skilled labor, and new roads and canals. In 1820 there were at least 33 glasshouses operating in the United States (McKearin and Wilson 1978:68–70, 230; Scoville 1948:7, 50). By 1880 there were 169 glasshouses in operation, with an annual output of bottles approximately seventy times greater than in 1820 (Scoville 1948:7, 64). Innovations in bottle manufacturing increased productivity. Full-size piece molds, adopted in America circa 1810, facilitated uniformity and speed (McKearin and Wilson 1978:216, 219, 293, 410). Refinements in the division of labor culminated in the shop system, introduced around 1860 and dominant after 1870. During the same period, workers began to be paid by the piece instead of by the day, and the limit on the day's output was abolished (Scoville 1948:22; Anonymous 1905a:6). After 1880, productivity was augmented by the adoption of gas fuel, the tank furnace, and the annealing lehr (Scoville 1948:28–29, 76–77, 176–77, 337). In 1892, semi-automatic machinery was introduced into the production of wide-mouth glass containers (Scoville 1948:155). In 1899, U.S. glass container production totalled 7,780,000 gross, compared to 1,480,000 gross just twenty years earlier (Davis 1949:221; Anonymous 1955:3).

Growth in bottle manufacturing was accompanied by a decline in bottle prices (McKearin and Wilson 1978:223–24; Scoville 1948:48, 213, 249). Lower prices combined with changes in American life to expand the bottle market. Urbanization and a rising standard of living expanded substantially the markets for products that were formerly produced at home, such as liquor and canned food, and for products that were previously consumed in small quantitites, such as patent medicines and carbonated beverages. Glass container use grew along with the increased demand for packaging of all kinds. With the development of roads, canals, steamboats, and railroads, more packaging was needed to protect and preserve goods during shipment. Sealed glass containers helped to assure consumers that the contents were pure and sanitary. Brand names on bottles reinforced consumer confidence. Packaging was also adopted to make it easier for customers to bring home and store their purchases.

Glass bottles were common by the end of the

19th century. What was the effect on their value? In 1899, beer, soda, and whiskey bottles were valued at $3.75 per gross, roughly half their cost earlier in the century, but this was still expensive compared to other products (Scoville 1948:213). The skilled labor required in glassblowing kept the cost high: in the 1870s the wages of skilled glassmen were one-third to two-thirds greater than the wages of other skilled craftsmen, and two to three times greater than the wages of ordinary laborers (Scoville 1948:32–33). Furthermore, the demand for bottles had grown so much that it was still greater than the supply. To meet this demand in 1899, a number of houses petitioned the bottle blowers' union to operate part of the summer, when glassworks traditionally closed due to the heat (Anonymous 1899a:1). More than a billion new bottles were produced that year, but old bottles retained enough value to be saved and used again.

The Secondhand Bottle Business

In the first decades of the 19th century, people continued to reuse bottles much as they had during the 18th century. In the 1830s it was still customary for consumers to bring empty bottles directly to merchants in return for cash (McKearin and Wilson 1978:232, 289). Druggists continued this custom into the 20th century, charging customers for new prescription bottles, then refunding the charge if the bottle was returned, or omitting the charge if the bottle was refilled. Customers also brought their own bottles to druggists to be filled; sometimes these were medicine bottles, sometimes they were not (Anonymous 1903a:487; Hague 1913:135; Leslie 1840:211; Anonymous 1899b:11; Anonymous 1902a:18). Merchants such as druggists who used large numbers of bottles kept many as permanent store furnishings, refilling them as needed. The "shop furniture" used by druggists was even passed on from father to son (Munsey 1970:174). Similarly, bars and saloons served whiskey from bottles but purchased it by the barrel. It was the bartender's job to fill bottles from the barrel, as described in an 1869 manual:

"The most unpleasant duties of the bartender are in the morning, when the bottles and decanters, reduced by the draughts of the day and night previous have to be refilled; the tumblers, used just previous to closing, washed, and everything put in order for the day's operations (Anonymous 1869; preparatory).

These simple cycles of bottle reuse were overshadowed by the growth of large businesses devoted to the trade in used bottles. As American commerce developed, the distance between manufacturers, merchants, and consumers increased, and middlemen moved in to facilitate the transfer of goods between them. In this case, used bottle dealers transferred empty bottles from consumers back to merchants and manufacturers. Information on the origin and early development of the secondhand bottle trade is elusive. First, there had to be enough used bottles to make the business profitable. A dealer named George Bartholf claimed to have started the first used bottle business in New York City in the late 1840s (Anonymous 1928:109–10). By 1878, soda bottlers were organizing against secondhand bottle dealers who unethically sold their bottles (Anonymous 1878:36). The secondhand bottle trade in Pittsburgh was reportedly founded in 1883 (Anonymous 1899c:7). The largest bottle dealer in Detroit started out in 1885 (Anonymous 1957:6). By the 1890s the secondhand bottle business was firmly established and thriving in America's cities.

In an 1896 report, New York City's Department of Street Cleaning described a flourishing business in used bottles:

> The trade in old bottles, for example, is enormous, several large establishments being devoted to it. At one store I was told that 5,000,000 bottles were kept in stock, that carload lots were received from different large cities, and that expensive exports were made to Europe (Department of Street Cleaning 1896:70–71).

In 1908 the secondhand bottle trade in New York state handled an estimated 2,000,000 gross bottles a year, at a value of $4,500,000 to $6,500,000 (Anonymous 1908a:32). Dealers received bottles from servants and employees who recovered them from private residences, restaurants, saloons, and hotels. Hotels were an important source, regularly collecting empty bottles even from the guest rooms and sending them to dealers by the wagon load. Many bottles arrived at the secondhand bottle dealer via pushcart men and junk shops. Large numbers of bottles were recovered from the dumps (Department of Street Cleaning 1896:34, 70–71; Anonymous 1903b:74; Anonymous 1905b:1; Anonymous 1899d:18). In New York city, "scow-trimmers" collected bottles from the waterfront garbage dumps. They set aside registered bottles belonging to soft drink and beer bottlers, and sold the remaining "mixed" bottles to bottle dealers for $1.50 a barrel. In 1896, New York's scow-trimmers collected approximately 500 barrels of mixed bottles a week, or 26,000 barrels a year (Department of Street Cleaning 1896:117).

Secondhand bottle dealers paid from one-half to two cents each for bottles around the turn of the century and sold the bottles for fifty cents less per gross than new bottles (Anonymous 1903b:74; Anonymous 1905b:1). Customers for used bottles were varied and widespread. In 1899 Jacobson Brothers of Pittsburgh sent an eight carload shipment of wine and champagne bottles to Puerto Rico and Cuba (Anonymous 1899c:7). The market for wine bottles was particularly good since few were manufactured in the United States. Secondhand bottle dealers distributed used European wine and champagne bottles to American wineries and to the fruit juice and gaseous water industries in upstate New York (Anonymous 1903b:74; Anonymous 1934a:10; Anonymous 1908b:13). Distilleries, bucket shops, and saloons provided a ready market for used whiskey bottles; illegal refilling of branded bottles with cheap whiskey was widespread (Anonymous 1903b:74; Anonymous 1908c:17). The South Carolina Dispensary, a legitimate customer, used as many secondhand whiskey bottles as possible for economy (Anonymous 1905c:88). Empty liquor bottles were also traditionally used in the sale of linseed oil, turpentine, and similar products (Anonymous 1938a:7). Embossed patent medicine bottles were purchased by the original medicine manufacturers or by imitators, and were used for bluing and ammonia (Anonymous 1903b:74; Blanc 1913:39). Large ink and mucilage bottles were returned to the manufacturers; cologne and perfume bottles went to the cheap scent manufactories on New York's East Side (Anonymous 1903b:74).

The Returnable Bottle System

The returnable bottle system complemented the used bottle business in the recovery of empty bottles. Returnable soda water bottles were used in New York city as early as the 1840s but did not become common until bottled soda became popular following the invention of the Hutchinson stopper in 1879 (McKearin and Wilson 1978:242–43; Riley 1958:97–98). Similarly, returnable beer and milk bottles became common after the 1870s. Lager beer was first bottled successfully in 1873, and the first known delivery of milk in glass containers was in 1878 (Anonymous 1909a:4; Munsey 1970:191). Under the returnable system, bottles were considered the legal property of the bottler, and customers were obligated to return them to the bottler for refilling. Bottles were embossed with the bottler's name, and frequently the reminder "This Bottle Not To Be Sold" or "This Bottle To Be Washed And Returned" (Wilson and Wilson 1968:170–77; McKearin and Wilson 1978:179, 242). Returnable bottles were practical when distribution was localized, as was generally the case with soda pop, beer, and milk. Their advantage was elimination of the cost of the bottle from the price of the product. Products such as patent medicine were expensive enough to absorb the price of the bottle, but a few cents added to the price of a bottle of soda would hurt sales. In the early 1900s a bottle of soda sold for 5¢; selling the bottle with the contents would have added an additional $2\frac{1}{2}$¢ (Scoville 1948:213). The returnable bottle system seemed sensible for these inexpensive, rapidly-consumed products, but it established "the bottle question" as the number one bottler headache.

The *National Bottlers' Gazette* called the bottle question "the monstrous evil which every year saps the life from this otherwise prosperous trade (Anonymous 1882:3). In 1883 bottle loss was estimated at roughly 65 percent (Anonymous 1883:25). An 1896 report on the bottling business in the United States reported a total capital investment of $41,573,469 and an annual loss in bottles of more than $3,500,000 (Department of Street Cleaning 1896:119). To fight bottle loss, bottlers banded together in trade associations. The Pennsylvania Bottlers' Association, the Maryland Bottlers' Association, the Missouri Bottlers' Association and their counterparts throughout the United States secured the passage of state laws protecting the property rights of registered trademark bottles. They organized the recovery of bottles from other bottlers, private households, and dumps, setting up central bottle exchanges and clearing houses where bottles were sorted and returned to their rightful owners. Bottle exchanges received the most bottles from member bottlers who acquired other members' bottles mixed with their own empties. With many small soda and beer bottlers operating in one area, empties were inevitably scrambled. The exchange was foremost a means of getting these bottles back to their proper owners.

Bottle exchanges also directed the recovery of bottles lost to careless and illegal users. In an 1855 advertisement in the *Savannah Daily News*, one bottler warned: "I hereby caution all persons particularly those engaged in bottling against either buying, selling, using or in any way depriving me of my bottles bearing my name John Ryan" (Schmeiser 1968:8). Seventy years later the *National Bottlers' Gazette* was still deploring the activities of the "bottle louse" who used competitors' bottles (Carr 1926:122). The bottle louse had plenty of opportunity to appropriate bottles left for collection or simply abandoned by customers. Dishonest dairymen ensured a supply of milk bottles by collecting their competitors' empties from the doorsteps when they made their morning deliveries (Hagerman 1912:68). Saloons sold a large proportion of the bottled soda in the 19th century, and the bottling trade papers bitterly criticized the "always careless and too often unscrupulous" saloon keeper who sold soda and beer bottles to used bottle dealers, who sold them in turn to the bottle louse (Anonymous 1878:36). The Trade-Mark Act of 1876 prohibited the refilling of

bottles that had registered trademarks blown in the glass, and subsequent state laws prohibited the sale of these bottles (Anonymous 1878:36; Peters 1902:24). By 1906, twenty-one states had laws imposing fines for dealing in registered bottles (Anonymous 1906a:30). The laws reduced, but did not eliminate the sale and reuse of registered bottles, and bottle exchanges hired detectives to track down violators (Anonymous 1905d:66; Carr 1926:122). Under the protective laws, bottlers were able to seize their property in raids and prosecute the violators. In 1921, within four months, the Massachusetts Bottlers' Exchange took more than 60,000 bottles in raids and prosecuted 30 bottlers for illegally using registered bottles (Anonymous 1921:34). Though dramatic, raids actually brought back fewer bottles than member exchanges and dump collections.

Large numbers of beer and soda bottles were lost to housekeepers who kept them for their own use, particularly in the fall (Anonymous 1900:56). "That period of the year when the good housewife begins to bottle her ketchup and make her preserves is at hand, and it is also the season when the Pennsylvania Bottlers' Protective Association makes its greatest efforts to prevent the bottles of its members from being utilized for purposes that necessitate hiding them in cellars and closets until gentle spring comes around again" (Anonymous 1902b:84). The shapes of beer and soda bottles made them particularly popular for home preserving. In 1901 the Pennsylvania Bottlers' Association found in Philadelphia homes over one million bottles filled with ketchup, sauces, corn beer, root beer, fruit wines, and other "exhilirating drinks" (Anonymous 1902b:84). Bottlers seldom prosecuted housewives, but they did confiscate the bottles (Anonymous 1902b:84; Anonymous 1905d:66). In the 20th century, bottle loss to home preserving declined, except during Prohibition. In 1922 the *National Bottlers' Gazette* attributed a shortage of soft drink bottles almost entirely to their use for home brew (Anonymous 1922:18).

Bottles taken by housekeepers and competing bottlers were lost to their legitimate owners, but they were still in use. Many bottles, however, were simply discarded. A bottle detective observed in 1905:

> Beer bottles are treated very much the same as boxes in which fried oysters are taken home. As soon as the box is done with it is thrown to one side to find the ash heap and finally the dump. The same is true with beer bottles. Many a man will take home a bottle or two of beer with his box of oysters and when the bottle is emptied it is thrown out with the oyster box (Anonymous 1905d:66).

Whereas saloon keepers legally or illegally returned bottles for refilling, consumers were more likely to throw bottles away. Archaeologists excavating late 19th century dumps in Atlanta found only fragments of beer bottles at a tavern dump but found whole bottles at domestic dumps (Dickens and Bowen 1980:54). Bottle exchanges followed the example set by used bottle dealers in recovering bottles from city dumps. In the 1890s a contractor for the New York Bottlers' and Manufacturers Association paid the scow-trimmers 50¢ a barrel to collect soda bottles, which he washed, sorted, and delivered to the exchange (Department of Street Cleaning 1896:119–20; Anonymous 1899:18). In 1895 the New York Association recovered 1,132,018 beer, soda, and siphon bottles from New York city and Brooklyn dumps. Milk bottlers were recovering 100,000 bottles a year from the New York dumps during the same period (Department of Street Cleaning 1896:119–20). In 1905, 453,475 milk bottles and 1,915,354 beer and soda bottles were recovered from the New York dumps (Anonymous 1906b:36; Anonymous 1906c:34). The New York Association found that dump bottles accounted for a consistently higher percentage of small soda bottles than of other bottles. In 1909 dump bottles accounted for 7% of the siphon bottles recovered, 20% of the quart-size bottles, 27% of the weiss beer bottles, 41% of the lager beer bottles, and 62% of the soda bottles recovered. Customers were understandably more careless with the smaller, cheaper bottles (Anonymous 1909b: 46–48). By the early 1900s, all of the state associations were recovering bottles from the dumps.

Reuse and Disposal ca. 1900

In 1900 a bottle manufacturer wrote:

> In no other country in the world is the consumption of glass bottles so great as in the United States. The reason for this is to be found in the greater material prosperity of the people of this country as compared with those of the old world. Here it is not the custom to preserve a bottle after it has once served the purpose for which it was originally intended (Tatum 1900:8).

Bottlers and bottle dealers recovered many bottles only after they were discarded, and recovery was far from complete. Used bottle dealers operated primarily in cities, even as far west as San Francisco, but the cost of collecting and shipping bottles from sparsely populated areas was generally too high to make the business profitable. Similarly, long distance "shipping brewers" found it too expensive to retrieve bottles used to ship beer across the Rocky Mountains (Cochran 1948:177; Kurtenacker 1914:58). In western mining towns, empty beer and liquor bottles were so abundant that in some towns they were used to build houses and sidewalks (Starry 1968:20–23; Baron 1962:254). In others they were just dumped. Even within the cities, bottles did not always make it to the city dumps, where they might be recovered, but were frequently broken or deposited in backyard dumps and vacant lots. A bottle detective described this scene in 1906: "In the various empty lots, especially those adjoining flat houses, many bottles, the greater number of them broken, can be found. It is so much easier to throw bottles out of the window." He noted that few bottles bearing the dates 1903 and 1904 were still in use (Brand 1906:28).

Consumers discarded empty bottles because they accumulated more than they needed. Housewives still used large quantities of glass containers for storage, home brewing, and preserving, but the number of bottles coming into the home was increasing. In 1910, twenty glass containers were produced for every person in the United States (Anonymous 1910a:1). Some of these glass containers contained prepared foods that the housewife formerly made herself, so the need for glass containers in the home was decreasing while the supply was increasing. A thrifty homemaker observed in 1916: "There is a vast array of bottles and jars accumulated in the course of a few months in the average home, in which pickles, cream cheese, dried beef, and various other kinds of edibles are sold, and there is a vast array of uses to which they can be put instead of being thrown away." (Farmer 1916:89–90). That same year, *Scientific American* noted that a very large portion of the bottles manufactured annually in the United States were thrown away after one use (Anonymous 1916a:56). Even where bottles were redeemable for cash, many people did not bother to redeem them. As the New York City Department of Street Cleaning reported:

> Old bottles are handled in every junk-shop, besides forming the sole stock in trade of a considerable number of dealers, large and small. But although they can be used over and over again, and are always exchangeable for cash, bottles are to be found in very load of garbage that reaches the dump (Department of Street Cleaning 1896:117).

Impact of the Bottle Machine

In 1903, when Michael Owens began marketing his automatic bottle manufacturing machine, the *New York Post* estimated that half of the bottles used in a year were lost and half were used again (Anonymous 1903b:74). Machine manufacturing did not at first affect this balance, although the effects on cost and productivity were immediate. The first Owens machines produced 35.4 gross pint beer bottles in an $8\frac{1}{2}$ hour day, while a shop of glassblowers and assistants produced 15 to 20 gross in the same time. Furthermore, the Owens machine could operate around the clock to produce at least 100 gross pint beer bottles in 24 hours. Productivity increased in subsequent models of the Owens machine; a 1917 model produced about five times as many bottles per day as a 1905 model. Greater productivity and the elimination of skilled bottle blowers combined to reduce the cost of production. Machine operators were paid $.20 an hour in 1906, compared to glass blower wages of $7.00 a day. The total labor cost for one gross of pint beers produced by an Owens machine between 1903 and 1907 was approximately $.10, compared

to $1.50 by manual production. In 1916, factories using glassblowers paid 51.49% of the sales value of their annual product in wages. Owens machine licensees paid 31.38% of their product sales value in wages and machine royalties (Scoville 1948:65, 155–56, 159–62, 205, 211).

By 1917, when the Owens Bottle Machine Company opened the first completely mechanized glass factory, Owens machines accounted for 50% of the glass containers produced in the United States (Meigh 1960:25; Scoville 1948:184). There were also more than 300 semi-automatic bottle machines in use. Comparatively simple and inexpensive, semi-automatic machines were more practical for small orders and helped to fill the gap in machine supply created by the Owens Bottle Machine Company's limited licensing policy. Gob feeding devices that could be attached to semi-automatic machines to make them fully automatic were available for jars in 1915 and for bottles in 1918 (Scoville 1948:162, 180–89; Meigh 1960:36–38). In the 1922–23 glassblowing season, automatic machines, either Owens or gob-feeding, produced 80% of the glass containers made in the United States. In 1924–25, automatic machines accounted for 90% of glass container production (Davis 1949:213).

When machine manufacturing began, the growing bottle market readily absorbed the additional output. Machine manufacturing actually increased the demand for bottles by producing bottles that were notably more uniform in weight and capacity than bottles hand blown into molds. Uniform size assured both retailers and consumers that they were not being cheated in the sale of bottled products and encouraged the use of glass containers in place of bulk containers. While the growing demand was thus helping to prevent overproduction, the Owens Company was limiting the number of its licensees toward the same end (Scoville 1948:212, 214). In 1909 the president of the bottle blowers union reported optimistically: "Even with all the machines in operation last season, and every bottle maker in the country employed, the stocks of ware now on hand are lighter than at any former time" (Anonymous 1909c:1). Instead of lowering prices, machine users turned lower production costs into extra profits, even charging 50¢ to $1.00 more per gross because of the superior quality of their product (Scoville 1948:212; Anonymous 1910b:1; Anonymous 1909d:10).

In 1909 this balance began to falter. The bottle blowers took wage cuts of 20% in 1909 and another 20% in 1912, hoping to preserve the market for handblown bottles by reducing the price. Owens licensees retaliated by reducing their bottle prices (Scoville 1948:212–13). In 1911 the Owens Bottle Machine Company reported average price reductions for the company and its licensees of 10 to 20% over 1908 (Anonymous 1911a:1). One licensee, the American Bottle Company, reduced its pint beer bottles from $3.75 to $2.60 per gross before Word War I ended the price war. During the war years, 1914 to 1918, prices rose throughout the glass industry, though less rapidly than prices in general (Scoville 1948:213–14).

Meanwhile, machines with ever-increasing productive capacity were steadily replacing the bottle blowers. Overproduction was inevitable. In 1911, the *National Glass Budget* reported that there would be a delay in the resumption of bottle blowing following the summer break: "The longer a general resumption is delayed, the better it will be for the market as the year advances, since there is a producing capacity in excess of consumptive requirements" (Anonymous 1911b:1). In 1919, glass container production reached 22,295,000 gross, more than three times the number of glass containers produced in 1899 (David 1949:221). The Owens Company discontinued a machine that produced three hundred four-ounce prescription bottles per minute because its output was too great for the market (Anonymous 1942:10). Nevertheless, in 1934 the automatic bottle machines in use were capable of producing 100,000 bottles a day, or 700,000 a week, and *Modern Packaging* reported: "You seldom have call for a full week's production on any single bottle, except in such exceptional instances as that caused by the legalization of beer and liquor" (Anonymous 1934b:35). In 1936, standard twelve-ounce returnable beer bottles cost $2.80 per gross, the equivalent of $1.73 in 1911 dollars (Anonymous

1936a:3; U.S. Bureau of the Census 1975:210–11). By comparison, pint beer bottles in 1911 cost $2.75 per gross (Scoville 1948:213). Machine manufacture accelerated the steady increase in bottle supply and decrease in bottle value that began during the 19th century, bringing the industry to the critical point where the supply of bottles surpassed the demand.

Decline of the Secondhand Bottle Business

Bottle manufacturers had always viewed used bottle dealers as a nuisance, but the competition took on new meaning with the arrival of machine manufacturing and overproduction. When the bottle blowers felt threatened by machinery, they channeled much of their anger toward their old enemies the bottle dealers. In 1905 the Glass Bottle Blowers Organization of the United States and Canada resolved to send a circular to all labor organizations in the country, asking them to encourage their families and friends to break all bottles before throwing them away (Anonymous 1905b:1). In the end, neither the bottle blowers nor the bottle dealers could compete with the bottle machines. While machine manufacturing was reducing the cost of producing new bottles, rising labor costs were increasing the cost of recovering old bottles. In *Municipal Refuse Disposal*, the American Public Works Association cited the high cost of labor for collecting and sorting materials as the primary cause of the decline of all forms of waste salvage (American Public Works Association 1961:308–9).

While the price advantage of used bottles was slipping, legislation to regulate the liquor industry crippled the secondhand bottle trade. Liquor bottles and imported wine bottles were the staples of the secondhand bottle business. In 1914, 2,689,000 gross liquor bottles and flasks were manufactured in the United States. The Eighteenth Amendment was ratified on 29 January 1919, and went into effect the following year. By 1919 liquor bottle production had already dropped to 993,000 gross (Barnett 1926:89). With liquor bottles practically eliminated, many bottle dealers undoubtedly went out of business, like the Kansas junk dealer who had to quit the bottle business in 1916 after Prohibition took effect in his state (Anonymous 1916b:73). On the other hand, there was a great demand for bottles suitable for bootleg liquor. Before 1920, the consumption of bottled liquor increased where local prohibition laws forced the closing of saloons (Anonymous 1910c:3). When Atlantic City began to enforce its Sunday Closing Law in 1913, the beaches became littered with bottles: "In a search made from Young's Ocean Pier to the Million Dollar Pier by one of the employees, 232 flasks of the pint and half-pint variety were discovered. This condition prevails only on Monday, following 'dry' Sundays" (Anonymous 1913:38). During Prohibition, bottle dealers who were able to maintain supplies of suitable bottles and were willing to deal with bootleggers must have flourished.

On 5 December 1933, the Eighteenth Amendment was repealed. Liquor boards prohibited the sale of bulk liquor in casks in the effort to establish tight control and prevent the resurgence of anything resembling the old time saloon (Anonymous 1933:32). Liquor was sold only in bottles, and well-established bootleggers took up the old practice of refilling the branded bottles of legitimate dealers (Anonymous 1935a:23; Anonymous 1935b:12). In 1934, a Federal Alcohol Control administrator estimated that one gallon of illegal liquor was sold for every legal gallon (Anonymous 1934c:13). On 1 January 1935, the federal government enacted legislation prohibiting the resale, purchase, or use of used liquor bottles, even by the original filler. All liquor bottles were embossed "Federal Law Forbids Sale or Re-Use of This Bottle." Used bottles were supposed to be destroyed. Before mid-January, one million empty liquor bottles were seized in a raid on three New York secondhand bottle dealers (Anonymous 1935a:23; Anonymous 1935d:92). By August the price of bootlegged bottles had reportedly increased 500%. Sales of legal liquor and new liquor bottles increased: 5,663,000 gross liquor and wine bottles were shipped for domestic consumption in 1935, 7,447,000 gross were shipped in 1936 (Anonymous 1935d:483; Anonymous 1936b:3;

Glass Container Manufacturers Institute 1960:54). By 1938 the law was pronounced successful in largely curtailing bootlegging (Anonymous 1938b:705). As an aside, *Business Week* noted: "So far no one has worried about the problem of final destruction. The old liquor bottle may become as bothersome an outcast as the dulled razor blade" (Anonymous 1935a:23).

After 1935 the secondhand bottle business survived on a greatly reduced scale. In 1938 New York city's used bottle dealers did a million dollar annual business, a fraction of their sales volume at the beginning of the century. They dealt primarily in wine bottles, with a large share of food and beer bottles (Anonymous 1938c:16). Used bottle dealers tried to collect and sell the nonreturnable beer bottles introduced in 1935. These special lightweight beer bottles were strong enough for one filling but not necessarily for two; some broke when returned to the fillers (Anonymous 1940a:12; Anonymous 1940b:15). Lightweighting was applied to other glass containers, and, combined with the use of faster filling machinery, may have contributed to the decline of the used bottle business.

Public health was another contributor. People had long been concerned about using bottles recovered from dumps. In the early 1900s, some customers required secondhand bottle dealers to deliver their bottles packed in boxes as if they were new bottles from the glass factories (Anonymous 1903b:74). In 1899, the Pennsylvania legislature passed a law prohibiting the collection of bottles from refuse and the sale of any goods in previously used bottles (except for milk, soft drink, beer, and prescription bottles). The stated purpose of the bill was to protect the public health, but the state's important glass manufacturing industry was reported to be behind the bill (Anonymous 1899c:7; Anonymous 1905e:54). Although this particular law was not enforced, it shows an awareness of possible health hazards from bottle reuse. In the 1930s, state pharmacy boards began issuing regulations requiring new bottles for all liquid prescriptions (Husa 1941:653).

After World War II, new methods of waste collection and disposal further discouraged the recovery of old bottles (Darnay and Franklin

1972:14, 22, 98). In 1961, *Municipal Refuse Disposal* cited only one company that salvaged bottles, and their efforts were limited to returnable deposit bottles (American Public Works Association 1961:308–9). Apart from some trade in returnables, the used bottle market no longer existed. In the late 1960s, when consumers concerned about solid waste began voluntarily bringing their used bottles to recycling centers, the bottles were crushed and used for cullet.

Deposits on Returnable Bottles

During the period when the used bottle business was declining, the returnable bottle system was actually growing stronger through the use of deposits. As early as 1877, the trade journal *Carbonated Drinks* proposed a deposit system as the solution to the bottle loss problem (Anonymous 1877:3). No one questioned the wisdom of deposits. Without them, only a sense of honesty and responsibility motivated customers to return bottles, and this had proven insufficient. Customers actually had more incentive to sell bottles to dealers than return them to bottlers. A deposit provided incentive for return and defrayed the cost of the bottle when it was not returned. But bottlers delayed adopting a deposit system for fear that they would lose business, particularly if neighboring bottlers continued to ''give bottles away'' (Anonymous 1931:118). When significant numbers of bottlers began to charge deposits they usually adopted the system at the state or regional level to minimize unfair competition. In 1903 Milwaukee brewers began charging deposits on all bottles leaving the city (Anonymous 1903c:70). The Bottlers Association of (Washington) D.C. began placing a 2¢ deposit on every bottle in 1906 (Anonymous 1906d:31). Nebraska bottlers adopted a deposit system in 1909, followed by Kansas bottlers in 1911, and so forth (Anonymous 1911c:51). The trade journal *American Bottler* chronicled the spread of deposits and their benefits. One example cited was a Massachusetts brewery which used an average of 16.6 bottles to bottle a barrel of beer before they began charging depos-

its, and only 13.8 bottles per barrel with deposits (Nicholson 1916:39).

Deposits were widespread in the soft drink industry by the 1920s. Under the 1934 National Recovery Act Code of Fair Competition for the Bottled Carbonated Beverage Industry, deposits became mandatory (Carr 1926:122; Anonymous 1934d:39). The Code required a deposit no less than one-third of the replacement value of bottles and cases (Anonymous 1934e:11). In practice, 2¢ per bottle became normal. Following repeal, the brewing industry adopted deposits as standard practice, although they posed a problem for long-distance shipping brewers (Anonymous 1934f:3). Dairies were also using deposits in the 1930s, particularly for milk purchased at retail stores (Anonymous 1938d:3, 7; Anonymous 1946:65). Combined with more organized systems of pick-up and delivery, deposits reduced bottle loss far more effectively than bottle exchanges and dump collections, which were generally discontinued. When a Virginia bottler recovered bottles from the city dumps in 1949, the *National Bottlers Gazette* reported it as a curious incident (Anonymous 1949:39). Bottle loss was 3 or 4% in 1947, not insignificant, but still a fraction of the loss typical at the turn of the century (Comptroller General of the U.S. 1980:40).

Decline of Returnable Bottles

Returnable bottles for soda pop, beer, and milk were at their strongest during the 1930s and 1940s. The value of a 2¢ deposit encouraged bottle returns during the Depression; materials shortages enforced returns during World War II. In 1947, beer bottles travelled an average of 32 round trips from brewer to market, and soda pop bottles travelled an average of 24 round trips (Comptroller General of the U.S. 1980:40; Organization for Economic Cooperation and Development 1978:39). Yet it was during this period that nonreturnable containers began to threaten the use of returnable bottles. Paper milk bottles were used as early as 1902, but it was the square paper carton, introduced in 1934, that became a serious competitor to glass (Anonymous 1902c:68; Anonymous 1934g:50; Anonymous 1935e;125; Anonymous 1936c:16). Non-returnable bottles and cans for beer were introduced in 1935 (Beer Can Collectors of America 1976:3; Anonymous 1935f:3). After World War II, nonreturnables progressed rapidly and steadily. By 1952, nonreturnable containers accounted for 30% of packaged beer and 37% of packaged milk (Anonymous 1959:79; Anonymous 1953:14). In the soft drink market, the progress of nonreturnables was slower; nonreturnable bottles were first used for soft drinks in 1948, and soft drink cans were not used successfully until 1953 (Anonymous 1948:107; Anonymous 1961:25). In 1978, nonreturnable containers accounted for 62% of packaged soft drinks and 89% of packaged beer (Comptroller General of the U.S. 1980:31). In 1976, nonreturnables already held 98% of the packaged milk market (Serchuk 1978:37).

Conclusions

When reuse is taken into account, as it must be, site interpretation based on bottles is more difficult. At the least there is the possibility of time lag between the dates of manufacture and disposal of bottles, reducing their usefulness in dating sites. Trade networks based on names and places marked on bottles are subject to error because bottles were often reused by different people in different locations. Furthermore, bottles can no longer be seen as an easy guide to consumer behavior. The relationship of what people consume to what they discard to what the archaeologist ultimately finds is complex. When efficient bottle collection systems are present, the evidence that a person drank a lot of soda pop, for example, would be removed or reduced. Of course an archaeologist would not base conclusions only on the absence of physical evidence. However the presence of a bottle, such as a wine bottle, does not necessarily indicate that wine was consumed for the bottle might have contained something else.

Despite these difficulties, archaeologists can still use bottles in site analysis. To begin with, awareness that reuse is a possibility will help to avoid simplistic interpretation. When a bottle must be

dated, archaeologists should look for wear such as scratches and abrasions to indictate how long a bottle was used, as well as the way it was used. Wear patterns on bottles could be analyzed as they are on ceramics. Bottles can help to determine trade networks when conclusions are based on a sample rather than on isolated instances, particularly when evidence from bottles is combined with evidence from other artifacts and from historical research. For example, historical research shows that in the early 20th century the South Carolina Dispensary used secondhand liquor bottles, an important clue to archaeologists at early 20th century South Carolina sites. When commercial and industrial sites are excavated, archaeologists should note the variety of packages found there; excavation of a dairy site might yield bottles from other dairies in the area, or from other areas. Although the shape or label of a bottle is not an automatic indicator of its contents, in some cases traces remain of the last product it held, traces that can be analyzed. Again, historical research provides clues: European wine bottles were used to bottle fruit juices and gaseous waters in upstate New York, liquor bottles were customarily reused for paint products, and so forth. Site-specific historical research should provide more clues.

There are some rough guidelines as to where bottles were more likely to be reused than discarded. Bottle dealers were most active within and between cities. In contrast, large numbers of beer and liquor bottles shipped full to frontier mining towns were discarded when empty. Commercial users seem to have been more inclined than consumers to return bottles, at least at urban sites. One might hypothesize that at rural domestic sites, where packaged products were less common than in cities, bottles had greater value for reuse in the home. Analysis of dump sites has shown that small bottles were discarded more readily than large bottles.

If bottles seem less useful in determining dates, trade networks, and consumption patterns, consider that the decision whether to reuse or discard a bottle is itself an aspect of consumer behavior. If an archaeologist observes that the occupants of a site were discarding whole, usable bottles, that may reveal something about those occupants. Perhaps they were too wealthy, or too careless, to care about redeeming bottles for cash. It could be a sign that scavengers and bottle exchanges were absent in that particular area. Conversely, absence of usable bottles in a trash deposit might be linked to immigrant status; there is historical evidence that European immigrants were more accustomed than Americans to reusing bottles (Department of Street Cleaning 1896:119; Tatum 1900:8). Multiple use reduces the certainty of bottle interpretation, but it adds dimension. With more careful and sophisticated analysis, the result can be a richer, more complete knowledge of an artifact and the society where it was used.

ACKNOWLEDGMENTS

I would like to thank LuAnn DeCunzo, Judith McGaw, George Miller, and Robert Schuyler for their comments on earlier versions of this paper. Thanks also to Joseph Gallagher, Olive Jones, Kevin Lunn, and Karl Roenke for sending information on bottle reuse.

REFERENCES

AMERICAN PUBLIC WORKS ASSOCIATION, COMMITTEE ON REFUSE DISPOSAL
  1961 *Municipal Refuse Disposal*. Public Administration Service, Chicago.

ANONYMOUS
  1869 *Steward and Barkeepers' Manual*. Jesse Handy & Company, New York.
  1877 The Bottle Question. *Carbonated Drinks: An Illustrated Quarterly Gazette* 1(1):2–3.
  1878 Protect Your Bottles. *Carbonated Drinks: An Illustrated Quarterly Gazette* 1(4):36.
  1882 A New Proposition to Bottlers. *National Bottlers' Gazette* 1(1):3–4.
  1883 Recovering Lost Bottles. *Carbonated Drinks: An Illustrated Quarterly Gazette* 6(3):24–25.
  1899a The Glass Market. *National Glass Budget* 15(3):1–2.
  1899b Familiar Bottles. *Meyer Brothers Druggist* 20(1):11.
  1899c Pittsburg's Junk Bottle Industry. *National Glass Budget* 15(11):7.
  1899d The Trade in Old Bottles. *Liquor Trades' Review* 7(26):18.
  1900 Recovery of Bottles in Auburn, N.Y. *American Carbonator and American Bottler* 20(235):56.

  1902a Unlawful Filling of Bottles. *American Carbonator and Bottler* 22(253):18.
  1902b Bottles Lost by Thousands. *American Carbonator and American Bottler* 22(261):84.
  1902c Paper Bottles for the Bottling Trade. *American Carbonator and American Bottler* 22(261):68.
  1903a A Grave Source of Danger. *Bulletin of Pharmacy* 17(12):487.
  1903b A Bottle Establishment. *American Carbonator and American Bottler* 23(266):74.
  1903c Pay for Bottles. *American Carbonator and American Bottler* 23(263):70.
  1905a A Government Bottle Report. *National Glass Budget* 21(18):6.
  1905b Out-Gazams the Gazabos. *National Glass Budget* 21(12):1.
  1905c To Buy Bottles. *American Carbonator and American Bottler* 25(290):88.
  1905d The Washington Bottle Exchange. *American Carbonator and American Bottler* 25(288):66.
  1905e Pennsylvania Law Against Refilling Bottles. *American Carbonator and American Bottler* 25(295):54.
  1906a The Bottle Laws of the States. *American Bottler* 26(6):30–31.
  1906b Milk Bottlers' Federation. *American Bottler* 26(3):36.
  1906c Bottlers' and Manufacturers' Association. *American Bottler* 26(1):32–35.
  1906d Washington's New Deposit System. *American Bottler* 26(11):31.
  1908a Property Rights in Plain Bottles. *American Bottler* 28(6):32–33.
  1908b Second-Hand Bottles. *Bar and Buffet* 6(25):13.
  1908c Whisky Bottles Too Often Refilled. *Bar and Buffet* 5(20):17.
  1909a The Export Beer Bottle. *National Glass Budget* 25(7):4.
  1909b Association Affairs. *American Bottler* 29(11):46–48.
  1909c The March of Progress. *National Glass Budget* 25(4):1–2.
  1909d Thatcher Milk Bottle Catalogue. *National Glass Budget* 25(12):10.
  1910a Bottles and Their Making. *National Glass Budget* 25(36):1.
  1910b Bottle Machine Statistics. *National Glass Budget* 25(50):1.
  1910c A Very Short Bottle "Crop." *National Glass Budget* 26(10):3.
  1911a The Owens Bottle Machine. *National Glass Budget* 27(29):1.
  1911b The Glass Bottle Situation. *National Glass Budget* 27(15):1–3.
  1911c Kansas Bottlers Enforce the Deposit System. *American Bottler* 31(5):51–52.
  1913 Bottles Strew the Beach. *American Bottler* 33(8):38.
  1916a Glass Bottles. *American Bottler* 36(12):55–56.

1916b Bottle Business Slumps in Western Kansas. *American Bottler* 36(9):73.

1921 Exchange Saves Bottles. *American Bottler* 41(3):31.

1922 Curbing Bottle Losses. *National Bottlers' Gazette* 41(489):118.

1928 Forty Years Ago. *National Bottlers' Gazette* 47(557):109–112.

1931 Forty Years Ago. *National Bottlers' Gazette* 50(590):117–19.

1933 John Barleycorn Dresses Up. *Modern Packaging* 7(4):29–43.

1934a Glass Container Officials Report on Its Activities. *National Glass Budget* 50(22):3.

1934b The Materials of Packaging, No. 2: Glass Containers. *Modern Packaging* 8(2):33–39.

1934c Change Our Control Methods and Curb the Bootlegger. *National Glass Budget* 50(1):13.

1934d Code Approved! *National Bottlers' Gazette* 53(628):39–42.

1934e Rules Governing Deposits on Soft Drink Bottles. *National Glass Budget* 50(19):11.

1934f Business Holding Despite Adverse Conditions. *National Glass Budget* 50(6):3.

1934g New Paper Milk Bottle. *Scientific American* 151(1):50.

1935a Outlaw Empties. *Business Week*, January 12:23.

1935b Non-Refillable Bottles. *Business Week*, March 16:12.

1935c Fight to Stop Illegal Liquor Business Continues on Front of Package Control. *Glass Packer* 14(2):92–93.

1935d Bulk Liquor Means Bootlegging. *Glass Packer* 14(8):483–84.

1935e Paper Containers. *Food Industries* 7(3):125–26.

1935f New No-Deposit Beer Bottle Makes Its Bow to the Trade. *National Glass Budget* 51(16):3.

1936a The "Steinie" Joins "Stubby" in Defense Against Cans. *National Glass Budget* 52(19):3.

1936b Glass Bottle Sales Active; But Beer Bottle Menaced. *National Glass Budget* 51(40):3.

1936c Container Conflict. *Business Week*, March 21:16.

1938a No Early Improvement Seen in the Container Industry. *National Glass Budget* 54(7):3.

1938b 10 Years Progress in Glass Packaging. *Glass Packer* 17(11):668–71.

1938c Glass Containers Continue to Gain in Popularity. *National Glass Budget* 54(27):16.

1938d Glass Container Industry Faces an Uncertain Year. *National Glass Budget* 53(37):3.

1940a Annual Report of Glass Container Association by Ackerman Constructive. *National Glass Budget* 56(4):3.

1940b News and Notes Relative to the No-Deposit Beer Bottle. *National Glass Budget* 56(1):14–15.

1942 Recent Developments in Glass Container Litigation. *National Glass Budget* 57(38):3.

1946 Raise the Bottle Deposit? *National Bottlers' Gazette* 64(768):64–67.

1948 One-Way for Soda. *Modern Packaging* 22(3):106–8.

1949 Bottler Combs City Dumps for Empties. *National Bottlers' Gazette* 67(804):39.

1953 Milk Packaging Trend in Glass—Paper Containers. *National Glass Budget* 69(14):3.

1955 O–I Provides Pertinent Glass Container Facts. *National Glass Budget* 71(27):3

1957 Max Jacob Prominent Cullet Dealer for Sixty Years. *National Glass Budget* 73(12):6.

1959 Bottles and Cans Make Vast Strides. *Modern Brewery Age* 59(17):79.

1961 Marketing-Packaging Trends. *National Bottlers' Gazette* 80(956):25–26

BARNETT, GEORGE F.

1926 *Chapters on Machinery and Labor*. Harvard University Press, Cambridge; reprint ed. 1969, Southern Illinois University Press, Carbondale.

BARON, STANLEY

1962 *Brewed in America: A History of Beer and Ale in the United States*. Little, Brown and Company, Boston.

BLANC, JOEL

1913 When Truth Telling Does Not Advertise. *The American Bottler* 33(9):39–40.

BRAND, JOSEPH

1906 Where Do the Bottles Go? *American Bottler* 26(1):28.

CARR, FRANK P.

1926 How to Operate a Bottle Exchange. *National Bottlers' Gazette* 44(528):122.

COCHRAN, THOMAS C.

1948 *The Pabst Brewing Company*. New York University Press, New York.

COMPTROLLER GENERAL OF THE UNITED STATES.

1980 *States' Experience with Beverage Container Deposit Laws Shows Positive Benefits*. PAD-81-08. General Accounting Office, Washington, D.C.

CUMMINGS, ABBOTT LOWELL (EDITOR)

1964 *Rural Household Inventories*. Society for the Preservation of New England Antiquities, Boston.

DARNAY, ARSEN AND WILLIAM E. FRANKLIN

1972 *Salvage Markets for Materials in Solid Wastes*. U.S. Environmental Protection Agency, Washington, D.C.

DAVIS, PEARCE

1949 *The Development of the American Glass Industry*. Harvard University Press, Cambridge.

DEPARTMENT OF STREET CLEANING

1896 *A Report on the Final Disposition of the Wastes of New York*. Department of Street Cleaning, New York.

DOW, GEORGE FRANCIS

1927 *The Arts and Crafts in New England, 1704–1775*. Wayside Press, Topsfield, Mass.

FARMER, LIZZIE C.

1916 *A-B-C of Home Saving*. Harper and Brothers, New York.

GLASS CONTAINER MANUFACTURERS INSTITUTE
1960 *Glass Containers, 1960.* Glass Container Manufacturers Institute, New York.

HAGEMAN, E. F.
1912 The Bottle Question. *American Bottler* 32(11):68–69.

HAGUE, GEORGE W.
1913 Practical Suggestions. *Meyer Brothers Druggist* 34(5):135.

HUSA, WILLIAM J.
1941 *Pharmaceutical Dispensing.* 2d ed. Husa Brothers, Iowa City.

KELSO, WILLIAM M.
1979 *Captain Jones's Wormslow.* University of Georgia Press, Athens.

KURTENACKER, CARL
1914 The Desirability of the Plain Bottle. *American Bottler* 4(5):58–59.

LESLIE, ELIZA
1840 *The House Book: or, A Manual of Domestic Economy.* Carey and Hart, Philadelphia.

MCKEARIN, HELEN AND KENNETH M. WILSON
1978 *American Bottles and Flasks and Their Ancestry.* Crown Publishers, New York.

MEIGH, EDWARD
1960 The Development of the Automatic Glass Bottle Machine. *Glass Technology* 1(1):25–50.

MUNSEY, CECIL
1970 *The Illustrated Guide to Collecting Bottles.* Hawthorn Books, New York.

NICHOLSON, JAMES R.
1916 Deposit Saves Large Sums. *American Bottler* 36(5):39.

NOEL HUME, IVOR
1962 Excavations at Rosewell, Gloucester County, Virginia, 1957–59. *United States National Museum Bulletin,* no. 225. Contributions from the Museum of History and Technology, paper 18, Washington, D.C.
1974 *All the Best Rubbish.* Harper and Row, New York.

ORGANIZATION FOR ECONOMIC CO-OPERATION AND DEVELOPMENT
1978 *Beverage Containers: Re-Use or Recycling.* OECD Publications, Paris.

PETERS, W. A.
1902 Trade Marks in the Bottling Industry. *American Carbonator and American Bottler* 22(251):24.

RILEY, JOHN J.
1958 *A History of the American Soft Drink Industry: Bottled Carbonated Beverages, 1807–1957.* American Bottlers of Carbonated Beverages, Washington, D.C.

SCHMEISER, ALAN
1968 *Have Bottles Will Pop.* Michalan Press, Dixon, California.

SCOVILLE, WARREN C.
1948 *Revolution in Glassmaking: Entrepreneurship and Technological Change in the American Industry, 1880–1920.* Harvard University Press, Cambridge.

SERCHUK, ALAN
1978 Milk Packaging Still in Transition. *Modern Packaging* 51:37–40.

STARRY, ROBERTA W.
1968 Bottle Houses. *Old Bottle Magazine* 1(11):20–23.

TATUM, C. A.
1900 Druggists Glassware. *National Glass Budget* 15(47):8.

U.S. BUREAU OF THE CENSUS
1975 *Historical Statistics of the United States, Colonial Times to 1970.* Bicentennial ed., part 1. Government Printing Office, Washington, D.C.

WILSON, BILL AND BETTY WILSON
1968 *Spirits Bottles of the Old West.* Wilson and Wilson, Wolfe City, Texas.

JANE BUSCH
WESTERN RESERVE HISTORICAL SOCIETY
10825 EAST BOULEVARD
CLEVELAND, OHIO 44106

LAURIE A. WILKIE

Glass-Knapping at a Louisiana Plantation: African-American Tools?

ABSTRACT

During the analysis of glass artifacts recovered from undisturbed archaeological contexts at Oakley Plantation, West Feliciana Parish, Louisiana (16WF34), a number of glass sherds were found to have retouching and edge damage consistent with wear found on utilized lithics. Of these, 35 sherds were determined to exhibit significant evidence of use as tools. These tools were recovered from four African-American assemblages dating from the 1840s through the 1930s. This paper discusses the analysis of these tools, whether variations among the tools are representative of distinct types, a review of the occurrence of similar tools at other sites, and whether the tools can be considered to be of uniquely African-American origin.

Introduction

During archaeological excavations in 1991 and 1992, 35 utilized glass sherds were recovered from assemblages dating from the 1840s to the 1930s at Oakley Plantation, West Feliciana, Louisiana (Table 1). These investigations were conducted as a follow-up to an earlier surface survey by Holland and Orser (1984), and further explored several features identified by them. In each instance of glass tool occurrence at the site, strong oral historical or documentary evidence associates the archaeological assemblages with African-American occupants.

Oakley Plantation was founded in 1796 as a cotton plantation in Feliciana Parish of Spanish West Florida. At its economic peak in the 1840s, the plantation comprised over 3,000 acres of land and over 200 slaves (Wilkie 1994). The plantation remained in the ownership of the same family and was continuously farmed by African Americans until the 1940s. In 1947, 100 acres of the plantation, including the planter's house and plantation yard area, were sold to the State of Louisiana for preservation and interpretation as the Audubon State Commemorative Area.

Three loci excavated during the 1991 and 1992 field seasons provided the archaeological materials for this study (Figure 1). These areas were defined as features in the Holland and Orser (1984) surface collection, and to maintain continuity for management purposes, feature numbers used by Holland and Orser were retained. Each of Holland and Orser's (1984) features—better thought of as loci—represented clusters of archaeological features associated with two house areas. The loci investigated included a cabin and yard area which were occupied throughout the antebellum and postbellum periods (Features 5, 29) and a house built by 1920 and occupied until 1949 by Sam Scott and his wife Nettie Scott (Feature 30). Specific details of excavations at each of these areas are given in the following discussion.

Mean Artifact Dates, a variation on South's Mean Ceramic Date method, which incorporates datable artifacts such as metals and glass in addition to ceramics, were used to date the assemblages. The author has found that manufacturing date ranges on artifacts such as glass, plastic, and rubber can provide tighter chronological control for late 19th- and early 20th-century sites than ceramics alone. For a detailed discussion of individual features and strata, see Wilkie (1994) and Wilkie and Farnsworth (1992, 1993).

TABLE 1
NUMBER OF TOOLS RECOVERED FROM EACH
AFRICAN-AMERICAN
ASSEMBLAGE AT OAKLEY

Assemblage	Mean Artifact Date (MAD)	Number of Tools Found
Features 5 and 29 (Antebellum)	1842–1843	5
Feature 5 (Silvia Freeman family)	1897	22
Feature 5 (Delphine and Eliza Freeman family)	1923	8
Feature 30 (Samuel and Nettie Scott)	1938.5	0

Historical Archaeology, 1996, 30(4):37–49.
Permission to reprint required.

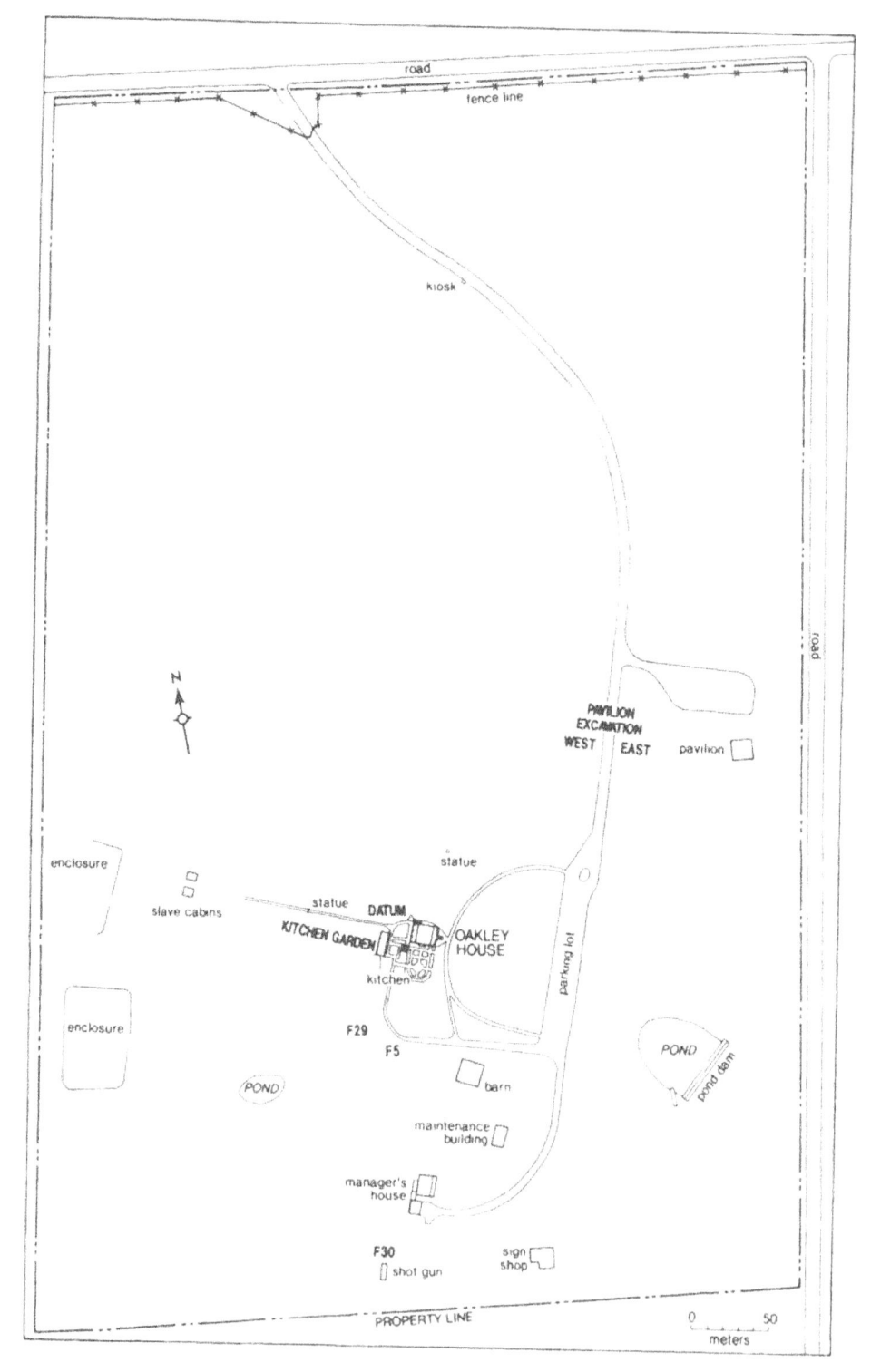

FIGURE 1 Archaeological Features at Oakley Plantation associated with African Americans

Feature 5

The area designated Feature 5 was described by Holland and Orser (1984) as a possible house site. In 1991 the area was tested with four 1-m units and three shovel test pits. The brick foundation of a pier and beam house were identified in association with mid- to late 19th- and early 20th-century materials.

Further testing was undertaken in 1992 to determine the preservation of the structural remains and the extent of the yard area deposits. A 7-x-9-m excavation grid (Grid A) of 1-m units was laid out and oriented along the brick foundations found in 1991 to insure that as far as possible, excavation units outside versus under the structure would be distinct. Both a second 3-m square grid (Grid B) was laid out to the west of Grid A and three additional 1-m units were placed to the south of Grid A to examine further a major artifactual concentration found in 1991.

During the course of excavation, a number of archaeological features were encountered at this locus, including three shallow trash pits, 25 postholes representing the extent of the house, a brick-mining pit, and three trenches. Each of these components was excavated separately, and color, diameter, shape, and depth recorded. This information was important in establishing the chronology of, and associations between, archaeological features at this locus.

Large quantities of material cultural remains were recovered from undisturbed contexts immediately around and under the house, and in the western yard area of the house. Materials recovered from stratigraphic levels and archaeological features determined to be of the same age through their *termini post quem* have been treated as single assemblages. In this way, three assemblages representing activities related to three occupations of the house were identified archaeologically.

Antebellum materials were recovered in the southwestern area of Grid A from a dark grayish-brown mottled clay overlying the sterile clay level and from two small trash pits and provided a Mean Artifact Date (MAD) of 1842.5 (Wilkie 1994:178). Above this level was a yellowish-brown to dark yellowish-brown mottled loam which contained artifacts dating to the end of the 19th century. Additional materials from this time period were recovered from postholes and another small pit. Materials from this level provided a MAD of 1897 (Wilkie 1994:180–181). A brownish-yellow loam overlying the 19th-century strata contained early 20th-century materials which provided a MAD of 1923 (Wilkie 1994:182–183).

Historical Context for Feature 5

The construction of the cabin at Feature 5, based upon its architectural style and archaeological remains, probably took place in the 1840s (Wilkie 1994). Given the proximity of the cabin to the planter residence, the antebellum materials recovered from Feature 5 are most probably associated with an enslaved family that worked in the great house.

Henry Cummings and John Hulbert, former tenants of Oakley, both described this feature during interviews as corresponding to the location of the "cook's house" which was lived in by the African-American Freeman family (Cummings 1991; Hulbert 1992). Most clearly, they remembered a woman named Delphine Freeman working in that capacity during the 1920s and 1930s but thought that her mother had also been a cook. Delphine Freeman had inherited the position from her mother, Silvia Freeman (Wilkie 1994:199–201).

Silvia Freeman and her family worked as domestic servants for the Matthews family through the late 19th and early 20th centuries. The late 19th-century materials from Feature 5 are most likely associated with their occupation of the cabin. Silvia Freeman's employment began sometime in or prior to 1886, when William Wilson and Isabelle Matthews owned the plantation. After Isabelle Matthews's death, Silvia Freeman and her family continued to work as domestics for Lucy and Ida Matthews.

The earliest documentary evidence available for Silvia Freeman is found on her marriage license. On 5 June 1875, Lewis Freeman paid

$50.00 for a license to marry Sylvia [sic] Hill. The date of their actual marriage was not recorded by the parish (West Feliciana Parish Records 1875). Lewis Freeman's family is known to have lived in this ward and parish as early as 1870, but Silvia Hill does not appear in the 1870 West Feliciana census (U.S. Bureau of the Census [USBC] 1870). In 1880, the census shows Silvia Freeman living with Lewis Freeman and their two sons, Joseph and John, at Oakley. Lewis Freeman's occupation was listed as "planter" and Silvia Freeman's as "farming" (USBC 1880).

The earliest reference to Silvia Freeman working in the house as the cook is an 1886 ledger entry in the Oakley Collection. No mention of Lewis Freeman is made in the ledger; however, Silvia Freeman's youngest child was born in 1889 and bears the last name Freeman, suggesting that Lewis Freeman had passed away no earlier than 1888. By 1900, Silvia Freeman is listed as a widow in the manuscript census (USBC 1900).

Silvia Freeman appears to have passed away between 1900 and 1910; she does not appear in the 1910 census. By 1910, Eliza Freeman, presumably "Lizzie" in the 1900 census, and Delphine Freeman were both still living at Oakley. Eliza was working as a servant and Delphine as a cook (USBC 1910).

The Freeman daughters appear in the 1920 census as well; Eliza is listed as "Louisa" Freeman, and still employed as the Matthews house servant (USBC 1920). Henry Cummings (1991) remembers Eliza and Delphine Freeman living together at the plantation through the 1930s but had no clear recollection of their daughters. The 20th-century materials recovered from Feature 5 are most probably related to the Freeman sisters' occupation.

Feature 29

Feature 29 was not previously identified by Holland and Orser (1984). During the 1991 surface collections, a concentration of mid-19th-century artifacts was found eroding at a tree base located to the northwest of, and in close proximity to, Feature 5. A 1-m unit was subsequently excavated to a depth of 40 cm below the surface at this locus. Large quantities of household refuse dating to the 19th century were recovered (Wilkie and Farnsworth 1992). Two additional 1-m units were excavated in 1992 to define further the deposit. Both 1992 units were excavated to depths of 40 cm below the surface and contained concentrations of antebellum household materials. No evidence of architectural remains was found at this loci. Intact, antebellum deposits including pearlwares, shell-edged whitewares, and green-glazed redwares, were recovered, concentrated between 20 and 30 cm deep. These materials place the MAD of this locus at 1843 (Wilkie 1994:185), comfortably within the antebellum period and very close to the 1842.5 date for the antebellum materials recovered at Feature 5.

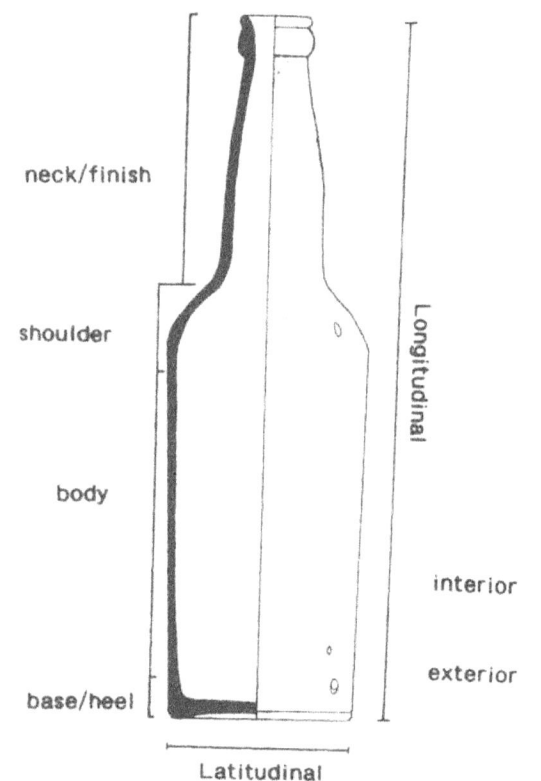

FIGURE 2. Terms used to describe bottle anatomy and sherd orientation during analysis.

TABLE 2
CONTINGENCY TABLE: RETOUCH VERSUS
ANGLE EDGE

Edge Angle	Retouched	Not Retouched
Less than 35°	0	11
Greater than 35°	24	0
Total	24	11

Although it has not been possible to determine which enslaved family may have been associated with the antebellum deposits at Features 5 and 29, the spatial and chronological proximity of these deposits suggests that the two groups of artifacts may both represent the activities of the same enslaved African-American family. Accordingly, glass tools from the antebellum period deposits at Features 5 and 29 were analyzed as a single group.

Feature 30

Feature 30 is the location of the only standing tenant house remaining in the park, and excavations in this area were directed in relationship to this architectural feature. During testing in September 1991, a 5-m grid was excavated north of the house to test the extent of a midden deposit first identified in the summer of 1991. These units contained large quantities of glass, plastic, ceramic, and metal artifacts dating between the 1920s and the 1940s, all concentrated in a soft, black oily midden soil that was 15 cm thick close to the building, and thinning to only a couple of cm thick at the west and north edges of the grid. The back room of the house served as the kitchen, thus likely explaining the large concentration of artifactual materials behind it. The MAD for this feature is 1938.95 (Wilkie 1994:187).

This house is known to have been built about 1920 by African-American Sam Scott. Henry Cummings (1991) remembered Sam, also called Sammy, living in the house with his wife, and for a time, his father. Sam and his wife had no children. John Hulbert (1992), the Scotts' nephew, was also able to provide information about the family. According to Hulbert (1992) and Cummings (1991), the Scotts were the only family to live in this house; therefore, the assemblage recovered here must be associated with them. While no glass tools were recovered from this assemblage, this feature was the only one at Oakley Plantation to produce steel razor blades. The possible impact of razor blades on glass-knapping traditions will be discussed below.

Description of the Glass Tools

In analyzing the 35 glass tools—nearly all made from fragments of glass bottles or jars, it was necessary to define descriptive terms that both reflected the nature of the raw materials used to construct the tools as well as those attributes of the tools which were functionally meaningful. To achieve this end, a standardized set of descriptive terms was used during analysis to describe the portion of the original bottle being utilized, the orientation of the sherd in the original vessel, and the interior and exterior of the bottle. The description of bottle components is drawn from Jones and Sullivan (1985:77, Figure 52) and is comprised of finish, neck-finish, shoulder, body, heel, and base.

In lithic analysis, flake tools typically are described and measured relative to the bulb of percussion (Keeley 1980; Vaughan 1985). Since glass sherds lack such a percussion bulb, it is necessary to use other means to describe them. The form and use of bottle sherds as tools is in part dictated by the original shape of the vessel. To describe the orientation of the utilized edge relative to the sherd's original position in the bottle, the circumference of the bottle is called the latitudinal plane, and the vertical aspect of the bottle is called the longitudinal plane. Therefore, utilized edges that would have been parallel to the base or finish of the intact bottle are referred to as longitudinal edges, and those that would have been perpendicular to the base and finish are referred to as latitudinal edges (Figure 2).

Other variables considered as potentially important attributes include the presence/absence of retouching, the angle of the utilized edge, the shape of the utilized edge, the distribution of use wear along the utilized edge, and placement of the contact edge or leading aspect (Keeley 1980:21) relative to the interior or exterior of the original vessel. To determine whether different attributes were meaningfully linked, contingency tables were constructed to determine if there were meaningful relationships between attributes and, therefore, typological differences between the tools (Sackett 1989).

This level of analysis formed the foundation for microwear analysis and for identifying relationships between use and morphology. Through this analysis, meaningful relationships were established between retouching, edge angle, and sherd orientation. In addition, some patterns related to the portion of the bottle utilized, and the nature of the tools has been established.

Correlating Attributes

Visual observation indicated that the tools fell into two rough groups, including those that had no retouching (n = 11) and those that were unifacially retouched (n = 24). To determine whether retouching may have served a functional purpose, a contingency table was constructed comparing the presence of retouch and the angle of the utilized tool edge. A general relationship has been established by lithic researchers be-

TABLE 4
CONTINGENCY TABLE: EDGE ANGLE AND ASSEMBLAGE OF RETOUCHED TOOLS[a]

	Assemblage		
Edge Angle	Antebellum	Silvia Freeman	Delphine and Eliza Freeman
40°	0	1	0
50°	0	3	6
60°	1	6	2
70°	0	5	2
80°	1	0	0
Total	2	15	7

[a] Retouched tools listed in Table 3 comprise these tools.

tween angle edge and use. For instance, whittling activities are usually associated with acute angles, whereas planing is usually associated with more obtuse edge angles (Keeley 1980:16–17). These criteria were compared, since edge angles had been observed to cluster below 35 degrees and above 45 degrees. The contingency table relating these two variables demonstrated that all of the tools with retouch had edge angles of greater than 35 degrees, while all tools lacking retouch had edge angles smaller than 35 degrees (Table 2). When a second contingency table was constructed relating longitudinal/latitudinal edge utilization with presence/absence of retouching, a correlation was found. All tools with retouching, a total of 24, were utilized on the latitudinal edge of the sherd, while all of the unretouched sherds were utilized on their longitudinal edge (Table 3). A comparison of edge angle by assemblage demonstrated that 60 degrees was the most common edge angle, with Silvia Freeman's assemblage demonstrating the greatest variation (Table 4).

Glass bottles/jars served as the raw material for all but two of the tools, with wine bottles being the most commonly used. The other two tools were made from tumbler sherds. Addi-

TABLE 3
CONTINGENCY TABLE: RETOUCH VERSUS LONGITUDINAL/LATITUDINAL UTILIZATION

Utilization	Retouched	Not Retouched
Latitudinal Edge	0	11
Longitudinal Edge	24	0
Total	24	11

tional comparisons were made to determine whether certain components of the bottles were preferred for retouched versus unretouched tools. Components of the bottles used for tools fell into the categories heel and base, neck and finish, shoulder, and body. Both heel and base and neck and finish are combined because tools were derived from both of these elements, as compared to body and shoulder sherds, which did not contain portions of any other bottle part. This analysis demonstrated that body sherds were most often used for tools. Base and heel sherds were only used to manufacture retouched tools (Table 5), but were by no means the exclusive choice for these tools.

Given the variety of bottle parts represented, several tables were then constructed to compare the distribution of bottle parts being utilized. Within each of the assemblages, body sherds were the most common. Shoulder sherds, used for both retouched and unretouched tools, were only associated with the assemblage of Silvia Freeman (Table 6). Whether the selection of the shoulder sherds represented a personal preference or a functional decision may be clarified when microwear analysis is conducted.

Visual observation suggested that the shape of the contact edge, in addition to edge angle, may be an important attribute for the retouched tools. Retouched tools were found to have concave-or convex-shaped contact edges. Comparison of the shape of the contact edge with bottle part (Table

TABLE 6
CONTINGENCY TABLE: ASSEMBLAGE VERSUS BOTTLE ANATOMY

Bottle Part	Antebellum	Silvia Freeman	Delphine Freeman
Heel and Base	1	1	2
Neck and Finish	1	2	1
Shoulder	0	4	0
Body	3	15	5
Total	5	22	8

7) demonstrated that convex edges were almost exclusively associated with body sherds. Analysis of edge angle with the shape of the contact edge (Table 8) demonstrated that convex contact edges were associated with edge angles of 50–70 degrees, while concave contact edges were associated with a broader range of edge angles (40–80°).

Other correlations failed to reveal meaningful trends. A comparison of edge angles with bottle parts found no correlations. An ambiguous correlation is related to the orientation of leading edges. The majority of the recovered tools utilized the exterior wall of the bottle as its leading or contact edge. However, five examples of interior wall contact edges were included in the assemblage of Silvia Freeman (Table 9). The use of interior versus exterior walls may represent a personal preference, as this decision affects how one grips the tools.

Exploring Potential Functions

Several conclusions can be drawn from the above analysis. First, there are clear correlations between the presence/absence of retouch, edge angle and utilized sherd edge, suggesting the presence of at least two tool types. The first type can be defined primarily as retouched, the second type as unretouched (Figure 3).

All retouched sherds are worked on a latitudinal edge and have an edge angle of greater than

TABLE 5
CONTINGENCY TABLE: RETOUCH AND BOTTLE ANATOMY

Bottle Part	Retouched	Not Retouched
Heel and Base	4	0
Neck and Finish	1	3
Shoulder	3	1
Body	16	7
Total	24	11

35 degrees. The steep edge angle that these tools possess suggest that they functioned as scrapers. The reason for the selection of the latitudinal edge for working may be related to comfort in gripping the finished tool or may reflect differences in ease of knapping along the edges. Given that these tools are retouched, their production required a certain degree of knapping ability and investment of time. They appear, therefore, to be intentionally produced tools.

Convex and concave contact surfaces were noted among the retouched tools; however, it is unclear whether these are meaningful attributes. Concave edges had a broader range of edge angles and bottle body sherds associated with them than did the convex edges. Further exploration of these issues through microwear analysis and comparison with other assemblages is necessary further to define the significance, if any, of these differences.

Bottle bases and heels were used exclusively for retouched tools. Bottle body sherds were the

most common (24 of the 35 tools). Shoulder sherds (n = 4) were only utilized by Silvia Freeman's family. Likewise, Silvia Freeman's assemblage is the only one to include contact edges on the bottle interior. Without an additional level of analysis, such as microwear, or the comparison of these tools with similar examples from other sites, it is not possible to determine which patterns reflect the preferences of the tool knappers/users or represent functional differences.

All of the unretouched sherds exhibit edge wear damage—scarring, pitting, and chipping—on their longitudinal or utilized edges, and all have edge angles of less than 35 degrees. Longitudinal edges are potentially longer and straighter than are latitudinal edges, suggesting that such tools may have been used for cutting rather than scraping. Since longitudinal tools lack retouching, it is not clear whether they were intentionally produced or if glass sherds from broken bottles were selected to be used as expedient tools when necessary. They may, in fact, represent tools of convenience rather than forethought.

Examination of the unretouched tools demonstrates that the wear damage on eight of the 11 was irregularly distributed along the length of both surfaces. This form of wear is typically associated with longitudinal motions, such as sawing or cutting (Vaughan 1985:20). The remaining three examples exhibit dense scarring on both edge surfaces. The motion associated with this distribution is less clear, for such wear has been found associated with both transverse and longitudinal motions (Vaughan 1985:20–21). However, the general pattern suggests that these tools were likely to have been used for cutting rather than scraping.

Putting the Tools in Context

Oral history and an evaluation of other cutting tools recovered from the African-American assemblages at Oakley can provide some insight into tool use. Mintz and Price (1976:48) have documented the use of broken bottles by Africans during the middle passage to shave tradi-

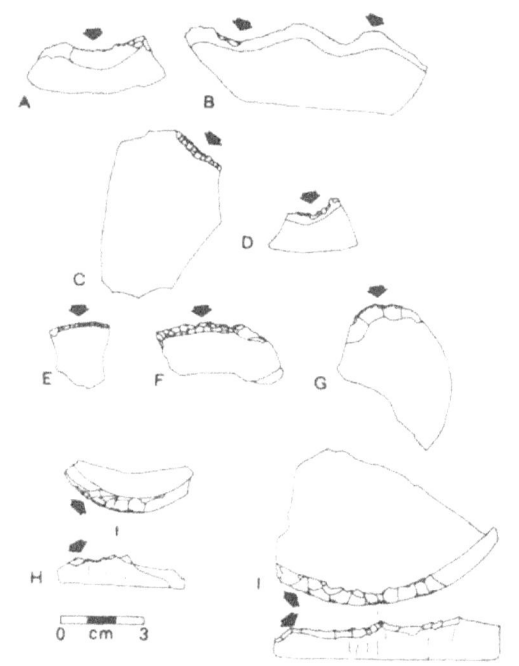

FIGURE 3. Examples of retouched and unretouched tools from Oakley Plantation. A-B, unretouched tools. C-I, retouched tools. Arrows indicate utilized edges.

0　cm　3

TABLE 7
CONTINGENCY TABLE: CONTACT EDGE SHAPE
VERSUS
BOTTLE PART ANATOMY, RETOUCHED TOOLS[a]

Bottle Part	Contact Edge Shape	
	Convex	Concave
Base and Heel	0	4
Shoulder	1	2
Body	10	6
Neck Finish	0	1
Total	11	13

[a]Table 3 comprises this same sample.

tional designs in their hair. The practice of using broken glass as a razor was common in the Bahamas until the 1930s (Ferguson 1995).

In Louisiana, John Hulbert (1992), a former tenant of Oakley, remembers glass tools used on the plantation to smooth axe and hoe handles in the 1930s. He indicated that making such tools was not a skill he possessed, stating that some people on the plantation knew how to break glass in a certain way to make a tool. He compared the use of these tools to the way a razor blade was used for the same purpose. His description suggests that the production of these tools was a specialized skill not shared by the entire tenant population.

John Hulbert's comment that only a few people had the skill to create these tools suggests that by the 1930s, when he was a child, this glass tool tradition may have been becoming less common. The Scott assemblage, Feature 30, contains none of these artifacts but does contain an artifact type not found in the other assemblages: razor blades. Razor blades are a versatile tool that can be used for cutting as well as scraping, depending upon the angle at which they are held. This metal tool can perform the tasks of the glass tools and maintains a functional edge for a longer period of time.

To determine whether there may be a relationship between the appearance of razor blades and the disappearance of glass tools in the Scott assemblage, a review of Oakley Plantation commissary ledgers from the 1890s to 1920 was conducted. These ledgers did not include any purchases of razor blades (Matthews 1889–1891, 1890–1901a, 1890–1901b, 1890–1901c; Matthews and Matthews 1902–1920a, 1902–1920b). The ledgers are nearly complete through the 1890s, and less complete for the remainder of this time period. However, enough of the records are available to demonstrate that razor blades, if available during this time period, were not commonly purchased. Archaeologically, the only other evidence of cutting tools recovered were two broken pairs of scissors from Silvia Freeman's assemblage.

The lack of razor blades in Oakley's commissary records may be related to the cost of purchasing these items. Razor blades, or blades for safety razors, were relatively expensive when first introduced. The 1897 Sears, Roebuck catalog ran the following advertisement for the Star Safety Razor:

An invention which obviates all danger of cutting the face. It is especially adapted to old and young, and is indispensable to travelers, miners and persons camping out. Blades of best steel and fully concave, which can be easily removed and placed in handle for strapping (Israel 1968:112).

The Star Safety Razor sold for $1.50, and extra blades for $1.00. Similarly, straight blade prices started at $.60, and single-bladed pocket knives at $.25, although both items were most commonly available in the $1.50 price range (Israel 1968:112). In 1891, Silvia Freeman was earning $4.00 a month, and had been working at that salary for at least two years (Matthews 1889–1891). The purchase of a knife or razor would therefore represent a significant portion of her monthly income.

No safety razors are listed in the 1900 Sears, Roebuck catalog (DBI Books 1970). By 1908, 10 safety razor blade replacements could be purchased through Sears, Roebuck and Company for a price of $.50 (Schroeder 1971:775). Straight razors were still the razor most commonly available through the catalog, with the cheapest option costing $.96 (Schroeder 1971:773). Prices for pocket knives are not available in this edition of the catalog. The 1927 Sears, Roebuck Catalog advertised 10-packs of razor blades for as low as $.54 (Mirkin 1970:529). Straight razors could be purchased for no less than $1.25 (Mirkin 1970:529), while pocket knives ranged in price from $.79 to $1.89 (Mirkin 1970:510).

The cost of razor blades dropped relative to straight razors and pocket knives between the 1890s and the 1930s. It is possible that the availability of this cheap, commercially-made alternative eventually rendered glass-knapping obsolete. It is also possible that the Scotts, as an individual family, simply did not possess the knapping skills or chose not to participate in this practice. An understanding of glass tools in a broader regional and chronological context is necessary before such conclusions confidently can be drawn.

Razor blades are commonly used today by African Americans in rural Louisiana for cutting, scraping, and whittling (Bibens 1994). If kept in the proximity of the house, razor blades can be

TABLE 8
CONTINGENCY TABLE: CONTACT EDGE SHAPE AND
EDGE ANGLE, RETOUCHED TOOLS[a]

Edge Angle	Contact Edge Shape	
	Convex	Concave
40°	0	1
50°	3	3
60°	5	4
70°	3	4
80°	0	1
Total	11	13

[a] Table 3 comprises this same sample.

TABLE 9
CONTINGENCY TABLE: LEADING EDGE FACE AND ASSEMBLAGE

Assemblage	Leading Edge Face	
	Interior Edge	Exterior Edge
Antebellum	0	5
Silvia Freeman	5	17
Delphine and Eliza Freeman	0	8
Total	5	30

easily stored and used. Pocket knives are certainly a safer portable option. While not the focus of this paper, it is interesting to note that preliminary analysis by the author of artifacts from a late 19th- to early 20th-century trash pit at Crawford Park, 1MB99, an African-American midwife's house site in Mobile, Alabama, has also identified glass tools. All of the tools from that site are retouched and, given the outcome of the Oakley analysis, were probably used as scrapers. While no glass knives have been identified as yet, two pocket knives have been recovered. Again, razor blades may be present at the Scott house instead of glass tools because they may have represented a functional substitution of one artifact type for another.

Glass Tools: A Distinctive African-American Trait?

Intentionally worked glass artifacts are not a new phenomenon and have been recovered from both Native American and other African-American archaeological sites. This discussion will focus upon examples recovered from plantation contexts. Two antebellum and two postbellum planter assemblages were recovered from Oakley Plantation. Neither glass tools nor razor blades were recovered from any of the planter contexts, and Native Americans have not been clearly associated with the sites where these particular tool types were recovered.

TABLE 10
ARCHAEOLOGICAL SITES WHERE WORKED GLASS HAS BEEN
RECOVERED FROM NON-NATIVE AMERICAN CONTEXTS

Site	State	Site Type	Date	Ethnic Affiliation
Oakley Plantation[a]	Louisiana	Plantation	1840s–1940s	African American
Riverlake Plantation[b]	Louisiana	Plantation	1840s–1990s	African American
St. Rose Plantation[c]	Louisiana	Plantation	1790–1810	African American and Euroamerican
Bennett House[d]	Louisiana	Plantation	1840–1860	African American and Euroamerican
Crawford Park[e]	Alabama	Urban house	1890–1910	African American
Garrison Plantation[f]	Maryland	Plantation	early 19th c.	African American
Monticello[g]	Virginia	Plantation	18th–19th c.	African American
Levi-Jordan Plantation[h]	Texas	Plantation	?	African American and Euroamerican

[a] Wilkie (1994)
[b] Site currently under study by the author
[c] Wilkie and Tannert (1994)
[d] Port Hudson State Commemorative Area Archaeological Collections, Louisiana
[e] Site currently under study by the author
[f] Klingelhofer (1987)
[g] Patten (1992)
[h] Anonymous SHA manuscript reviewer (1995, pers. comm.)

In Maryland, Klingelhofer (1987:114–115) found an intentionally chipped tumbler at Garrison Plantation, and reported that similar artifacts had been recovered in Virginia. Patten (1992:6) reports the recovery of chipped glass from Monticello, as well as from other Virginia tidewater sites. The author has identified isolated examples of glass tools from the Bennett House and St. Rose Plantation, both in Louisiana. As noted earlier, significant numbers of these tools are currently under analysis by the author from Crawford Park, and from Riverlake Plantation, Pointe Coupee Parish, Louisiana. Excavations at Riverlake Plantation were focused on the African-American quarters buildings, which have been continuously occupied from the 1840s until the 1990s. Analysis of these materials is ongoing, but the glass tools from these sites will be compared with those from Oakley to determine if broader regional patterns are visible. Of the sites known to the author to contain glass tools, the vast majority come from contexts that are either clearly African American or from contexts which may have been used jointly by African Americans and Euroamericans (Table 10). Such tools have been recovered from both rural and urban settings. At this point, however, published reference to glass tools recovered from strictly Euroamerican contexts has not been found.

What is not clear, however, is whether glass tools are more likely to be recognized in African-American assemblages by archaeologists aware of their presence in other African-American sites. It is important that non-African-American contexts for such tools be explored so that it can be determined whether their production and use is tied to a distinct ethnic heritage or whether they were broadly used by many ethnic groups. The association of such tools with predominately female contexts at both Oakley Plantation and Crawford Park also suggests that glass flake tools, like prehistoric lithics (Gero 1991), deserve further attention for their potential engendered meanings.

Conclusion

Thirty-five utilized glass sherds from African-American contexts have been recovered from Oakley Plantation, West Feliciana Parish, Louisiana. Attribute analysis of these glass sherds has demonstrated that the sherds easily divide into two major groups which seem to be functionally significant, one group of unretouched sherds serving as knives, and the other group of retouched sherds serving as scrapers. Additional differentiations may be identifiable in conjunction with microwear analysis.

The tools were recovered from three different African-American assemblages at Oakley Plantation dating 1840–1930. No glass tools were recovered from the latest African-American assemblage, dating 1920–1940. It is unclear if the absence of tools from this context represents the abandonment of the tradition by this time period or simply represents the nonparticipation of this family. It is suggested that cheaper, commercially manufactured cutting tools such as razor blades may have replaced glass tools at this time.

In closing, the tools discussed in this paper were drawn from strictly African-American contexts. It is unclear at this juncture whether these tools are distinctly African American in nature or if they have only been recognized in African-American contexts. The majority of glass tools reported in the literature have been recovered from rural settings, and it may be that closer examination of glass from Euroamerican rural contexts will reveal the presence of similar practices.

ACKNOWLEDGMENTS

The author would like to thank the Louisiana State Division of Archaeology and the National Park Service for funding archaeological research at Oakley Plantation. Additional assistance was provided by the University of California, Los Angeles, Friends of Archaeology, and students from UCLA and Louisiana State University, who participated in field schools at the site. Finally, I would like to thank Paul Farnsworth, Christopher R. DeCorse, Daniel G. Roberts, and two anonymous reviewers for their comments on this manuscript.

REFERENCES

BIBENS, DAVID
1994 Interview at Riverlake Plantation. Notes on file, Department of Geography and Anthropology, Louisiana State University, Baton Rouge.

CUMMINGS, HENRY
1991 Videotaped Interview at Oakley Plantation. On file, Department of Geography and Anthropology, Louisiana State University, Baton Rouge.

DBI BOOKS
1970 Sears, Roebuck and Co. Consumer Guide, Fall, 1900. DBI Books, Northfield, IL.

FERGUSON, "PAPA D"
1995 Oral History Interview. Crooked Island Bahamas. Notes on file, Department of Anthropology, University of California, Berkeley.

GERO, JOAN M.
1991 Genderlithics: Women's Roles in Stone Tool Production. In Engendering Archaeology: Women and Prehistory, edited by Joan M. Gero and Margaret W. Conkey, pp.163–193. Blackwell, Cambridge.

HOLLAND, CLAUDIA C., AND CHARLES E. ORSER, JR.
1984 A Preliminary Archaeological Investigation of Oakley Plantation, Audubon State Commemorative Area, West Feliciana Parish, Louisiana. Report on file, State Division of Archaeology, Baton Rouge, Louisiana.

HULBERT, JOHN
1992 Interview in Baton Rouge. Notes on file, Department of Geography and Anthropology, Louisiana State University, Baton Rouge.

ISRAEL, FRED L.
1968 1897 Sears, Roebuck Catalogue. Chelsea House, NY.

JONES, OLIVE, AND CATHERINE SULLIVAN
1985 The Parks Canada Glass Glossary. Government Publishing Centre, Québec.

KEELEY, LAWRENCE
1980 Experimental Determination of Stone Tool Uses. University of Chicago Press, Chicago, IL.

KLINGELHOFER, ERIC
    1987   Aspects of Early Afro-American Material Culture:
            Artifacts from the Slave Quarters at Garrison
            Plantation, Maryland. *Historical Archaeology*
            21(2):112–119.

MATTHEWS, ISABELLE
    1889–   Plantation Ledger Kept by Isabelle Matthews. Oakley
    1891   Collection. Audubon State Commemorative Area, St.
            Francisville, LA.
    1890–   Store Receipts. Oakley Collection. Audubon State
    1901a   Commemorative Area, St. Francisville, LA.
    1890–   Store Receipts. James Pirrie Bowman Papers.
    1901b   Louisiana and Lower Mississippi Valley Collections.
            Hill Memorial Library, Louisiana State University,
            Baton Rouge.
    1890–   Store Receipts, Turnball-Slocum Papers. Louisiana
    1901c   and Lower Mississippi Valley Collections. Hill Memorial
            Library, Louisiana State University, Baton Rouge.

MATTHEWS, LUCY, AND IDA MATTHEWS
    1902–   Store Receipts. Oakley Collection. Audubon State
    1920a   Commemorative Area, St. Francisville, LA.
    1902–   Store Receipts, Turnball-Slocum Papers. Louisiana
    1920b   and Lower Mississippi Valley Collections. Hill Memorial
            Library, Louisiana State University, Baton Rouge.

MINTZ, SIDNEY, AND RICHARD PRICE
    1976   *The Birth of African-American Culture*. Beacon Press,
            NY.

MIRKIN, ALAN (EDITOR)
    1970   *1927 Edition of the Sears, Roebuck Catalogue*. Bounty,
            NY.

PATTEN, DRAKE
    1992   Mankala and Minkisi: Possible Evidence of African-
            American Folk Beliefs and Practices. *African-
            American Archaeology* 6.5–7.

SACKETT, JAMES R.
    1989   Statistics, Attributes, and the Dynamics of Burin
            Typology. In Alternative Approaches to Lithic
            Analysis, edited by Donald O. Henry and George H.
            Odell. *Archaeological Papers of the American
            Anthropological Association* 1:51–82.

SCHROEDER, JOSEPH J.
    1971   *1908 Sears, Roebuck Catalogue*. DBI Books,
            Northfield, IL.

UNITED STATES BUREAU OF THE CENSUS (USBC)
    1870   Population Census, West Feliciana Parish, Louisiana.
            U.S. Government Printing Office, Washington, DC.
    1880   Population Census, West Feliciana Parish, Louisiana.
            U.S. Government Printing Office, Washington, DC.
    1900   Population Census, West Feliciana Parish, Louisiana.
            U.S. Government Printing Office, Washington, DC.
    1910   Population Census, West Feliciana Parish, Louisiana.
            U.S. Government Printing Office, Washington, DC.
    1920   Population Census, West Feliciana Parish, Louisiana.
            U.S. Government Printing Office, Washington, DC.

VAUGHAN, PATRICK C.
    1985   *Use-Wear Analysis of Flaked Stone Tools*. University
            of Arizona Press, Tucson.

WEST FELICIANA PARISH RECORDS
    1875   Marriage License of Lewis Freeman and Silvia Hill.
            Marriage Book C, No. 161. Recorded 5 June 1875.
            West Feliciana Parish, LA.

WILKIE, LAURIE A.
    1994   *"Never Leave Me Alone": An Archaeological Study
            of African-American Ethnicity, Race Relations and
            Community at Oakley Plantation*. Ph.D. dissertation,
            Archaeology Program, University of California, Los
            Angeles. University Microfilms International, Ann
            Arbor, MI.

WILKIE, LAURIE A., AND PAUL FARNSWORTH
    1992   National Register Testing at Oakley Plantation
            (16WF34), West Feliciana Parish, Louisiana, 1991.
            Report on file, State Division of Archaeology, Baton
            Rouge, LA.
    1993   National Register Testing at Oakley Plantation
            (16WF34), West Feliciana Parish, Louisiana, 1992.
            Report on file, State Division of Archaeology, Baton
            Rouge, LA.

WILKIE, LAURIE A., AND STEPHANIE TANNERT
    1994   An Archaeological and Historical Investigation of
            Site 16SC77 Discovered During Construction of State
            Project No. 700-19-0001 F.A.P. No. HES-373-1(004),
            St. Rose-Destrehan Highway Route LA 48, St. Charles
            Parish. Report on file, State Division of Archaeology,
            Baton Rouge, LA.

LAURIE A. WILKIE
DEPARTMENT OF ANTHROPOLOGY
UNIVERSITY OF CALIFORNIA
BERKELEY, CALIFORNIA 94720–3710

RODERICK SPRAGUE

Glass Trade Beads: A Progress Report

ABSTRACT

The use of glass trade beads as a good chronological marker has been hampered by a lack of precise terminology and uniform description. There has also been a profound lack of appreciation of what is in reality a large series of complex manufacturing techniques that vary with time and geography. The several manufacturing techniques can be grouped into drawn, wound, mold-pressed, fired, blown, and a few minor techniques. Suggestions are made for describing the physical appearance of beads. Suggested levels of analysis include laboratory analysis, historical analysis, and cultural analysis.

Introduction

It has become customary in historical archaeological reports for the section on glass trade beads to contain a perfunctory statement on bead manufacturing techniques. These statements are invariably condensations from one of several available secondary sources. Since each secondary source is usually based on one primary source, the secondary sources as well as the tertiary statements are usually descriptions of one specific time period in one specific country, and more often than not, they have little or no relationship to the beads being described. Too often, the bead descriptions do not follow any established format and include new and confusing terminology. The data presented in one report will not be comparable to another, thus making any comparative analysis virtually impossible. It is in response to these and other problems that this work is addressed.

What follows is not another typology or classification but rather a statement of the current status of bead description and analysis. For classification studies see the works of Beck (1928); Stone (1970:288–294, 1974:88–89); Kidd and Kidd (1970); Bass et al. (1971); Lugay (1974); Smith and Good (1982); and Meighan (n.d.). Any use of Kidd and Kidd (1970) must also include Karklins (1982); however, Smith (1983:4) has expressed additional concerns.

Bead Manufacturing

Before glass trade beads can be truly appreciated, it is necessary to understand the various techniques of manufacture. Virtually all analytical classifications found in the trade bead literature utilize manufacturing techniques as the first level of analysis. Meighan (n.d.: 37) using size, shape, and color; and DiPeso et al. (1974: 228) using shape are the major modern exceptions. The terms applied to the basic technology unfortunately have not been standardized, and very different terms are used by equally knowledgeable researchers. The major advantage of the several basic terms suggested here over many of the others is that they refer to the process of manufacturing not to a geometric description of the bead after it is manufactured (Karklins, pers. comm.). For example, what is called a drawn bead here is often called a tubular or cane bead. Tubular and cane imply the shape, but not all tubular beads are necessarily made by the drawn process. This work is based on a three page summary formulated over 15 years ago (Sprague 1966) and has been distributed among students and bead researchers ever since.

As the bead making industry has progressed, it has advanced through several broad evolutionary stages. Specific techniques such as "baked" beads and some geographical areas such as the Middle East have been more conservative than others. While not using these specific terms, Francis (1983b:193–194) suggested a three stage bead making development of cottage industry, large-scale industry, and mechanization.

Drawn Beads

The most commonly occurring bead in most archaeological sites is the drawn bead (Figure

1a–1e) also known as tubular drawn, cane, hollow-cane (Harris and Harris 1967:135), tube (Kidd and Kidd 1970:50), and cut (Storm 1976:106). The major process involved in making drawn beads has been described many times; however, three publications in English have priority as the best compilation *from* the primary sources: Murray (1964), van der Sleen (1967), and Kidd and Kidd (1970). One of the best primary sources in the English language is a work edited by Dionysius Lardner, the earliest edition of which is 1832. It bears a striking similarity to an even earlier work (Anonymous 1825). Lardner's (1832) description of drawn bead manufacturing on the island of Murano in the Bay of Venice reads:

> When upon inspection the coloured glass is found to be in a fit state for working, the necessary quantity is gathered in the usual manner upon the rod, and is blown into a hollow form. A second workman then provides himself with an appropriate instrument, with which he takes hold of the glass at the end which is farthest from the extremity of the rod, and the two men running thereupon expeditiously in exactly opposite directions, the glass is drawn out into a pipe or tube, in the manner of those used for constructing thermometers, the thickness of which depends upon the distance by which the men separate themselves. Whatever this thickness may be, the perforation of the tube is preserved, and bears the same proportion relatively to the substance of the glass as was originally given to it by the blower.
>
> Tubes striped with different colors are made by gathering from two or more pots lumps of different coloured glass, which are united by twisting them together before they are drawn out to the requisite length.
>
> As soon as they are sufficiently cool for the purpose, the tubes are divided into equal lengths, sorted according to their colours and sizes, packed in chests, and then dispatched to the city of Venice, within which the actual manufacture of the beads is conducted.
>
> When they arrive at the bead manufactory, the tubes are again very carefully inspected, and sorted according to their different diameters, preparatory to their being cut into pieces sufficiently small for making beads.
>
> For performing this latter operation, a sharp iron instrument is provided, shaped like a chissel, and securely fixed in a block of wood. Placing the glass tube upon the edge of this tool at the part to be separated, the workman then, with another sharp instrument in his hand, cuts, or chips, the pipe into pieces of the requisite size; the skill of the man being shown by the uniformity of size preserved between the different fragments.
>
> The minute pieces thus obtained are in the next process thrown into a bowl containing a mixture of sand and wood ashes, in which they are continually stirred about until the perforation in the pieces are all filled by the sand and ashes. This provision is indispensable, in order to prevent the sides from falling together when softened by heat in the next operation.
>
> A metallic vessel with a long handle is then provided, wherein the pieces of glass are placed, together with a further quantity of wood-ashes and sand; and the whole being subjected to heat over a charcoal fire, are continually stirred with a hatchet-shaped spatula. By this simple means the beads acquire their globular form.
>
> When this has been imparted, and the beads are again cool, they are agitated in sieves, in order to separate the sand and ashes; this done, they are transferred to other sieves of different degrees of fineness, in order to divide the beads according to their various sizes. Those of each size are then, after being strung by children upon separate threads, made up into bundles, and packed in casks for exportation.

A work published slightly later (Anonymous 1835:78–80) describes the hollow sphere as two cones made by two workers and put together. The softening of the broken edges (heat finishing) is done by tumbling in "a sheet iron cylinder about eighteen inches in length and a foot in width, with an iron handle to it . . . thrust into the furnace and subject to a rotatory motion." This source also states that the beads were polished by rubbing them with cloth. Knight (1874:254) has an excellent drawing of a rotary heat finishing furnace. Gasparetto (1958:198) lists 1817 as the date for the introduction of the tumbling type of finishing. Tayenthal (1900:21) gives "the end of the 80's" (1880s) as the date for the introduction of the Italian drawn bead techniques into Jablonec (Gablonz).

A later work (Pellatt 1849) not only gives a description for drawn bead manufacture similar to Lardner (1832) but also presents excellent illustrations, which have been reproduced frequently in secondary sources, to show the drawing process as well as the process for making striped beads. This procedure, known as casing or flashing (Kidd 1979:57), is lucidly described in a still later work (Lock 1879:1073–1074) but using the same illustration:

> A mass of molten glass attached to the blow-pipe is pressed into a circular open mold, around and inside of which, short lengths of coloured cane have been arranged. The mass is withdrawn with the canes adhering to its surface, and after being rolled upon the marver to effect

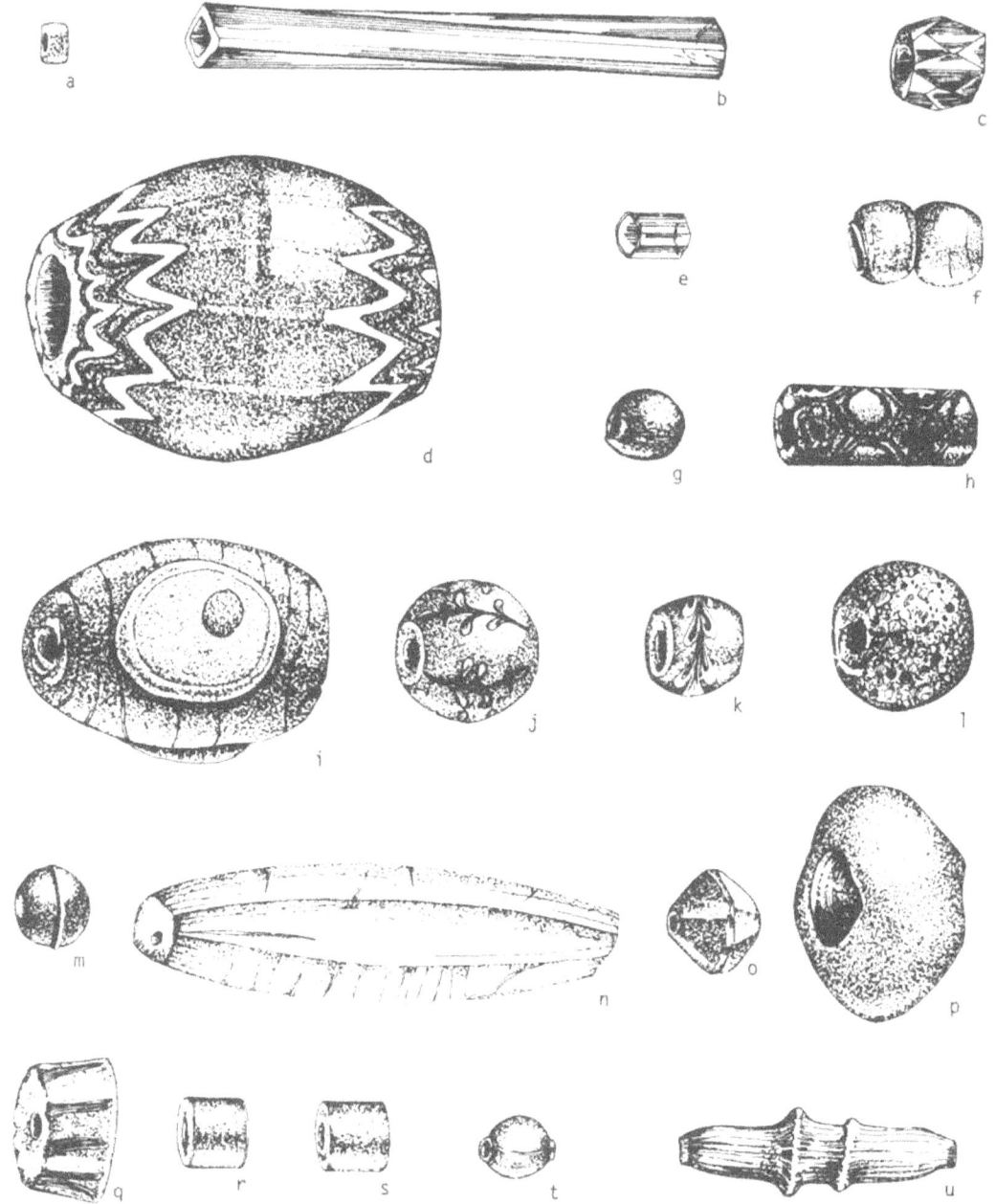

FIGURE 1 Examples of major bread types discussed in the text. a, drawn pony bead; b, drawn square, striped, and twisted bead; c, drawn, facetted "Russian" bead; d, drawn chevron bead; e, drawn short bugle bead; f, double wound bead; g, wound bead showing projection; h, wound *millefiorri* bead; i, wound eye bead; j, wound floral spray or arabesque bead; k, wound squiggle bead; l, wound crumb bead; m, pressed round bead; n, pressed elongated faceted bead; o, mandrel pressed bead; p, donkey bead; q, African baked bead; r, tile bead, smooth end; s, tile bead, rough end; t, blown collared bead; u, blown fancy bead.

amalgamation, is drawn out in the usual manner. If short lengths of variegated cane be used in the above process, in the place of plain coloured cane, the section of the cane produced will bear some resemblance to a flower.

An excellent 20th century work (Anonymous 1919) presents a picture of improvements through mechanization. One major difference in this later description is that the gather is not blown hollow; rather, a cup-shaped area is scooped out and pressed into the glass and then blown (Anonymous 1919:606). The final polishing in this report is called "lucidation" and was accomplished "with emery paste or other grinding material, or even sawdust" (Anonymous 1919:608). Two recent publications (Francis 1979b; Kidd 1979) list several other alternatives to these procedures and suggest that each master craftsman had his own variations on the basic technique.

Allen (1983b:27) makes the disarmingly simple but vitally important observation that there are four major ways in which drawn beads can be finished from the basic cane. These are: "1) beads finished in a cold state, individually; 2) beads finished in a cold state, *en masse;* 3) beads finished in a warm state, individually; and 4) beads finished in a warm state, *en masse.*" While Allen's concern was with rosetta beads, the four classes still hold true for all drawn beads. Type 1 involves alteration by grinding on wheels. Type 2, according to Allen (1983b:28), is a late process involving cold tumbling in an abrasive. Tayenthal (1900:21) mentions the use of sandstone. Type 3 is a poorly known process of working canes on a spit within a flame, a process discussed in more detail below. Type 4 is the typical drawn bead process discussed in detail above.

Francis (1982, 1983b) has reported two quite different drawing techniques from India. In one process the gather is drawn out by one person rather than two. This is accomplished after "the free end of the glass is quenched in a bucket, an iron rod is stuck into this end, and the rod is put in a sand pile or on hooks driven into the ground" (Francis 1982:14). The other process (Francis 1982:17) is an ingenious one involving the creation of a vacuum "not unlike that used by modern automatic drawing machines such as the Danner method" discussed below.

Certain characteristics are found in different beads depending on their manufacturing technique and help to identify the bead. The small bubbles found as inclusions in the glass tend to be elongated in the same direction as the perforation in drawn beads since the originally round bubbles have been distorted by the drawing process.

Any number of additional variations can be made on the basic technique. The gather of molten glass, before being drawn out, can be shaped on a marver or marvering surface (i.e., a flat, or in some cases corrugated piece of marble, bronze, or cast iron), or the gather can be formed in a mold into square or other geometric shapes and can even be twisted as it is drawn out to give a combination of traits such as a square, striped, and twisted bead (Figure 1b).

To define the structure of drawn beads, in the past, strong support has been given to the terms "simple" for one layer of glass, "compound" for two or more layers, and "complex" as having decorative designs made of glass elements pressed into the bead as suggested by Duffield and Jelks (1961:40–41). Stone (1974:88–89) solved the basic weakness of this system by setting up four levels of structure: 1) simple—composed of one layer; 2) compound—composed of two or more layers; 3) complex—utilizing applique or inset designs; and 4) composite—involving both compound and complex attributes.

The abbreviations recommended by Duffield and Jelks (1961:41) are still valid despite their lack of acceptance over the past 20 or so years:

In the following descriptions of the beads an abbreviated set of terms is employed for designating the structure of the compound and complex (and composite) specimens. The term used for a tubular bead made up of two or more concentric layers of glass lists the layers by color, beginning with the exterior layer and ending with the central core. For example, a bead with a blue glass core and an exterior layer of white glass would be termed White/Blue (this may be read as white over blue). A bead with three layers might be designated Clear/Red/Green, or a more complex form might be labeled Red-and-White (swirled)/Green/Red. Some of the beads have stripes, dots, or other designs formed by tiny glass rods or dots that are embedded in one of the constituent layers. This feature is indicated by the use of the symbol <. For example, many of the Cornaline d'Aleppo beads are listed as Clear/Red<White Stripe/Green, which may be translated as: a clear glass exterior layer, a second layer of red glass into the surface of which are inlaid white rods that form stripe patterns, and a central core of green glass. White<Blue Dots/Blue would indicate a bead with a blue glass core and a white exterior layer into which are embedded blue dots.

It is true this technique combines elements of structure, color, and ornamentation, but it is still useful for reducing bead descriptions. The order of layer description is illogical. It makes more sense to describe them in the order they were manufactured; however, the convention appears to be established.

Most drawn beads are used in beaded work and are often given the designation embroidery beads. It is hoped that the term garter bead as used by Harris et al. (1965) will not gain widespread acceptance beyond its two or three other uses in the literature. The smaller embroidery beads are usually called seed beads. Francis (1979a; 1981a:9) also lists micro bead, sand bead, and bead–work bead and indicates that what are called seed beads would be better not called by that name, because they are not made from seeds. The larger varieties of drawn beads for bead work are often called pony beads or pound beads (Figure 1a). Conn (1972:7–8) defines seed beads as 0–2 mm, pony beads as 3–5 mm, and an undesignated group, 2–3 mm as intermediate.

Nesbitt (1878) and Francis (1979b) divide 16th century Italian drawn bead makers into two classes: 1) *Margariteri*, makers of small beads such as seed beads; and 2) *Perlai* or *Paternosteri*, makers of larger beads that are further finished by hand techniques. Gasparetto (1958:186) gives greater detail on the history of these and other terms such as *conterie*. Originally *conterie* refered to *perle a lume* or lamp beads made by winding as described below and from large tubes. From the 1800s *conterie* replaces *margarite* as the term for small drawn beads (Gasparetto 1958:235–236). There is a complex and contorted history of the specializations within the Italian bead industry to

which the recent works in English on the subject (Kidd 1979; Francis 1979b) do not do justice. Francis has presented unpublished summaries of the Italian bead industry chronology (Allen 1980:3) that would be welcome in print.

A little noticed statement by Gasparetto concerning the second class of large drawn beads *(Paternoster)* has been referred to in English only, very briefly by Francis (1979b:8). Gasparetto (1958:186) describes this process for heat finishing drawn beads as contrasted to the iron pan or rotary furnace: "sections of hollow tubes of larger thickness, strung on a 'spit,' were softened in the fire of the furnace." (The original quote reads: " . . . *si ammollivano dei pezzetti di canna forata di grosso spessore, infilati in una sorta di spiedo, al fuoco della fornace . . .*)." It is interesting that Gasparetto (1958:186) uses *spiedo* (spit) rather than *mandrino* (mandrel). However, elsewhere he also states that "the pontil of the smaller size is called spit" (Gasparetto 1958:242). The original reads: "*Il 'pontello' pi'u piccolo chianasi anche 'speo' (spiedo) . . . .*" The final shaping was done with hand tools or a bronze mold (Gasparetto 1958:187). This method corresponds to Allen's (1983b:28) Type 3 finishing technique. More research is needed to place this technique in its proper chronological position.

The large, blue, facetted beads (Figure 1c), popularly called Russian trade beads, are made according to one theory by marvering six, seven, or eight sides to a drawn bead gather (Woodward 1964, pers. comm.). However, examination of these beads shows striations, concave facets, and other surface textures that argue logically against this hypothetical manufacturing technique. It has been suggested by Ross (1975, pers. comm.) that these beads are made by some undefined extrusion technique. Gasparetto (1958:241) states that facetted beads are made by placing the gather in a metal mold.

According to a similar but doubtful theory of marvering, the rosetta bead (Figure 1d); also known as chevron, star, star chevron, *Paternoster*, aggry, or sun bead (Karklins and Sprague [1980] found chevron the most common and accepted term in the literature, but Allen [1983a:19; 1983c:177] gives a convincing argument for rosetta as generic, star as unground, and chevron as ground.) was made by dipping two colors of glass, one after another, and then marvering across a corrugated surface, followed by two more colors and marvering again until the number of desired layers had been built up. After being drawn out and cut into segments the star beads were often ground on the ends to expose the various layers and give the traditional chevron appearance (Neuburg 1949:54, 1962:22). Kidd (1979:14) reverses his earlier work (Kidd and Kidd 1970:49) and concludes that rosetta and square beads, like faceted beads, were made by blowing the gather in a mold of the proper shape. Smith and Good (1982:17) go into even more detail in reference to Nueva Cadiz square beads and conclude that "the hollow bubble of molten glass, either in one or multiple layers, is blown into an open, square, bucket-like mold to form a square cross section." Thus the evidence is becoming stronger that rosetta, square, multi-sided, and even melon beads were all formed in a mold, not by marvering. Allen (1983c:185) disagrees to the extent that he says the gather is formed in a mold, not blown. Allen (1983a:22) clearly points out, however, that all descriptions of "rosetta bead manufacture are *essentially speculative in nature*" (original italics). He (Allen 1983b:24) summarizes the most likely process thus: "1) forming of the core layer of the *gather*, that surrounds the bubble of air, 2) layering the gather with additional glass (*casing* [plating]), 3) molding the gather, and 4) drawing the gather." Steps 2 and 3 may be repeated. According to Revi (1959:262) the term plated is more appropriate than casing when the "casing" is external.

The large, faceted beads often have additional facets ground on the ends at approximately a 45° angle to the axis of the bead. These were apparently ground by hand on stone wheels. This is an example of Allen's (1983b:27–28) Type 1 finishing technique. Other faceted drawn beads were not hot tumbled but sold with sharp and irregular edges (Figure 1e). These might be thought of as a fifth technique of "no finish." Woodward (1965:11) calls these short bugles. The 17th century great bugles were much longer, one to four inches. It is difficult to interpret him without illustrations, but Woodward (1965:11–12) seems to imply that the typical blue faceted beads were called short bugles, "O.P." beads, or rods.

According to Désiré F. deTremaudan (1969, pers. comm.), a major importer of beads in Victoria, British Columbia, during the 20th century, seed beads were packaged in special units of measure: 10 threads = 1 tassle and 10 tassles (100 strings) = 1 bunch. Gasparetto (1958:200) lists units of measure used by the women stringing beads, but these apparently were not used outside the stringing process. Terms used in the selling of strung beads to the next processor could be translated as: 20 strings = 1 bunch, 12 bunches (240 strings) = 1 complete bunch [bundle?]. A source early in the century (Anonymous 1919:607) states that "for very small beads the string was about 10 in. long and for longer beads about 18 in. long. A bundle then consisted of 480 strings." This source also gives some indication of how beads were sold at that time:

> Some classes of beads are bunched for weight and others for number. Many of the small beads are sold by number. Such beads are sometimes referred to as "count beads," while those sold by weight are known to the English trade as "pound beads" [Anonymous 1919:608].

Some seed beads are made today, especially in Japan, by a machine technique that among other things can produce a round seed bead with a square hole (Hoffman and Ross 1974:74). The first successful automatic system was invented by Edward Danner in 1917 (Douglas and Frank 1972:46–51). The Danner process as defined in his three basic patents (Danner 1917a, 1917b, 1917c) is clearly a mechanized process for producing drawn beads. The fact that the machine can include a rotating mandrel (see below) should in no way lead to the erroneous conclusion of some researchers that this is a wound process. Danner (1917a) in his first patent titles it a "process of drawing" and describes the drawing of both tubes and rods.

Wound Beads

In terms of the number of beads that have been recovered archaeologically, the second most common technique of manufacture is the wound bead (Figure 1f–1m), also known as wire wound, wire wrapped, mandrel wound, turned (Anonymous 1884:819), or coiled. By spun, Cleland (1972:184) presumbaly means wound. Because wound beads are usually strung rather than sewn to a backing, they are often called necklace beads. Francis (1979b:9) calls Italian–made wound beads, lamp beads (*perle a lume*), and Kidd (1979:21) calls them *suppialume*, a term better applied to the makers of lamp beads (Gasparetto 1958:245). The spiral bead of van der Sleen (1967:26) is also in reality just another type of wound bead.

In the wound process a cane or rod of glass without a central hole, made in essentially the same manner as the drawn bead, is heated over a small flame until it is in a plastic state and is then wound around a wire or mandrel. The mandrel may be coated with graphite, clay, or other materials to aid in removal of the beads after cooling. A German patent in 1922 was for a coating of half aluminum oxide and half koalin (Paisseau 1922). The winding can be once around with a fairly noticeable joint, or it can be done with very fine filaments several times around. During some periods a slight projection will be left where the rod is broken loose from the bead (Figure 1g). A dexterous worker can make beads in this manner very quickly. Often the beads were made so close together that they occasionally became fused together forming a variant form of a double or multiple bead (Figure 1f). The Bonnet bead making machine (Cousen 1924), an improvement of the 1920s, is little more than a machine rotating the wire in contrast to the former practice of the worker manipulating the glass and the wire.

As mentioned above, inclusion bubbles in drawn beads elongate in the direction of the perforation. On the other hand, bubbles in wound beads tend to elongate around the axis of the perforation. It is also often possible to observe the separate filaments used in the winding or to observe the juncture of the winding. It has been assumed in the past that there is also a tendency for wound beads from Italy to show black graphite or iron oxide inside the perforation while those from China tend to have accumulations of white clay; however, Francis (1983b:202) has shown this to be less than accurate. The most common Chinese beads, also popularly known as Canton or Peking beads, are wound beads characterized by numerous bubbles and an especially glossy surface. According to Liu (1975:14) the process for making wound Chinese beads as explained by Chu and Chu (1973) would explain the presence of clay inclusions within the actual glass of the bead. Chu and Chu (1973:138) state:

> One man who remembers watching his aunts at work in South China not far from Canton [Guangzhou] (for glass beads were made in many locations throughout China) told us that long bamboo reeds were dipped into troughs of wet clay slip, then taken out and dried. When the reeds were ready—and it is assumed that large piles of them were prepared in advance—two people would hold one reed as a third poured threads of molten glass at intervals on it. The two end people twirled the reed, making the glass form into beads. When the glass had hardened but not yet cooled, the reed was laid on a bed of dry clay. When completely cool, the beads were shaken off into water to be washed.

Francis (1979c:12) has shown an important distinction between the usual European wound bead technique described above using solid glass rods over a flame and two other techniques involving molten glass. In one the workers "wind the mandrel directly into the molten glass in the furnace," and in the other, they "draw the glass out and wind it onto the mandrel outside of the furnace." Francis (1981b:39) described these processes in another source thus: 1) "made by dipping the mandrel into the glass box in the furnace and twirling the mandrel until sufficient glass is gathered" and 2) "the scoop wound (glass drawn out by scoop and dripped over a rotating mandrel) method." Pazaurek (1911:1) lists the "at the glass furnace" winding as the oldest technique and "today no longer popular." He fails to mention more advanced methods for making wound beads.

Francis (1983b:194) has also reported an important difference in the smoothing of wound beads with a pincher tool or a half–mold. Italian beads with the pincher tool will not have the ends smoothed so that the winding will still show while Czechoslovakian and Japanese beads, made with a half–mold, will be smoothed over the entire surface. Chinese beads must have been smoothed by a technique similar to the latter method. According to Francis (1982:11) in one area of India, wound beads are also smoothed on a half–mold:

> While still hot, the beads are shaped to near perfection in iron half–molds. These are dies made of small metal cubes with depressions on one face corresponding to half the ultimate section of the bead. Grooves running from the center of the depression to the edge of the die allow the wire to rest in them. The bead and wire are laid on the half–mold and the wire is twirled, shaping the bead by this rolling action in the depression.

The wound bead is also the basic background for many forms of additional work in inlay or appliqué for forming "fancy" or "polychrome" beads. Allen (1982) presents the most detailed discussion of mosaic beads. Francis (1979b:14–15) lists special types of wound beads as: *millefiori* (thousand flowers; Figure 1h), eye (Figure 1i; see Smith 1982 for a full discussion of drawn construction eye or "flush–eye" beads), floral spray or arabesque (Figure 1j), combed, and squiggle (Figure 1k). The crumb or frit surface bead (Figure 1l) is still another probable Italian fancy bead found in the 19th century. As early as A.D. 200–552 the Japanese are reported to have been "inserting bits of hard glass into the bead while still soft" (Salmon 1976:48).

The best description of the making of fancy beads in English is found in an anonymous source (Anonymous 1867:760):

> The art of bead-making at the lamp, "Perle alla Lucerna," is, as we have said before, quite a separate business. In working at the lamp, tubes and rods of glass and enamel are used. It is impossible to describe all the manipulations of this ingenious art, over which the taste and dexterity of the artist so entirely preside. But we may give an example: a black bead, decorated with roses, forget–me–nots, and leaves of aventurine. The artist first takes a rod of black glass, and melting it in the blow pipe flame of the lamp, twists it about an iron wire until he has made a small ball of the required size, rolling it on a kind of iron mould with a circular groove, and smoothing it with an iron tool until it has acquired a perfectly spherical shape. He then takes a small rod of aventurine, and softening it in the flame, traces on the black glass ball leaves of [or] any other pattern that may be required, and smooths it again with the iron tool. He next traces with a small rod of rose–coloured enamel the roses on the ball, smoothing it as before with the smoothing tool. The forget–me–nots are next traced on the bead with a small rod of blue and white enamel, that has been previously twisted together spirally in the flame, and drawn out to about the diameter of a shawl pin. The bead thus completed is taken off the wire, and left to cool in a box filled with sand.

A series of beads obtained in 1976 from a dealer included a defective one with the hole filled by a copper wire. This was a spherical bead made to imitate turquoise, perhaps a modern example of one of the so–called Hubble class of beads. It was speculated that such wound beads could be left on the copper wire and the wire removed by nitric acid or other strong acids. A film observed in Rochester, New York in 1982 also showed modern Italian beads being made according to this procedure. This technique is referred to as an older, less satisfactory method of manufacture in a 1922 German patent issued to a Parisian, Paisseau (1922). A 1925 German patent (apparently also 1924 in France) to the same individual (Paisseau 1925) describes the use of multiple wire cores and asbestos wire covered with sodium or potassium silicate. The requirement was for a core that was easily dissolved chemically but still able to withstand torsion, flexion, and the lateral pressure of mechanical bead manufacture. Beads wound on a wire *could* be finished with a pincer type of mold, perhaps the mold actually cutting the wire.

The special type of bead, popularly called a *Cornaline d'Aleppo*, was made during the 19th and 20th centuries by both drawn and wound methods. From personal observation, the chronology for this ancient bead type in western North America begins with a two–color bead composed of a light green core that appears almost black without sufficient backlighting; this is covered by a brick red outer layer. By 1830 this had been replaced by a dark ivory center still with a brick red outer layer. Around 1860 the core had become white, and by 1880 the outer layer had become a much more brilliant red due to the introduction of modern dyes. This bead, in the drawn form, often has a third layer of clear glass over the red. The chronology and the term Hudson's Bay for this bead as suggested by Francis (1979a:39, 58, 66) are not supported by the evidence in the Northwest. The source of this confusion may be Orchard (1929:88–89). More Northwest collectors call the blue facetted ''Russian'' bead a ''Hudson's Bay'' bead than use the term for the *Cornaline d'Aleppo*. No less than nine times, Quimby (1978) equates ''Russian'' beads with ''Hudson's Bay'' beads.

The inherent problem with rigid classifications for beads such as the one suggested by Kidd and Kidd (1970) is illustrated by one *Cornaline d'Aleppo* type recovered from the Ozette site on the coast of Washington. This bead type, which has been personally observed, is composed of a drawn white core with a wound red exterior. Karklins (1982:95), working from the same specimens, calls these ''wound-on-drawn'' and suggests that it is a manufacturing class separate from both drawn and wound. Karklins (1982) also suggests how to expand the Kidd and Kidd system to include entirely new forms. Smith (1983:4) however casts doubt on the complete success of Karklins' proposal.

Mold-Pressed Beads

Utilizing dictionary definitions, the terms molded (moulded) and pressed are obviously interchangeable. Mold or molded can mean ''to give shape to [a] malleable substance,'' ''to form by pouring or pressing into a mold,'' or ''blown in a mold'' (Gove 1976:1454). Pressed is defined as ''compacted or molded by pressure: squeezed together into some form'' (Gove 1976: 1795). To further confuse the situation, pressed glass is defined as being manufactured ''by being pressed into a mold while still plastic'' (Gove 1976:1795). My translator of Pazaurek (1911:19) suggested ''stamped bead'' for the German *Druckperlenerzeugung*, a possible term to be added to the literature. An earlier draft of this work attempted to make a distinction between molded and pressed, an effort now abandoned as not meaningful. The suggestion is made that they only be used together as mold-pressed (Karklins, pers. comm.).

The techniques used for separating a bit of viscous glass for mold-pressing beads includes several of those used for basic bead manufacturing such as drawing, winding, folding, or blowing. This gives some weight to the contention of Kidd and Kidd (1970:48) that all beads originally were drawn or wound (or both). While the inspection of mold-pressed beads will sometimes indicate the first stage in manufacturing, more often than not there will be no clue hence the need for the mold-pressed bead class. There is also no reason why the proper quantity of glass can be measured out only through drawing or winding. Karklins (1982:96) makes a distinction between mold-pressed beads made from one piece of glass and those made from two pieces brought together in a two piece mold. Often in the second type the two gathers may show a noticeable boundary line.

Mold-pressed beads as noted, can be called molded, pressed, pinched, tong molded (Francis 1979a:111), or a special variety described by Ross (1974:17) as mandrel pressed. After the middle of the 19th century the manufacture of mold-pressed beads in Bohemia within today's Czechoslovakia became much more important in the world market of trade beads.

The process as described in 1886 (Schwarz 1886:350) for the manufacture of small glass objects in Bohemia was undoubtedly applicable to bead manufacture. Glass canes were heated and ''the softened end is fastened upon by a pair of pincers, drawn out a little, and introduced into a mold in which is carved the figure of the object into which it is designed to be formed, and which is firmly snapped upon it by closing the mold and the application of pressure.'' At about the same time another author (Anonymous 1884:820) stated clearly that ''the manufacture of pressed beads is effected by pincers of suitable form.'' Pazaurek (1911:1) says that mold-pressed beads were made from ''bars (rods, canes) . . . with molded iron tongs and perforated at the same time.''

Mold-pressed beads usually can be identified by the ridge formed where the two halves of the mold come together (Figure 1m). Some beads, especially elongated shapes, will have the seam parallel to the axis of the perforation rather than the normal equatorial seam (Figure 1n). This type could be made as suggested by Beck (1928:61–62) for the double strip bead:

> in this method two strips of glass were taken and placed on top of each other with a rod between them. They were then pressed together and cut off at the correct length to form the diameter of the bead, which was finished by rounding it to shape by pressure whilst the glass was still plastic.

Some expensive varieties, usually faceted and especially of the elongated shape, will have the seam ground down (Figure 1n). Mold–pressed beads also tend to have tapered perforations.

Mandrel pressed beads have all of the characteristics of other mold–pressed beads including an even more tapered hole plus a chipped scar or "bulb of percussion" around the small end of the perforation (Figure 1o). Recent radiographic work shows the hole to be a regular cone.

Ross (1974:17, 20) has postulated a technique for the manufacture of these beads:

> they were made by pressing two pieces of molten (or plastic) glass together in a mold. The resultant bead blank had a conical hole which did *not* pass through the entire bead. This blank was placed upon a mandrel and random facets were ground over the entire surface, and after faceting, the remaining portion of the hole was punched through the bead.

Based on his prior experience with glass, Robert Elder (1976, pers. comm.) of the Smithsonian Institution vehemently disagrees with Ross's hypothesis but has offered no alternative theory. Possible support for Ross's hypothesis is offered in an anonymous German source dated 1913. The beads of unknown type were apparently pressed in iron forms from glass rods which had been remelted. The description (Anonymous 1913:61) goes on to say: "Since the beads were only partly pierced, they had to be singly perforated with a punch" ["*Da die Perlen nur teilweise durchstochen wurden mussten sie einzeln mit einen Dorn durchschlagen werden*"]. It should be added however, that the same source stated: "For several years machines have been employed which press and pierce the bead with a single application of pressure" (Anonymous 1913:61).

The process of modifying drawn, wound, and blown beads with hand tools that do not destroy the basic perforation but alter to some degree the shape has been called marvering. To be absolutely correct, marvering is only that shaping done by rolling the glass on the marver. Any shaping done with paddles or other tools should be called modeling. This is not another manufacturing class but only an additional process added to the basic manufacturing process. Francis (1979a, 1979b) apparently would apply the term impressed to some such secondary modification of a pressed bead from a drawn or wound bead. He also suggests that this procedure is more typical of the Italians than the Czechoslovakians.

Fired Beads

It is suggested here that the class of beads manufactured from granular material that is compressed and further heated be called fired beads. This process is sometimes called sintering or fritting; however, some fired processes are not sintering, and fritting is actually the process of reducing the raw material to small–sized pieces so that it can be sintered. Fired is the manufacturing process formerly called molded (Sprague 1966.). The term compressed bead could be used, but fired beads can be made by pressing in molds or by hand modeling, hence confusion would still be possible with mold–pressed beads. The important distinction is between molten glass being treated (pressed) *vs.* glass constituents or frit being compressed and then subjected to heat (fired). The terms baked and porcelain have been used (Gibson 1976:104), but the first of these, in the Old World literature, usually refers to one specific type of African process, and the second is in the popular literature in reference to any glass beads, usually opaque white, of a high quartz content.

Fired beads have a great antiquity, perhaps the oldest glass making technique known. The Middle Eastern donkey bead (not to be confused with the pony bead) is still being made as it probably was in ancient Egyptian times by modeling damp quartz sand and an alkaline flux, such as potash or borax, into globules by hand or pliers, inserting a thorn, or sun drying and drilling with a bow drill to make a perforation. The beads were then fired in a furnace. A blue salt-glazed surface was achieved by throwing copper salts into the fire or packing the beads in powdered ingredients before firing (Figure 1p; Wulff et al. 1968). It can be argued that such beads are more correctly called faience than glass.

Another fired bead technique is found today in Africa (Figure 1q). According to Liu (1974) ground glass is placed in clay molds, fired and then sometimes ground, especially on the ends. Some are made in individual holes in the mold (Wild 1937) while others are made in a grooved mold and then broken apart (Sinclair 1939). Such beads are called powder–glass beads (Francis 1979a:88), pot beads (Liu 1974:8), or baked beads (van der Sleen 1967:27). Van der Sleen also suggests that this technique was used in ancient Egypt to make faience beads. This may be close to the technique used by the Arikara Indians for making beads as well as their better known native glass pendants (Stirling 1947; Ubelaker and Bass 1970).

For many years, the appearance of so-called tile beads (Figure 1r,s) had been disturbing, and as a result they became the subject of a conference paper (Sprague 1973). These beads are generally classified along with glass trade beads but have a ceramic, mold-made appearance (Sprague 1983). Several years ago in a discussion with DiAnn Herst of the National Historic Parks and Sites Branch, Ottawa, the Prosser process for making ceramic buttons was described. A review of the literature suggested that tile beads and some other molded beads, usually round, are probably made by a process similar to that for making Prosser buttons.

The Prosser process was patented in 1840 by Richard Prosser in England and by his brother, Thomas Prosser, in the United States in 1841. Slightly moist clay is impressed in steel or iron dies of the proper shape and compressed to about one-fourth its original bulk. The buttons are then fired at high temperature to produce a bisque object that is then glazed and refired.

Prosser beads (Sprague 1973), or Prosser molded beads, the term used by Ross (1974:18), are characterized by a very smooth, round appear-ance at one end of the bead (Figure 1r) and a rough pebbly or orange peel appearance at the other end (Figure 1s). Not only is the hole tapered, but in the case of tile beads, the whole bead is slightly tapered. The term tile generally is limited to the cylindrical type of bead; however, Karklins (1982:99) implies that all Prosser beads are called tile. Tile beads appear to have a granular structure not typical of true glass, but chemically they are virtually identical to glass (Sprague 1983:172).

Blown Beads

Blown beads are also called hollow blown, hollow sphere, and hollow bubble. Again, these alternative terms imply the geometry of the bead rather than simply the technique of manufacture. Blown beads can best be likened to small Christmas tree ornaments (Figure 1t). Because of their fragile nature they are not often found in an archaeological context. Ross (1976:766–767) has described several different styles of blown glass beads found at Fort Vancouver. Good (1977:32) summarizes the literature on proposed methods of manufacturing blown beads. These four hypothesized techniques include those in which 1) small spheres were blown and perforated on opposite sides before cooling (Harris and Harris 1967:137); 2) a closed, grooved tube was formed by blowing glass into a mold, and an expanded central portion was created by heating only a section of the tube and blowing air into it (Ross 1974:18, 21); 3) either a small bubble (Type 3a) or a portion of a glass tube (Type 3b) was blown into a bead, forming a smooth ball, or (Type 3c) it was blown into a mold that had a more decorative form; 4) tubing was heated in a mold and air was blown into the tube, forming a connecting chain of beads broken apart after being removed from the mold.

Karklins (1982:98) classifies these several techniques more logically and suggests (Karklins 1981, pers. comm.) correlations with Good (1977): 1) free blown bubble on a blow tube (cf., Good's Type 1 and Type 3a); 2) tube blown in a mold (cf., Good's Type 2, Type 3c, and Type 4);

and 3) bubbles in a blown glass tube (cf., Good's Type 3b).

Karklins' Type 2 is described in more detail by Francis (1982:9) including the use of a foot pedal to close the brass two–piece mold. A mechanism for blowing six to ten Type 3 beads at one time is described in a 1927 German source (Anonymous 1927).

Examples of additions to these basic processes include such variations as multiple (chain) production and fancy work (Figure 1u) such as that hypothesized by Ross (1974:18):

> . . . a closed, grooved tube was formed by blowing glass into a mold. Next, a single upset (in some cases two) was produced by heating one portion of the tube while rotating and forcing air into the tube. Finally, the ends were formed by heating and crimping the tube, snapping off unwanted portions and subsequently fire polishing the broken edge [Figure 1u].

Round blown beads made in imitation of pearls were first made in 1656 (Lardner 1832:235–236; Beckman 1846:265–268). M. Jaquin, a French inventor, filled the inside of blown glass beads with a coating made from fish scales and then filled the beads with white wax. The first description in English of this process appears to be Rees (1819); however he does not describe the making of the actual glass beads. The blowing of such "false pearls" is described by Sauzay (1870:245–249). He states that the blowing is done by hand from glass tubes without the use of molds, "the only exception to this is for pearls called fluted, which must be done in a mould."

Pazaurek (1911:19), probably after Tayenthal (1900:23–24), states that the chronology for blown beads in the Jablonec (Gablonz) region is "first manufactured with a blowpipe, later with the bellows, and most recently at the 'blowtable;' no longer singly but in molds up to 30 pieces." These molds were invented in 1876 (Tayenthal 1900:23). The silvering of blown beads was made practical by "Dr. Weiskopf" in the 1850s (Tayenthal 1900:23).

Other Processes

Additional minor techniques for the manufacture of glass beads can be found throughout the world. Van der Sleen (1967:26) lists folded beads as a manufacturing type. Oftentimes, a folded bead is just a poorly or incompletely wound bead, however some beads *are* clearly made in this way as shown by Beck (1928:61) and Neuburg (1949:54).

Francis (1979a:113) describes the manufacture of a twirled bead thus: "The method of making small beads like seed beads [is] by putting a bit of glass on a wire and twirling it around quickly so that the glass can obtain a spherical shape."

Van der Sleen (1967:27) also lists hand perforated beads which he suggests are made thus: "drops from a molten rod of glass on a soft earthenware dish are perforated with the aid of a hot iron nail, while plastic." Francis (1983a:5) clearly points out that van der Sleen was basing his conclusions on the writings and observations of M. G. Dikshit.

The " 'Allen book of beads', a 32 page booklet issued by Allen's Boston Book Shop" and dating about 1920 (Liu 1975b) relates still another way in which fancy beads were made in Italy:

> The glass which forms the bead comes in bars or rods (sometimes called glass "canes"), approximately the diameter of the bead to be made. The bars are placed in a small furnace over an open fire, until the end becomes sufficiently soft. With a pair of plyers, a piece is pinched off large enough to form one bead. The bead, being now in a semi–fluid state, is pierced with a long wire or needle and is then turned and twisted over the hot flame till it can be shaped into either a round, lozenge shape, square, octagonal or olive shape.

Again, it should be pointed out that this is not marvering but modeling. Recently such beads have been reported from South America and have also been produced experimentally (Harris and Liu 1979:60).

Gibson (1976:104) and Bone (1977:17) suggest facetted beads as a manufacturing type; however, facetting is a by–product of the basic manufacturing process in the case of mold–pressed beads and a finishing modification during or after the basic manufacturing process in the case of facetted drawn beads. Nevertheless, the literature review by Gibson (1976:104–106) on the possible methods for the manufacturing of facetted beads is the most complete in print.

Physical Appearance

The shape or geometry of beads can be determined best through reference to the basic source by Beck (1928) or the more recent summary by van der Sleen (1967). There are several levels of bead shape or geometry, the first of which is standard geometric description using such terms as sphere or cylinder. When they are used, such terms should be geometrically accurate. For example, the term "round" is not round at all, but spherical. Spheres and disks are both called round but are very different shapes. Karklins' (1982:101–102) recent discussion of shape has only added to the confusion, a point also made by Francis (1984) in his review of Karklins' work. This is not to suggest that historical terms should not be noted but that the specific description should be accurate; in other words the emic and etic descriptions should be kept separate. In addition to the standard geometric shapes there are specialized names such as melon, raspberry, collared, corn, etc. Contrary to Kidd and Kidd (1970), the term "doughnut" is not a specialized shape but rather should be designated "torus," a specific and quite common geometric shape. The difference between a spherical bead and a torus bead is a good example of the importance of perforation size. Most geometric terms ignore the perforation, but some terms, such as torus or ring, do consider the perforation, hole, or bore, usually when it is relatively large.

Since each bead factory had its own set of screens for determining sizes there is no standard or objective way of establishing common sizes today that correspond to those used by the factories (e.g., 000, 00, 0, 1, 2, 3, etc). The trend among serious researchers of trade beads is to measure them in millimeters giving length, greatest diameter, and hole diameter. Among flattened beads, the maximum and minimum width should be recorded. Karklins (1982:109) calls these width and thickness. Most researchers working with large quantities of beads have gone beyond the "small, medium, and large" stage suggested earlier by Kidd and Kidd (1970:66). Personal experience with this (Sprague 1971) led to ridiculous subdivisions including "very small, extra very small, super extra very small," etc. The small, medium,

and large designations are of little or no help for statistical analyses to determine factory bead sizes such as Ross (1976) has been able to do with the Fort Vancouver material, but they are of some use for describing relative bead sizes.

In the past the use of standard screen mesh sizes, standard twist drill sizes, or even knitting needle sizes has been suggested (Sprague 1969), but these are now rejected as inadequate. Measurement to the nearest 0.1 mm with a micrometer or dial caliper is recommended as is the use of a flat scale gauge graduated in 0.1 mm increments which is useful for measuring bead perforation diameters. A jewelry tool supply house can provide one of these gauges for under $100.

Some objection has been raised to measuring the bead hole or bore, but until more is known about bead manufacture and dating, it is important to include this information for all bead classes except perhaps for the more common varieties of drawn beads.

Bead color should be designated by general and widely understood terms such as red, green, robin's egg blue, etc., but when possible they should also be given a Munsell color designation. The Munsell charts are very expensive but can often be borrowed through interlibrary loan or from university or scientific laboratories. The Munsell color charts remain the standard of both industry and science, hence one must view as very unfortunate, the use by some of lesser known, out of print, or less discriminating charts such as the Container Corporation of America Chart, the Bustanoby Chart, the Maerz and Paul Dictionary of Color, or the Letraset Pantone Letracolor Color Paper Picker (Motz and Schulz 1980:50). One reasonably priced substitute for the Munsell chart that is also easily available and should continue to be so is the ISCC-NBS Centroid Color Chart, available with the *Color Universal Language and Dictionary of Names* (Kelly and Judd 1976) from the National Bureau of Standards. Smith and Good (1982:17) recently demonstrated the practical use of ISCC-NBS Centroid Color Charts *but* in conjunction with Munsell designations.

Bead color is oftentimes best determined by wetting the surface while making the color determination. Motz and Schulz (1980:50) make all determinations while the bead is wet. Karklins (1982:106) suggests wetting the bead if it is "eroded, dull or slightly patinated." It is also advisable to have a consistent light source. Kelly and Judd (1976:5–6) recommend a north facing window as a light source. Artificial light, unless a special and expensive color–corrected system, should be avoided. An old fashioned gooseneck lamp with a hole punched in the center of the shade just above the light bulb is useful so that very dark glass beads (e.g., black and deep purple) can be held over the hole to determine the color of the transmitted light. Both transmitted and reflected light have been proposed for determining bead color. Good (1976:242–243) suggests the term "diaphenetic color value" from the Munsell designation "when held to the light." The more easily understood terms "reflected light color" and "transmitted light color," are preferred.

The capacity of beads to transmit light, technically called diaphaneity, should be noted for each bead. The usual designations are opaque, translucent, and transparent. Opaque beads do not transmit light. Translucent beads transmit light but do not permit vision through the glass. Transparent beads permit vision through the glass. Motz and Schulz (1980:50) define translucency as when "any part of the glass is capable of transmitting light when back-lighted by a frosted 100-watt incandescent lamp." Smith and Good (1982:21) present criteria for making all three levels of diaphaneity as follows:

> A bead is classified as transparent if its perforation is visible when it is held sideways to the light, and/or if there is little variation in the Munsell color classification when the color of the bead in reflected light is compared to its color in transmitted light. Likewise, it is considered translucent when light does penetrate the bead, and opaque when it does not.

Any special ornamentation on the bead must be noted. These include ground facets as already mentioned but also such techniques as painting, glazing, inlay, overlay, or appliqué. Francis (1979a) best defines these modifications. Karklins (1982:109) also discusses internal decoration, defined as "decorative elements, such as coloured cylinders, spiral bands, and metal foil, located within the body of the bead."

Closely related to ornamentation and color is luster. Karklins (1982:109) defines luster as "the appearance of the bead in reflected light." His basic types are "dull" and "shiny" (glossy). Bead luster can be altered significantly by weathering in the soil, sandblasting in a surface site, absorption of oil through wearing and handling both before and after excavation, and other factors of aging. Luster also may involve specialized descriptive terms such as pearl, opal, metallic, greasy (vaseline glass), and satiny; the last is said by Karklins (1982:109) to be "characterized by a fibrous structure." Luster can be recorded conveniently with the descriptions of bead color and ornamentation.

Laboratory Analysis

The laboratory analysis of beads is limited only by the imagination and budget of the researcher. The first and most obvious analysis is the chemical composition of the bead. This can be determined by any number of chemical and physical techniques including, among others, spectographic analysis, x-ray diffraction, or ion activation. Other laboratory analyses can reveal micromorphology, index of refraction, fusability, fluorescence, specific gravity, etc. Eventually, such studies should result in the determination of the place of bead manufacture; however, for the most part, studies of this type thus far have been less than rewarding. Kidd (1982) quite correctly points out that for such studies to be of any utility thousands of determinations are needed not just the few hundred now available. Inexpensive and non-destructive techniques such as energy dispersive x-ray fluorescence should make this possible.

Historical Analysis

A basic question that constantly confronts a researcher in bead analysis is the original source of its manufacture. Research in the last ten years has shown that the locations of bead manufacturing are much more widespread than was formerly thought. The older notion that all beads came only from Venice and Czechoslovakia is no longer accepted by the serious researcher. On the other hand, it is probable that not as many beads were made in Holland as van der Sleen (1967) would have had one believe. The source of manufacture should not be confused with the country making the sale to the trader, the country of origin of the trading company, the flag under which the trading ship sails, or the nationality of the trader.

The second question in historical analysis is the chronological one. The age of a specific bead can be approached from several levels including the date of manufacture, the date of initial trade, and the date of use. Even the questions of trade and use can involve several levels including multiple use and thus different dates. Beads were (and still are) often considered important heirlooms handed down from generation to generation. Take also for example, the prevalent story among bead merchants in the first half of the 1970s concerning "old and rare" beads being found in warehouses in Venice and/or New York and sold for the "hippie" trade.

The next level of historic analysis following the temporal, is that of spatial distribution. Distributional research involves comparative analysis, often on a worldwide basis. Although some researchers have argued that site reports need to give more consideration to the provenience of each bead in the description so that intrasite chronology can be seen, sites with beads in the western United States tend to be single component thus the intersite relationships are more important for chronology building.

Cultural Analysis

The final, and to the anthropologist, the ultimate level of analysis is the cultural use of the artifact or in Linton's (1936) terms the form, function, use, and meaning of the bead in each specific culture. It is impossible to reach even the level of historical

analysis, let alone the level of cultural analysis; however, until an adequate descriptive system has been developed. It is not suggested that the system given here represents the only method for the description of beads but only that it is one system that takes into account all of the bead varieties found in world wide historical research. Nor is it implied that the terminological suggestions made here are absolute or final, but only that they are a step in the direction of establishing terminology that uses one logical and basic criterion for the naming of manufacturing techniques. Aside from some terminological differences with this work, the Guebert site by Mary Elizabeth Good (1972) is a published example of excellent bead descriptions worthy of emulation.

It is obvious that as yet there is not enough known about the basic bead manufacturing methods to even list them in outline form, not to mention, a detailed analysis of the many variations through time and space. What has been attempted here is a summary of the state of our knowledge and to separate out the speculations and hypotheses from the more reliable and first-hand accounts contained in the literature. One can only agree with the warning recently sounded by Kenneth Kidd (1982) in reference to historical research on glass trade beads: "there are all kinds of pit falls, one can not be too careful."

ACKNOWLEDGMENTS

First and foremost I must thank Arthur Woodward who introduced me to glass trade beads and Kenneth E. Kidd who introduced me to trade bead research. Extensive discussion on bead matters with Karlis Karklins has influenced both of our writing and is gratefully acknowledged. Extensive and helpful comments on the manuscript have come from Karklins as well as Peter P. Pratt, Lester A. Ross, and Marvin T. Smith. In addition to those mentioned above, discussion or correspondence (more or less in chronological order) with the following has contributed to my thoughts on trade beads: John D. Combes, Richard Conn, Robert Murray, Carling Malouf, the late W. G. N. van der Sleen, Wayne Davis, Martha Kidd, Mac Pullen, Cloyd Sorensen, George I. Quimby, the late Charles Fairbanks, Dick Hsu, Linda Ferguson

Sprague, the late Emory Strong, David H. Chance, Mary Elizabeth Good, G. B. Fenstermaker, George Phebus, Robert Elder, L. B. Jones, Richard Polhemus, Peter Francis, Jr., Jamey D. Allen and Albert Summerfield. Translations of German sources were provided by James R. Reece and Lori Keenan. The late John B. Sita assisted in the translation of Italian sources, and John's Old World approach to scholarship will be missed. The Reverend Wilfred P. Schoenberg, S.J. is responsible for asking me to write the initial draft of this work. Through no fault of his own, the manuscript was not published as originally planned, but still, without Father Schoenberg's insistence, it would not have been written in the first place. Cathy Lubben, Claire Worth, Tracy Iverson, and Tommi Blevins typed several drafts of the manuscript. The illustrations were done by Jennifer Chance. Innumerable interlibrary loan personnel have processed an infinite number of requests over the past 20 years without complaint.

REFERENCES

ALLEN, JAMEY D.
1980 Reviews. *Northern California Bead Society Bulletin* 3(4):2–5.
1982 Cane Manufacture for Mosaic Glass Beads: Part I. *Ornament* 5(4):6–11.
1983a Chevron–Star–Rosetta Beads: Part I. *Ornament* 7(1):19–24.
1983b Chevron–Star–Rosetta Beads: Part II. *Ornament* 7(2):24–29, 40.
1983c The Manufacture of Intricate Glass Canes, and a New Perspective on the Relationship between Chevron–Star Beads and Mosaic-Millefiori Beads. In *Proceedings of the 1982 Glass Trade Bead Conference*, edited by Charles F. Hayes, III, pp. 173–91. *Research Records* No. 16. Rochester Museum & Science Center, Rochester, New York.

ANONYMOUS
1825 On the Manufacture of Glass Beads. *American Mechanics' Magazine* 2(34):120.
1835 Miscellaneous Communications from an American Naval Officer, Travelling in Europe; Forwarded from the Mediterranean, May 1834. *American Journal of Science and Arts* 27(1):74–84.
1867 The Glass Works of Venice and Murano. *Journal of the Society of Arts* 15:758–60.
1884 Manufacture of Glass Beads. *Journal of the Society of Arts* 32:819–20.
1913 Von der Fabrikation der böhmischen Glasperlen. *Keramische Rundschau und Kunst–Keramik* 21(6):61–62.
1919 Bead-Making at Murano and Venice. *Journal of the Royal Society of Arts* August 8, pp. 605–09.
1927 Eine Perlenblasemaschine. *Glas und Apparat* 8(25):215.

BASS, WILLIAM M., DAVID R. EVANS, AND RICHARD L. JANTZ
1971 *The Leavenworth Site Cemetery: Archaeology and Physical Anthropology*. University of Kansas Publications in Anthropology No. 2., Lawrence, Kansas.

BECK, HORACE C.
1928 Classification and Nomenclature of Beads and Pendants. *Archaeologia* 77:1–76.

BECKMAN, JOHN
1846 *A History of Inventions, Discoveries, and Origins*, vol. 1. Henry G. Bohn, London.

BONE, KENNETH JOHN
1977 A Preliminary Analysis of Beads from Mission San Jose, Alameda County California; Ala-1, A New System of Classifying and Typing Glass Trade Beads based on Manufacture Techniques, 3rd revised edition. Ms. on file, The Anthropology Museum, California State University, Hayward.

CHU, ARTHUR AND GRACE CHU
1973 *Oriental Antiques and Collectibles Guide*. Crown Publishers, New York.

CLELAND, CHARLES E.
1972 The Matthews Site (20 CL 61), Clinton County, Michigan. *Michigan Archaeologist* 18(4):174–207.

CONN, RICHARD G.
1972 The Pony Bead Period: A Cultural Problem of Western North America. *Society for Historical Archaeology Newsletter* 5(4):7–13.

COUSEN, A.
1924 The Machine Manufacture of Beads. *Journal of the Society of Glass Technology* 8:306–07.

DANNER, EDWARD
1917a Process of Drawing Molten Material in Cylindrical Form, Patent No. 1,218,598; 6 March 1917. *Official Gazette* 236:245.
1917b Process for Forming Molten Material in Cylindrical Form, Patent No. 1,219,709; 20 March 1917. *Official Gazette* 236:300.
1917c Bar and Tubing Feeding and Severing Means, Patent No. 1,220,201; 27 March 1917. *Official Gazette* 236:909.

DiPESO, CHARLES C., JOHN B. RINALDO, AND GLORIA J. FENNER
1974 *Casas Grandes, A Fallen Trading Center of the Gran Chichimeca*, vol. 8. Northland Press, Flagstaff.

DOUGLAS, R. W. AND SUSAN FRANK
1972 *A History of Glassmaking*. G. T. Foulis & Co., Oxfordshire.

DUFFIELD, LATHAL F. AND EDWARD B. JELKS
1961 *The Pearson Site. Archaeology Series* No. 4. University of Texas, Austin.

FRANCIS, PETER, JR.

1979a *A Short Dictionary of Bead Terms and Types.* The World of Beads Monograph Series No. 4. Lake Placid, New York.

1979b *The Story of Venetian Beads.* The World of Beads Monograph Series No. 1. Lake Placid, New York.

1979c *Third World Beadmakers.* The World of Beads Monograph Series No. 3. Lake Placid, New York.

1981a Bead Nomenclature: Some Sources and Some Proposed Criteria, Part One: The Source of Bead Nomenclature. *Northern California Bead Society Bulletin* 4(2):5–9.

1981b Bead Report V: Beads in Turkey, Part 1. *Ornament* 5(2):38–39, 58.

1982 *The Glass Beads of India.* The World of Beads Monograph Series No. 7. Lake Placid, New York.

1983a Early Post–contact Native–made Glass Beads in America. *Bead Forum* 2:5–6.

1983b Some Thoughts on Glass Beadmaking. In *Proceedings of the 1982 Glass Trade Bead Conference,* edited by Charles F. Hayes III, pp. 193–202. *Research Records* No. 16. Rochester Museum & Science Center, Rochester, New York.

1984 Review of "Guide to the Description and Classification of Glass Beads," by Karlis Karklins, 1982. *Historical Archaeology* 18(2):130–32.

GASPARETTO, ASTONE

1958 *Il vetro di Murano.* Neri Possa, Venice. Manuscript tranlsation of chapter 4 by John Sita and Roderick Sprague, 1980. Ms. on file, University of Idaho, Laboratory of Anthropology, Moscow, Idaho.

GIBSON, R. O.

1976 A Study of Beads and Ornaments From the San Buenaventura Mission Site (VEN-87). In *The Changing Face of Main Street,* edited by Roberta S. Greenwood, pp. 77–166. Redevelopment Agency City of San Buenaventura, Ventura, California.

GOOD, MARY ELIZABETH

1972 *Guebert Site: An 18th Century, Historic Kaskaskia Indian Village in Randolph County, Illinois. Memoir* No. 2. Central States Archaeological Societies.

1976 Glass Beads from the First Hermitage. In *An Archaeological and Historical Assessment of the First Hermitage,* edited by Samual D. Smith, pp. 237–248. *Research Series* No. 2. Tennessee Department of Conservation, Division of Archaeology.

1977 Glass Bead Manufacturing Techniques. In *Beads: Their Use by Upper Great Lakes Indians,* pp. 27–34. Grand Rapids Public Museum Publication No. 3, Grand Rapids.

GOVE, PHILIP BABCOCK (EDITOR)

1976 *Webster's Third New International Dictionary of the English Language. Unabridged.* G. & C. Merriam, Springfield.

HARRIS, ELIZABETH J. AND ROBERT K. LIU

1979 Identification: Mold-made (?) Glass Beads from Ecuador/Peru. *Ornament* 4(2):60.

HARRIS, R. KING AND INUS M. HARRIS

1967 Trade Beads, Projectile Points, and Knives. In *A Pilot Study of Wichita Indian Archaeology and Ethnohistory,* edited by Robert E. Bell and others, pp. 129–58. Southern Methodist University, Anthropology Research Center, Dallas.

HARRIS, R. KING ET AL.

1965 Preliminary Archeological and Documentary Study of the Womack Site, Lamar County, Texas. *Bulletin of the Texas Archeological Society* 36:287–363.

HOFFMAN, J. J. AND LESTER A. ROSS

1974 Fort Vancouver Excavations—VIII, Fur Store. Ms. on file, Fort Vancouver National Historical Site, Vancouver, Washington.

KARKLINS, KARLIS

1982 Guide to the Description and Classification of Glass Beads. Parks Canada, Ottawa, Ontario. *History and Archaeology* 59:83–117.

KARKLINS, KARLIS AND RODERICK SPRAGUE

1980 *A Bibliography of Glass Trade Beads in North America.* South Fork Press, Moscow, Idaho.

KELLY, KENNETH L. AND DEANE B. JUDD

1976 *Color: Universal Language and Dictionary of Names.* National Bureau of Standards Special Publication No. 440.

KIDD, KENNETH E.

1979 Glass Bead-Making from the Middle Ages to the Early 19th Century. *History and Archaeology* No. 30. Parks Canada, Ottawa, Ontario.

1982 Comments following Some Problems in Trade Bead Research. Paper presented 12 June 1982 at the Glass Trade Bead Conference. Rochester Museum & Science Center, Rochester, 12–13 June 1982.

KIDD, KENNETH E. AND MARTHA A. KIDD

1970 A Classification System for Glass Beads for the Use of Field Archaeologist. *Canadian Historic Sites: Occasional Papers in Archaeology and History* 1:45–89. Ottawa.

KNIGHT, EDWARD H.

1874 *American Mechanical Dictionary,* vol. 1. Houghton, Mifflin and Company, Boston.

LARDNER, DIONYSIUS (EDITOR)

1832 *A Treatise on the Progressive Improvement and Present State of the Manufacture of Porcelain and Glass.* Longeman, Rees, Orme, Brown, and Green and John Taylor, London. Reprinted 1972 by Noyes Press, Park Ridge, New Jersey.

LINTON, RALPH

1936 *The Study of Man.* Appleton-Century-Crofts, New York.

LIU, ROBERT K.
1974 African Mold-Made Glass Beads. *Bead Journal* 1(2):8–14.
1975a Cover Story/Chinese Glass Beads and Ornaments. *Bead Journal* 1(3):10–28.
1975b Early 20th Century Bead Catalogs. *Bead Journal* 2(2):31.

LOCK, CHARLES G. WARNFORD (EDITOR)
1879 *Spons' Encyclopaedia of the Industrial Arts, Manufactures and Commercial Products.* E. & F. N. Spon, London.

LUGAY, JOSE B.
1974 Determination of the Methods of Manufacture of Glass Beads. In *Proceedings of the First Regional Seminar on Southeast Asian Prehistory and Archaeology, Manila, 1972,* pp. 148–81. National Museum of the Philippines, Manila.

MEIGHAN, CLEMENT W.
n.d. Glass Trade Beads in California. Ms. on file, Department of Anthropology, University of California, Los Angeles.

MOTZ, LEE AND PETER D. SCHULZ
1980 European "Trade" Beads from Old Sacramento. In *Papers on Old Sacramento Archeology,* edited by Peter Schulz and Betty J. Rivers, pp. 49–68. California Archeological Reports No. 19, Sacramento.

MURRAY, ROBERT A.
1964 Glass Trade Beads at Fort Laramie. *Wyoming Archeologist* 8(3):13–19, reprinted in 11(4):27–33 (1968).

NESBITT, ALEXANDER
1879 *Glass.* Chapman and Hall, London.

NEUBURG, FREDERIC
1949 *Glass in Antiquity,* translated by R. J. Charleston. Salisbury Square, London.
1962 *Ancient Glass,* translated by Michael Bullock and Alisa Jaffa. Barrie & Rockliff, London.

ORCHARD, WILLIAM C.
1929 *Beads and Beadwork of the American Indians.* Contributions from the *Museum of the American Indian, Heye Foundation,* No. 11, New York.

PAISSEAU, JEAN
1922 Verfahren zur Hestellung von Glas- oder Email-leperlen. Deusches Reich Reichspatentampt Patenschrift, No. 443,013; 22 February 1922.
1925 Verfahren zur Hestellung von Perlen aus Glas oder anderen glasigen Massen. Deusches Reich Reichspratentampt Patenschrift, No. 449,541; 8 April 1925.

PAZAUREK, GUSTAV E.
1911 *Glasperlen und Perlen-arbeiten in alter und neuer Zeit.* Verlags-anstalt Alexander Koch, Darmstadt.

PELLATT, APSLEY
1849 *Curiosities of Glass Making.* David Bogue, London.

QUIMBY, GEORGE I.
1978 Trade Beads and Sunken Ships. In *Archaeological Essays in Honor of Irving B. Rouse,* edited by Robert C. Dunnell and Edwin S. Hall, Jr., pp. 231–46. Mouton, The Hague.

REES, ABRAHAM
1819 *The Cyclopaedia; or Universal Dictionary of Arts, Sciences, and Literature.* Longeman, Hurst, Orme, and Brown, London.

REVI, ALBERT CHRISTIAN
1959 *Nineteenth Century Glass, Its Genesis and Development.* Thomas Nelson and Sons, New York.

ROSS, LESTER A.
1974 Hudson's Bay Company Glass Trade Beads: Manufacturing Types Imported to Fort Vancouver (1829–1860). *Bead Journal* 1(2):15–22.
1976 Fort Vancouver, 1829–1860: A Historical Archeological Investigation of the Goods Imported and Manufactured by the Hudson's Bay Company. Ms. on file, Fort Vancouver National Historic Site, Vancouver, Washington.

SALMON, PATRICIA
1976 The Little Known Field of Japanese Glass. *Arts of Asia* 6(2):47–56.

SAUZAY, ALEXANDER
1870 *Wonders of Glass-Making in All Ages.* Charles Scribner & Co., New York.

SCHWARZ, HEINRICH
1886 Bohemian Glass. *Popular Science Monthly* 29(111):346–52.

SINCLAIR, G. E.
1939 A Method of Bead-making in Ashanti. *Man* 39(111):128.

SLEEN, W. G. N. VAN DER
1967 *A Handbook on Beads.* Musée du Verre, Liège, Belgium.

SMITH, MARVIN T.
1982 "Eye" Beads in the Southeast. *The Conference on Historic Site Archaeology Papers* 14:116–27. Columbia, South Carolina.
1983 An Unusual Glass Bead from Southern Florida. *Bead Forum* 2:3–4.

SMITH, MARVIN T. AND MARY ELIZABETH GOOD
1982 *Early Sixteenth Century Glass Beads in the Spanish Colonial Trade.* Cottonlandia Museum Publications, Greenwood.

SPRAGUE, RODERICK
1966 Toward a Chronology of Glass Trade Beads. Paper presented at the 19th Annual Northwest Anthropological Conference, Banff, Alberta.

1969 A Suggested Standardized System for the Identification of Glass Bead Color and Size. Paper presented at the 2nd Annual Meeting of The Society for Historical Archaeology, Tucson.

1971 Review of *Canadian Historic Sites: Occasional Papers in Archaeology and History* No. 1. *Historical Archaeology* 5:128–29.

1973 Molded Ceramic Beads. Paper presented at the 26th Annual Meeting of the Northwest Anthropological Conference, LaGrande, Oregon.

1983 Tile Bead Manufacturing. In *Proceedings of the 1982 Glass Trade Bead Conference*, edited by Charles F. Hayes III, pp. 167–72. *Research Records* No. 16. Rochester Museum & Science Center, Rochester, New York.

STIRLING, MATTHEW W.
1947 Arikara Glassworking. *Journal of the Washington Academy of Sciences* 37(8):257–63.

STONE, LYLE M.
1970 *Archaeological Research at Fort Michilimackinac, An Eighteen Century Historic Site in Emmet County, Michigan: 1959–1966 Excavations.* Ph.D. dissertation, Michigan State University, East Lansing, Michigan. University Microfilms, Ann Arbor.

1974 Fort Michilimackinac, 1715–1781. An Archaeological Perspective on the Revolutionary Frontier. *Publications of the Museum, Michigan State University, Anthropological Series* Vol. 2., East Lansing, Michigan.

STORM, J. M.
1976 The Beads. In *Kanaka Village/Vancouver Barracks 1974*, by David H. Chance and Jennifer V. Chance, pp. 106–115. *Reports in Highway Archaeology* No. 3, University of Washington, Seattle.

TAYENTHAL, MAX VON
1900 *Die Gablonzer Industrie und die Produktivgenossenschaft der Hohlperlenerzeuger im politischen Bezirke Gablonz. Wiener Staatswissenschaftliche. Studien* 2 (2). Wien, Austria.

UBELAKER, DOUGLAS AND WILLIAM M. BASS
1970 Arikara Glassworking Techniques at Leavenworth and Sully Sites. *American Antiquity* 35(4):467–475.

WILD, R. P.
1937 A Method of Bead-making Practised in the Gold Coast. *Man* 37(115):96–97.

WOODWARD, ARTHUR
1965 *Indian Trade Goods. Publication* No. 2. Oregon Archaeological Society.

WULFF, HANS E., HILDEGARD S. WULFF, AND LEO KOCH
1968 Egyptian Faïence: A Possible Survival in Iran. *Archaeology* 2(2):98–107.

RODERICK SPRAGUE
ALFRED W. BOWERS LABORATORY OF ANTHROPOLOGY
UNIVERSITY OF IDAHO
MOSCOW, IDAHO 83843

LINDA FRANCE STINE
MELANIE A. CABAK
MARK D. GROOVER

Blue Beads as African-American Cultural Symbols

ABSTRACT

Blue beads are consistent finds at African-American sites. Archaeologists acknowledge these artifacts were used for adornment, yet some researchers also propose beads possessed additional cultural meaning among African Americans. For this study bead data from African-American sites in the South are analyzed. The results indicate blue is the predominant bead color. The prevalence of these items suggests they may indeed have been an important yet unrecognized aspect of African-American culture. The multiple underlying meanings assigned to blue beads are considered through reference to ethnographic information, folklore, and oral history associated with West and Central Africa and the Southeast.

Introduction

Although almost always recovered in small quantities, historical archaeologists have nevertheless noted that glass beads, especially blue beads, are typical finds at African-American sites. These artifacts have been interpreted in several ways. At a minimal level, beads are considered to be merely clothing or personal artifacts. Several archaeologists suggest beads were primarily used by women (Smith 1977:160–161; Drucker and Anthony 1979: 79; Otto 1984:73, 174–175; Yentsch 1994a, 1994b) and reflect cultural practices derived from West Africa (Handler et al. 1979:15–18; Armstrong 1990:272; Yentsch 1994a, 1994b). Concerning blue beads, Ascher and Fairbanks (1971:8) suggest they are similar to trade beads highly valued in Africa. Smith (1977:161) and Otto (1984:75) propose they are ethnic markers for sites occupied by African Americans. Adams (1987:14) argues blue beads were symbolically meaningful artifacts for slaves between the 18th and 19th centuries. An alternative

interpretation is that the cultural meaning assigned to blue beads is a creation of archaeologists and has had little historic validity among African Americans in the past (e.g., Wheaton 1993:80).

The following essay evaluates the assumptions that blue is the most common bead color on slave sites and that these objects were symbolically laden artifacts for African Americans. Interpretation is based upon five interrelated facts: (1) between the 16th and 19th centuries Central and West African cultural groups used beads, in addition to other items, for adornment and as personal charms for protection from misfortune and illness; (2) these African-derived practices were in turn transplanted and reinterpreted by African Americans in the South; (3) enslaved African Americans participated in informal economies that provided limited access to material goods such as beads; (4) belief in the evil eye was present among slaves in the study region; and (5) the color blue, a recurring and abundantly documented motif in African-American folklore along the Sea Islands, is considered to be a potent form of spiritual protection. The role of blue beads considered in this essay is anthropologically relevant because these items provide insight concerning the African-American worldview they embodied. Hence, these artifacts and their related meanings offer an emic perspective regarding African-American material culture during the slavery era.

The results of archaeological data analysis are first presented followed by a brief overview of bead use in Africa. A discussion of how African Americans may have obtained beads is then offered. This study then considers the multiple functions of beads among slaves. This paper concludes with a discussion of the worldview and cultural processes illustrated by the use of blue beads by African Americans.

Archaeological Data

In plantation archaeology a systematic or synthetic study of beads from African-American sites has yet to be conducted. A data set based on the distribution of beads at African-American sites was

Historical Archaeology, 1996, 30(3):49–75.
Permission to reprint required

therefore assembled to determine if blue was indeed the most common bead color at these sites. Artifact analysis was conducted at both national and regional levels. Data from North American sites illustrate general trends of bead use. To provide finer grained analytical resolution and a regional perspective, beads from South Carolina and Georgia sites are in turn considered in greater detail. Archaeological data incontrovertibly demonstrate blue beads are consistently represented more often than any other bead color on African-American sites.

Preliminary data were collected by placing a bead survey form in the spring 1994 issue of *African-American Archaeology* (No. 10). The survey form listed frequency of beads found by color, probable date range, and context. Beads were recovered from rural and urban sites, and the contexts consisted of burials, middens, and structural features. Information provided in the survey responses was supplemented with published testing and excavation reports. The survey responses were from Alabama, California, Georgia, Kentucky, Louisiana, North Carolina, South Carolina, Tennessee, Virginia, Montserrat, and Barbados. These data are from a total of 51 temporal components and 26 sites. As illustrated in Table 1, considerable variety exists within this sample. Blue beads comprise 27 percent of the total site sample (n = 1,676). Blue is the most prevalent bead color and blue beads are present in 63 percent of the components. No other color is as uniformly represented. The difference in the distribution of beads by color at these sites proved to be statistically significant ($X^2 = 1,462.29$, $df = 10$, $p = <.001$). The unidentified bead category was removed before calculating this statistic for glass beads. The assembled information clearly illustrates that although blue is not always the most prevalent bead color at each African-American site across the country, blue nevertheless is the most consistent bead color present at each African-American site. No other bead color is as uniformly represented in the national site sample.

To provide finer grained analytical resolution, a data set based on beads from a specific geographic region was assembled. Beads from African-American sites in South Carolina and Georgia were ex-

TABLE 1
BEAD COLOR DISTRIBUTIONS FOR AFRICAN-AMERICAN SITES

Bead Color	Bead		Components	
	N	%	N	%
Blue	448	26.73	32	62.75
Black	64	3.82	6	11.76
Green	50	2.98	5	9.80
Clear	343	20.46	14	27.45
White	139	8.29	16	31.37
Multicolor	200	11.93	9	17.65
Red	79	4.71	10	19.61
Purple/Pink	17	1.01	3	5.88
Amber	12	0.72	3	5.88
Yellow	15	0.89	6	11.76
Brown	232	13.84	4	7.84
Stone	4	0.24	4	7.84
Shell	11	0.66	4	7.84
Unidentified	62	3.70	12	25.53
Total	1,676	99.98		

Sources: Survey responses supplemented by Ascher and Fairbanks (1971); Smith (1975, 1977); Good (1976); Handler and Lange (1978); Drucker and Anthony (1979); Wheaton et al. (1983); Carnes (1984); Zierden et al. (1986); Gardner (1987); Watters (1987); Babson (1989); Shogren et al. (1989); Wayne and Dickinson (1990); Pogue and White (1991); Norrell and Meyer (1992); Praetzellis and Praetzellis (1992); Stine (1993); Heath (1994); Stine et al. (1994); O'Malley (1995); Steen (1995).

amined in greater depth due to the larger number of African-American sites that have been investigated in these states. The geographic setting of the majority of the study sites was the lower coastal plain and coastal areas in South Carolina. The level of investigation for the site sample was either intensive testing or excavation. Archaeological investigations that relied only on survey methods were not considered since survey methods usually result in low recovery rates for small artifacts. Data were obtained primarily from published books and compliance reports. Information concerning the geographic setting, site function, excavation methods, temporal periods, bead colors, bead types, counts, and authors' interpretations of the beads was tabulated. Frequency and color were the most consistently recorded attributes of analysis. Bead type and size were not always recorded or comparable. The

TABLE 2
BEAD COLOR BY SITE FUNCTION ON AFRICAN-AMERICAN SITES IN SOUTH CAROLINA AND GEORGIA

Bead Color	Domestic		Kitchen		General		Total	
	%	(N)	%	(N)	%	(N)	%	(N)
Blue	47.6	(101)	24.4	(10)	20.9	(29)	35.7	(140)
Black	15.6	(33)	2.4	(1)	10.8	(15)	12.5	(49)
Green	9.0	(19)	4.9	(2)	3.6	(5)	6.6	(26)
Clear	6.6	(14)	12.2	(5)	2.2	(3)	5.6	(22)
White	4.2	(9)	36.6	(15)	45.3	(63)	22.2	(87)
Multicolor	3.8	(8)	7.3	(3)	7.2	(10)	5.4	(21)
Red	2.8	(6)			2.9	(4)	2.6	(10)
Unidentified	3.3	(7)	7.3	(3)	3.6	(5)	3.8	(15)
Purple/Pink	2.8	(6)					1.5	(6)
Amber	1.4	(3)	4.9	(2)			1.3	(5)
Yellow	1.4	(3)					0.8	(3)
Stone	0.9	(2)			0.7	(1)	0.8	(3)
Gray	0.5	(1)					0.3	(1)
Gold					0.7	(1)	0.3	(1)
Brown					0.7	(1)	0.3	(1)
Shell					1.4	(2)	0.5	(2)
Total	99.9	(212)	100	(41)	100	(139)	100.2	(392)

Sources: Rayfield Plantation (Ascher and Fairbanks 1971); 38BK160 (Drucker and Anthony 1979); 38CH109 (Carrillo 1980); 38BK75, 38BK76, and 38BK245 (Wheaton et al. 1983); Cannon Plantation (Otto 1984); 38CH322 (Brockington et al. 1985); 38DR38 (Zierden et al. 1985); Midway Plantation (Smith 1986); 38BK202 (Zierden et al. 1986); 38BU805 (Trinkley 1986); 9CM172, 9CM183, and 9CM194 (Adams 1987), 38GE267 (Michie 1987); 38AB9 (Orser et al. 1987); 38GE306 (Michie and Mills 1988), 38BU96 (Trinkley 1990); 38CH1081, 38CH1083, and 38CH1086 (Wayne and Dickinson 1990); 38GE410 (Weeks 1990); 38BU805 (Espenshade and Grunden 1991); 38BU966 and 38BU967 (Kennedy et al. 1991); 38BU1214 (Trinkley 1991); 38CH1100 and 38CH1101 (Wood 1991); 38CH1098 (Gardner 1992); 38CH1199/38CH1200 (Gardner and Poplin 1992); 38RD397 (Groover 1992); 38BK1608 (Steen 1992); 38LU323 (Trinkley et al. 1992); 38GE377 (Adams 1993); 38BU880 (Kennedy et al. 1993); Bowers Housesite (Paonessa et al. 1993); 38CH127 (Trinkley 1993a); 38GE294, 38GE297, and 38GE340 (Trinkley 1993b); 38FL240 (Trinkley et al. 1993); 38CH812 and 38CH1214 (Wheaton 1993); 38BU791 (Eubanks et al. 1994); 38BU890 (Garrow 1994); 38BU647 (Kennedy et al. 1994); 38BR522, 38BR619, and 38BR629 (Crass and Brooks 1995); 38BK38 (unpublished).

bead data were placed in three broad temporal periods: the colonial period—18th century; the antebellum period—19th century, pre-Civil War; and the postbellum-modern period—post Civil War to 1950. Recovery locations and contexts were separated according to the categories of African-American residences—slave quarters, tenant and yeoman farms; plantation kitchens; and plantation complexes. The plantation complex category refers to excavations around the main house or excavations that did not firmly determine the specific functional context yet contained a large proportion of Colono Ware. It is assumed this distinctive ware indicates an African-American presence (Ferguson 1992).

The South Carolina and Georgia study sample is composed of 392 beads recovered from 50 sites that possessed 58 temporal components (Table 2). Within this site sample, beads were recovered at 42 sites, and blue beads were found at 34 sites representing 81 percent of the sites that contained beads. Glass is the primary material type but plastic, shell, and stone beads were also recovered. The sample contained a wide range of bead colors including red, green, yellow, pink, blue, gray, and white. There were also several polychrome beads—i.e., two-toned, striped, and floral—within the sample. The results clearly indicate blue is the predominant color of beads found on sites inhabited by African Amer-

TABLE 3
BEAD COLOR BY TEMPORAL PERIOD ON AFRICAN-AMERICAN DOMESTIC SITES IN SOUTH CAROLINA AND GEORGIA

Bead Color	Period					
	Colonial		Antebellum		Postbellum	
	%	(N)	%	(N)	%	(N)
Blue	51.1	(24)	52.2	(60)	34.0	(17)
Black	2.1	(1)	15.7	(18)	28.0	(14)
Green	6.4	(3)	7.0	(8)	16.0	(8)
Clear	6.4	(3)	8.7	(10)	2.0	(1)
White	4.3	(2)	2.6	(3)	8.0	(4)
Multicolor	12.8	(6)			4.0	(2)
Red	2.1	(1)	2.6	(3)	4.0	(2)
Unidentified	12.8	(6)	0.9	(1)		
Purple/Pink			3.5	(4)	4.0	(2)
Amber			2.6	(3)		
Yellow			2.6	(3)		
Stone	2.1	(1)	0.9	(1)		
Gray			0.9	(1)		
Total	100.1	(47)	100.2	(115)	100.0	(50)

Sources: Rayfield Plantation (Ascher and Fairbanks 1971); 38BK160 (Drucker and Anthony 1979); 38BK75, 38BK76, and 38BK245 (Wheaton et al. 1983); Cannon Plantation (Otto 1984); 38CH322 (Brockington et al. 1985); 38BK202 (Zierden et al. 1986); 38BU805 (Trinkley 1986); 9CM172, 9CM183, and 9CM194 (Adams 1987); 38GE267 (Michie 1987); 38AB9 (Orser et al. 1987); 38GE306 (Michie and Mills 1988); 38BU96 (Trinkley 1990); 38CH1081, 38CH1083, and 38CH1086 (Wayne and Dickinson 1990); 38GE410 (Weeks 1990); 38BU805 (Espenshade and Grunden 1991); 38BU966 and 38BU967 (Kennedy et al. 1991); 38BU1214 (Trinkley 1991); 38CH1100 and 38CH1101 (Wood 1991); 38BK1608 (Steen 1992); 38GE377 (Adams 1993); 38BU880 (Kennedy et al. 1993); Bowers Housesite (Paonessa et al. 1993); 38GE297 and 38GE340 (Trinkley 1993b); 38FL240 (Trinkley et al. 1993); 38BU791 (Eubanks et al. 1994); 38BU890 (Garrow 1994), 38BU647 (Kennedy et al. 1994), 38BR522, 38BR619, and 38BR629 (Crass and Brooks 1995); 38BK38 (unpublished).

icans in the South Carolina and Georgia region. Blue beads comprise 36 percent (n = 140) of the total sample. For the analysis category of location, blue beads comprise 48 percent of the sample from African-American residences, 24 percent of the sample from plantation kitchens, and 21 percent of the sample from general plantation contexts (Table 2). A chi-square test of association indicates the difference in the distribution of blue beads between African-American domestic components and other plantation areas is significant (X^2 = 28.7784998, df = 1, p = < 0.01). This comparison indicates while blue beads were typically lost in a variety of locations on plantations, these beads were predominantly lost or intentionally discarded in and around African-American residences.

Consideration of African-American sites, consisting of slave, tenant, and yeoman domestic components, by temporal period, indicates blue beads were much more prevalent during the colonial and antebellum periods than after the Civil War (Table 3). Blue beads represent 51 percent of the sample during the colonial period and 52 percent during the antebellum period. During the postbellum period both blue (34%) and black (28%) are the predominant bead colors. A chi-square test demonstrated the difference in the distribution of blue beads between the colonial-antebellum and postbellum periods is statistically significant (X^2 = 4.88138515, df = 1, p = < 0.05).

Analysis results firmly demonstrate that blue beads were deposited most often in African-American domestic areas, particularly during the colonial and antebellum periods in South Carolina and Georgia. If the distribution of blue beads was only a result of availability and not cultural preference, blue beads should have been found equally in all areas of the plantation.

West and Central African Antecedents

In order to achieve an enhanced understanding of bead use among African Americans in the South, the African antecedents of this practice must first be considered. Among the estimated 10 million Africans brought to the New World between the 16th and mid-19th centuries (Blassingame 1974:3), approximately 40 percent originated in Kongo and Angola (Thompson 1993:56). These areas of Africa included many different tribes such as the Ibo, Ewe, Biafada, Bakongo, Wolof, Bambara, Ibibio, Serer, and Arada (Blassingame 1974:2). Since African-American slaves originated from such a wide range of cultural groups, it is difficult to associate specific African cultural groups with specific regions in the South. Also, slave traders and holders were aware of ethnic differences (Littlefield 1981:115–173) and therefore often intentionally broke up ethnic groups and families (Genovese 1974). Consequently, specific, as opposed to regional, origins for individual plantation inhabitants are very difficult, if not impossible to reconstruct.

Many South Carolina slaves, a regional focus of this study, originated from the Kongo-Angola region and the rice growing areas of Gambia and the Windward coast. A study of slaves imported to Charleston from 1733 to 1807 records six major source areas for slaves: Senegambia (19.7%); the Windward Coast (23.3%); Gold Coast (13.4%); Whydah-Behhin-Calabar area (3.7%); Congo (16.9%); and Angola (23%) (Pollitzer 1975:268; cf. Littlefield 1981:109–114; Creel 1988:16–44; Ferguson 1992:61; Kernan 1993:30; Thompson 1993:56). Africans from Gambia were desired by South Carolina planters because they already had specialized knowledge needed for the successful cultivation of rice and indigo, which were important regional cash crops (Creel 1988:34–36; Ferguson 1992:61).

Due to the demographic realities of the African slave trade, discussed above, African-American culture in the South during the era of slavery should therefore be regarded as a fusion of African-inspired cultural forms and practices. Hence, it is expected that bead use among enslaved African-Americans represents a pan-cultural phenomenon derived from African origins. It is not only difficult but counterproductive to attempt to identify direct, one-to-one correspondences between artifact patterning and artifact types at specific plantation sites and specific ethnic groups in Africa. However, it is not unreasonable to anticipate that broadly based practices and beliefs associated with beads and personal ornamentation, in addition to other aspects of the material domain, both survived the middle passage and were eventually transformed into new cultural traits by enslaved African Americans in the South.

Long before the arrival of Europeans, beads were an important aspect of West and Central African material culture. Beads had many religious and secular uses in Africa. Lois Dubin (1987:122), who has collected and studied beads from around the world, notes that ''beads are central to the lives of all Africans'' and have a wide variety of functions. Historic travelers to West Africa recorded that people used beads to adorn their body, as jewelry, to adorn ceremonial costumes, and to decorate everyday clothes. Today, and in the past, West Africans wear beads in their hair, on clothing, and as necklaces, bracelets, waistbands, and anklets. Beads were a form of personal adornment and perhaps more importantly, they conveyed social meaning and denoted information concerning wealth, age grade, marital status, artistic attitudes, and political, religious, and cultural affiliation. Beads were also important trade items often used as currency. These items were also associated with myths, with ceremonies such as rites of passage, and with religious cults, and were made into sculptural beadwork and worn as amulets and charms (Rattray 1923:147, 187, 1927:22, 46, 62, 66, 171; Ellis 1964:232, 235, 237, 240; Farrow 1969:47; MacDonald 1969:58–61; Courlander 1975:120–123; Fisher 1984:67–106; de Marees 1987; Dubin 1987:119–151). Furthermore, different regions or cultural groups had particular preferences for certain bead types and colors (Erikson 1969:59; de Marees 1987:56; Nourisson 1992:29). In contemporary West Africa, beads manufactured in the 19th century are often curated and highly valued (DeCorse 1989:44; Steiner 1990:59). For example, although Côte d'Ivoire women of West Africa wear modern European-style jewelry manufactured from gold, silver, and plastic, glass trade beads are nevertheless still valued and purchased for their spiritual potency (Steiner 1990:59).

The manner in which West and Central Africans incorporated beads into charms, amulets, and fetishes is particularly relevant to this study. Charms, considered to have spiritual power, are used to insure success in all aspects of life, including journeys, hunting, farming, and romance, as well as to ward off evil, sickness, and misfortune, and to gain material goods (Kingsley 1897:448; Nassau 1904: 78, 83; Lowie 1924:269–270; Wallis 1939:33–34; Farrow 1969:122–124). Some charms are used to avert witchcraft, particularly as manifested through illness and misfortune. Amulets therefore have an important function in health care among West and Central African groups. For example, among various West African groups, where infant mortality is high, it is thought that mothers and children particularly require the protection provided by charms and amulets (Rattray 1927:22; Ellis 1964:232; Janzen 1982:55–56; de Marees 1987:25, 75). Farrow (1969:84) notes that among the Yoruba *Abiku* cult, to prevent harm from the vengeful spirits of children that died in infancy, "iron rings, waist belts, anklets, and wristlets of beads and other charms are put upon young children from their earliest days." A string tied around the waist of a child is also a widespread West African charm (Milligan 1912: 220). American writer Era Bell Thompson (1954: 26) observed a Liberian infant encircled by a string of blue beads (cf. DeCorse [1997]). This amulet is worn throughout childhood for good health. In Kongo terms, this practice keeps the child's soul round, or rich, with life's possibilities. A mother would "fashion a small round disk from wood or a seed, perforate it, and attach it to a string to hang over his heart or tie around her neck, waist, or ankle. This would become a guide and charm to the child's soul, guarding its round boundaries, charting the

child's safe circuit to maturity and old age" (Thompson 1993:57).

Charms were expressed verbally, through ceremony or as material objects (Milligan 1912:220; Farrow 1969:121). Amulets, charms, and fetishes are any material object that is thought to contain spiritual power (Lowie 1924:268–270; Wallis 1939:33–34; Hoebel 1966:487). Many items are used for charms including beads, animal bones or teeth, stones, iron, broken pottery, feathers, bits of skin, leaves, hair, and fingernails (Nassau 1904:76, 84–85; Puckett 1975:172, 217–218). There are principally two types of charms, consisting of personal and household amulets (Burton 1864:361; Baudin 1885:83; Ellis 1894:118; Parrinder 1957:114–115, 1961:160–161; Farrow 1969:123; Awolalu 1979: 79). Personal amulets are worn around the neck, arm, wrist, or ankle. These objects protect the wearer. Household amulets are placed on the house or on household property to protect the actual structure, its contents, and residents (Parrinder 1957: 114–115, 1961:160–161; Nassau 1969:85; Ellis 1970:92).

Beads were, and still are, typically used for making amulets and charms among many African cultures (Baudin 1885:83; Rattray 1927:22; Nassau 1969:82). However, within some regions, such as southern Togo, beads are rarely used in charms (Nourisson 1992:32). Among the people of the Gold Coast, bead charms were often worn by pregnant women on their wrists, ankles, and neck to avert harm (Ellis 1964:232). Among the Ewe, a Popo bead and human tooth worn around the neck prevented sickness (Ellis 1970:93). In 17th-century Guinea, the traveler de Marees (1987) recorded that shirts fashioned like nets were worn by small children. The children's parents would:

> drape the Net extensively with their Fetissos, such as little golden crosses, tie strings of beads around the children's hands, feet and neck, and fill their hair with little shells, which they greatly esteem; for they say that as long as the young child is draped with this Net, the Devil cannot catch the child or carry it away; but without it would be carried away by the Devil. They highly esteem the Fetisso of the Beads which they hang around the neck of the little child and they consider it protection against vomiting, falling, bleeding, harmful animals, unhealthiness, and for sleeping well (de Marees 1987:25).

In contemporary Guinea, this custom persists and parents still adorn and protect their infants with various amulets, beads, cowrie shells, and bangles (de Marees 1987:25).

The above review illustrates that in West Africa beads were often used in amulets for protection from harm and illness. The archaeological data gathered for this study indicate blue beads are associated with African-American sites. To understand the role of these artifacts in the lives of African Americans it is, in turn, necessary to consider the meaning and uses of blue beads in West Africa.

European visitors to West Africa between the 15th and 19th centuries observed that certain blue beads were highly valued. The most well-known bead is the aggri or akori bead, which was possibly blue (Fage 1962; Landewijk 1970; Davison et al. 1971; Kalous 1979). Magical and mythical qualities were associated with this bead. Aggri beads were incorporated into jewelry, but they were also used in ritual and placed in burials. Among the Ashanti aggri beads were often placed in containers during offerings and divination (Parrinder 1961:67). Along the Gold Coast this bead was worth its weight in gold, and a person's wealth could be determined by the number of aggri beads they owned (MacDonald 1969:58–61).

Upon initial consideration the aggri appears to be an appropriate example of blue bead use in West Africa that could demonstrate continuity with African-American practices. However, as a caveat it should be emphasized that West and Central African groups exhibited tremendous cultural variation. DeCorse ([1997]) also emphasizes that beads had numerous uses and meanings among cultural groups involved in the Atlantic slave trade, and likewise slaves may have had a range of uses and meanings for blue beads. In summary, this section has attempted to illustrate that beads in West and Central Africa were important social, economic, and religious items that were used for a wide range of purposes.

Bead Sources and Availability of Goods

Archaeological data indicate the distribution of beads at South Carolina and Georgia sites is sta-

tistically significant in terms of differences in color, context, and time periods. This section considers the crucial element of acquisition—or how enslaved African Americans, tenants, and freed persons may have obtained beads. Archaeological interpretation of personal artifacts such as beads is usually based on the assumption that they were bought by planters for African Americans, were hand-me-downs from the planter family, or were stolen (e.g., Kelso 1984: 190, 201). A few reports indicate that some personal items may have been curated heirlooms or were produced by slaves for their own use (e.g., Drucker and Anthony 1979; Wheaton et al. 1983; Otto 1984: 73, 174–175; Zierden et al. 1986). If slaves indeed had little or no influence in the items they used in daily life, then the distribution of beads identified in this study may merely reflect the tastes or economies of planters and overseers. If slaves were able to make decisions concerning their material life, then bead color preferences should be viewed as an aspect of African-American consumerism within the informal slave economy.

Conversely, beads from African-American sites may merely reflect availability and manufacturing trends rather than slave or planter choices or cultural preferences. In order to explore these issues, the color distributions of glass beads that were produced, sold, and traded between the 17th and 19th centuries were investigated. This proved a daunting task, since published reports detailing production types and numbers are not readily available. Numerous glassmakers produced beads throughout Europe, Asia, and the Middle East and most kept information about processes, amounts, and other manufacturing arts secret (e.g., Moore 1924:48–50; Robertson 1969:38; Kidd 1970; Smith and Good 1982:12–15; Harris 1984; DeCorse 1989:41–44). Two published bead catalogs suggest that manufacturers offered more varieties of blues, blue-greens, and greens than other colors (Karklins 1985: 12, 43). This trend could be the result of consumers purchasing more shades of blue and green, or merely bead manufacturing technology. In discussing glass production, Jones and Sullivan (1989:14) state that "cobalt is one of the strongest colorants available to glass manufacturers." Nonetheless, if bead consumers refused to purchase, trade, or use blue beads, it is doubtful that so many varieties would have been available in bead catalogs.

Concerning bead sources, colonial merchants and planters often participated in both the African and Indian trade. Deeply involved in the mercantile system, merchants and planters ordered goods on credit from factors in colonial ports such as Charleston, or directly from factors in London (Rawley 1981; Stine 1990; Braund 1993). During the 17th century, Amsterdam was the "... great entrepôt for western Europe. To it came the products needed in the slave trade: cloths from many nations, beads, copper, iron, brandy, and tobacco, and numerous other commodities. Slave ships from foreign nations, notably England, often put into Amsterdam to acquire wares for the African trade" (Rawley 1981: 81). Traders and planters often purchased goods from the same London merchants (Stine 1990:27). Late 18th-century Bristol slave trader James Rogers mentions his captain buying trade goods at "the bead store" in London. There he "found beads plentiful, but he had not determined the price for cowries" (Rawley 1981:186).

Bristol slave ships carried numerous slaves to Virginia and the Carolinas. Some local traders waited and purchased leftover goods from African slave dealers in Virginia ports. Travelers and traders, in the words of John Lawson, "came often to a good Market, at the Return of the *Guinea*-Ships for Negro's, and the Remnant of their Stores, which is very commodious for the *Indian*-Trade" (Lefler 1967:94). Their merchandise likely included beads. This information suggests that a variety of goods were available in the colonies for the Indian trade as well as for resale to plantation owners, local storekeepers, and the general population.

Lists of trade goods, account books, and published histories of some of the great trading houses were consulted to gain a sense of the amounts and types of beads shipped to North America (e.g., Crane 1928; Coker 1976; Coker and Watson 1986; Wright 1986; Weisman 1989; Stine 1990; Merrell 1991; Braund 1993). Unfortunately, most trade lists merely record the price of strings of beads in number or weight of deerskins without mentioning color (e.g., Crane 1928:331–332). Occasionally a record with a little more detail is encountered, such as a listing that enumerated "5 strings barley seeds, 5

strings common beads, 10 strings white enameled beads" (Weisman 1989:67, Table 4).

Consumer Choice

The above discussion illustrates that primary and secondary information concerning the range and types of beads produced in the Old World and shipped to North America is not abundantly available. However, a substantial amount of information regarding the types of items preferred by traders and merchants, and perhaps more importantly, the influence exerted by consumers, has been recorded since the 17th century. The influence of local demand on the types of goods offered by European traders is illustrated in Senegal, West Africa (Opper and Opper 1989:5–6). In 1678 French voyager Jean Barbot noted that specific beads were preferred by certain African buyers. Some trade goods were purchased by inhabitants and remade into items that conformed to local taste (Opper and Opper 1989:7). West Africans in Senegal were willing to pay more for certain types of beads and often refused to purchase goods made in unpopular colors or shapes (Opper and Opper 1989:5–8).

In North America there are numerous examples of the effect of consumer choice on the types and varieties of colonial and antebellum trade goods, particularly for Native American contexts. Traders and factors often complained of kettles that were too large or of receiving shipments of beads and blankets that were the wrong colors—items that Native Americans, in turn, adamantly refused to purchase (e.g., Peake 1954:70; Stine 1990; Braund 1993: 121). William Byrd (in Tingling 1977:63–64) wrote to merchants Perry and Lane in 1686 complaining, "Your duffeilds this year proved indifferent onely narrow & some too light a blew . . . beads you sent me [were] large white instead of small. I can by no means put them of, pray (if it's not too late) send me none but small white this year." Braund (1993: 121) writes that "Creek spokesmen were very specific about what they needed and wanted in exchange for their deerskins." Thus, among Native Americans during the colonial period there existed a clear pattern of consumer choice that affected the quality, range, and types of goods that were traded, including beads. For example, in a recent study of Plains Indian bead use and ethnicity, researchers discovered that many tribal groups used similar colors and types of beads. The selection of design elements, however, was directly related to the ethnicity of the maker and the time period of manufacture (Logan and Schmittou 1995). Archaeological data likewise substantiate this interpretation. Beads from trading posts across North America illustrate the extent of variation in consumer demand that existed among Native Americans. Consequently, the distribution of beads recovered at individual posts was undoubtedly influenced by the cultural preferences of the native groups that were trading at specific posts (DeVore 1992:61). For example, 72 percent of the beads recovered from Fort Michilimackinac, Michigan, for contexts dating between 1714 and 1781, were white (Stone 1974). At Fort Vancouver, British Columbia, for contexts dating between 1829 and 1860, 57 percent of the beads found in the fort and 74 percent of the beads from the Indian trade store were white (Ross 1990). The most prevalent bead color from Fort Union, North Dakota, occupied between 1829 and 1865, was blue, comprising 43 percent of the bead assemblage (DeVore 1992).

Archaeological studies of Native American groups in the Eastern Woodlands indicate a similar pattern. The same bead types were traded throughout the area, but Native American groups firmly preferred specific colors and bead types (Smith 1983:151). For example, in the Northeast, red beads predominate at archaeological sites (Hamell 1983; Kenyon and Kenyon 1983:69; Smith 1983:151). Conversely, in the Chesapeake, blue beads and blue and white striped glass beads are by far the most prevalent on 17th-century Native American and trader-planter sites (Miller et al. 1983:133, Table 3). In Jamestown, between 1607 and 1608, Captain John Smith traded 4 lb. of beads for 600 bu. of corn, since he had convinced local leaders that blue beads were used by only the most high-status chiefs (Miller et al. 1983:127). Fourteen years and a rebellion later, "20,000 blue beads were paid for some mats," indicating blue beads were no longer viewed as scarce, high-status items (Miller et al. 1983:127). As the period of intense Indian trade

declined, so too did the number of blue and other beads in regional sites (Miller et al. 1983:130–132).

In a study that compared 19th- and 20th-century Upper Creek towns in Alabama and Georgia to Creek towns in Oklahoma, Good discovered a contrasting pattern in bead use. In Oklahoma Creek artifact assemblages "anything other than blue and 'white' faceted beads is in limited quantities; and of the faceted beads, there are always a greater number of blue ones." Varieties of blue beads were also the most prevalent in the Alabama and Georgia study sites (Good 1983:160, 162). Seminole sites dating to the 1830s also often contain large proportions of blue beads (Piper and Piper 1982; Piper et al. 1982; Weisman 1989:69–76).

The North Carolina Occaneechi, who were middlepersons in the southern piedmont trade between 1680 and 1710 (Stine 1990), did not prefer blue or even red beads, but white (Carnes 1987:151). Sissipahaw villagers between 1660 and 1680 preferred blue and white seed beads (Carnes 1987:151; Ward and Davis 1993:109, 141). In the village of Upper Saratown along the Dan River, the Sara also decorated their clothes with sewn white and blue seed beads, and occasionally wore necklaces and bracelets of large white, blue, and blue and white striped beads (Ward and Davis 1993:423–428).

Although blue was a common bead color used by Native Americans and Euroamericans, it is not the most prevalent color at all non-African-American sites. Native Americans displayed pronounced variation in bead use and preferences, especially during periods of culture contact and change. If Native Americans and Euroamericans could significantly influence the types of beads obtained from traders, then it is not unreasonable to infer that the distribution of beads characteristic of African-American sites is likewise quite possibly the result of cultural preferences and consumer choice rather than mere market availability. Consideration of the informal slave economy reinforces this interpretation.

The Informal Slave Economy

The idea that enslaved peoples had some control over their symbolic and material world has been discussed in recent archaeological studies (Single-ton 1991; Orser 1994). However, the notion of slaves as consumers appears contradictory. Archaeologists typically think about enslaved African Americans as producers, but seldom as consumers. One can infer that if slaves were also consumers, they may have influenced the types of goods made available for sale. In order to resolve this issue, archaeologists must first determine if slaves exercised decision-making in the acquisition of material goods such as beads. What were their opportunities to purchase them, and did they have the means to do so?

Although planters provisioned slaves, the quality and quantity of goods differed by individual inclination and wealth. On many plantations slaves were expected to contribute towards their own provisioning—from garden plots and wild foodstuffs (Berlin and Morgan 1990:3–4; McDonald 1990:187; Gasper 1991:134–135). As a consequence of this practice, an informal barter economy quickly developed in which slaves exchanged surpluses with each other, with plantation owners, and with local storekeepers (Berlin and Morgan 1990:12). In many regions slaves, and later tenants, excelled at poultry production, selling eggs and fowls both on and off the plantation (Schlotterbeck 1990:170, 189; Pulsipher 1991:150–155). Sunday markets were also commonplace, where slaves sold poultry, garden produce, fish, and handcrafts (Mintz and Hall 1960; Price 1966; Berlin and Morgan 1990:9–11, 13; Pulsipher 1990, 1991; Schlotterbeck 1990:173; 189). In the early 19th century, South Carolina slaves often personally sold goods at public markets (Campbell 1990:147).

Many slaves also labored extra hours during official rest periods, such as holidays, during the evening, on Saturday afternoons, and Sundays. They worked in their gardens or at their crafts, but some also toiled additional hours both on their own and on the planter's cash crops. Through these efforts they earned cash, either by direct wages or selling bales of cotton, cords of lumber, or other commodities. Some planters arranged for slaves to work for other planters as skilled laborers. In some cases, slaves received a portion of the wages. Over time occasional work privileges were viewed as entitlements (Berlin and Morgan 1990:4; Campbell 1990:134, 141; McDonald 1990:187).

Several laws were passed in various regions to stop or control these practices but had little success (Berlin and Morgan 1990:10; Campbell 1990: 143–144; Schlotterbeck 1990:171). Slaves sold their legal—and illegal—goods to yeomen, to local storekeepers, to itinerant peddlers, and to planters (Berlin and Morgan 1990:12; Campbell 1990:140; McDonald 1990:195–197; Schlotterbeck 1990:173, 175, 190–191). During the later antebellum period some planters regained more control over their slaves' purchasing activities by issuing credit instead of cash. Planters also became factors for their slaves' goods (Campbell 1990:151). This modification of the informal economy in turn reduced direct access to markets.

Slaves rarely accumulated large sums of cash or credit. They could only marginally participate in personal enterprises outside the heavy demands of plantation labor. For example, Guignard Plantation slaves in upcountry South Carolina made about three dollars a year between 1802 and 1804. Campbell (1990:135) estimates the typical field hand earned between $3 and $8 annually. At the Gay Plantation in Louisiana, slaves in 1844 earned between $1 and $82. Between 1858 and 1859 slaves at Tureaud's Plantation earned between $1 and $170 (McDonald 1990:191, 199).

Slaves purchased a great variety of items, especially "tobacco, alcohol, cloth, clothing, bowls, pots, and other utensils" as well as jewelry, watches, and other personal goods (Berlin and Morgan 1990:13; McDonald 1990:135–136, 200–201; Schlotterbeck 1990:177). Larger commodities such as stock animals and furniture were also purchased, but less frequently (Berlin and Morgan 1990:13). When comparing Georgia and South Carolina plantation task labor systems, Joseph (1987) discovered a generalized pattern of slave purchases. The three general categories of purchased goods were improved subsistence items, high-status objects, and luxury consumables. He states, "Items which reflect personal/individual status, such as finer quality clothing, beads, elaborate buttons, eyeglasses, . . . or [artifacts which demonstrate] the success of entire households and families, such as wagon and buggies, decorative ceramics, mirrors, more elaborate furniture, and perhaps window glass, would be another means of expressing financial accomplishments through a material medium'' (Joseph 1987: 5). These items may have been multifunctional, communicating more than economic information within slave society.

Historical studies of the informal slave economy do not list the entire range of items that were purchased or traded. They do, however, mention many primary sources that list these goods. For example, *Negro Account Books* maintained by merchants and plantation records offer a wealth of information for future research. Besides urban merchant houses and stores, colonists could purchase goods from local stores. These stores became more plentiful in the antebellum period.

In the postbellum period, local stores gained an important role in the economic system, replacing many of the large urban factors (Stine 1989). Some of the larger landowners also operated commissaries for laborers (Campbell 1990:147). The store ledgers for Oakley Plantation, Louisiana ''demonstrate that African-American tenants bought 'lace,' 'trim,' 'beads,' and 'buttons' to ornament their clothing'' (Wilkie 1994:4; cf. Bell 1994:9). Likewise, an 1871 account book lists items purchased by an African-American servant from a Pike County, Georgia, store. She purchased a number of items on credit, including ''one string of beads'' worth $0.25 (Fincher 1871).

Extant information therefore underscores the fact that many enslaved individuals participated in local, informal economies. During the last four centuries, people of African descent have therefore had access, albeit differential and circumscribed, to material goods. These men and women often maintained exchange relations with individuals on other plantations, as well as traders, peddlers, and storekeepers. It is not far-fetched to consider they may have exercised influence on the varieties of items sold and bartered, such as beads. Since people of African descent were able to pick and choose *some* of the things in their lives—certain material items like beads, other objects for personal adornment, and perishable or curated luxury goods—then it follows that slaves could also influence the types

and varieties of goods stocked by merchants. Also, due to the autonomy represented by purchasing decisions, the personal artifacts encountered at slave sites may possess social and symbolic significance not usually recognized by archaeologists.

Beads and African Americans in the South

African-American culture developed and was transformed from West and Central African antecedents within the rural South, and beads illustrate one aspect of this historical process. Beads and their related meanings offer an emic understanding of rural African-American culture. In order to explore the role of beads among slaves, African-American belief systems must first be considered. While many slaves embraced Christianity and Islam, the forms of worship, organization of churches, tenets, and symbolic systems were often translated into a specifically African-American worldview (Herskovits 1962:207–260; Thompson 1993:74–95).

An appreciable degree of consistency existed with the rural, African-American worldview. This level of consistency suggests that the development of African-American culture from West and Central African antecedents and influences from European and Native American elements was a process characterized by selection and amplification (Herskovits 1962). This same cultural process has been documented by Joyner (1984:14) concerning the way a distinctive form of Christianity emerged from diverse West African belief systems and European influences among African Americans along the South Carolina and Georgia coast. Ferguson (1992) has likewise explored the fusion of cultural forms within African-American material culture during the colonial period. Thompson has also examined how this process is expressed in African-American art (Thompson 1993).

African and rural African-American belief systems were characterized by an animistic orientation in which the world was inhabited by both benign and malign spirits (Folklore Project [1930s]; Works Progress Administration [WPA] 1974[1940]; Puckett 1975; Joyner 1984). Individuals could both benefit and suffer from the whims of these forces, and conjurers were seen as powerful people who could control the supernatural. Illness and misfortune were typically explained through the actions of malevolent spirits.

Ex-slave interviews, compiled during the 1930s by the Works Progress Administration, convincingly demonstrate the persistence of West and Central African inspired animism in the South. The interviews were conducted among rural African Americans in a number of southern states. Although researchers using these collections have to be aware of the cultural context and biases in the oral history data, certain common themes emerge from these sources. As illustrated in the interviews, concern with good and bad spiritual forces was a central element in the rural African-American worldview. The mediator between the human and spiritual world was the minister and the conjurer. Besides prayer, one of the most efficient means for influencing the spiritual world was through the use of charms and amulets obtained from conjurers (WPA 1974[1940]:7, 20–21, 92, 124–125). The role of these individuals figured prominently in the culture of rural African Americans in the South. Blassingame (1974:45) notes, "Often the most powerful and significant individual on the plantation was the conjurer." For example, in 1822, Gullah Jack drew some of his charisma as a leading rebellion figure for Lowcountry slaves from his use of powerful charms (Herskovits 1962:138).

Like their West and Central African predecessors, conjurers claimed they could influence all aspects of life, such as causing and preventing sickness and death and influencing romance and success. Healers also had extensive knowledge of the medicinal qualities of roots and herbs which were used to cure the sick. Reliance upon conjurers, their spiritual knowledge, and the charms they manufactured extended to all practical affairs of life within southern African-American culture. Charms and amulets were manufactured from a wide range of materials, represented by bluestone, blue glass, lodestone, red pepper, graveyard dirt, horseshoes, red flannel, hairpins, copper, silver, human hair and nails, nutmeg, buckeyes, *beads*, finger rings, wrist or ankle bands of various materials, and perforated coins (Botkin 1966:630–632; WPA 1974[1940]:74; Puckett 1975:235, 237, 240–241).

Personal charms in the South were typically worn on the neck, finger, wrist, waist, or ankle, tied or sewn to garments, and carried in the pockets, shoes, or hats (WPA 1974[1940]; Puckett 1975). Household charms were also distributed about the house, under or around the doorstep, placed under the bed or pillow, placed on a gatesill or doorsill, or over the door (Botkin 1966; WPA 1974[1940]). Personal charms, as noted in the ex-slave narratives, were used to prevent illness, ward away evil, and bring good luck in all aspects of life. Examples of personal charms consist of metal wire, heavy cord, or a leather strap worn on the ankle, wrist, or neck (WPA 1974[1940]:20–21; Rawick 1972a:235; Puckett 1975:314), nutmeg worn on a string around the neck to cure headaches (Rawick 1972b:244–245), and a silver coin worn around the ankle, neck, or in the shoe (WPA 1974[1940]:92, 125; Rawick 1972b:245, 1972c:31; Puckett 1975:288, 314; Escott 1979:109). In recent years archaeological examples of personal charms have been identified at numerous African-American sites (e.g., Adams 1987; McKee 1992; Patten 1992; Samford 1994; Young 1994; Singleton and Bograd 1995:23; Wilkie 1995; Russell 1996). Examples of likely house charms have likewise been documented at the Eno Quarter and Stagville Plantation, both near Durham, North Carolina, and at Prestwould Plantation in Mecklenburg County, Virginia (Samford 1996: 107–109).

The above information suggests that charms were a fundamental element of African-American material culture and belief systems. For example, Liza, a former slave from Harris Neck, Georgia, remembered that "most of the folks carry something for protection" (WPA 1974[1940]:125). Further, given their significance in West Africa, beads were probably a typical item used for charms in the South. African-American slaves, like their African predecessors, wore beads in jewelry or affixed to clothing. Although the role of beads among African Americans in the South was poorly documented, a few observations were recorded in the Caribbean. Griffin Hughes, a Caribbean planter, remarked in

1750 that his slaves adorned their bodies with beads, but he did not offer an explanation for their purpose (Handler and Lange 1978:147; Karklins and Barka 1989:75). Europeans in Barbados and Jamaica also observed plant material, such as seeds, that were used for beads (Handler and Lange 1978:147). Eighteenth-, 19th-, and 20th-century engravings, portraits, and photographs depict African Americans adorned with beads. Beads have likewise been worn by African-American women, and some men, since the colonial period, and are still worn today. Illustrations may be found in Hughes and Meltzer (1968), Wesley (1968), Johnson and Dunn (1986), Welty (1989), Gasper (1991: 134–135), Singleton (1991:163), and White (1991: 102).

Ex-slaves in Georgia during the 1930s recalled that beads were worn for adornment (Rawick 1972c:217, 312, 1972d:71). Callie Elder, an ex-slave from Athens, Georgia, stated that "them blue and white beads what the grown woman wore was just to look pretty. They never meant nothing else" (in Rawick 1972c:312). The response provided by Callie Elder is interesting, since it implies that the interviewer thought blue and white beads had symbolic meaning. As Callie Elder noted in the 1930s, beads were often used for adornment. However, it is clear from ethnographic information that beads were more than mere ornaments in Africa. The role of beads as socially meaningful objects probably continued in the South, particularly among African Americans along coastal South Carolina and Georgia. This inference is supported by several examples which suggest that bead charms were often used by African Americans to avert misfortune and illness. Beads were also used during prayer by Muslim and Catholic African Americans.

Botkin (1966:630), a folklorist, recorded that beads were worn as charms in the South. Further, blue beads on African-American sites have been interpreted to be indicative of the evil eye belief (Adams 1987). Blue beads are considered to be particularly effective in warding away the evil eye in many cultures (Maloney 1976). The persistence of the evil eye belief in the study region is confirmed by the presence of practicing Muslim slaves, his-

torical references to the evil eye, and archaeological evidence.

Ex-slave narratives collected during the Depression contain several direct references to Muslim religious practices (WPA 1974[1940]:76), including the use of prayer beads by Muslim African Americans. A former slave recalled that people would "pray on duh bead" (WPA 1974[1940]:166) and that "duh beads is on a long string. Belali he pull bead" as he prayed (WPA 1974[1940]:161). Former slave Charles Ball also spoke of Muslim practices on the plantation where he resided. Ball recalled that one slave prayed five times a day to the east (Frazier 1930:202). The presence of Muslim religious practices in the Southeast may have included the use of blue beads to ward away the evil eye. Christian tradition is also another source for the evil eye concept. Both the books of Proverbs and Ecclesiastes contain references to the evil eye (Dundes 1981:41–43).

Laura Towne, a reconstruction-era schoolteacher on St. Helena Island, South Carolina, recorded in her diary that the Gullah "believe in the evil eye, and also in the power of a good eye for healing" (Creel 1988:315). Likewise, C. R. Tredman, a writer for the WPA Folklore Project in South Carolina, recorded from an informant in the 1930s that, among African-American residents of Edisto Island,

> some would rather encounter the devil himself than the [witches] known as hags, for if one of them should cast her eye in their direction bad luck would overtake them. Some believe that a hag can bewitch a person by merely looking at them. This is known as the "evil eye" and is very much feared (Folklore Project [1930s]:1655, D-4–27A:2).

Puckett (1975:188) also recorded that African Americans used charms and amulets to avert the Judas eye, another name for the evil eye. Beads, then, were probably a typical element of charms that were worn and used for the prevention of illness and misfortune. The firmest archaeological evidence to date for the presence of the evil eye belief at a single plantation has perhaps been recovered from the Hermitage in Nashville. In addition to a predominance of blue beads—25 of 71 beads, comprising 33 percent of the total bead sample—three brass *figas*, which figure prominently in the evil eye complex (Distasi 1981), have been recovered from slave residences (Smith 1976; McKee 1992; Russell 1996).

In addition possibly to being used to avert the evil eye, beads were also used to bring good luck and prevent illness. Former slave Mollie Dawson recalled, "Most all de young girls had what we called a charm string. Dey was a lot pettier den dese beads we buys at de store now. Dis charm string was suppose ter bring good luck ter de owner of it" (Singleton 1991:163). As late as the 1930s, African Americans continued to wear beads to prevent illness. This practice is illustrated by an elderly African-American woman photographed by a fieldworker with the Farm Services Administration. The photograph's caption states that the woman wore "black beads to prevent heart trouble" (Nixon 1938). Mrs. Holmes, from Amite County, Mississippi, remembers her grandfather praying on a long string of beads. He would then put one of the beads in a cup of tea which he said would cure rheumatism (Rawick 1972d:254).

Besides the use of beads in daily life, archaeologists have discovered beads in African-American interments. These mortuary contexts provide additional information concerning symbolic bead use. During the excavations at Parris Island, South Carolina, an African-American graveyard was encountered (South et al. 1988:163–165). This cemetery, called the Means Graveyard, was part of the Means Plantation which was occupied during the 18th and 19th centuries. Within the graveyard, a pit containing charcoal and 3,481 glass beads, predominately blue and polychrome—blue, white, and coral—was found. Archaeologists found two more cremated, bead-filled pits located some distance from the African-American graveyard, but in the Means Plantation. These pits date between the late 17th and 19th centuries. By conducting interviews with members of the nearby African-modeled Yoruba ceremonial center, South was informed that West African inspired funerals involve two ceremonies, one in which the physical body is buried and another in which material possessions are cremated. South suggests these pits may represent the "practice of cremating material possessions" and offer firm evidence of African beliefs regarding the burial of the dead in the past (South et al. 1988:165).

In contrast to the Means Graveyard, most excavated African-American cemeteries do not contain very many beads. For example, excavation at seven cemeteries demonstrates burials containing beads average less than 5 percent of the total excavated burials (Handler and Lange 1978; Handler et al. 1979; Rose 1985; Parrington 1987; Watters 1987; Shogren et al. 1989; Cotter et al. 1992; LaRoche 1994). A good example of the mortuary distribution of beads is Elko Switch Cemetery which was in use between 1850 and 1920. This cemetery contained relatively few graves with beads (4% or two of 56 excavated burials). A middle-aged African-American woman over 50 years old (Burial 3), interred between 1850 and 1870, was buried with a necklace composed of 33 black wire-wound beads and one blue glass bead. Interestingly, the faceted blue bead was located in the center of the strand (Shogren et al. 1989:46–49, 143). Burial 24, an infant interred in 1895, contained 300 clear glass beads. Twenty-four of the beads are large necklace beads, and the rest are seed beads. This burial contained an ornately decorated coffin (Shogren et al. 1989:91–93).

Recently recovered information from the African Burial Ground in New York city also illustrates the persistence of African-derived cultural practices and bead use. Seven interments out of a sample of over 400 individuals contained beads. Interestingly, the burials containing beads were the remains of three women and two infants—the sex of the other two individuals was not determined. One woman exhibited dental mutilation, an African form of body decoration, and was buried with a waist strand composed of over 100 beads. One of the infants also possessed a waistlet. The beads associated with the other infant appear to have been worn in a necklace. The functional context of the beads interred with the other four individuals was not determined. Interestingly, blue and turquoise beads comprise 58 percent of the total sample (LaRoche 1994:3–20).

Mortuary information therefore illustrates beads were not typically an aspect of African-American burial practices. However, interments that do have beads appear to be associated more often with the graves of children, women, and conjurers (Handler et al. 1979; Rose 1985; Shogren et al. 1989; La-Roche 1994). Finally, although only quantifiable at the African Burial Ground, Newton, and Elko Switch cemeteries, blue beads in interments represent less than 30 percent of the beads by color. This distribution differs significantly with the number of blue beads (48%) from African-American domestic contexts ($X^2 = 14.34$, $df = 1$, $p = < 0.01$). More detailed analysis of burial data could refine these insights, but in general it appears that different colors of beads may have been used in daily life and burial practices by African Americans.

Future archaeological research pertaining to bead use in both mortuary and daily life contexts should be conducted. This study examined only beads contained in published reports and books. In these reports the only consistently recorded bead attribute is color. Additional research should encompass the variables of manufacturing techniques, shape, diaphaneity, color, and size. A detailed comparison of bead data from cemeteries may reveal that age, gender, and status are important variables related to bead use.

Color Symbolism

Color symbolism is a central aspect of Central and West African religious beliefs (Farrow 1969; Janzen 1977, 1982; Gleason 1987). Concern with the spiritual qualities attributed to specific colors was also reestablished in the New World, in both South (Sturm 1977; Gleason 1987; Omari 1994) and North America. In North America, colors are often imbued with meaning in African-American traditions. Florida author Zora Neal Hurston (1978) writes in *Mules and Men* that 20th-century candle colors had symbolic meaning as follows: blue provided protection and success, or in an inversion could cause death. White was used for peace, weddings, or "to uncross"; red represented victory; pink, love and drawing away success; green aided success, or helped to "drive off" [haints]; yellow and brown brought money; lavender "caused harm"; and black "always [represented] evil or death" (Wahlman 1993:113). Color continues to be a key element in the modern novels of African-

American writers such as Toni Morrison. Baby Suggs in *Beloved* contemplates blue and yellow, because "that don't hurt nobody" (Morrison 1988: 179).

In studies of quilts made by African Americans in North Carolina, researchers found that strong, contrasting color choice was an important aesthetic (McDonald 1986:36, Roberson 1988:5). Twentieth-century quilter Pecolia Warner used blue to symbolize truth, red for blood, white or silver for peace, yellow or gold for love, and brass for trouble. Black, although representing mourning in clothes, was used more for aesthetics by Warner as a contrast color in her quilts (Wahlman 1993:113). Various sources suggest that combined colors, such as red and white, in clothing and other textiles were often worn to ward away spirits (Wahlman 1993:113). In her folklore study of the Sea Islands, Twining (Wahlman 1993:113; 129 fn. 51) states that four colors—blue, black, red, and white—are "linked to a deeper set of values and meanings in culture." These colors are often used by African Americans in combinations that express binary oppositions such as good and bad or safe and dangerous. Color choice is important in African-American aesthetics, and certain colors used in specific contexts carry specific symbolic meaning.

The archaeological data compiled for this study clearly indicate that blue beads are the predominant bead color associated with African-American residences in the study area between the 18th and 19th centuries. It is, in turn, proposed that the predominance of blue beads at African-American slave sites was due to intentional selection. Their meaning reflects both aesthetics and religious beliefs. Blue beads were used as adornment and probably worn, in part, as amulets for protection from illness and misfortune. This interpretation is supported through consideration of the meaning attributed to the color blue in rural African-American belief systems. These belief systems are particularly apparent within folklore and art.

A wide array of items were used to make charms in the Southeast, and the color blue was commonly used for items incorporated into personal charms. Concerning the qualities attributed to the colors used in charms, a sheriff in the Beaufort area of

South Carolina in the late 1960s wrote that root doctors "deal in tokens or charms of varying colors, and powders. A token of one color may cast a spell while another color is reputed to take it off" (McTeer 1970:72). Further, the Beaufort sheriff noted that blue charms are used for protection against evil and misfortune (McTeer 1970:24). In the South, powdered blue glass and bluestones were used in charms (Botkin 1966[1949]:632; Rawick 1972e:34; Puckett 1975:237, 240), blue ribbons are used in love charms (Hughes and Bontemps 1958: 194; Hurston 1978:283), and according to McTeer (1970:24) blue amulets are often used for romance. Jay Mills (1991, pers. comm.) has collected similar African-American oral histories about the importance of blue for protection and blessings in the Carolina Lowcountry.

In addition to personal charms, household charms and furnishings that contained the color blue were also used to protect the residences of rural African Americans. For example, in South Carolina and Georgia, African Americans in the past and present sometimes paint the attic louvers, gables, doors, and window molding blue for protection from spirits and witches (Folklore Project [1930s]: 1655, D-4–27A(1), D-4–27B(1); 1885, D-4–27A, F-2–18A; Crum 1968:85; Joyner 1984:153; Creel 1988:321; Conroy 1990:29; Wahlman 1993:113). During the 1930s, C. S. Murray, a Folklore Project writer, recorded that

> The color blue is a sure charm against both ghosts and lightning, the Sea Island negroes hold. This is one reason why the doors and windows of almost every negro cabin are painted bright blue . . . ghosts are afraid of this particular color because it reminds them of heaven. . . . They cannot face the sunlight, and neither can their eyes bear the sight of the color blue, for blue is the color of heavens. . . . Lightning too is an evil spirit. Holy blue has the power to divert it from harm, if the bolt should enter the cabin while the doors and windows are open and the blue charm is temporarily hidden. In fact the color blue is a charm against almost any kind of evil, for the negroes like to think God himself prefers blue. (Folklore Project [1930s]:1655, D-4–27A).

Concerning this practice, Creel likewise states that

> interviewers for the Federal Writers Project observed that nearly all the doors and windows of Gullah cabins were painted blue, the color of the heavens. One theory was that the custom of painting doors and windows blue was an

unconscious holdover from the early days of slavery in the Sea Islands when Gullahs were given the residue from indigo vats to use on the doors and windows of their cabins. However, this does not explain the fact that Gullah conjurers concocted pills for their patients, the color of which was usually blue also. Perhaps then, the shade blue was effective in keeping out spirits (Creel 1988:321).

A resident of Georgia recently stated he still trims his house in this color to honor his elders' beliefs that they warded their homes from spirits by "painting the shadows" (Joel Jones 1994, pers. comm.). Mrs. Elizabeth Porcher Mahoney, a native of Porcher's Bluff near Mt. Pleasant, South Carolina, also indicated that the blue trim around many local residences was to "keep out the hags" or witches (Elizabeth Porcher Mahoney 1995, pers. comm.). Mailboxes painted blue are also thought to keep away bad news (Steen 1992:53). Within the house, blue candles for furnishings are thought to provide success and protection (Hurston 1978:287). Similarly, when houses are cleaned, blue-colored scrub water is sometimes used to protect the residents (Hurston 1978:284, 286).

Bottle trees can be seen in Alabama, Georgia, Louisiana, and Mississippi. Brightly colored bottles, often blue, serve as protection from spirits (Melissa Beasley and John Cottier 1994, pers. comm.). Bottle trees, mirrors, and other objects could bless the person of good heart, or drive away those of evil intent (Thompson 1993:82–83; Vernon 1993:158). On a recent trip through Cleveland, Alabama, a decorated bottle tree placed in an African-American man's backyard was observed. Blue painted Clorox bottles were hung on a tree close to the property's boundary with a cemetery (Stine 1994, pers. observation). In a number of illustrations of African-American yards and graves blue is likewise a prevalent color (Thompson 1993:79, 86 Plates 70, 71, 72; 91 Plates 62, 83; 94 Plate 93).

Conclusion

Through consideration of archaeological, ethnographic, and historical information, the preceding study attempted to demonstrate that blue beads served as both jewelry for personal adornment and charms among African Americans. Concerning general trends, several observations are apparent. Analysis of archaeological data demonstrated that blue is the predominant color of beads recovered from African-American domestic sites occupied during the colonial and antebellum periods in South Carolina and Georgia. Archaeological data clearly indicate that while only a few beads are typically recovered at African-American sites and cemeteries, the differences in color distributions are significant. For the entire South Carolina and Georgia site sample, blue beads comprise 36 percent, or represent on average eight beads per site. Mortuary data indicate beads are usually associated with women and infants, which parallel the preventive role of beads in West and Central Africa. Ethnographic information and folklore studies also demonstrate a strong degree of continuity existed between African Americans and their West and Central African predecessors in both their general animistic belief systems and the use of charms to influence the world they perceived. Archaeologically derived interpretations are supported by historical observations and folklore.

Our interpretation described the distribution of a specific artifact type and the beliefs, or emic worldview, possibly expressed by these artifacts. However, information presented in this essay has archaeological and anthropological relevance concerning historical processes of cultural continuity and change that extend beyond an artifact study. Diverse Central and West African groups exhibited staggering variation in material culture related to ornamentation and associated belief systems. Within the colonial and antebellum South an amalgam of West and Central African groups were forced to survive in a new and often hostile setting. A consequence of this experience was that previous and specific cultural elements were selected, rejected, modified, and magnified by African Americans and a largely uniform African-American culture emerged, particularly along coastal South Carolina and Georgia.

The pervasive aspect of blue within the African-American worldview and material domain illustrates this process. From a multitude of cultural traditions and possibilities, African Americans along the Sea Islands of South Carolina and Georgia apparently selected blue as a socially meaningful cultural element. The symbolic role of this color, in the absence of clear African parallels, possibly represents the development of a uniquely African-American practice. The underlying reasons why this color was specifically selected are unknown, yet research conducted by psychologists indicates blue exhibits beneficial, curative qualities and has been used around the world to prevent illness and cure diseases (Birren 1961[1950]:37, 57, 109, 260, 1978:95; Mahnke and Mahnke 1987:13). These qualities parallel the role of blue as a form of protection from misfortune and sickness documented in the South. The selection of this culturally meaningful element was in turn amplified and expressed within the material domain of rural African Americans between the 18th and 20th centuries. This folk belief also persisted differentially to the present. Ex-slave Callie Elder stated that blue beads had no particular meaning but were merely for decoration. Conversely, former slave Mollie Dawson recalled that beads were worn for good luck. The elderly African-American woman photographed in the 1930s stated that black beads were worn to prevent heart trouble. These examples illustrate that the folk beliefs considered in this essay persisted among some African-American people and not others in the South. The meaning attributed to blue survived in several material domains, yet was lost or forgotten in others, such as the realm of personal ornamentation. Oral history and folklore reveal that quilts, window trim, scrub water, mailboxes, and candles were imbued with the beneficial quality attributed to blue. The prevalence of blue beads at African-American sites offers compelling evidence these items were likewise vested with this characteristic during the colonial and antebellum periods.

ACKNOWLEDGMENTS

Earlier versions of this paper were presented in 1994 at the annual meetings of the Southeastern Archaeological Conference in Lexington, Kentucky, and the American Anthropological Association in Atlanta, Georgia. The authors thank Christopher De-

Corse, Leland Ferguson, and Jay Mills for constructive suggestions on the subject. We also thank Thomas Wheaton for including the bead survey form in *African-American Archaeology* and appreciate the response from the newsletter's readers. Keith Derting of the South Carolina Institute of Archaeology and Anthropology was instrumental in helping locate reports and site information that formed the basis of the data set. Support for this study was provided by the Savannah River Archaeological Research Program. The authors assume responsibility for any errors in the essay.

REFERENCES

ADAMS, NATALIE
1993   Archaeological Investigations at 38GE377: Examination of a Deep Creek Phase Site and a Portion of the Eighteenth-Century Midway Plantation. *Research Series* 37. Chicora Foundation, Columbia, South Carolina.

ADAMS, WILLIAM H. (EDITOR)
1987   Historical Archaeology of Plantations at Kings Bay, Camden County, Georgia. *Reports of Investigations* 5. Prepared by the Department of Anthropology, University of Florida, Gainesville. Submitted to the Naval Submarine Base, Kings Bay, Georgia.

ARMSTRONG, DOUGLAS
1990   *The Old Village and the Great House: An Archaeological and Historical Examination of Drax Hall Plantation, St. Ann's Bay, Jamaica.* University of Illinois Press, Chicago.

ASCHER, ROBERT, AND CHARLES H. FAIRBANKS
1971   Excavations of a Slave Cabin: Georgia, U.S.A. *Historical Archaeology* 5:3–17.

AWOLALU, J. O.
1979   *Yoruba Beliefs and Sacrificial Rites.* Longman Group Limited, Burnt Mill, United Kingdom.

BABSON, DAVID W.
1989   Pillars on the Levee: Archaeological Investigations at Ashland-Belle Helene Plantation, Geismar, Ascension Parish, Louisiana. Report prepared by Midwestern Archaeological Research Center, Normal, Illinois. Submitted to Division of Archaeology, Louisiana Department of Culture, Recreation, and Tourism, Baton Rouge.

BAUDIN, REV. P.
1885   *Fetichism and Fetich Worshipers.* Benziger Brothers, New York.

BELL, ELIZABETH Y.
1994   Buttons as Reflections of Plantation Culture. Paper presented at the Annual Meeting of the Southeastern and Midwestern Archaeological Conference, Lexington, Kentucky.

BERLIN, IRA, AND PHILLIPS A. MORGAN (EDITORS)
1990   *The Slaves' Economy: Independent Production by Slaves in the Americas.* Frank Cass, London.

BIRREN, FABER
1961   *Color and Psychology and Color Therapy: A Factual Study of the Influence of Color on Human Life.* Reprint of 1950 edition. University Books, Secaucus, New Jersey.
1978   *Color and Human Response.* Van Nostrand Reinhold, New York.

BLASSINGAME, JOHN W.
1974   *The Slave Community: Plantation Life in the Antebellum South.* Reprint of 1972 edition. Oxford University Press, New York.

BOTKIN, B. A.
1966   *A Treasury of Southern Folklore: Stories, Ballads, Traditions, and Folkways of the People of the South.* Reprint of 1949 edition. Crown, New York.

BRAUND, KATHRYN E. HOLLAND
1993   *Deerskins and Duffels: The Creek Indian Trade with Anglo-America, 1685–1815.* University of Nebraska Press, Lincoln.

BROCKINGTON, P., M. SCARDAVILLE, P. GARROW, D. SINGER, L. FRANCE, AND C. HOLT
1985   Rural Settlement in the Charleston Bay Area: Eighteenth- and Nineteenth-Century Sites in the Mark Clark Expressway Corridor. Report prepared by Garrow and Associates, Atlanta, Georgia. Submitted to South Carolina Department of Highways and Public Transportation, Columbia.

BURTON, RICHARD F.
1864   *A Mission to Gelele, King of Dahome.* Tinsley Brothers, London.

CAMPBELL, JOHN
1990   As "A Kind of Freeman"?: Slaves' Market-Related Activities in the South Carolina Upcountry, 1800–1860. In *The Slaves' Economy: Independent Production by Slaves in the Americas*, edited by Ira Berlin and Phillips A. Morgan, pp. 131–169. Frank Cass, London.

CARNES, LINDA F.
1984   Archaeological Investigations of Third Halifax Jail, Historic Halifax. North Carolina Historic Sites Division, Department of Cultural Resources, Raleigh.
1987   Euroamerican Artifacts from the Fredricks, Wall, and Mitchum Sites. In The Siouan Project: Seasons I and II, edited by Roy S. Dickens, Jr., H. Trawick Ward,

and R. P. Steven Davis, Jr. *Research Laboratories of Anthropology Monograph* 1:141–165. University of North Carolina, Chapel Hill.

CARRILLO, RICHARD F.
1980   Green Grove Plantation: Archaeological and Historical Research at the Kinlock Site (38CH109). Charleston County. Report submitted to South Carolina Department of Highways and Public Transportation, Columbia.

COKER, WILLIAM S.
1976   Entrepreneurs in the British and Spanish Floridas, 1775–1821. In *Eighteenth-Century Florida and the Caribbean*, edited by Samuel Proctor, pp. 15–39. University Presses of Florida, Gainesville.

COKER, WILLIAM S., AND THOMAS D. WATSON
1986   *Indian Trader of the Southeastern Spanish Borderlands: Panton, Leslie and Company and John Forbes and Company, 1783–1847.* University of West Florida Press, Pensacola.

CONROY, PAT
1990   *The Water Is Wide.* Reprint of 1972 edition. Old New York Book Shop Press, Atlanta, Georgia.

COTTER, JOHN L., DANIEL G. ROBERTS, AND MICHAEL PARRINGTON
1992   *The Buried Past: Archaeological History of Philadelphia.* University of Pennsylvania Press, Philadelphia.

COURLANDER, HAROLD
1975   *A Treasury of African Folklore: The Oral Literature, Traditions, Myths, Legends, Epics, Tales, Recollections, Wisdoms, Sayings, and Humor of Africa.* Crown, New York.

CRANE, VERON W.
1928   *The Southern Frontier, 1670–1732.* Duke University Press, Durham, North Carolina.

CRASS, DAVID C., AND MARK J. BROOKS (EDITORS)
1995   Cotton and Black Draught: Consumer Behavior on a Postbellum Farm. *Savannah River Archaeological Research Papers* 4. South Carolina Institute of Archaeology and Anthropology, University of South Carolina, Columbia.

CREEL, MARGARET WASHINGTON
1988   *"A Peculiar People": Slave Religion and Community-Culture Among the Gullahs.* New York University Press, New York.

CRUM, MASON
1968   *Gullah: Negro Life in the Carolina Sea Islands.* Negro Universities Press, New York.

DAVISON, CLAIRE, ROBERT GIAUQUE, AND DESMOND CLARK
1971   Two Chemical Groups of Diachronic Glass Beads from West Africa. *Man* 6(4):645–659.

DECORSE, CHRISTOPHER
1989   Beads as Chronological Indicators in West African Archaeology: A Reexamination. *Beads: Journal of the Society of Bead Researchers* 1:41–54.
[1997] Oceans Apart: African Perspectives on New World Archaeology. In *"I, too, Am America": Studies in African American Archaeology*, edited by Theresa A. Singleton. University Press of Virginia, Charlottesville, forthcoming.

DE MAREES, PIETER
1987   *Description and Historical Account of the Gold Kingdom of Guinea (1602)*, translated by Albert van Dantzig and Adams Jones. Oxford University Press, New York.

DEVORE, STEPHEN LEROY
1992   *Beads of the Bison Robe Trade: The Fort Union Trading Post Collection.* Friends of Fort Union Trading Post, Williston, North Dakota.

DISTASI, LAWRENCE
1981   *Mal Occhio [evil eye]: The Underside of Vision.* North Point Press, San Francisco, California.

DRUCKER, LESLEY M., AND RONALD W. ANTHONY
1979   The Spiers Landing Site: Archaeological Investigations in Berkeley County, South Carolina. Report prepared by Carolina Archaeological Services, Columbia, South Carolina. Submitted to U.S. Department of Interior, Heritage Conservation and Recreation Services, Interagency Archaeological Service, Atlanta, Georgia.

DUBIN, LOIS
1987   *The History of Beads. From 30,000 B.C. to the Present.* Harry N. Abrams, New York.

DUNDES, ALAN (EDITOR)
1981   *The Evil Eye: A Folklore Casebook.* Garland, New York.

ELLIS, A. B.
1894   *The Yoruba-Speaking Peoples of the Slave Coast of West Africa.* Chapman and Hall, London.
1964   *The Tshi-Speaking Peoples of the Gold Coast of West Africa.* Reprint of 1897 edition. Benin Press, Chicago, Illinois.
1970   *The Ewe-Speaking Peoples of the Slave Coast of West Africa.* Reprint of 1890 edition. Anthropological Publications, The Netherlands.

ERIKSON, JOAN M.
1969   *The Universal Bead.* W. W. Norton, New York.

ESCOTT, PAUL D.
1979   *Slavery Remembered: A Record of Twentieth-Century Slave Narratives.* University of North Carolina Press, Chapel Hill.

ESPENSHADE, CHRISTOPHER, AND RAMONA GRUNDEN
1991   Contraband, Refuge, and Freedman: Archaeological

and Historical Investigations of the Western Fringe of Mitchelville, Hilton Head Island, South Carolina. Report prepared by Brockington and Associates, Atlanta, Georgia. Submitted to Greenwood Development Corporation, Hilton Head Island, South Carolina.

EUBANKS, ELISE, CHRISTOPHER ESPENSHADE, MARION ROBERTS, AND LINDA KENNEDY
1994   Data Recovery Investigations of 38BU791, Bonny Shore Slave Row, Spring Island, Beaufort County, South Carolina. Report on file, Brockington and Associates, Atlanta, Georgia.

FAGE, J. D.
1962   Some Remarks on Beads and Trade in Lower Guinea in the Sixteenth and Seventeenth Centuries. *Journal of African History* 3(2):343–347.

FARROW, STEPHEN S.
1969   *Faith, Fancies and Fetich or Yoruba Paganism.* Reprint of 1926 edition. Negro Universities Press, New York.

FERGUSON, LELAND
1992   *Uncommon Ground: Archaeology and Early African America, 1650–1900.* Smithsonian Institution Press, Washington, D.C.

FINCHER, JOSEPH TRAVIS
1871   Account Book of Mr. Joseph Travis Fincher of Pike County, Georgia. On file with Fincher's great-granddaughter, Linda Fincher Wood, Birmingham, Alabama.

FISHER, ANGELA
1984   *Africa Adorned.* Harry N. Abrams, New York.

FOLKLORE PROJECT
[1930s]Folklore Project, Works Progress Administration, No. 1655, D-4-27A(1), D-4-27B(1); No. 1885, D-4-27A, F-2-18A. Manuscripts Division, South Caroliniana Library, University of South Carolina, Columbia.

FRAZIER, E. FRANKLIN
1930   The Negro Slave Family. *Journal of Negro History* 15(2):198–259.

GARDNER, JEFFREY W.
1987   The Hunter's Hill Project: Historical and Archaeological Research at the Shute-Turner Farm, Davidson County, Tennessee. Ladies Hermitage Association, The Hermitage, Hermitage, Tennessee.
1992   Historic Adaptations Through Time: Archaeological Testing of Five Sites, Francis Marion National Forest, Berkeley and Charleston Counties, South Carolina. Report prepared by Brockington and Associates, Charleston, South Carolina. Submitted to the U.S.D.A. Forest Service, Francis Marion National Forest, Columbia, South Carolina.

GARDNER, JEFFREY W., AND ERIC POPLIN
1992   Wappo Plantation (38CH1199/1200): Data Recovery at an Eighteenth-Century Stono River Plantation in Charleston County, South Carolina. Report prepared by Brockington and Associates, Charleston, South Carolina. Submitted to the U.S.D.A., Agriculture Research Service, South Atlantic Area, and U.S. Vegetable Laboratory, Charleston, South Carolina.

GARROW, PATRICK
1994   Postbellum Life on Hilton Head Island: The Frazier Cabin Site. Paper presented at the Annual Meetings of Southeastern Archaeological Conference and Midwest Archaeological Conference, Lexington, Kentucky.

GASPER, DAVID BARRY
1991   Antigua Slaves and Their Struggle to Survive. In *Seeds of Change: A Quincentennial Commemoration,* edited by Herman J. Viola and Carolyn Margolis, pp. 130–138. Smithsonian Institution Press, Washington, D.C.

GENOVESE, EUGENE D.
1974   *Roll, Jordan, Roll: The World the Slaves Made.* Vintage Books, New York.

GLEASON, JUDITH
1987   *Oya: In Praise of the Goddess.* Shambhala, Boston, Massachusetts.

GOOD, MARY E.
1976   Glass Beads from the First Hermitage. In An Archaeological and Historical Assessment of the First Hermitage, edited by Samuel D. Smith. *Research Series* 2:237–248. Division of Archaeology, Tennessee Department of Conservation, Nashville, and Ladies Hermitage Association, The Hermitage, Hermitage, Tennessee.
1983   A Comparison of Glass Beads from Upper Creek Indian Towns in the Southeast and in Oklahoma. *Proceedings of the 1982 Glass Trade Bead Conference. Rochester Museum and Science Center Research Records* 16:159–166. Charles F. Hayes III, editor. Rochester, New York.

GROOVER, MARK D.
1992   Of Mindset and Material Culture: An Archaeological View of Continuity and Change in the 18th-Century South Carolina Backcountry. *Volumes in Historical Archaeology* 20, edited by Stanley South. South Carolina Institute of Archaeology and Anthropology, University of South Carolina, Columbia.

HAMELL, GEORGE R.
1983   Trading in Metaphors: The Magic of Beads. *Proceedings of the 1982 Glass Trade Bead Conference, Rochester Museum and Science Center Research Records* 16:5–28. Charles F. Hayes III, editor. Rochester, New York.

HANDLER, JEROME S., AND FREDERICK W. LANGE
1978   *Plantation Slavery in Barbados: An Archaeological and Historical Investigation.* Harvard University Press, Cambridge, Massachusetts.

HANDLER, JEROME S., FREDERICK W. LANGE, AND CHARLES E. ORSER
1979   Carnelian Beads in Necklaces from a Slave Cemetery in Barbados, West Indies. *Ornament* 4(2):15–18.

HARRIS, ELIZABETH
1984   Late Beads in the African Trade. *Archaeological Research Booklets* 19. Center for Books on Beads, G. B. Fenstermaker, Lancaster, Pennsylvania.

HEATH, BARBARA J.
1994   An Interim Report on the 1993 Excavations: The Quarter Site at Poplar Forest, Forest, Virginia. Manuscript on file, Poplar Forest State Historic Site, Poplar Forest, Virginia.

HERSKOVITS, MELVILLE J.
1962   *The Myth of the Negro Past.* Reprint of 1941 edition. Beacon Press, Beacon Hill, Boston, Massachusetts.

HOEBEL, E. ADAMSON
1966   *Anthropology: The Study of Man.* McGraw-Hill, New York.

HUGHES, LANGSTON, AND ARNA BONTEMPS
1958   *The Book of Negro Folklore.* Dodd, Mead, New York.

HUGHES, LANGSTON, AND MILTON MELTZER (EDITORS)
1968   *A Pictorial History of the Negro in America.* Third edition, revised by C. Eric Lincoln and Milton Meltzer. Crown, New York.

HURSTON, ZORA NEALE
1978   *Mules and Men.* Indiana University Press, Bloomington.

JANZEN, JOHN M.
1977   The Tradition of Renewal in Kongo Religion. In *African Religions: A Symposium,* edited by Newell S. Booth, Jr., pp. 69–116. NOK, New York.
1982   *Lemba, 1650–1930: A Drum of Affliction in Africa and the New World.* Garland, New York.

JOHNSON, THOMAS L., AND PHILLIPS C. DUNN (COMPILERS)
1986   *A True Likeness: The Black South of Richard Samuel Roberts, 1920–1936.* Bruccoli Clark, Columbia, and Algonquin Books, Chapel Hill, South Carolina.

JONES, OLIVE, AND CATHERINE SULLIVAN
1989   *The Parks Canada Glass Glossary for the Description of Containers, Tableware, Flat Glass, and Closures.* Studies in Archaeology, Architecture, and History. Environment Canada-Parks, Ottawa, Ontario.

JOSEPH, J. W.
1987   Highway 17 Revisited: The Archaeology of Task Labor in the Lowcountry of Georgia and South Carolina.

Paper presented at the Annual Meeting of the Society for Historical Archaeology Conference on Historical and Underwater Archaeology, Savannah, Georgia.

JOYNER, CHARLES
1984   *Down by the Riverside: A South Carolina Slave Community.* University of Illinois Press, Chicago.

KALOUS, MILAN
1979   Akorite? *Journal of African History* 20:203–217.

KARKLINS, KARLIS
1985   *Glass Beads: The 19th-Century Levin Catalogue and Venetian Bead Book and Guide to Description of Glass Beads.* Studies in Archaeology, Architecture, and History. Environment Canada-Parks, Ottawa, Ontario.

KARKLINS, KARLIS, AND NORMAN BARKA
1989   The Beads of St. Eustatius, Netherlands Antilles. *Beads: Journal of the Society of Bead Researchers* 1:55–80.

KELSO, WILLIAM M.
1984   *Kingsmill Plantations, 1619–1800: Archaeology of Country Life in Colonial Virginia.* Academic Press, New York.

KENNEDY, LINDA, CHRISTOPHER T. ESPENSHADE, AND RAMONA GRUNDEN
1991   Archaeological Investigations of Two Turn-of-the-Century Farmsteads (38BU966 and 38BU967), Hilton Head Island, South Carolina. Report prepared by Brockington and Associates, Atlanta, Georgia. Submitted to the Greenwood Development Corporation, Hilton Head Island, South Carolina.

KENNEDY, LINDA, MARION D. ROBERTS, AND CHRISTOPHER T. ESPENSHADE
1993   Archaeological Data Recovery at River Club (38BU880), Hilton Head Island, Beaufort County: A Study in Late Eighteenth-/Early Nineteenth-Century African-American Lifeways. Report on file, Brockington and Associates, Atlanta, Georgia.
1994   Archaeological Data Recovery at Colleton River Plantation (38BU647), Hilton Head Island, Beaufort County, South Carolina: A Study of an Early 19th-Century Slave Settlement. Report on file, Brockington and Associates, Atlanta, Georgia.

KENYON, IAN, AND THOMAS KENYON
1983   Comments on Seventeenth-Century Glass Trade Beads from Ontario. *Proceedings of the 1982 Glass Trade Bead Conference, Rochester Museum and Science Center Research Records* 16:59–74. Charles F. Hayes III, editor. Rochester, New York.

KERNAN, MICHAEL
1993   The Object at Hand. *Smithsonian* 20:30–32.

KIDD, KENNETH E.
1970   Glass Bead-making from the Middle Ages to the Early
        19th Century. *History and Archaeology* 30. Ottawa.

KINGSLEY, MARY H.
1897   *Travels in West Africa.* Macmillan, New York.

LANDEWIJK, J. E. J. M. VAN
1970   What Was the Original Aggrey Bead (a New Aggrey
        Bead Hypothesis)? *Ghana Journal of Sociology* 6(2):
        89–99.

LANGE, FREDERICK W., AND JEROME S. HANDLER
1985   The Ethnohistorical Approach to Slavery. In *The Ar-
        chaeology of Slavery and Plantation Life,* edited by
        Theresa Singleton, pp. 15–32. Academic Press, New
        York.

LAROCHE, CHERYL J.
1994   Beads from the African Burial Ground, New York
        City: A Preliminary Assessment. *Beads: Journal of
        the Society of Bead Researchers* 6:3–20.

LEFLER, HUGH TALMAGE (EDITOR)
1967   *A New Voyage to Carolina by John Lawson.* Univer-
        sity of North Carolina Press, Chapel Hill.

LITTLEFIELD, DANIEL C.
1981   *Rice and Slaves: Ethnicity and the Slave Trade in
        Colonial South Carolina.* Louisiana State University
        Press, Baton Rouge.

LOGAN, MICHAEL H., AND DOUGLAS A. SCHMITTOU
1995   With Pride They Made These: Tribal Styles in Plains
        Indian Art. *Occasional Paper* 12. Frank H. McClung
        Museum, University of Tennessee, Knoxville.

LOWIE, ROBERT H.
1924   *Primitive Religion.* Boni and Liveright, New York.

MACDONALD, GEORGE
1969   *The Gold Coast, Past and Present: A Short Descrip-
        tion of the Country and Its People.* Negro Universities
        Press, New York.

MAHNKE, FRANK H., AND RUDOLF H. MAHNKE
1987   *Color and Light in Man-Made Environments.* Van
        Nostrand Reinhold, New York.

MALONEY, CLARENCE (EDITOR)
1976   *The Evil Eye.* Columbia University Press, New York.

MCDONALD, MARY ANNE
1986   Jennie Burnett: Afro-American Quilt Maker. In *Five
        North Carolina Folk Artists,* edited by Charles G. Zug
        III, pp. 27–39. Ackland Art Museum, University of
        North Carolina Press, Chapel Hill.

MCDONALD, RODERICK A.
1990   Independent Economic Production by Slaves on An-
        tebellum Louisiana Sugar Plantation. In *The Slaves'
        Economy: Independent Production by Slaves in the
        Americas,* edited by Ira Berlin and Phillips A. Mor-
        gan, pp. 182–208. Frank Cass, London.

MCKEE, LARRY
1992   Summary Report on the 1991 Hermitage Field Quar-
        ter Excavation. *Tennessee Anthropological Associa-
        tion Newsletter* 18(1):1–17.

MCTEER, J. E.
1970   *High Sheriff of the Low Country.* Beaufort Books,
        Beaufort, South Carolina.

MERRELL, JAMES H.
1991   *The Indians' New World: Catawbas and Their Neigh-
        bors from European Contact Through the Era of Re-
        moval.* Second edition. W. W. Norton, New York and
        London.

MICHIE, JAMES L.
1987   Richmond Hill and Wachesaw: An Archaeological
        Study of Two Rice Plantations on the Waccamaw
        River, Georgetown County, South Carolina. *Research
        Manuscript Series* 203. South Carolina Institute of
        Archaeology and Anthropology, University of South
        Carolina, Columbia.

MICHIE, JAMES L., AND JAY MILLS
1988   The Search for Architectural Remains at the Planter's
        House and the Slave Settlement, Richmond Hill Plan-
        tation, Georgetown County, South Carolina. *Research
        Manuscript Series* 205. South Carolina Institute of
        Archaeology and Anthropology, University of South
        Carolina, Columbia.

MILLER, HENRY, DENNIS POGUE, AND
MICHAEL SMOLEK
1983   Beads from the Seventeenth-Century Chesapeake.
        *Proceedings of the 1982 Glass Trade Bead Confer-
        ence, Rochester Museum and Science Center Re-
        search Records* 16:127–144. Charles F. Hayes III,
        editor. Rochester, New York.

MILLIGAN, ROBERT H.
1912   *The Fetish Folk of West Africa.* Fleming H. Revell,
        New York.

MINTZ, SIDNEY W., AND DOUGLAS HALL
1960   The Origins of the Jamaican Internal Marketing Sys-
        tem. In *Papers in Caribbean Anthropology* 57, edited
        by Sidney W. Mintz. Yale University Publications in
        Anthropology, New Haven.

MOORE, N. HUDSON
1924   *Old Glass: European and American.* Tudor, New
        York.

MORRISON, TONI
1988   *Beloved.* Plume Contemporary Fiction, New York.

NASSAU, ROBERT H.
1904   *Fetishism in West Africa.* Charles Scribner's Sons,
        New York.
1969   *Fetishism in West Africa.* Negro Universities Press,
        New York.

NIXON, HERMAN CLARENCE
1938 Forty Acres and Steel Mules. University of North Carolina Press, Chapel Hill.

NORRELL, ROBERT J., AND CATHERINE C. MEYER
1992 History and Archaeology of Nineteenth-Century Alabama. Report of Investigations 64. Report prepared by Division of Archaeology, University of Alabama. Alabama Museum of Natural History. Submitted to Transcontinental Gas Pipe Line Corporation of Houston, Texas

NOURISSON, PASCALE
1992 Beads in the Lives of the People of Southern Togo, West Africa. Beads: Journal of the Society of Bead Researchers 4:29–38.

O'MALLEY, NANCY
1995 Archaeological Investigations in Kinkeadtown, a Post-Civil War African-American Neighborhood in Lexington, Kentucky. Department of Anthropology, University of Kentucky, Lexington

OMARI, MIKELLE SMITH
1994 Candomlé: A Socio-Political Examination of African Religion and Art in Brazil. In Religion in African Experience and Expression, edited by Thomas D. Blakely, Walter E. A. van Beek, and Dennis L. Thomson, pp. 135–159. Heinemann, Portsmouth, New Hampshire.

OPPER, MARIE-JOSE, AND HOWARD OPPER
1989 Diakhite: A Study of the Beads from an 18th- to 19th-Century Burial Site in Senegal, West Africa. Beads: Journal of the Society of Bead Researchers 1:5–20.

ORSER, CHARLES E., JR.
1994 The Archaeology of African-American Slave Religion in the Antebellum South. Cambridge Archaeological Journal 4(1):33–45.

ORSER, CHARLES E., JR., ANNETTE M. NEKOLA, AND JAMES L. ROARK
1987 Exploring the Rustic Life, Multidisciplinary Research at Millwood Plantation, a Large Piedmont Plantation in Abbeville County, South Carolina, and Elbert County, Georgia. Report prepared by Mid-American Research Center, Loyola University, Chicago, Illinois. Submitted to U.S. Army Corps of Engineers, National Park Service, Atlanta, Georgia.

OTTO, JOHN SOLOMON
1984 Cannon's Point Plantation, 1794–1860: Living Conditions and Status Patterns in the Old South. Academic Press, New York.

PAONESSA, LAURIE J., SCOTT K. PARKER, AND LYNNE G. LEWIS
1993 "I Was Born and Raised Here": Investigations at the Bowens House Site, Drayton Hall, Spring 1992. National Trust Archaeological Research Center, Monograph Series 6. Montpelier Station, Virginia.

PARRINDER, GEOFFREY
1957 African Traditional Religion. Hutchinson House, New York.
1961 West African Religion: A Study of the Beliefs and Practices of Akan, Ewe, Yoruba, Ibo, and Kindred Peoples. Epworth Press, London.

PARRINGTON, MICHAEL
1987 Cemetery Archaeology in the Urban Environment: A Case Study from Philadelphia. In Living in Cities: Current Research in Urban Archaeology, edited by Edward Staski. Special Publication Series 5:48–55. The Society for Historical Archaeology, California, Pennsylvania

PATTEN, M. DRAKE
1992 Mankala and Minkisi: Possible Evidence of African American Folk Beliefs and Practices. African American Archaeology 6:5–7.

PEAKE, ORA BROOKS
1954 A History of the United States Indian Factory System, 1795–1822. Sage, Denver, Colorado.

PIPER, HARRY M., KENNETH W. HARDIN, AND JACQUELYN G. PIPER
1982 Cultural Responses to Stress: Patterns Observed in American Indian Burials of the Second Seminole War. Southeastern Archaeology 1(2):122–137.

PIPER, HARRY M., AND JACQUELYN G. PIPER
1982 Archaeological Excavations at the Quad Block Site, 8-Hi-998; Located at the Site of the Old Fort Brooke Municipal Parking Garage, Tampa, Florida. Report on file, Piper Archaeological Research, St. Petersburg, Florida.

POGUE, DENNIS J., AND ESTHER C. WHITE
1991 Summary Report on the "House of Families" Slave Quarter Site (44 Fx162/40–47). File Report 2. Report on file, Mount Vernon Ladies' Association, Mount Vernon Plantation, Mount Vernon, Virginia.

POLLITZER, W. S.
1975 The Negroes of Charleston (S.C.): A Study of Hemoglobin Types, Serology, and Morphology. In Man and Nature, Studies in the Evolution of the Human Species, edited by Frederick S. Hulse, pp. 266–283. American Book-Stratford Press, Brattleboro, Vermont.

PRAETZELLIS, MARY, AND ADRIAN PRAETZELLIS
1992 "We were there too": Archaeology of an African-American Family in Sacramento, California. Report on file, Anthropological Studies Center, Sonoma State University, Rohnert, California

PRICE, RICHARD
  1966   Caribbean Fishing and Fishermen: A Historical
          Sketch. *American Anthropologist* 68:1363–1383.

PUCKETT, NEWBELL NILES
  1975   *Folk Beliefs of the Southern Negro.* Reprint of 1926
          edition. Negro Universities Press, New York.

PULSIPHER, LYDIA M.
  1990   They Have Saturdays and Sundays to Feed Them-
          selves: Slave Gardens in the Caribbean. *Expedition*
          32(2):24–33.
  1991   Galways Plantation, Montserrat. In *Seeds of Change:
          A Quincentennial Commemoration,* edited by Herman
          J. Viola and Carolyn Margolis, pp. 139–159. Smith-
          sonian Institution Press, Washington, D.C.

RATTRAY, R. S.
  1923   *Ashanti.* Clarendon Press, Oxford.
  1927   *Religion and Art in Ashanti.* Clarendon Press, Oxford.

RAWICK, GEORGE P.
  1972a   *The American Slave: A Composite Autobiography.*
          Vol. 6, *Alabama and Indiana Narratives.* Greenwood,
          Westport, Connecticut.
  1972b   *The American Slave: A Composite Autobiography.*
          Vol. 4, *Texas Narratives, Parts 1 and 2.* Greenwood,
          Westport, Connecticut.
  1972c   *The American Slave: A Composite Autobiography.*
          Vol. 12, *Georgia Narratives, Parts 1 and 2.* Green-
          wood, Westport, Connecticut.
  1972d   *The American Slave: A Composite Autobiography.*
          Supplement Series 1. Vol. 6, *Mississippi Narratives,
          Part 1.* Greenwood, Westport, Connecticut.
  1972e   *The American Slave: A Composite Autobiography.*
          Vol. 4, *Georgia Narratives, Part 1.* Greenwood,
          Westport, Connecticut.

RAWLEY, JAMES A.
  1981   *The Transatlantic Slave Trade: A History.* W. W.
          Norton, New York and London.

ROBERSON, RUTH HAISLIP (EDITOR)
  1988   *North Carolina Quilts.* North Carolina Quilt Project,
          University of North Carolina Press, Chapel Hill.

ROBERTSON, ROBERT ALEXANDER
  1969   *Chats on Old Glass.* Dover, New York.

ROSE, JEROME C. (EDITOR)
  1985   Gone to a Better Land: A Biohistory of a Rural Black
          Cemetery in the Post-Reconstruction South. *Arkansas
          Archeological Survey Research Series* 25. Arkansas
          Archeological Survey, Fayetteville.

ROSS, LESTER A.
  1990   Trade Beads from Hudson's Bay Company, Fort Van-
          couver (1829–1860), Vancouver, Washington.
          Beads: Journal of the Society of Bead Researchers
          2:29–68.

RUSSELL, AARON E.
  1996   "Spiritual" Artifacts from Hermitage Slave Dwell-
          ings. Paper presented at the Annual Meeting of the
          Society for Historical Archaeology Conference on
          Historical and Underwater Archaeology, Cincinnati,
          Ohio.

SAMFORD, PATRICIA
  1994   West African Cultural Traditions in the Archaeolog-
          ical Record. Paper presented at the Annual Meetings
          of the Southeastern Archaeological Conference and
          Midwest Archaeological Conference, Lexington,
          Kentucky.
  1996   The Archaeology of African-American Slavery and
          Material Culture. *William and Mary Quarterly,* third
          series, 53(1):87–113.

SCHLOTTERBECK, JOHN T.
  1990   The Internal Economy of Slavery in Rural Piedmont
          Virginia. In *The Slaves' Economy: Independent Pro-
          duction by Slaves in the Americas,* edited by Ira Berlin
          and Phillips A. Morgan, pp. 170–181. Frank Cass,
          London.

SHOGREN, MICHAEL G., KENNETH R. TURNER, AND
JODY C. PERRONI
  1989   Elko Switch Cemetery: An Archaeological Perspec-
          tive. *Report of Investigations* 58. Division of Archae-
          ology, Alabama State Museum of Natural History,
          Moundville.

SINGLETON, THERESA A.
  1991   The Archeology of Slave Life. In *Before Freedom
          Came: African-American Life in the Antebellum
          South,* edited by Edward D. C. Campbell, Jr., with
          Kym S. Rice, pp. 155–175. Museum of the Confed-
          eracy, Richmond, and University Press of Virginia,
          Charlottesville.

SINGLETON, THERESA A., AND MARK D. BOGRAD
(COMPILERS)
  1995   The Archaeology of the African Diaspora in the
          Americas. *Guides to the Archaeological Literature of
          the Immigrant Experience in America* 2. The Society
          for Historical Archaeology, California, Pennsylvania.

SMITH, MARVIN T.
  1983   Chronology from Glass Beads: The Spanish Period in
          the Southeast, 1513–1670. *Proceedings of the 1982
          Glass Trade Bead Conference, Rochester Museum
          and Science Center Research Records* 16:147–158.
          Charles F. Hayes III, editor. Rochester, New York.
  1986   Archaeological Testing of Sites 2 and 3, Heritage
          Plantation, Georgetown County, South Carolina. Re-
          port prepared by Garrow and Associates, Atlanta,
          Georgia. Submitted to Heritage Plantation, Pawleys
          Island, South Carolina.

SMITH, MARVIN, AND MARY ELIZABETH GOOD
  1982   *Early Sixteenth-Century Glass Beads in the Spanish
          Colonial Trade.* Cottonlandia Museum, Greenwood,
          Mississippi.

SMITH, SAMUEL D.
1975   Archaeological Explorations at the Castalian Springs, Tennessee, Historic Site. Tennessee Historical Commission, Nashville.
1976   An Archaeological and Historical Assessment of the First Hermitage. *Research Series* 2. Tennessee Division of Archaeology, Nashville.
1977   Plantation Archaeology at the Hermitage: Some Suggested Patterns. *Tennessee Anthropologist* 2(2):152–163.

SOUTH, STANLEY, RUSSELL K. SKOWRONEK, AND RICHARD E. JOHNSON
1988   Spanish Artifacts from Santa Elena. *Anthropological Studies* 7. Occasional Papers of South Carolina Institute of Archaeology and Anthropology, University of South Carolina, Columbia.

STEEN, CARL
1992   A Preliminary Report on the 1992 Excavations at Pine Grove Plantation, Berkeley County, South Carolina. Report on file, Diachronic Research Foundation, Columbia, South Carolina.
1995   Archaeological Investigations at Somerset Plantation, Washington County, North Carolina. Report prepared by Diachronic Research Foundation, Columbia, South Carolina. Submitted to the North Carolina Historic Sites Division, Department of Cultural Resources, Raleigh, North Carolina.

STEINER, CHRISTOPHER
1990   West African Trade Beads: Symbols of Tradition. *Ornament* 14(1):58–61.

STINE, LINDA FRANCE
1989   Raised Up in Hard Times: Factors Affecting Material Culture on Upland Piedmont Farmsteads, circa 1900–1940s. Unpublished Ph.D. dissertation, Department of Anthropology, University of North Carolina, Chapel Hill.
1990   Mercantilism and Piedmont Peltry: Colonial Perceptions of the Southern Fur Trade, circa 1640–1740. *Volumes in Historical Archaeology* 14, edited by Stanley South. South Carolina Institute of Archaeology and Anthropology, Columbia.
1993   Archaeological Testing at the Saddlebag Cabin, Forks of Cypress Plantation, Lauderdale County, Alabama. Report prepared by RUST International, GIS Labs, Samford University, Birmingham, Alabama. Submitted to Heritage Preservation, Florence, Alabama.

STINE, LINDA F., PAUL BROCKINGTON, JR., AND CONNIE HUDDLESTON
1994   Searching for the Slave Village at Snee Farm Plantation: The 1987 Archaeological Investigations. Report prepared by Brockington and Associates, Atlanta, Georgia. Submitted to the Southeastern Regional Offices, National Park Service, Atlanta, Georgia.

STONE, LYLE M.
1974   *Fort Michilmackinac, 1515–1781: An Archaeological Perspective on the Revolutionary Frontier.* Publications of the Museum, Michigan State University, East Lansing.

STURM, FRED GILLETTE
1977   Afro-Brazilian Cults. In *African Religions: A Symposium*, edited by Newell S. Booth, Jr., pp. 217–240. NOK, New York.

THOMPSON, ERA BELL
1954   *Africa: Land of My Fathers.* Doubleday, New York.

THOMPSON, ROBERT FARRIS
1993   *Face of the Gods: Art and Altars of Africa and the African Americas.* Museum for African Art, New York, and Prestel, Munich.

TINGLING, MARION (EDITOR)
1977   *The Correspondence of the Three William Byrds of Westover, Virginia, 1684–1776.* Virginia Historical Society, University Press of Virginia, Charlottesville.

TRINKLEY, MICHAEL (EDITOR)
1986   Indian and Freedmen Occupation at the Fish Haul Site (38BU805), Beaufort County, South Carolina. *Research Series* 7. Chicora Foundation, Columbia, South Carolina.
1990   Archaeological Excavations at 38BU96, a Portion of Cotton Hope Plantation, Hilton Head Island, Beaufort County, South Carolina. Chicora Foundation, Columbia, South Carolina.
1991   Further Investigations of Prehistoric and Historic Lifeways on Callawassie and Spring Islands, Beaufort County, South Carolina. *Research Series* 23. Chicora Foundation, Columbia, South Carolina.
1993a   The History and Archaeology of Kiawah Island, Charleston County, South Carolina. *Research Series* 30. Chicora Foundation, Columbia, South Carolina.
1993b   Archaeological and Historical Examinations of Three Eighteenth- and Nineteenth-Century Rice Plantations on the Waccamaw Neck. *Research Series* 31. Chicora Foundation, Columbia, South Carolina.

TRINKLEY, MICHAEL, NATALIE ADAMS, AND DEBI HACKER
1992   Plantation Life in the Piedmont: A Preliminary Examination of Rosemont Plantation, Laurens County, South Carolina. *Research Series* 29. Chicora Foundation, Columbia, South Carolina.

TRINKLEY, MICHAEL, DEBI HACKER, AND NATALIE ADAMS
1993   Life in the Pee Dee: Prehistoric and Historic Research on the Roche Carolina Tract, Florence County, South Carolina. *Research Series* 39. Chicora Foundation, Columbia, South Carolina.

VERNON, AMELIA WALLACE
1993   *African Americans at Mars Bluff, South Carolina.* Louisiana State University Press, Baton Rouge.

WAHLMAN, MAUDE SOUTHWELL
1993   *Signs and Symbols: African Images in African-American Quilts.* Studio Books, Museum of American Folk Art, New York.

WALLIS, WILSON
1939   *Religion in Primitive Society.* F. S. Crofts, New York.

WARD, H. TRAWICK, AND R. P. STEPHENS DAVIS, JR.
1993   *Indian Communities on the North Carolina Piedmont, A.D. 1000 to 1700.* Reprint of 1978 edition. Cleveland Museum of Art, Cleveland, Ohio.

WATTERS, DAVID R.
1987   Excavations at the Harney Site Slave Cemetery, Montserrat, West Indies. *Annals of Carnegie Museum* 56:289–318.

WAYNE, LUCY B., AND MARTIN F. DICKINSON
1990   Four Men's Ramble: Archaeology in the Wando Neck, Charleston County, South Carolina. Report prepared by SouthArc, Gainesville, Florida. Submitted to Dunes West Development Corporation, Mount Pleasant, South Carolina.

WEEKS, WILLIAM M.
1990   The John H. Allston House Site: An Initial Occupation of Richmond Hill Plantation, Georgetown County, South Carolina. *Volumes in Historical Archaeology* 10, edited by Stanley South. South Carolina Institute of Archaeology and Anthropology, University of South Carolina, Columbia.

WEISMAN, BRENT RICHARDS
1989   *Like Beads on a String: A Culture History of the Seminole Indians in North Peninsular Florida.* University of Alabama Press, Tuscaloosa.

WELTY, EUDORA
1989   *Eudora Welty Photographs,* forward by Reynolds Price. University Press of Mississippi, Jackson.

WESLEY, CHARLES HARRIS
1968   *In Freedom's Footsteps: From the African Background to the Civil War.* International Library of Negro Life and History. Publishers Company, New York.

WHEATON, THOMAS R.
1993   Archaeological Testing of Willow Hall and Walnut Grove Plantations, Francis Marion National Forest. Report prepared by New South Associates, Stone Mountain, Georgia. Submitted to U.S.D.A. Forest Service, Francis Marion National Forest, Columbia, South Carolina.

WHEATON, THOMAS R., AMY FRIEDLANDER, AND PATRICK GARROW
1983   Yaughan and Curriboo Plantations: Studies in Afro-American Archaeology. Report prepared by Soil Systems, Marietta, Georgia. Submitted to U.S. Army Corps of Engineers, Charleston District.

WHITE, DEBORAH GRAY
1991   Female Slaves in the Plantation South. In *Before Freedom Came: African-American Life in the Antebellum South,* edited by Edward D. C. Campbell, Jr., with Kym S. Rice, pp. 101–121. Museum of the Confederacy, Richmond, and the University Press of Virginia, Charlottesville.

WILKIE, LAURIE A.
1994   Archaeological Evidence of an African-American Aesthetic. *African-American Archaeology* 10:1, 4.
1995   Magic and Empowerment on the Plantation: An Archaeological Consideration of African-American Worldview. *Southeastern Archaeology* 14(2):136–148.

WOOD, KAREN G.
1991   Site Evaluation on Three Sites at Historic Clayfield Plantation, Wambaw Ranger District, Francis Marion National Forest, South Carolina. Report prepared by Southeastern Archaeological Services, Athens, Georgia. Submitted to U.S.D.A. Forest Service, Francis Marion and Sumter National Forest, Columbia, South Carolina.

WORKS PROGRESS ADMINISTRATION (WPA)
1974   *Drums and Shadows: Survival Studies among the Georgia Coastal Negroes.* Savannah Unit, Georgia Writers' Project, Work Projects Administration. Reprint of 1940 edition. Reprint Company, Spartanburg, South Carolina.

WRIGHT, J. LEITCH, JR.
1986   *Creeks and Seminoles: The Destruction and Regeneration of the Muscogulge People.* University of Nebraska Press, Lincoln.

YENTSCH, ANNE E.
1994a   *A Chesapeake Family and Their Slaves: A Study in Historical Archaeology.* Cambridge University Press, Cambridge.
1994b   Beads as Silent Witnesses of an African-American Past: Social Identity and the Artifacts of Slavery in Annapolis, Maryland. Paper presented at the Annual Meeting of the Society for Historical Archaeology Conference on Historical and Underwater Archaeology, Vancouver, British Columbia.

YOUNG, AMY L.
  1994   Change and Continuity in African-Derived Religious
          Practices on an Upland South Plantation. Paper pre-
          sented at the 51st Southeastern Archaeological Con-
          ference, Lexington, Kentucky.

ZIERDEN, MARTHA A., JEANNE CALHOUN, AND DEBI
HACKER-NORTON
  1985   Archdale Hall: Investigations of a Low Country Plan-
          tation. *Archaeological Contributions* 10. Charleston
          Museum, Charleston, South Carolina.

ZIERDEN, MARTHA A., LESLEY M. DRUCKER, AND
JEANNE CALHOUN
  1986   Rural Life on Daniel's Island, Berkeley County,
          South Carolina. Report prepared by Carolina Archae-
          ological Services, Columbia, and Charleston Mu-
          seum, Charleston. Submitted to South Carolina De-
          partment of Highways and Public Transportation,
          Columbia.

LINDA FRANCE STINE
1801 15TH STREET
SILER CITY, NORTH CAROLINA 27344-2131

MELANIE A. CABAK
SAVANNAH RIVER ARCHAEOLOGICAL RESEARCH
    PROGRAM
P. O. DRAWER 600
NEW ELLENTON, SOUTH CAROLINA 29809-0600

MARK D. GROOVER
UNIVERSITY OF TENNESSEE
DEPARTMENT OF ANTHROPOLOGY
252 SOUTH STADIUM HALL
KNOXVILLE, TENNESSEE 37996-0720

ANN SMART MARTIN

The Role of Pewter as Missing Artifact: Consumer Attitudes Toward Tablewares in Late 18th Century Virginia

ABSTRACT

Ceramic assemblages have long been scrutinized by archaeologists. Yet, remarkably little attention has been given to
food-related objects not found in the archaeological record.
This study assesses the role of pewter—one such "missing
artifact"—as an alternative and companion to ceramics,
and thus provides a documentary framework of consumer
choice amidst social and marketing pressures. Probate
inventories of Albemarle County, Virginia, from 1770 to
1799 reveal a nearly standard presence of pewter in households of varying economic levels even after the introduction
of the "fashionable" creamware, and the slow addition of
ceramics to—not substitution for—pewter in more wealthy
households. Comparing pewter and creamware purchases at
contemporary retail stores estimates the time between an
object's purchase and its recording in the probate process,
and demonstrates real regional variability and rural conservatism. Finally, a consumer's view of pewter is attempted
through an understanding of its economic and symbolic
value and its uses within a household.

Introduction

Archaeologists have long used ceramics as primary evidence for the study of historic cultures.
The technical and decorative variation of ceramic
artifacts, their widespread use, and their availability in a large continuum of cost provides important
evidence about choices of acquisition and use.
Recent excellent publications in historical archaeology have also focused upon ceramics as sensitive
barometers of social and economic status and
ethnicity (Miller 1980; Felton and Shultz 1983;
Herman 1984). Certainly well-suited to examine
the role of ceramics, these studies are nonetheless
restricted by a reliance on archaeologically retriev-
able goods and fall short in the study of the full

range of behavioral patterning. Of course, while
the limitations of the archaeological record cannot
be changed, what can be altered is the analytical
focus. By considering the social and economic
value of using certain kinds of ceramics within a
framework of the full range of available choices,
perhaps some more sophisticated statements can be
made about the materials and behavior that are
recovered.

In a sense, ceramics have become a proxy for all
tablewares, a fatally simplistic assumption. For
example, pewter, a major component of tableware
items for two centuries, is seldom recovered in
archaeological excavations. Three simple reasons
explain its absence. First, pewter's durability prevented significant breakage and discarding and,
second, its resale value for recasting provided a
major outlet for its disposal. Finally, if discarded,
as a metal alloy it suffered varying degrees of
decomposition in the ground.

The absence of pewter tablewares, and to a far
lesser extent, those of wooden and silver, skews
our archaeological data in important ways. A brief
example will suffice. John Otto's now-famous
study of planter, overseer and slave sites in Cannon's Point, Georgia, revealed some compelling
differences in "social status and access to material
resources" through ceramic distribution. Because
the evidence of the slave population indicated a
greater reliance on hollow table wares, one inference was that they had a greater reliance on stews
than roasts (Otto 1975:120,360).

While not directly reflective of Otto's sample
population, a study of Albemarle County probate
inventories from 1770 to 1799 raises some important questions about "missing artifacts." For example, when both pewter and ceramic items were
combined, there was no correlation between
wealth and the number of hollow wares, such as
bowls and basins. One could not predict the other.
More important, 88 per cent of those particular
hollow ware forms were pewter, leaving few
bowls and basins likely to even become part of an
archaeological assemblage. Hence a change in the
patterning of ceramic forms did not necessarily
represent a change in all forms.

Analysis of these probate inventories demonstrates that until the opening decades of the 19th century, pewter was the common, if not predominant, material of serving items in Albemarle County, Virginia. This study will examine patterns of pewter ownership within different economic groups and look for changes after the introduction of the certainly less expensive and allegedly more fashionable creamware—tablewares so appropriate for the high-style dining behaviors documented among the elite in long-settled and urban regions. Comparing pewter sales at local retail stores will help assess the lapse in time between the purchase of an object and its recording in probate inventories, as well as estimate regional preferences in purchasing patterns. Finally, an attempt will be made to re-create the consumer's view of pewter through its market and symbolic value and its uses within the household.

Tablewares in Probate Inventories

Historical archaeologists have begun to stress the need for studying evidence discrete from the archaeological record (for example, see Beaudry et al. 1983). Probate documents from county courts are particularly popular data as they enumerate and evaluate slaves and household goods upon the death of an encumbered county resident. A 1774 guide for procedures of probate in Maryland listed the items to be inventoried:

> All the singular goods, chattels, wares, and merchandise such as ready money, household furniture, clothing, negroes, stock of cattle, corn, the crop on hand begun in the lifetime of the deceased and every sort of property in and about the house what kind soever, not being a freehold or parcel of it or fixed to it (the convenient apparel of the widow according to her degree excepted) (Vallete 1774:3).

Custom seemed to allow a widow her clothing, and at least protected a bed and a pot from eager creditors. Virginia law also provided that all food and liquor set aside for family use should not be sold or accounted for. Other exclusions included gifts and legacies made before death even though bequests made through wills remained a part of the estate until settlement (Hening 1823:150). Even though quite inexpensive items were listed, others were lumped or excluded.

The major problem with the study of probate records is not the quality and quantity of information available in the extant inventories. The overall possibility of retrieving accurate information from existing records is excellent. But because Virginia law provided several ways to bypass the probate process, the nagging problem remains of the actual representation of those whose estates reached probate. Under-representation of the very poor skews probate evidence towards the wealthy. Yet even if every estate was appraised, inventories would be further biased towards the wealthier population merely due to the recording of goods owned at death, an event which usually occurred at a later stage in the goods accumulation cycle (Carr and Walsh 1980). Thus the probate population is not a perfect reflection of the living population.

Overriding these considerations of bias, however, is the rich detail of their evidence of past household consumption. The data chosen for this study represented a 30 year period, 1770–1799, in Albemarle County, lying in the central piedmont of Virginia (Figure 1). One hundred and seventy households reached probate in those years, and their estates contained 2872 items relating to food preparation and serving (see Table 1 and Appendix).

Lying west of the fall line and at the eastern base of the Blue Ridge Mountains, present-day Albemarle County contains some 735 square miles, widely varying from east to west in topography, soils, drainage, and climate. Most of the area is within the Piedmont Physiographic Province characterized by rolling hills dissected by many small streams. The western portion, however, contains higher elevations and steeper slopes where many small, rapidly flowing streams cut narrow valleys. Most of these streams drain into the Hardware or the Rivanna Rivers, both tributaries of the James, which forms the southern border of the county (Hantman 1985:9–11). These waterways served as crucial linkages eastward, especially before the improvement of roads leading to the fall line. One late 18th century traveller reported that the area's temperate climate created what some called "the garden of the United States" (Weld 1799:206).

TABLE 1
FOODWAYS OBJECTS IN PROBATE INVENTORIES: ALBEMARLE COUNTY, VIRGINIA, 1770–1799

CERAMIC ITEMS:

Baking pan	Slop bowl	Dough chest	Shaving basin
Basin	Spoon boat	Dripping pan	Sieve
Bottle	Stand	Dutch oven	Sifter
Bowl	Sugar bowl	Ewer	Skillet
Breakfast plate	Sugar pot	Fat Jafr	Skimmer
Butter boat	Sweet meat dish	Fat pot	Soup spoon
Butter pot	Tea Canister	Flask	Spice mortar
Can	Tea pot	Flesh fork	Spinder
Chamber pot	Tureen	Fork	Spoon
Coffee cup	Twiffler	Frying pan	Spit
Coffee pot	Water jug	Funnel	Square bottles
Cream pot	Water vessel	Glass	Stand
Creamer		Grater	Stew pan
Crock	OTHER FOOD—	*Gravy Spoon*	Stilliards
Cruet	WAYS	Grid iron	Sugar box
Cup	ITEMS:	Hand dish	Sugar dish
Custard Cup		Hook	Sugar tongs
Desert plate	Baking pan	Jack	Tankard
Dish	Basin	Kettle	Tea board
Ewer	Basket	Kitchen furniture	Tea cannister
Fruit basket	Beer glass	Knife	Tea kettle
Jar	Bird roast	Ladle	Tea kitchen
Jug	Bottle	Measure	Teapot
Lid	Bowl	mortar and pestle	Teaspoon
Milk pot	Bread baker	Mug	tin
Muffin plate	Bread toaster	Mustard pot	Tongs
Mug	Bread tray	Nutmeg grater	Tray
Mustard pot	Butter tub	oven	Trivet
Ointment pot	Cannister	Pan	Tumbler
Oval dish	Canteen	Pan Handle	Vessel
Oval plate	Case knife	Patty pan	waiter
Pan	Cask	Pepper box	Warming pan
Pap boat	Castor	Phial	Wash basin
Patty pan	Chafijkn dish	Plate	Wash bowl
Pickle bottle	Chamber pot	Plate holder	Wash noggin
Pickle leaf	Cheese toaster	Plate warmer	Water polate
Pickle pot	Coffee Mill	Porringer	Wine glass
Pitcher	Coffee pot	Pot	
Plate	Collander	Pottle Pot	
Platter	Cork screw	Punch bowl	
Pot	Cover	Punch lakde	
Punch bowl	Crute	Rack	
Salad dish	Cup	salt cedllar	
Sauce boat	Decanter	Salt glass	
Saucer	Dish	Salver	
	Divided spoon	Sauce pan	

The piedmont region of Virginia was one of the first great frontiers of the Chesapeake. Previously held back by fears of Indians and frontier policy, the colony began to expand in the early 18th century past the fall line up the James River Valley. Beginning in the 1720s, large land grants were made to wealthy eastern planters in what was then the western portion of Goochland County, but another decade would pass before owners regularly settled their families there. By the time the sepa-

TABLE 2
LAND AND SLAVEOWNING: VIRGINIA AND MARYLAND, 1782–1783

Region	Piedmont Va	Shenandoah Valley, Va	Southside Va	Northern Neck Va	Western Shore, Md
County	Albemarle[a]	Frederick	Charlotte	Richmond	Calvert
Land					
% owning land	87.0	60.0	67.0[b]	70.0	49.0
% of all landowners:					
100 acres or less	8.5	8.0	8.0	23.5	29.2
1000 +	8.0	4.0	7.0	5.5	2.8
Slaves					
% owning slaves	54.0	20.0	63.5	62.5	56.0
% of slaveowners:					
12 or more slaves	9.0	3.5	10.5	16.5	10.0

Sources: [a]Data from Ayres, 1966. All other from Risjord, 1978.
[b]Land ownership in 1790.

rate county of Albemarle was established in 1744, much of the prime land in its present boundaries, especially along the rivers, had already been patented and a quarter of the landowners owned nearly three-quarters of the land (Watts 1947:15). Devereux Jarrett, a tutor moving from New Kent County to Albemarle in the 1750s, found an employer who owned "great possessions in lands, slaves, etc. etc." that he feared as "gentlefolk," one who moved in a different world from simple men of poor beginnings like himself. Yet despite the early establishment of a landed aristocracy, Jarrett found Albemarle County in those early years to be "nearly a frontier county," and the "manners of the people were generally more rough and uncivilized than in the more interior parts of the country (Matthews 1957: 23,20). As "nearly a frontier county," Albemarle remained a land of some opportunity for those of limited means. Many gained land and moderate prosperity, and by 1765 moderate sized farms (under 400 acres) were the homes of over 70 per cent of the landowners (Ayres 1966:47). Tobacco was the prime crop, although by no means the only one, and many farmers dragged their weighty hogsheads to the nearest creek or river where it was floated down the James. Others, enticed by high prices at the fall line at Fredericksburg, carried their produce overland. But the rapidly expanding population soon encouraged local marketing facilities, a process

eased in 1789 when two tobacco inspection stations were established in the county (Moore 1976).

By this time, however, many Albemarle County residents had begun moving in earnest toward the cultivation of wheat and other crops especially suited to the deep upland clays. Economic diversification and entrepreneurial activities added to the wealth of long-established families, as well as that of the sons of the tidewater that were increasingly pushed westward. The population in Albemarle County swelled so rapidly that the county was divided twice before the Revolution. By 1790, 12,000 residents made their home within the present day boundaries, blacks forming just under half of that number. The population would increase by nearly a quarter before the century's end.

Rapid population growth suggests that many who came were able to prosper. Table 2 demonstrates that the wealth of Albemarle County at the end of the Revolution was remarkably well distributed compared to many regions of Virginia and Maryland. Nearly 90 per cent of the households owned some form of land, and over half had slaves. There were few small farms, although planters owning more than 1000 acres were perhaps more prominent than in the other sample counties. A comparison of the size of landholdings between Albemarle and the coastal counties of Middlesex, Gloucester, Elizabeth City, Princess Anne, Accomac, and Northampton further high-

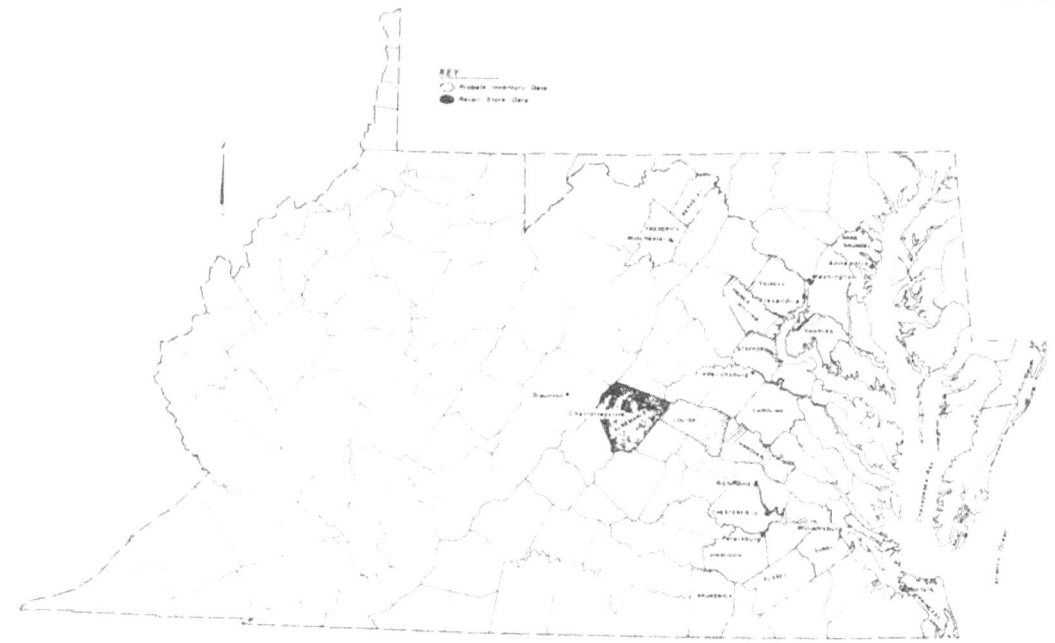

FIGURE 1. County locations of probate inventory and retail store data base.

lights the relatively equal prosperity of the Piedmont region. While two-thirds of the farms in Albemarle County were between 100 and 400 acres, less than half of those in those tidewater counties were of a similar size. The number of upper middling landowners—those owning 400 to 1000 acres—was doubled in Albemarle. Finally, there were four times the number of small farms (under 100 acres) in the long-established region than in Albemarle (Main 1954; Ayres 1966).

Thus, many residents of Albemarle County had access to capital in the form of farms and enslaved labor at least by the 1780s. Yet the expansion and opportunity for poorer men in a "frontier" society was to a large extent over. As population pressures and improvement pushed land prices higher, mobility in the piedmont became more restricted, just as it had in the tidewater. So too, a small group of elite consolidated their wealth and political power into a network linked by kinship and friendship. Joining that small group was increasingly limited to those men born to wealth (Kulikoff 1986: 160–161).

Tablewares in Retail Stores

Additional data for this study was gathered from the records of 19 Virginia and Maryland merchants in business between 1740 and 1800 (see Appendix and Figure 1). Like the village shops of England, these stores supplied the colonists with "every individual article necessary in life such as linens, woollens, silks, paper, books, iron, cutlery, hats, stockings, shoes, wine, spirits, sugars, etc. and even jewelry" (Smyth 1784:II,99). Such objects were usually purchased on credit, with payment made in crops, cash, or services. Thus, someone like Devereux Jarrett, the Albemarle County tutor, could begin to "get some credit in a store" and venture into debt for a new suit of clothes (Matthews 1957:32).

These kinds of year-round facilities mushroomed across the two colonies after the Tobacco Inspection Acts of Virginia in 1730 and Maryland in 1747, keenly jostling for customers and their crops. While even some of the wealthier planters were abandoning the consignment system of marketing—selling their own crops and obtaining goods on account in England—the patrons of local retail stores were most likely lesser farmers. These men and women did not usually have the capital to risk the vagaries of slow trans-Atlantic trade against potentially higher profits on their crops, and thus turned to a local storekeeper, often an agent for an English or Scottish firm. One Virginia merchant wrote in 1767 that the "best customers a store can have" were "those people who have one or two h[ogsheads] to dispose of" and who wanted goods instead of cash (Gill 1984:IV,4). The demand of these customers was for local access to consumer goods in the latest styles at reasonable prices, and twice-yearly it was customary for local merchants to complete an extensive order of the goods necessary for the following season's trade (Price 1954,1980).

While the organizational details of these retail businesses differed, a common problem faced both Scottish factor and local entrepreneur. By the eve of the Revolution, nearly one-quarter of all titheables may have been merchants (Bergstrom 1980: 219). So many merchants made competition fierce to obtain business at all. As early as 1743, Francis Jerdone reported 25 stores within 18 miles of his own in piedmont Louisa County, and four or more were expected in the next year (Jerdone 1743). Yet, in the west, Cumberland was deemed "a very proper place for a Merchant" in 1752 because it was on navigable water and there was no store within 10 miles (O'Mara 1983:233). Soon, however, competition for crops and customers would be felt even in backcountry places where stores moved in "to supply the real and imaginary necessities" of settlers and their wives. Thus, as "wealth and population increased, wants were created, and many considerable demands, in consequence, took place for the various elegancies as well as necessaries of life" (Eddis 1969:51–52).

As markets became more competitive, the selection of goods for sale became even more important for attracting and keeping business. John Mair's popular *Book-keeping Modernized* recommended varied stock for an 18th century retail store in Virginia or Maryland, and "the greater variety . . . the better; for wherever planters find

they can be best suited and served, thither they commonly resort" (Mair 1905:89). If one merchant could not provide the desired goods, there were always other stores for customers to patronize. Richard Blow's storekeeper in Charlotte Court House wrote in 1785 complaining that several new stores had opened there. He explained that his customers had grown choosy and "now if you do not exactly suit them in every article they may want they go immediately to some of our neighbors and there lay out there [*sic*] tobacco" (Teute 1976:81). William Allason of Falmouth had the same problem: he needed a "good assortment in order to keep my customers to myself without allowing them to go to my neighbors for trifles" (Allason 1760).

Invoices recording goods ordered by these merchants complement the probate data in several important ways. Although these particular lists of goods cannot answer questions of household consumption (i.e. *who* bought what), they can help override a major problem of probate evidence: the accumulation of goods over a lifetime or even several generations. Merchants' records thus provide much better dating control. Secondly, if stores in a number of communities have similar patterns in the goods they stocked, a horizon in material culture is suggested and the representativeness of the Albemarle County data may be confirmed.

Changes in Anglo-American Society and Tableware Production

The temporal limits of this study were chosen for several reasons. The most important was the testing of the impact of a specific historical process on 18th century Virginians. An alleged radical transformation of English consumer attitudes towards objects resulted in a spending boom that reached "revolutionary proportions" by the third quarter of the century. Large and small, inexpensive and dear, consumer goods representing the pursuit of fashion and conspicuous consumption were becoming a part of life for all but the indigent, each group participating to their own ability. The propellants of this tidal wave of mass consumption were rumbles of social and economic change, beginning in England and spreading to the colonies. Seemingly disjointed in their genesis, widespread economic, cultural and structural changes would come together by the end of the century to produce new abilities, desires, and methods of obtaining goods. One signal of this new consumer society was the demand for fashionable new ceramic items, a desire created by intense and innovative marketing of Josiah Wedgwood and other Staffordshire potters (McKendrick et al. 1982).

How did these changes in the cosmopolitan center affect consumers across the Atlantic? The American colonies had emerged as a significant foreign market for British manufactured goods, the destination, in fact, for almost half of the glass and earthenware exported in 1770 (McCusker and Menard 1985:284). Even after England lost the monopoly on her colonial market, the Staffordshire industry maintained a dominant position as supplier of ceramics. One Englishman observed just after the American Revolution that there would be little competition with British production of "Porcelain and Earthen ware of all Qualities, except the most Gross and Common . . . The importation has been and must be made from Great Britain, on account both of the quality and price" (Sheffield 1783:7). By no means were all of these items utilitarian; Benjamin Franklin claimed in 1766 that the greatest part of all British exports were "mere articles of fashion, purchased and consumed, because the fashion in a respected country" (Larabee 1969:143). Ceramics clearly matched his description, at least as seen in orders from some Virginia merchants. For instance, John Wilkins was insistent in his 1773 London order: he wanted "one dozen fashionable sugar dishes, newest fashion ware" (Wilkins c. 1773). Current ceramic vogue was the paramount concern, for whatever the coming fashion would soon be demanded by his Northampton County customers.

Archaeological and documentary sources should reflect these supposed profound changes. Archaeological evidence seems to show that the rise of the Staffordshire pottery industries made ceramics so

inexpensive, plentiful, and desired that they filled virtually every white home in the British Empire. Ivor Noël Hume points out, for instance, that creamware is present on "most American sites of the late 18th and early 19th centuries" (Noël Hume 1969:125). Evidence from 18th century retail stores demonstrates that consumers flocked to purchase the new creamwares in a variety of dining and tea forms, leaving older styles languishing on store shelves (Martin 1988). One would believe that ceramics, and especially creamware, had become the predominant tableware item.

"Quite new in its appearance, covered with a rich and brilliant glaze, bearing sudden alternations of heat and cold, manufactured with ease and expedition and consequently cheap," creamware could naturally outpace its rivals like the oldfashioned and expensive pewter (Coombe 1790: VI, 934). As a matter of fact, Neil McKendrick claims that by the third quarter of the 18th century "one no longer spoke of common pewter but of common Wedgwood" (McKendrick et al. 1982:103). The creamware of Wedgwood and others was arriving in this country "in such quantities and so cheaply that it was supplanting all other tablewares and crowding the pewter plate right off the table" (Sprackling 1958:7).

To best evaluate how—if—and when this hypothetical pewter plate came to fall of the household table requires a bit of background. Other scholars have shown that a majority of households in 17th century Virginia and Maryland used pewter plates (Beaudry et al. 1983:25). Indeed, Gloria Main discovered that pewter ware was the third "priority" in Maryland households of young fathers between 1650 and 1720, falling in frequency only behind beds and iron cooking utensils. This choice cross-cut class lines, forming a continuum with over 90 per cent of those in the top two-thirds of wealth owning pewter, and even half in the bottom five per cent of the population. Overall, 88 per cent of these households contained at least one item of pewter (Main 1982:242).

The dominance of pewter in Virginia and Maryland households before 1700 seemed to be representative of much of the British empire. The unfortunate result was a virtual saturation of the

British and American markets by the mid 18th century (Hatcher and Barker 1974:280). The pewterers had a compound dilemma: the durability of their product limited replacement demand by those who already owned it, and the nature of their medium limited the ways designs could be used to make it fashionable. Even if the forms were slightly modified, a more important problem was the restriction of surface decoration, for it was just this surface ornament that differentiated ceramic prices and popularity. While there were two basic grades of pewter, common and hard, there were many levels of price—and hence social status—in ceramic items (Miller 1980) (see Figures 2 and 3).

Another change lay far beyond the pewter industry itself. A transformation in the drinking habits of British and American society did not favor pewter. Between 1722 and 1833 British beer consumption decreased an estimated 50 per cent per capita, with pewter vessels preferred by many for its drinking. In the same period, per capita tea consumption rocketed from one ounce to two to three pounds. Hot beverages were the potter's domain. While the British liked their beer warm, they did not want their tea cold. Pewter conducted heat, especially to human lips, and cooled tea. Despite production of pewter tea and coffee pots, the influx of tea drinking was highly detrimental to the pewterer; he could never emulate delicate china teacups, and with changing tastes his own wares looked increasingly bulky (Hatcher and Barker 1974:281).

The final cause contributing to pewter's downfall was the aforementioned wooing of public taste by Staffordshire entrepreneurs. The tensions felt in the pewter industry as its popularity waned and that of its competitors rose can be seen through the reaction of the Cornwall tin miners, the first and major link in the chain of pewter production. As tin prices plummeted, an Exeter paper of 1776 reported a mob of tinners which rose "in consequence of the introduction into that country of large quantities of Staffordshire and other earthenwares." The crowd went to a neighboring town and broke all the wares for sale. From there they went to the next town where "because they could not force their way into the Town Hall where large

FIGURE 2 Pewter plate, London, Thomas Chamberlain, 1750–1770 (Photograph courtesy of the Colonial Williamsburg Foundation)

amounts of Staffordshire and other wares were lodged," set about to burn it down, a job only averted by the town alderman going with them to a pewterer's and ordering a quantity of pewter dishes and plates. Josiah Wedgwood himself noted in his journal of June 5, 1775 that he had been advised "not to trust myself among the miners of Cornwall, the tin trade being then low, and they being persuaded that the use of Queen's ware was the cause of it" (Hatcher and Barker 1974:286).

A rough scenario is set. A transformation occurred in the production of ceramics just as the British pewter industry was struggling, perhaps even providing the catalyst for pewter's demise. According to historical accounts of British tableware production, a simple change had occurred: innovatively marketed and technologically improved ceramics replaced pewter as the common tableware.

Part of the appeal of these new ceramics was their social value. Josiah Wedgwood's acquisition of royal patronage for his new creamware was brilliant marketing that sent consumers scrambling. By 1767 Wedgwood's experience with such patronage had taught him that "if a Royal, or Noble introduction be as necessary to the sale of an

FIGURE 3. Creamware plate, overglaze transfer print of the seal of Virginia, 1770–1785 (Photograph courtesy of the Colonial Williamsburg Foundation).

Article of Luxury as real Elegance & beauty, then the Manufacturer . . . will bestow as much pains, and expence too, in gaining the former of these advantages, as he wd. on bestowing the latter'' (McKendrick et al. 1982:108). First royalty was impressed, then nobility flattered, then the wishes of the common people to be like their betters were finally realized—each group's purchases separated by the appropriate quality, decorations, forms, and hence price. The powerful engine of social emulation was in high gear in mid 18th century society. As Henry Fielding complained, ''the nobleman will emulate the Grandeur of the Prince and the Gentleman will aspire to the proper state of a Nobleman; the tradesman steps from behind his Counter into the recent place of the Gentleman. Nor doth the confusion end there: It reaches the very Dregs of the People, who aspire still to a degree beyond that which belongs to them'' (McKendrick 1985:21–22). Soon such complaints would be echoed across the Atlantic where one post-war traveller blustered that ''this mania for luxury has reached such an extent that the wife of the laboring man wishes to vie in dress with the wife of the merchants, and the latter does not wish to be inferior to the wealthy women of Europe'' (Bayard 1950:130–131). From the wish for ease and comfort sprang emulative spending—the common man's ''petty vanity for tricking out himself

and his family in the flimsy manufactures of Britain'' (Lemay 1987: 847).

These complaints illustrate the material effects of the challenge to traditional ideas about class structure and relations in 18th century Anglo-American society (Corfield 1987). Focusing on the Chesapeake colonies, the evidence has also mounted exponentially for sweeping changes in the economy, social structure, architecture, and material culture of the region (Kulikoff 1986; Isaac 1982; Neiman 1978; Carr and Walsh 1985, 1988). Social stratification and the importance of social rituals as class delineators are a major tenet of these recent studies. Specialized spaces in manorial brick houses provided an appropriate environment for such social rituals as the fashionable, elaborate serving of labor-intensive and exotic foods on fine ceramic tablewares; an elegant atmosphere and a genteel activity to demonstrate one's enhanced position to the lesser classes and reinforce one's membership in a colony-wide political and economic elite (Bushman 1984:345–383; Douglas and Isherwood 1979:66). All of these behaviors—and their props— became demarcators of class membership, visible indicators of the way people lived at the top of the social hierarchy. Not institutionally disbarred, the lesser classes at least perceived the chance to be received in the circles above, further spurring social emulation to close the gap to those above and increase the distance from those below.

In this process, fine ceramics, like the socially-correct creamware, gained heightened importance as social symbols. If a new concern for fashionable and elaborate dining had emerged among the middling ranks, the demand for the appropriate supporting artifacts—such as fine ceramic tablewares—should be seen in their household inventories. Thus, both from society and the market, historical evidence suggests change, not continuity, in the use of pewter or ceramics in 18th century Virginia.

Albemarle County Probate Records

But are those changes reflected in the household possessions of those that lived and died in late

8th century Albemarle County, Virginia? The answer from the probate evidence of 170 households is clear: despite large-scale changes in British tableware production and the heightened importance of fine ceramics in dining, pewter was not immediately replaced by ceramics in Albemarle County homes.

The number of households containing some type of ceramic remained static from 1770 to the end of the century; there was no large influx as would be produced by the revolutionary and universal introduction of creamware by 1762 and later refined earthenwares. Similarly, pewter remained a standard presence in households of all economic levels. Eighty per cent of all the households represented in Albemarle County probate inventories in those three decades contained pewter, 80 per cent contained ceramics, and about 70 per cent contained both pewter and ceramic.

The ubiquitous ownership of pewter reported between 1650 and 1720 seems to have remained surprisingly constant for households of the next several generations. Does this mean that dining behaviors remained unchanged? One way to test this proposition is to examine the presence of pewter and ceramic serving items in those households of varying economic ranks and through time. Plates were the most basic and numerous item, and those inventories listing at least one plate—either pewter or ceramic—were selected as test cases. Of that group of plates found in Albemarle County probate inventories, about two-thirds were pewter. Each household contained a median of about a dozen plates, and only a quarter of these were ceramic. However, the large number of ceramic plates in *some* households pulled the mean to 21, of which almost half were ceramic. The continued predominance of pewter in Albemarle County is again suggested.

Did the frequency of pewter change in households of differing wealth? Cautioning that the very poorest were probably not represented in the probate process, the percentage of households in each wealth category that owned at least one pewter plate did not change greatly as one progressed up the economic scale. At no economic tier did fewer than 70 per cent of the households own pewter,

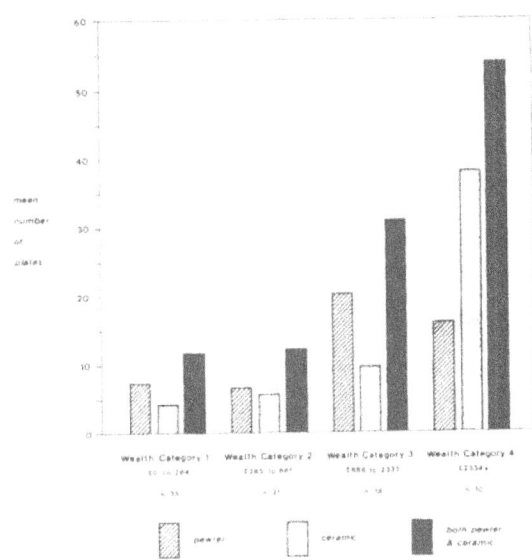

FIGURE 4 Mean number of plates by wealth category, Albemarle County, 1770–1799

and the percentages were nearly identical at the top and bottom end of society.

Nevertheless, the frequency of ceramics does suggest some differences among economic groups: the presence of ceramics markedly increased as one's wealth increased. While little more than a third of the bottom tier owned ceramic plates, that number steadily increased to two-thirds in the top echelon. Thus, even though pewter was standard in all groups, the frequency of ceramics increased up the economic scale. The poorest households were most likely to have pewter, but the richest chose both pewter and ceramic.

Turning from presence/absence of pewter plates to the mean number of plates, these patterns are again confirmed. Figure 4 presents the mean numbers of plates in these probate records, while Table 3 presents the basic statistical data to evaluate those averages. The most obvious trend is expected: the wealthier a household, the more plates of all categories owned. Within each group there was also significant variation in the quantities owned, a characteristic which increased significantly with wealth. For example, the marked

TABLE 3
DESCRIPTIVE STATISTICS FOR PLATES IN HOUSEHOLDS OF VARYING WEALTH: 1770–1799

	WEALTH GROUP 1	WEALTH GROUP 2	WEALTH GROUP 3	WEALTH GROUP 4
ALL PLATES				
MEAN	11.5	12.2	30.7	53.8
MEDIAN	7.0	7.0	19.0	38.0
STD DEV	12.1	9.5	25.6	57.3
MAXIMUM	66.0	36.0	97.0	156.0
PEWTER PLATES				
MEAN	7.3	6.6	21.0	15.7
MEDIAN	6.0	6.0	14.0	12.0
STD DEV	5.2	6.5	22.6	13.0
MAXIMUM	21.0	23.0	97.0	45.0
PRESENCE[a]	85.7	71.4	100.0	90.0
CERAMIC PLATES				
MEAN	4.2	5.6	9.7	38.1
MEDIAN	0.0	3.0	5.0	18.5
STD DEV	9.4	8.4	11.1	54.2
MAXIMUM	48.0	36.0	30.0	144.0
PRESENCE[a]	37.1	52.4	63.1	70.0
N[b]	35	21	19	10

[a]Percentage of households
[b]Number of inventories listing at least one plate

difference between the mean and median figures in the richer households suggests a tendency to own either large numbers of ceramic plates or perhaps none at all. The number of ceramic plates rose rapidly with one's wealth level, increasing nine-fold from top to bottom. In contrast, the number of pewter plates, although naturally increasing in wealthier households, did not increase in such large numbers. The mean number of pewter plates showed a much smaller increase from top to bottom, and it was the third wealthiest group that owned the largest number.

The bottom 70 per cent of the population, Wealth Groups 1 and 2, were remarkably similar in their ownership of pewter plates. An average of about a dozen plates graced their tables. These plates were most often pewter. Yet if an Albemarle County resident's rank moved just above the bottom half of the population to Wealth Group 2, one in two added a half dozen ceramic plates to the pewter ones in his home. However, it was in the top third of the population that dining behavior

may have become quite different. The inventories of those households just below the economic elite, Wealth Category 3, contained at least twice the number of plates as those less wealthy below them. While every householder in this group had pewter plates, two-thirds also had ceramic.

Yet, the wealthiest households in Albemarle County, the top nine per cent of the decedent population, still managed to separate themselves from those below through their material goods. The number of plates jumped so dramatically that ownership of several sets of ceramics is suggested. Men and women in this group could choose between three dozen ceramic plates or more than a dozen pewter ones. While the group below had more pewter plates on average, more of Wealth Group 4 chose ceramics—and in large numbers. It is only at the top of the economic scale that ceramic plates outnumbered pewter ones.

Were there changes in pewter ownership as a generation matured and died in the late 18th century? While the retention of pewter from an earlier era might be expected for those dying in the beginning years of the sample, part of the group setting up a household in 1770 may have just been entering the probate population by the end of the century. This cohort would not necessarily have already made the initial investment into pewter as ceramics had become more popular. Yet while there were differences between the consumer choices in the estates of *some* of these men or women and those of the previous generation, no clear picture of change emerges. Mean numbers of all plates decrease, as well as the mean number of ceramic and pewter plates. But large differences between mean and median numbers and large standard deviations, particularly in ownership of ceramics, imply quite different choices within these households in each time period. There may have been a transitional period, or variability among economic groups may have masked changes across time.

Attempting to divide the population into economic groups by decade produces a sample size too small to be statistically significant, but one quite tentative generalization might be offered. While the number of pewter plates remains steady in households at each tier of the economic hierarchy in each time period, the mean number of ceramic plates among the elite tripled after 1780. Yet the median number of ceramic plates remained constant in this group in the same periods. It seems again that some households, particularly at the top of the economic scale, were acquiring large numbers of ceramic plates, but by no means were all making such purchases. This addition of ceramic to—not substitution for—pewter after the Revolution helps explain another trend over time. While fewer than half of the plates between 1770 and 1779 were ceramic, two-thirds were ceramic in the final decade of the century.

But, again, what of the seeming lack of change over time in the vast majority of the population—the middling and lower ranks that continued to choose pewter over ceramic? Perhaps this later generation were investing in differing ceramic *forms* than their fathers, evidence that would be hidden in considering plates alone. If so, ownership of *any* ceramics should increase by the end of

the century. Combining all forms into a simple presence/absence test also enables the inclusion of "parcels" of pewter and ceramic in the probate lists, lumped groupings of goods where no form was designated.

Even so, the ownership of pewter, ceramic or both pewter and ceramic is relatively static in these 30 years, although there was some slight decrease in the number of households owning tablewares at all (Figure 5). Perhaps there was a change in the population itself: for example, more probate inventories in this time period did not include a full range of household goods and thus fewer decedents may have succeeded in setting up their own household after the Revolution.

Two sample years, 1815 and 1825, were arbitrarily chosen to test if a significant decline in pewter ownership took place in households in Albemarle County in the early 19th century. About half of those 26 households that entered probate in 1815 had some form of pewter. A decade later, however, fewer than a quarter of the dozen inventories listed pewter. The slight decreases occurring in the 18th century quickly accelerated by the first quarter of the 19th century. Pewter was then no longer common in Albemarle County households.

Two salient patterns are seen in this data. First, there are no significant changes in pewter ownership in probate inventories through the end of the 18th century, although a slight decrease may be indicated. Pewter remained standard for most families, while some households were slowly adding ceramic plates. Changes in production and marketing in the late 18th century were not immediately reflected in the consumer behavior of the Albemarle County probate population. According to the probate data, there were fewer ceramic plates than pewter ones in the last three decades of the 18th century in Albemarle County, but this would markedly change in the coming generation.

The second important evidence is that there were distinct differences in the patterning of ceramic and pewter usage by varying economic groups. If those in the wealthier groups owned ceramic plates, they owned large numbers. But only in the uppermost echelon of society did ceramic plates outnumber pewter ones. Many in

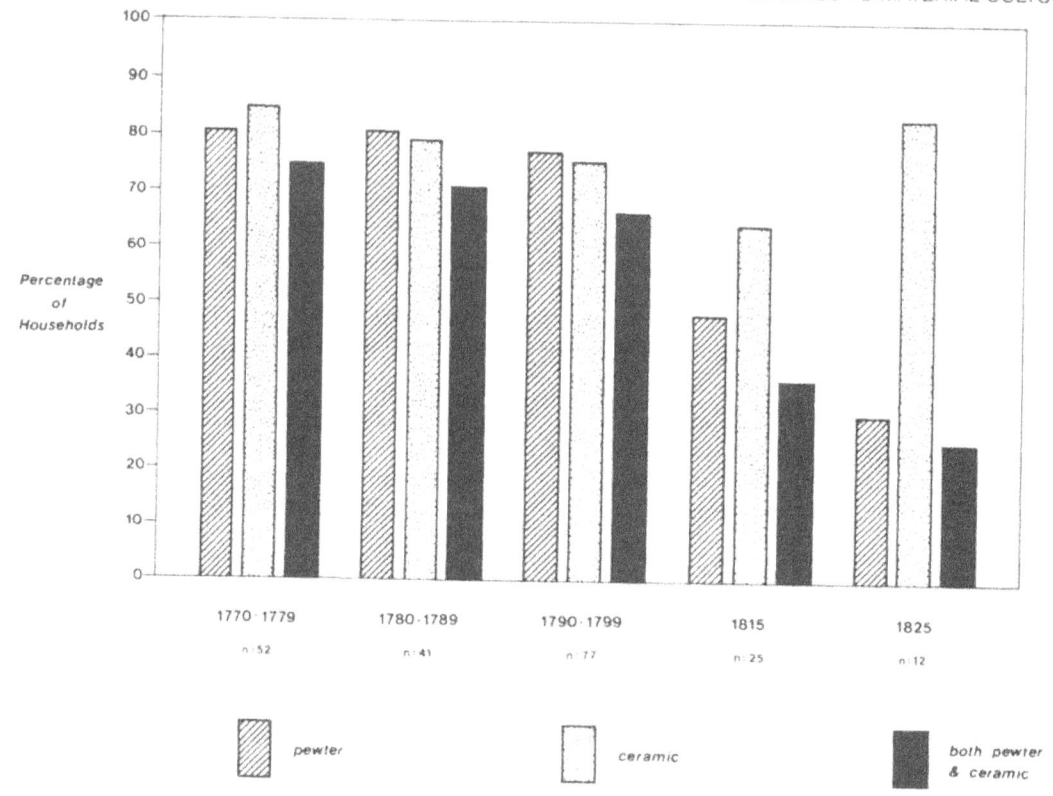

FIGURE 5. Presence of pewter and ceramics in Albemarle County households, 1770–1825.

this elite group acquired a large number of the more fashionable new ceramic wares so appropriate for large-scale entertaining, and here ceramic plates outnumbered pewter ones. Looking to those just below the elite, the upper middling ranks that may also have had disposable income to invest in items of social display, some did certainly choose to separate themselves from those below through the investment in more ceramic tablewares. But most still selected pewter, albeit in far larger numbers that their less wealthy neighbors. If the proposition is valid that the purchase of ceramic tablewares suggests a participation in the consumer frenzy promoted by Wedgwood, then the middling ranks of Albemarle County do not seem to have been fooled by such fashion manipulation. Similarly, if the ownership of fine ceramic tablewares suggests an attempt to emulate elite fashionable high-style dining behaviors, then those households do not seem to have been participating in the anxious social drama of the 18th century Chesapeake colonies.

Virginia and Maryland Retail Stores

Such answers only open a Pandora's box of questions. Is the inventory evidence so blurred with the lifetime accumulation of objects that changes in consumer behavior are masked? Were Albemarle County residents representative of Virginia society as a whole? One way to answer both of these questions is through the use of independent historical documents. While probate inventories represent the acquisitions of one household for many years, invoices of goods sent to Virginia and

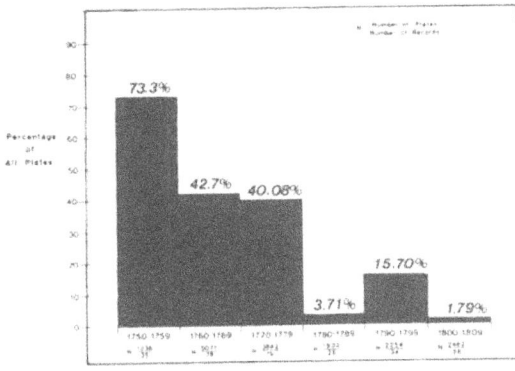

FIGURE 6. Pewter plates ordered in 19 sample Virginia and Maryland stores, 1750–1810: Percentage of all plates.

Maryland merchants record the acquisitions of many households at one time. These records provide a more precise tracking of the introduction and popularity of items throughout the general population. Similarly, by studying the inventories of stores in other places, we can better judge the consumer behavior of Albemarle County.

The decline in the importance of pewter plates in 19 sample stores is dramatic (Figure 6). Between 1750 and 1759, three-fourths of the plates were pewter. Fifty years later that number was less than two per cent. With each decade, fewer of the plates imported were pewter, their number particularly plummeting during the chaos of the Revolution and its immediate aftermath. A partial explanations for this abrupt plunge may lie in the materials of pewter, tin and lead. Both were necessary to the war effort. In any event, total exports of pewter from Britain dropped 75 per cent between 1772 and 1780 (Schumpeter 1960).

Even as the sale of pewter declined, that of creamware skyrocketed. The trickle of creamware that began in the late 1760s would become a flood in the Chesapeake in only a few years, pushing aside not only pewter but white salt glazed stonewares and tin-enameled earthenwares as well (Martin 1988). The purchase of creamware by so many people in so short a time could not have merely been for functional reasons. Even if all had

the same ability to buy, each consumer carried into these different stores certain cultural, social, and behavioral norms that may have led one to purchase a certain item, another to abstain. Some modes were general, others were personal. A different mix of cultural values—some matching a social norm, some varying—led some customers to respond positively to certain artifacts or aspects of artifacts while neglecting others. The decisions to purchase creamware or pewter in a handful of stores, each catering to a differing assortment of middling backcountry farmers, small tidewater planters, and the urban service sector create aggregate purchasing patterns that demonstrate the degree to which each locality ascribed to one such cultural value—the emulation of elite behaviors and the appeal of fashion.

Residents of Albemarle County shopped at one such local store, owned by Dr. Thomas Walker. A physician, merchant, politician and entrepreneur in Albemarle County, he held multiple political offices and was trustee for laying out the fledgling town of Charlottesville beginning in 1763 (Woods 1900:53). By the 1780s he seems to have ranked among the wealthiest men in the county (Moore 1976:84). Walker's store was in operation in the new county seat at least by 1768 and his family papers from 1764 to 1769 included invoices for his retail business. During this time he imported 30 dozen plates—two-thirds pewter and the remainder of white salt glazed stoneware. His customers were probably the middling ranks of Albemarle County society, and he would have extended credit for their purchases throughout the year, answering requests like "please send by the Bearer a quart stone or earthen Bowl and one of your largest Tumblers" (Maury 1768).

Even though later data is not available for this store, we can assume from other merchants' records that the percentage of ceramic plates in his stock should have increased over time. The customers that came in the 1770s to purchase sugar or salt or coarse osnaburg would undoubtedly see the gleaming creamware plates, so delicate and refined and new. Did they buy them, carefully tucking them in straw or carrying them in their laps across the jolting back country roads?

FIGURE 7. Locations of four sample merchants. c. 1760–1784.

While some were won by the new fashions, as a group they were not. The number of pewter tablewares in households of the lower 70 per cent of the Albemarle County probate population, those most likely to have been local store customers, remained almost static from 1770-1799—ranging from 55 to 65 per cent of all tablewares, matching the stock of Walker's store as much as 30 years earlier. If the middling sorts purchased creamware in large amounts instead of pewter in the 1770s, perhaps it was by the young setting up household,

for such behavior was not seen in the middle-aged ranks that died by the end of the century. But the wealthy Dr. Walker was not so immune to a sense of status display, purchasing queen's ware serving items in quantities in 1772 and 1773 for his own use. Walker's seven queen's ware dishes, however, were not to become probate evidence for some 24 years.

Did the consumer behavior of Albemarle County represent Virginia society at the end of the 18th century? The stock of retail stores demonstrates some local, or perhaps regional, variation in consumer demand. Four contemporary stores with excellent documentation can serve as quick examples (Figure 7). William Allason was a merchant in Falmouth, Virginia from 1760 to 1774. On the fall line of the Rappahanock River, his store drew a large number of customers from the piedmont and the upper Shenandoah Valley, nearly a quarter travelling the 80 miles from Frederick County. The importance of the consumers of that western market led Allason to open a satellite store in Winchester before a feared Indian attack forced him to withdraw (Spoede 1973). Between 1760 and 1774 the majority—about two-thirds—of the plates stocked in his store were pewter. Allason ordered tin-glazed earthenware (delft) in the 1760s, sold in small but constant quantities until he introduced creamware in 1770. After that time, the leftover delft plates lingered on his shelves until the closing of his store.

In contrast, creamware plates sold quickly; his customers purchased 172 plates in only three years. Porcelain, by far the most expensive ceramic plate, had no buyers for three years, and even then Allason could only rid himself of half of his original order of twelve. Pewter was the workhorse of his tablewares—demand was high and he re-ordered it consistently even after adding creamware to his stock. While 270 creamware plates were ordered in 1770 and none after, he added twice that number of pewter in the next four years.

Just down the Rappahanock River was the store of Edward Dixon. A retired sea captain, gaining land and slaves through a well-placed marriage, Dixon had settled in Port Royal in Caroline County as an agent for an English mercantile firm. A merchant with an extensive commission trade in tobacco and grain exports, he also managed the inspection warehouse, as well as keeping a blacksmith shop. (Bergstrom 1980:211). An invoice and inventory book records store transactions there from 1767 to 1774. In that first year he ordered 96 delft and 144 pewter plates, of which about half of each remained in stock a year later. After another year a little more than a third of the original delftware plates remained, and he would only sell

seven in the next two years. But his pewter sold out and he replenished his stock of it in March.

So far the transactions at his store are not so different from those at William Allason's. But after the introduction of creamware, Dixon ordered no more pewter plates. His customers instead chose 28 dozen creamware plates in the next four years. The patrons of Dixon's store were demanding expensive and fashionable ceramics, and in his store is the earliest creamware documented in Virginia: enameled cream colored teas in 1768. Enameled porcelains and copper plated (overglaze transfer printed) coffee pots were all available to his customers.

A third example is the firm of Hooe, Stone and Company, running a commission house and store in prosperous Alexandria, with satellite stores on both sides of the Potomac at Dumfries, Virginia, and Portobacco, Maryland. Invoice books, extant from 1771 to 1784, record large-scale dealings in grains to Europe, Britain, and the West Indies. Their transactions were only slowed by the Revolution; shipments of ceramics continued through neutral countries (Preisser 1977).

The first plates Hooe and Stone received in 1771 were three dozen "white stone barley corn plates," followed by two dozen more of "white stone" two years later. During this same time their suppliers also shipped four dozen pewter plates. By 1774, 80 per cent of the white salt-glazed plates had been sold, as well as half of the pewter. As in Edward Dixon's store, there was little demand for other types of plates after the introduction of creamware. The first creamware was top-of-the-line: over four dozen "gold-bordered" queen's ware table and desert plates, costing two to three times undecorated creamware and more than blue-and-white porcelain. While these luxuries were slow-sellers, Hooe, Stone and Company ordered more than 500 plain creamware plates in the next 11 years, as well as six dozen porcelain ones. They also stocked two "compleat dining setts Queens Ware," each containing 240 pieces. Such matched sets included all the props for the serving of abundant and elaborate foods in the highly-schematic diagrams illustrated in contemporary cookbooks. With the inclusion of items such as barrel-shaped mugs "painted and gilded with the four parts of the world," an impressionistic picture arises of truly urban difference in lifestyle, a "level of conspicuous consumption almost never matched in the countryside" (Walsh 1983:112).

This impression is only reinforced by the items for sale in other urban places. The partnership of Wallace, Davidson, and Johnson formed in Annapolis in March 1771. With £1000 capital contributed by each partner, Joshua Johnson was dispatched to London to purchase goods for a new store. Despite increasing competition in the Annapolis trade, Johnson felt their business would have the advantage, "our goods being better in quality, more fashionable and better chosen . . . for my having time and seeing them myself." He instructed his partners to "enumerate the articles and describe them but leave the fashion and quality to me" (Papenfuse 1975; Price 1979:21,11).

His first shipment of goods was equal to the firm's whole capital, forming at once an inventory about three times the value of William Allason's. That initial order included 11 dozen creamware table, dessert, and soup plates, and six dozen more table plates were re-ordered a few months later. Yet no pewter plates were included in the two schemes of goods requested or shipped that year. Annapolis residents wanted not only creamware plates, but a wide assortment of the proper matching serving pieces: three different varieties of salad dishes (oblong, octagonal, and pierced), cruets for condiments, egg cups and pickle stands and salts. Marketed separately, their price would be in reach of a far greater part of the population than the complete sets sold by Hooe, Stone, and Company. Perhaps they are evidence that those of lesser economic abilities were also concerned with the kinds of high-style dining dictated in contemporary cookbooks. Aptly enough, one such recipe book, Hannah Glasse's *The Art of Cookery Made Plain and Easy*, was included in the first shipment, containing instructions for preparation of the kind of "side or corner dishes" those forms would contain (Glasse 1797:134). Creamware was the overwhelming tableware of choice for the residents of Annapolis.

The customers of these stores differed in their demands for expensive and fashionable goods. Although Allason successfully added creamware to his stock, it was in addition to pewter. In contrast, creamware replaced pewter to a large extent in Edward Dixon's store. Pewter was insignificant in the stock of Hooe, Stone, and Company in Alexandria, while two grades of creamware were available there; a small number of gold-bordered plates were sold as well as a huge volume of common creamware plates. But Wallace, Davidson and Johnson did not even stock pewter plates in their new store in Annapolis. They sold several sizes of creamware plates for a soup, main, and dessert course, as well as a large complement of matching serving pieces.

The bulk of customers at stores in places like Annapolis and Alexandria were not the wealthiest urban elite, many of whom continued to make direct requests to an agent in England, but those that catered to the elite themselves; artisans, ordinary keepers, and the broad range of a growing service sector (Papenfuse 1975:28). It was in these more urban places that sociability, both private and public, was an important part of daily life (Clark 1988). Even the 800 residents of declining Yorktown, Virginia spent their time "dining together, drinking punch and playing billiards" at the end of the 18th century. One function of this conviviality was social display, an opportunity for the rich man "to shew the stranger his splendid furniture, his fine English glass, and exquisite china" (La Rochefoucauld 1799:II,21,38). Nor was this limited to the wealthy: one early 19th century critic lampooned urban society as a citadel of bandboxes where "fashion intermeddled with everything and descended to all ranks to seek for votaries" (*Norfolk Gazette and Publick Ledger*, January 26, 1814). For example, in early 19th century Williamsburg, Virginia, over one-third of the lower-middling ranks of society owned some portion of a group of luxury goods related to entertaining at dinner or tea parties, such as table or tea wares of silver, plate or cut glass, or mahogany dining tables, sideboards or chairs. Yet only three per cent of the same economic group in surrounding rural York County had such items in their households (Smart 1986:84). These urban/rural contrasts are clearly documented in the types of goods purchased at local urban stores.

A second distinction may be found even between rural areas. While many of William Allason's customers were drawn from the western piedmont and "backcountry," Edward Dixon's patrons were mostly drawn from established tidewater families. Creamware was becoming increasingly common and popular for those of the "middling and lower sorts" in the east. Lorena Walsh and Lois Carr found that even one-third of the poorest Talbot County households on Maryland's Eastern Shore had some creamware by the 1790s, and among the richest, sets of 100 or more pieces of ceramic were common. Pewter continued at all levels of wealth, but with far less frequency than in Albemarle County (Lorena Walsh 1984, pers. comm.).

The predominant tableware items in late 18th century Virginia and Maryland were pewter and ceramics. Most ceramics were less expensive and perhaps more fashionable than pewter. But if the unbreakable pewter was already owned, the purchase of a dozen creamware plates—no matter what the cost—was unnecessary, even frivolous. If none other than functional meanings were attached, new products would only slowly move into a community, mainly as new households made their purchasing decisions based on long- or short-term economic value. But if *social* value was attached to their real value; if prestige could be consolidated by their purchase; then innovation would take place more quickly. Thus the acquired social value of queen's ware plates—the successful status marketing by Wedgwood and others and the desire for social emulation—was recognized most markedly in Annapolis, Alexandria, and the tidewater region. In the more recently settled piedmont and backcountry, however, such fashion trends and social desires were more muted. Thus, the data from Albemarle County probate inventories, though blurred by time, cannot be dismissed as anomalous.

What forces in Albemarle County and other Virginia regions mitigated against the replacement of pewter? For a product, such as creamware, to be generally adopted in a region, it must be afford-

able, available, and desirable. As discussed above, Albemarle County was marked by a large number of "middling" farmers, as well as quite a few rich landowners compared to many more eastern regions of the state. Many householders had already gained land and slaves to produce capital and enter commercial agriculture. Isaac Weld (1799:206) observed that the county's common people were able to "procure the necessaries of life upon very easy terms." Pewter was certainly purchased by those common people, and the few shillings necessary to purchase a dozen of the less expensive creamware plates was not beyond the means of most of the population.

In addition, the product must be available. First, creamware was stocked in each of the sample stores after the early 1770s, despite their location. Second, while no specific estimates are available for the number of stores in late 18th century Albemarle County, her inhabitants most likely had access to ample retail facilities. Charles Farmer's study of country stores in the Virginia southside demonstrates a wide range of facilities for the purchase of goods. Although Farmer did not study variation within a general stock of goods, he found that these smaller stores sold items not unlike those at fall line towns, although prices were slightly higher and finding a particular item at any given time was more difficult. In addition, there was extensive shopping at higher order retail places, like the towns at the fall line. Business and agricultural products moved regularly between frontier and established regions, not only among the wealthy, but among the cast of wagoners, herdsmen, and tobacco rollers who made purchases for neighbors and friends (Farmer 1984). It is unlikely that creamware was not available to Albemarle County residents.

It seems, therefore, that consumer desire probably played the paramount role in the acquisition of ceramic tablewares in places like Albemarle County. The county elite were certainly mirroring the lifestyles of their tidewater peers even before the Revolution, when one of the wealthiest residents paid for dancing lessons for the children of relatives and neighbors (Moore 1976). At the end of the century, Isaac Weld found "several gentlemen of large landed property, who farm their own estates, as in the lower parts of Virginia.'' Yet, he also thought the ''common people'' of the county to be ''of a more frank and open disposition, more inclined to hospitality, and to live more contentedly on what they possessed than the people of the same class in any other part of the United States I passed through'' (Weld 1799:205–206). If the common people of Albemarle County ''lived more contentedly on what they possessed,'' does this suggest that they did not choose to purchase items that were unnecessary or beyond their means? Thus, even if those at the top like Thomas Walker or Thomas Jefferson lived and moved in a world not unlike that of established tidewater society, perhaps those of the middling ranks chose a different set of cultural values, tied to the relative simplicity and egalitarianism of a prosperous piedmont economy.

Pewter's Value and Use

The rejection of mere fashion or conspicuous consumption in Albemarle County as one explanation for the continued presence of pewter fits nicely, but begs one final question. What was the function of the pewter recorded there? The final answer must lie in an object's use and value: its cost in the marketplace, its long-term worth for resale or reuse, its function or functions, and its ''meaning,'' if any, to those who used it.

The cost of new pewter to an Albemarle County consumer can easily be established in Thomas Walker's store in the late 1760s. A dozen white salt glazed stoneware plates cost him a modest two-and-a-half shillings while the same number of pewter plates ranged from eight to fourteen shillings. Assuming a constant mark-up for Mr. Walker's profit, a customer choosing pewter would spend four to six times more than had he or she chosen white salt glaze. The new fashionable creamware was no less a bargain to that customer. Between 1770 and 1779 the cost of pewter plates was consistently three to four times the cost of creamware plates, and even a bit higher than

porcelain ones in stores throughout Virginia and Maryland.

This initial start-up cost, however, was offset by pewter's durability and resale value. Suppose that hypothetical customer dropped a new ceramic plate a few weeks later. It could be repaired and placed on a shelf, but re-use was far less certain. In contrast, if the new pewter plate had been dropped, it would not have suffered more than a dent and could continue in use for years. If it had become a bit too battered, its owner could send it off to a pewterer to be recast, and for about half of his original cost could have a new plate in perfect condition (Greene 1965:1060). Perhaps he or she would sell it to a tradesman like James Haldane, who advertised that he gave ''the best prices for old . . . pewter'' or perhaps pass it on to an itinerant peddler (*Virginia Gazette,* February 6, 1772). One tradesman offered about 40 per cent of the retail cost of a new pound of pewter in the early 1770s, and a similar ratio was used for ''old pewter'' or ''pewter unfit for use'' in probate inventories throughout the century (Carter 1773: 26; York County Wills and Inventories 12:277, 23:414). In contrast, even intact ceramic items retained little value in probate inventories.

Thus pewter cost more initially but was a wise long-term investment. Was it perceived that way? According to James Deetz (1973: 28), pewter was a traditional symbol of wealth in 17th century America, its display serving as both ornament and social statement. Evidence from travellers' records, literary sources, and contemporary prints demonstrate some continuation of that tradition throughout the next century. For instance, upon entering a small log cabin in Connecticut in 1744, a wealthy traveller was horrified to find ''several superfluous things which showed an inclination to finery in these poor people,'' such as six pewter plates ''old and wore out but bright and clean.'' His suggestion that they sell the pewter—''too fine for such a cottage''—and substitute wooden plates which would be ''as good for use, and, when clean . . . almost as ornamental'' clearly articulates pewter's multiple role with utilitarian, decorative, and social functions (Bridenbaugh 1948:55). The description of the interior of a 14 by 18 foot cabin in 1800 still included brightly shining pewter, where make-shift shelves supported by pins driven into the logs displayed "in ample order a host of pewter plates, basins, dishes, and spoons, scoured and bright." More formal arrangement was on a "kind of sideboard or dresser with shelves called the pewter rack. Women prided themselves on keeping the whole [dinner set] brilliant as silver" (Montgomery 1973:16,14).

Even the famous tale of "The Legend of Sleepy Hollow" contains evidence of pewter's symbolic role. In this story, Washington Irving sets the scene of the home of a traditional wealthy Dutch family in New York. As the poor schoolmaster enters the hall "which formed the center of the mansion and the place of usual residence . . . rows of resplendent pewter, ranged on a long dresser, dazzled his eyes" (Irving 1978:781). Perhaps the immediate acknowledgment of wealth and material abundance dazzled Ichabod Crane as much as its gleaming metal. New fashions in refined earthenwares were less likely to impress in these traditional rural pockets of wealthy conservatism, where yeoman values were reinforced by religion and ethnicity. An 1816 description of Dutch and Quaker households in Virginia acknowledges the material culture of such conservatism where "the dresser[s] glistening with pewter-plates, still stand their ground, while the baseless fabrics of fashion fade away" (Paulding 1835:109). Thus, pewter for some may have represented both a solid economic investment and an accepted realm for display of one's wealth as late as the early 19th century.

Obviously some who could easily have afforded to purchase a dozen creamware or even porcelain plates chose to do so; yet others did not. Their foodways carried clear social meaning, and that message may have been remarkably conservative. Jack Goody points to the "nature and order of meals and courses, and the etiquette of eating" as an important factor for this conservatism in foodways (Goody 1977:151). Thus an early 19th century English poet lamented the disintegration of the traditional common table "Where master, son, and serving-man and clown/Without distinction daily sat them down," in households "where bright rows of pewter by the wall/Served all the pomp of

kitchen or of hall." The author chose these images as the final evidence of the transformation of ancient agrarian relationships and scorned the modern farmer who ate alone with his family, aspiring "to ape the country squire" (Snell 1985: 67).

Contemporary prints also confirm the display of pewter on shelves or in cupboards. In some households, however, ceramics and pewter stood side-by-side. Thus, acquired ceramics were not necessarily in competition with pewter as status symbols but actually reinforced the metal's statement about wealth. For instance, a household scene illustrated in 1796 depicts both pewter and ceramic gleaming from the parlor corner cupboard (Figure 8). Irving's wealthy Von Tassel "knowingly left open" his corner cupboard to display "old silver and well-mended china" while pewter dazzled in his hall (Irving 1978:782).

Just as the display of pewter and ceramic were not exclusive, neither were their functions in daily usage. Open cabinets were for storage of items as well as showmanship. As only the upper groups seemed to have more than enough plates than were required for daily usage, these scenes of display in most households could only have been one part of pewter's role. When a family owned both pewter and ceramics, what was the function of each?

Personal choice may have dictated that pewter still be used at the household table despite the introduction of more refined earthenwares. John Hancock, for one, claimed that pewter was preferable for "the contents of the plates were not so apt to slide off" and the use of them "caused no clatter in contact with knives and forks" (Montgomery 1973:13). A village clergyman refused to give up his pewter because, he explained, "I can't sharpen my knife on the new stuff" (Sprackling 1958:7). If Von Tassel displayed his pewter in the great hall and his china in the parlor he may have preferred the traditional pewter.

An alternative to uses of display or at the family table may have been the passing of pewter tablewares down for kitchen usage. A 1770 print depicts both black and white servants dancing below a shelf of pewter in the kitchen (Figure 9). As early as 1757 pewter dishes, plates, and basins

FIGURE 8. "Diligence and Dissipation", London, 1796–1797, engraving by Gaugain and Hellyer after a painting by James Northcote, 1746–1831 (Photograph courtesy of the Colonial Williamsburg Foundation).

were included with "kitchen furniture" in 15 general categories of goods for stocking stores (Gill 1984:III, 7). In addition, the inventory data often distinguished between "old" and "new" pewter, and the older pewter is often listed in the constellation of kitchen, or food preparation, objects.

Yet, these kinds of impressions do not completely bear quantification from the probate data. If pewter replaced either food preparation or food serving ceramics, the ratio of items within these functional categories should change with the ownership of pewter. Overall some 60 per cent of the ceramics in the 170 Albemarle households fell in a loosely-defined food preparation/storage category while the other 40 per cent were tablewares. This ratio of ceramic table and kitchen wares was nearly the same in households with or without pewter. Pewter did not seem to take the place of either ceramic classification, or thus to be confined to one function.

Second, the pewter may have descended even farther down the household hierarchy and slaves, overseers, or servants could have used the cast-offs in their own homes. A 1797 Albemarle County probate inventory gives an enticing hint of slave usage, for on the second day of inventory taking only eleven slaves and "sundry pewter in basins and porrangers" were listed, despite an earlier extensive kitchen listing. Parker Potter found in

FIGURE 9. "High Life Below Stairs", England, 1770 (Photograph courtesy of the Colonial Williamsburg Foundation).

19th century Rockbridge County, Virginia, inventories that pewter is often listed in association with items from the "outside" realm, such as dairying items, farm equipment, and specialized tools (Potter 1983). This could also suggest slave use. Finally, excavation at slave structure 'S' at Thomas Jefferson's Monticello in Albemarle County revealed a large pewter basin, evidence suggesting at least some form of usage by the structure's occupants. It should be cautioned, however, that this phenomenon may not have been related to the introduction of newly-fashionable earthenwares. A precedent can be found as early as 1704 in the York County inventory of Joseph Ring, where a parcel of old pewter was found in the "Mattapany Quarter" assumedly for the use of overseer or slave (York County Deeds and Wills 12:285).

Thus the relationship between pewter and ceramic tableware items was complex. First, the assumption cannot be made that pewter had one

"meaning" that was shared across time, space, and the social hierarchy. As Sidney Mintz (1985: 122) has vividly demonstrated in the case of sugar, differing social groups may transform or recast "meanings specific to the social and cultural position of the users." Second, alternative usages within the household may provide a partial explanation for a coexistence of pewter and ceramics in probate inventories. Pewter may have retained its function as a symbol of conservative stability and wealth long after its daily usage had passed. It may have been merely personal preference that dictated the continued usage of pewter in households that could afford to replace it. If ceramics were purchased, pewter may have become designated a less prestigious kitchen ware, continuing in standard service while ceramic plates and their supporting serving items graced the new mahogany dining table increasingly requisite for an elite lifestyle. Perhaps as these plates grew more derelict they were even passed down to slaves or servants for their own household. The puzzling anomaly in that case must lie in the curation of pewter despite its resale value as metal, and the seeming lack of desire within these households to regain part of their investment in cash or kind. Yet, whatever the use of the pewter recorded in Albemarle County inventories, other constraints balanced the pressures of marketing and social emulation to obtain new ceramic items.

The evidence presented here is not necessarily contradictory, but points to a period of transition within Virginia society in which many were unable—or in some cases, unwilling—to participate in a particular kind of behavior. Food and its presentation carried a strong message about one's place in the social hierarchy. Dining was undoubtedly ceremonial and gracious in the elite world of Thomas Jefferson (1790), who returned home to Albemarle County from Paris in 1790 with four cases of porcelain. But few on the farms and plantations there lived in the world of their famous neighbor. While some may have tried to imitate the gentry, food and food serving for others was still simple and hearty in the yeoman tradition. For the less fortunate, foodways were repetitious and mundane. Eating, not dining, was the norm, and that eating was often done from pewter plates.

Creamware plates were relatively inexpensive, but if the ubiquitous pewter plate was already owned, the purchase of ceramics was an "amenity." In urban or more established tidewater society, the upper and middling classes were clearly being wooed and won by the Staffordshire manipulation of fashion in the 18th century. There too the middling ranks were purchasing supporting artifacts of elite social behavior. Yet, less wealthy Virginians, or the more rural, frontier, or conservative of varying ranks, may not have been so easily convinced. Pewter remains an important "missing artifact" until the early 19th century.

ACKNOWLEDGMENTS

Research in merchants' records was funded by a 1986–87 grant from the National Endowment for the Humanities: "English Ceramics in America: Prices, Availability and Marketing"(# RO-21158-86), directed by George L. Miller. Research in Albemarle County probate records was partially funded by the Thomas Jefferson Memorial Foundation in 1983 when William M. Kelso incorporated the original probate study into the archaeology program at Monticello. James P. Whittenburg of the College of William and Mary guided my stumbling steps in 1983 and 1984 into the world of computer analysis with patience and enthusiasm, and carefully read the final product. J. Mark Wittkofski similarly made helpful comments on the original paper, and provided certain research materials on Albemarle County. Many on the staff of the Colonial Williamsburg Foundation have since helped refine and expand this research. My faithful partner George L. Miller read numerous drafts and made helpful suggestions for improvement. John Davis, Curator of Metals, was generous with his time and information, and arranged for all photographs. Harold Gill kindly provided me with his draft manuscript on the Virginia retail trade and Lorena Walsh shared probate data from her research. Marley R. Brown III helped inestimably through his critical insights of an earlier draft, and Greg Brown patiently proofed the final manuscript. Graphics were prepared by Virginia Caldwell Brown and Tamera Mams of the Department of Archaeological Research.

REFERENCES

ALBEMARLE COUNTY, VIRGINIA
1752– Will and Inventory Books 2–4, Albemarle County
1809 Courthouse, Charlottesville, Virginia.

ALLASON, WILLIAM
1760 Letter to James Mitchell, August 19. Letter Book 1757–1770, Allason Papers, Virginia State Library, Richmond. Microfilm Holdings, Colonial Williamsburg Foundation.

AYRES, S. EDWARD
1966 Albemarle County, 1744–1770: An Economic, Political, and Social Analysis. *Magazine of Albemarle County History* 25:37–72.

BAYARD, FERDINAND
1950 *Travels of a Frenchman in Maryland and Virginia with a Description of Philadelphia and Baltimore in 1791.* Translated and edited by Ben C. McCary. Edward Brothers, Ann Arbor, MI.

BEAUDRY, MARY C., JANET LONG, HENRY M. MILLER, FRASER D. NEIMAN, AND GARRY WHEELER STONE
1983 A Vessel Typology for Early Chesapeake Ceramics: The Potomac Typological System. *Historical Archaeology* 17(1):18–43.

BERGSTROM, PETER VICTOR
1980 *Markets and Merchants: Economic Diversification in Colonial Virginia, 1700–1775.* Ph.D. Dissertation, Department of History, University of New Hampshire, University Microfilms, Ann Arbor.

BRIDENBAUGH, CARL (EDITOR)
1948 *Gentleman's Progress: The Itenerarium of Dr. Alexander Hamilton in 1744.* University of North Carolina Press, Chapel Hill.

BUSHMAN, RICHARD L.
1984 American High-Style and Vernacular Cultures. In Jack P. Greene and J.R. Pole, editors. *Colonial British America: Essays in the New History of the Early Modern Era,* pp. 345–383. Johns Hopkins University Press, Baltimore.

CARR, LOIS GREEN AND LORENA WALSH
1988 The Standard of Living in the Colonial Chesapeake. *William and Mary Quarterly* 3rd series 45 (1):124–134.

1985 Changing Life Styles and Consumer Behavior in the Colonial Chesapeake. Paper presented at the Conference on Anglo-American Social History, Williamsburg, Virginia.

1980 Inventories and the Analysis of Wealth and Consumption: Patterns in St. Mary's County, Maryland, 1658–1777. *Historical Methods,* 13(2):81–104.

CARTER, ROBERT
1773 Day Book. Volume XIII (1773–1776). Manuscript Division, Duke University Library. Typescript, Foundation Library, Colonial Williamsburg Foundation.

CLARK, PETER
1988 Clubs and Sociability in Britain and the American Colonies in the 18th Century. Paper presented at an Institute of Early American History and Culture Colloquium, Williamsburg, Virginia.

COOMBE, WILLIAM
1790 *Anderson's Historical and Chronological Deductions of the Origin of Commerce . . . A History of the Great Commercial Interests of the British Empire.* revised and continued to the year 1789. P. Byrne, Dublin.

CORFIELD, P.J.
1987 "Class by Name and Number in Eighteenth-Century Britain." *History,* 72(234):38–61.

DEETZ, JAMES F.
1973 Ceramics from Plymouth, 1635–1835: The Archaeological Evidence. In Ian M.G. Quimby, editor, *Ceramics in America,* Winterthur Conference Report 1972. Charlottesville, Virginia. pp. 15–40.

DOUGLAS, MARY AND BARON ISHERWOOD
1979 *The World of Goods: Toward an Anthropology of Consumption.* W. W. Norton and Company, New York.

EDDIS, WILLIAM
1969 *Letters from America,* edited by Aubrey C. Land. Belknap Press of Harvard University, Cambridge.

FARMER, CHARLES JAMES
1984 *Country Stores and Frontier Exchange Systems in Southside Virginia During the Eighteenth Century.* Ph.D. Dissertation, Department of Geography, University of Maryland.

FELTON, DAVID L. AND PETER D. SCHULZ
1983 *The Diaz Collection: Material Culture and Social Change in Mid-Nineteenth Century Monterey.* California Archaeological Reports, No. 23. California Department of Parks and Recreation, Sacramento.

GILL, HAROLD
1984 The Retail Business in Colonial Virginia. Draft ms. on file, Colonial Williamsburg Foundation.

GLASSE, MRS. [HANNAH]
1797 *The Art of Cookery, Made Plain and Easy.* Reprint edition, 1945. Randolph Carter Williams, Richmond.

GOODY, JACK
1977 *Cooking, Cuisine and Class: A Study in Comparative Sociology.* Cambridge University Press, New York.

GREENE, JACK P. (EDITOR)
1965 *The Diary of Colonial Landon Carter of Sabine Hall, 1752–1778.* The University Press of Virginia, Charlottesville.

HANTMAN, JEFFREY
1985 *The Archaeology of Albemarle County: Results of a Systematic Survey of Proposed Development Areas in Albemarle County, Virginia.* Laboratory of Archaeology, Department of Anthropology, University of Virginia. Submitted to the Virginia Division of Historic Landmarks, Richmond, Virginia.

HATCHER, JOHN, AND T. C. BARKER
1974 *A History of British Pewter.* Longman, London.

HENING, WILLIAM WALTER
1823 *The Statutes at Large: Being a Collection of all the Laws of Virginia, from the First Session in the Legislature to 1823.* Richmond, Virginia.

HERMAN, BERNARD L.
1984 Multiple Materials, Multiple Meanings: The Fortunes of Thomas Mendenhall. *Winterthur Portfolio* 19(1):67–86.

IRVING, WASHINGTON
1978 The Legend of Sleepy Hollow. In *Anthology of American Literature,* edited by George McMichael. McMillan, New York, pp. 575–595. Originally published 1819.

ISAAC, RHYS
1982 *The Transformation of Virginia: 1740–1790.* University of North Carolina Press, Chapel Hill.

JEFFERSON, THOMAS
1790 Memorandum of the Objects Made and Furnished by me Grevin Master Boxmaker for Mr. de Jefferson minister of the United States of North America. July 17. Typescript on file, Thomas Jefferson Memorial Foundation, Charlottesville, Virginia.

JERDONE, FRANCIS
1743 Letter to Neill Buchanan, August 4. Jerdone Letter book, 1736–1744. E.G. Swem Library, College of William and Mary, Williamsburg, VA.

KULIKOFF, ALLAN
1986 *Tobacco and Slaves: The Development of Southern Cultures in the Chesapeake 1680–1800.* University of North Carolina Press, Chapel Hill.

LARABEE, LEONARD W. (EDITOR)
1969 *The Papers of Benjamin Franklin.* Vol. 13. Yale University Press, New Haven.

LA ROCHEFOUCAULD, FRANCOIS ALEXANDRE FREDERIC
1799 *Travels through the United States of North America, the Country of the Iroquois, and Upper Canada in the Years 1795, 1796, 1797.* Translated by Henry Norman. R. Phillips, London.

LEMAY, J.A. LEO (EDITOR)
1987 *Benjamin Franklin: Writings.* The Library of America, New York.

MCKENDRICK, NEIL, JOHN BREWER AND J.H. PLUMB
1982 *The Birth of a Consumer Society: The Commercialization of the Eighteenth Century.* University Press, Bloomington, Indiana

MCKENDRICK, NEIL
1985 The Cultural Response to a Consumer Society: Coming to Terms with the Idea of Luxury in Eighteenth Century England. Paper presented at the Conference on Anglo-American Social History, Williamsburg, Virginia.

MCKUSKER, JOHN J. AND RUSSEL R. MENARD
1985 *The Economy of British North America, 1607–1789.* University of North Carolina Press, Chapel Hill.

MAIN, GLORIA
1982 *Tobacco Colony: Life in Early Maryland, 1650–1720.* Princeton University Press, Princeton, New Jersey.

MAIN, JACKSON TURNER
1954 The Distribution of Property in Post-Revolutionary Virginia. *Mississippi Valley Historical Review* 41: 241–258.

MAIR, JOHN
1905 "The Produce and Commerce of Virginia and Maryland." Extract from *Book-keeping Modernized* (3rd Edition, 1784) *William and Mary Quarterly,* 1st Series, XIV (2):87–93.

MARTIN, ANN SMART
1988 *To Supply the Real and Imaginary Necessities. The Retail Trade in Table and Teawares, Virginia and Maryland, c. 1750–1810.* Submitted to the National Endowment for the Humanities, Grant No. RO-21158-86.

MATTHEWS, ELIZABETH
1957 *The Life of Reverend Devereux Jarrett.* Master's thesis, Department of History, College of William and Mary.

MAURY, J.
1768 Letter to T. Walker, January 21. Dr. Thomas Walker Papers, Library of Congress. Microfilm Holdings, Colonial Williamsburg Foundation.

MILLER, GEORGE L.
1980 Classification and Economic Scaling of Nineteenth Century Ceramics. *Historical Archaeology* 14(1):1–40.

MINTZ, SIDNEY W.
1985 *Sweetness and Power: The Place of Sugar in Modern History.* Viking Penguin, New York.

MONTGOMERY, CHARLES
1973 *A History of American Pewter.* Praeger, New York.

MOORE, JOHN HAMMOND
1976 *Albemarle: Jefferson's County, 1727–1976.* University Press of Virginia, Charlottesville.

NEIMAN, FRASER D.
1978 Domestic Architecture at the Clift's Plantation: The Social Context of Early American Buildings. *Northern Neck of Virginia Historical Magazine:* 3096–2138.

NOEL HUME, IVOR
1969 *A Guide to Artifacts of Colonial America.* Alfred A. Knopf, New York.

NORFOLK GAZETTE AND PUBLICK LEDGER
1814 January 26. Norfolk, VA.

O'MARA, JAMES
1983 *An Historical Geography of Urban System Development: Tidewater Virginia in the Eighteenth Century.* York University Geographical Monographs 13. York University Press, York, Canada.

OTTO, JOHN SOLOMON
1975 *Status Differences and the Archaeological Record.* Ph.D. dissertation, Department of Anthropology, University of Florida. University Microfilms, Ann Arbor.

[PAULDING, JAMES]
1835 *Letters from the South by a Northern Man.* 2nd edition, Harper and Brothers, New York.

PAPENFUSE, EDWARD C.
1975 *In Pursuit of Profit: The Annapolis Merchants in the Era of the American Revolution: 1763–1805.* Johns Hopkins University Press, Baltimore.

POTTER, PARKER, JR.
1983 *Down the Rabbit Hole: An Application of the Structuralist Principal of Binary Opposition to a Historical Material Culture Problem.* Ms. on file, Historic Annapolis.

PREISSER, THOMAS M.
1977 *Eighteenth-Century Alexandria, Virginia, before the Revolution, 1749–1776.* Ph.D. Dissertation, Department of History, College of William and Mary.

PRICE, JACOB L.
1980 *Capital and Credit in British Overseas Trade: The View from the Chesapeake, 1700–1776.* Harvard University Press, Cambridge.
1979 *Joshua Johnson's Letterbook: Letters from a Merchant in London to his Partners in Maryland.* London Record Society, London.
1954 The Rise of Glasgow in the Chesapeake Tobacco Trade, 1707–1775. *William and Mary Quarterly,* 3rd series, XI: 179–199.

RISJORD, NORMAN K.
1978 *Chesapeake Politics, 1781–1800.* Columbia University Press, New York.

SCHUMPETER, ELIZABETH BOODY
1960 *English Export Trade Statistics.* Clarendon Press, Oxford.

SHEFFIELD, JOHN BAKER HOLROYD
1783 *Observations on the Commerce of the American States with Europe and the West Indies; including the Several Articles of Import and Export.* Reprint edition, Research Reprints, Inc. New York, 1970.

SMART, ANN MORGAN
1986 *The Urban/Rural Dichotomy of Status Consumption. Tidewater, Virginia 1815.* Master's thesis, Program in American Studies, College of William and Mary

SMYTH, J.F.D.
1784 *A Tour in the United States of America.* G. Robinson, London.

SNELL, K.D.M.
1985 *Annals of the Labouring Poor. Social Change and Agrarian England, 1660–1900.* Cambridge University Press, Cambridge, England.

SPOEDE, ROBERT WILLIAM
1973 *William Allason: Merchant in an Emerging Nation.* Ph.D. Dissertation, Department of History, College of William and Mary.

SPRACKLING, HELEN
1958 *Customs on the Table Top: How New England Housewives Set Out Their Tables.* Old Sturbridge Village Booklet Series

TEUTE, FREDERICKA J.
1976 *The Commercial Endeavors of a Virginia Merchant during the Confederation Period: The Rise and Fall of Richard Blow.* Master's thesis, Department of History, College of William and Mary.

UNITED STATES BUREAU OF THE CENSUS
1975 *Historical Statistics of the United States, Colonial Times to 1970, Bicentennial Edition, Part 1,* Series E 52–63:202. Government Printing Office, Washington, D.C.

VALLETE, ELIE
1774 *The Deputy Comissary's Guide Within the Province of Maryland Together with Plain and Sufficient Directions for Testators to Form and Executors to Perform their Wills and Testaments, for Administrators to Compleat their Administrations and for Every Person any Way Concerned in Deceased Person's Estates, to Proceed Therein with Safety to Themselves and Others.* printed by Ann Catherine Green and Son, Annapolis.

VIRGINIA GAZETTE
1772 February 6. Williamsburg: Purdie and Dixon, publishers.

WALSH, LORENA S.
1983 Urban Amenities and Rural Sufficiency: Living Standards and Consumer Behavior in the Colonial Chesapeake, 1643–1777. *Journal of Economic History* XLIII (1) 109–117.

WATTS, CHARLES WILDER
1947 Land Grants and Aristocracy in Albemarle County, 1727–1775. *Magazine of Albemarle County History* 8:6–26.

WELD, ISAAC
1799 *Travels Through the States of North America.* Reprint edition, 1968. Johnson Reprint Corporation, New York.

WILKINS, JOHN
c. Letter to John Norton. John Norton and Sons Papers.
1773 Colonial Williamsburg Foundation.

WOODS, EDGAR
1900 *Albemarle County in Virginia.* C.J. Carrier Company, Bridgewater, Virginia.

YORK COUNTY, VIRGINIA
1702– Deeds, Orders, and Wills Book 12. Typescript. Foun-
1706 dation Library, Colonial Williamsburg Foundation, Williamsburg, Virginia.
1783– Wills and Inventories Book 23. Typescript. Founda-
1811 tion Library, Colonial Williamsburg Foundation, Williamsburg, Virginia.

ANN SMART MARTIN
DEPARTMENT OF ARCHAEOLOGICAL RESEARCH
COLONIAL WILLIAMSBURG FOUNDATION
WILLIAMSBURG, VIRGINIA 23185

APPENDIX

For the purpose of this study, food-related items were all those ceramic, glass, pewter, brass, tin, copper, bell metal, iron, flint, horn, lead, silver, silver plate and wooden items used in the preparation, storage, and serving of foods. Table 1 lists the broad range of vessels and utensils found in Albemarle County probate inventories between 1770 and 1799. Excluded were agricultural implements or large-scale storage containers, as well as textiles. Descriptive statistics were generated by SAS on an IBM mainframe at the College of William and Mary.

The problem of price fluctuations and inflation was a serious one, especially with the depreciation of paper money in the Revolutionary war era and after. A crude weighting was performed using Warren and Pearson's wholesale price indices found in U.S. Bureau of the Census (1975:202). While the total effects of national price trends on Albemarle County is debatable, its participation in a market economy predicts a smoothing relationship. A price series from probate data was beyond the scope of this work.

Wealth groups were devised based on the statistical profile of the probate population. Those households below the median wealth level were designated the bottom group (50 per cent of the population with weighted estate valued between £0 and £284); those above the median and below the mean became the second wealth level (22 per cent, £284 to £887 estate values); between this line and one standard deviation lay an upper middle group (20 per cent, £888 to £2333); and those beyond this point were the wealthiest elite, Wealth Group 4 (9 per cent, £2333 +). My thanks to James Whittenburg of the College of William and Mary for his suggestion of this method.

A listing of sources of merchants' records follows.

Microfilm Holdings, Foundation Library, Colonial Williamsburg Foundation, Williamsburg, Virginia:

William Allason Papers, Virginia State Library.

Edward Dixon Papers. Library of Congress.

Eilbeck, Ross and Company Papers. Miscellaneous Collections, Duke University.

John Glassford and Company Papers, Library of Congress.

Frederick Hall Account Books. Southern Historical Collection, University of North Carolina at Chapel Hill.

Hooe, Stone, and Company Papers. Invoice Book. New York Public Library.

Neil Jamieson Account Books, Library of Congress.

James Lawson-John Semple Accounts, Scottish Record Office, Currie-Dal Misc. Bundle 20.

Logan, Dunmore and Company Inventory. Original: P.R.O./A.O. 13/30 Loyalist Claims 1782–1790, Reel 252.

John Norton and Sons Papers, London. 1769–1780.

Wallace, Davidson and Johnson Order Book, Annapolis. Maryland Hall of Records.

Dr. Thomas Walker Papers, Rives Papers, Library of Congress.

Willison, Stewart and Company Invoice. U.S. Circuit Court, Eastern District of Virginia Records—Record Books # 1 A–# 2 B. 1790–November 1794.

Swem Library, Manuscripts Department, College of William and Mary, Williamsburg, Virginia:

Henry Bedinger Invoice Book, 1785–1796.

Briggs and Blow Letter Book, Blow Family Papers.

Virginia State Library, Richmond, Virginia:

William Allason Papers, Loose papers.

Dramgoole Family Papers.

JAMES T. ROCK

Cans in the Countryside

ABSTRACT

The mining frontier was "a curious blending of the new and the familiar, of innovation and imitation" (Paul 1963:7). The truth of this assertion is reflected in the artifacts present in early Anglo sites found in northern California. One artifact class that documents this blending of the familiar with the new is the tin can.

The study of tin cans and their associations with other artifacts can provide a key to understanding the dependence of settlers on the outside world. The same artifacts, of course, also mirror technological advances in the canning industry. This study discusses one example of the mutual ties that settlers in northern California maintained with the larger, industrialized society from which they had come.

Introduction

The material culture remains left by those who came to northern California between 1825 and the early 1900s is ample proof (if such is needed) that these settlers also brought their socio-cultural "baggage" with them. The material remains reflect the supply and transportation systems that maintained contact with homeland areas left behind. Material evidence for connections between the larger parent society and its offspring in northern California are exemplified by the "tin can."

The relationships maintained with the outside world as settlement, communication and supply systems developed in Siskiyou County, California, form the central focus of this article. Of equal interest are the technological and industrial stages that the canning industry achieved as the direct result of increased demand created by western expansion and national industrial growth. The physical evidence suggests that between 1825 and 1900 eastern industry responded to demand from those who migrated to the Far West by increasing both the quantity and quality of the goods they supplied. The positive feedback system between suppliers and consumers must be examined to understand the interplay among the social, technological and economic forces operating in this period.

The tin can is a perfect example of an artifact type that reflects the interrelationship between man and one attribute of his material culture. Detailed analysis of such mundane artifacts can contribute to a wider understanding of the ways in which mankind adapts to new and challenging social and natural environments while retaining many elements of an already familiar cultural repertoire.

Settlement of the American Far West depended to a large degree on the established culture of the East. The demand for eastern goods triggered a response in an individual society adjusting to meet new needs and markets. Relationships between East and West were dynamic; the development of the American West was always closely linked to the production capacities of the American East.

The Area

The first recorded Anglo contact in Siskiyou County, California, was via the trappers and traders of the Hudson's Bay Company who brought trade goods with them in their quest for pelts. In the 1820s and 1830s a number of trapping parties explored this area of California exchanging beads, knives, axes, blankets, etc., with the Shasta and Karok Indians in return for beaver pelts and the skins of other animals.

By the 1850s, a new group of Anglos had arrived who had not come to trade but to search for gold. The first miners brought very little with them to the Klamath, Scott and Salmon rivers and withdrew when winter weather became too severe. Beans, flour, sugar and coffee were frequent dietary staples, but liquor and tinned goods did not lag far behind in frequency of use. Prospectors needed these supplies to live, and this need was met by the development of trade routes and supply systems (Figure 1).

In the early 1850s, steamboats carried supplies into the northern part of the central valley of California. The goods were transferred from boats to mule trains which journeyed north into the mountains, mining camps and towns of Siskiyou

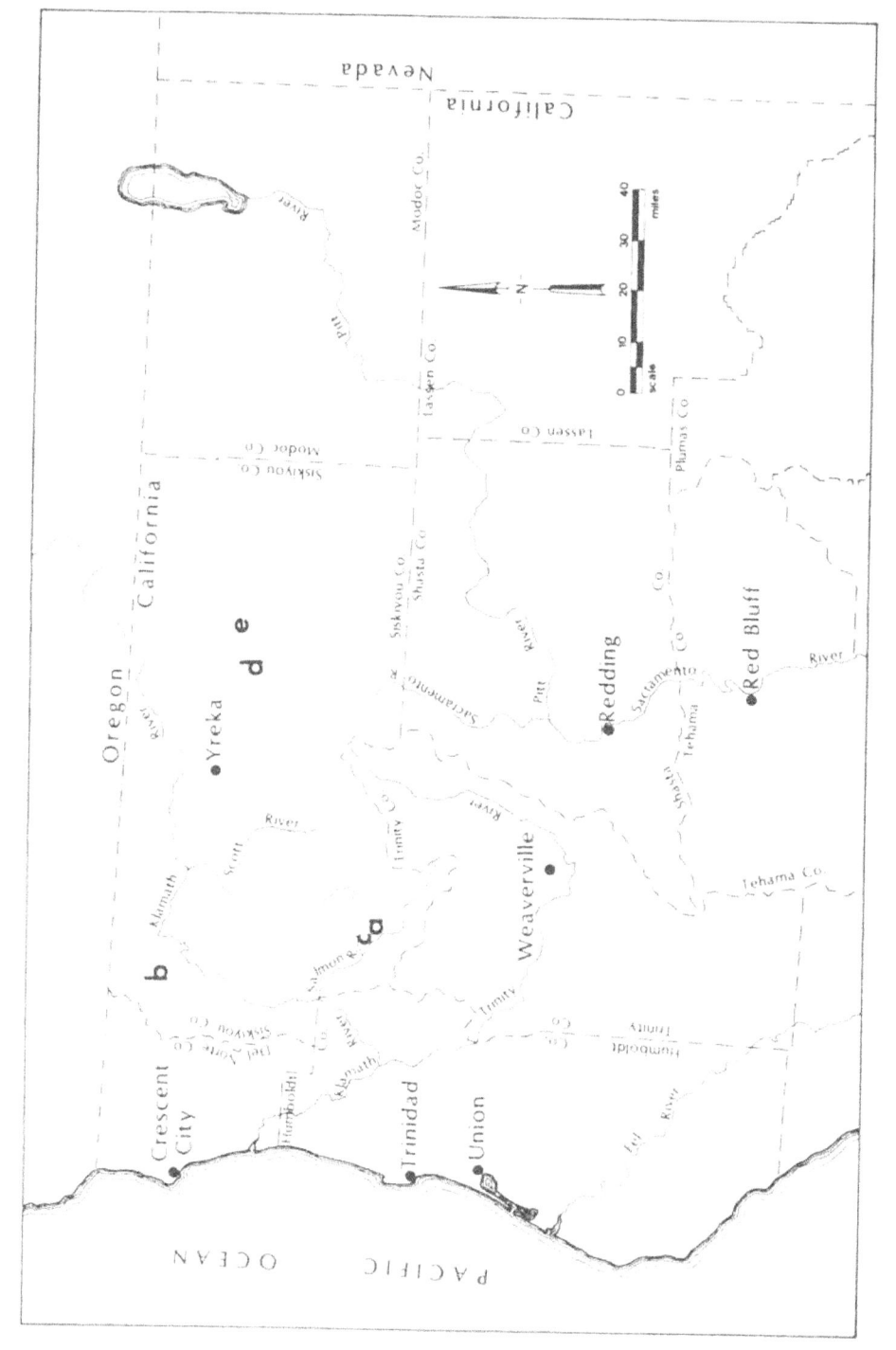

FIGURE 1 Far northern California Letters indicate locations of sites discussed in Table 2 a Wadsten mining claim b Cassic Hill mine c White Bear mine d Abner e Kellum railroad logging camp

County. Some supplies also came from the coast; they were shipped by sea to Trinidad, Union and Crescent City and were then brought inland by packers. Mule trains brought the tents, gold pans, shovels, picks and foods such as fruits, vegetables, flour, sugar and coffee into the county. Consumer practices by the time of the Gold Rush assured that northern California's immigrants were already familiar with canned goods. Many necessities were packaged in tin when this chapter in the expansion of the American frontier opened.

Settlement of the northern California gold fields was hastened by many who originally came for gold but who quickly turned to ranching, homesteading, logging or supply occupations. Towns such as Yreka, California, developed into inland supply centers from which pack trains conveyed stores to more remote areas. By the late 1850s, prospecting as well as individual small-scale placer mining were on the wane; large-scale operations were replacing them. Larger mining operations required increased capital, labor and material goods that could be met only by increased interaction with the "outside" world.

Steamboat and coastal trade were greatly affected when railroad transportation reached Siskiyou County from the Sacramento Valley in the mid-1880s. The railroad's arrival promoted a marked population increase. Supply shipments became more predictable at the same time that shipment predictability itself became more critical. Of course, rail transportation also meant that a new class of bulk goods could be brought into the county and that products could also be exported efficiently.

Large-scale logging began in northern California in the 1890s as mining activity continued to expand. Operations of larger scope naturally employed more people who had to be supplied with non-perishable foods. Industrialized logging and mining businesses thereafter became a part of Siskiyou County's economic and social milieu (Anonymous 1886; Cox 1974; McDonald 1979; McGown 1949; Reichman 1957; Rock 1980; Schrader 1949; Stumpf 1979; Wells 1881).

The Canning Industry

As the Far West continued to industrialize, complementary changes were occurring in those parts of the country that already had experienced this economic, technological and social revolution. This is exemplified in the canning industry and in the manufacture of tin cans (Table 1). Originally, metal food can bodies were cut out by hand; shaping and soldering of the side seam and ends were operations also performed by hand. The finished products had flush ends or ends that were crimped by hand and plumb or lap side seam joints (Figure 2). The cans were almost always filled through an opening in the center of one end. Once filled, a cap was soldered into place to close the can which, logically enough, became known as the hole-and-cap can (Busch 1979:3, 1981:96; Cobb 1919:5; Collins 1924:32; Fontana et al. 1962:69-70; Hunt 1902:464; May 1937:28, 435; MacNaughtan and Hedges 1935:41; Stevenson 1914:92; Woodward 1958:37).

An improvement to the hole-and-cap can was the addition of a small hole in the center of the cap; this was known as the hole-in-cap can (Figure 3). Hole-in-cap cans allowed filled containers to be closed and then heated to drive off excess moisture and air through the small hole. Sealing by this process reduced the number of "leakers," i.e., cans that swelled or burst. The "match-stick" filler hole in the center of the cap was closed and sealed by a drop of solder after the can and its contents had been heated. These cans were made by a slow, labor intensive process that produced only 60 crude cans per day per tinsmith (Sacharow and Griffin 1970:9).

The hole-in-cap can served a need, but manufacturers worked to improve both its dependability and availability. By the 1840s, large-scale canneries were in operation in both Baltimore, Maryland, and Boston, Massachusetts. If folklore is correct, it was at the William Underwood Company's Boston plant that bookkeepers shortened the term *cannister* to *can* (Fontana et al. 1962:67; May 1937:12; Woodward 1958:35).

TABLE 1
CAN CHRONOLOGY AND TERMINOLOGY

Term	Description	Approximate Date for Onset of Manufacture	Comments	References
tin canister	containers made from tin plate or iron plate	1810	Augusta de Heine and Peter Durand patented iron and tin plated containers in England at this time. Durand patented his tin plate containers in the United States in 1818. Thomas Kensett patented an improved tin canister in 1825.	Clark 1977:13; Sacharow and Griffin 1970:9.
hole-and-cap	cans with a filler hole in one end that is closed by a cap	1810	These cans were used for a very brief period and were quickly improved upon. They often swelled or burst.	Collins 1924:34; MacNaughtan and Hedges 1935:40; Sacharow and Griffin 1970:9.
hole-in-cap	tin containers with a filler hole in one end sealed with a tin plate cap that has a pinhole vent in its center (see Figure 3)	By 1820	The introduction of the pinhole vent in the filler hole cap greatly reduced can failure. The terms hole-in-cap, hole-in-top and hole-and-cap are often used interchangably in the literature.	Clark 1977:14; Fontana et al. 1962:68; Sacharow and Griffin 1970:9.
stamped can ends	machine made can ends with extended edges that fit over the can body (see Figure 4)	1847	Allen Taylor invented a drop press to convert flat discs into vertically flanged caps. In 1849, Henry Evans invented a machine for pressing can tops and bottoms, rendering them more quickly and efficiently made.	Collins 1924:32; May 1937:28, 435; MacNaughtan and Hedges 1935:41.
key-wind opened	This is a closure mechanism in which a scored band on the side	1866	The sardine can is the most familiar example of this closure method in which nearly the	MacNaughtan and Hedges 1935:42–44; Sacharow and Griffin 1970:10.

Term	Date	Description	Reference
		or top of a can can be removed by rolling or tearing it away with the use of a key (see Figure 10).	entire can end is removed. There are many variations on this theme.	
tapered tin	1875	The base of this tin is larger than its top. The original tapered tins were rectangular in shape	Arthur A. Libby and J. Wilson of Chicago, Illinois, purchased the patent rights for this container in 1875 and began using it for their processed meat products.	May 1937:437; Pulati 1973:16.
double side seam	1888	This is a seam that locks the parts of a can together (see Figure 9).	Max Ams of the Max Ams Machine Company of New York, New York, invented and produced tin products using this seam.	Sacharow and Griffin 1970:9.
key-wind opened tapered tins	1895	This is a closure mechanism in which a scored strip was placed on the can body near its larger end. The scored strip was removed with a key (see Figure 6).	Edwin Norton of Chicago, Illinois, perfected this closure method which soon was in use on tapered tins. Later, the key-wind mechanism was most frequently found on cylindrical coffee cans.	Cobb 1914:94; Lee 1914:44.
Ams can	1898	This term denotes cans without internal solder and which have their side seam, top and bottom closed by double seams.	The Max Ams Machine Company first produced these cans for the Cobb Preserving Company of Fairport, New York, at this time. Ams' employees called these containers "sanitary cans."	Collins 1924:39; May 1937:88.
hole-in-top	After 1900	This is a can with a single pinhole or "match-stick" filler hole no larger than 1/8 inch in the center of one end. This hole is closed by a drop of solder (see Figure 8).	By ca. 1920, evaporated milk tins were almost exclusively hole-in-top cans. These cans were also known as venthole cans.	Hunziker 1914:90; Pulati 1973:28-29.
sanitary can	1904	Sanitary cans are made using double seams. They are airtight and need no solder to fasten the side seam, top, or bottom (see Figure 11).	Sanitary Can Company cans were completely made by machines, the interiors were lacquered to prevent chemical reaction of the product with the metal. American Can Company took over the four Sanitary Can Company plants in 1908.	Clark 1977:18; Collins 1924:36-37; Cruess 1948:37-38; Kopetz 1978:87ff; May 1937:91-95, 440

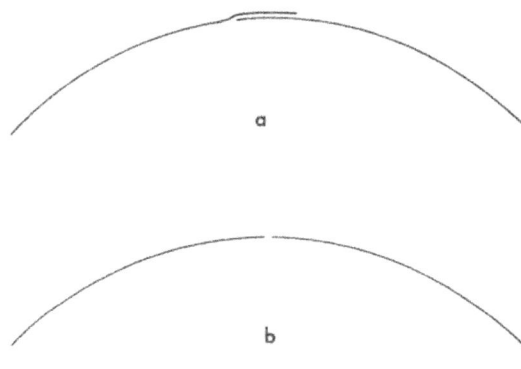

FIGURE 2. Can side seam types: a. lap side seam. b. plumb joint. The lap side seam was the dominant side seam type on cans until 1888

A major technological improvement in the tin can was the process that permitted stamping the can ends (Figure 4). Allen Taylor patented a drop-press to flange the edges of can ends in 1847. In 1848, William Numsen and Son of Baltimore, Maryland, improved the machine that stamped flat discs into can tops and bottoms. Numsen and Son patented their foot–powered pendulum press in 1849. This machine consisted of a "combination die" that not only formed flanged can ends but also cut the filler hole in the cap at the same time (Busch 1981:96; Clark 1977:13; Fontana et al. 1962:69–70; May 1937:12, 28; Sacharow and Griffin 1970:9).

An example of the variety of foods available in cans by 1863 is apparent by examining a list of the foodstuffs packaged by Ezra A. Edgett of Camden, New York, who was then a supplier for the Union Army. These products included sweet corn, chickens, turkey, ducks, geese and beef (May 1937:24).

At the same time that soldiers in the Civil War were learning of the existence of canned foods, a demand for fish was being met at the opposite end of the country by William Hapgood and the Hume Brothers. They established a salmon cannery in Sacramento, California, in 1864 (Collins 1924:140; May 1937:103, 436; Stevenson 1899:512). Cans for the Hapgood and Hume cannery were cut out and shaped by hand; however, the ends of their cans were stamped. All seams were hand–soldered (Figure 5). The interior of

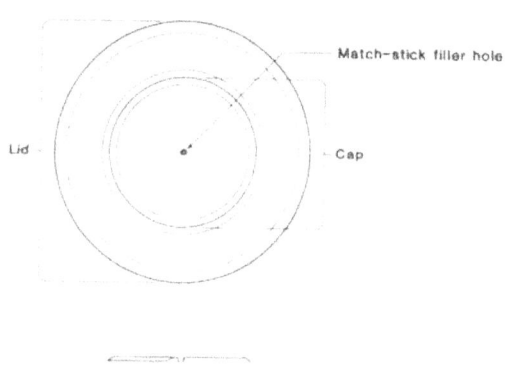

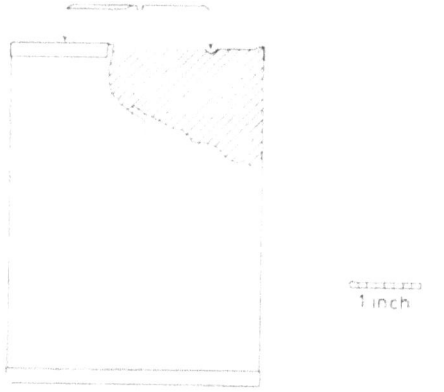

FIGURE 3. Hole–in–cap can. These were the first cans used for commercially produced food in the United States

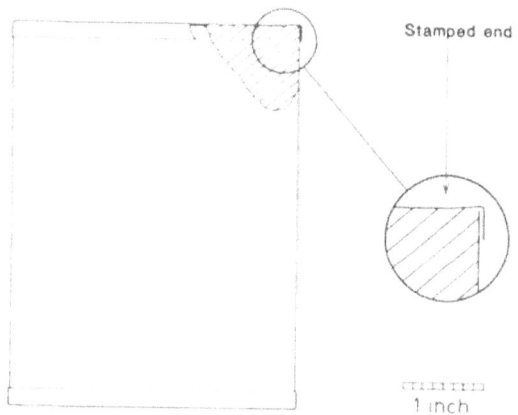

FIGURE 4. Stamped or flanged can ends. This process was patented in 1847

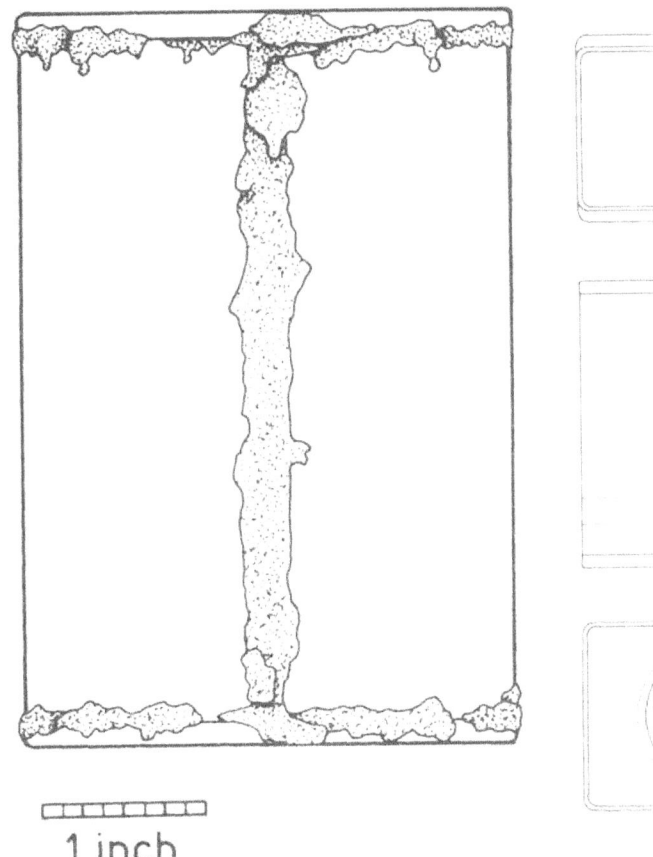

1 inch

FIGURE 5. Hand-soldered hole-in-cap can. This can type was common until the 1880s.

Top

Bottom

1 inch

FIGURE 6. Tapered tin. A patent for the tapered tin was obtained by Libby and Wilson of Chicago in 1875.

these hole-in-cap cans was painted with a mixture of red lead paint, turpentine and linseed oil in an attempt to prevent the fish from chemically reacting with the tin (Bitting 1937:850).

In 1875, Arthur A. Libby and W. J. Wilson of Chicago, Illinois, obtained rights to use a rectangular can for their products (Figure 6). This tapered tin allowed removal of the can's contents in a single piece. Libby and Wilson's canned corn beef rapidly gained popularity (Collins 1924:153; Fontana et al. 1962:73–74; May 1937:437).

Labor problems stimulated improvements in can soldering techniques during the 1870s. The "Howe Floater" system was introduced to canneries in 1876. This system rolled the cans at an angle in a solder bath and sealed the ends (Busch

1981:97; May 1937:28–29; Fontana et al. 1962:70).

The Norton Brothers of Chicago, Illinois, introduced a semi-automatic machine for soldering can side seams in 1883. This improvement meant that all processes of can-making could now be done by machines (Figure 7). Automatic can construction permitted up to 2500 cans to be made per machine in a single hour (Busch 1979:5, 1981:97; Clark 1977:18; Hunt 1902:464; May 1937:351; Stevenson 1914:92; Woodward 1958:37).

John B. Meyenberg began to use hermetically sealed cans for evaporated milk in 1885 (Bitting 1937:737; Hunziker 1914:9, 13; May 1937:184; Rock 1983). Many of Meyenberg's cans had a flush profile and a small (½ inch or ¼ inch) cap

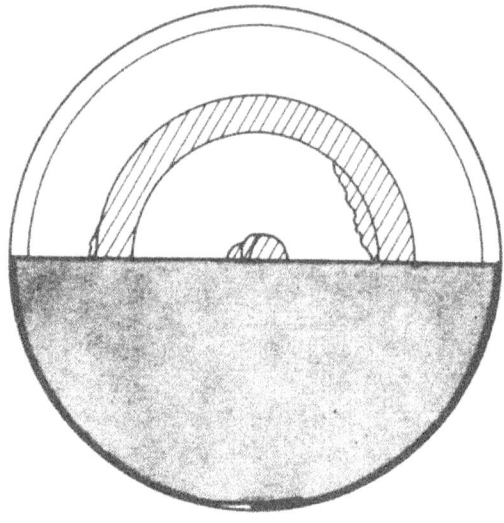

1 inch

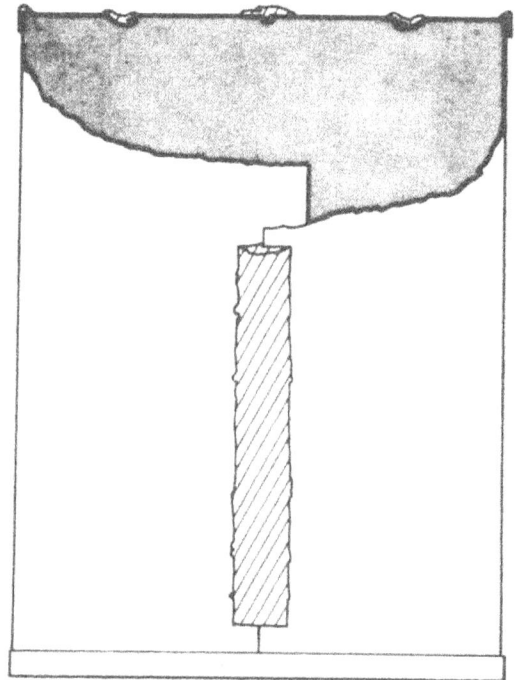

FIGURE 7 Machine-soldered side seam hole-in-cap can with flush profile ca 1883

with a "match–stick" filler hole in the center of the top. The tops and bottoms of Meyenberg's cans had lips that overlapped the can body (Fontana et al. 1962:74). After 1900. Carnation introduced the

hole–in–top can which has stamped ends and a match–stick filler hole in one end. This can is still dominant in the evaporated milk industry today (Figure 8).

Until the mid–1880s, can-making was a part of the canning business itself and was linked to the processing plant. The demand for tin cans had be-

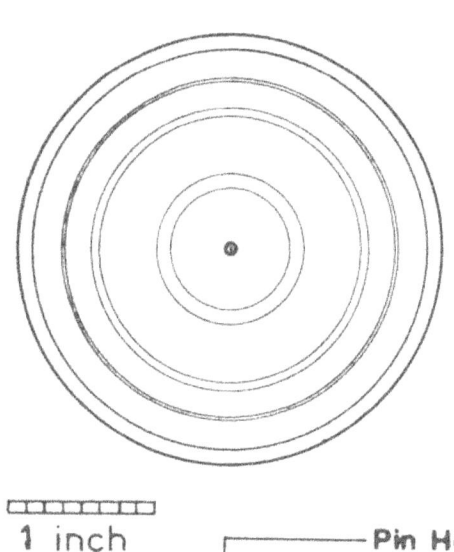

1 inch   **Pin Hole**

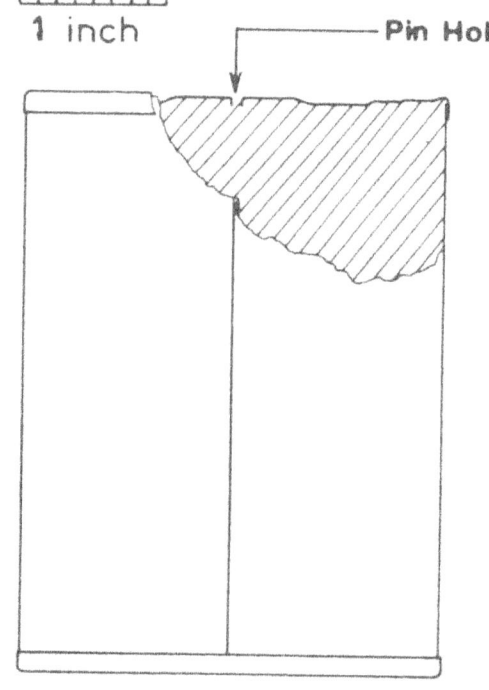

FIGURE 8 Hole–in–top can with a so-called match–stick filler hole. This is an example from an evaporated milk can, post-1900

come sufficiently great by about 1885 that a separate can–producing industry became necessary. Many technological advances in can manufacture were made as a result of this specialization. Such businesses could focus on the problems of can production, improving their products and advancing their position in the marketplace without the added responsibility of undertaking successful foodstuff processing (Collins 1924:36; Fontana et al. 1962:74–75; Pulati 1973:28–29).

Max Ams of the New York based Max Ams Machine Company made a major technological breakthrough for the canning industry in 1888. He introduced the double seam method for side seaming cans. This locking seam held the sides of a can together far more satisfactorily than the earlier plumb and lap seams had been able to do (Figure 9). Can failure during the build–up of internal pressure was greatly reduced (Sacharow and Griffin 1970:9).

The key–opened, rolled, scored strip can was used by Edwin Norton in Chicago in 1895 (Figure 10). This can opening method had been known previously, but it was not employed to any great extent until Norton adapted it for his processed meat tins (Cobb 1914:94; Fontana et al. 1962:71, 73–74; Lee 1914:44; MacNaughton and Hedges 1935:43–44; Teague 1980:107).

In 1897, Charles Ams and Julius Brenzinger improved their can sealing equipment by crimping both the top and bottom thus forming a sealed double seam. In 1896 Charles Ams had patented a

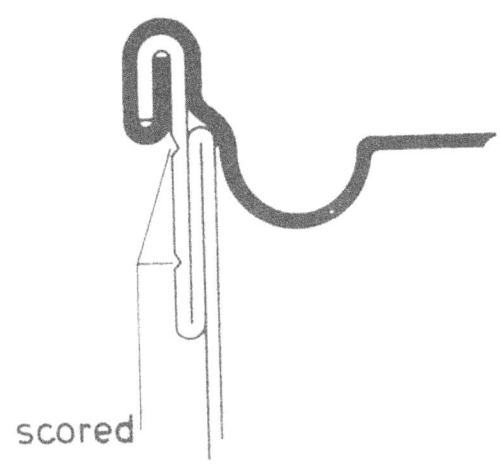

FIGURE 10 Cross section of key-opened tin introduced by Edwin Norton of Chicago in 1895.

liquid sealing compound of rubber and gum that replaced the rubber gaskets previously used. The combination of Am's double side seam method of closure, the double seam crimp top and bottom, exterior solder and automatically applied sealing compound produced what became known as the "solderless can" (Collins 1924:38; May 1937:439).

The first so–called solderless cans were under production at the Max Ams Machine Company for the Cobb Preserving Company of Fairport, New York, by 1898 (May 1937:88). The solderless can also became known as the "Ams can." Between 1900 and 1902 Cobb's Fairport cannery shifted from using the older hole–in–cap can to the open–top can (May 1937:90) which by this time had become a commercially viable commodity.

The Sanitary Can Company was formed in Fairport, New York, in 1904, and thereafter sanitary cans rapidly replaced hole–in–cap cans. Sanitary cans were the first tin–plated cylindrical food containers that were air–tight and did not use solder for sealing and fastening their side seam, top and bottom (May 1937:91). Sanitary cans replaced the Ams can when the double seam process became completely mechanical. By 1904, sanitary cans were being made at the rate of 25,000 in a 10–hour day (Figure 11). The American Can Company purchased and took over the plants of the Sanitary Can Company in 1908.

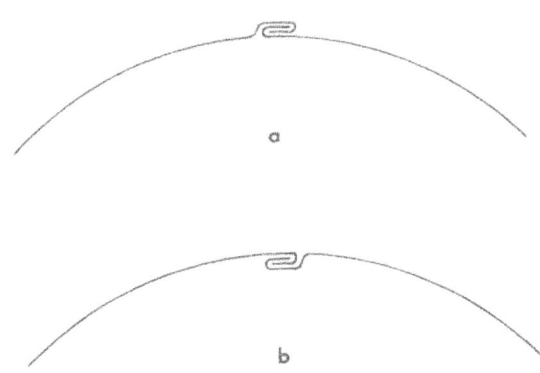

FIGURE 9 Double side seams a external b internal. Double side seams were introduced in 1888 and were being commercially produced by the late 1890s.

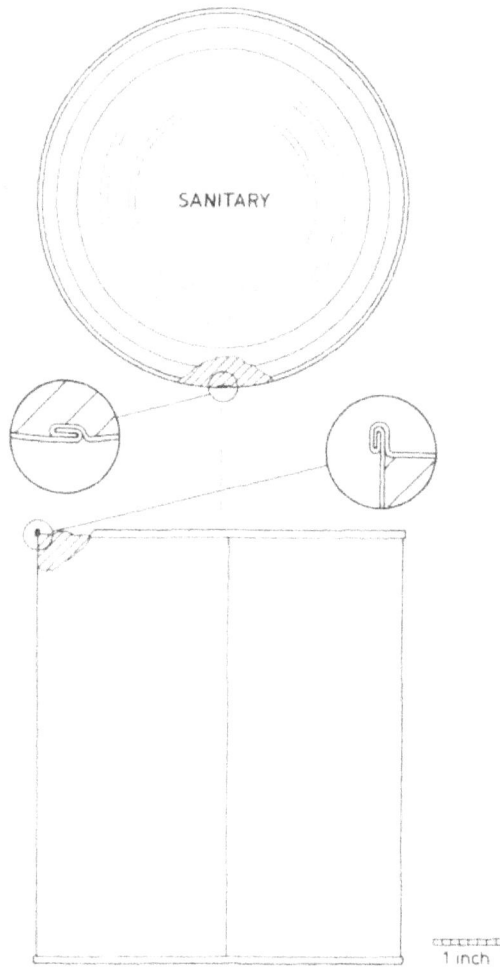

SANITARY

1 inch

FIGURE 11 The double seam or sanitary can commercially produced in 1889. The illustrated example is from a Weed Lumber Company camp in Siskiyou County, California, and dates between 1910 and 1914

By 1910, California canners were incorporating into their production new elements in canning technology developed in the East. The sanitary can dominated the West Coast industry by the end of 1911 (Busch 1979:6, 1981:98; Clark 1977:11, 18; Cobb 1914:94, 96; Collins 1924:36–40; Cruess 1948:37, 38; Fontana et al. 1962:72–75; Kopetz 1978:87; May 1937:91–95).

Northern California Evidence

Material culture remains left by the settlers of northern California between 1825 and the early 1900s indicate that frontier development was accompanied by the extension of products and processes already developed in the East. The first Anglos in the area left only trade goods including Hudson's Bay Company axes, beads, traps, buttons and an occasional musket. Clearly, the traders and trappers who came to northern California were themselves part of a larger social and economic unit, the international trading company.

The first miners brought with them very little but their clothes, gold pans and shovels, but as time went on, there is material evidence of greater contact with other segments of American culture. One example, and one that reflects an outside source of supply, is the hand–formed, hand–soldered hole–in–cap can with lap side seams. Soldering on the California specimens is ordinarily quite crude even though the tops and bottoms usually had been manufactured by stamping (Table 2).

Supplies of all kinds were imported into northern California in increased amounts to meet growing demand in the 1870s and 1880s. The logging industry was still comparatively small but grew throughout this period. Mining continued as the major occupation in northern California. Artifact inventories from the sites of small–scale operations frequently contain recycled tin cans. Cans were made into cups by adding a handle or were punctured to form strainers.

As a rule, big mining operations required more goods and more complex equipment. Population in northern California increased rapidly, and this is at times seen not only in the extensive alteration of the land but in the greater variety and increased quantity of consumer goods found on sites occupied after the time of initial exploration.

Distinguishing features of larger, more complex mining and logging sites are tins of greater volume than those on sites of individual habitations or small–scale businesses. The No. 10 tin and the evaporated milk can are quite common artifacts on sites where big mines and logging operations fed large numbers of workers (Figure 12).

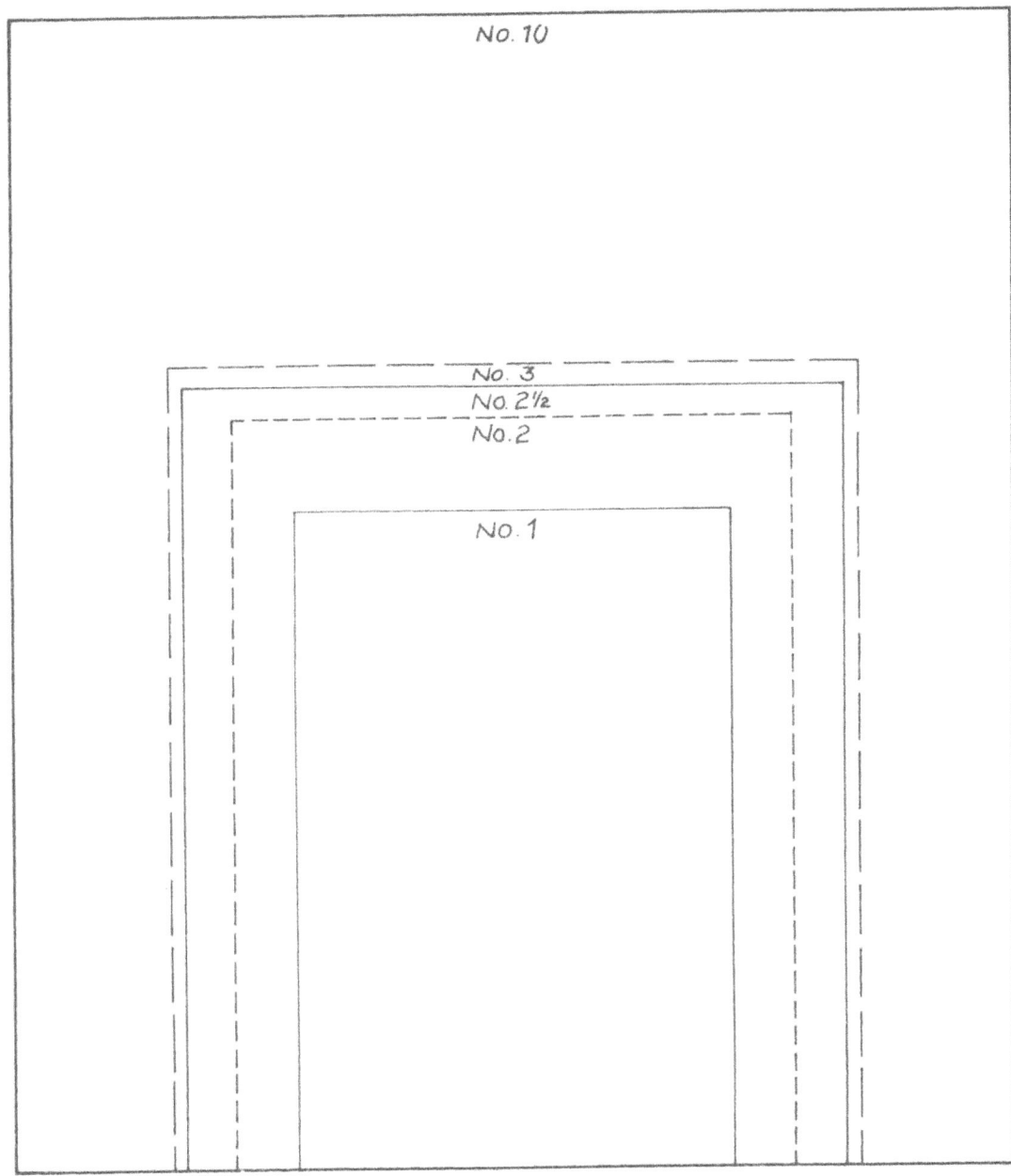

No. 10

No. 3

No. 2½

No. 2

No. 1

1 inch

FIGURE 12. Numerical designations for tin cans and their profile sizes.

TABLE 2
EXAMPLES OF ARCHAEOLOGICAL SITES PRODUCING CANS IN SISKIYOU COUNTY, CALIFORNIA

Site Name Number	Location	Other Names	Years of Operation	Comments
Wadstein Mining Claim (three archaeological sites)	Eddy Gulch (Figure 1a)	Burnes Brothers Placer John Frank 1&2 Placer Mines Judge Hydraulic Mine	ca. 1870s ca. 1900–1920 ca. 1920–1940	One site in this complex has yielded hole-in-cap evaporated milk tins, several sizes of lap side seam hole-in-cap cans, and opium tins, in addition to shoe parts, cooking utensils, ceramics, etc. The other two sites in the complex include a post-World War II cabin and a hydraulic mining pit with crane, single drum, beam and box hydraulic balance, sluice boxes, flume, and plank wing dams.
Classic Hill Mine	Indian Creek (Figure 1b)	Classic Claim 1873 Howard Placer Mine	land patented 1877 by Classic Hill land patented 1880 by Howard Placer	The site includes the collapsed James Camp cabin, the dwelling of the original claimant, as well as mining ditches, a dump with fragments of lap seam hole-in-cap cans, wine bottle fragments, ironstone plate fragments, porcelain, and cut nails.
White Bear Mine	Callahans Gulch (Figure 1c)	White Bear May Land Mining Co.	1890 1920s	This site consists of Adits, office, domestic, and work buildings, and a five stamp mill location. 15 structures in all, in addition to an ore car track. Various powder

cans, cooking and washing containers, sanitary cans, evaporated milk hole-in-top cans, vegetable cans of various sizes, including No. 10 tins in association with bottles and bottle fragments, wire nails, corrugated iron, etc. The mine dump is quite large and diffuse rather than concentrated in one area

| Abner | Grass Lake (Figure 1d) | Weed Lumber Co Abner Camp | 1908–1911 |

This site has yielded several thousand cans, about one-half of which are No. 10 tins. The remainder are dominated by hole-in-cap evaporated milk tins and rectangular tins in association with bottle fragments, handleless white ceramic cups, plates, saw-cut cattle bones, lumber, horseshoes, etc.

| Kellum | Butte Creek (Figure 1e) | Weed Lumber Co Kellum Wye | 1917–1920 |

This railroad logging camp site has yielded amethyst glass, a sanitary can with the letter "C" embossed on one end, ca. 100 small hole-in-cap food cans, a H. J. Heinz octagonal bottle base, white ceramics marked "Grindley Hotel Ware, England, Vitrified," and Lea & Perrins machine-made bottles, tobacco tin lunch pail, etc. There are no No. 10 tins present. Sanitary cans are the dominant can type present in the artifact inventory.

From the preceding discussion, it is clear that cans made after the 1880s reflect a major technological change in soldering techniques. The hole–in–cap can predominated, but more uniform application of solder to the can ends and to the side seams is apparent in more recent specimens. The cap and vent hole in the 1880s were still hand–soldered. Many hole–in–cap can sizes are represented at northern California sites of this time period.

After 1890 and into the early 20th century, industrial improvements in northern California continued as the railroad opened a two–way flow of products and the lumber industry established large camps. Cookhouse foods in the lumber camps came out of large–volume containers and were served on ironstone plates. Concentrations of No. 10 tins, evaporated milk cans and condiment tins with double side seams are often all that remain at logging camp sites. For recreation, it appears from the evidence of empty cans that the men smoked or chewed tobacco. Pocket tobacco tins and tobacco tins designed for reuse as lunch boxes are common. Mining sites and other company-controlled operations reflect similar artifactual components. As noted above, the tin can was improved in this time period by the introduction of the open top, by the adoption of double seam side seams and finally by the development of double seam ends. Sanitary cans dominated can production in the United States by 1910, and by the mid–1930s, the hole–in–cap can had all but passed from the scene.

Conclusions

The humble tin can formed one important link between the developing western frontier of the United States and the industrialized East which supported the expansion of that frontier. The technological, economic and social significance of the tin can is recognized only by examining the material culture record within a theoretical framework that acknowledges the dependence of the West on the products of the East. The artifacts left by miners, settlers and others who moved into far northern California after 1825 clearly reflect the level of this dependence. The canning industry is but one example of rapid technological development in response to increasing demand for canned products. The effect of market on producer is reflected in both the increased variety and the types of tins recovered in northern California archaeological contexts. In the final analysis, the tin can and its development is but one key to understanding larger anthropological problems of the interrelationships and mutually reinforcing feedback mechanism that existed between East and West, that is, between producer and consumer. Ultimately, it is those behind the can—the makers of the products and the consumers—whose behavior and motivations one may hope to fathom by the systematic study of these physical remains.

ACKNOWLEDGEMENTS

The author would like to thank Joseph W. Hopkins III for his help in developing the symposium we held in 1981 at the Society for American Archaeology meetings in San Diego, California, from which this paper developed. Thanks also are extended to Tim Nilsson for creating the illustrations.

REFERENCES

ANONYMOUS
    1886   *List of Names on the Great Register of Siskiyou, State of California.* Yreka Semi-Weekly Journal Book and Job Office, Yreka, California.

BITTING, A. W.
    1937   *Appetizing or the Art of Canning: Its History and Development.* The Trade Pressroom, San Francisco.

BUSCH, JANE
    1979   Sardines to Beer: An Introduction to the Tin Can. Ms on file, Klamath National Forest, Yreka, California.
    1981   An Introduction to the Tin Can. *Historical Archaeology* 15(1):95–104.

CLARK, HYLA M.
    1977   *The Tin Can Book.* New American Library, New York.

COBB, GEORGE W.
    1914   The Development of the Sanitary Can. In *A History of the Canning Industry,* edited by Arthur I. Judge, pp. 94–97. The Canning Trade, Baltimore.

COBB, JOHN N.
1919 *The Canning of Fishery Products*. Millen Freeman, Seattle.

COLLINS, JAMES H.
1924 *The Story of Canned Foods*. E. P. Dutton and Company, New York.

COX, THOMAS R.
1974 *Mills and Markets: A History of the Pacific Coast Lumber Industry to 1900*. University of Washington Press, Seattle.

CRUESS, WILLIAM V.
1948 *Commercial Fruit and Vegetable Products*. McGraw-Hill, New York.

FONTANA, BERNARD L., J. CAMERON GREENLEAF, CHARLES FERGUSON, ROBERT WRIGHT AND DORIS FREDERICK
1962 Tin Cans. In Johnny Ward's Ranch: A Study in Historic Archaeology. *The Kiva* 28(1–2):67–78.

HUNT, ARTHUR L.
1902 Canning and Preserving, Fruit, Vegetable, Fish and Oysters. In *Twelfth Census of the United States, Part III*, pp. 463–513. Washington, D.C.

HUNZIKER, OTTO F.
1914 *Condensed Milk and Milk Powder*. Privately published. Lafayette, Indiana.

KOPETZ, ARNOLD A.
1978 Metal Cans: Types, Trends and Selected Factors. Modern Packaging 1978/1979. *Encyclopedia and Buyers Guide* 51(12):87–91.

LEE, C. T.
1914 A History of the Canned Meat Industry. In *A History of the Canning Industry*, edited by Arthur I. Judge, pp. 40–42. The Canning Trade, Baltimore.

MACNAUGHTAN, D. J. AND ERNEST S. HEDGES (EDITORS)
1935 The Evolution of the Sealed Tinplate Container. *Bulletin of the International Tin Research and Development Council* 1:40–56.

MAY, EARL CHAPIN
1937 *The Canning Clan: A Pageant of Pioneering Americans*. The MacMillan Company, New York.

MCDONALD, JAMES A.
1979 Cultural Resource Overview. Ms. on file, Klamath National Forest, Yreka, California.

MCGOWN, JOSEPH A.
1949 *Freighting to the Mines in California 1849–1859*. Unpublished Ph.D. dissertation, Department of History, University of California, Berkeley.

PAUL, RODMAN
1963 *Mining Frontiers of the Far West, 1848–1880*. Holt, Rinehart and Winston, New York.

PULATI, EVALENE
1973 *Illustrated Tin Container Guide*. Privately published. Santa Ana, California.

REICHMAN, GUS
1957 The Farmers Mill. *The Siskiyou Pioneer* 2(8):3–8.

ROCK, JAMES T.
1980 *What's Out There: Railroad Logging's Material Culture Remains*. A Paper Presented at the Society for California Archaeology Meeting, Redding, California, April 4.

1983 *The Swiss Connection*. A Paper Presented at the Society for Historical Archaeology Meeting, Denver, Colorado, January 8.

SACHAROW, STANLEY AND ROGER G. GRIFFIN
1970 *Food Packaging: A Guide for the Supplier, Processor and Distributor*. The AVI Publishing Co., Inc., Westport, Connecticut.

SCHRADER, GEORGE R. (EDITOR)
1949 *Yearbook* 1(4). Siskiyou County Historical Society, Yreka, California.

STEVENSON, CHARLES H.
1899 The Preservation of Fishery Products for Food. In *Bulletin of United States Fish Commission*, edited by George M. Bowers, pp. 335–563. U.S. Government Printing Office, Washington, D.C.

STEVENSON, W. H. H.
1914 Cans and Can-Making Machinery. In *A History of the Canning Industry*, edited by Arthur I. Judge, pp. 92–93. The Canning Trade, Baltimore.

STUMPF, GARY D.
1979 *Gold Mining in Siskiyou County 1850–2900. Siskiyou County Historical Society Occasional Paper 2*.

TEAGUE, GEORGE
1980 *Reward Mine and Associated Sites. Western Archaeological Center Publications in Anthropology 11*.

WELLS, HARRY L.
1881 *History of Siskiyou County, California*. D. J. Stewart & Co., Oakland, California.

WOODWARD, ARTHUR
1958 *Appendices to the Report on Fort Union 1851–1891*. Ms. on file, Western Archaeological Center, Tuscon, Arizona.

JAMES T. ROCK
KLAMATH NATIONAL FOREST
YREKA, CALIFORNIA 96097

D.B.S. MAXWELL

Beer Cans: A Guide for the Archaeologist

ABSTRACT

Beer cans are potentially useful as tools for dating later
components in historical sites, and for determining the time
of intrusion into prehistoric sites. Changes in major and
minor design features are sufficiently documented to yield
age estimates accurate to within five years of production.
Even in cases of poor can preservation, general trends in
shape and construction should provide an estimate accurate
to within a decade. This article details both morphological
and stylistic changes for the purpose of providing a basic
guide to the dating of beer cans.

Introduction

Busch (1981) provides an overview of the history of the tin can. The research herein serves to
expand her work on a specific subject—the beer
can. Beer cans are of potentially great value for
dating both later historic sites and intrusive components in prehistoric sites. Changes in beer can
morphology and design are well documented,
meaning that determining the age of a beer can to
within a few years of production is a distinct possibility. Beer can collectors have done a great deal
of research into the history and development of the
beer can, and much of the terminology used in this
article is taken from beer can collecting literature.

Origins

In 1909, a brewer in Montana first suggested
that beer be put in cans. The American Can Company of Greenwich, Connecticut, experimented
with this idea briefly, but had little success (Beer
Can Collectors of America [BCCA] 1985:3). The
technology available at that time simply made
canned beer an impossibility. While ordinary tin
cans are designed to withstand internal pressure of

between 24 and 35 p.s.i., the pasteurization process used on beer creates pressures of 80 p.s.i. and
requires a more sturdy container (BCCA 1976a:1).
Another obstacle to canning beer was the necessity
of developing an internal coating for the can (Martells 1976).

With the coming of prohibition in 1920, further
canning experiments were discontinued. However,
towards the end of prohibition the American Can
Company resumed its experiments in making a
stronger container (*Fortune* 1936). The weakness
problem was solved by using rephosphorized steel
for the can top and bottom, and by soldering each
layer of metal in the fold of the side seam.

The second problem was that beer reacts with
metal, producing precipitated salts—referred to by
brewers as metal turbidity (*Fortune* 1936)—ren-
dering the beer discolored and undrinkable (BCCA
1985:3). To address this problem, a number of
experimental can linings were tried, and several
proved to be suitable. The American Can Company had settled on a combination of enamel and
brewer's pitch, similar to a keg, which was trademarked "Keglined." The trademark lasted although the material itself was replaced by a synthetic vinyl (known as "vinylite") prior to large-
scale production. The Continental Can Company
of New York City and the Cork, Crown, and Seal
Company of Philadelphia both developed wax
coatings, while National Can and Pacific Can each
developed enamel coatings for their containers
(BCCA 1985:4).

The first cans filled were "Kruger's Special
Beer," a 3.2 percent alcohol beer made during the
partial lifting of prohibition in 1933 (Christensen
1976:3). Two thousand of these cans were filled,
but none was sold. On 24 January 1935, in Richmond, Virginia, Kruger Cream Ale became the
first brand of canned beer sold commercially.
These cans were the standard 12-oz. size, similar
in design to cans sold today.

Dating Cans

Unfortunately, there are few foolproof guides
for dating beer cans. Very few brewers ever in-

Historical Archaeology, 1993, 27(1):95–113.
Permission to reprint required.

TABLE 1
CHRONOLOGY OF STYLISTIC DEVELOPMENT OF THE BEER CAN

Date	Feature Introduced
1980s	–UPC computer codes standard feature on all cans.
	–Multiple neck-in chimes present on cans produced in the early years of the decade.
	–Single, longer neck-in chimes prevalent during latter years of the decade.
1989	–Government alcohol warning labels introduced.
1984	–Straight-sided steel cans cease production.
1983	–Production of ring-pull cans ceases.
1970s	–Production of 11-oz., 15-oz., and gallon cans ceases.
	–UPC computer codes introduced.
1977	–Coors phases out push-button cans.
1975	–American Can Company begins producing push-button cans.
1974–1979	–Cans issued commemorating the U.S. bicentennial.
1972	–Oregon bans the use of ring-pull cans. Push-button can openings introduced by Coors.
	–Cans with specialized shapes first marketed.
1967	–Tin-free steel (TFS) cans introduced.
1966	–Welded-seam cans introduced.
	–"Neck-in chime" cans (lid smaller than can body) introduced.
1965	–First "ring-pull" can marketed.
1964	–Continental Can's "U-tab" design introduced.
	–Tab-tops with "smile" beads introduced.
	–Gallon cans introduced.
1963	–In January, Schlitz becomes first national brewer to use tab-top cans. By August, 65 brands are available in this design.
	–First 12-oz. all-aluminum can issued.
	–Plastic six-pack holder (yoke) introduced.
1962	–First self-opening can ("snap-top" or "tab-top") introduced by Pittsburgh Brewing Company.
1960	–Cones completely phased out by this time.
1950s	–Crowntainers phased out by mid-decade.
	–Cones largely phased out by mid-decade.
	–Odd-size cans marketed include 7-, 8-, 10-, 11-, 14-, and 15-oz. sizes.
	–Aluminum lids used on steel-bodied cans. These are often described on can labels as "soft-tops."
	–Pastels and metallic colors become common features of can labels.
1959	–Coors markets 7-oz. all-aluminum can.
1958	–Primo markets 11-oz. paper-labeled, all-aluminum can.
1954	–Schlitz markets the first 16-oz. punch-top can.
1950	–"Internal Revenue Tax Paid" marking removed from can (and bottle) labels, March 30.
1942–1947	–Domestic canned beer production ceased due to World War II. Over 18 million cans of beer produced for military use.
	–Military beer cans are silver or olive drab in color.
	–Military cans are not marked "Internal Revenue Tax Paid" but, rather, "Withdrawn Free of Tax for Exportation."
1940	–J-spout cans phased out of production.
	–Introduction of crowntainer, which replaces the J spout.
1930s	–Most cans feature heavy paint and lacquer, resulting in good label preservation.
	–The word "beer" is usually as prominent as the brand name, owing to the novelty of having beer in cans.
	–Opening instructions, usually with illustrations, are included as part of the label (usually near the seam).
	–Contents are often described as "contains 12 fluid ounces—same as a bottle."
1937	–Cones produced after this date have concave bottoms and long cones ("high-profile").
	–J-spout cans introduced.
	–Quart-size cones introduced in July.
1935	–First can marketed on January 24 in Richmond, Virginia. Eighteen breweries are canning beer by end of year.
	–Beginning June 28, all cans produced are marked "Internal Revenue Tax Paid."
	–Cone-top cans first marketed in September. These have flat bottoms and short cones ("low-profile").

Note. It is often difficult (if not impossible) to document the dates when various features are eliminated or removed from use, due primarily to the fact that old stock is frequently utilized after changes have been made. The presence of multiple suppliers (and in some cases, brewery locations) will also result in the simultaneous usage of different styles of cans (i.e., a single brewing company may produce aluminum and crimped-steel cans in different plants).

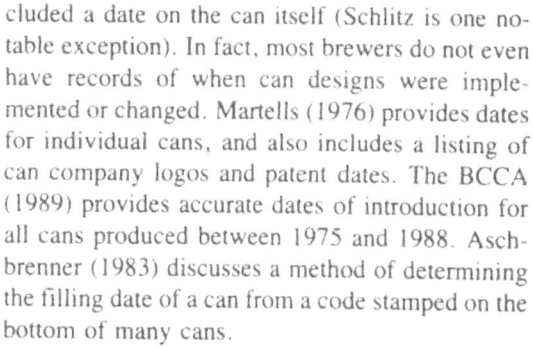

FIGURE 1.   A standard 12-oz., punch-top beer can.

FIGURE 2.   "Internal Revenue Tax Paid" (IRTP) marking on a pre-1950 can.

cluded a date on the can itself (Schlitz is one notable exception). In fact, most brewers do not even have records of when can designs were implemented or changed. Martells (1976) provides dates for individual cans, and also includes a listing of can company logos and patent dates. The BCCA (1989) provides accurate dates of introduction for all cans produced between 1975 and 1988. Aschbrenner (1983) discusses a method of determining the filling date of a can from a code stamped on the bottom of many cans.

The techniques and information utilized by these authors may not always be obtainable from a beer can, owing to problems such as preservation. However, there are a number of guidelines for determining the age of any given can to within a few years. The majority of this information comes from BCCA (1976a, 1985, 1989), Martells

(1976), and from personal observation and experience. Table 1 summarizes the major events in the beer can's history.

The Pre-World War II Era

Pre-World War II era cans are divisible into three primary categories: punch tops, cone tops, and crowntainers. Each category is discussed below.

Punch-Top Cans

The 1930s and 1940s saw the greatest variety of types of beer cans. The first type marketed was

FIGURE 3. Cone-top can depicting side seam and "Cap-Sealed" logo.

FIGURE 4. A short cone or "low-profile" can, produced only prior to World War II.

American Can's "punch-top" or "flat-top"—so named because its flat top required a punch opener. An early punch-top can stands 12–12.5 cm (5 in.) high, has a diameter of 7 cm (2¾ in.), and a soldered side seam 2.5 cm (1 in.) wide. Cans produced by the American Can Company all bear the trademark "Keglined" (Figure 1). Continental Can, National Can, and Pacific Can all marketed similar 12-oz. cans.

By the end of 1935, 18 breweries were canning beer in punch-top cans; by the late 1930s, at least 78 breweries were doing the same (Garard 1978). Cans first appeared on the west coast in late 1936 (Maloney 1973:4).

All cans (and bottles), with the exception of those designated for military use, produced be-tween 28 June 1935 and 30 March 1950 were marked "Internal Revenue Tax Paid" (IRTP) (Figure 2). The IRTP marking is an important horizon for determining the production date of a can.

Cone-Top Cans

Cone-top cans were manufactured by the Continental Can Company, and were trademarked "Cap-Sealed" (Figure 3). These were first marketed in September of 1935 by the Schlitz Brewing Company of Milwaukee, Wisconsin (BCCA 1985: 9).

Cone-top cans have been described as looking like tin bottles—complete with a cap—and thus as

Cone-top cans came in three sizes: 12 oz., 16 oz. (rare), and 32 oz. (U.S. quart). There are three varieties of cones on standard 12-oz. cans: short cone, referred to as "low-profile" (Figure 4) which stands a total of 14 cm (5½ in.) high (12 cm [4¾ in.] to the base of the cone); a standard long cone or "high-profile" (Figure 5), which also stands 14 cm (5½ in.) high (11.5 cm [4½ in.] to the base of the cone—see Garard 1981:18); and a type produced by the Crown, Cork, and Seal Company referred to by collectors as a "J spout" because of its straight, narrow neck which flares into a wide base (Cameron 1983b:28). These cans all have a basal diameter of 7 cm (2¾ in.), and a soldered side seam that is 2.5 cm (1 in.) wide.

FIGURE 5.   A long cone or "high-profile" can, produced after World War II.

being more likely to be accepted by beer drinkers. In fact, early advertisements claim that "the public preferred the shape of the Continental can two to one over American's flat-top can" (BCCA 1976a: 41). Indeed, the appeal of the can to both brewers and beer drinkers does appear to have been its familiar bottle-like shape. However, Clark (1977: 32) feels that this attraction was primarily for the brewer, as the shape of this can meant that it could be filled with only minor modifications to existing bottling lines, thus eliminating the need to purchase American Can's expensive (ca. $25,000) flat-top canning line. As a result, smaller brewers tended toward using cone-top cans. Garard (1981) lists 102 breweries using cone-top cans by the end of 1939. Only one of these, Schlitz, was a national brewer.

FIGURE 6.   The silver crowntainer lacks a side seam.

FIGURE 7. Early Brown Derby can (ca. 1937) shows the word "beer" as prominently as the brand name.

FIGURE 8. Early cans often had opening instructions as part of their label.

Crowntainers

In 1940, the Crown, Cork and Seal Company introduced a new and very distinctive can design. This was known as the crowntainer (Figure 6), and was often referred to as a "Silver Growler" or "Silver Bumper" (BCCA 1985:21). This design replaced the "J spout" described above. The crowntainer "was formed by drawing the sides and top from one piece of steel sheet, and attaching the concave bottom by the standard rolled flange method" (BCCA 1985:21). The method of drawing involved would not allow for the use of tin-plated steel, and plating the can after forming was very expensive, so an aluminum coating was used on the steel body. The bottom was tin-plated, and the internal lining was wax (BCCA 1985). A crowntainer stands 13 cm (5 in.) high, and has a 7.2 cm (2¾-in.) diameter at the base and no side seam. Crowntainers were used by a number of brewers until the mid-1950s, when they were phased out. These cans were either silver- or cream-colored and were available only in the 12-oz. size and east of the Rocky Mountains.

Dating Cans from Prior to 1950

Because of Internal Revenue tax laws, beer cans from prior to 1950 can be easily distinguished from those produced after this date. Developments prior to this date are described subsequently.

FIGURE 9   An early 16-oz. can (ca. 1958).

FIGURE 10.   Two different versions of the 8-oz. can (ca. 1980).

Punch Tops

Cans of this time period have a number of distinguishing features. Both the paint and the lacquer used on the can were very heavy, especially during the 1930s, as can manufacturers did not know exactly how much of each was necessary to preserve the label. Thus, early cans often have very good paint preservation.

Can labels from the 1930s often display the word "beer" as prominently as the brand name (Figure 7), because the idea of canned beer was still unfamiliar to many customers. Cans produced up to the early 1940s usually had opening instructions (Figure 8) along the seam of the can (Cameron 1983b). Also common on early cans was the practice of describing the contents, e.g., "contains 12

fluid ounces—same as bottle." Many of these practices had been discontinued by the early 1940s.

Cone Tops

Many of the stylistic label variations found on cone-top cans are similar to those found on punch tops made at the same time. However, some features are unique to cones.

Cones made prior to 1937 have flat bottoms. Those produced after this date have concave bottoms. Cones produced prior to World War II are described as "low-profile"—that is, they have a short cone (Figure 4). Post-war cones are called "high-profile," because the cone is longer (Figure 5). J-spout cones were produced only from 1937 to 1940 (Cameron 1983a). The quart-size cone was introduced in July 1937 (White 1978:17) and continued until the early 1950s.

Crowntainers

Crowntainers and growlers have a much more limited history, having been produced only be-

FIGURE 11. Ten-oz. can.

FIGURE 12. Eleven-oz. can (ca. 1960).

tween 1940 and the middle 1950s. The presence or absence of an IRTP marking should differentiate these two time periods. There were no major changes in the construction of crowntainers (BCCA 1976a). As is mentioned earlier, most cone-top cans and all crowntainers were obsolete by the mid-1950s.

The World War II Era

Canned beer production for the U.S. domestic market ceased in 1942 because of restrictions in the availability of tin plate, which was reserved for military use (Martells 1976; Rock 1980). However, the military purchased huge quantities of canned beer—at least 18 million cans (BCCA 1976b:29)—for overseas consumption. According to the BCCA (1985:21), over one billion cans of beer were supplied to the armed forces. Military cans, which were produced by 40 different breweries, have two distinct features that set them apart from other cans. First, rather than reading "Internal Revenue Tax Paid," all military beer cans read "Withdrawn Free of Tax for Exportation." Second, these cans are camouflaged—olive drab (or grey) in color, with the brand's standard logo in black. Advertisements of the time describe these cans as "lusterless—will not reflect the sun's rays—and of olive-drab color, like tanks, army trucks, etc." (Beer Cans Monthly 1979:26). A number of olive-drab cans have turned up in North

FIGURE 13. Fourteen-oz. can.

America (California, Texas, and Washington State), suggesting that not all were shipped overseas (Kirkpatrick 1980:4). Domestic production of canned beer resumed in 1947.

The 1950s

On 30 March 1950, the U.S. Bureau of Alcohol, Tobacco, and Firearms lifted the regulation of paying internal revenue tax on beer prior to shipping it from the brewery (Henderson [1976]:2). Thus, the words ''Internal Revenue Tax Paid'' were re-

FIGURE 14.   Fifteen-oz. can (late 1950s).

moved from the labels of all beer packages including cans, which is an important guide for dating cans. Most beer cans lacking these words (or ''Withdrawn Free of Internal Revenue Tax'') were produced after this date, as discussed above.

The 1950s also saw the demise of cone-top cans and crowntainers. Most brewers canning beer had reached the point where sales revenue exceeded the expense of installing canning lines. Since cone-

FIGURE 15. Schlitz can with "Super Softop" logo advertizing an aluminum top for easier opening (1960).

FIGURE 16. Two varieties of 7-oz. cans (mid-1970s).

top cans and crowntainers were slower to fill than punch-top cans, they became too costly and thus obsolete (Martells 1976:9; BCCA 1985:22). The Rice Lake Brewing Company was the last brewer to use cone-top cans, which were completely phased out of the brewing industry by 1960 (BCCA 1985). Cone-top cans continued to be used for oil and gasoline additives until the 1980s.

While punch-top cans were the standard of the 1950s, the 12-oz. size was by no means universal. Schlitz issued 16-oz. cans (Figure 9) in 1954, in an effort to make up revenue lost during a 1953 Milwaukee strike (Martells 1976). Other sizes were also introduced: Goebel of Detroit began marketing beer in 8-oz. cans; and 10-, 11-, 14-, and 15-oz. cans were also brought to market (Figures 10–14). Eleven- and 15-oz. cans were used in the western states, while 10- and 14-oz. cans were popular in the southern states. Thirty-two-oz. cans continued to be produced on a small scale (e.g., New York's Ballentine brewery made quart punch-top cans). Many of these sizes continue to be produced at present.

Aluminum also found its way into beer cans during the 1950s. The Adolf Coors Company of Colorado began to use cans with aluminum tops; these were billed as "soft-tops" and were designed to make opening the can easier. Schlitz and a number of other brewers continued this practice beginning in 1960 (Figure 15). All-aluminum cans followed shortly. Primo, a Hawaiian brewer, marketed an 11-oz. paper-labeled, all-aluminum can in 1958 (Martells 1976:100). Coors issued an all-aluminum 7-oz. can in 1959 (Figure 16; BCCA 1985: 22).

Another distinctive change found in the 1950s was a wider variety of label colors, as can manufacturers exploited improved printing methods. Pastels and metallic colors were quite common.

The 1960s

The decade of the 1960s was a time of great innovation in the canning industry, and a number of new types of cans became available.

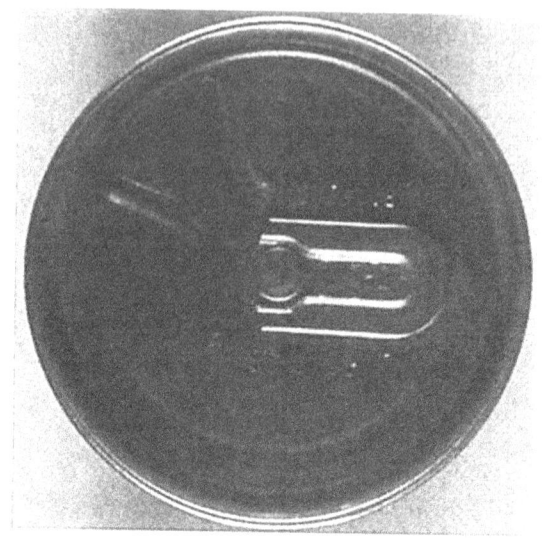

FIGURE 18.   An early version of the "tab-top," with the tab still in place (can unopened). Occasionally early tab-top cans will be found with the tab in place, and holes punched either through the tab or the bottom of the can, apparently by a beer-drinker who did not approve of the new innovation.

FIGURE 17.   Hamm's produces the first all-aluminum 12-oz. can.

In the early years of the decade, soft-top cans became very common, in an attempt to increase convenience for the buyer (*Modern Packaging* [*MP*] 1962a:33–34, 1963a:159–160). The presence of the soft-top was usually advertized on the cans label using words such as "super soft-top."

All-aluminum cans also became an important part of the market. While such cans had been introduced in the 1950s, they were available only in the 7-oz. size (Primo notwithstanding). In 1963, 12-oz. aluminum cans became a reality. Hamm's beer was the first brand available in this package (Figure 17) and was quickly followed by Budweiser (*MP* 1963b:150, 1963c:210). These are two-piece aluminum cans. In 1966, aluminum cans with a lid smaller than the body of the can (known as a "neck-in chime") appeared on the

market (*MP* 1966a). Many early aluminum cans include slogans such as "New! All-Aluminum Can" on their labels.

The single most significant change in beer cans during the 1960s was the introduction of the self-opening can, frequently described as the "pop-top" or "snap-top" can (Figures 18, 19), first used in 1962 when the Pittsburgh Brewing Company test-marketed their "Iron City" label with the new self-opening device (BCCA 1985:22). *Modern Packaging* (1962b:102, 1963d:66–67) also treats this type, which met with immediate popularity. Schlitz was the first national brewer to use the device, beginning on 17 January 1963 (BCCA 1973:6), and by March 1963, the "tab-top" was used on all cans produced by Schlitz and Pittsburgh. Forty brands were using "tab-tops" by July of that year, 65 by August, and by 1965, 70 percent of all canned beer featured this item (BCCA 1985:22).

The actual design of the "tab-top" underwent a

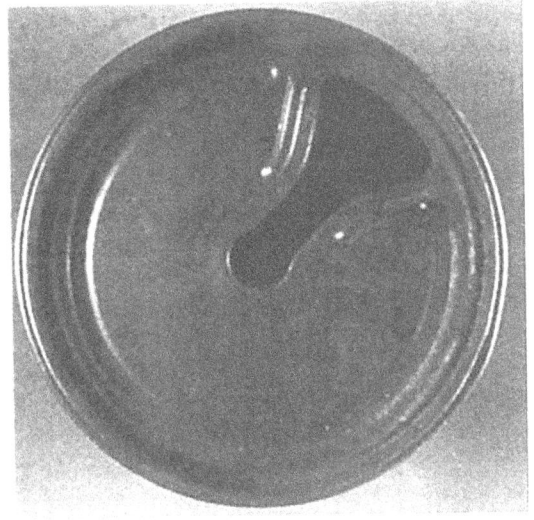

FIGURE 19. Early "tab-top" can, after the tab is removed and the can opened.

FIGURE 21. The "ring-pull" or "pull-ring" opener.

FIGURE 20. Continental Can's "U-tab."

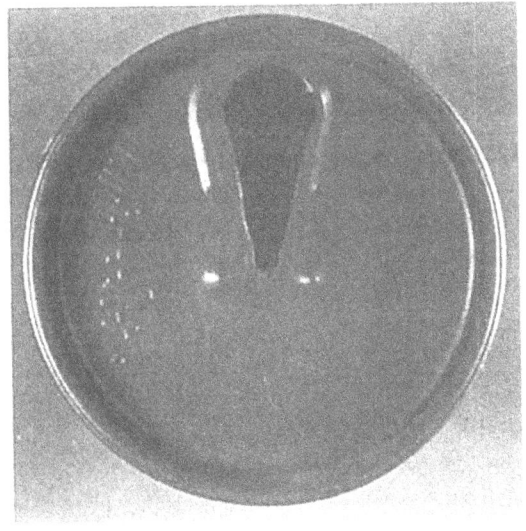

FIGURE 22. A "tear-drop shaped" opening, with "smile"
beads along the side to prevent spillage.

considerable number of changes over the years.
These changes were primarily associated with convenience and safety for the consumer. Early tabs
were quite sharp, often resulting in cut fingers, and
so, by early 1964, the American Can Company
had introduced a tab that had no sharp edges (*MP*
1964a:58). Continental Can produced an almost
identical version, called the "U-Tab" (Figure 20),

FIGURE 23. Iron City can has both a welded side seam and neck-in chimes (crimps at top and bottom) (ca. 1980).

FIGURE 24. A tin-free steel (TFS) can with wrap-around graphics, known as MiraForm II. Seam can be seen along the center line of the can (ca. 1978).

later that year (*MP* 1964b:back cover). Also at this time, both companies introduced "smile beads," raised lines alongside the opening which helped to prevent spillage (*MP* 1964c:60).

In 1965, Continental Can introduced the first "ring-pull" can (Figure 21) (*MP* 1965:back cover). This opening design allowed the consumer to insert a finger into the ring and pull open the can. The initial version of this device produced a rather narrow opening which was soon expanded from a tear-drop (Figure 22) to a more triangular shape (*MP* 1966b:back cover). Martells (1976) provides an excellent pictorial overview of the development of the tab-top and pull-ring. It is interesting to note that although self-opening beer cans were not produced until 1962, the idea had been

well developed and patented as early as 1943 (Gordon 1984:22–23).

In 1961, the Continental Can Company began experimenting with a welded side seam (Figure 23) for their steel cans. This seam is narrower than the conventional soldered seam that had been in use up to that time (Kelsey 1961:147). Welded-seam cans did not appear on the market until 1966 (*MP* 1966c:54). Roth (1981:158) provides an illustrated comparison of seam types. At the time, this seam was only used on 12-oz. cans, although other sizes such as 8- and 16-oz. cans followed shortly.

In 1967, tin-free steel (TFS) cans first appear on the market (*MP* 1967). TFS cans allow the side seam to be cemented, rather than soldered or welded (although welding was still possible),

FIGURE 25. Hamm's Draft barrel can, the only widely produced beer can with a custom shape.

FIGURE 26. Standard and tall 12-oz. cans.

which allows for wrap-around graphics (Figure 24). TFS cans were produced under different trade names by different companies, including American Can's "Miraseam" and Continental Can's "Conoweld" (*MP* 1968a). TFS cans were available in both the traditional straight-sided style, and the neck-in chime style (*MP* 1968b).

The ubiquitous plastic six-pack holder (yoke) was first introduced by Anheuser-Busch in 1963 (*MP* 1963e:121–124, 199).

A final innovation of the 1960s was the introduction of U.S. gallon-sized cans, beginning in 1964 (*MP* 1964d:119).

The 1970s

Aluminum cans became most common during the 1970s, due primarily to the fact that aluminum cans weigh less than steel cans and so are more economical for the brewer to ship. To combat this situation, steel can manufacturers began to market "crimped-steel" cans (Figure 23)—cans with end pieces smaller than the body of the can (*MP* 1970). These cans are lighter in weight and require less shipping space than straight-sided steel cans. "Crimped-steel" cans also have a more narrow side seam (5 mm) than most straight-sided steel cans (those which are not welded).

The "Miraform" can (Figure 24) was developed by the American Can Company in 1972 (BCCA 1972a:2), as an attempt by steel manufacturers to regain the market lost to aluminum. This was a two-piece, drawn-steel can, referred to by collectors as "seamless steel" (BCCA 1985). It resembles an aluminum can in appearance but is more robust, and thus less likely to dent.

A short-lived phenomenon was the use of specialized shapes for beer cans. The idea of having different can shapes dates at least to the late 1960s (*MP* 1968c:back cover). In 1972, the Theodore Hamm Brewing Company of Minnesota introduced their draft beer in a 12-oz. can shaped like a

FIGURE 27. The push-button can lid. This design was implemented in Oregon after pull-rings were banned for creating excess litter.

FIGURE 28. The StaTab. This early design was replaced because it was difficult to open.

barrel (Figure 25) (BCCA 1972b:3). These cans were quite popular, but production costs were higher than the profit made from selling the beer, and they were gone from the market by 1978. At least two other brands were produced in cans of this shape, although these were never marketed (Cameron 1982). Some brewers, including Schlitz, began to use a taller, more narrow version of the standard 12-oz. can (Figure 26). This practice continued until the mid-1980s.

A number of types of self-opening cans became available during the 1970s. Pull-rings were common throughout most of the decade, although they were phased out beginning in the late 1970s as a response to lobbying by environmentalists who objected to the additional litter created by the rings. In 1972, Oregon banned the use of pull-rings on cans (BCCA 1972c:20). This law meant that canners needed to develop a new type of self-opening can without a separate pull tab.

That same year, Coors of Colorado introduced a push-button can lid (Figure 27) (BCCA 1972d:2). This type of lid found a wider market in 1975,

when the American Can Company began to produce a similar style of opening device (BCCA 1975:4). Coors phased out the push-button top in late 1977 (BCCA 1977:40).

Later, the "StaTab"—an opening device that remained with the can—was introduced (BCCA 1985:23) by the Reynolds Aluminum Company, and it has become the standard of today's canned beverage. A number of varieties of "stay-with-the-can" openers were used during the 1970s, and many of these are pictured in Martells (1976) (Figures 28, 29, 30).

The 1970s also saw the widespread production of beer cans which commemorated both local and national events (Figure 31). These cans will often bear the date of the event on their label. However, it may be misleading to assume that all cans produced for an event were used at the time of the event itself. For example, cans commemorating the U.S. bicentennial were produced from 1974 until 1979, widely bracketing the event itself.

The production of 11-oz., 15-oz., and gallon-sized cans ceased by the mid-1970s.

FIGURE 29   StaTab's second stage, with solid tab structure.

FIGURE 31.   One of Falstaff's bicentennial commemorative cans.

FIGURE 30   StaTab's current design, with a ring-like tab structure.

The 1980s

During this decade, the brewing industry changed to the exclusive use of cans with ''stay behind'' tops (although pull-ring cans were produced as late as 1983), which have a less detrimental effect on the environment, theoretically cutting in half the amount of litter produced by cans.

Production of straight-sided steel cans—the same design as the original beer can—ceased in 1984 (BCCA 1985:23). Crampton (1988:119) suggests that steel cans may make a comeback in the next few years, owing to improvements in the manufacturing of thin steel cans (comparable in strength to aluminum) combined with the escalating cost of aluminum.

A phenomenon occurring throughout the 1980s is decreasing the diameter of the can lid. It is less expensive to produce a can with a small diameter lid and a tapering neck than to produce a can lid

FIGURE 32. Multiple neck-in chimes

FIGURE 33. Single, long neck-in chimes.

equal in diameter to the base of the can. Early tapered cans featured a number of neck-in chimes (Figure 32), while those from the later years of the decade (1985 and later) feature a single, longer neck-in chime (Figure 33).

Cans produced in the 1980s are also notable for the presence of UPI computer codes and, beginning in 1989, government warning labels detailing the harmful effects of drinking alcoholic beverages (Figure 34).

landscape also suggests that it should be employed by archaeologists interested in inferring the age of historic deposits, or the date of intrusion on prehistoric sites. While it may not be possible to determine the exact production date of the can, it should be well within the abilities of anyone to provide an age range within about five years. This range, combined with other datable materials from sites, should provide abundant information for firmly establishing the age of a given deposit.

Conclusion

Changes in beer can design are sufficiently well documented to render this artifact very useful as a dating tool. Its presence on virtually all parts of the

ACKNOWLEDGMENTS

The author gratefully thanks Michael B. Schiffer, William L. Rathje, Tim Jones, David V. Burley, Jim Rock, and two anonymous reviewers for their comments and suggestions regarding this manuscript.

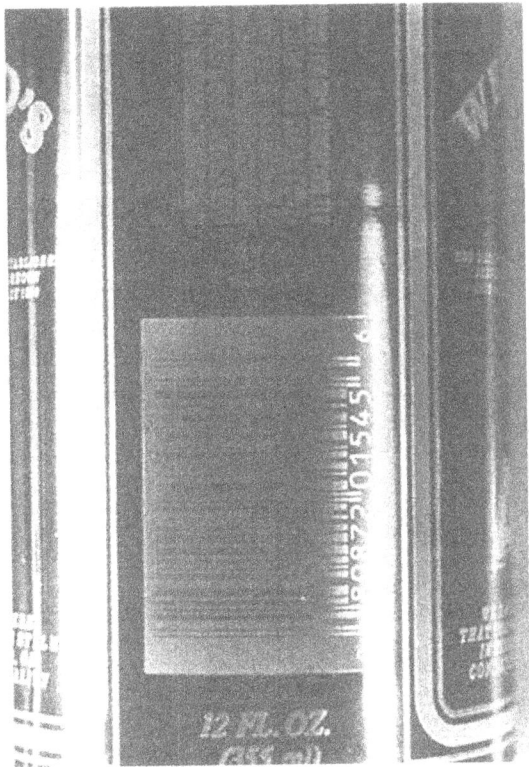

FIGURE 34. Computer price code and government warning about alcohol consumption.

However, omissions and errors remain entirely the responsibility of the author. Thanks also to W. Karl Hutchings for his invaluable darkroom assistance. Special thanks is due to Thomas, Sheilah, and Susan Maxwell for their continued encouragement and enthusiasm. Partial funding for this research was provided by the Educational Fund, Department of Anthropology, University of Arizona, Tucson.

REFERENCES

ASCHBRENNER, LEIGH
  1983 Cracking the Code. *Beer Can Collectors News Report* 13(1):4–5.

BEER CAN COLLECTORS OF AMERICA [Fenton, Missouri] (BCCA)
  1972a American Can Announces Patented Two-Piece Can. *Beer Can Collectors of America News Report* 2(3):2.

1972b ConCan's Conoweld Making News. *Beer Can Collectors of America News Report* 2(3):3.
1972c Oregon Cans the Can! *Beer Can Collectors of America News Report* 2(4):20.
1972d Coors to Introduce Revolutionary New Can. *Beer Can Collectors of America News Report* 2(1):2.
1973 10 Years Ago Today. *Beer Can Collectors of America News Report* 3(2):6.
1975 Next: Beer Can with Buttons. *Beer Can Collectors of America News Report* 5(5):4.
1976a *The Beer Can: A Complete Guide to Beer Can Collecting.* Great Lakes Living Press, Matteson, Illinois.
1976b Million Camouflage Cans? *Beer Can Collectors of America News Report* 6(5):29.
1977 New Tab Junked by Coors Beer. *Beer Can Collectors of America News Report* 7(6):40.
1985 The Golden Anniversary. *Beer Can Collectors News Report, Special Edition.* St. Louis, Missouri.
1989 *American Beer Cans, 1975–1987.* Pressworks, Denver, Colorado.

BEER CANS MONTHLY [Buckner, Missouri]
  1979 Gangway for G.I. Beer. *Beer Cans Monthly* 1(11):26–32.

BUSCH, JANE
  1981 An Introduction to the Tin Can. *Historical Archaeology* 15(1):95–104.

CAMERON, JEFFREY C.
  1982 *The Class Book of U.S. Beer Cans.* Class, Souderton, Pennsylvania.
  1983a J Spouts. *Brewery Collectibles* 1(3):28–31.
  1983b Opening Instruction Cans. *Brewery Collectibles* 1(4):32–36.

CHRISTENSEN, BILL
  1976 The Prewar Krueger Cans or the Riddle of the "World's First Beer Can" Resolved. *Beer Can Collectors of America News Report* 6(3):3–9.

CLARK, HYLA M.
  1977 *The Tin Can Book.* Tree Communications, New York.

CRAMPTON, NORM
  1988 *Complete Trash: The Best Way to Get Rid of Practically Everything Around the House.* M. Evans, New York.

FORTUNE [New York]
  1936 Beer into Cans. *Fortune* 13(1):75–80.

GARARD, MICHAEL
  1978 The Early Flats—1935. *Beer Cans Monthly* 1(1):12–13.
  1981 Early Cone Tops. *Beer Cans Monthly* 3(7):18–19.

GORDON, DENNIS W.
  1984 Early "No Opener Needed" Cans. *Beer Can Collectors of America News Report* 14(4):22–23.

HENDERSON, BILL
  [1976] Why They Did That. *Beer Can Collectors of Amer-*
         ica News Report, New Member Issue. Beer Can Col-
         lectors of America, St. Louis.

KELSEY, ROBERT J.
  1961   Continental Can Experimenting with Welded Seam.
         Modern Packaging 35(1):147.

KIRKPATRICK, ROGER
  1980   OD Military Cans Revisited. *Beer Can Collectors of*
         America News Report 10(4):4.

MALONEY, JOHN
  1973   Homage to the Beer Can. *Beer Can Collectors of*
         America News Report 3(5):4–5.

MARTELLS, JACK
  1976   *The Beer Can Collectors Bible.* Ballantine, New
         York.

MODERN PACKAGING [New York City] (*MP*)
  1962a Advertisement for Alcoa Aluminum. *Modern Pack-*
         aging 36(2):33–34.
  1962b New Importance of Convenience. *Modern Packag-*
         ing 36(3):101–107.
  1963a Advertisement for Alcoa Aluminum. *Modern Pack-*
         aging 36(7):159–160.
  1963b Hamm's Beer First in the New 12-Ounce All-Alu-
         minum Can. *Modern Packaging* 37(4):150.
  1963c 12-oz. Aluminum Cans Now Used for Beer. *Modern*
         Packaging 37(4):210.
  1963d Advertisement for Alcoa Aluminum. *Modern Pack-*
         aging 36(9):66–67.
  1963e All-Plastics Multipack that Saves Thousands. *Mod-*
         ern Packaging 36(11):122–124, 198–199.
  1964a Improved Beer-Can Tear-Tab Top. *Modern Packag-*
         ing 37(7):58.
  1964b Advertisement, Continental Can Company. *Modern*
         Packaging 37(10):back cover.
  1964c Equipment and Materials. *Modern Packaging*
         37(12):60.

1964d Gallon Can of Beer Converts to Refrigerator-Storage
       ''Keg.'' *Modern Packaging* 38(1):119.
1965   Advertisement, Continental Can Company. *Modern*
       Packaging 39(1):back cover.
1966a Neck-in Chime on New Aluminum Cans (Equipment
       and Materials). *Modern Packaging* 39(11):66.
1966b Advertisement, Continental Can Company. *Modern*
       Packaging 40(4):back cover.
1966c Welded-Seam Can Is Now Commercially Available
       to Packagers (Equipment and Materials). *Modern*
       Packaging 39(12):54.
1967   Here Comes the Tin Free Steel Can (Ideas in
       Action). *Modern Packaging* 40(9):96.
1968a Look at the Action in Metals. *Modern Packaging*
       41(10):100–105.
1968b Advertisement, Continental Can Company. *Modern*
       Packaging 41(4):back cover.
1968c Advertisement, Continental Can Company. *Modern*
       Packaging 41(7):back cover.
1970   New Economy in Shrink-Wrapped Six-Packs for
       Double-Neck-In TFS Beer Cans. *Modern Packaging*
       43(1):71.

ROCK, JAMES
  1980   Beverages: Canned Beer and Soda Notes. Ms. on
         file, U.S. Forest Service, and with the author,
         Yreka, California.

ROTH, LASZLO
  1981   *Package Design; An Introduction to the Art of Pack-*
         aging. Prentice-Hall, Englewood Cliffs, New Jer-
         sey.

WHITE, KEN
  1978   Collecting Quart Conetops. *Beer Cans Monthly* 1(6):
         17.

D.B.S. MAXWELL
DEPARTMENT OF ANTHROPOLOGY
UNIVERSITY OF ARIZONA
TUCSON, ARIZONA 85721

ERICA HILL

Thimbles and Thimble Rings from the circum-Caribbean Region, 1500–1800: Chronology and Identification

ABSTRACT

This paper provides an overview of literature on the subject of thimbles. Particular attention is devoted to the identification of functional categories and determining the gender and age composition of a site using thimbles. Major innovations in construction, decorative patterning, and shape are identified as well. Archaeologically, thimbles are often recovered at European domestic sites, in aboriginal burials, and as trade goods. This omnipresent artifact has considerable potential for general dating and demographic purposes.

Introduction

Although thimbles are often recovered at post-contact sites in the Americas, very little scholarly research is devoted to identification and dating and even less to the gender and age implications of these artifacts. Most information on thimbles has been compiled by collectors, often with impressive attention to historical and archaeological detail, yet these data are circulated among a very specialized audience and are either unknown or unavailable to the professional archaeologist. Due to the specialized nature of the pursuit and the limited number of scholarly publications, an overview of the topic is due. The collections of the Florida Museum of Natural History, primarily those from the Spanish sites of Florida and the circum-Caribbean region, were used to develop a typology and identify key characteristics.

Historical Background

The original purpose of thimbles was to protect the tip of the finger of the tailor or seamstress from injury by the blunt end of the needle. In this regard, some form of thimble has probably been in use since the origins of sewing. Thimble rings—or sewing rings as they are sometimes called—served the same purpose as thimbles, but protected the side of the finger instead of the tip. Their construction and design reflect their use by tailors, who typically sewed using the palm side of the finger to propel the needle through fabric.

Leather thimbles have been documented from the medieval period in Europe (Moorhouse 1971: 60), although such examples rarely are preserved archaeologically. Bone, horn, and wooden thimbles also have been recovered, especially in contexts in which metal was unavailable or undesirable as a construction material. This discussion, however, will focus on thimbles of metal—brass in particular—since this is the type most frequently recovered archaeologically.

The earliest metal thimbles or thimble rings with reliable archaeological provenience have been traced to the site of Corinth (Holmes 1985:19). Over one hundred bronze thimble rings were recovered, all of which date to the 9th through the 12th centuries A.D. (Davidson 1952:178).

While various types of thimbles were probably in use prior to the medieval period, two distinct types with definite regional associations have been identified. The distinctive Hispano-Moresque thimbles, conical in shape and constructed of bronze, are too heavy to have been used for tailoring or mending. Instead, Holmes (1985:20–21) suggests that they were used to make and repair horse trappings. A second early type is the Turkish-style domed thimble suggestive of the onion dome so prominent in architecture of the Near East. Thimble rings of Byzantine origin display a similar rounded shape.

Holmes ([1987b]:1) dates the earliest metal thimbles in England to A.D. 1350, and thimble rings to A.D. 1450, although metal thimbles were in use on the Continent at least a century earlier. This temporal delay is due most likely to the fact that Britain lacked a native brass industry because the island had no workable deposits of copper. An alloy of copper and zinc, brass was imported in sheets in the late Middle Ages (Steane 1984:225).

Historical Archaeology, 1995, 29(1):84–92.
Permission to reprint required.

TABLE 1
MORPHOLOGICAL CHARACTERISTICS

Time Period	Morphological Characteristics	Manufacturing Technique	Location of Production
Medieval (pre-1500)	Domed, irregular indentations, squat shape	Casting indicated by either a small hole in crown or by four notches in the rim	
1500–1600	Elongated, rectangular indentations, Spiralling punctation around crown	Single-piece casting, annealing indicated by folds of metal near rim	
Late 1500s	Edges folded over	Deep drawing	
Prior to 1650	"Tonsured" crown (no indentations on crown)		Nuremberg
1650–present	Machine-made indentations that are evenly spaced and sized		
Post-1650	Two-piece assembly crown may be attached separately		
Late 1700s	Edges folded over outside of rim	Deep-drawing	England

By the 1500s, brass thimbles had become a major import to Britain. It was not until the 17th century that Britons began producing sufficient brass to rival the well-developed industries of Germany and the Low Countries (Holmes 1985:37, [1987b]: 1). Primary sources of copper on the Continent included Spain, Bohemia, Saxony, Hanover, and Sweden (Holmes 1985:133).

Although the majority of thimbles recovered archaeologically are of brass, customs records from this period demonstrate that smelted iron was imported to Britain in large quantities for the manufacture of thimbles. However, due to the poor preservation properties of the metal, iron thimbles are rarely recovered archaeologically.

Iron was only one of many types of construction material used to manufacture thimbles. The flow of gold and silver from the Americas into the metals markets of Europe created an exceptional demand for thimbles of these heretofore scarce materials. Although popular as collectibles, thimbles of gold or silver are seldom recovered archaeologically, probably because as expensive and elite goods they were carefully guarded against loss.

Holmes (1985:133) suggests that the increased availability of brass directly contributed to the growth of the thimble-making industry at the end of the 15th century. The hallmark of the medieval thimble is the dome shape. Due to the casting pro-

cess by which they were produced, medieval brass thimbles are frequently squat and heavy with very irregular indentations (Groves 1966:36). A small hole in the top of a domed thimble or four small notches encircling the rim are indications that a thimble has been cast (Holmes 1985:134–135; cf. Greif 1984:28). Since the technique of casting had been refined by the 1500s, such characteristics date thimbles of this type securely within the Middle Ages (Table 1).

Noël Hume (1969:256) has identified additional characteristics of early thimbles. The rim is not rolled, nor are the indentations regularly patterned. Rather, thimbles through A.D. 1600 display uneven punctation, often in a spiralling pattern which terminates before reaching the center of the crown (Noël Hume 1969:256; Holmes [1987b]:2). Thimbles with crowns that have no indentations—"tonsured" thimbles—date prior to A.D. 1650 (Holmes [1987b]:3). Such design may reflect the use of the side of the finger, rather than the tip, to propel the needle through fabric. The disappearance of tonsured thimbles thus suggests not only an alteration in design, but also a change in patterns of usage.

One of the most distinctive characteristics of thimbles produced before A.D. 1600 was single-piece construction. The casting process produced a thimble which, when cooled, was composed of a single piece of brass. A second early construction technique employed hammering and stamping sheet metal into the desired shape. The process involved frequent heating of the cooled metal in order to soften it and thus make it more malleable. This technique, called annealing, often caused the metal to settle in folds, usually near the rim (Holmes 1985:133, 135, [1987b]:2).

By the late 1700s in England, the technique of deep-drawing had become widespread. Deep-drawn thimbles were made by pressing sheet metal, a "form of mechanical stamping" (Holmes [1987b]:2). The edges were then folded over the outside of the rim. In contrast, cast thimbles of this period have edges which project outward but which are solid. In Germany the process of deep-drawing had been in use over two centuries earlier (Greif 1984:12, 29–30; Holmes 1985:26). The city of Nuremberg jealously guarded the means of refining brass and so was the only European producer of deep-drawn thimbles (Greif 1984:28–29). This process is depicted in a 1564 woodcut by Jost Amman (Holmes 1985:27) in which a thimble-maker hammers brass sheets into a mold while a second craftsworker punches indentations into the newly wrought thimbles.

Identification of Thimbles Recovered from circum-Caribbean Sites

Hand-punched indentations are a distinguishing feature of 16th-century thimbles recovered archaeologically from the circum-Caribbean region. A well-dated example from the site of Nueva Cadíz, Venezuela, has evenly spaced elongated indentations which spiral from the rim to the crown (Figures 1, 2). Settled by the Spanish in 1515, Nueva Cadíz was destroyed by an earthquake in 1541 (Deagan 1987:9), securely dating this thimble to the early 16th century.

A second example of the same type was recovered from the site of Convento de San Francisco in the Dominican Republic. Although this site is not as narrowly dated as Nueva Cadíz, the recovered thimble bears a striking resemblance to the one discussed above. The indentations are virtually identical in size and shape to the thimble from

FIGURE 1. Side view of deep-drawn thimbles from Convento de San Francisco (*left*) and Nueva Cadiz (*right*). Note elongated, rectangular indentations. (Courtesy of Florida Museum of Natural History.)

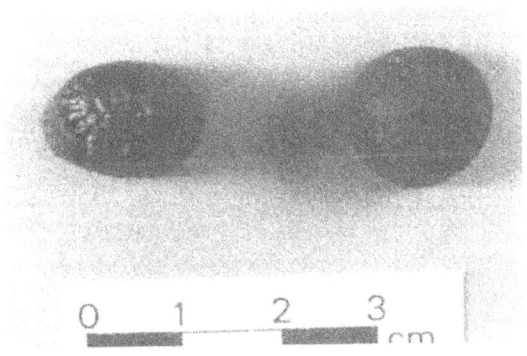

FIGURE 2. Top view of thimbles from Convento de San Francisco (*left*) and Nueva Cadiz (*right*). Note spiraling around crown. (Courtesy of Florida Museum of Natural History.)

Venezuela (Figures 1, 2); however, the indentations are not as evenly spaced nor as finely made. In both examples, the vertical indentations spiral to the crown and terminate in the center.

Despite differential quality in production, both thimbles appear to have been deep-drawn. This process was monopolized by the city of Nuremberg until the late 18th century. Only when the technique of producing metallically pure zinc was acquired by England and the rest of Germany did Nuremberg lose its control of the market for deep-drawn thimbles (Greif 1984:28–30). Therefore, the two thimbles recovered from Venezuela and the Dominican Republic probably were produced in Nuremberg and exported to Spain.

Historical records indicate that trade in thimbles between Spain and Germany developed as early as 1428 (Feldhaus 1931, cited in Holmes 1988), well before links between the two countries were solid-ified by the Hapsburg presence in 1520. Deagan notes that Spain was unable to supply the increas-ing demands of its colonies for manufactured goods and thus relied heavily upon imports from Genoa and northern Europe. Goods were shipped first to Seville, then exported to the colonies. As a result, "the material assemblages of the Spanish colonies ought to be of multiple Old World origins from 1503 onward" (Deagan 1987:20). Not sur-prisingly, then, Nuremberg thimbles appear ar-chaeologically at early Spanish sites throughout the circum-Caribbean region.

The use of nautical archaeology for dating thim-bles has been extensively explored by Holmes (1986). A particularly interesting example was re-covered from a mid-16th-century Portuguese wreck in the Seychelles. The brass thimble illus-trated by Blake and Green (1986:18) displays in-dentations which are strikingly similar to those of the Nueva Cadíz and Convento sites. Punch marks are unevenly spaced and sized and encircle the crown; indentations are square or rectangular in shape.

A second group of early thimbles, also securely dated archaeologically, have circular or reversed D-shaped indentations. Two examples from Puerto Real, Haiti, display indentations spiralling around the crown. Like the two Nuremberg examples, these thimbles have been hand-punched or drilled. The dates of 1503–1578 for the Puerto Real site (Deagan 1987:8–9) correspond to the period that predates mechanical stamping. A third brass thim-ble of this type was recovered from Panama la Vieja, Panama (PA-3), 1519–1671 (Deagan 1987). However the hand-made spiralling indentations date this artifact to the 16th century (Figure 3). Like the examples above, indentations are circular in shape, rather than the elongated or rectangular type which characterizes the Nuremberg examples.

By 1620, the technique of hand punching, or

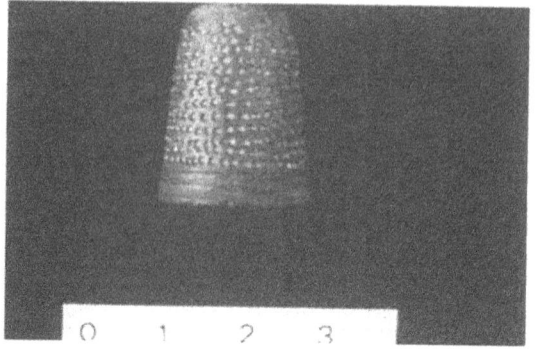

FIGURE 3. Sixteenth-century hand-indented thimble from Panama la Vieja. (Courtesy of Florida Museum of Natural History.)

drilling, indentations was disappearing with the ad-vent and spread of mechanical knurling—the pro-cess of indenting a thimble mechanically rather than by hand. By 1650, virtually all indentations were machine-made (Holmes 1987a:9). Therefore, all thimbles with evenly spaced and sized indenta-tions were manufactured sometime after 1600.

By the beginning of the 17th century, the Nuremberg monopoly on thimble production was in decline. At the same time, the Dutch casting industry was steadily expanding. Large numbers of Dutch thimbles were exported to France and to the Dutch colonies in North America throughout the 1600s (Holmes 1985:135–136; cf. Greif 1984:42).

A tall domed thimble found during an unprove-nienced surface collection in Haiti displays several features typical of the Dutch industry (Figure 4). Recovered from the site of En Bas Saline, which was originally a contact-period Taino village, this thimble is cast brass, which distinguishes it from earlier deep-drawn Nuremberg thimbles. Noël Hume (1969:256) noted that thimbles produced until ca. 1650 may be characterized by tonsuring. This example from Haiti displays a bald spot in the very center of the crown. The tonsured crown grad-ually declined in frequency and entirely disap-peared by around 1650 (Holmes [1987b]:3). The high dome and large, regularly shaped circular in-dentations are characteristic of thimbles produced in the Netherlands during this period.

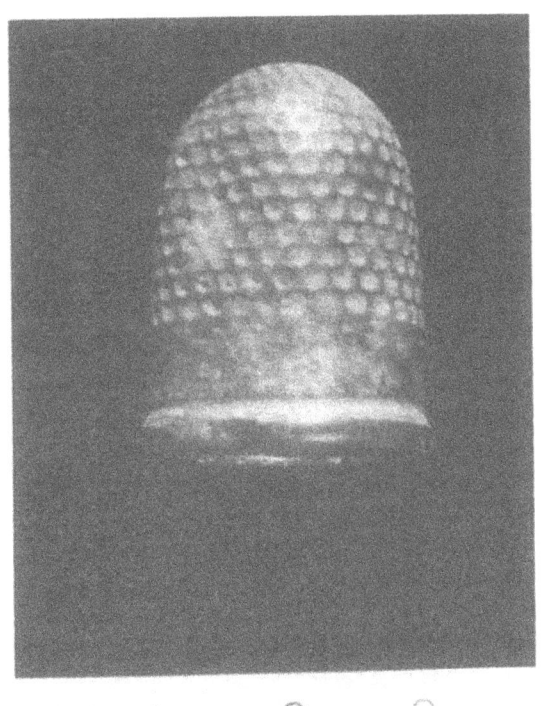

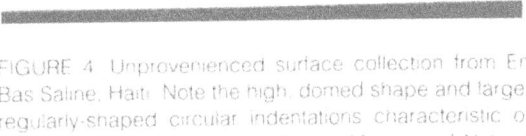

FIGURE 4. Unprovenienced surface collection from En Bas Saline, Haiti. Note the high, domed shape and large, regularly-shaped circular indentations characteristic of Dutch thimbles. (Courtesy of Florida Museum of Natural History.)

Thimbles of this type are frequently referred to as "French" (Holthuizen 1984:14–15), perhaps because of the large number exported to that country during the 17th century. Although the Spanish were a formidable presence on Hispaniola in the first half of the 16th century, by the 1600s their settlements were largely abandoned. This Dutch thimble, then, may have originated at a French sugar plantation called Montholon, established in 1650 on the site of the original Taino village.

In contrast to the spiral pattern featured by hand-punched thimbles of the 1500s, thimbles from the 17th century display circular indentations aligned in concentric circles. Indentations on the crown and those encircling the sides may be separated by a ring of unmarked brass or may be distinguished by differential size. Note, for example, the small size of the crown indentations in Figure 4 in comparison to those marking the sides.

In the Spanish examples analyzed for this study, circular indentations spiralling around the crown disappear by the mid-17th century. While thimbles after 1650 may have circular indentations on the crown, they are arranged in rows or concentric circles rather than in a spiral design.

Dutch thimbles of the 17th century are rarely decorated and maintain a simplicity of design thereafter. One possible explanation is the increased popularity of silver thimbles. Attention to design and ornamentation was lavished upon 17th-century silver thimbles, while brass thimbles acquired a reputation as common needleworking tools (Holmes [1987b]:3), useful rather than decorative.

With the apparent exception of the Dutch industry, thimbles were becoming increasingly straight sided by the 1600s (Woodfield 1981:157). The dome shape was gradually abandoned, and thimbles began to acquire the shape which they retain to this day. Excavations at the Jamestown site, inhabited between 1607 and 1699 (Cotter and Hudson 1957:16), yielded both brass and silver thimbles (Cotter and Hudson 1957:50). Several examples have waffle crowns and vertical sides and are undecorated for the most part. Although the dates for the site encompass an entire century, stylistically these thimbles date to the latter part of the 1600s, and probably to the last quarter, ca. 1675–1700.

Two thimbles from the site of Aldgate, London, which have been dated contextually to ca. 1670–1720, also display honeycomb patterning and hatched crowns. Measuring 2.1–2.4 cm, both thimbles are straight sided (Thompson et al. 1984:114–115). Thompson, Grew, and Schofield observe that one thimble was constructed in two separate pieces, the crown being attached to the body. This two-piece construction can be traced to technological change in manufacturing and may parallel the switch to machine-made indentations. Holmes

(1985:137) notes that some 17th-century brass thimbles were constructed in two pieces by applying the crown to the inside rim of the body of the thimble.

Thimbles recovered from Spanish sites dating to the 1700s display a uniformity of shape and design which is unmistakable, and they closely resemble the British thimbles discussed above. The de Hita-Gonzales domestic site (SA 7–4) at St. Augustine, Florida, yielded several brass thimbles. Although artifacts from the 18th through the 20th centuries were recovered, the closed context of the second of two stratigraphic zones has been securely dated to the 1700s (Shephard 1975:20, 32, 1983:71).

Even, honeycomb-patterned indentations characterize thimbles from this period (Figure 5). The indentations encircling the sides of these thimbles are regular and closely spaced. The crowns are distinguished by a hatched waffle pattern spatially distinct from the indented sides. A virtually identical example was recovered from the late 18th- to early 19th-century context of the site of Spaulding's Lower Store (8Pu23) in central Florida. This thimble was probably an item of trade between the Seminole and British colonists. It displays the three primary characteristics of machine-made thimbles of the 18th century: honeycomb indentations, waffle crown, and outwardly rolled rims.

This period of intense production and increased uniformity makes identification more difficult, but not impossible. The two-piece construction of the Aldgate thimble may be an excellent dating feature. At the Second Spanish period domestic site of de León (SA 26–1), St. Augustine, the crown of a thimble was recovered. It had been separately manufactured and attached, since it was fully intact with no evidence of corrosion. Two-piece construction of thimbles originated in the latter half of the 17th century; however, this feature demands further research before a secure date can be determined.

While thimbles of this period usually have rolled edges, the best identifying characteristic of late 17th- to 18th-century thimbles are the even pattern-stamped indentations. The hatched pattern in conjunction with honeycomb indentations originated sometime during the 1600s and has remained fairly consistent.

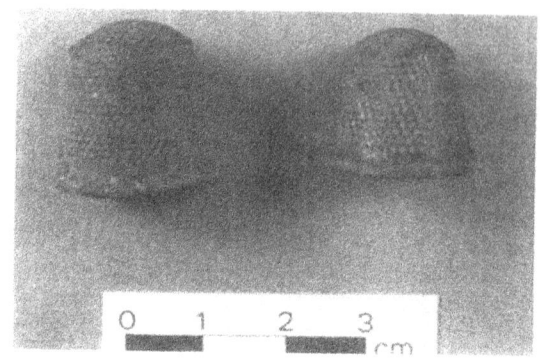

FIGURE 5. Two 18th-century thimbles recovered from the de Hita site (SA 7–4), St. Augustine, Florida. Note the even, honeycomb-patterned indentations, waffle crown, and outwardly-rolled rims. (Courtesy of Florida Museum of Natural History.)

One example from the de Hita site displays evenly spaced indentations, however the pattern begins halfway up the sides of the thimble. The lower portion of the body is not indented, nor are the edges rolled. A similar example was recovered by Hale Smith (1965:114) at the excavation of the town of Santa Rosa Pensacola, 1722–1752. Concentric rings of small circular indentations abruptly end three-quarters of the way down the length of the sides. A series of rings completes the design to the unrolled rim. The settlement of Santa Rosa was destroyed by a tropical storm in 1752 after 30 years of habitation (Smith 1965:4).

The dates for this site dovetail neatly with those of the de Hita site. The historical reconstruction of the genealogy of early St. Augustine families has revealed that, in 1736, Gerónimo José de Hita y Salazar married Juana de Avero and thereafter resided on the de Hita property (Deagan 1983:69). Evidence such as this, which details family composition in terms of both gender and age, can be positively correlated with material remains recovered archaeologically.

Gender and Age Correlation

Fundamentally, historical archaeology contributes to analyses of socially constructed relationships through material remains. Material goods such as sewing implements may potentially be used to address questions of household organization and production, status, and the division of labor (Conkey and Gero 1991:17). McEwan (1991: 34) has noted that "[t]he archaeological correlates of Spanish women are associated mostly with their domestic responsibilities." Sewing, a major occupation of European women in the Spanish colonies, is represented archaeologically in the omnipresence of thimbles at domestic sites. Closely associated with the role of women in household production—at least in European contexts—thimbles have the potential to illuminate both the presence and role of women archaeologically. At historic colonial sites in particular, the correlation of thimbles with the documented residence of women and children confirms their reliability as material indicators of gender and age.

In contrast, open-topped thimble rings, such as those recovered in quantity from the site of Concepción de la Vega, are most often the tool of the tailor. At least two thimble rings were also recovered at Jamestown; both displayed large indentations (Cotter and Hudson 1957:51) more suitable for heavy leather work than for embroidery or fine sewing. Other pursuits which also required thimble rings included harness-making, saddlery, upholstery, and shoemaking (Holmes 1985:163). In European and colonial contexts, at least, these were occupations associated primarily with males.

Less obvious, perhaps, is the correlation which exists between thimbles and the presence of female children. As part of their domestic education and perhaps also as a reflection of their role in household production, young girls were provided with the tools of their mothers and other female relatives in miniature form. Thus, children's thimbles approximating 1 cm in height abound at Spanish colonial sites (Figure 6) (Holmes 1985:169).

Two children's thimbles were recovered from the de Hita site, where five children grew to maturity in the 18th century (Deagan 1983:69). The relative invisibility of children in terms of material culture demands innovation and detailed study of artifacts which may indicate their presence. Greater attention to thimbles as age and gender

FIGURE 6. Three 18th-century childrens' thimbles (*left*), and an adult's thimble (*right*) for comparison. All thimbles were recovered at the de Hita site with the exception of the second specimen from the right, recovered from Useppa Island, Florida. (Courtesy of Florida Museum of Natural History.)

correlates may help to alleviate this bias in materials recovered archaeologically.

Thimbles Recovered from Native American Sites

Although this discussion has focused on thimbles recovered from Spanish sites in the circum-Caribbean region, thimbles also have been documented in Native American contexts. Beyond the confines of European patterns of use, thimbles as indicators of gender and age are no longer valid. McEwan (1991:34) writes that "Spanish women were important purveyors of Spanish culture among Native American . . . domestics with whom they sustained daily contact." Such culture was material as well as socioreligious. As a result, thimbles are recovered rather frequently in Native American contexts. The impact of trade on the indigenous material assemblage compounded the effects of cultural exchanges occurring within Spanish households.

The use of thimbles as tiny bells by Native American populations has been fairly well documented. Thimble bells of different sizes adorned clothing, bags, and pouches (Holmes 1985:234).

Noël Hume (1969:256) noted that holes were punched in the crown of trade thimbles, which were then strung on thongs over glass beads. The result was both ornamental and musical. Holmes (1985:234) dates this innovation to the late 18th century.

The design of a waffle-crowned thimble (Figure 6, second from the right) recovered from Useppa Island in southern Florida is consistent with this date. The thimble has no provenience, but was most certainly fashioned as a child's thimble. While the size and patterning place this thimble securely within the 1700s, the tiny circular hole through the center of the crown suggests Native American decorative use rather than an educational purpose in the European tradition.

Another interesting example was recovered from the Philip Mound site, Polk County, central Florida. This Native American burial site was looted; however, a silver thimble was recovered with the crown pierced, probably for suspension (Benson 1967:126).

Conclusion

Thimbles, so often an item of exchange in the historic colonial period, are highly context-specific. Size, indentations, and subsequent alteration of thimbles, when closely observed, may indicate not only patterns of use, such as fine needlework or tailoring, but also the age and gender of the owner. Outside of historic European contexts, thimbles acquired though trade may be used as ornaments.

As an artifact commonly recovered from domestic sites, thimbles are potential date markers. The well-documented history of the thimblemaking industry in Europe, from small medieval workshops where metalsmiths wrought thimbles by hand to the machine-stamping of the 18th century, and the parallel changes in form and design provide a framework for typing and identification of European thimbles recovered archaeologically.

ACKNOWLEDGMENTS

Sincere thanks to Kathleen Deagan for advice and encouragement, and to Elise LeCompte-Baer for her patient assistance. Ryan J. Wheeler gave generously of his time and brought several sources to my attention. I would also like to thank Barbara J. Little for her careful reading and valuable comments.

REFERENCES

BENSON, CARL A.
1967 The Philip Mound: A Historic Site. *Florida Anthropologist* 20(3&4):118–132.

BLAKE, WARREN, AND JEREMY GREEN
1986 A Mid-XVI-Century Portuguese Wreck in the Seychelles. *International Journal of Nautical Archaeology and Underwater Exploration* 15(1):1–23.

CONKEY, MARGARET W., AND JOAN M. GERO
1991 Tensions, Pluralities, and Engendering Archaeology: An Introduction to Women and Prehistory. In *Engendering Archaeology: Women and Prehistory*, edited by Joan M. Gero and Margaret Conkey, pp. 3–30. Basil Blackwell, Oxford.

COTTER, JOHN L., AND J. PAUL HUDSON
1957 *New Discoveries in Jamestown*. National Park Service, Washington, D.C.

DAVIDSON, GLADYS R.
1952 *Corinth*. Vol. 12, *The Minor Objects*. Princeton University Press, Princeton, New Jersey.

DEAGAN, KATHLEEN
1987 *Artifacts of the Spanish Colonies of Florida and the Caribbean, 1500–1800*. Vol. 1, *Ceramics, Glassware, and Beads*. Smithsonian Institution Press, Washington, D.C.

DEAGAN, KATHLEEN (EDITOR)
1983 *Spanish St. Augustine: The Archaeology of a Colonial Creole Community*. Academic Press, New York.

FELDHAUS, FRANZ MARIA
1931 *Die technik der antike und des mittelalters*. Akademische verlagsgesellschaft Athenaion, Wildpark-Potsdam.

GREIF, HELMUT
1984 *Talks about Thimbles: A Cultural Historical Study*. Fingerhutmuseum Creglingen, Klagenfurt, Austria.

GROVES, SYLVIA
1966 *The History of Needlework Tools and Accessories*. Country Life Books, London.

HOLMES, EDWIN F.
1985 *A History of Thimbles*. Cornwall Books, London.
1986 Nautical Archaeology. *Thimble Collector's International Bulletin*, July:2–5.
1987a Early Brass Thimbles. *Thimble Collector's International Bulletin*, July:3–11.

[1987b]Finds Research Group, 700–1700. Datasheet 9. On file, Archaeology Department, Castle Museum, Norwich, England.

1988   Letter from Edwin F. Holmes to Elise V. LeCompte, 29 October. On file, Florida Museum of Natural History, University of Florida, Gainesville.

HOLTHUIZEN, HENNY
1984   Working Thimbles in Amsterdam, 1550–1700. *De Vingerhoed*, June:13–15. Amstelveen.

McEWAN, BONNIE G.
1991b The Archaeology of Women in the Spanish New World. *Historical Archaeology* 25(4):33–41.

MOORHOUSE, STEPHEN
1971   Finds from Basing House, Hampshire (ca. 1540–1645): Part Two. *Post-Medieval Archaeology* 5:35–76.

NOËL HUME, IVOR
1969   *A Guide to Artifacts of Colonial America*. Knopf, New York.

SHEPARD, STEVEN J.
1975   The Geronimo José de Hita y Salazar Site: A Study of *Criollo* Culture in Colonial St. Augustine. Unpublished M.A. thesis, Department of Anthropology, Florida State University, Tallahassee.

1983   The Spanish *Criollo* Majority in Colonial St. Augustine. In *Spanish St. Augustine: The Archaeology of a Colonial Creole Community*, edited by Kathleen Deagan, pp. 65–97. Academic Press, New York.

SMITH, HALE
1965   Archaeological Excavations at Santa Rosa Pensacola. Florida State University. *Notes on Anthropology* 10. Tallahassee.

STEANE, JOHN
1984   *The Archaeology of Medieval England and Wales*. University of Georgia Press, Athens.

THOMPSON, ALAN, FRANCIS GREW, AND JOHN SCHOFIELD
1984   Excavations at Aldgate, 1974. *Post-Medieval Archaeology* 18.1–148.

WOODFIELD, CHARMAIN
1981   Finds from the Free Grammar School at the Whitefriars, Coventry, ca. 1545–1557/58. *Post-Medieval Archaeology* 15:81–159.

ERICA HILL
DEPARTMENT OF ANTHROPOLOGY
UNIVERSITY OF NEW MEXICO
ALBUQUERQUE, NEW MEXICO 87131

TOM WELLS

Nail Chronology: The Use of Technologically Derived Features

ABSTRACT

A technology-based nail chronology is presented. This chronology is derived from a typology based on a combination of general information about the historical developments of the technology applied by the nail manufacturing industry and the periods of actual use for each of twelve basic nail types presently identified as having been used in Louisiana. The author believes that the approach used to establish the Louisiana Nail Chronology can also be used to establish accurate nail chronologies in other regions.

Introduction

Nails are artifacts commonly found at historic sites. The frequency of their occurrence has encouraged archaeologists to use them as dating tools, supplementing chronologies based on ceramics, glass, and other artifacts. The nail chronologies in common use among archaeologists; however, have not been as reliable as the glass and ceramic chronologies. A reliable chronology is needed to make nails more useful as dating tools. To be reliable the nail chronology should be based on accurately dated nail types, and it should be useful for archaeologists in the field and in the laboratory. To answer this need the Louisiana Nail Chronology has recently been developed. This chronology is based on twelve basic types of nails, sampled from dated buildings. The nail types are readily identifiable and are based on the structure and the physical characteristics of the nails (here called features) that result from dateable technological developments in the history of nail manufacture. Each of the general methods of nail manufacture leaves readily identifiable features on nails. These features are indicative of the technology used in the manufacture of nails, thus because nail manufacturing technology changed over the course of time, the features are temporally significant.

A standard nail chronology used today is one developed by Lee H. Nelson in 1968 (Nelson 1968). This chronology was severely simplified by Ivor Noël Hume (1972). In his chronology Nelson uses the style (referred to here as "form") of the nail, burrs, and head style to date nails. To use his chronology one compares a nail to those illustrated in the pamphlet to find the closest match. An earlier work, by Henry C. Mercer (1924), is based on samples of nails from several houses in Pennsylvania; however, this pioneering work provides some misinformation. For instance, Mercer shows a photograph of a selection of cut nails that are incorrectly identified as "hammer-headed" (Mercer 1924:9). These nails are completely machine-made by a process that will be discussed later. Mercer does illustrate burrs (1924:7), though his conclusions about the dates of the appearance of these are not necessarily applicable beyond the houses he studied. These chronologies were a good start, based on such information as was available at the time. One of the best attempts at establishing a nail chronology is that by Maureen Phillips (1989). She used nails from dated structures to establish the actual time that a nail type was used. Her nail typology is primarily based on manufacturing features, though it is limited to the houses she studied and may not have a general or regional application.

While cataloging a collection of several thousand nails from a house built in the 18th century and continuously occupied since, the author was faced with nails that could not be matched with any of those illustrated or described by either Nelson or Mercer. In addition, numerous nails that appeared to be hand-made had burrs, presumably a feature of cut nails.

Experiences with the problems of existing nail typologies and chronologies lead the author to collaborate with Jay D. Edwards, of Louisiana State University, in the study of nails. The results of that study were published in a general interest monograph devoted to 19th century-nails in Louisiana (Edwards and Wells 1993). The

Historical Archaeology, 1998, 32(2):78–99
Permission to reprint required.

following article is based in part on research for that publication and on additional research not included in the book. The chronology presented here differs from that published in our book in one respect: the nail designated as Type 9 is replaced with a different nail. The reason for eliminating it is discussed below. The scope of this article is limited to ferrous house nails. The chronology presented here is based heavily on the historical development of nail manufacture, thus a brief technological history is first presented, followed by a general description of the various types of nails produced by methods employed in each stage of technological development of the nail industry. Finally, the Louisiana Nail Chronology is presented. This section briefly discusses the method used to develop the chronology, which can also be applied in other localities. A short lexicon of some technical terms used here is appended.

A Brief History of Nail Manufacturing Technology

Beginning in the late 18th century great changes began in the technology of nail manufacturing. Through the course of the 19th century the American nail industry developed from small, often part-time, cottage-level concerns to large industrial establishments. The technological development of the nail industry closely followed developments in other fields of iron manufacturing technology. Improvements in iron production, synchronized machinery, steam power, iron casting, and eventually steel manufacture were soon followed by changes in nail manufacturing technology. Each stage of nail manufacturing technology has left readily observable, temporally significant evidence on the nails so produced. This evidence is found in the metal used and the characteristic features resulting from the various changes in the production of nails. These pieces of temporally significant evidence may properly be called "features" (from Latin *facere* "to make") rather than "attributes" (*ad + tribuere*

"to bestow") because each piece of evidence is characteristic of a stage in the development of nail manufacturing technology rather than a value that is ascribed to aspects of the appearance of a given nail. Identification of the nail types in the Louisiana Nail Chronology is based on these nail features. Historical background is included in a brief review of the evolution of the technology of the nail manufacturing industry.

Metals

Common house nails were made from one of two types of iron: wrought iron or steel. Determining which of these two forms of iron is used and the salient features of each is the first step in establishing the temporal significance of any nail sample. A brief history of 18th and 19th century iron and steel manufacturing technology is presented to introduce the reader to this subject.

Wrought Iron

Wrought iron is a ductile two component metal consisting of almost pure metallic iron and moderate amounts of a siliceous slag (Aston and Story 1939:1). There are traces of other elements which are regarded as contaminants. This form of iron is "wrought," meaning worked rather than cast in its final shape by pouring liquid iron into molds. In the 18th century one of two methods was generally employed to reduce iron ore into metallic iron. These are referred to as the direct method and the indirect method. Which of these two methods was used cannot be discerned in the final product. The entire process, from mining to extraction and refinement, may be found in Georgius Agricola's *De Re Metallica* (Agricola 1950), originally published in 1556.

The roughly consolidated blooms, sometimes called "muck bars," were further refined in the chaffery into "merchant bars" that were next drawn into commonly used stock sizes of bars

FIGURE 1. Surfaces of iron (left) and steel (right) (Edwards and Wells 1993)

bars over and stacking several of these, one on the other, then welding them all together to produce a higher quality, cleaner iron (Mott 1983:28, 35-36).

The last step in whatever process was used was to draw out the iron into stock sizes of bars, flat stock, and rods. Until the 1780s the drawing out process was accomplished by forging the bars using a water powered helve hammer and hand labor, with swedges used to size and shape the stock. In 1784 an English patent was issued for turning out stock using grooved rollers (Mott 1983:37-39). The grooved rollers both consolidated and shaped the hot iron.

When cleaned to bare metal wrought iron can be readily identified by its wood-like grain (Figure 1). The wood-like grain is caused by the silicious slag that could not be removed from the bloom; it was drawn out with the iron, becoming longitudinal glassy veins in the bar. The metallic part of wrought iron is chemically almost pure iron. Typically, a wrought iron bar may have 1% to 3% mixed slag and traces of other impurities (Aston and Story 1939:2, 20-26). Batches of wrought iron may vary considerably in both chemical constituents and their proportions. Even iron samples from the same ores and the same bloomery may differ significantly from bar to bar, depending on the proportions of flux mixed with the ore, the temperature at which the iron was worked, how long it was held at high temperature, and the worker's diligence in the refining processes.

Steel

Steel is an alloy of iron and carbon. A low carbon steel, called mild steel, is usually used for nail manufacture. Steel has a crystalline structure, contains insignificant amounts of slag, and does not have the wood-like grain that is characteristic of wrought iron. Steel may be recognized by its fine uniform surface. When rusty steel is cleaned to bare metal, a surface covered with small circular pits is revealed, in contrast

and plates. Some bars were next sent to the rolling and slitting mill to be made into nail plates and then nail rods.

During the 15th century an additional refining step was added. It involved the reheating of the iron to a welding heat and again hammering it to consolidate the iron better by working out as much of the slag and impurities as possible. Another step in the refining of iron was added in the late 18th century. It consisted of folding the with wrought iron's longitudinal striations (Figure 1).

Though small quantities of steel have been made for millennia, large scale mass production of steel began in the late 1870s with the adoption of a modified Bessemer process. Until the perfection of the industrial processes steel had been made by carburizing high grade wrought iron. In the late 1880s and 1890s the various Bessemer and open hearth methods of steel making were being developed and perfected. Both Bessemer and open hearth processes involved melting pig iron and blowing oxygen through it, generating an extremely high heat that burns out nearly all of the impurities. Carbon content of the steel was controlled by adding it to the molten steel. The molten metal was next poured into ingot molds (Campbell 1940:5-14). The ingots were then sent to rollers to be formed into rods, sheets, or other shapes. By the middle 1890s steel production, being less labor intensive than wrought iron production, began to replace it in most applications, including nail manufacture.

The Manufacture of Nails

Each of the methods of nail manufacture leave readily identifiable features on the nails produced.

FIGURE 2 An eighteenth century rolling and slitting mill (Diderot 1765)

FIGURE 3 Detail of a rolling and slitting machine (Diderot 1765).

These features are indicative of the technology used in the manufacture of nails and because the manufacturing technology changed over the course of time, these features are temporally significant. There are two important divisions of nail manufacturing technology: hand forged and machine made. The earliest of these two, hand forged, will be presented first.

Hand Forged Nails

Hand forged nails were made from iron nail rods. The older way of making nail rods was by drawing out large bars to a smaller size. This was accomplished by the smith, using a hand hammer or with a helve-hammer. This is a rather slow, labor-intensive process, but it continued to be used even after later technological developments had made it obsolete. Its advantage was that no specialized equipment other than basic blacksmith tools was required. Nails made from forged nail rods are generally square in cross section and have evidence of hammering on all sides and the head.

After their development in the 17th century, rolling and slitting mills made most nail rods (Figure 2). In the mills, bars were heated and run through water powered rollers until they had rectangular cross sections and were about one quarter to one half inch thick, according to the size nail rod that was to be produced. These were called nail bars. Each nail bar varied from 6 to 8 in. wide and roughly 12 ft. long. The rectangular nail bar was then sent through the slitter (Kauffman 1966:34-35). This machine consisted of intermeshing hardened disks that cut the nail plate lengthwise into nail rods (Figure 3).

Nail rods made in slitting mills often do not have perfectly square sides; they are often rectangular, rhomboid, or trapezoid in cross section. The rectangular section is the result of feeding a thin plate through the cutters. Rhomboid and trapezoid cross sections are caused by the pulling action of dull cutter disks. As the nailer, the smith who makes nails, draws out the point of a trapezoidal cross section of nail rod, a valley is sometimes formed in the wider face in the upper part of the shaft. A rhomboid cross section will not have marked effect. The cross section of the original nail rod may extend from under the head down the shaft for a quarter of the length of the nail.

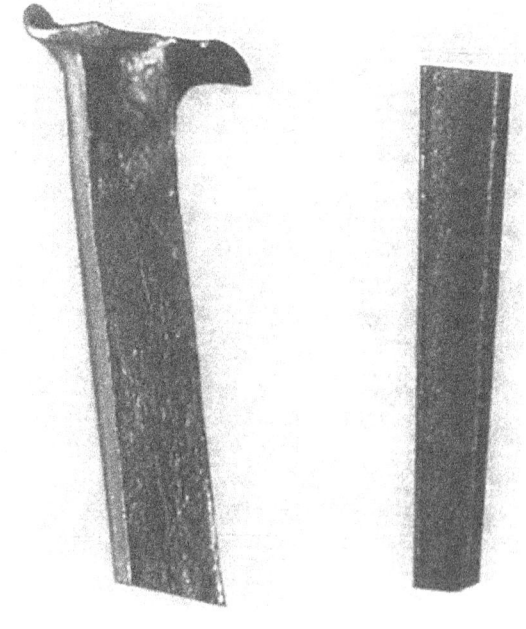

FIGURE 4   Burrs on a forged nail (left) and a cut nail (right)

Hand forged nails may have burrs on the trailing edge of the rod on the same face (Figure 4). The burrs are caused by the cutters dragging a small amount of iron into the slight gap between the cutter disks. The burrs will often be visible on the unmodified part of the shaft below the head and above the tapered part that was drawn to form the point.

Nails were forged using specialized versions of standard blacksmithing tools, including hammer, anvil, and header. The header is a tool that is pierced by a tapered hole that is slightly smaller than the nail rod employed. A standard method used by smiths to forge a nail began with heating the end of a nail rod in the fire. The end was then pointed and the shaft was drawn to a diameter that would slip into the header, a shoulder being left to catch in the header where the head was to be formed. While the rod was still showing color it was nicked above the shoulder and twisted off in the header, leaving the shaft in the hole and a little of the rod projecting above the header. Finally, this projecting piece was "upset," mushrooming it to form the head, completing the nail.

A common feature on nails made from slit stock is a slight depression under the head on one face. This feature suggests an alternative method of heading the nail. Instead of leaving a shoulder to catch in the header, the smith struck the rod on its face, bulging the sides at the place the shaft was to catch the header. The nailer might do this when the nail rod size was the same size or slightly smaller than the hole in the header. On nails made in this way the original unmodified nail rod can be seen between the head and the point taper.

All hand-made nails exhibit hammering on the head and all four sides in the point taper. It is not always possible to tell if a nail is made from forged rods or slit rods, if the nail was drawn from a large slit rod down to a smaller size. This is because the distinct features of the slit rod will be obliterated by the smith's hammering. Shafts often do not taper uniformly from head to point; however, there may be valleys, cold shuts, or other evidence that suggests the use of slit rods. A cold shut is an unconsolidated fold of metal hammered against the shaft. Nails may have burrs or vertical drag marks immediately under the head, the result of seating the nail in a tight header. The heads exhibit hammer marks and are somewhat irregular. There are numerous styles of head which may represent functional types. Head styles and functional types, however, are beyond the scope of this study.

Forged nail technology antedates the colonization of America, and limited numbers of forged nails were still being made well into the 19th century. The use of forged nails became progressively less common as cut nail technology improved. Nails and nail rods were imported into the European colonies from the time of their establishment in the New World and were manufactured in limited numbers in the United States into the 19th century, making forged nails not especially useful for dating. Their presence at a site can only suggest the early 19th century or earlier.

Machine-Made Nails

IRON CUT NAILS

All cut nails are made from strips of iron or steel called nail plates. The length of the nail is determined by the width of the nail plate, and the thickness of the nail is the same as the thickness of the nail plate. The surface of the nail plate is the surface of the nail's face. The body of the nail, the nail blank, is sheared off the end of the nail plate at an angle so the nail blank describes an acute, usually truncated, triangle. The small end is the point and the large end will be upset to form the head. In cutting the blank from the nail plate the shearing action leaves two features on the nail that are of interest here: the cut face and the burr (Figure 5). All cut nails taper on two sides, the cut faces, and have a uniform thickness on the opposite faces below the pinched area. Though cut nails rarely have

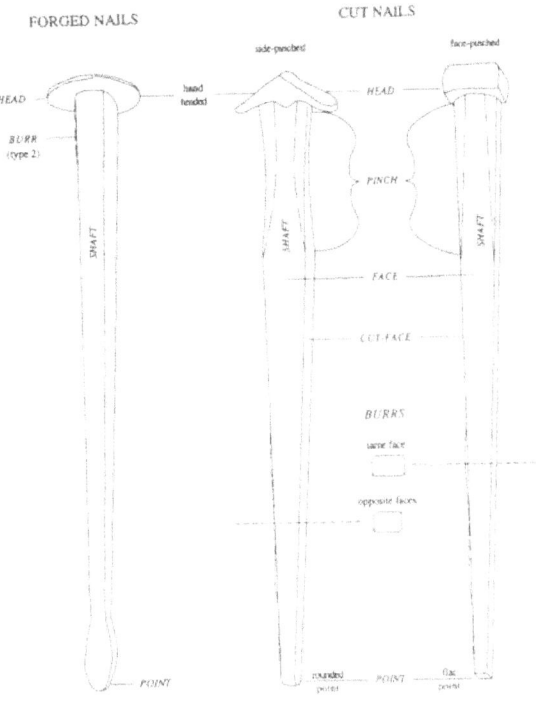

FIGURE 5. Nail nomenclature.

sharp points, some are to be found, usually on early cut nails.

Beginning in the late 18th century, early cut nail manufacture was accomplished in two steps, beginning with the shearing of the nail blank. Then the blank was held in a clamp and headed by hand. The earliest nail cutting machines, like Nathaniel Reed's (Loveday 1983:13, 18), were manually powered and the nail plate was fed into the shear by hand. After the nail blank was cut off it was put in a vice-like header, leaving a short section of the shaft projecting above the header. This device grasped and crushed the cut faces, resulting in a side-pinched nail. The nailer then struck the projecting part of the shaft with a hand hammer to form the head.

The first successful combined cutting and heading machines were developed and used in the northeastern United States in the early 19th century. The factories used water power to drive the machinery rather than human power, thereby increasing the speed of production and uniformity of the product. Some early, fully machine-made, nails can be hard to distinguish from hand-headed cut nails. Both are generally strongly side-pinched, the burr is on opposite faces, both have points that are rounded from front face to back face, and are cross-grained. The heads of machine-headed nails, however, tend to be more

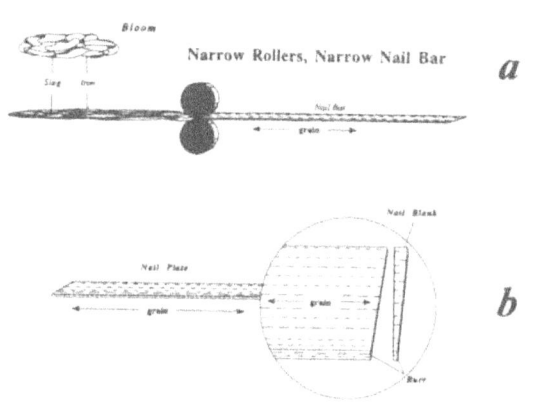

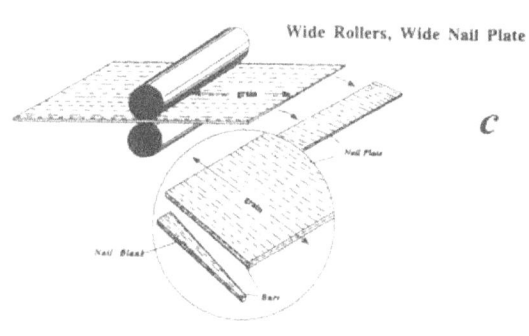

FIGURE 7. Points of cut nails compared. The top point is that of a nail that was cut from a nail plate which was sheared from a sheet. The bottom point is from a nail cut from a narrow nail plate (Edwards and Wells 1993).

regular and thicker than hand-headed nails, and the shafts tend to be uniform in pinch, shearing angle, and general appearance.

Both hand-headed and machine-headed early cut nails were cross-grained. They were cut from narrow nail plates which were produced by rolling mills using narrow rollers (Figure 6). The grain of the iron in these plates runs the length of the plate so the grain of the nail blank, cut from the end of the nail plate, ran across the nail. The rounded edge of the nail plate usually survives at the point. Nails cut from such plates will have points that are rounded from the front face to the back face (Figure 7).

In the hand-fed nail machines the nail plate had to be repositioned for each cut to produce

FIGURE 6. Wrought iron grain and methods of making nail plates. a, slag in the bloom is drawn out with the iron, narrow rollers form the narrow nail plate with the grain running the length of the bar, nails cut from narrow nail plates are cross-grained; b, narrow rollers form the narrow nail plate with the grain running the length of the bar, nails cut from narrow nail plates are cross-grained; c, wide rollers produce sheets, which are then sheared across the grain to produce nail plates, nails made from such plates are in-line-grained (after Edwards and Wells 1993).

the necessary angle for the nail blank. The inevitable, though slight, variation in feed angle resulted in nails that are of variable breadth. With the perfection of the automatic feeder came greater uniformity in shaft breadth and taper. Most of the early cut nail types have burrs on opposite faces, evidence that the nail plates were inaccurately repositioned after each cut.

A major drawback of all cross-grained nails is their tendency to break when clinched, bent, or extracted from the wood. This is because wrought iron is laterally weakened by the slag running across the shaft. Cross-grained cut nails break cleanly along the slag inclusions in the grain. The superior performance of grain-in-line nails, such as hand forged nails, was well understood by Jacob Perkins who advertised, in 1795, a machine that he claimed could produce such nails (Phillips 1989:91). That Perkins' nail machines did not dominate the nail market may be ascribed either to the unreliability of the machines or to the expense of making wide plates before the technology had matured. Grain-in-line cut nails dating from before 1834 have not been found in Louisiana, though they may have been used in Boston before the turn of the century (Phillips 1989).

Large scale manufacture of grain-in-line cut nails awaited the full development of other technologies, especially the art of iron casting and steam power. The narrow rollers of the old water-powered rolling mills were unable to produce wide plates and sheet iron. Though wide rollers had been used since the 18th century they were flexible because of their small diameter, limiting their use to the softer non-ferrous metals (Daumas 1964:252). The demand for wide sheet iron for steam engine boilers was met at first by hammering thick narrow plates under a water powered helve hammer until they were sufficiently wide. By 1803 in England, iron casting technology improved enough that large diameter, rigid, wide rollers could be made of cast iron. It was also there that steam power was first applied to drive machinery (Dickinson 1939). After those developments, wide rollers powered by reliable steam engines could economically produce wide plate and sheet iron. These technologies were soon brought to America (Binning 1938:88).

Steam engines provided reliable power, permitting factories to be established away from the falls of the eastern seaboard rivers to the western coal and iron producing areas. There were three advantages realized from the use of steam power. First, factory layout could be directed for manufacturing efficiency rather than being limited by access to the river and the axle that transferred power from the water wheel. Second, power to the machines was no longer limited by the river's flow rate, rate of fall, and seasonal availability of water. And finally, beginning in the early decades of the 19th century, factories could be located in the west where the greatest demand was. In the west, boats communicated with every town in the Mississippi valley, quickly transporting nails for the ever expanding market.

In 1810 a plant in Pennsylvania had water driven rollers 3-4 ft. long and 16-18 in. in diameter; the following year steam power was first used in a Pittsburgh rolling mill (Mackintosh-Hemphill Company 1953:31-32). In 1832 one of the first cut nail factories was established in Wheeling, (West) Virginia, a town that was soon to be the center of the cut nail industry. In this factory, sheets were rolled and cut into nail plates (Heitmann 1989:311). It appears that by 1830 wide roller technology had come into common use by American nail makers to make an improved, in-line-grained nail.

By the second decade of the 19th century some manufacturers were producing nail plates that were cut from sheets or wide plates (Ure 1865:255; Martineau 1866:613). With this new method, wide rolled plates were cut across the grain-producing nail plates that had the grain running across them. Nails cut from the end of cross-grained nail plates had the grain running from point to head. These nails could be successfully clinched without breaking. All nails that were made by this method have flat points with four sharp corners (Figure 7).

In the more technologically advanced machines the angle of the nail blank was established without the necessity of repositioning the plate after each cut. A reciprocating cutter, having two cutting edges, each set at the correct angle, came into use at about the same period as the transition from cross-grained to grain-in-line nails. These machines produced nails having the burrs on the same face. This single feature, however, should not be used by itself for establishing the nail date; there are cross-grained nails that have burrs on the same face.

After the nail blank is cut it is mechanically grasped for heading. Grasping by the header clamp deforms the upper end of the shaft just below where the head will be formed. This is another feature of cut nails referred to as the "pinch" (Edwards and Wells 1993). Most of the later nails are face-pinched, though side-pinched nails have been continuously produced from the beginning of cut nail mass production to the present. The most common in-line-grain nail is face-pinched so the edges of the faces are nearly straight from head to point. The heads are usually small, either square or rectangular when viewed from the top and rather blocky. Two functional types of cut nails do not have a pinch: sprigs, which are left unheaded, and brads, whose heads are cut simultaneously with the shaft.

Heading was done cold or at a low heat, putting great stress on the iron, often resulting in small cracks that run with the grain on the face side of the head. The cracks result from the iron separating along the grain under the force of heading. It is common to find long cracks on the cut faces of all iron cut nails, indicating that the iron was poorly consolidated. As iron producers adopted better iron making techniques, the quality of wrought iron improved so that such cracks are less often seen in nails made after the 1840s.

IRON WIRE NAILS

Wire was made by pulling a rod through successively smaller holes in a draw plate until the desired diameter was reached. At the end of each drawing the leading end of the wire had to be reduced to the next smaller size and started through the hole so it could be grasped by the clamp that pulled the wire (Ferguson 1965:90-94). In iron wire the grain runs the length of the shaft, allowing it to be bent without breaking.

Wire making technology changed little from medieval times until the middle of the 19th century, though water and then steam took the place of human power to pull the wire. Steam was not employed in American wire making until the 19th century (Binning 1938:88-89). Although wrought iron wire had been made for a long time it was not considered suitable for nail making for two main reasons: wrought iron wire could not be made as cheaply as nail plates, and because of their narrow, un-tapered sides, and the softness of iron, wire nails could not be driven into hardwoods without pilot holes. Even so, small iron wire nails called "French points" were made in this country beginning in 1875 with imported French machines. In 1880, the first American wire nail manufacturer began commercial scale operation in Kentucky (The Iron Age 1898).

The manufacture of wire nails begins with feeding the end of a roll of wire into clamps which grasp the length of the shaft with a short length projecting past the clamp. The wire is held in place by teeth in the clamp that make a series of lateral scores found on the upper shaft immediately below the head. The wire projecting from the clamp is mechanically upset to form the head. While still in the clamp, cutter dies squeeze the point on to the shaft, while separating it from the wire roll, then the clamp opens and drops the finished nail; the process begins again as more wire is fed into the machine (Clark 1978:192-193). The same basic design of machine is used in steel wire nail manufacture.

Distinguishing wrought iron wire from steel wire can be difficult. Iron wire for iron wire nails was highly refined and the grain is noticeable only after it has been acid-etched. Recognizing steel wire nails can also be difficult. As steel is drawn through the reducing dies the crystalline structure becomes stretched. This, com-

...ined with the minute longitudinal abrasion of the die, often gives the steel a striated appearance similar to that of iron. It is also possible to tell the difference between iron and steel using powerful microscopes, microphotographs, spectral analysis, and other metallurgical techniques.

STEEL CUT NAILS

After the steel making processes were perfected and the price for steel was less than that of wrought iron, cut nail manufacturers began to use steel for nails. From the late 1880s through the 1890s steel gradually replaced wrought iron in the manufacture of cut nails (Heitmann 1989:30). From 1884 through 1886 only 5% of cut nails were made of steel. By 1891 three quarters of all cut nails were made of steel. Before the end of the century all cut nails were made of steel. Steel cut nails are still made in small quantities, some on old machines. The manufacturing process is the same for steel and iron cut nails and because there are styles of steel cut nails that resemble early 19th century-nails, it is necessary to determine whether the nail is made from iron or steel.

STEEL WIRE NAILS

The processes for the manufacture of steel wire nails is essentially the same as that for iron wire nails, though more abrasion resistant materials are now available for use in the dies (Committee of Rod and Drawn Wire Producers 1969:7-9). Though manufacturers began to produce steel wire in the 1860s, the wire was used mostly for telegraphs, seat springs, and crinolines. Steel wire nails do not seem to have been available until the late 1870s (Loveday 1983:136), possibly because of the expense of steel manufacturing of the day. Steel wire nails were not produced in competitive quantities until the late 1880s and early 1890s (Loveday 1983:137). By the turn of the century most nails that were sold were wire nails. By 1920, wire nails had taken over the nail market, leaving cut nails with only 8% of the market.

The Louisiana Nail Chronology

The Louisiana Nail Chronology represents an attempt at establishing a system for dating sites and standing structures using nails as dating tools. One of the problems with existing nail chronologies is that they are form-based: their use requires one to compare a sample nail with illustrations of nails to find one that looks similar. The assumption is that similar form indicates similar dates of manufacture and use. This method can be misleading because nails with the same form have been made for over a century. This problem is slightly ameliorated by the brief descriptions of burr location and grain direction.

Mention should be made here of other systems of categorizing nails. The least useful of these, for dating purposes, is by functional type. Functional types are based on the intended or customary use of a particular kind of nail. Functional types are of little use for establishing dates. Additionally, the actual use of any particular nail cannot be known out of its original context. Functional types may be of limited use in describing some nails, in the same manner and with the same skepticism as "arrow head" or "adz" are used to describe prehistoric stone artifacts.

Closely related to functional types is classification by means of head and point style, which meets with the same objection: style has not proved useful for establishing a chronology, though it may be useful in establishing a nail typology. The English used such classifications as "clout" and "rose head" to describe nails and sometimes this may indicate their use; however, not all such terms need to be discarded. There are useful English terms that have specific and limited use, such as "brad" and "sprig." Such terms may be used to describe the form of specific nail classes. For instance, a sprig is a nail made without an apparent head. Care must be taken because one cannot always be certain that a pointed shaft is a sprig. In the case of "brad," both forged and cut brads have a "7" shape, but modern wire brads have a small round head that slightly overhangs the shaft around its diameter. Although functional types and head and point styles are not reliable temporal indicators, functional types can be valuable for other purposes. Even after having visited and sampled nails from many late 18th and early 19th century-buildings the author can only make very broad generalizations about how any particular functional type was actually used in that period.

The use of "penny" is avoided because of its vagueness. "Penny" can mean the number of nails that could be bought for a penny, the price per pound of a size of nail, or the price, in pence, for a hundred nails. Today the term has been standardized to describe a size of nail. An additional objection is that "penny" is culture-specific; it is an English system not shared by the French or Spanish in Louisiana. For instance, among the supplies requested from France for the colony in 1759 are "twenty *quintals* of double caravel nails; thirty *quintals* of half caravel nails; thirty *quintals* of caravel nails; forty *quintals* of shingling nails, a little longer than half-deck nails." The list goes on to describe a total of seven varieties of nail by using named types. The list, however, also includes "twenty *quintals* of 6-, 7- and 8-inch nails" (Rowland and Sanders 1984:57), a description of nails by length. Interestingly, none of the names of the above types is used by Diderot (1765) to describe nails.

Using patented designs of machines or patent dates for nail machines have been found to be of no use in dating. It is doubtful that it will ever be possible to tell that a particular nail was made by a given machine based on its patent, or even if the machine were built and actually put into service. Many patents were taken out on plausible ideas, often in hopes of making money from litigation against successful manufacturers who could be sued for patent infringement.

Another danger results from using references on the British nail industry for generalizing about nail manufacture in the United States. It should be remembered that throughout the 18th and 19th centuries, the manpower and economic forces of the two countries differed greatly. In Great Britain, and in Europe generally, there was a surplus of manpower. In the U. S. there was a chronic shortage of labor. In England there was considerable resistance, on the part of skilled labor, to the adoption of machinery that could threaten their employment. This resistance retarded the technological development of certain other industries in England, for instance, boots, clothing, and locks. Labor resistance to "labor-saving" machinery has been cited as the chief reason that England continued to produce nails by hand into the late 19th century (Habakkuk 1962:172). In the late 19th century an English nailer could make, by traditional hand forging, about 112 pounds of larger size nails in a day. In a week he earned about 16 shillings ($3.87). At the same time, an American nailer, operating three machines, could produce 54 kegs of 10d nails, and earn $5.00 a day (Schoenhof 1974:226-227).

Historical research may indicate that a particular nail was being manufactured, but how does one tell if it was used in a particular region? Taking Lee Nelson's suggestion that local chronologies be developed, the author and Jay Edwards did just that; however, the nail typology on which the Louisiana Nail Chronology is based depends on the identification of significant features. These features include the physical structure or characteristics of the nails that result from dateable manufacturing technology. Each stage in the history of technological development may be discerned on the nail. The use of iron or steel, grain direction, and so on result from stages in the development of nail manufacture technology and thus, indicate a general date for the manufacture of the nail. This method; however, assumes that earlier technologies were discarded as more efficient technologies were developed.

The nail typology derived from technology-based dates is of general applicability only. Such dates do not allow for the use of nails made from obsolete technologies, differences in trade routes, or old nails used in new structures. In order to obtain dates of actual use specific to Louisiana, another method was used to develop a regional chronology. This method follows that of Mercer (1924) and Maureen Phillips (1989) by using dated standing structures as sources of dateable nails. Technological features were used to establish nail types; however, dates-of-use were determined by sampling dated historic buildings. Nails selected for this study were functional parts of the structure, pulled from original, permanent parts of the building such as the roof truss, knee walls, jack rafters, sills, purlins, and rafters. Roofs may be replaced several times over the lifetime of a building, thus they were not (with one exception) used as sources for nails. Nails from later additions or repairs, unless they were well dated, were not sampled. Thus, structural nails drawn from the original parts of an 1840 house could be assumed to date from 1840 or earlier.

As the historical background research and nail study began to take shape, houses were selected for dates that coincided with documented changes in nail manufacturing technology. This was done to obtain nail samples that would sharpen the transition period from one nail type to another. Of particular interest was the transition from hand-headed cut nails to fully machine-made nails that started near the beginning of the 19th century. Also of special interest was the period of transition from cross-grained nails to grain-in-line nails that took place in the first two decades of the 19th century. Documenting the periods of transition from the use of iron to steel and of cut nails to wire nails was considered less vital because by the late 19th century-interstate transportation made the shipment from factory to carpenter a matter of weeks, if not days. The transition period can be reliably documented by historical research; however, several buildings from the end of the 19th century were sampled to verify the historical evidence.

The resulting data base used to develop the chronology is summarized in Table 1. The name of the building is followed by the date of the building's construction. The date is followed by a letter scale from "A" to "D" designating confidence in the accuracy of that date. An "A" indicates a firm documentary record from the time of construction; "B" is a building dated to within two years by a combination of documentation and other methods; "C" indicates that the

building is dated to within five years by a combination of methods; the scale ends with "D" indicating a building whose construction can be dated to within a decade by a combination of methods. Nails from buildings that could not be dated to within a decade were not used to establish the chronology. Obviously, the "A" buildings are to be preferred as sources for nail samples; however, "A" buildings dating from the years of interest were not always available.

Nail dates based on their use in buildings should be understood to be probabilities; there are abundant opportunities for sample error, especially for the early cut nail dates. Few of the structures built in the 18th century and early 19th century are still standing. Nails from archaeological sites were beyond the scope of the survey. The eventual inclusion of archaeological sites as a source for nail samples may improve the accuracy of the chronology.

How to Determine the Age of a Nail

As many nails as possible (or as many as the owner will allow!) should be sampled to establish the uniformity of the sample and the types used. In addition, nails should be drawn from as many parts of the original structure as possible, again to establish the uniformity of the sample and, eventually, to develop a functional type system based on nail use.

Diagnostic Features

Nails should be cleaned of all oxides to expose the bare metal and in order to reveal the diagnostic features. The important features are: material (iron or steel); general uniformity (or lack of it) of the head and shaft; shaft shape, cross section, and taper; the pinch, if present; shape of the point; burr, if present; cold shuts or cracks; and heading method. No one of these features should be relied on for determining the age of a nail. Except for the use of iron or steel none of these features is, in its self, chronologically significant. When the nail features are used together, one may determine the nail type and its time of use.

TABLE 1
DATA BASE

Source of Nail Samples	Nail Types	1	2	3	4	5	6	7	8	9	10	11	12
LaCour (1731 D)		X											
Godchaux-Reserve (1764 D)		X											
St. Gabriel Church (1769 A)	X	X											
Wells (1776 C)	X	X											
Madam John's Legacy (1788 B)	X												
Destrehan (1790 A)	X	X											
Graugnard (1790 C)		X											
Cabildo (1791 A)	X	X											
Magnolia Mound (1791 B)		X	X										
Merieult (1793 A)		X	X										
Pitot (1799 A)		X	X										
Kleinpeter-Knox (1800 C)			X										
Roque (1805 D)		X			X								
Whitney (1805 B)		X	X										
Michael Prudhomme (1809 B)				X									
Magnolia Mound (1810 C)			X	X		X							
Jaque-Duprée (1811 B)									X				
Planter's Cabin (1818 D)					X	X							
Cabildo (1813 A)				X		X							
Bucvalt (1815 D)		X		X		X							
Zeringue (1815 C)		X	X		X								
Kroll (1816 C)			X										
Destrehan, Garconnières (1818 A)					X								
Merieult (1818 A)				X									
Pentagon Barracks, Bldg. B (1819 A)		X	X										
Pentagon Barracks, Bldg. D (1819 A)			X		X								
River Lake (1820 C)					X	X							
Wycliffe (1820 B)		X				X							
Bucvalt (1820 C)								X					
Graugnard (1820 C)								X					
Oakland (1820 D)								X					
Pentagon Barracks, Bldg. B (1823 A)				X	X								
Pentagon Barracks, Bldg. D (1823 A)						X		X					
Aillet (1830 B)					X	X		X					
Moniotte (1830 C)						X							
Estorge (1830 B)						X							
Austerlitz (1832 A)						X							
Evergreen (1832 D)					X								
Riverland (1832 C)								X					
Jackson Barracks, Bldg. 2 (1834 A)				X		X							
Jackson Barracks, Bldg. 4 (1834 A)							X	X					
Live Oak (1835 C)						X							
Lindsey (1835 D)								X					
Kleinpeter (1836 C)			X		X	X							
Bozant-Hart (1836 B)					X	X		X					
Jackson Barracks, Magazine (1837 A)								X					
Kroll (1840 C)								X					
Oaklawn (1840 C)						X		X					
Little Texas (1840 C)								X					
Presbytere (1847 A)							X	X					
Cabildo (1848 A)								X					
Pontalba (1849 A)								X					
Bond (1850 D)								X					
Lobell (1862 C)								X					
Palo Alto, Overseer's (1880 C)								X					
Baytree (1892 D)								X					
Wilbert (1891 B)								X		X		X	
Curole (1891 B)											X		
Curole (1893 A)												X	

To determine if the nail is iron or steel the distinctive characteristics of iron are important; these include grain and possibly a poorly consolidated structure such as cold shuts and cracks described below. The absence of the typical characteristics of iron probably indicates steel. The transition from the use of iron to steel in the nail industry was not immediate, having begun in the mid-1880s and continued into the 1890s.

Though not itself a dating factor, the general uniformity of the head and shaft, especially in a collection of similar nails from a site, usually indicates improved production methods, and therefore a later date. Heads located eccentrically on the shaft, misshapen heads, and shafts that have several tapers or diameters indicate early nails. The judgment of uniformity can be rather subjective, thus it is desirable to obtain a large nail sample.

The shape of the shaft, its cross section, and taper can be used to distinguish among wire, cut, and hand-made nails. Cut nails have parallel faces but cut faces that taper straight towards the point. Wire nails have parallel sides extending from the head to the point. Hand-made nails, naturally, exhibit the greatest variation in all aspects of shaft form. Generally, hand-made nails tend to taper on all sides to the point and maintain a square cross section, though many such nails have a rectangular cross section, with parallel sides, on the upper one-third to one-half before they gradually taper to the point. Hand-made nails often exhibit hammer marks on the shaft and head, or other evidence of hand work.

Except for sprigs and brads all cut nails are grasped by a clamp at the upper end of the shaft for heading. The clamp leaves a deformation, referred to as the "pinch," under the head. De-

TABLE 2

FEATURES OF LOUISIANA NAIL TYPES

Feature: Nail Type:	1	2	3	4	5	6	7	8	9	10	11	12
Shaft Section:												
square/rect	X	X	X	X	X	X	X	X	X			
square	X	X										
Round											X	X
Material:												
Iron	X	X	X	X	X	X	X	X	X		X	
Steel										X		X
Grain (iron only)												
Cross	X	X	X	X	X	X			X			
In-Line							X	X			X	
Rounded Points			X	X	X							
(cut face view)												
Shaft Shape:												
Four Sides Taper	X	X										
Two Sides Taper		X	X	X	X	X	X	X	X	X		
No Taper											X	X
Burr												
Same Face		X			X	X	X	X		X		
Opposite Faces			X	X					X			
Header Clamp Pinch												
Side-Pinched			X	X	X		X					
Face-Pinched						X		X	X	X		
Hand-Headed	X	X	X									
Used: Beginning	1699	1699	1791	1809	1805	1810	1834	1820	1811	1891	1875	1891
Ending	1805	1820	1836	1834	1836	1840	1847	1891	1812	1893	1880s	present

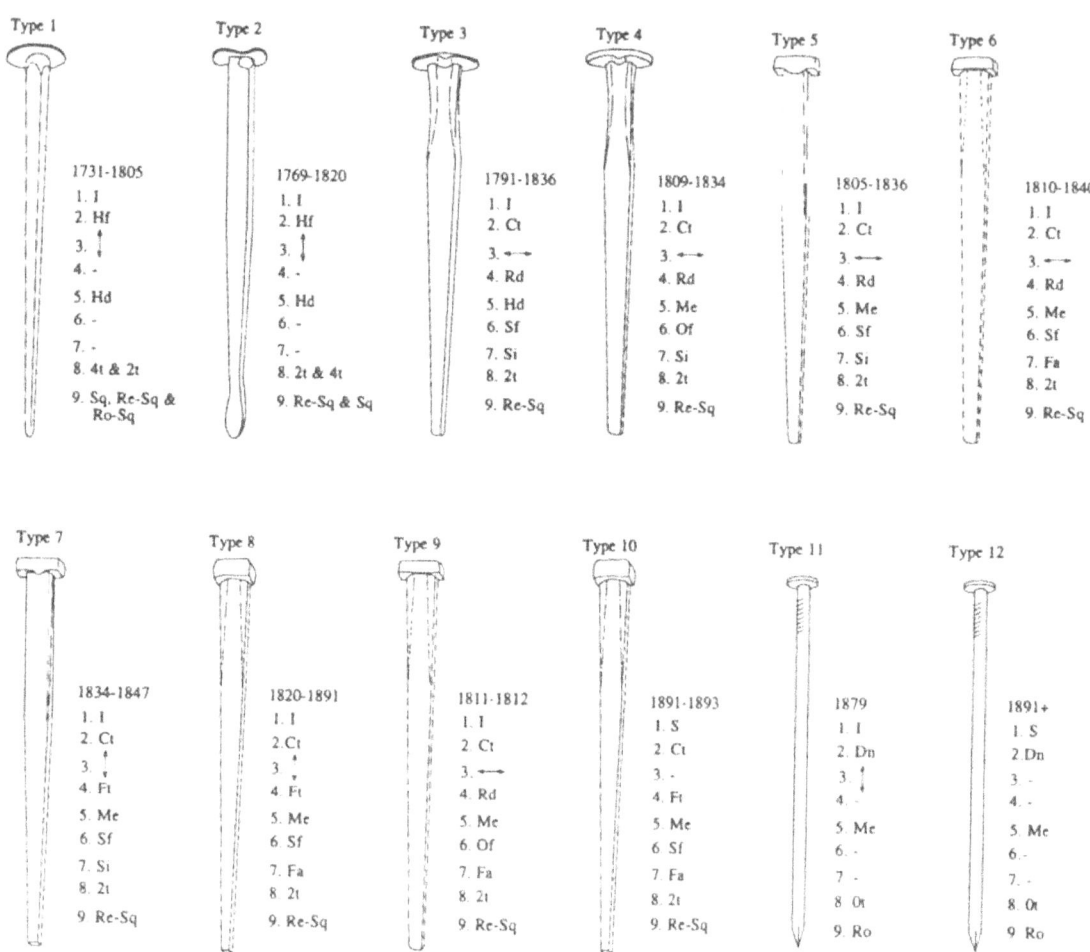

Diagnostic Nail Features

Feature	Symbol	Meaning
1. Metal:	I, S	Iron, Steel
2. Mfg. Method	Hf, Ct, Dn	Hand-forged, Cut, Drawn
3. Grain (iron only)	↕ ↔	In Line, Cross
4. Point (cut only)	Rd, Ft	Round, Flat
5. Head Mfg.	Hd, Me	Hand, Machine
6. Burr (cut only)	Sf, Of	Same faces, Opposite faces
7. Pinch (cut only)	Si, Fa	Side, Face
8. Shaft Taper	4t, 2t, Ot	Taper on 4 sides, 2 sides, no taper
9. Shaft Section	Sq, Re, Ro	Square, Rectangular, Round

FIGURE 8. Louisiana Nail Types

pending on the length of nail, the pinch usually extends down the shaft, generally for about one-eighth to one-quarter of its length. The pinch is relatively shorter on large nails and longer on small nails. Only cut nails are pinched, thus this feature is useful for establishing the type of nail. The earliest cut nails in Louisiana are pinched on their cut faces (side-pinched). Nails pinched on their faces (face-pinched) began to appear in Louisiana in the 1820s, though there is one face-pinched type that was used on a house in 1811. The pinch, however, is not chronologically significant by itself: similar nails were made throughout the 19th century, and are still manufactured, though now they are made of steel.

Variation in the point of wire nails does not appear to be temporally significant, though the point can be of great significance on cut nails. Generally, cut nails have a blunt point: the cut faces form an acute triangle that extends from the head and ends abruptly before meeting. Where the faces end, the flat point, is the edge of the nail plate. The point can indicate whether the nail was made from the early style nail plate or the later nail plates cut from sheets. The points of nails cut from narrow nail plates are slightly rounded from the front face to the back face. Nails made from nail plates that were cut from sheets have four sharp corners at the point. This feature can be used to help distinguish between cross-grained nails and grain-in-line nails, a difference that can be temporally significant. Among hand-made nails there is great variation in point styles. Some hand-made nails have burrs and a rectangular cross section, and can easily be mistaken for early hand-headed cut nails. It is here that the point type can be of use to the archaeologist. The points of cut nails are almost always blunt, while those of hand-made nails are generally either sharply pointed or chisel-shaped. In addition, the point is formed by opposite faces tapering until they meet. Except for distinguishing between cut nails and hand-made nails, these variations do not appear to have any temporal value, though they probably had functional significance.

The burr can cause some unnecessary confusion. Burrs are found on the shafts of cut nails and may be present on some hand-made nails made from slit nail rods. The burr on cut nails indicates whether the cutting of the nail blank from the nail plate was done from the same side or opposite sides. Most of the early nail machines cut the nail blank from the same side of the nail plate, leaving the burr on opposite edges of the nail shaft. Most of the later machines cut the nail from opposite sides of the nail plate, leaving the burrs on the same face of the shaft. Burrs on the same face may indicate a more developed technology: either the nail plate was turned over after each cut or, more likely, the nail plate was fed into a nail machine having a reciprocating cutter with two cutting surfaces. The burr on hand-made nails made from slit stock is often obliterated during the forging of the nail, especially where the shaft is tapered to form the point. Sometimes it may be discerned along the edge as a cold shut, as noted below.

Cracks and cold shuts are characteristic of wrought iron. Cracks result from the fibers of unconsolidated iron opening as the metal is worked. The cracks occur along the grain, where the slag prevented a perfect union of the metal. On cross-grained nails the crack will run across the face, while on grain-in-line nails the cracks will run length-wise on the face. On the cut face of both kinds of nails there may be a crack, or even separation, running length-wise down the shaft. The heads of either kind can be cracked across the top in the direction of the cut faces. Cold shuts are unconsolidated metal folded against the body of the stock. There are numerous causes of cold shuts, but for the purposes of defining nails, they occur on hand-forged nails when the burr is hammered flat against the nail shaft.

All hand-made nails and early cut nails were hand-headed. Hand-formed nail heads are found in a plethora of styles. Though these styles may have a functional significance, they are not useful for establishing temporal significance. For instance, on cut nails, hand-heading indicates an early date of manufacture. Hand-formed nail heads tend not to be uniform and, on cut nails, are usually thinner than machine-formed heads. There will also be evidence of hammering on the head. Caution is advised, however, because the presence of shallow hammer marks on the heads of cut nails may be caused by the carpenter driving the nail rather than the nailer forming the head.

Louisiana Nail Types

Nails are assigned to one of the various types based on their possession of the requisite diagnostic features. The number assigned to any particular type has no significance, though it will be noticed that the first eight numbered types are also in chronological order; this is a reflection only of the evolution in the development of this system. Newly identified types can be added to this list by assigning the next vacant number. The dates of use given should be understood as a general period that a type was used because the dates are based on a limited survey of standing structures. The following list differs from that of Edwards and Wells (1993) by dropping their Type 9 nail. Edwards and the author think that the original Type 9 nail should probably be considered a variant of Type 7 nails. In its place a recently collected nail has been given the designation of Type 9, which is discussed under that heading below.

In the following section descriptions of some of the nail types include elements of the superficial appearance of the nail type. These superficial elements are included to aid the researcher in identifying the nail type to augment, and not to limit, the type description. In the cases in which the type description includes elements about the appearance it must be remembered that superficial elements are merely characteristic of many of the samples observed. In addition, there are some features that may have chronological significance, though these are not representative of technological developments. One of these is the length of pinch on side-pinched nails; the early nails tend to have a rather short

pinched area compared to later nails. The intent is to illustrate a method of establishing a chronologically significant nail typology based on manufacturing and structural features, rather than on the appearance of a nail. Some examples of Louisiana nail types are illustrated in Figure 8.

Type 1. These are hand-made nails made from forged or drawn nail rods. Included in this type are Type 2 nails that do not exhibit burrs and other evidence characteristic of that type. A Type 1 nail is forged from an iron nail rod and exhibits hammer marks on both the shaft and head. The shaft is usually square and tapers evenly on all sides to the point. Heads are generally rather thin and may occasionally bend or even break loose from the shaft if pulled forcefully from the timber. The numerous head and point varieties have no temporal significance other than indicating that the nail is hand made.

Type 2. These nails are similar to the Type 1 except that they are made from slit nail rods and have burrs. Nails of this type are often rectangular from under the head to where the point taper begins. Cold shuts may be present on the shaft. Type 1 and Type 2 nails are found in many varieties, but no temporal value can be attached to the varieties. The technology that produced these nails pre-date the European settlement of Louisiana, so an early date for this type begins with the establishment of the French colony in 1699 at Mobile. Though hand-made nails may have been manufactured well into the 19th century, the latest date of use in Louisiana is 1820.

Type 3. These nails are machine cut and hand-headed. Because they were made from narrow rolled nail plates they are cross-grained and have points that are slightly rounded from the front face to the back face. The shaft is usually strongly side-pinched and the heads are thin. Depending on the size of the nail, the pinch extends only about one-fifth or one-sixth of the way down the length of the shaft from below the head. Burrs are on opposite faces of the shaft.

Within a sample of nails of the same length and thickness from the same building there can be considerable variation in the width of the shaft and its degree of taper. This unevenness is an indication that the nail plate was fed into the shear by hand. The heads are generally a flat disk. Also a common sub-type of Type 3 was manufactured by hammering the heads from two angles, producing a narrow head that overhangs the cut faces, leaving a roof-like peak centered on the shaft. Type 3 use in Louisiana extends from 1791 to 1836.

Type 4. Nails of this type are entirely machine-made cut nails. They are cross-grained and have points that are slightly rounded from front face to back face. Type 4 nails are side-pinched and usually have a flat, discoid head. Some samples of this type are distinguishable from Type 3 nails only by their thicker heads and general uniformity. Burrs are on opposite faces. In Louisiana these nails appear to have been used from 1809 to 1834.

Type 5. These are entirely machine cut nails. They are cross-grained and have points that are slightly rounded from the front face to back face. They are uniformly cut and headed. The heads are roughly square, small, and thick. These are side-pinched nails. The pinch is rather long and shallow, making the upper one-third of the nail appear parallel when viewed from the face. The faces, when viewed from the cut face, bulge slightly. Though not common, these nails saw a rather long use in Louisiana from 1807 to 1836.

Type 6. Nails of this type are cross-grained cut nails and, like the other cross-grained nails, have points that are slightly rounded from the front face to back face. Type 6 nails are face-pinched and, depending on the size, the area deformed by the header extends one-fifth to one-tenth of the length of the nail. Burrs are on the same face. The outline and superficial appearance of these nails is often indistinguishable from that of later Type 7 iron nails and Type 10 steel nails, demonstrating the need for careful attention to the temporally significant features. These nails were used in building construction from 1810 to 1840 in Louisiana.

Type 7. These are side-pinched cut nails; however, the grain runs the length of the shaft, and all four corners of the point are flat. This indicates that the nail blanks were cut from nail plates that were sheared from wide, rolled sheets. Nails in a typical sample of Type 7 nails are uniform, have heads of moderate size, and have a long pinch extending nearly one-half down the shaft. A cross section through the shaft at the pinch describes a square with rounded corners. In Louisiana these nails saw use from 1834 to 1848.

Type 8. These nails are grain-in-line, face-pinched cut nails. Early nails of this type are more often found with cracks or even grain separation on the cut face than later nails. Their form is similar to that of Type 6 nails as well as Type 9 nails. Nails of this type are perfectly uniform and consistent within a sample. There are several styles of head, varying from small and rectangular to large and oval. This is the most common 19th century-nail, seeing long use in Louisiana from 1820 to 1891.

Type 9. This is a cross-grained and face-pinched nail. It exhibits the point rounding common to cross-grained nails. The burrs are on opposite faces, otherwise it is indistinguishable from Type 6 nails. Its head is small, rectangular, and rather thin. This nail type has been found in only one house in Louisiana, dated 1811 or 1812. This is a recently collected type of nail and replaces the former Type 9 nail of Edwards and Wells (1993).

Type 10. These are cut nails made of steel. In general outline this type resembles the earlier face-pinched cut nails (Types 6, 8, and 9). It is distinguishable from the Type 8 only in that it is made of steel rather than iron. The earliest appearance of Type 10 nails in Louisiana is 1891. Steel cut nails are currently available at many hardware stores.

Type 11. These are iron wire nails. The form is indistinguishable from modern steel wire nails. This type is poorly represented in Louisiana, and the provenience of the sample is highly questionable; so far only one house has provided nails of this type, and they were drawn from a roof lath in an 18th century house. Interestingly, this lath also had Type 1, Type 2, and Type 8 nails. The building is believed to have been re-roofed in the late 1870s as a part of a general rebuild of the structure.

Type 12. These are modern steel wire nails. The earliest example found in Louisiana is from 1891.

Conclusion

The establishment of a useful and accurate nail chronology requires a nail typology that is based on readily observable, objective criteria. Each of the evolving methods of nail manufacture leaves readily identifiable features that are indicative of the technology used in the manufacture of nails. The manufacturing technology changed over the course of time, therefore these features are temporally significant. A typology based on these features provides the best basis for the establishment of a nail chronology.

The Louisiana Nail Chronology was developed from samples of nails drawn from houses in southern Louisiana and Natchitoches Parish, Louisiana. The survey provided dates of actual use for the types of nails collected. These data supplemented information derived from historical research into the development of nail manufacturing technology. Investigation further afield indicates that the chronology may have a general applicability to the greater Mississippi and Ohio Valleys. That the Louisiana Nail Chronology can be applied to those areas may be hypothesized, based on the existence of the extensive river-born and coastal trade that linked Louisiana with nail manufacturing centers in Pittsburgh, Wheeling, and elsewhere. The development of similar, locally adjusted, nail chronologies on the

East Coast and the Mississippi Valley using the methods outlined here can test this hypothesis.

Nail Terms

*denotes terms developed by the author and Jay Edwards

Alloy: A molecular combination of two or more metals: iron + carbon = steel. Wrought iron is a mixture, not an alloy.

Brad: A forged or cut nail that is "7" shaped. Cut brads do not go through an additional heading step because the head is sheared with the shaft. This type of nail has been made from antiquity, but may be dated on technological features. One of the few traditionally named types included here because it is clearly defined.

Burr: Burrs may be found on cut nails and nails made from slitted rods. The cutting tool leaves a sharp, rough flange of metal on the lower side of the shaft as it cuts through the metal stock. The edge above the burr may be slightly beveled or rounded. Burrs may also be found on hand-made nails. Such burrs are found on nails made from slit nail rods. In some cases, burrs can be left on hand-made nails if they were seated in a poorly fitted header.

Clinch: To bend and hammer the nail's exposed point end flat against the wood; done to prevent its loosening.

Cold shut: An unconsolidated fold caused by hammering the burr against the shaft at a too low heat to weld it to the body of the nail.

Cross-grained nails: Cut nails sheared from the end of a narrow nail plate that has the grain running length-wise. The earliest cut nails are cross grained. See "grain."

Cut face:* The two opposite surfaces of a cut nail that show the dragging of the shear. The upper edge may be slightly rounded where the shear entered the nail plate; lower edge will have the burr. See "face."

Cut nail: A machine-made nail. Cut nails are made by cutting the blank off the end of a long strip of iron or steel. The blank is wider at one end than the other. The wide end is mechanically held and is then headed by hand or by machine. The point is left flat.

Drag marks: Striations below the head of hand-made nails caused when being seated in the header. Drag marks are also seen on the cut face of cut nails. These are caused by the shear as it slices through the metal, pulling the metal in the direction of the burr. The burr is also the result of dragging.

Drawn, Draw-out: Blacksmith term for lengthening and narrowing the metal. A point is drawn on a nail shaft by hammering the rod on two sides 90° apart. The opposite of "upset."

Face*: The surface of the shaft that is 90° from the cut face, and is the wider of the two pairs of faces. No distinction is made between front and back faces. See "cut face."

Forged nail: A hand-made nail. The shaft is formed from an iron rod using a hand hammer and an anvil. One end is pointed and then inserted into a header. The head is formed by hammering down on the end of the shaft that projects out of the header.

Grain: Striations in the metal that are characteristic of wrought iron. Iron is strongest when the load is applied across the grain because the slag that forms the grain prevents the metal from having a uniform bond over its whole surface. This is why grain-in-line nails can be clinched reliably and cross grained nails cannot. Steel has no grain because it has a crystalline structure.

Head: That part of a nail that is driven by the carpenter's hammer. Sprigs have no apparent head. Hand-formed heads are usually faceted by the numerous blows made during the heading process. Machine-headed nails will have a flat, smooth surface except for some modern cut nails that have a hemispherical knob centered on the head.

Header: 1. A tool used to form the head of hand forged nails. The most common form of header is a flat bar pierced with a hole the size of the nail shaft. The shaft is inserted into the hole and the header is rested over a hole (the pritchel hole) in the anvil, with the shaft point down. A part of the shaft projects above the header and is hammered down to form the head. 2. A machine or a part of a machine that grasps the shaft of a nail for heading.

Nail bar: A wrought iron strip from which nail rods were slit.

Nail plate: The stock from which cut nails are cut. These were originally produced in the early rolling mills with the grain running their length. Nails cut off these early nail plates are cross grained. Nail plates were later cut from sheet iron in such a way that the grain of the iron of nails cut from them ran the length of the nails. See "grain."

Nail rod: Square or rectangular rods from which some hand-made nails were made. Some nail rods were produced by rolling and slitting mills. Nails made from such rods may exhibit burrs on the same face, between the head and part of the shaft that is drawn out for the point.

Penny, penny weight: English system of nail sizing. It has several meanings: number of nails per pound, price in pence for a hundred nails, number of nails one could get for a "dinar" or penny (hence the abbreviation "d" as in 16d). Today it is standardized to describe the size of a wire nail. Because the term is vague it is not used here.

Pinch*: On cut nails: the area under the head that is grasped for heading. When the unheaded shaft of a cut nail is mechanically held for the heading operation, the part held is deformed on the shaft under the head. Earlier nails are generally deformed on the cut face and are described here as being "side-pinched." Later nails are deformed on the front and back and are described as being "face-pinched."

Point: The end opposite the head. Points may be sharp (all four sides meet), blunt (sides stop abruptly before meeting, forming a square or rectangle when viewed from above), or chisel (two opposite faces meet).

Rolling and slitting: Two stages in the process of making nail rods. The early rollers were about 8-10 in. wide and 10-12 in. thick. By the 1830s rollers were 3 ft. or more wide and over 2 ft. in diameter. To make a flat nail bar the iron ingot was fed into the rollers at a high heat. Slitting follows rolling; it is the longitudinal cutting of the flat nail bar into several long nail rods.

Rose head: English term for a faceted discoid head on a hand-made nail. This term is not used here because it is too vague to be useful for describing the enormous variation in head styles.

Shaft: Body of a nail extending from under the head to the point.

Shear: A cutting tool, usually with one moving edge and a lower stationary edge. Shearing is cutting across the width.

Slit: To cut a bar down its length. A slitter is a machine tool used in the manufacturing of nail rods consisting of an upper and a lower set of interlocking, disk-shaped cutters. The slitter cuts the nail plate longitudinally into nail rods. Though nails made from these rods often exhibit cut faces, they may be distinguished from early machine-made nails by the slitted nail's hand forged heads and grain running the length of the shaft.

Spike: A large nail. Imprecise term standardized too recently to be useful for describing hand-made and cut nails.

Sprig: A headless nail. This term can be defined clearly enough to be useful for describing hand-made and cut nails.

Steel: An iron-carbon alloy, usually having less than 2% carbon. The steel used in nails usually has less than 0.1% carbon. Steel began to supplant wrought iron in nail manufacturing in the 1880s. All modern wire nails are steel. Etched steel shows a very fine crystalline structure.

Upset: Blacksmith term for making the iron shorter and thicker. The head of a hand-headed nail is formed by upsetting the end of the shaft.

Wire nail: Machine-made nails made from round wire. In the 19th century these were called "French Points" and "French nails," after the country in which they were developed.

Wrought iron: Iron/silica amalgam produced by working a lump (bloom) of iron using a silicious flux as a part of the manufacturing process. Wrought iron is soft and more resistant to corrosion than steel. When etched the metal reveals a wood-like grain structure.

REFERENCES

AGRICOLA, GEORGIUS
     1950   *De Re Metallica*, translated and edited by Herbert Clark Hoover and Lou Henry Hoover. Reprint of 1912 edition, originally published in 1556. Dover, New York.

ASTON, JAMES, AND EDWARD B. STORY
     1939   *Wrought Iron.* A. M. Beyers, Pittsburgh.

BINNING, ARTHUR CECIL
     1938   *Pennsylvania Iron Manufacture In the Eighteenth Century.* Pennsylvania Historical Commission, Harrisburg.

CAMPBELL, HARRY L.
     1940   *The Working, Heat Treating, and Welding of Steel.* John Wiley & Sons, New York.

CLARK, DONALD (EDITOR)
1978   The Encyclopedia of How It's Made. A & W Publishers, New York.

COMMITTEE OF ROD AND DRAWN WIRE PRODUCERS
1969   Designer's Handbook: Steel Wire. American Iron and Steel Institute, New York.

DAUMAS, MAURICE
1964   A History of Technology and Invention, Vol. 2, translated by Eileen Hennessy. Crown Publishers, New York.

DICKINSON, H. W.
1939   A Short History of the Steam Engine. Cambridge University Press, Cambridge.

DIDEROT, DENIS
1765   Recueil de Planches, sur les Sciences, les Arts Libéraux, et les Arts Méchaniques, Aves Leur Explication. Paris.

EDWARDS, JAY D., AND TOM WELLS
1993   Historic Louisiana Nails: Aids to the Dating of Old Houses. Geo-Science Publications, Louisiana State University, Baton Rouge.

FERGUSON, EUGENE S. (EDITOR)
1965   Early Engineering Reminiscences (1815-1840) of George Escol Sellers. Smithsonian Institution, Bulletin 238. Washington.

HABAKKUK, H. J.
1962   American and British Technology in the Nineteenth Century: The Search for Labour-Saving Inventions. Cambridge University Press, Oxford.

HEITMANN, JOHN A.
1989   Peter Shoenberger. In Iron and Steel in the Nineteenth Century, edited by Paul Paskoff, pp. 309-311. Facts on File and Bruccoli Clark Layman, New York.

THE IRON AGE
1898   The Pioneer Wire Nail Manufacturer. The Iron Age 62(8).

KAUFFMAN, HENRY J.
1966   Early American Ironware. Charles E. Tuttle, Rutland, VT.

LOVEDAY, AMOS J., JR.
1983   The Rise and Decline of the American Cut Nail Industry: A Study in the Relationships of Technology, Business Organization, and Management Techniques. Greenwood, Westport, CT.

MACKINTOSH-HEMPHILL COMPANY
1953   Rolling Mills, Rolls, and Roll Making. Mackintosh-Hemphill, Pittsburgh.

MARTINEAU, R. F.
1866   Birmingham and Midland Hardware District, edited by Samuel Timmins. Robert Hardwicke, London.

MERCER, HENRY C.
1924   The Dating of Old Houses. A Paper Read by Dr. Henry C. Mercer, of Doylestown, Pa. at a Meeting of the Bucks County Historical Society, at New Hope, Bucks County, Pa., October 13, 1923. Bucks County Historical Society Papers, 5.

MOTT, R. A.
1983   Henry Cort, the Great Finer, edited by Peter Singer. The Metals Society, London.

NELSON, LEE H.
1968   Nail Chronology as an Aid to Dating Old Buildings. American Association for State and Local History, Technical Leaflet No. 48. Nashville.

NOEL HUME, IVOR
1972   A Guide to Artifacts of Colonial America. Alfred Knopf, New York.

PHILLIPS, MAUREEN KATHLEEN
1989   A Revised Chronology of Cut Nails in New England 1790-1820: A Case Study of the Spencer-Pierce-Little House Addition. Unpublished Master's thesis, Boston University, Boston.

ROWLAND, DUNBAR, AND A. G. SANDERS
1984   Mississippi Provincial Archives, French Dominion, 1749-1763, Vol. 5, revised and edited by Patricia Kay Galloway. Louisiana State University Press, Baton Rouge.

SCHOENHOF, JACOB
1974   The Economy of High Wages. Reprint of 1892 edition. Garland, New York.

URE, ANDREW
1865   A Dictionary of Arts, Manufactures, and Mines, Vol. 2. D. Appleton, New York.

TOM WELLS
838 AMERICA STREET
BATON ROUGE, LA
70802

NANCY KENMOTSU

Gunflints: A Study

ABSTRACT

A study of gunflints was undertaken to determine if a uniform use wear pattern is present on gunflints which would assist in the identification of small rectangular or sub-rectangular lithic artifacts from historic sites as gunflints. The study also sought better to understand how these patterns were formed. Both modern and archaeological specimens were employed in the study. Background information on the history, technology, and use of gunflints is summarized as a key to understanding the use wear patterns.

Introduction

Gunflints are a relatively common artifact recovered at many historic Indian and early European archaeological sites. However, the identification of these artifacts as gunflints, especially those which were native-made, is not always easy. The present study was designed, first, to determine if uniform use wear patterns exist which can assist in identifying small rectangular and sub-rectangular lithic artifacts as gunflints and, second, to understand how these patterns were formed. To achieve these goals a study of gunflint manufacturing and reduction sequences, oral and archival documentation on the history, technology, and use of gunflints, and an examination of used gunflints from modern and archaeological contexts was conducted.

Thirty-eight gunflints from archaeological and modern contexts were utilized in the study. Gunflints from archaeological contexts include five of the 11 gunflints recovered from the Pearson site (41RA5) at Lake Tawakoni Reservoir in Texas and 17 of the 114 recovered from the Gilbert site (41RA13) at nearby Lake Fork Reservoir (Figure 1). The 16 modern gunflints for the study consist of three obtained from black-powder contestants at an annual summer rendezvous in the Cascade Mountains of Washington State in July 1987; six from Leland Bement, an archaeologist and black-powder enthusiast employed by the Texas Archae-ological Research Laboratory of the University of Texas at Austin; and seven used and unused gun-flints purchased from McBride's Guns, a local store in Austin, in June of 1987.

Use wear experimentation studies in the past 20 years have shown that a number of variables affect resulting wear patterns on lithic tools. Given the constraints imposed by the function and size requirements of flintlock guns and the ability of the user to reposition the gunflint in the cock to allow for defects in the shape of the gunflint, a number of these variables (hardness of the material worked, edge angle, edge thickness, etc.) were not considered in this study. Two variables—method of manufacture and duration of tool use—were, however, considered. Methods of tool manufacture may result in microscars that can be mistaken for use wear (Tringham et al. 1974:90), whereas duration of tool use will affect the quantity of use wear evidence (Keeley 1980; Odell and Odell-Vereecken 1980:90).

In order to address the question of tool manufacture, a review of reports describing the history of gunflints and the reduction sequences used in their manufacture was conducted. General information on reduction sequences was also derived from a number of archaeological reports together with considerable advice from lithic specialists. Information gleaned from the literature was also used to determine the length of the time the gunflint was used. In addition, informant data from black powder enthusiasts were gathered.

Once these data were acquired, use wear analysis proceeded with a microscopic inspection of used flints from both modern and archaeological contexts. The results were recorded on a Lithic Analysis Data Sheet (Figure 2) modeled after Ahler (1979:318), and compared to data acquired during literature and oral informant studies of gunflints. It shall be argued that there is a wear pattern that can be associated with gunflints.

The Gunflint Industry: Its History, Development, and Study

This section briefly reviews the history and development of the gunflint industry from 1600 to

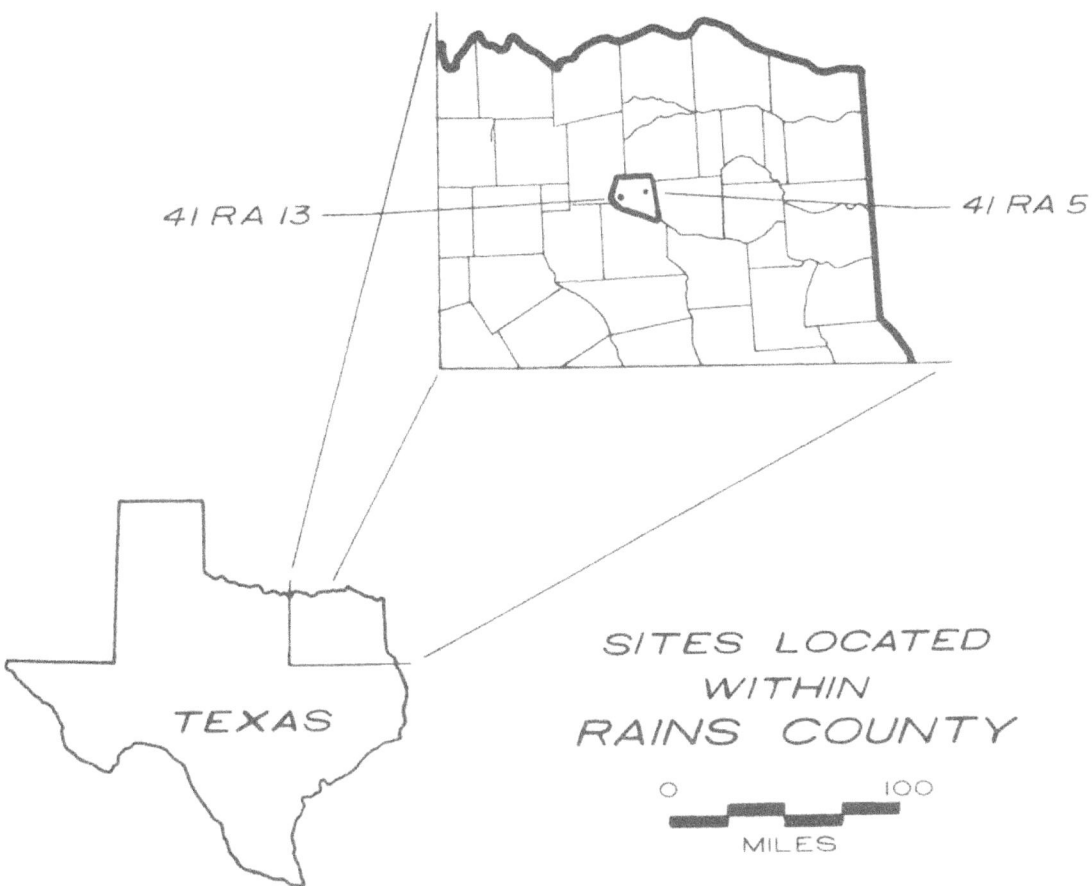

41 RA 13

41 RA 5

TEXAS

SITES LOCATED
WITHIN
RAINS COUNTY

0   100

MILES

FIGURE 1 Locations of sites referred to in text.

1880, the approximate date when flintlock guns were largely replaced by repeating rifles. The section also provides an overview of the raw material for the gunflints used in Texas and a summary of gunflint manufacturing techniques. Descriptive in nature and taken from a number of other sources, this section is included as necessary background to understanding what manufacturing microscars might be present, how gunflints would have been used, and what wear patterns might be expected.

Gunflints were first employed as the sparking instrument in snaphance guns that were invented around A.D. 1600 (Lenk 1965:29). Much experimentation in gun manufacture and powder ignition

systems followed, and by A.D. 1650 true flintlocks were being manufactured (Chapel 1962:40–45, Rosebush 1962:5–7). This flintlock design was only slightly modified over the next 230 years. Essential to these weapons was the gunflint itself, a small sub-rectangular, wedge-shaped artifact manufactured from flint or chert (Figures 3, 4), a cryptocrystalline silicious rock (Crabtree 1972:51).

European and North American quarries have been identified as source material for gunflints used in North America and Texas (Hamilton and Emery 1988:210, 235). In France the quarries were generally confined to the Seine and Marne

LITHIC ANALYSIS DATA SHEET: GUNFLINT STUDY

SITE NUMBER _____   ARTIFACT NO. _____ LOT NO._____

DATE _____   ANALYZED BY _____

MAX. LENGTH _____ MAX WIDTH _____   MAX. THICKNESS _____

RAW MATERIAL TYPE _____   SOURCE MATERIAL _____

WEAR NOTED	AREA	COMMENTS
X-Section		
Rounded	_____	_____
Faceted	_____	_____
Stepped	_____	_____
Concave	_____	_____
Wear Type		
Grinding	_____	_____
Blunting	_____	_____
Smooting	_____	_____
Polishing	_____	_____
Step Flake	_____	_____
Crushing	_____	_____
Flat Flake	_____	_____
Striation	_____	_____
Pitting	_____	_____
Heating	_____	_____
RESIDUE	_____	_____
Outline		
Irregular	_____	_____
Normalized	_____	_____

Number of working edges:

1   2   3   4   5   6   7   8

FIGURE 2. Lithic Analysis Data Sheet, modeled after Ahler (1979:318).

River valleys in calcareous formations of superim-posed horizontal beds of chert nodules of varying quality (Dolomieu [1797] 1960:58). In England the flint is found in the Dover chalk deposits in several thick horizontal strata at depths varying between 3–30 ft. below the surface (Skertchly

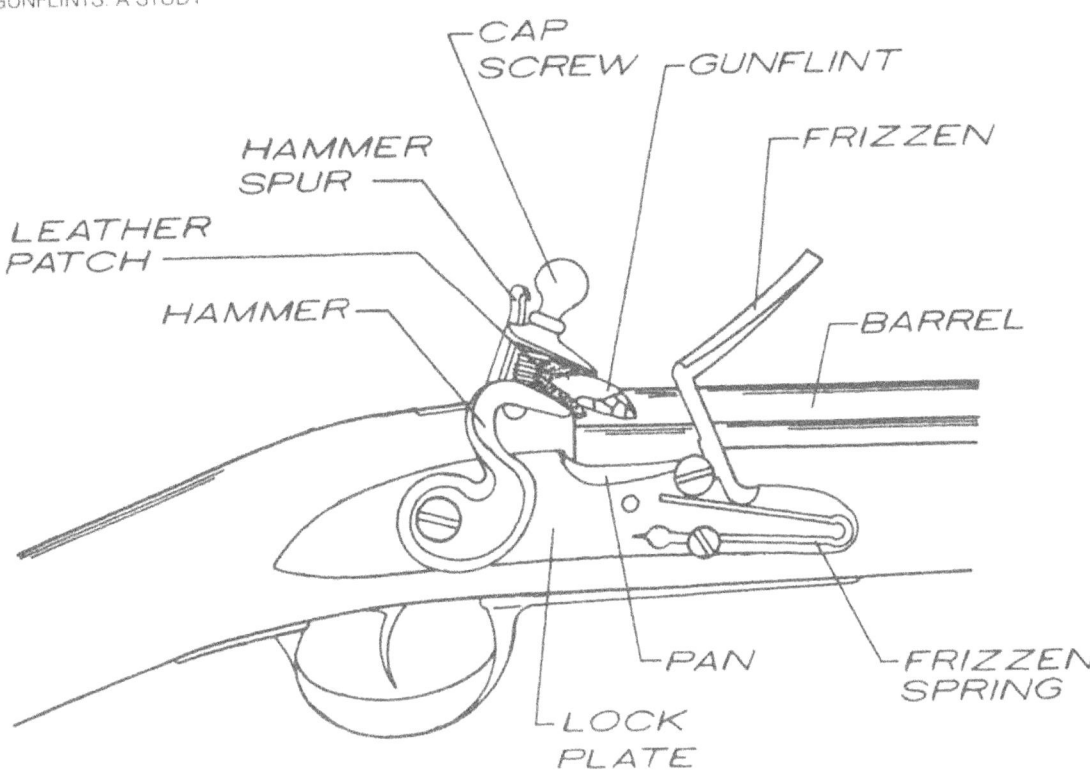

FIGURE 3 Sketch of firing mechanism of flintlock musket

[1879] 1984:21–22). In the United States historic Indian groups extracted chert from quarries that they also had used as source material for other lithic tools (Hamilton 1960:73).

Gunflints from English, French, and American quarries have two primary distinguishing characteristics: physical qualities of the source material, and the manufacturing technique. Probably the best described source material is from an area centered around Brandon, in Suffolk County, northeast of London. Brandon flint grades from one that is a very dark, nearly black, translucent fine-grained flint to a gray, opaque flint with inclusions. Descriptions of this flint and its variations can be found in Hamilton and Fry (1975) and Skertchly (1984). The sample of Brandon flints purchased from McBride's Guns in Austin reflects this variation (Figure 5).

Until recently it was believed that this dark Brandon flint was quarried from Neolithic to modern times (Woodward 1960:29; Skertchly [1879] 1984:79). Recent research, however, indicates the quarries were not extensively mined for gunflints until the Napoleonic Wars of the 1790s (de Lotbiniere 1984:vii–viii). Presence of black English flints on an archaeological site would indicate a date of later than A.D. 1790. The Pearson sample contains a black musket flint from the Brandon quarries, indicating a terminal date after A.D. 1790. Prior to 1790 the English imported gunflints from France. Others were locally produced from quarries of Southern England. One distinctive brown, banded gunflint from the Pearson site (Figure 8a), identified by Duffield and Jelks (1961: 56) as an English flint, may represent one of these earlier non-Brandon gunflints. It is unique in the

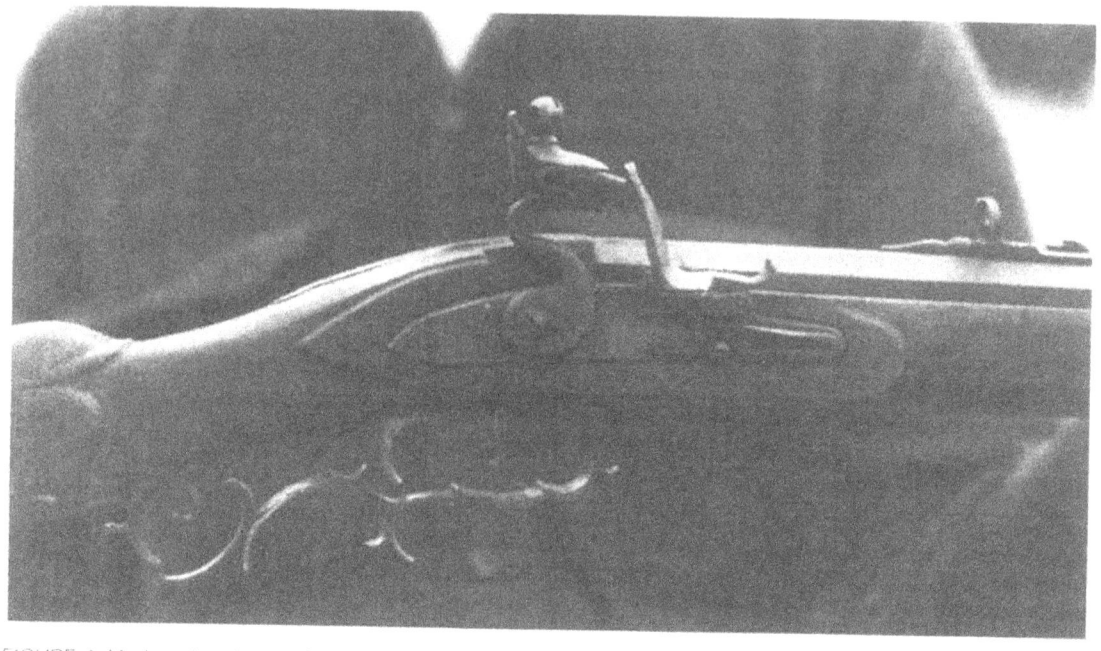

FIGURE 4 Modern, hand-made flintlock rifle with details of cock plate and gunflint visible; flint is just striking frizzen; note leather pad holding gunflint in jaws of cock.

sample, and similar source material was not found; Jay Blaine (1987, pers. comm.), an historic gun authority from Texas, believes it represents a gunflint manufactured by the British.

French gunflints (Figure 6) are distinguished by a honey-yellow or blond flint which often contains white inclusions and occasionally a whitish chalk cortex. The honey-colored French flints are translucent and fine-grained cherts (Dolomieu [1797] 1960:53). This chert has often been called chalcedony to distinguish it from the fine-grained English flint (Hamilton 1960:73).

French blond gunflints date to at least A.D. 1675 (Hamilton 1960:74). These were the most commonly used gunflints in England, France, and the American colonies prior to A.D. 1800. Witthoft (1966:22) notes, "over 95% of the gunflints found in camps occupied during the American Revolution, including even British camps, are of French origin." Once the Brandon quarries were opened about 1790, however, English gunflints began to dominate archaeological collections in the United States (Hamilton and Fry 1975:109).

Native American gunflints are less easily distinguished by source materials. These gunflints were knapped from locally available or non-local source material, resulting in substantial source variation. In the present study, it is assumed that all archaeological specimens that could not be typed as French or British were of Native American source material and locally manufactured. This assumption is at odds with some conclusions made by Hamilton and Emery (1988:242–243). Hamilton and Emery state that three Gilbert specimens (120F3, 134F4, and 181F5), which were also used in the present study, are French flakes reworked by the Indians. This may be correct. However, there are a number of other artifacts from Gilbert (not made available to Hamilton and Emery) which were manufactured from the same source materials, suggesting these three were manufactured with local material. Too, the three were concluded by

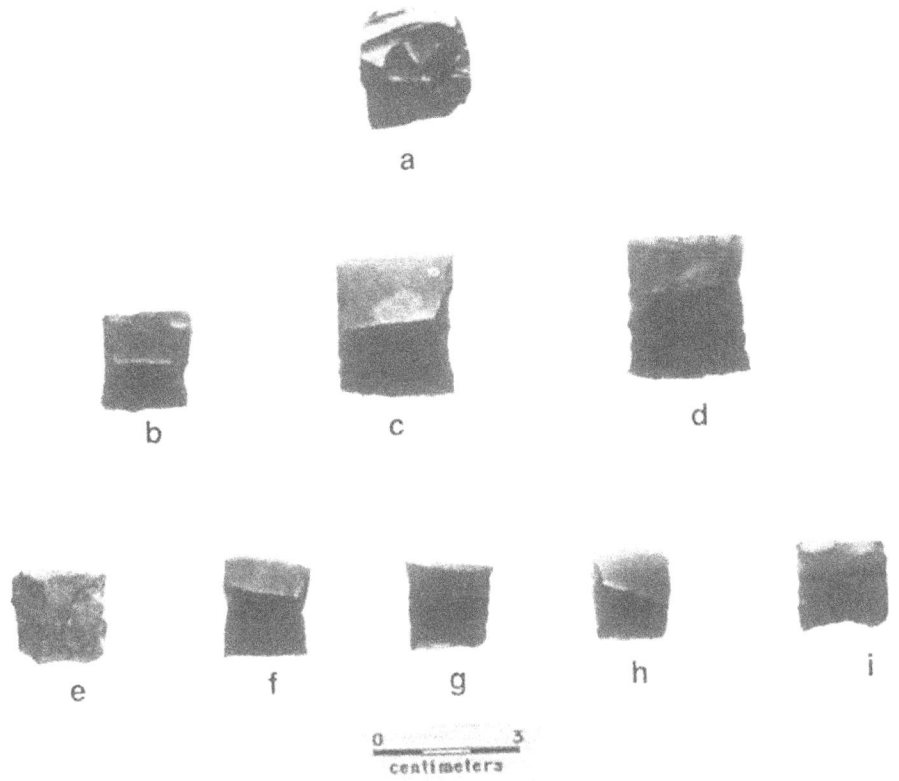

FIGURE 5. English Brandon gunflints used in this study. a, specimen 41-1, Pearson site; b, specimen 1, Other Modern Gunflints; c, specimen 6, Other Modern Gunflints; d, specimen 10, Other Modern Gunflints; e, specimen 5, Other Modern Gunflints; f, specimen 4, Other Modern Gunflints; g, specimen 9, Other Modern Gunflints; h, specimen 8, Other Modern Gunflints; i, specimen 7, Other Modern Gunflints.

Larry Banks (1988, pers. comm.) to be manufactured from Ouachita Mountains chert. In the absence of petrographic analysis, a North American source designation was given to these specimens for the present study.

Native American manufacture of gunflints began with the introduction of guns into a given region and generally continued until an accepted and reliable source of European gunflints was available. Prior to A.D. 1700 most gunflints on Native American sites were aboriginally knapped and are characterized as being more square than European gunflints, with "all four edges carefully worked to an edge by secondary chipping" (Witthoft 1966: 22). After A.D. 1700 Native American manufac-

ture of gunflints continued in individual tribes until there was an accepted source of European flints. This variable time frame is based upon the archaeological record. For example, the Osage in Missouri continued to manufacture gunflints until about A.D. 1730 (Hamilton 1960:77; Hamilton and Emery 1988:233). In the Upper Missouri River Basin, European flints began to increase around A.D. 1750 (Hamilton 1960:77; Witthoft 1966:22), and at the Tunica Treasure site in Louisiana, dated before A.D. 1740, only one of 44 flints is of native manufacture (Hamilton 1979: 210). Once available and accepted, then, a rapid transition to European gunflints seems to have occurred.

FIGURE 6. French gunflints used in this study: a, specimen 134, Feature 4; b, specimen 27–14, Feature 3; c, specimen 152, Feature 6 (all from the Gilbert site).

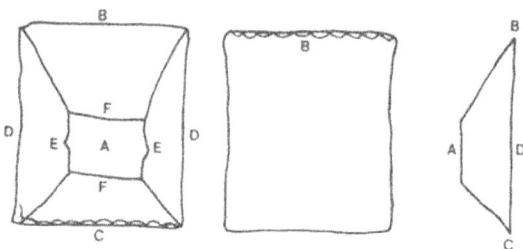

FIGURE 7. Snap-blade gunflint terminology: a, back; b, working edge; c, heel; d, sides; e, aris lip (not always present); f, blade scars.

The other distinguishing characteristic of gunflints is their method of production or reduction. Reduction sequences are used both to date gunflints from a given archaeological context (Hamilton 1964) and to confirm their manufacturing origin and source of trade (Hamilton 1964, 1979). In the present report, reduction sequences were studied to reduce potential errors in the use wear interpretations.

At this juncture it is necessary to briefly discuss standard gunflint terminology. This terminology dates to the 18th century and continues to be used both by contemporary weaponry experts and by authors of archaeological reports describing gunflints. The terminology can be confusing as it sometimes ignores, and at other times contradicts, terms of modern lithic technology. Perhaps most confusing are the terms for two types of European gunflints: gunspalls and gunflints. Gunspalls are wedge-shaped, non-lenticular gunflints (Hamilton 1960:73–79) ancestral to the prismatic gunflint in France and England. The term gunflint is employed to refer to the prismatic gunflints manufactured in Europe through a blade technology. It is also employed to refer to the entire artifact class regardless of when, where, how, or by whom manufactured. In addition to these general terms, there exists a fairly complete nomenclature for the various parts of the body of gunflints and gunspalls. Figure 7 illustrates these terms (face, back, ridge, etc.). In this report the terms of Figure 7 are used

where possible. Use of these terms, when applied to European gunspalls and aboriginally knapped gunflints can be problematical. Therefore, while Skertchly's terms are used, modern lithic terminology has been used or parenthetically added where appropriate.

Gunspalls are produced by removing individual flakes (spalls) from flint nodules or prepared cores through direct percussion (Hamilton 1979:210). They typically have positive bulbs of percussion on the ventral surface, opposed by a relatively flat dorsal surface. The working edge of a gunspall is the roughly straight margin formed on its distal edge. This straight edge is sometimes formed naturally during the reduction process, and sometimes formed by removal of small thinning flakes. The edge of the gunspall opposite the striking edge is called the heel, and it was left unmodified in English gunspalls. In French spalls the heel was "nibbled" or reduced through pressure flaking into a semi-circular form described as "D-form" (Hamilton 1979:211; de Lotbiniere 1984:vi). Sides of English and French gunspalls also tend to have been retouched to form relatively straight, albeit thick, sides.

In the present sample only the British banded flint from Pearson is confidently classified as a European gunspall. One French gunflint from the Gilbert site (Figure 6b) may be a gunspall but has little remaining evidence of the original reduction technique due to subsequent attempts to reduce its thickness through percussion and pressure flaking along its margins.

Gunspall manufacture is believed to have produced greater quantities of waste material than did gunflint manufacture, eventually leading to the demise of the gunspall. In 1836 an English informant described his recollections of the spall production as a "waste of material, and only a small number could be made in a short time" (de Lotbiniere 1984:vii). Often one core would produce only one or two gunspalls. In contrast, with blade technology, large cores are typically used to produce long, slender flakes. Each flake in turn produced a number of flints. Historic documents indicate substantial production increases with gunflint manufacture (Hamilton 1960:74; Woodward 1960:32; Blackmore 1961:138; Skertchly [1879] 1984:33).

The exact date of the introduction of blade technology is unclear. Information gathered from archaeological sites in Canada indicates it had been developed in France by A.D. 1663 (Blanchette 1975) but was probably not perfected until about A.D. 1750. Four blade gunflints were recovered along with 35 "spall or 'wedge-shaped' " gunflints at Chicoutimi, a Canadian site destroyed in 1663 (Blanchette 1975:49). The 44 gunflints from Louisiana's Tunica Treasure site, believed to be occupied from about A.D. 1730 to 1760 (Brain 1979: 1), consist of one native made gunflint, 11 French gunflints, and 32 French gunspalls (Hamilton 1979: 210). Gunflints from the French Louisbourg Fortress in Canada contained a cache of 541 gunflints, only 20 of which were gunspalls (Hamilton and Fry 1975). While the fortress was occupied from 1713 to 1768, several documents from Louisbourg and France indicate the cache probably relates to a time around A.D. 1740. The documents contain several letters from fortress commanders noting the poor quality of gunflints shipped to them "for the last several years" (Hamilton and Fry 1975: 111–113). The presence of both gunflints and gunspalls in the collections from these sites indicates use of both technologies during that period. Further, it would appear that in France blade technology began before A.D. 1663 but was not perfected until some time after A.D. 1740.

Gunflint production consists of removal of a series of fairly long, thick blades from a prepared core using direct percussion. The earliest descriptions of gunflint production were written in France in 1797 (Dolomieu [1797] 1960; Gillet-Laumont [1797] 1960), and a comprehensive English study was made in 1879 by Skertchly ([1879] 1984). The following description of gunflint manufacture has been drawn from these sources. In France, the flint tended to be contained in large nodules of up to 20 pounds (Gillet-Laumont [1797] 1960:62–65). English flint, however, is contained in thick, horizontal beds (see Skertchly [1879] 1984 for illustrations).

Gunflint makers used metal tools with wooden handles for the reduction process. Workers rejected "those which do not have a good color, or which have white inclusions or which contain chalk at the center" (Dolomieu [1797] 1960:65). Critical in the reduction process was removal of a series of long, narrow blades, with the quartering hammer. French and English authors concur that operation requires the "greatest craftsmanship and surest hand" (Dolomieu [1797] 1960:59; Skertchly [1879] 1984:28). The ventral surface of these flakes is slightly convex, tapering to a pointed or rounded distal end (Dolomieu [1797] 1960:60; Skertchly [1879] 1984:29), with one or two dorsal ridges called "single" or "double"-backed. Dorsal ridges were essential to the final forms of the gunflint: flakes without ridges were discarded (Dolomieu [1797] 1960:60) or used for other purposes (Skertchly [1879] 1984:29). For efficiency all flakes were removed until the core was exhausted.

The final process, knapping, was accomplished with the blade resting upon a stake or cutter with the ventral surface up. Several cuts at regular intervals were made along the ventral surface of the blade, producing from one to four gunflints from each blade. The edge and heel were formed by the sides of the long blade. The primary difference between French and British reduction is that French sides and heel were often trimmed by removing small pressure flakes.

In the present sample two French gunflints from the Gilbert site and the English Brandon gunflint from the Pearson site appear to have been manufactured using the blade technology. The black Brandon flint appears to have been the proximal segment of the blade based on the presence of the bulb of percussion resulting from a blow with a hard hammer and the single, irregular dorsal ridge (Figure 8e). A snap fracture from final artifact preparation, as described above, is present on one side. Some light nibbling along one edge appears to represent reverse trimming, produced by rasping the artifact with a hard surface (such as a file) during final gunflint manufacture, and evidenced by the presence of irregular and very small flake scars removed from both surfaces. Based on the side snap fracture, erailluer flake, and dorsal ridge, it is concluded that this is a gunflint rather than a gunspall.

The two French specimens from the Gilbert site are problematical and generally of poor quality (Figure 9o, p). Each appears to have double ridges along its back (dorsal surface), but the ridges are quite close together. In one specimen the ridges have been partially obscured by pressure flaking along the heel. The other specimen has a highly irregular face (ventral surface) produced by removal of several pressure flakes from the sides. However, the two are classified here as gunflints based on the presence of elongated front bevels, lack of bulbs of percussion, and their possible dorsal ridges. The presence of French blade gunflints at Gilbert, together with the absence of any Brandon gunflints among the 114 recovered from the site, suggests a date prior to 1790. In addition both the poor quality of these two gunflints and the presence of a possible French gunspall at the site indicate that a date prior to 1750 may be reasonable.

Native American gunflint production was most similar to that of gunspalls. That is, reduction was initiated by direct percussion to a core, producing a flake subsequently modified to a sub-rectangular form. In the present sample these modifications seem to fall into two groupings. In one group flake modification takes the form of pressure flaking along one or more margins; the remaining ventral and dorsal surfaces are left intact. This type of modification appears in the present sample on five specimens, two from Pearson (Figure 8a,c), and three from Gilbert (Figure 9b, c, d). These specimens were produced from prepared cores struck to

FIGURE 8 Gunflints used in this study from Pearson site. a. specimen ?-11; b. specimen 87-5; c. specimen 66-1; d. specimen ?-11; e. specimen 47-1

remove fairly small flakes. Bulbs of percussion are usually evident, and each is plano-convex in form with a roughly wedge shape. One Pearson specimen also has a series of percussion flakes removed from its back (dorsal surface). The specimens also evidence pressure flaking along one or more sides, sometimes bifacially. Both Pearson specimens appear to have been manufactured from different varieties of flint from the Ouachita Mountains, one possibly from Johns Valley Shale (Larry Banks 1988, pers. comm.).

Similar to the Pearson specimens in method of reduction, the Gilbert specimens are lumped with European gunspalls by Blaine and Harris (1967: 81–82), primarily on the basis of their form. In the present study these three are assumed to be native-made from North American source material. One of the three is of the same raw material as several scrapers in the Gilbert collection. Another specimen has bifacial pressure flaking of high quality along two margins, something more typical of Native American than European workmanship. Finally, Larry Banks (1988, pers. comm.) has viewed the specimens and believes they were probably manufactured from several varieties of chert from the Ouachita Mountains.

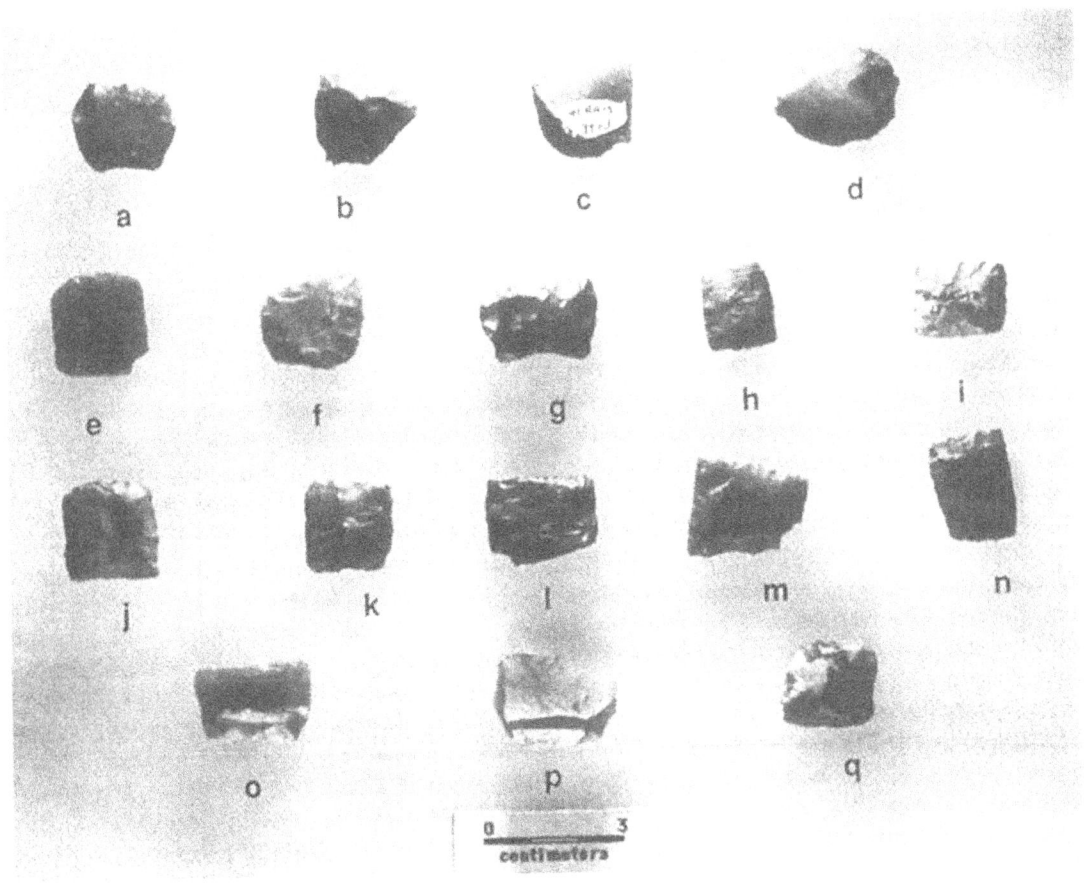

FIGURE 9. Gunflints used in this study from Gilbert site: a, specimen 120, Feature 3; b, specimen 110, Feature 3; c, specimen 94, Feature 3; d, specimen 94, Feature 3; e, specimen 208, Feature 7; f, specimen 9, Feature 15; g, specimen 98, Feature 3; h, specimen 181, Feature 5; i, specimen 134, Feature 4; j, specimen 117, Feature 3; k, specimen 281, Feature 3; l, specimen 29, Feature 3; m, specimen 281, Feature 3; n, specimen 197, Feature 3; o, specimen 27-14, Feature 3; p, specimen 152, Feature 6; q, specimen 134, Feature 4.

The other type of Native American gunflint flake modification is overall bifacial reduction, often followed by careful bifacial retouch along all four sides. Thirteen gunflints in the present sample fall into this grouping. Most initial flake attributes (bulb of percussion, fissures, etc.) have been removed through the reduction process. Typically all four margins are bifacially pressure flaked, and the gunflints are biconvex in cross section with subrectangular outlines. Two contain cortex along one or more surfaces: one has cortex covering its dorsal surface, and one has a small central area containing cortical material. Nine of the specimens appear to be of Ouachita Mountain flints (Larry Banks 1988, pers. comm.).

In summary, the gunflint industry began in the 17th century in response to a need for a more uniform flint for flintlock guns. French gunflints dominated the market in France, England, and North America until the Napoleonic wars of the 1790s. After 1790, English Brandon flint mines began to dominate. Native American gunflints were common on historic Indian sites until an available and accepted source of gunflints was found and tend to reflect the bifacial reduction technology commonly associated with arrowpoint production.

The Sample, the Goals, the Methods

Gunflints from an archaeological context are from the Pearson site (41RA5) at Tawakoni Reservoir and the Gilbert site (41RA13) at Lake Fork Reservoir. Recorded in 1957, the Pearson site consists of about 25 acres in the floodplain of the Sabine River (Johnson 1957:2). In March 1960, the Texas Archaeological Salvage Project conducted machine-aided site excavation, sketch mapping, and an unsystematic surface collection (Duffield 1960; Duffield and Jelks 1961:11–12). The authors conclude Pearson was a late 18th-century Tawakoni village (Duffield and Jelks 1961:68). This conclusion was largely based on a comparison of the Pearson site's native and European artifacts with those from other historic Indian sites in north central Texas.

Eleven gunflints were recovered from the site and analyzed by Dr. Carlyle S. Smith and Mr. C. Malcolm Watkins. The report describes all as rectangular to square in outline, with five of European manufacture and eight "evidently manufactured by the Indians" (Duffield and Jelks 1961:56). Duffield and Jelks note that most of the gunflints show "breakage on one edge" and many evidence secondary retouch on one or more edges. Most gun parts from the site were English, dating from about 1780 to 1835, although some gun fittings could date slightly earlier (Smith, quoted in Duffield and Jelks 1961:77). For the present study, five of the 11 gunflints were selected by the author in a subjective manner. The 11 were placed on a table and five appearing distinct from each other in color and/or physical shape, including two classified by Duffield and Jelks as British, were selected.

The remaining gunflints from an archaeological context were taken from the Gilbert site (41RA13) located on a tributary of the Sabine River (Davis et al. 1967:1). The Gilbert site was first recorded in 1957 and investigated in 1962 by members of the Texas Archaeological Society (TAS). Based on its similarity to other historic Indian sites, the authors conclude that the site was occupied by Yscani, Tawakoni, or Kichai Indians from about A.D. 1750 to 1775. As at the Pearson site, ethnic affiliation and age of the site was largely reliant upon an artifactual assemblage similar to other sites in north central Texas (Duffield and Jelks 1961:69–75) and upon identification of European artifacts which could be reliably dated.

Among the artifacts, 114 gunflints were recovered at 41RA13. Studied by Jay C. Blaine and R.K. Harris, the gunflints were subdivided into 32 spall, 13 conventional, and 69 native-made gunflints. It is the authors' opinion that Gilbert gunspalls tend to exhibit prepared platforms in the heel area and were produced from prepared cores rather than cobbles (Blaine and Harris 1967:82–83). Blade gunflints were all determined to be French due to the source material, a honey-yellow flint, and rounded heels. The 69 native-made gunflints "were produced from flakes by secondary flaking. Specimens of good workmanship are generally square to rectangular thin and biconvex in cross section; all four sides are usually worked to a fine edge" (Blaine and Harris 1967:84). At least two of the native gunflints were produced from Kay County, Oklahoma, flint and most of the others are from Ouachita Mountain cherts (Larry Banks 1988, pers. comm.).

As with Pearson, the sample of 17 Gilbert site gunflints was chosen subjectively. All gunflints in the collection at the Texas Archeological Research Laboratory were laid out, and an attempt was made to choose a range of specimens representing a variety of source materials and possibly different reduction strategies. Three of the 17 are of French origin. The remainder are considered to have been native made, based on raw material and type of reduction.

Gunflint specimens from non-archaeological contexts also were studied. Seven flints from Brandon, England, were purchased (at $1.00 each) from McBride's Guns in Austin. These seven range in size and purity of the Brandon flint and in quality of the finished product. Three used gunflints were obtained in July 1987 from an informant at the Pine Creek Rendezvous in the Cascade

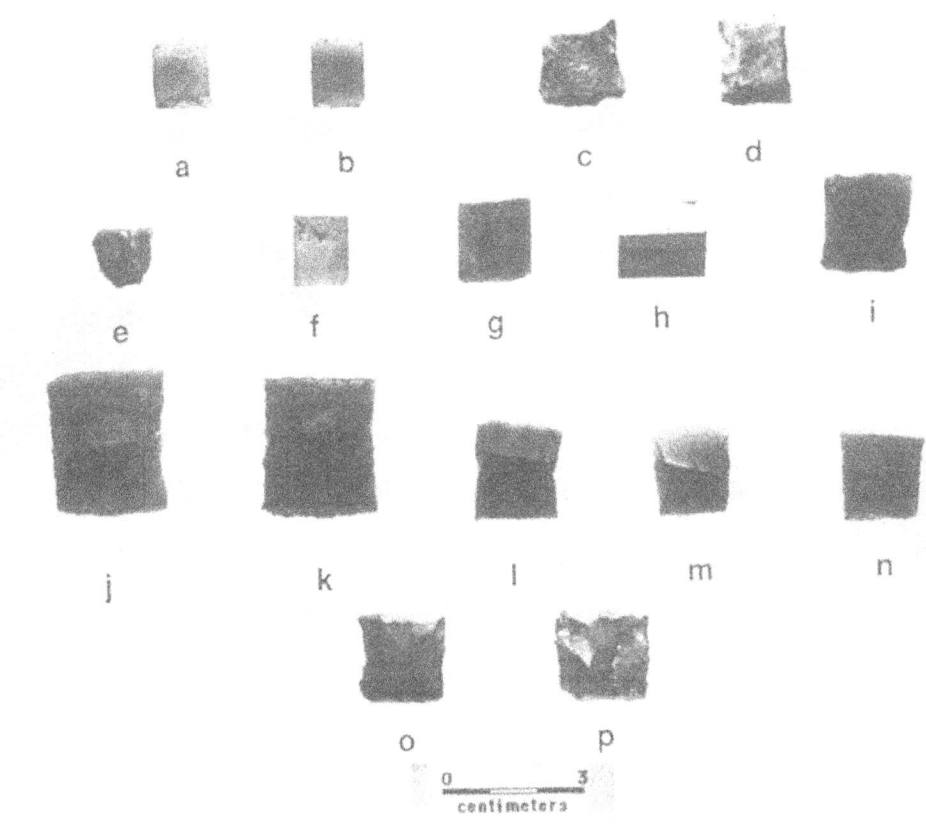

FIGURE 10. Modern gunflints used in this study. Lee Bement specimens include: a, specimen 1; b, specimen 4; c, specimen 2; d, specimen 3; e, specimen 6; f, specimen 5. Pine Creek specimens include: g, specimen 2; h, specimen 3; i, specimen 1. Gunflints purchased from McBride's Guns include: j, specimen 6; k, specimen 10; l, specimen 4; m, specimen 7; n, specimen 8; o, specimen 5; p, specimen 9.

Mountains of Washington State, a shooting competition of black-powder enthusiasts. Six used flints were obtained from Lee Bement, an archaeologist and black-powder enthusiast who provided much valuable information and advice for this study (Figure 10).

It had been hoped that an equal number of used, modern specimens could be obtained. This was not possible for two reasons. First, relatively few black powder enthusiasts use gunflints, most preferring the simpler percussion/cap system. Second, those who use flints are able to maintain a much longer gunflint life expectancy than was maintained for flints used 300 years ago. Informants in the Pine Creek Rendezvous stated one flint would typically last for an entire meet, about 200 rounds. Lee Bement (1987, pers. comm.) confirmed that flints could last for a substantial number of shots. Historically, however, 20 rounds were considered average. The U.S. Army in 1846 issued one flint per 20 rounds (Chapel 1962:71). One plausible explanation of this difference was suggested, that gunflints with potential flaws can continue to be used without prejudice at a competition; potential flaws in the wilderness or war could mean the difference between life and death (Robert Mallouf 1987, pers. comm.).

As stated in the introduction, the goal of this study was to determine if typical wear patterns on gunflints can be identified and to better understand how those wear patterns are formed. The methods employed to reach the goals are detailed below.

Lithic Reduction Sequences

First, a study of lithic reduction strategies employed in gunflint manufacture was undertaken to ensure that remnants of the manufacturing process were not misidentified as use wear (Cotterell and Kamminga 1987:675–676). Historic accounts of the manufacturing process were sought. These accounts detail how the process changed through time, e.g., from core/flake technique to a blade technology. Second, general sources on lithic technology were reviewed, especially Crabtree (1972), Girard (1982), Patterson (1978), and Cotterell and Kamminga (1987). Other sources pertinent to the study are Bruseth and Perttulla's 1981 report of subsequent investigations at Lake Fork Reservoir and discussions with lithic specialists. Third, characteristics of the reduction strategy for each gunflint were studied and recorded (Appendix A). The table format of Appendix A presents a brief description of each gunflint. The data recorded were then summarized and compared with data from gunflint literature, informant accounts, and Crabtree (1972) and Girard (1982). Much of the reduction data was presented in the preceding section.

Use Wear Analysis

To understand better how gunflint wear patterns are formed, and to attempt to define a "typical" gunflint wear pattern, background research on gunflints and use wear studies was conducted, including a review of pertinent literature. Subsequently wear patterns for each specimen were recorded using a 10–70 power microscope; some patterns were further verified with other lithic analysts.

Informant data offered several variables that needed to be considered during the use wear study. First an informant at the Pine Creek Rendezvous stressed that a relatively uniform and even gunflint working edge presented to the frizzen will ensure its smooth run down the frizzen and will maximize the quantity of sparks reaching the pan. Similarly, Bement (1987, pers. comm.) stressed the need for an equal distribution of force to ensure the greatest quantity of sparks and even wear of the gunflint. To equalize the force, the gunflint should have a relatively flat lower surface, permitting its snug fit in the cock. This does not mean the working edge should be perfectly smooth, as the light serrations created during the knapping process are believed to increase the number of sparks. However, edges with deep (1–2 mm) serrations or irregularly spaced gaps in the working edge can, according to informants, hasten wear of both the gunflint and the frizzen. Likewise the narrower the contact point with the steel frizzen, the more concentrated the force as the gunflint moves down the frizzen. Small irregular projections on the working edge would concentrate that force unevenly and tend to spall off.

The main spring of the flintlock may also be important in this action. Instrumental in producing the firing of a flintlock, these springs can have a tripartite life span (Bement 1987, pers. comm.). New, they can sometimes be tight, driving the cock too forcefully into the frizzen, shattering or causing undue wear on the gunflint. As the spring is used it may gradually loosen and develop an efficient action that ensures predictable movement and spark. Over time the metal of the spring can lose tensile strength and again become unpredictable, subjecting the gunflint to undue wear. Informant data, then, suggest the optimum striking action occurs when the striking edge of the gunflint has only slight irregularity, as would be produced by pressure flake retouch. It also appears that a number of factors influence this optimum.

Another aspect of the sparking action which affects gunflint wear patterns is the overall size and shape of the gunflint itself. Modern gunflint No. 3 (Appendix A) from the Pine Creek Rendezvous informant was considered by him to be exhausted, *i.e.*, no longer effective in producing sparks. He noted the bevel was rather steep and short, and could not be resharpened. Thus, bevel angle and distance from the working edge to the bevel impose some outside limits on gunflints. Bement uses gunflints in a flintlock pistol and noted the length of the gunflint determined whether he used it with its bevel down or up. Too, he noted absolute thickness will be determined by the height allowance within the cock. All of these factors will affect the lifespan of the gunflint and hence the quantity of wear imposed on it. On the other hand some caution should be interjected. Flintlock guns, even when produced in factories, were hand-made. Consequently, individual guns from the same factory vary somewhat. Exact parameters for optimum gunflint size would be difficult to establish and are usually expressed as ranges (Stone 1974: 253, Table 46).

The type and manufacture of the gun is another factor affecting wear patterns. Bement noted there is a shortened strike in pistols simply because of their smaller overall size. Therefore, the first action is one of impacting the frizzen rather than rasping down it. The impact tends to remove flakes from both the top and bottom more quickly than on larger guns. This action may result in more blunting than in large guns. Too, Spanish Miquelets produce a unique wear pattern because of their harsh spring action (Blaine 1987, pers. comm.; Hamilton and Emery 1988: 202). Since the archaeological specimens in this study were likely used in French or British weapons rather than Spanish Miquelets, the potentially heavier wear was not anticipated for this sample.

Pertinent archaeological literature on lithic use wear analysis was also reviewed during this phase of the study. While not exhaustive, most attention was given to articles concerned with tools used in scraping activities (Tringham et al. 1974; Ahler 1979; Odell and Odell-Vereecken 1980; Odell 1981; Girard 1982). From these sources, the background on gunflints and informant data, five expectations of gunflint wear patterns were developed. These are listed below with their rationale.

Expectation No. 1: *The working edge will consistently exhibit crushing and/or heavy step flak-*

ing. Small hinge-terminated, irregular step flaking along an edge has consistently been documented on lithics experimentally used in scraping motions (Ahler 1979:313; Odell and Odell-Vereecken 1980: 99). The material contacted by the flint in the case of gunflints is steel, a material sufficiently hard to be especially resistant to the flint and likely to cause a high incidence of hinge and step fractures (Odell 1981:200). Further, the contact with the steel frizzen is confined to the edge, suggesting scars would be concentrated there, as shown by Tringham et al. (1974:189). Finally, as ignition action is repeated, step flaking should increase until the edge has a crushed appearance. It was thus anticipated that step flaking and crushing would be present.

Expectation No. 2: *The working edge will exhibit a relatively uniform pattern of wear across the margin*. Frison's experiment (1979:264) in bison butchering suggested that any repeated activity with lithic tools would tend to result in a relatively uniform wear pattern across the working margin. Odell and Odell-Vereecken (1981:99) note that transverse scraping use wear tends to occur over a wide area of the tool edge, although projections are worn down first. An informant at the Pine Creek Rendezvous remarked that flints are exhausted when working edges become irregular. His ideal was to achieve a uniform strike down the frizzen surface for two reasons: a uniform edge will provide the largest quantity of sparks, and it will also prevent early deterioration of the frizzen. It was expected, then, that whatever wear pattern was found to be typical, it would be present uniformly across the used edges since the action is repetitive and the artifacts restricted to a single purpose.

Expectation No. 3: *Step flaking will be confined to the upper surface of the working edge; striations, smoothing, or polish will be present on the inferior surface of the working edge of the gunflint*. "Step flaking occurs on tool edge and flake ridge elements. Step flake scars are almost always wider than they are long and terminate in a transverse fracture" (Ahler 1979:309). These types of flake scars have been demonstrated to occur in scraping activities where the scars are concentrated on the upper surface of the tool (Tringham et al.

1974:189; Odell and Odell-Vereecken 1980:99; Odell 1981:200). Girard (1982:268) noted that nearly all use wear on unifaces and unifacially edge-modified spalls at the Deshazo site (41NA27) was unifacial. Based on his replication studies, he concluded that the single margin, edge modified spalls with unifacial wear had been used in scraping motions (Girard 1982:239). Tringham et al. (1974:188) note that these step scars are unifacially formed because "only one surface of the flake [receives] pressure from the worked material." This pressure produces microflakes in a manner similar to intentional retouch (Odell 1980: 198). Given the type of scraping motion involved in the rasping of the gunflint down the frizzen, it was anticipated that step flaking would be unifacial and confined to upper surfaces of working edges. It should be noted that the terms "upper" and "lower" surfaces of a gunflint cannot be equated to the terms "face" or "back" (Figure 7). Gunflints are used today with the bevel up or down, and are frequently turned over. Historic accounts also document variation in gunflint position, especially with regard to whether the bevel is up or down.

At the same time, it was believed that the rasping could result in other types of wear, specifically striations, smoothing, or polish on the inferior surfaces of the working edge. A previous study of the Mayhew site (41NA21) gunflints revealed striations on one surface of two of the five specimens (Kenmotsu 1987). Tringham et al. (1979:189) note that on hard materials "scars do occasionally occur on the surface of the flake nearest the worked material," especially short striations at the immediate edge and oriented perpendicular to the worked edge. Girard (1982:239) notes striations and smoothing present on some inferior surfaces of edge-modified spalls concluded to have been used in a transverse scraping motion. With the rasping of the gunflint down the hard steel frizzen, it was expected that striations and/or smoothing on the inferior surface of the working edge might be present. Since polish is a more intense form of smoothing (Ahler 1979:308), its presence should reflect longer use of the gunflint.

Expectation No. 4: *Blunting will be present on*

the working edge. The first action on Bement's pistol was one of the flint impacting the frizzen. This would cause blunting of the projections of the working edge. Other informants stated that gunflints improperly mounted strike the frizzen too forcefully and shatter. Normal contact with the frizzen, then, should result in blunting defined as "the presence of unpatterned fracturing or pulverization of the worn tool surface" typically found only on flake ridges and edge elements (Ahler 1979:308). Blunting is believed caused by "contact with work material hard enough to produce fracturing of the stone tool, but not necessarily of greater hardness than the stone tool" (Ahler 1979:308). Girard (1982:267) recorded a fairly high proportion of blunting on his Functional Group 5 tools "with steep unifacial marginal retouch and/or use-wear" and inferred they had been used in scraping activities. He noted that blunting often occurred on tools used on hard material (Girard 1982:229). It was therefore anticipated that blunting would be present on the working edges of gunflints.

Expectation No. 5: *Rejuvenation of the gunflint will be evidenced by multiple working edges and edge retouch.* At the Pine Creek Rendezvous two types of gunflint rejuvenation were noted. One informant from Oregon, who used gunflints cut by lapidary saws, stated that he had turned his flint upside down and revolved it 180° that morning in order to use the other available edge. In the other instance, a wooden billet was used lightly to tap the edge of the flat surface of a Brandon flint, removing small thinning flakes on the beveled edge. This was performed with the flint still in the jaws of the cock. Bement's specimens were acknowledged to have multiple working edges; his hand-made specimens tended to have wear along all four edges. Bement's methods of rejuvenation were: (1) revolve the gunflint in the cock, taking advantage of other edges; (2) lightly tap along the edge of the bottom of thinner gunflints with a small chunk of sandstone; and (3) retouch, via percussion, thicker gunflints. Some archaeological and historical reports also document multiple incidents of gunflint rejuvenation (Stone 1974:255; Hanson and Hsu 1975:73). Given this background,

SITE NUMBER: MODERN USED GUNFLINTS

WEAR NOTED X-Section	Total	% of wear on working edge		WEAR NOTED Wear Type	Total	% of wear on working edge
Rounded	0	0		Grinding	0	0
Faceted	6	22		Blunting	5	19
Stepped	14	52		Smooting	17	63
Concave	2	7		Polishing	0	0
				Step Flake	27	100
RESIDUE	10	37		Crushing	12	44
				Flat Flake	12	44
Outline				Striation	3	11
Irregular	14	52		Pitting	0	0
Normalized	2	7		Heating	0	0

Number working edges per gunflint:

1 2 3 4 5 6 7 8	TOTAL
1 4 2 3	27

FIGURE 11. Results of use wear study for modern gunflints; sample size is 17.

it was anticipated that the archaeological specimens in the sample would evidence rejuvenation.

After development of the preceding expectations, all gunflints were studied under a 10-70 power microscope, beginning with the modern specimens. It should be emphasized that the microscopic study of the modern gunflints was critical to all interpretations, because their wear could be orally verified or was observed in the field. While still open to some subjectivity (i.e., hazy remembrances of informants, inaccurate note taking, etc.), the subjectivity was assumed to be less than that which might be imposed on a sample of archaeological specimens only. It was anticipated that wear on modern specimens would be duplicated to a large degree in archaeological specimens. Wear patterns noted during this microscopic inspection were recorded on the Lithic Analysis Data Sheet (Figure 2), adapted from Ahler (1979: 318). Definitions of wear patterns were taken from Ahler and will not be redefined here. Once the

analysis was complete, results were totaled to determine the presence/absence of trends of use wear. In turn, any trends were compared to informant and archival data.

Results of the Analysis

This section presents results of the analysis of wear patterns on 38 gunflints. Figures 11, 12, and 13 present the summary results of the use wear analysis. Each sample has been totaled individually and simple percentages are provided. The figures also provide information on the quantity of working edges for each gunflint. Each expectation described in the preceding section will be discussed, relating how well the data did or did not conform to those expectations. Comparisons to the modern sample will be detailed in these discussions, and relevant informant and archival data noted.

SITE NUMBER: PEARSON SITE 41RA5

WEAR NOTED X-Section	Total	% of wear on working edge
Rounded	2	22
Faceted		0
Stepped	5	56
Concave	0	0
RESIDUE	4	44
Outline		
Irregular	1	11
Normalized	0	0

WEAR NOTED Wear Type	Total	% of wear on working edge
Grinding	0	0
Blunting	0	0
Smooting	6	67
Polishing	1	11
Step Flake	9	100
Crushing	2	22
Flat Flake	1	11
Striation	0	0
Pitting	0	0
Heating	0	0

Number working edges per gunflint:

1 2 3 4 5 6 7 8	TOTAL
3 2	9

FIGURE 12. Results of use wear study for Pearson site gunflints; sample size is 5.

Expectation No. 1: *The working edge will consistently exhibit crushing and/or heavy step flaking.* The motion of the flint down the frizzen is one of scraping. Scraping activities of experimental tools have been documented to result in step flaking wear patterns (Odell and Odell-Vereecken 1980:99). As the action is repeated, the pattern should intensify. It was thus anticipated that step flaking and crushing would be present.

Step flaking clearly dominated the wear for modern gunflints, being present in 100% of the cases of working edges (Figure 14). In the modern sample, all edges known to have been used as a working edge exhibited step flaking, although intensity varied from very heavy to light. Both Lee Bement and an informant at the rendezvous noted constant wearing of edges as the flint is drawn down the frizzen to release sparks. Similar patterns of step flaking also were present on nine margins of the five gunflints from the Pearson site and 38 margins of the 17 Gilbert site specimens. These margins were concluded to represent working edges. Stepped cross sections were also fairly well represented on working edges of all three samples, as were irregular outlines. Fourteen (52%) of 27 working edges of modern flints exhibited a stepped cross section and irregular outlines. Five (56%) of the nine Pearson working edges had stepped cross sections and one was irregular in outline. Twenty-five (66%) of 38 Gilbert working edges were stepped in cross section and 17 were irregular in outline. While the samples are quite small and not statistically drawn or valid, it is interesting that the percentages for stepped cross sections of the archaeological specimens so closely approximate those of the modern sample.

Crushing, however, was not as prominent as expected. Fourteen (50%) of the modern sample's working edges had evidence of crushing. In the archaeological sample even less crushing was present: two (22%) of the nine working edges from the Pearson site and four (11%) of 38 working edges from the Gilbert site evidenced crushing. In general, crushing from the gunflint movement

SITE NUMBER: GILBERT 41RA13

WEAR NOTED X-Section	Total	% of wear on working edge
Rounded	7	18
Faceted	0	0
Stepped	25	66
Concave	1	3
RESIDUE	15	39
Outline		
Irregular	17	45
Normalized	5	13

WEAR NOTED Wear Type	Total	% of wear on working edge
Grinding	0	0
Blunting	7	18
Smooting	24	63
Polishing	0	0
Step Flake	38	100
Crushing	4	11
Flat Flake	14	37
Striation	0	0
Pitting	0	0
Heating	0	0

Number working edges per gunflint:

1 2 3 4 5 6 7 8	TOTAL
6 4 4 3	38

FIGURE 13. Results of use wear study for Gilbert site gunflints. sample size is 17

down the frizzen appears to have a lower incidence than step flaking, especially in the archaeological samples. The lower incidence in the archaeological samples may relate to differences between archival and informant accounts of the average number of shots feasible per flint. Twenty rounds per flint was the U.S. Army estimate in 1846 (Chapel 1962: 71), yet all informants reported modern flints lasted from 50 to 100 rounds. Such a difference in life spans may be sufficient to induce crushing on modern flints but not on archaeological specimens.

Possible reasons for shorter gunflint life spans during historic times are several. Gunflints may have been so cheaply produced, in terms of time and money, that any slight flaw was sufficient to cause its discard. The present sample may represent specimens with inherent material flaws detected during early use. Too crushed edges may have been resharpened, removing evidence of crushing, and subsequently used insufficiently to produce crushing.

Expectation No. 2: *The working edge will exhibit a relatively uniform pattern of wear*. This expectation assumed that whatever wear pattern was found to be typical, it would be present uniformly across the working edges since the action is repetitive and artifacts restricted to a single purpose. During analysis it quickly became apparent that this expectation was poorly defined and hard to quantify. Many unanticipated variables affected the expectation. The gunflint may have been rejuvenated several times, obscuring "uniform wear patterns." At least two Gilbert specimens—one French blade flint and one native made gunflint (Figure 9o and e, respectively)—exhibited fresh pressure flakes along their edges, suggesting they were undergoing rejuvenation, obscuring step flaking and uniform wear patterns when they were discarded or lost. Another problem in qualifying this expectation is that flaws in the raw material could cause small, irregular and deep snap fractures (Figure 9n, l; Figure 10c). These flaws also will confuse the evidence for clear uniform wear

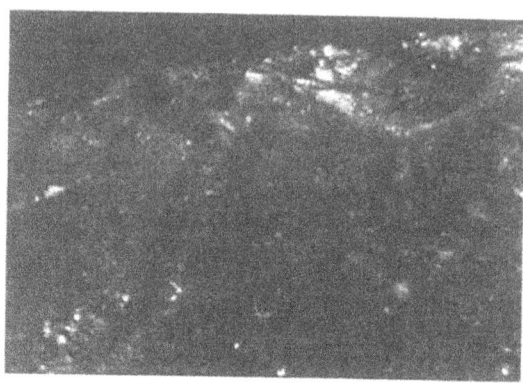

FIGURE 14. Microphotograph of step flaking on upper surface or working edge of modern gunflint. note smoothing of points at the edge of the gunflint. Pine Creek specimen (photo by N. Kenmotsu, 16X).

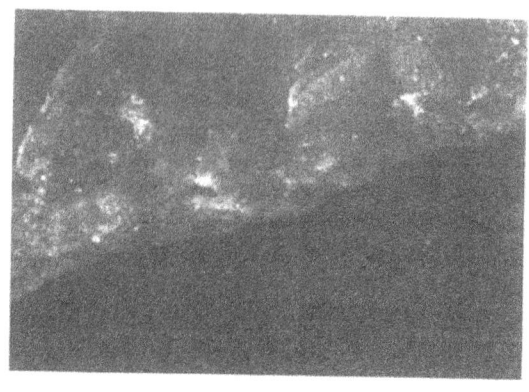

FIGURE 15. Microphotograph of Gilbert specimen 29, Feature 3, with unifacial step flaking and some blunting and smoothing along the edge; dark colored stains represent residue (photo by N. Kenmotsu, 16X).

patterns. In short the expectation was not very helpful and was finally abandoned because it was too broad and inconclusive.

Expectation No. 3: *Step flaking will be confined to the upper surface of the working edge; striations, smoothing, or polish will be present on the inferior surface of the working edge of the gunflint.* Given the type of scraping motion involved in the rasping of the flint down the frizzen, it was anticipated that flaking would be unifacial and confined to the back (upper surface) of the working edge. If present, striations, smoothing, or polish would occur on the face (lower surface) contacting the frizzen.

As expected working edges of all modern specimens exhibited step flaking on their upper surfaces (Figure 14). Archaeological specimens also exhibited unifacial step flaking (Figures 15, 16) in all but one case, and it was concluded that the step flaking represented the upper surfaces of what had been the working edges. One specimen (Figure 8d) from the Pearson site contained some light step flaking on the inferior surface. No clear explanation of this case was found, although it may simply represent turning the flint to obtain a better striking edge on the opposing surface.

Striations were present on three modern gunflints, but none of the archaeological specimens

evidenced this attribute. The small sum of incidents of striations may not, however, be unusual. Tringham et al. (1974:189), Odell and Odell-Vereecken (1980:99), and Odell (1981:201) concur that striations are not commonly found on artifacts used in transverse scraping motions, and imply that intensity of use may be involved in creating this wear pattern on inferior surfaces. Hence, its presence on only modern specimens may again relate to a higher intensity of use of those gunflints over archaeological specimens.

Smoothing and polish are related types of abrasive wear (Ahler 1979:308). Smoothing causes a rounded, less coarse appearance of artifact surfaces than the appearance of surfaces with fresh flake scars. Polish is a higher degree of smoothing where light is reflected.

Seventeen (63%) of the 27 working edges in the modern sample exhibited smoothing (Figure 14) while no occurrences of polish were noted. Six (67%) of nine working edges of the Pearson sample exhibited smoothing with one occurrence of polish noted on one specimen (Figure 8d). This specimen is morphologically distinct from all others in the sample and its classification as a gunflint is questionable (see Appendix A). Twenty-four (63%) of the 38 working edges of the Gilbert sample exhibited smoothing; no occurrence of polish

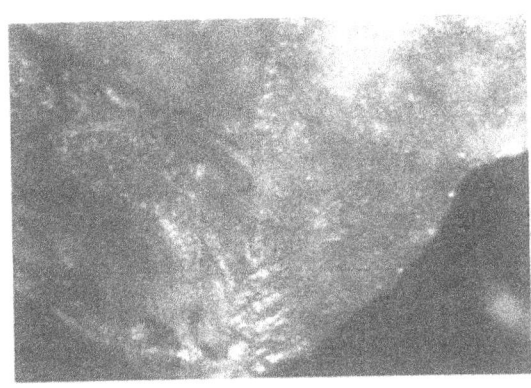

FIGURE 16. Microphotograph of Gilbert specimen 134, Feature 4, with unifacial step flaking on left working edge, bottom of microphoto shows small portion of the burin-like flake removed to rejuvenate the gunflint; the opposing margin of the burin-like flake is very similar to the step flaking on the left margin; left margin's reverse side had burin removed (photo by N. Kenmotsu, 16X).

was recorded. Once again the similarity of the percentages between modern and archaeological samples is striking. Further study of more statistically valid samples would be needed to determine whether this is a fortuitous similarity. Regardless, the results of the analysis tend to suggest a high incidence of smoothing on gunflints. However, the location of this wear pattern is not confirmed by the analysis. Only three of the working edges of the modern sample and one of the Gilbert specimens exhibited smoothing only on inferior surfaces. The remaining occurrences of smoothing were either on both surfaces or on the superior surfaces of the working edges. On reflection, the distinction may be more apparent than real. Evidence for smoothing is along the immediate edge where divisions between superior and inferior are fairly arbitrary. It seems more significant that in all three samples smoothing is second only to step flaking in its occurrence, is located on the working edge, and that the anticipated unifacial step flaking is confirmed in the microscopic inspection of the artifacts. The presence of striations on only three modern specimens and near absence of polish suggests that the intensity of use is generally insufficient to form these wear patterns on gunflints.

Expectation No. 4: *Blunting will be present on the working edge*. The first contact of the gunflint with the frizzen is one of impact. This impact, evidence of blunting from the Deshazo site, 41NA27 (Girard 1982), and use wear studies (Ahler 1979:308) suggested that blunting would be identified on the gunflints inspected microscopically.

Blunting was present, but not to the extent anticipated. Five (19%) working edges of the modern sample evidenced blunting as did seven (18%) of 38 working edges from the Gilbert site (Figure 15). Again the percentages are similar. One modern used gunflint appeared to have blunting on the heel, perhaps due to a loose fit in the cock. Two of the modern occurrences on working edges were from a single specimen. It is possible that the specimen was of a softer chert than the remaining specimens, or that the main spring of the pistol was relatively tight, enhancing the gunflint's impact with the frizzen.

The archaeological occurrences of blunting (Figure 9g, l, o) all appear to have more intense use than the modern sample. Heavy step flaking is present on these specimens on all working edges, and all but one of their working edges is stepped in cross section. All but the French specimen (Figure 9o) have multiple working edges (see Expectation No. 5); several working edges exhibit normalized outlines. This combination of wear attributes is not present in specimens without evidence of blunting. For example, specimens with less intense step flaking do contain evidence of smoothing, but not blunting. On the other hand, crushing is present in the Gilbert sample on two other working edges. If crushing is indicative of intensity of use, then blunting is curiously absent from these two specimens (Figure 9f, m). No simple explanation is offered. It is possible that intensity of use may result in more than one set of wear attributes; or evidence for blunting on the crushed edge may have been missed in the analysis. Nonetheless, each specimen has other working edges with moderate amounts of step flaking (sometimes with smoothing) and yet without evidence for crushing. In sum, while present and apparently not an overly common wear associated with gunflints, blunting

TABLE 1
QUANTITY OF WORKING EDGES PER GUNFLINT

| | No. Working Edges | | | | | | | | |
	1	2	3	4	5	6	7	8	Total
Modern Sample	3	7	2	3					35
Pearson (41RA5)	3		2						9
Gilbert (41RA13)	3	4	4	3					35
Total	9	11	8	6					79

is present in the sample. Blunting may be the result of attributes unique to individual guns, or, as appears to be the case with the archaeological specimens, to reflect the degree and extent of use.

Expectation No. 5: *Rejuvenation of gunflints will be evidenced by multiple working edges and edge retouch.* During the course of this study, modern informants and gunflint literature documented the ease of gunflint rejuvenation. This rejuvenation can occur by turning the gunflint to use another edge, turning the flint over, or edge retouch using a wooden billet or another instrument such as antler, bone or lithic tools, or copper.

Quantity of working edges on the modern gunflints was a known (Table 1). From established wear patterns for these modern specimens, the number of working edges on each archaeological specimen was determined by identifying those with patterns similar to modern specimens. The results indicate a high percentage of rejuvenation by simply revolving the flints in the cock. Three Pearson specimens had evidence of use on one edge; two had evidence of use on three edges. Those from the Pearson site with multiple worked edges are the brown banded English gunspall and one native gunflint, each having three margins that appear to have been used as working edges. At Gilbert three gunflints had only one working edge, four had two working edges, four had three working edges, and three had four working edges. One French and 10 native-made Gilbert specimens contain this evidence of multiple use. The total number of working edges on the 19 archaeological specimens from both sites is 44, suggesting a fairly high incidence of rejuvenation by simply turning the gunflint.

Other types of rejuvenation also are present in the samples. The used French blade flint (Figure 9o) from Gilbert has intermittent pressure flaking along its working edge. These pressure flakes appear to interrupt step flaking formed by use wear and are here concluded to represent resharpening of the working edge. Two other Gilbert specimens (Figure 9e, q) have similar evidence of retouch interrupting step flaking.

Still another type of retouch appears to have been employed as gunflint rejuvenation. Two Gilbert specimens have evidence of burin and burin-like flake removal. One is a native-made gunflint (Figure 16) with two working edges on opposing surfaces, which contains an elongated, narrow flake scar down the lower surface of one working edge. The possible French gunspall (Figure 9q), also contains a burin-like flake removed from the lower surface of one working edge. While not common, burin-type retouch seems to have been employed on inferior surfaces of working edges of relatively thick gunflints and is here tentatively suggested to have been a method of improving the striking action of thicker specimens. It would appear then that there is considerable evidence of gunflint rejuvenation within the three samples.

In addition to the above expectations, two other use attributes of gunflints were discovered through the use of Ahler's analysis sheet: evidence of flat flakes and residue. Flat flakes, confined to the lower surfaces of the working edges and evidenced by wide, flat flakes with feathered or hinged terminations, were present on 14 (38%) of 35 modern working edges. One occurrence (11%) of flat flaking was present in the Pearson sample, and 14 (38%) of 38 working edges in the Gilbert sample contained flat flakes. Photographs in Hamilton and Emery (1988: Figures 46, 52) appear to document the removal of flat flakes on the inferior surfaces of working margins as well. Bement (1987, pers. comm.) suggested flat flaking may be related to the shock to the gunflint of the initial impact when striking the frizzen. At any rate, this type of wear, while not ubiquitous, is more frequent than blunting and polishing and appears to be part of overall gunflint wear patterns.

Finally, residue was present on all but three specimens and was identified on all surfaces as well as along edges and sides. Residue falls into three loosely defined types. First there are shiny silver or gold iridescent flecks (visible only at 40+ power under the microscope) on the artifacts. Believed to be metal, these flecks may have resulted from filing of edges performed during terminal stages of manufacture of both modern and European archaeological specimens, or they may be small chips of the steel frizzen. Another type of residue on the gunflints was a black substance sufficiently thick that it is was often visible macroscopically (Figure 17). Although not analyzed, this residue may be fragments of leather used to pad the gunflint in the cock. Informants noted that the gun powder reacts with leather resulting in its moistening. Two of Bement's specimens had this substance, and he identified it as leather.

The third type of residue noted has a very burned, powdery appearance and was especially apparent along edges (Figure 18). Quite distinctive, these may represent hot sparks released from the frizzen which were relatively large and which burned on the gunflint surface. Although outside of the scope of the present inquiry, further analysis would be needed to verify the true nature of the residues. For the purposes of this present study, it is sufficient to note the high incidence of residues which may assist in assessing whether small subrectangular lithic tools in an archaeological assemblage are gunflints.

Summary

Gunflints are frequently recovered from historic Indian sites. Since these artifacts are still manufactured and used today, a study was conducted to

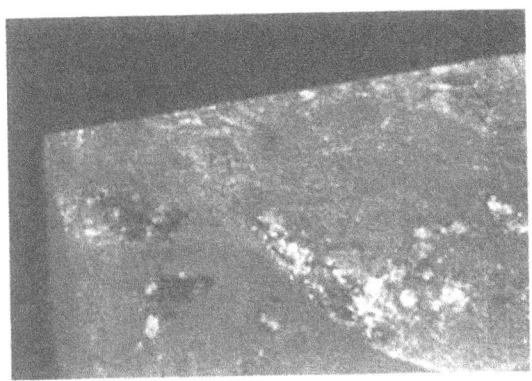

FIGURE 17. Microphotograph of Lee Bement specimen 1 with flat flake removed from inferior surface, dark stains are leather residue (photo by N. Kenmotsu, 64X).

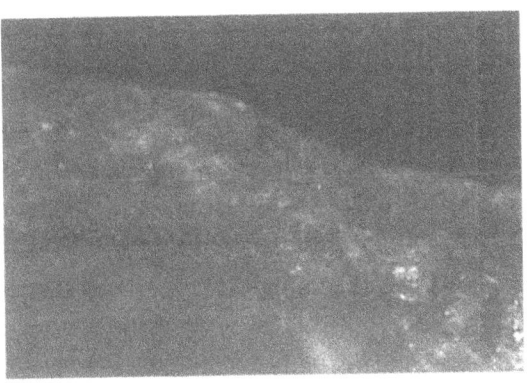

FIGURE 18. Microphotograph of Gilbert site specimen 110, Feature 3, with evidence of light step flaking, unifacial in pattern, and blunting on the central projection; note dark colored area which represents the third type of residue (photo by N. Kenmotsu, 16X).

determine whether typical wear patterns can be established for gunflints to aid in their identification in archaeological assemblages, and to understand better how these patterns formed.

In the course of the study, background data were gathered on the history of gunflints, including data pertinent to methods of manufacture. The gunflint industry began during the 16th century and continues today. French gunflints dominated the market in North America until the Napoleonic wars of the 1790s, when the British began gunflint production at Brandon. These French gunflints were initially manufactured by a core-flake technology whereby each core yielded from one to several flakes suitable for individual gunflints. Commonly called gunspalls, these specimens have a wedge-like shape and often retain a bulb of percussion and exhibit retouch around the heel. Sometime prior to A.D. 1663, the French developed a more efficient blade technology which was perfected by about A.D. 1750. Distinctive from the earlier gunspalls, gunflints are prismatic and a bevel is formed by the blade scars on the dorsal surface. It was this blade technology which was used at Brandon. Brandon quarries dominated the gunflint trade in North America after A.D. 1790. Native American gunflints were common on historic Indian sites until an available and accepted source of commercial gunflints was found. Native-made gunflints tend to reflect the bifacial reduction technology commonly associated with arrowpoint production.

Based on this background 38 gunflints from black-powder enthusiasts in Washington and Texas and from the Gilbert and Pearson archaeological sites in Rains County, Texas, were studied. All specimens were subjected to microscopic inspection to detect wear patterns. The goal was definition of typical wear patterns, and modern specimens were inspected first since their wear could be orally verified or observed. Results of the microscopic study were recorded on the Lithic Analysis Data Sheet (Figure 2) modeled after Ahler (1979). Once complete, the results were totaled and compared with five expectations developed from the background information.

Several expectations of wear patterns were verified by the study, while others were shown to not apply or to be less common for gunflints. Based on these results it appears that a wear pattern for gunflints can at least be outlined at this time. The pattern consists of unifacial step flaking often associated with smoothing of the working edges and some flat flaking on lower surfaces of the working edge. Blunting, while not as common, may be present. Occasional working edges may also exhibit crushing. Rejuvenation is common in the gunflints studied. Lastly, metal and leather residues are characteristically present on gunflint surfaces.

ACKNOWLEDGMENTS

A number of persons have greatly assisted in this study Dr. Jeremiah Epstein, T. M. Hamilton, and Jay C. Blaine read and offered valuable advice on the direction of the study as well as on constructive changes in the paper, and their assistance is deeply appreciated. Robert Mallouf, James E. Bruseth, and Wayne Bartholomew also provided advice and encouraged completion of the study. Daniel Prikryl and Leland Bement were especially helpful in sharing their knowledge of lithic technology. The source material for native gunflints could not have been accomplished without the help of Larry Banks of the Southwest Region, Corps of Engineers. David Hafernik kindly drafted the map, the gunflint, and the flintlock drawing, and Deborah Smith and Helen Simons graciously edited the manuscript.

Finally, deep appreciation is given to Ray and Jeannie Kenmotsu without whose patience and encouragement nothing would have been accomplished

REFERENCES

AHLER, STANLEY A.
1979 Functional Analysis of Non-Obsidian Chipped Stone Artifacts: Terms, Variables and Qualification. In *Lithic Use-Wear Analysis*, edited by Brian Hayden, pp. 301–328. Academic Press, New York.

BLACKMORE, H. L.
1961 *British Military Firearms, 1650–1850*. Herbert Jenkins, London.

BLANCHETTE, JEAN-FRANCOIS
1975 Gunflints from Chicoutimi Indian Site (Quebec). *Historical Archaeology* 9:41–54.

BLAINE, JAY C., AND R. K. HARRIS
1967 Guns. In The Gilbert Site, a Norteno Focus Site in Northeastern Texas. *Bulletin of the Texas Archeological Society* 37:33–86. Dallas.

BRAIN, JEFFERY P.
1979 The Tale of the Tunica Treasure. In *Tunica Treasure*, edited by Jeffery P. Brain, pp. 1–32. Papers of the Peabody Museum of Archaeology and Ethnology. Vol. 71. Peabody Museum of Archaeology and Ethnology, Cambridge, Massachusetts.

BRUSETH, JAMES E., AND TIMOTHY K. PERTTULA
1981 *Prehistoric Settlement Patterns at Lake Fork Reservoir*. Southern Methodist University, Dallas.

CHAPEL, CHARLES EDWARD
1962 *U.S. Martial and Semi-Martial Single Shot Pistols*. Coward and McCann, Inc., New York.

COTTERELL, BRIAN, AND JOHAN KAMMINGA
1987 The Formation of Flakes. *American Antiquity* 52: 675–708.

CRABTREE, DON E.
1972 *An Introduction to Flintworking.* Occasional Papers of the Idaho State University Museum 38. Pocatello, Idaho.

DAVIS, E. MOTT, KATHLEEN GILMORE, LOYD HARPER, R. K. HARRIS, EDWARD B. JELKS, AND BILL YANCY
1967 The Site. In The Gilbert Site, a Norteno Focus Site in Northeastern Texas. *Bulletin of the Texas Archeological Society* 37:33–86. Dallas.

DE LOTBINIERE, SEYMOUR
1984 Introduction, Updating Skertchly. In *The Manufacture of Gunflints,* by Sydney B.J. Skertchly, pp. i–viii. Museum Restoration Service, Alexandria Bay, New York.

DOLOMIEU, CITIZEN
1960 Report on the Art of Making Gunflints (Fire-Flint). (Reprint of 1797 article.) *The Missouri Archaeologist* 22:50–61.

DUFFIELD, LATHEL R.
1960 Field Notes. On file at the Texas Archeological Research Laboratory, Balcones Research Center, University of Texas, Austin.

DUFFIELD, LATHEL R., AND EDWARD P. JELKS
1961 The Pearson Site, a Historic Indian Site in Iron Bridge Reservoir, Rains County, Texas. *Archaeology Series No. 4.* Department of Anthropology, University of Texas, Austin.

FRISON, GEORGE C.
1979 Observations on the Use of Stone Tools: Dulling of Working Edges of Some Chipped Stone Tools in Bison Butchering. In *Lithic Use-Wear Analysis,* edited by Brian Hayden, pp. 259–268. Academic Press, New York.

GILLET-LAUMONT, F. P. N.
1960 Extract from a Report by Citizen Salivet on the Making of Gunflints in the Departments of Indre and Loir-et-Cher. (Reprint of 1797 article.) *The Missouri Archeologist* 22:62–69.

GIRARD, JEFF SCOTT
1982 The Chipped Stone Collection from the Deshazo Site (41NA27): A Technological, Functional, and Typological Analysis. Unpublished M. A. thesis, Department of Anthropology, University of Texas, Austin.

HAMILTON, T. M.
1960 Additional Comments on Gunflints. *The Missouri Archaeologist* 22:73–79.
1964 Recent Developments in the Use of Gunflints for Dating and Identification. In *Diving into the Past, Theories, Techniques and Applications of Underwater*

Archaeology, edited by June D. Holmquist and Ardis H. Wheeler, pp. 52–58. Proceedings of a Conference on Underwater Archaeology. Minnesota Historical Society and the Council of Underwater Archaeology, St. Paul.
1979 Guns, Gunflints, Balls and Shot. In *Tunica Treasure,* edited by Jeffery P. Brain, pp. 206–216. Papers of the Peabody Museum of Archaeology and Ethnology, Vol. 71. Peabody Museum of Archaeology and Ethnology, Cambridge, Massachusetts.

HAMILTON, T. J., AND K. O. EMERY
1988 Eighteenth-Century Gunflints from Fort Michilimackinac and Other Colonial Sites. *Archaeological Completion Report Series* 13. Mackinac Island State Park Commission, Mackinac Island, Michigan.

HAMILTON, T. M., AND BRUCE W. FRY
1975 A Survey of Louisbourg Gunflints. *Occasional Papers in Archaeology and History* 12:101–128. National Historic Parks and Sites Branch, Parks Canada, Ottawa, Canada.

HANSON, LEE, AND DICK PING HSU
1975 Casemates and Cannonballs, Archaeological Investigations at Fort Stanwix, Rome, New York. *Publications in Archaeology 14.* National Park Service, Washington, D.C.

JOHNSON, LEROY, JR.
1957 *Appraisal of the Archeological Resources of Iron Bridge Reservoir, Hunt, Rains and Van Zandt Counties, Texas.* River Basin Surveys, National Park Service, Washington, D.C.

KEELEY, LAWRENCE H.
1980 *Experimental Determination of Stone Tool Uses, a Microwear Analysis.* University of Chicago Press, Chicago.

KENMOTSU, NANCY
1987 The Mayhew Site, 41NA21, a Possible Hasinai Caddo Farmstead in Bayou Loco, Nacogdoches County, Texas. Manuscript on file at the Texas Archeological Research Laboratory, University of Texas, Austin.

LENK, T.
1965 *The Flintlock: Its Origin and Development.* Bramball House, New York.

ODELL, GEORGE H.
1981 The Mechanics of Use-Breakage of Stone Tools: Some Testable Hypotheses. *Journal of Field Archaeology* 8:197–209.

ODELL, GEORGE H., AND FREIDA ODELL-VEREECKEN
1980 Verifying the Reliability of Lithic Use-Wear Assessments by 'Blind Tests': The Low Power Approach. *Journal of Field Archaeology* 7:97–120.

PATTERSON, PATIENCE E.
1978 A Lithic Reduction Sequence, a Test Case in the

North Fork Reservoir Area, Williamson County, Texas. *Bulletin of the Texas Archeological Society* 48:53–82. Austin.

ROSEBUSH, WALDO E.
1962 *American Firearms and the Changing Frontier.* Eastern Washington State Historical Society, Spokane.

SKERTCHLY, SYDNEY B.J.
1984 *The Manufacture of Gunflints.* (Reprint of 1879 edition.) Museum Restoration Service, Alexandria Bay, New York.

STONE, LYLE
1974 *Fort Michilimackinac 1715–1781, an Archaeological Perspective on the Revolutionary Frontier.* Publications of the Museum, Michigan State University, East Lansing.

TRINGHAM, RUTH, GLENN COOPER, GEORGE ODELL, BARBARA VOYTEK, AND ANNE WHITMAN
1974 Experimentation in the Formation of Edge Damage: A New Approach to Lithic Analysis. *Journal of Field Archaeology* 1:171–196.

WITTHOFT, JOHN
1966 A History of Gunflints. *Pennsylvania Archaeologist* 36:12–49.

WOODWARD, ARTHUR
1960 Some Notes on Gunflints. *The Missouri Archaeologist* 22:29–39.

NANCY KENMOTSU
TEXAS HISTORICAL COMMISSION
P.O. BOX 12276
AUSTIN, TEXAS 78711

Appendix A: Gunflint Specimen Descriptions

The following table provides descriptions of individual gunflint specimens. The table format was chosen for easy reference and to reduce bulk. Categories are: specimen number, provenience (if any), length, width, thickness, color, source, and reduction comments. While categories are self explanatory, some explanation of the data presented is in order. Specimen numbers for the Pearson and Gilbert gunflints reflect actual numbers on the artifacts. In both sets of numbers duplicates exist. The only way to compensate for the duplication was to use the same order consistently. Hence the order in the table is mirrored in the photographs of each sample. Numbers for modern flints are arbitrary; all but Bement's will be put on file at the University of Texas at Austin (UT) for future gunflint researchers. Length, width, and thickness are all in millimeters. It should be noted that, contrary to 18th-century practices, the length is the distance from the heel to the working edge, rather than the distance from side to side. Too, for native-made gunflints, length versus width is quite arbitrary, as several margins were often utilized.

Source material for European gunflints is based upon modern purchased samples and upon descriptions and photographs in Hamilton (1960), Witthoft (1966), and Hamilton and Fry (1975). Source material for native-made specimens was determined by comparing each specimen with UT mineralogical samples, and by the assistance of Larry Banks. Where the specimen was concluded to match a sample at UT, the mineralogical sample number is provided below the named source. Although a number of archaeological specimens state "unknown" as their source material, other lithic artifacts in the Gilbert or Pearson site collections on file at UT were produced from the same source material, reinforcing the conclusion that the specimens were native-made.

Reduction comments provide data concerning both overall general methods used to form each gunflint and any evidence of edge retouch. Where possible, percussion versus pressure flaking is noted. When dorsal versus ventral surfaces can be discerned, descriptions use these terms; where indiscernible just the term surface is employed. The term gunflint is restricted to the snap blade specimens, gunspall is restricted to the wedge-shaped English banded flint from Pearson, and flake is used to identify all non-European specimens. While not entirely satisfactory, this system was used to try to reduce confusion.

INDIVIDUAL SPECIMEN DESCRIPTIONS

SPECIMEN	PROVENIENCE	LENGTH (mm)	WIDTH (mm)	THICKNESS (mm)	COLOR	SOURCE	REDUCTION COMMENTS
41RA5 (PEARSON SITE)							
?-11	Surface	23	31	8	Gray with faint white mottling	Ouachita Mountains (Banks 1988. pers. comm.)	Flake from hard hammer percussion: bulb of percussion still evident on heel; no bifacial thinning of original flake; bifacial percussion retouch along irregular working edge; unifacial pressure flaked retouch along dorsal surface of one margin.
87-5	Surface	23	23	7	Buff with reddish inclusions	Ouachita Mountains (Banks 1988. pers. comm.)	Secondary flakes with central channel removed on ventral surface: all but two margins of dorsal surface covered with cortex; one small soft hammer platform present on another margin with only unifacial retouch; remnant bulb of percussion may be present on heel, but evidence is equivocal; may not be gunflint.
66-1	Surface	21	21	7	Tan with gray inclusions	Ouachita Mountains? (Banks 1988. pers. comm.)	Flake produced by percussion with part of bulb of percussion removed from heel; wedge-shaped, sub-rectangular in plan view. margins and working edge bifacially retouched by pressure flaking: size and overall shape may indicate this is a fire flint.
?-11	Surface	18	20	7	Banded tan and gray	English? John's Valley Shale? (Blaine 1987. pers. comm.; Banks 1988. pers. comm.)	Gunspall or flake: wedge-shaped with hard hammer bulb of percussion on ventral surface; relatively flat dorsal surface. unifacial percussion retouch along heel and one thick margin. light irregular pressure retouch along other two margins

(continued)

INDIVIDUAL SPECIMEN DESCRIPTIONS

SPECIMEN	PROVENIENCE	LENGTH (mm)	WIDTH (mm)	THICKNESS (mm)	COLOR	SOURCE	REDUCTION COMMENTS
47-1	Surface	24	26	7	Black	Brandon, England	Gunflint produced from proximal end of blade; retains hard hammer bulb of percussion with eraillure scar; another margin exhibits snap fracture with hinge; dorsal surface has single ridge or flake scar; heel has small flake scars alternating from dorsal to ventral surface (probably from filing); working edge has no intentional retouch.
41RA19 (GILBERT SITE)							
120	Fea 3	19	23	7	Blue gray	Ouachita Mountains? (Banks 1988, pers. comm.)	Octagonal shaped flake with overall bifacial reduction; bifacial pressure retouch on all margins; compression rings in central area of ventral surface.
110	Fea 3	20	23	9	Brown	Ouachita Mountains (Banks 1988, pers. comm.)	Relatively thick flake, roughly triangular in outline and wedge-shaped in cross section; irregular bifacial pressure flaking along margins; hertzian cone, unrelated to gunflint production, present in central area of one surface; no overall bifacial thinning.
94	Fea 3	20	23	7	Brown	Ouachita Mountains (Banks 1988, pers. comm.)	Flake without bifacial overall thinning; wedge-shaped; irregular bifacial percussion retouch present along all margins and surfaces; two thin margins appear to be working edges and have bifacial pressure retouch.
94	Fea 3	20	28	8	Tan/gray with white mottling	Ouachita Mountains, possibly John's Valley Shale (Banks 1988, pers. comm.)	Fairly thick flake with soft hammer platform at one end; bulb mostly removed; oblong in outline, no

							overall bifacial thinning; relatively flat dorsal surface; unifacial percussion flakes removed from all margins of dorsal surface.
208	Fea 7	21	22	9	Yellow gray	Georgetown (M41TV1); or Ouachita Mountains (Banks 1988, pers. comm.)	Sub-rectangular flake with overall bifacial thinning; may have old platform on one corner margin; one corner has aborted attempt to remove thick marginal area with a wrap-around flake; all margins bifacially pressure flaked for thinning.
9	Fea. 15	21	23	6	Light gray	Ouachita Mountains (Banks 1988, pers. comm.)	Sub-rectangular thin flake with bifacial retouch along three margins; roughly plano-convex in plan view; one margin is thick and contains evidence of old platform scars unrelated to the removal of this flake from its core.
981	Fea 3	17	26	7	Gray brown	John's Valley Shale (Banks 1988, pers. comm.)	Sub-rectangular flake; convex in cross section; cortex present along two margins; upper surface exhibits overall percussion reduction with fine, parallel pressure retouch along the two available margins; inferior surface has remnants of large percussion flake removal and fine parallel pressure along the long margin; the other usable margin exhibits single linear wrap-around or burin-like flake removed along entire margin, perhaps in re-sharpening attempt

(continued)

INDIVIDUAL SPECIMEN DESCRIPTIONS

SPECIMEN	PROVENIENCE	LENGTH (mm)	WIDTH (mm)	THICKNESS (mm)	COLOR	SOURCE	REDUCTION COMMENTS
181	Fea. 5	19	16	4	Tan gray	John's Valley Shale (Banks 1988, pers. comm.)	Sub-rectangular flake with overall bifacial reduction; some evidence of compression rings on one surface; very fine bifacial pressure flaking on all four margins.
134	Fea. 4	17	21	5	White	Ouachita Mountains (Banks 1988, pers. comm.)	Sub-rectangular flake with overall bifacial thinning; some faint compression rings on one surface; all margins bifacially pressure retouched and one margin deliberately rounded (perhaps for a heel?).
117	Fea. 3	23	21	6	White/tan	Ouachita Mountains (Banks 1988, pers. comm.)	Sub-rectangular flake with overall bifacial reduction, rings of compression evident in central portion of one surface; parallel bifacial retouch on all four margins.
281	Fea. 3	22	25	6	Pinkish gray	Ouachita Mountains (Banks 1988, pers. comm.)	Bifacially thinned flake with some faint compression rings on one surface; all margins bifacially pressure retouched; convex; sub-rectangular in outline; one corner has large flake removed, possibly from shovel, based on its relatively fresh appearance.
29	Fea. 3	19	25	6	Blue gray	Ouachita Mountains, possibly John's Valley Shale (Banks 1988, pers. comm.)	Sub-rectangular cortical flake with overall bifacial thinning; heel has brown cortex; other three margins exhibit bifacial pressure retouch.
281	Fea. 3	20	21	11	Gray	Georgetown (M41CM1 or M41CM2), or Ouachita Mountains (Banks 1988, pers. comm.)	Sub-rectangular flake with overall bifacial reduction; some cortex present on one surface; one point of which in center causes the thickness

							measurement; all margins bifacially pressure flaked.
197	Fea. 7	18	24	6	Gray blue	John's Valley Shale (Banks 1988, pers. comm.)	Sub-rectangular flake with overall bifacial thinning; small area of cortex on central portion of one surface; all margins bifacially pressure retouched with parallel flake removal.
27-14	Fea. 3	18	26	8	Honey-color with chalk heel	France	Probable blade gunflint with what may be two ridges formed by flake scars on dorsal surface; quasi-prismatic in cross section; percussion retouch on heel to form a steep bevel; pressure retouch on ventral surface of working edge.
152	Fea. 6	20	28	8	Honey-color	France	Probable blade gunflint with what may be two ridges formed by flake scars on dorsal surface; quasi-prismatic in cross section; ventral surface covered with percussion flake removals and light pressure flaking along left margin; may have shattered after only one to two firings.
134	Fea. 4	19	20	7	Honey-color with inclusions	France	Thick flake with irregular, bifacial retouch from a punch along margins; one margin has burin; another exhibits attempt to remove another burin; burins may be method of resharpening.

MODERN GUNFLINTS FROM LEE BEMENT

1	L. Bement	15	12	5	Clear	Unknown	Pistol gunflint cut with modern lapidary saw.

(continued)

INDIVIDUAL SPECIMEN DESCRIPTIONS

SPECIMEN	PROVENIENCE	LENGTH (mm)	WIDTH (mm)	THICKNESS (mm)	COLOR	SOURCE	REDUCTION COMMENTS
2	L. Bement	19	19	7	Tan	Georgetown Flint	Fairly thick, sub-rectangular flake with thick margins that have been retouched with hard hammer percussion using small quartzitic cobble; one percussion flake removed from ventral surface; knapped by Lee Bement.
3	L. Bement	20	15	9	Gray tan with faint white mottling	Ogallala cobble	Fairly thick, sub-rectangular flake with thick margins; cortex present on one margin, one large compression ring on one surface, percussion retouch used along margins; knapped by Lee Bement
4	L. Bement	17	11	6	Clear	Unknown	Pistol gunflint cut with modern lapidary saw
5	L. Bement	15	11	5	Clear/gray	Unknown	Pistol gunflint cut with modern lapidary saw
6	L. Bement	15	12	10	Blue gray	Georgetown Flint	Thin interior flake with bulb of percussion on ventral surface along with some concentric rings, both percussion and pressure flaking used on dorsal surface to thin flake and prepare thinner margins; knapped by Lee Bement.

OTHER MODERN GUNFLINTS

SPECIMEN	PROVENIENCE	LENGTH (mm)	WIDTH (mm)	THICKNESS (mm)	COLOR	SOURCE	REDUCTION COMMENTS
1	Pine Creek Rendezvous	22	20	7	Black	Brandon	Conventional rifle gunflint made from snap blade process; one dorsal ridge visible, another may be present but heel percussion retouch obscures the ridge; side margins exhibit manufacturing percussion

No.	Source				Color	Origin	Description
							retouch and filing largely obscuring snap fractures.
2	Pine Creek Rendezvous	24	16	5	Light brown with tan mottling	Germany	Rifle gunflint cut with modern lapidary saw
3	Pine Creek Rendezvous	17	19	6	Gray white	Ohio	Modern rifle gunflint manufactured in a mold and cut by lapidary type saw, has narrow medial ridge with two relatively uniform facets.
4	McBride's Guns, Austin	21	19	14	Gray banded	Brandon	Conventional rifle blade gunflint made from snap blade industry. ventral surface has remnant of one compression ring; white inclusion present on corner of margin of working edge; dorsal surface has one irregular ridge; if another ridge present, it has been obscured by pressure retouch along the heel. snap fractures on margins obscured by percussion retouch. impact scar present on one edge of medial ridge.
5	McBride's Guns, Austin	22	20	12	Tan with gray and black inclusions	Brandon	Very thick, irregular rifle gunflint possibly made from blade industry; ventral surface slightly convex, ridges very hard to define on dorsal surface, percussion retouch along all four margins.
6	McBride's Guns, Austin	31	30	16	Gray with tan inclusions	Brandon	Modern musket flint made from snap blade industry; ventral surface slightly convex with very fine pressure retouch along the working edge. side margins and heel of dorsal surface double backed or ridged.

(continued)

INDIVIDUAL SPECIMEN DESCRIPTIONS

SPECIMEN	PROVENIENCE	LENGTH (mm)	WIDTH (mm)	THICKNESS (mm)	COLOR	SOURCE	REDUCTION COMMENTS
7	McBride's Guns, Austin	19	17	11	Black	Brandon	aris lip present on one margin; working edge evidences no retouch. Conventional gunflint from snap blade industry; ventral surface slightly convex; dorsal surface with double ridges; heel and side margins' pressure retouch has removed some evidence of snap fractures.
8	McBride's Guns, Austin	22	21	13	Black	Brandon	Conventional gunflint from snap blade industry; ventral surface slightly convex; dorsal surface with double ridges; aris lip on one lateral margin snap; only heel exhibits pressure retouch, possibly to strengthen blade
9	McBride's Guns, Austin	24	23	17	Black	Brandon	Conventional gunflint from snap blade industry; ventral surface slightly convex; dorsal surface double ridged; aris lip on one marginal snap fracture; white cortex present along one-half the working edge.
10	McBride's Guns, Austin	34	30	16	Black	Brandon	Conventional musket gunflint from snap blade industry; ventral surface slightly convex and with concentric rings; very light retouch along the working edge. ventral surface; dorsal surface is double ridged; heel and two margins have been reduced through pressure retouch. aris lip visible on one marginal snap fracture.

JEFFREY A. BUTTERWORTH

Forming the Past

ABSTRACT

The water-logged components of five shoes from the 17th-century Nanny privy and one shoe and one boot from the 19th-century Mill Pond site were treated, shaped, and re-formed as part of the Central Artery Project. Four of the 17th-century shoes have an unusual square gap-toe and may have been made in Boston.

Introduction

The discoveries made possible by the Central Artery Project excavations at the Cross Street Back Lot Feature 4 (BOS-HA-13) and the Mill Pond site (BOS-HA-14) expand our knowledge of what people wore, both clothes and footwear, in historic Boston. Recovered along with textile fragments and botanical matter were the leather components of at least five shoes from the late 17th-century, as well as the pieces of a shoe and a boot from the late 18th and early 19th century

(Table 1). Footwear has a unique advantage in the realm of artifacts in that, while fashion alters the stylistic qualities of succeeding generations of shoes, the foot has not changed, and the requirements for its support and protection dictate footwear design. Everyone can relate to the experience of donning footwear both for protection and as some sort of fashion statement. While archaeologists and scientists are impressed by the survival of the proteinaceous fiber structures, or leather, in New England's environment, and shoe historians can rejoice in rare examples of quarters and uppers of the 17th century, the average person is more impressed by a relatively complete, three-dimensional object. The various leather components were reassembled into easily identifiable footwear artifacts, returned as near as possible to their original appearance, to give form to the past.

Conservation

The steps in reassembling the 17th-century shoes included: 1) drawing and photographing

TABLE 1
STRATIGRAPHIC LOCATION OF RECONSTRUCTED FOOTWEAR, FEATURE 4

Date MCD	TPQ	Subphase	Event	HN	Comments
		IV	Feature 1, late privy	92	
1745	1840	III	Close drain feature	98, 97	
1713	1670	II-3	Tub matrix	122	
1695	1700	II-2	Clay around tub drain	99, 91	
1697	1670	II-1	Percolation? fill	125	
1702	1670	I-10	Fecal deposit	100	6405-child's square gap-toe shoe w/4-hole vamp
		I-9	Construction	various	
1703	1690	I-8	Fecal deposit	146	6662A-adult's square gap-toe shoe
					6662C-child's square gap-toe shoe
					6580-young adult's or woman's roundtoe shoe
					6610-child's square gap-toe vamp
1699	1650	I-7	Privy modification & construction fill	149	
		I-6	Cleaning	164	
1695	1670	I-5	Fecal deposit	148	
		I-4	Cleaning	165	
1705	1630	I-3	Capping fill	151-153	
1699	1650	I-2	Fecal deposit	154	
		I-1	Privy construction	various	

Historical Archaeology, 1998, 32(3):91-98.
Permission to reprint required.

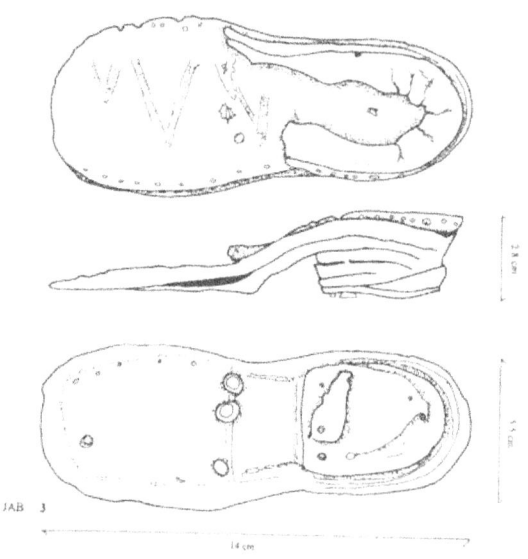

JAB 3

FIGURE 1 Ink renderings of the sole and heel of shoe
6662C (Cat. 36.089).

all components; 2) evaluation and historical placement of unassembled parts; 3) reshaping misshapen components; 4) creating the final mounts or forms; 5) adhering and assembling the components; and, 6) photographing the assembled objects and sketching speculation of missing pieces and original appearance. The procedures are chronological in that the information garnered from each step supplied knowledge and experience crucial to those that followed. All of the footwear was found in a water-logged condition in the Nanny privy and was treated with different molecular weights of polyethylene glycol (PEG) and freeze dried to relative shape by Doug Currie, objects conservator for the project. The pieces were stored in acid free boxes, transferred to the Textile Conservation Laboratory at the University of Rhode Island, and stored in a climate-controlled area.

All sixty-odd pieces of leather were studied and drawn in full scale with pencil. The convention of stippling represents a change of level. The pencil sketches were redrawn in ink (Figure

1). All of the pieces were photographed both on the flesh and hair sides, with close-ups of significant mechanical details or stylistic characteristics.

All known shoes with a 17th-century American provenience were located, studied, and photographed, such as the 1680 to 1710 shoe (No. 103,923) from the Peabody Essex Museum in Salem, Massachusetts, and the Leverett Shoe (No. 68,595) from the Museum of Fine Arts in Boston. Footwear from other archaeological contexts was sought. Photocopies of English, Dutch, French, and Italian paintings and prints of the 17th century were collected.

Sources for information concerning 17th-century shoemaking and tanning practices as well as the works of 20th-century scholars were located and studied. All of these sources helped to determine the original shapes of the Nanny privy shoes.

The leather components themselves also helped to determine the original shapes. The original stitch marks and in some cases original threads were still intact. Historically one of the steps in creating leather vamps and quarters (the single front and two back components that, when joined, comprise the upper of a shoe) was to wet the leather with water and partially shape them

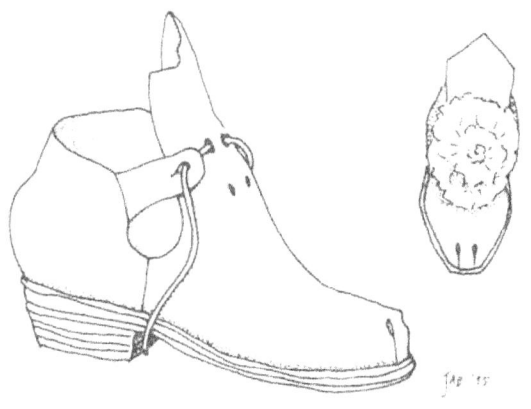

JAB '15

FIGURE 2 Ink sketch approximating original appearance of child's square gap-toe shoe 6405 (Cat. 36.089) with shoe bow.

with friction or heat on lapstones, large flat, round rocks (Hazard 1969:4). Moisture and heat cause the molecular structures of protein fibers to realign themselves into new positions that will not change until moisture and heat again are applied, much the same way that wool felt hats are blocked. The leather fragments from Feature 4 retained their original shapes on a molecular level. Softened with PEG and allowed to dry while supported by similar convex and concave curves carved of ethafoam, which acted as a cobbler's last, the pieces resumed their original shapes. Spontaneously created supports, such as small pebbles in protective plastic helped shape particularly difficult areas.

The shoes were reassembled with an ethyl methacrylate copolymer solution or "B-72." The leather that supported the original seams was fragile, and new skived-leather strips support the new center-back seam and quarter/vamp joins. The final ethafoam mounts were covered with the dull side of a brown silk crepe. Some of the forms are sectioned into three-parts to ensure future access to the artifact's inside. Once the shoes were assembled, images were drawn to approximate the footwear's original appearance (Figure 2). The two footwear artifacts from the early 19th-century Mill Pond site were treated with the same procedures as the artifacts from the Nanny privy.

Interpretation

One of the most important questions posed by the presence of the footwear found in the Nanny privy is one of origin. Early New England colonists had difficulty obtaining footwear. Captain John Smith wrote a letter to the Worshipful Society of Cordwainers of the City of London in 1624, pleading for experienced craftsmen to immigrate (Huntington Library 1946:20). Gleanings from Jay Mack Holbrook's (1980) *Boston Beginnings 1630-1699* suggest that some shoemakers heeded Smith's call and were rewarded with parcels of land. By 1647 several shoemakers had

banded together to form a company or guild, one of the first in the Colonies. Governor Winthrop accepted their charter in 1648 (Hazard 1969:171-173). The footwear produced in the Boston area was apparently inferior to that imported from England and elsewhere. The confederation of cordwainers was to regulate shoemaking and its charter was renewable in three years. The charter was renewed once in 1651 (Gannon 1912:12) but not again. Were the shoemakers of Boston capable of producing the Nanny family footwear? Research to answer this question is continuing.

The 17th-century shoes with American provenience extant in museums, for the most part, seem to have been imported into the country. All are very well-made, intricately constructed with exceptional detailing of fine leathers and luxury textiles, seemingly for a high-end market. Most are associated with legendary Colonial names and special events such as weddings. All were preserved and cherished as artifacts and eventually became part of museum or historical society collections.

The Nanny family shoes were found in a privy, and may manifest the stylistic characteristics of up to ten years prior to deposition. The leather used to create them is of a very high quality. Tanneries had been established in New York, Lynn, and Salem by 1640. The Nanny family had land in Barbados and were merchant-traders. Temple H. Croker (1765) in the 1764/5 edition of *The Complete Dictionary of Arts and Sciences* states "the operation of tanning is performed, on leather, better in the West Indies than in England." Perhaps the shoes, or at least their leather, came from the West Indies, signifying the owner's wealth and/or connections.

The footwear from the Nanny privy provides information concerning everyday 17th-century Bostonian foot fashion. When compared to other museum artifacts, the Nanny shoes, while of good quality leather, lack superfluous details, and maintain stylish elements. The fashionable characteristics manifested in the footwear appears to

FIGURE 3 Detail of vamp 6610 (Cat 36.086) featuring a
square gap-toe

neously is seen in Gerrand van den Eekhout's
"Four Officers of the Amsterdam Wine Coopers'
and Wine Racker's Guild" at the National Gallery in London.   Are the Nanny shoes physical
evidence of a missing link between the folded
toe and the pointed toe popular around 1700?
Or do they represent a parsimonious New
Englander's unique solution to a leather-wasting
popular style?

The components of shoe 6662A with a square
gap-toe (Figure 5) create an historically significant adult male's shoe from 1660 to 1680 (Figure 6).   The only other extant shoes from the

have been popular up to ten years prior to deposition, although the lag time of Colonial fashion
is not known.

Two of the shoes have a central vamp slash
that originated in the 16th century, but the most
curious stylistic element is the toe shape of four
of the shoes: a square gap-toe. Extensive research has not revealed another toe design like it.
This design feature is created by cutting two
equidistant triangular incisions on both sides of
the vamp's toe area (Figure 3).   The original
stitch marks indicate a butt to butt whip stitch (a
shallow diagonal stitch that joins two edges of
leather without seam allowance) that stops halfway up the triangular incisions. leaving a gap
above the stitching on both sides of the squarish
toe. A style popular during the second and third
quarters of the 17th century was the folded toe.
Contemporary portraits of children are one of the
only sources for good clear full-body depiction
including footwear (Figure 4).   The portraits of
the Mason children from the DeYoung Museum
in San Francisco; the National Park Service.
Adams Historical Site in Quincy, Massachusetts;
the Gibbs children from the Boston Museum of
Fine Arts; and private collections are all from the
Boston area in the 1670s. The children display
the stylish toe-shape variants, the folded toe and
the rounded toe, seemingly without gender differentiation.   Additional proof of different shoe
styles, round and folded toes, occurring simulta-

FIGURE 4   Portrait of Alice Mason. (Unknown. 1670.
courtesy of the National Park Service. Adams Historic Site.)

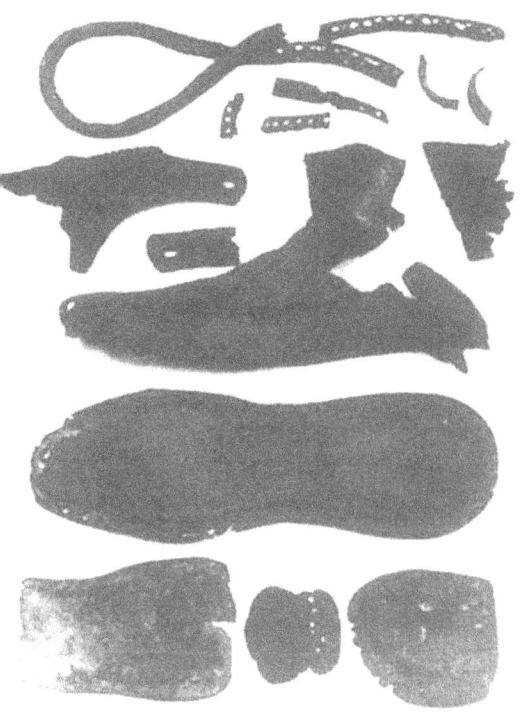

FIGURE 5. The leather components of shoe 6662A (Cat 36.088). Vamp dimensions: 20 cm side to side. 18.5 cm tongue to toe. Sole length: 24.9 cm.

period are the Boston Hotel site shoe (Bradley et al. 1983) and Sarah Coleman's shoe at the Memorial Hall Museum in Deerfield, Massachusetts, the latter is dated to 1677. Unfortunately, both of these shoes are incomplete in the toe area of the vamp. Shoe 6662A has a central vamp slash and the square gap-toe. The flaring tongue and the size of the side holes created by the join of the vamp and the quarter under the latchet (finger of leather extending from the quarter over the foot's arch usually supporting some sort mechanical closure: strap, ribbon, or buckle) support a date of around 1660 to 1670.

Was the adult shoe deposited in the privy because it had served its purpose? It is quite worn in the toe and sole, and the central slash had torn. The stylish quality of the shoe may indicate the taste of the intemperate, philandering Edward Naylor. J. D. de Saint-Jean's "Peasant from the Paris Region" (Bibliothèque National) depicts shoes that are similar to the adult Nanny shoe, but lack the square gap-toe. The deposit may date to the period when "Katherine Nanney alias Naylor" was dealing with the consequences of Naylor's flight to Maine with the pregnant

FIGURE 6. Adult male shoe 6662A of about 1670. Important stylistic elements are the latchets, side holes, central vamp slash, flaring tongue, and the square gap-toe. Sole length: 24.9 cm.

FIGURE 7 Child's shoe 6405 (Cat. 36.089) of about 1660 to 1670. Important stylistic elements are the flared tongue, square gap-toe, and the four latchet holes. Sole length 17.3 cm.

Mary Read—a good time to dispose of an old, but telling piece of footwear. On the other hand, Katherine's first husband, Robert Nanny, died in 1663; perhaps she waited ten years to dispose of her first husband's shoe.

The pieces of leather that filled bag number 6662C, 6405, and vamp 6610 (Figure 3), are all from children's shoes (Figure 7). The vamp (6610) has similar stylistic characteristics to the adult male shoe previously discussed: central vamp slashing and a square gap-toe. Shoe 6662C had the square gap-toe, but the tongue is square, not flared, with two latchet holes for a leather lace. Child's shoe 6405 had a square gap-toe and a tongue with more flare. It sports four vamp holes. The purpose behind the four holes is indicated by the Josiah Winslow baby shoes at The Pilgrim Hall Museum in Plymouth, Massachusetts, which date from 1600 to 1625. The top two holes are slightly almond-shaped from wear, and the bottom two holes are round, suggesting that while the top two holes were used as part of the latchet/closure mechanism, the bottom two holes were used to attach a decorative shoe rosette (Figure 2). The shoe rosette

was fashionable until the buckle replaced it about 1660. Samuel Pepys first put buckles to his shoes in January of 1660 (Pepys 1893:20). The Harris Number indicates that Bag 6405 was deposited at a later date than the other 17th-century shoes, but the shoe may be stylistically slightly earlier.

The death dates of all the children of Katherine Nanny were not obtainable, but only two of her eight children survived. Often, children's shoes are saved if they are not completely worn through, to be used by other children. Children's shoes also may be preserved for emotional reasons. David Hackett Fischer in *Albion's Seed* suggests that Puritan death ways included sustained grief for "constructive spiritual purposes" (Fischer 1989:114). Perhaps Katherine Nanny-Naylor saved her dead children's shoes until an emotional connection was no longer necessary, which explains the wide-range of stylistic elements.

The components of Bag 6580 assembled into a young adult and possibly female shoe (Figure 8). This shoe is very different from the other shoes from Feature 4; it is not particularly stylish and is the only shoe of the group with the practical skin-side-out finish; all of the other shoes have a suede finish. This style, or lack of style, creates problems in dating. This type of shoe is basic and appears in the paintings of Abel Grimmer (*Winter*, 1607) and the etchings of Jacques Callot (*Various Figures*, between 1617 and 1623) and

FIGURE 8 Young adult and possibly female shoe 6580 of around 1670. Important stylistic elements are the rounded toe, latchet closure, and a triangular tongue. Sole length 19 cm

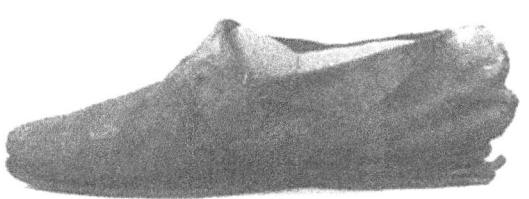

FIGURE 9. Adult male shoe of 1794 to 1805. Important stylistic elements are the pointed toe, tie closure, and pentagonal tongue. Sole length: 27.5 cm.

was worn by both males and females. This style continued as a plain shoe into the early decades of the 19th century and its echoes can be seen in current shoe styles. It is related to the non-provenienced male shoe from the Mill Pond site. It could have belonged to Katherine Nanny-Naylor, or one of the servants, including Mary Read, the servant accused of poisoning Katherine Nanny—since it was deposited around 1672.

Two footwear artifacts, a shoe (non-provenience) and a boot (Bag 8323)) from the Mill Pond site were selected for restoration. The leather components formed a shoe that stylistically dates from 1794 to 1805 (Figure 9). Both artifacts are from the Mill Pond Phase IV which is material from the filling of Mill Pond which started in this area in 1806 and ended by 1809. The fill could have come from anywhere in the Boston area. The 1802 portrait *Ephriam Starr* from the Wadsworth Athenaeum in Hartford, Connecticut, depicts a man wearing similar shoes. The Historical Society of Old Newbury has a similar, finer quality shoe from the later 1810 to 1820 period with a less pointed toe. The leather used to create the shoes is thick and of a quality that hints at moderate to meager means. The loose fit suggests a term associated with whaler's footwear—slip shod, or, quite literally, slipper shod.

The other leather components (Bag 8323) from the Mill Pond site formed a man's stylish boot dating from 1805 to 1813 (Figure 10). Specifically, it is a Wellington boot, a style popularized by the Duke of Wellington during the Napoleonic campaigns. A Wellington boot has seams on the sides as opposed to front and back seams. Men's boots were custom-made and were an expensive and important male accessory. This is a very well-made boot of fine leather. Many graphics represent gentlemen's boots from the first decade of the 19th century. A "Tammany" cartoon from 1800 at the New York Public Library, depicts a fashionable male attired in Cupid's-bow-top boots like that from Mill Pond. *Nathan Hawley and Family* painted in 1801, from the Albany Institute of History and Art, shows Mr. Hawley in boots with a top variation and extremely pointed toes, which were not as practical as the more rounded toe of boot 8323.

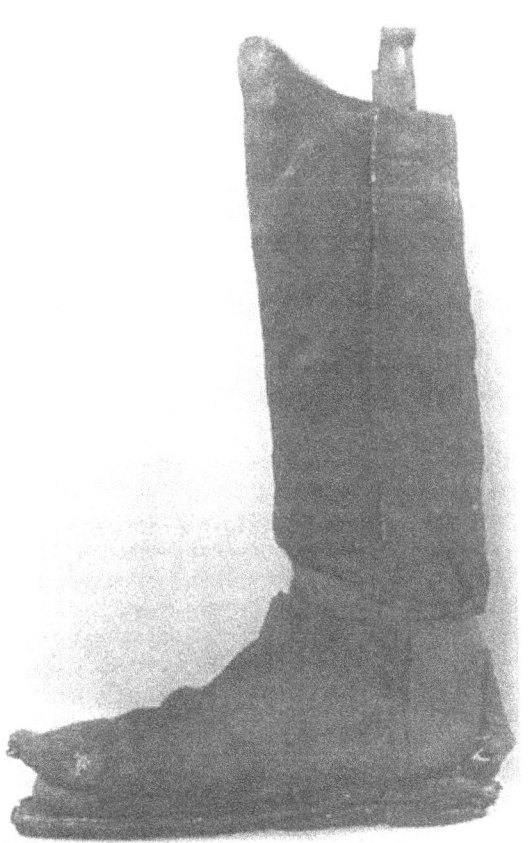

FIGURE 10. Adult male Wellington boot 8323 from 1805 to 1813. Important stylistic elements are the Cupid's bow top, side seams, and the slightly pointed toe. Sole length: 24 cm.

The less pointed toe also indicates a date of origin after 1805. The wide variety of boot styles available is clear in the 1807 *Shoeing Asses* (Northampton Museum, UK), drawn by the artist Isaac Cruikshank.

Conclusion

The shoes found in the 17th-century Nanny privy are some of the earliest extant examples of American-made footwear. The five restored shoes are sophisticated and divers in their design, representing both high and common styles. The footwear from the 19th-century Mill Pond site is also a study in contrasts: the large working man's shoe and the elegant boot of a gentleman. All of the footwear artifacts contribute to the understanding of people and their times. Most everyone has footwear experience and, while the styles represented by these artifacts are vastly different and from different times, "putting our feet in their shoes" can make those eras compellingly accessible. Shaping and assembling the footwear artifacts from the Central Artery Project close to the original appearances enhances that accessibility by giving form to the past.

ACKNOWLEDGMENTS

This was an internship project in partial fulfillment of a Master's degree with an emphasis in Textile Conservation from the Department of Textiles, Fashion Merchandising and Design, at the University of Rhode Island. I would especially like to thank Margaret Ordoñez of the University of Rhode Island, and Doug Currie of Timelines, Inc., the University of Connecticut, and the Mashantucket, Pequot Museum and Cultural Resource Center for their expertise, time and patience. I also would like to acknowledge: Mike Roberts and Martin Dudek of Timelines, Inc., Judith Dufault, Paula Richter, and the Peabody Essex Museum, Claudia Iannuccilli and the Boston Museum of Fine Arts; Karen Goldstein and the Plymouth Pilgrim Hall Museum; Suzanne Flint and the Memorial Hall Museum, Pocumtuck Valley Memorial Association; Judith McAlister and the National Park Service, Adams Historic Site; Trevor Johnson and the Boston Athenaeum; and the Massachusetts Historical Society.

REFERENCES

BRADLEY, JAMES W., NEILL DePAOLI, NANCY SEASHOLES, PATRICIA McDOWELL, GERALD KELSO, AND JOHANNA SCHOSS
    1983   Archaeology of the Bostonian Hotel Site. *Occasional Publications in Archaeology and History* 2. Massachusetts Historical Commission, Boston.

CROKER, TEMPLE H., THOMAS WILLIAMS, AND SAMUEL CLARK
    1765   *The Complete Dictionary of Arts and Sciences*, Vol. 2. Published by the authors, London.

FISCHER, DAVID HACKETT
    1989   *Albion's Seed: Four British Folkways in America*. Oxford University Press, Oxford, England.

GANNON, FRED A.
    1912   *A Short History of American Shoemaking*. Fred A. Gannon, Salem, MA.

HAZARD, BLANCHE EVANS
    1969   *The Organization of the Boot and Shoe Industry in Massachusetts Before 1875*. Reprint of the 1921 edition. Augustus M. Kelley, New York.

HOLBROOK, JAY MACK
    1980   *Boston Beginnings 1630-1699*. Holbrook Research Institute, Oxford, MA.

HUNTINGTON LIBRARY
    1946   *Newes from the New-World*. Friends of the Huntington Library, Pasadena, CA.

PEPYS, SAMUEL
    1893   *The Diary of Samuel Pepys*, Vol. 1, edited by Henry B. Wheatley. Random House, New York.

Jeffrey A. Butterworth
Community College of Rhode Island
400 East Avenue
Warwick, RI 02886-1807

JAMES P. P. HORN

"The Bare Necessities:" Standards of Living in England and the Chesapeake, 1650–1700

ABSTRACT

The domestic environment had a profound influence on the texture of everyday life in early modern England and America not only in terms of family interaction but also as a tangible reflection of broader social attitudes towards hierarchy, status and consumerism. This article compares standards of living in England and the Chesapeake between 1650 and 1700. Three regions are analyzed in detail: the Vale of Berkeley, Gloucestershire; St. Mary's County, Maryland; and part of the Northern Neck of Virginia. It is argued that a comparison of material culture and living standards reveals important aspects of the advantages and disadvantages of emigrating from England to the Chesapeake, and suggests significant differences between the two societies in this period.

Introduction

What were the gains and losses involved for the tens of thousands of men and women who left England in the 17th century to live "beyond the seas" in the Chesapeake colonies of Maryland and Virginia? Many factors influenced immigrants' adaptation to their new society: their own backgrounds, the environment they encountered, the timing of their arrival, the ebb and flow of the tobacco economy, and plain luck. This paper investigates one aspect of adaptation through a comparison of standards of living reflected in the household inventories of selected communities in England and the Chesapeake. It will focus on items of material culture not normally recovered by archaeologists, but which were central in determining the quality of life experienced by settlers. Analysis of probate inventories not only provides a means of drawing broad comparisons of living standards across time and place (Shammas 1980, 1982; Main 1982; Carr and Walsh 1985), but also suggests exciting possibilities for co-operation between historians and archaeologists engaged in the study of material culture in early America.

Standards of living, as examined in this paper, relate to the dwellings and domestic furnishings of householders who have been divided into five wealth groups: less than £10, £10–£49, £50–£99, £100–£249, £250 and over. Wealth is defined as the sum total of a decedent's moveable estate, including debts receivable; land is not included (Horn 1981; Main 1982; Carr and Walsh 1978, 1985). No attempt is made to assess living standards using other criteria, for example, work patterns, health or recreational opportunities. This paper is concerned only with the domestic environment. Dividing households of both societies into the same wealth categories raises problems about comparability. Does a person worth £100 in England occupy roughly the same social position as a person worth the same amount in Maryland or Virginia? Are we comparing like with like? Adjustments have been made for differing exchange rates, as will be explained later, but the subjective problem of comparison remains. It was decided to adopt the same wealth groups for the English and Chesapeake data because using different categories would raise even greater problems of comparability. Since these categories are approximations of social status, rather than precise definitions, distortions caused by this approach should not invalidate general conclusions.

Three regions are analyzed in detail: the Vale of Berkeley, Gloucestershire; St. Mary's County, Maryland; and Lancaster and Northumberland counties, Virginia. Two characteristics of the Vale of Berkeley make it suitable for this analysis (Figure 1). First, the Vale is representative of one of the main types of community from which colonists emigrated, that is, a wood-pasture district in the southern half of England (Horn 1979; Salerno 1979). Conclusions drawn from an analysis of living conditions in the Vale can be placed in the wider context of woodland parishes within Bristol's hinterland. Secondly, compared to other rural areas in England, the region provided large

FIGURE 1 Location of the Vale of Berkeley in England

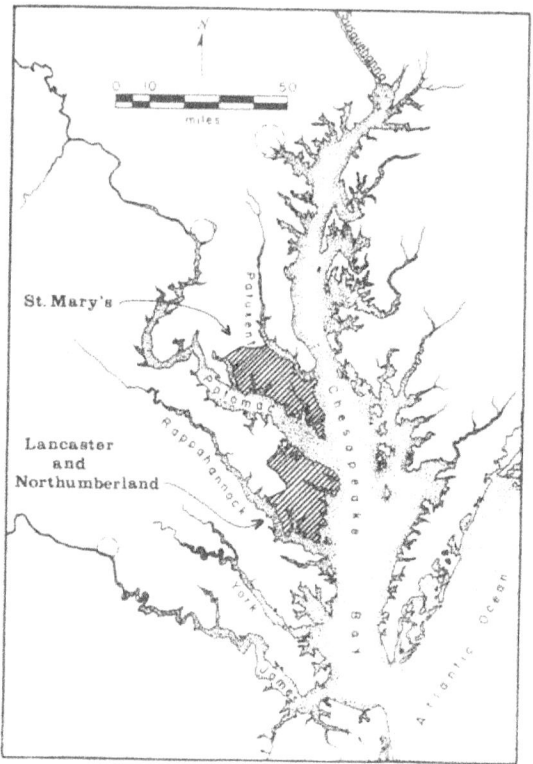

FIGURE 2 The Chesapeake Region showing the locations of St. Mary's County, Maryland and Lancaster and Northumberland Counties, Virginia

numbers of emigrants to the Chesapeake in the 17th century; several hundred between 1619 and 1690. The great majority of these were indentured servants who emigrated from Bristol during the second half of the century but there were also significant numbers of free emigrants who were connected to Bristol's mercantile community.

Because there is insufficient evidence to link the geographical origins of English immigrants in particular Chesapeake communities, two regions with especially complete local records were chosen as representative of mainstream social and economic developments along the tobacco coast (Figure 2). St. Mary's County, Maryland is one of the most intensely studied areas of the colonial Tidewater (St. Mary's City Commission). During the middle decades of the century, immigrants poured into the region from London, Bristol and other ports. Low to medium quality tobacco was produced locally and the county appears, on the

basis of both historical and archaeological evidence, to have had close links with Bristol merchants (Harris 1978; Miller 1983:83). Lancaster and Northumberland counties had closer ties with London merchants, but Bristol ships also traded along the Rappahannock and Potomac rivers. The region was a major receptor of immigrants in the 1650s and 1660s and produced medium to high grade leaf (Morgan 1975:227–28). No claim is made that these areas represent the entire range of regional variation in the early Chesapeake. Virginia and Maryland historians are aware of significant differences in local economic and social structures. However, while it is important not to overlook local variation, there can be little doubt that society in St. Mary's County and in the

Northern Neck had much in common with other major tobacco producing regions in terms of environment, economic base and social development.

Sources

Probate inventories comprise the most important data source in this study. Four hundred and eighty inventories were analyzed for the Vale of Berkeley, 372 for St. Mary's County, and 150 for Lancaster and Northumberland. Using probate records in a comparative context poses a number of technical difficulties relating to provenience and consistency of data across the three inventoried populations. At best, only about 30 percent of all adult male decedents from the Vale, who died between 1660 and 1700, are represented by an inventory. Periodically the proportion is far lower, and there are also considerable fluctuations from one parish to another (Horn 1981). As far as English probate sources are concerned, there is nothing unusual about this. Most communities have only a fifth to a quarter of all decedents appearing in probate records. Poorer groups in early modern England are grossly underrepresented and hence most of the surviving evidence relates to middling and wealthy householders (Riden 1985:18).

Inventory coverage was much higher in Maryland during the second half of the 17th century, possibly about 70 percent of the total decedent population (Menard 1976). People at all levels of society in Maryland appear to have been more assiduous than their English counterparts in having inventories drawn up for their kin, friends, or debtors (Carr and Walsh 1978). There are no reliable estimates for Virginia, but coverage appears closer to the English level than that of her sister colony.

In both England and the Chesapeake, probate inventories followed a similar format: a list with valuations of the decedent's clothes, household possessions, livestock, crops or shopwares, and debts receivable. Apart from leasehold properties, real estate is rarely mentioned and was not required to be included (Horn 1981:82; Main 1975:89–99).

In both societies the production of an inventory was an essential step in the process of proving a will or administration, and was designed to reduce the likelihood of embezzlement of the deceased's estate. Probate was supervised by the Church courts in England until the 19th century, and by secular county and prerogative courts in Maryland and Virginia (Main 1982:48–49).

Although there are a good many similarities in the form of inventories in England and the Chesapeake, there are also some notable differences. The importance of bound labor in colonial society is reflected by the high levels of planter investment in servants and slaves, which in monetary value sometimes comprised the bulk of an estate. Secondly, whereas valuations in English inventories are always in pounds sterling, in Maryland and Virginia various currencies were used, the most common being tobacco. Comparison of the price of particular items is further complicated by different exchange rates which fluctuated throughout the colonial period. To control these variations, all valuations in tobacco have been converted to sterling equivalents using Russell R. Menard's data on tobacco prices throughout the 17th century (Menard 1975: 465–79). Inflation and fluctuations in exchange rates were adjusted using data supplied by the St. Mary's City Commission. Wealth levels and values of individual items are standardized to the English rate of exchange.

Thirdly, Chesapeake inventories are frequently more detailed than English sources. It was customary in England for appraisers to value commodities of small worth together under general categories such as "For things unseen or forgotten" and "other old lumber." Small items, such as knives and spoons, or relatively inexpensive goods such as earthenware appear in Chesapeake inventories with much greater frequency than in the English sample. Undoubtedly householders in England owned these items, but they went largely unrecorded. Firm conclusions therefore can only be drawn from comparisons of goods that were normally included in inventories in both England and the Tidewater. These items are furniture, cooking equipment, linen and cloth, and expensive possessions.

Finally, English and Chesapeake inventoried

populations reflect the different age structures of the two societies. On average, men and women living along the tobacco coast died ten years earlier than adults in England (Walsh and Menard 1974; Smith 1978; Rutman and Rutman 1979). They therefore had less time to accumulate household goods and other possessions. Relatively short life spans account, in part, for the poverty exhibited in the inventories of most 17th century settlers (Main 1982:49).

Dwellings

The Vale of Berkeley was an important pasture-farming district in the 17th century and had much in common with dairying regions in Hampshire, Wiltshire, Dorset and Somerset (Thirsk 1967). Characterized by numerous family farms, scattered settlement and a good deal of rural manufacture, the Vale was considered a particularly fertile area (Smyth 1889:4; Defoe 1971:364). Although much of the region was enclosed, there were still pockets of commonland, generally on marginal soils, where villagers raised cattle and sheep. Availability of commons was vital to smallholders who earned a living partly from farming and partly from various by-employments, notably woollen manufacture (de Lacy Mann 1971; Perry 1945; Smyth 1902).

Housing in the region was characterized above all by diversity. In the upper part of the Severn valley, timberframe dwellings in the square-panelled tradition of the West Midlands remained common throughout the 17th and early 18th centuries (Hey 1974:122; Smith 1985;691). Further south, stone and rubble were the most common building materials, with bricks being generally reserved for chimneys. Roofing was usually of stone, tiles or thatch (Hall 1983:1, 3, 29, 33–34). Dwellings with a through-passage were the dominant type until the mid-17th century but thereafter, as rebuilding went on apace, other floor plans were adopted or adapted to suit local needs. Within the three basic types found in the area—through-passage, central-passage and no-passage—there

were literally scores of different floor plans (Hall 1983).

Little evidence survives about the dwellings of the poorest people living in the region. The most rudimentary were shacks and hovels erected on commons, heaths and woodlands which housed itinerant laborers and vagrants. A squatter's cottage dating from the late 17th or early 18th centuries found in the parish of Iron Acton, just north of Bristol, measured 10-foot square and had two stories (Hall 1983: 183–84). Eighteen cottages erected on wasteland in Urchfont, Wiltshire, in the late 16th and early 17th centuries ranged in size from 10 by 18 feet to 15 by 15. The average was fourteen by ten feet (Bettey 1983: 28–30).

It is improbable that these tiny, and often flimsy, structures were numerous by the post-Restoration period. It has been suggested that the two or three-roomed cottage was the smallest form of housing common in central and southern England in this period (Barley 1967: 762). Inventory evidence, although slight, bears out this view. Of 10 people who died in the Vale of Berkeley between 1660 and 1700 worth less than £10, 4 lived in two rooms, 2 in three rooms, 1 in four rooms and 3 in five rooms. The mean average was 3.3 rooms. People living in two rooms may have inhabited shacks such as those described above but, more likely, lived in parts of bigger tenements. Agricultural laborers from the Frampton Cotterell area, to the south of the Vale, usually lived in three-roomed cottages (Moore 1976: 35–36). Despite their small size (20 by 20 or 20 by 35 feet) such dwellings were often well constructed by local craftsmen and built to last (Hall 1983: 22).

The commonest housing in the region had between five and seven rooms. Two-thirds of the inhabitants who died worth £10 to £49 lived in dwellings of five or more rooms, while those worth £50 to £99 lived in houses of six to seven rooms. The mean number of rooms per house was 5.3 and 6.4 respectively. Room names provide clues to the layout of the dwellings. The larger number of different room names emphasizes the great variety of housing in the Vale but certain common features emerge. A 'typical' five-roomed house had a hall, kitchen and buttery on the ground floor and two chambers above, probably over the hall and kitchen. Larger dwellings usually had a hall, kitchen and buttery on the ground floor with three chambers over them, and possibly one or two lofts. Extra rooms did not necessarily imply greater domestic comfort since larger dwellings may have contained more storage rooms necessary for keeping foodstuffs, raw materials and working tools.

There was no sharp distinction between the dwellings of middling groups and those of rich householders. Parish gentry and substantial yeomen lived in houses of between eight and 15 rooms; wealthy retailers and artisans in dwellings of nine or 10 rooms. Many appear to have had a similar layout to smaller houses with the addition of a parlor, cellar, whitehouse, and extra lofts. They usually had more hearths, providing warmth and light to a larger range of chambers and ground floor rooms than in humbler structures. There was also greater potential for more specialized use of domestic space, but building materials and styles did not differ significantly from other housing. Only at the very pinnacle of society were differences in terms of style and size of dwellings striking. Smalcombe Court, owned by the Smyth family, stewards to the Lords Berkeley, had at least 27 rooms. Few but the county elite could afford to keep up with the latest fashions in architecture and ornamental gardens. Not only were their building materials different—dressed stone or brick—but the architecture owed as much to metropolitan taste as vernacular tradition.

A number of points from this brief survey of housing in the Vale of Berkeley are worth stressing. As in other parts of central and southern England, the medieval open hall house had given way during the 15th and 16th centuries to the multi-roomed, two story dwelling, allowing greater specialization in the use of domestic space and also more comfort (Smith 1985: 689–90). Apart from makeshift structures on wastes and in woodlands, the smallest houses were generally three-roomed cottages; sturdily built of local materials by village craftsmen. Most of the Vale's inhabitants, however, probably lived in larger dwellings of between four and seven rooms. Houses were made to last. Given reasonable maintenance they would stand for centuries. Built of rubble, stone, brick and tile, they were sufficiently well-constructed to be durable, but also sufficiently flexible in plan and structure to allow the addition of new rooms when necessary (Hall 1983).

The contrast with Chesapeake housing is stark. Typical Chesapeake dwellings were about 20 by 16 feet and, as Walsh points out, were very unlike vernacular buildings in England (Walsh 1977: 248–50). Settlers developed a structure appropriate to their needs and available materials. Houses were constructed entirely of wood with the whole of the outside covered with riven oak clapboards (Figure 3). Clapboards not only provided the exterior surface but also constituted an essential structural element of the dwelling. Such dwellings, termed "Virginia houses" by the third quarter of the 17th century, were easy and cheap to construct but did not last as long as English buildings (Carson 1974).

This latter aspect of Chesapeake housing has led some architectural historians to characterize the vernacular buildings of the region as "impermanent" (Carson, et al, 1981). "Tobacco barns and dwelling houses", says Walsh, "were intended by the builders to last only for a few years, and their construction was apparently such that it was almost invariably easier to put up a new building than to repair the old one" (Walsh 1977: 252). The nature of tobacco culture and land ownership also contributed to an "architecture of transience." When fields became exhausted, the owner sometimes simply moved to another part of the tract where a new dwelling could be quickly erected. The old building would be left to decay. Local building materials, the development of a distinctive Chesapeake form of architecture, ravages of climate, and the demands of tobacco culture all contributed to the short life-span of housing; perhaps no more than 20 to 25 years.

As far as domestic living standards are concerned, the most important aspect of the typical Chesapeake dwelling was its small size. The vast majority of houses had only one or two rooms.

FIGURE 3. Recreation of a 17th Century Chesapeake House in St. Mary's City, Maryland based upon historical, architectural and archaeological evidence.

Fewer than 50 out of a sample of over 1400 house-holders along the lower Western Shore of Maryland, between 1658 and 1705, owned dwellings with more than two rooms (St. Mary's City Commission). Except perhaps in summer when people could live partially outside, these were the physical constraints placed upon the daily domestic routine of the great bulk of planters. This factor in itself has a considerable bearing on a comparison of living standards in England and the Chesapeake.

Material Possessions of Poor and Lower-Middle Class Households Worth Less than £50

In both societies, poor and lower-middle class householders constituted the majority of the pop-ulation, accounting for about 60 percent of inhab-itants in the Vale and between 50 and 60 percent in Maryland and Virginia (Horn 1981:93, 101; forth-coming). There is little evidence concerning the standard of living of the very poor worth less than £10. In England, they included the aged, poor widows, paupers and laborers, but the vast major-ity did not go through probate (Horn 1981: 85–94). Planters who had not lived sufficiently long to get started or who had simply failed to make a living from growing tobacco comprise the majority of the very poor in the Chesapeake. Since the numbers are small, conclusions must remain tentative but the contrast between the Vale of Berkeley poor and the Maryland and Virginia samples is nevertheless striking. The most impres-sive feature of Table 1 is the difference in the proportions of people owning furniture in England

Table 1

STANDARDS OF LIVING OF HOUSEHOLDERS WORTH LESS THAN £50, VALE OF BERKELEY, GLOUCESTERSHIRE; ST. MARY'S COUNTY, MARYLAND; LANCASTER AND NORTHUMBERLAND COUNTIES, VIRGINIA, 1650-1700

Household	Vale of Berkeley		St. Mary's County		Lancaster and Northumberland	
	< £10 (N = 37) %	£10–£49 (N = 155) %	< £10 (N = 15) %	£10–£49 (N = 134) %	< £10 (N = 9) %	£10–£49 (N = 69) %
Boiling Equip.	73.0	63.9	86.7	86.6	100.0	100.0
Frying Equip.	10.8	23.2	53.3	53.7	44.4	63.8
Roasting Equip.	29.7	63.2	6.7	24.6	–	34.8
Other Cooking Equip.	–	3.9	6.7	0.7	–	–
Brass	81.1	94.8	20.0	30.6	33.3	47.8
Pewter	83.8	96.1	53.3	70.9	66.7	79.7
Earthen/Stoneware	–	9.7	13.3	35.1	33.3	36.2
Fine Ceramics	–	..	..	–	–	–
Glassware	–	2.6	–	0.7	–	1.4
Knives	..	–	–	0.7	–	2.9
Forks	–	–	–	–	–	–
Spoons	2.7	4.5	26.7	29.9	44.4	26.1
Table/Tableboard	81.1	92.3	6.7	34.3	–	37.7
Tableframe	35.1	52.3	–	–	–	–
Chair	40.5	79.4	26.7	28.4	–	33.3
Bench/Form	40.5	63.2	–	9.7	0	23.2
Stool	24.3	61.3	–	9.7	–	5.8
Settle	10.8	21.9	–	–	–	–
Couch	–	–	6.7	9.7	44.4	23.2
Other	–	–	–	–	–	–
No Seats	35.1	6.5	73.3	55.2	55.6	49.3
Table Linen	8.1	40.6	6.7	9.7	44.4	23.2
General Linen	29.7	74.2	33.3	36.6	–	46.4
Beds	97.3	100.0	66.7	87.3	66.7	92.8
Bedsteds	81.1	94.2	6.7	21.6	–	30.4
Sheets	29.7	47.1	20.0	20.1	–	30.4
Curtains/Valances	–	13.5	6.7	5.2	–	14.5
Warming Pan	5.4	23.9	–	5.2	–	7.2
Cupboard	29.7	33.5	–	9.0	–	4.3
Clothespress	–	20.6	–	–	–	1.4
Sideboard	10.8	29.0	–	–	–	–
Chest of Drawers	–	1.3	–	–	–	–
Desk	5.4	5.8	–	2.2	11.1	2.9
Chest/Trunk/Coffer	81.1	92.3	80.0	82.8	66.7	89.9
Lighting	2.7	29.0	20.0	26.9	11.1	30.4
Chamberpot/Closestool	5.4	13.5	–	10.4	–	5.8
Pictures	–	–	–	0.7	–	1.4
Books	5.4	20.6	27.7	17.2	11.1	49.3
Plate/Jewels	–	9.7	–	0.7	–	7.2
Clocks/Watches	–	1.9	..	–	–	–

Sources. Vales of Berkeley; GRO Probate Inventories, 1660–1699 PRO, PCC Inventories, PROB 4 and %; St. Mary's County inventories, 1658–1699 courtesy of SMCC; Lancaster and Northumberland, Probate inventories, 1650–1699, (copies), Virginia State Library, Richmond, Virginia.

and the Chesapeake. Although at the bottom of the social and economic ladder, the majority of the very poor in the Vale possessed what were considered the basic necessities of life. Virtually everyone had a bed (97.3%) and over 80% had bedsteads. People without bedsteads probably slept on mattresses on the floor in a similar fashion to that described by William Harrison in the 16th century (Harrison 1968: 201). Beds and bedding were cheap and unsophisticated. The mean value of a bed, bedstead and ''appurtenances'' (coverlets, rug, blankets, and possibly sheets) was £1.17, compared to £1.93 for all groups. Most of the very poor possessed tables and seats. Over 80% had a table or table board and two-thirds had some kind of seating. Chairs and forms were most common. Other furniture, however, was less frequently owned. Thirty percent had cupboards, although most of these must have been of crude construction since in no case were they worth more than a few shillings. Only 11% had sideboards, while more elaborate case furniture such as presses and chests of drawers were entirely absent. Very few poor owned goods that were not essential to everyday domestic life. Some possessed a few books, while chamberpots, lighting untensils, and warming pans—items which, although not essential, made home life a little more comfortable—were scarce.

If the very poor in the Vale owned the basic necessities, the poor in the Chesapeake did not. Seventeenth century colonists' standards of sufficiency, comfort and luxury were not simply more modest versions of those in England, they were different standards altogether. Apart from a few chairs and couches, furniture of any kind was entirely missing from the households of the very poor in Maryland and Virginia. Virtually all householders at this level were without bedsteads, and only two-thirds even owned a proper mattress. Rags or piles of straw perhaps served those who could not afford bedding. Over 70% of the St. Mary's group and 55.6% of the Virginia sample were without seating. They had to make do by sitting on the floor or using up-turned barrels, pails and chests. Other common domestic furniture was non-existent. Cooking equipment, for the most part, was limited to an iron pot or two for boiling mush and stew. Inventories less commonly mention a frying pan. As one might expect, non-essentials and luxury goods, with the important exception of books, were completely absent.

Living standards of the very poor have been described as ''remarkably, almost unimaginably primitive. . . . Equipment of any kind was so scarce that we must look to aboriginal cultures to find modern analogies that even approximate these pre-consumer living conditions of the seventeenth century'' (Carson and Carson 1976: 17). Barbara and Cary Carson provide a graphic illustration of the living conditions of the poor in southern Maryland:

> It is suppertime. A wife, husband, two children, and perhaps a servant are gathered together in the perpetual dusk of their shuttered cottage. This evening, like most evenings, their dinner is cornmeal mush boiled in an iron pot. The food is ladled into five plates or porringers, one for each person. The father sets his down on a large storage trunk which he straddles and sits on. His daughter is perched on the edge of a small chest, the only other piece of furniture in the room. The rest either stand or squat along the walls. They spoon up the food from the plates they must hold in their hands or place on the floor. They drink milk or water from a common cup, tankard or bowl passed around. No candle or lamp is lighted now or later when the room grows completely dark except for the glow of embers on the hearth. Nightfall puts an effective end to all the day's activities. While someone rinses the bowls in a bucket of water (there being only one pot), someone else drags out a cattail mattress and arranges it in front of the fire. The husband, wife, and daughter lie down there, covering themselves with a single canvas sheet and a worn-out bed rug. The son and servant roll up in blankets on the floor. For warmth all sleep in their clothes. (Carson and Carson 1976: 9–10).

As the Carsons point out, this is a fictional and in some respects an unprovable recreation of the most wretched conditions in which poor planters lived. But on the other hand, conditions such as these, or similar to them, were to be found among the poor throughout the Chesapeake. Evidence from Charles County, Maryland, and Lancaster and Northumberland counties, Virginia, confirms the Carsons' findings for St. Mary's County. Moreover, these conditions were not merely confined to the very poor. The above reconstruction could almost equally apply to a planter in the £10 to £49 wealth group.

Although it is possible to detect improvement in the standard of living of lower middle class compared to the very poor, the primitiveness of domestic conditions is nevertheless remarkable. In both Maryland and Virginia, half of the decedents worth between £10 and £49 lacked any seating, and between 70% and 80% were without bedsteads. Tables were to be found in only a third of the households. Other furniture was even less common. In the Virginia sample, there does appear to have been an important increase in the number of householders owning linen. Linen of any kind was missing from the under £10 group whereas nearly one-half of the £10–£49 group owned either table linen, sheets or both. This pattern is not repeated in the St. Mary's County sample. These differences may reflect regional variations in marketing by English manufacturers or possibly in living standards, but it is important to remember that in both samples the size of the under £10 group is small (15 in the case of St. Mary's and nine in Virginia) and therefore might be unreliable.

Sitting down at meals on furniture, or even standing at a table, as the Carsons suggest, was not yet a convenience that most planters worth less than £50 could afford. Sleeping arrangements were similarly crude. Few householders had the pleasure of sleeping on a bed and bedstead with proper bedding. In short, "these were people living at a subsistence level. In a life-time of hard work many were no better equipped than newly arrived indentured servants . . ." (Carson and Carson 1976:15).

Again, the contrast with householders in the Vale of Berkeley is striking. Houses of weavers, cloth-workers, poorer artisans and smallholders, who comprised the majority of the lower-middling groups worth between £10 and £49, in every case contained beds, bedsteads and bedding and generally had tables, chairs and other forms of seating. Mary Martimore, widow in the parish of Berkeley, died in the spring of 1663 worth about £16. She owned two beds and bedsteads, with pillows and sheets; two large tableboards with frames; a side cupboard; three coffers; a chair and another tableboard with a frame. Judging by the cooking utensils, she mainly boiled her food in a "brasspot" or iron kettles, and ate her meals from pewter dishes. Charles Smyth, a tailor also of Berkeley, died in the same year worth about £20. His house had at least five rooms: three on the ground floor, including his shop, and two chambers. He owned three beds, bedsteads and "appurtenances", several tables, and a range of seating consisting of chairs, forms and stools. He kept his clothes in a "presse" and stored household linen in a chest in the chamber over the hall. Both chambers appear to have been used solely for sleeping and storing of clothes and linen. The hall was probably Smyth's main living room, while the buttery served as a kitchen (Gloucestershire Records Office, Probate Inventories, 1663/51, 1663/67).

Cupboards, sideboards, and clothes presses—items of furniture rarely found in the households of Chesapeake planters worth less than £50—were much more commonplace in the Vale. These items provided a more convenient means of storing goods than the ubiquitous chest or trunk. There was also a greater readiness to invest in non-essential items. Nearly a quarter of the Vale of Berkeley sample possessed warming pans, testifying to the superiority of beds and bedding in the English sample, and just under 10 percent owned a small piece of silver or jewelry—perhaps a family heirloom. The main luxuries that poor and lower-middling Chesapeake planters allowed themselves were lighting equipment and books. Titles are not usually mentioned but most books appear to have been bibles and devotional works. Given the low incidence of apparent book ownership in the Vale, it may be that books, like other small items, were not generally appraised in English inventories. Discrepancies between the English and Chesapeake samples for small objects might possibly reflect differing recording practices in the two societies, rather than different consumer patterns.

Material Possessions of Middle and Upper-Middle Class Householders Worth £50 to £249

The living standards of Chesapeake planters worth above £50 show a gradual improvement

(Table 2). Householders of between £50 and £99 (better off leaseholders and small landowners) appear to have formed an intermediate group between the living standards of the poor and those of the middling and rich. There was generally more furniture. Between a half and three-quarters of decedents in the Maryland and Virginia samples owned tables and most householders (70% to 80) had seating of some kind. There was also a marked improvement in beds and bedding. Nearly 60% of the Virginia sample and 40% of St. Mary's householders in this wealth group owned bedsteads. A similar proportion (40% to 60%) were able to cover their beds with sheets, while approaching a third had curtains and valances.

Diet also appears to have improved. Most householders were equipped with boiling, frying and roasting implements. John Baley of Lancaster County, Virginia, who died in 1695 worth about £56, owned 2 brass kettles, 1 small spit and dripping pan, 2 iron kettles, 1 frying pan, 2 pots, potracks, and a pair of pothooks (Lancaster County Records, Wills 8:49). John Pearse, who died in neighboring Northumberland County in 1667 worth about £83, had 2 iron pots, 1 frying pan, 2 spits, 1 dripping pan, 1 brass pot and kettle "all very old", 2 pair of pothooks, and 1 pair of potracks (Northumberland County Records 1666-72: 220, 228). Along with a greater variety of cooking equipment, there was also a greater number of implements, in contrast to the one or two iron pots and occasional frying pan commonly found in the inventories of planters worth less than £50.

Another notable improvement was in dining habits. About half the householders of the £50–£99 wealth group in Maryland and Virginia were able to cover their tables with tablecloths, and almost everyone could set their tables with pewter plates and dishes. Nearly half the sample in both colonies owned earthen or stoneware, and few possessed glassware.

Non-essential items are also found in greater numbers in the households of the £50 to £99 group. Lighting equipment (candles, candlesticks, snuffers) was present in half the inventories of this group, compared to between 27% and 30% of the £10–£49 group, and 11% to 20% of the under £10 group. Being able to light the house artificially in the evenings must have made a substantial difference in the quality of life by lengthening the day's activities. The daily routine need no longer be circumscribed by the hours of daylight.

If the £50 to £99 group represents a transitory stage from poor to rich, the £100 to £249 group displays the first substantial improvement in living standards in both colonies. At this level most people owned basic furniture such as tables, seats, beds and bedsteads. The great majority owned sheets, as well as table linens, and between half and two-thirds possessed curtains and valances. More elaborate beds and bedding were reflected by their rising value. The average value of beds, bedding and bedsteads of all wealth groups in St. Mary's County across the period 1658 to 1700 was around £2.50 (SMCC, Inventories 1658-1700). Planters in the £100–£249 category, however, commonly owned beds of twice this value. Edward Fishwick, for example, owned six "feather beds and furniture" valued at £30 (SMCC Inventories, 637). John Tennison of the same county, who died in the following year worth £209, possessed "2 old feather pillows, 1 bolster, 1 feather bed, 2 blankets, 1 Worsted Rugg, Reg serge curtaines and vallens, and bedstead" appraised at £4 10s. 6d. (SMCC Inventories, 632). Clearly, as wealth and status increased, so there was a greater investment in more expensive and comfortable bedding.

Similarly, there were notable improvements in other aspects of everyday home life. Most people had boiling, frying and roasting equipment, but there was also a few specialized implements for preparing sauces, pastries, and fish. Almost everyone ate their meals from pewter dishes, and there is more evidence of the use of knives at the table. Furnishings were also more varied, with larger numbers of people owning cupboards and chests of drawers. The incidence of non-essential items also increased significantly in this wealth group. Warming pans, lighting equipment, chamberpots, books, plate, jewelry, and timepieces all become common.

A number of contrasts with English households stand out. In the Vale of Berkeley, middling and upper-middling wealth holders—mainly husband-

Table 2

STANDARDS OF LIVING OF HOUSEHOLDERS WORTH £50–£99 and £100–£249, VALE OF BERKELEY, GLOUCESTERSHIRE; ST MARY'S COUNTY, MARYLAND; LANCASTER AND NORTHUMBERLAND COUNTIES, VIRGINIA, 1650–1700

Household Item	Vale of Berkeley £50–£99 (N = 103) %	Vale of Berkeley £100–£249 (N = 111) %	St. Mary's County £50–£99 (N = 98) %	St. Mary's County £100–£249 (N = 67) %	Lancaster and Northumberland £50–£99 (N = 41) %	Lancaster and Northumberland £100–£249 (N = 19) %
Boiling Equip.	6.2	67.6	94.4	95.5	100.0	100.0
Frying Equip.	12.6	14.4	64.0	67.2	80.5	89.5
Roasting Equip.	73.8	77.5	44.9	73.1	68.3	78.9
Other Cooking Equip.	2.9	5.4	7.9	13.0	–	–
Brass	98.1	99.1	62.9	82.1	75.6	68.3
Pewter	98.1	96.4	89.9	95.5	92.7	100.0
Ironware	92.2	92.8	91.0	94.0	97.6	94.7
Earthen/Stoneware	8.7	11.7	49.4	64.2	46.3	31.6
Fine Ceramics	–	–	–	–	–	–
Glassware	1.0	2.7	4.5	4.5	4.5	5.3
Knives	–	–	2.2	16.4	2.4	15.8
Forks	–	–	–	1.5	–	–
Spoons	1.9	7.2	23.6	29.9	41.5	42.1
Table/Tableboard	95.1	97.3	52.8	88.1	75.6	84.2
Tableframe	48.5	61.3	–	–	2.4	–
Chair	86.4	86.5	52.8	82.1	63.4	68.4
Bench/Form	77.7	74.8	32.6	41.8	43.9	42.1
Stool	62.1	78.4	10.1	22.4	4.9	26.3
Settle	22.3	27.0	–	–	–	–
Couch	–	0.9	30.3	38.8	46.3	57.9
Other	–	–	–	–	–	–
No Seats	2.9	–	30.3	10.4	22.0	10.5
Table Linen	49.5	60.4	46.1	74.6	58.5	78.9
General Linen	75.7	84.7	64.0	83.6	82.9	89.5
Beds	100.0	100.0	97.8	98.5	95.1	100.0
Bedsteads	95.1	95.5	40.4	61.2	58.5	78.9
Sheets	45.6	40.5	43.8	67.2	61.0	84.2
Curtains/Valances	23.3	27.9	28.1	49.3	31.7	68.4
Warming Pan	31.1	38.7	20.2	35.8	24.4	57.9
Cupboard	40.8	37.8	12.4	31.3	9.8	31.6
Clothespress	33.0	29.7	–	–	2.4	5.3
Sideboard	28.2	38.7	1.1	3.0	–	–
Chest of Drawers	1.9	14.4	6.7	11.9	4.9	15.8
Desk	4.9	10.8	3.4	9.0	2.4	–
Chest/Trunk/Coffer	92.2	88.3	78.7	98.5	97.6	100.0
Lighting	36.9	40.5	48.3	61.2	53.7	63.2
Chamberpot/Closestool	15.5	17.1	15.7	34.3	17.1	26.3
Pictures	–	1.8	6.7	10.4	–	15.8
Books	22.3	26.1	39.3	52.2	58.5	68.4
Plate/Jewels	21.4	27.9	12.4	22.4	4.9	36.8
Clocks/Watches	6.8	13.5	–	10.4	–	5.3

Sources: See Table 1

men, yeomen, wealthy artisans and retailers (Horn 1981:93)—lived in houses of between five and eight rooms compared to the three to five rooms inhabited by their counterparts in the Chesapeake (Moore 1976:36; Main 1982:152). Problems of space accounts, in large part, for the smaller incidence of domestic furniture among middle class and relatively affluent Maryland and Virginia planters. Whereas basic furniture, such as chairs and tables, are to be found in virtually every household in the £50–£99 category in the Vale, between a half and a quarter of planters in this group still had to make do without (Table 2). Among the upper-middle class (£100–£249) the gap between the English and Chesapeake samples closes, but it is notable that the range of case furniture is usually less in Maryland and Virginia inventories. On the other hand, curtains and valances appear more frequently in Chesapeake households and were perhaps more important in providing privacy in a crowded dwelling than in England, where separate chambers were set aside exclusively for sleeping. Finally, there appears to have been a greater predisposition among tobacco planters to invest in non-essential items such as pictures and books, which may have helped to brighten up the home or perhaps served as reminders of England.

Material Possessions of Rich Householders Worth £250 and Over

The economic elite, as here defined, comprised about 10 percent of the population in the Vale of Berkeley and between 10 and 15 percent in Maryland and Virginia. Table 3 suggests that their domestic furnishings were quite similar. Ordinary furniture was present in every household and in larger numbers than lower wealth groups. Substantial wealth brought a more varied diet, greater comfort in dining and sleeping, and also a higher investment in non-essential items, particularly silver plate. Nearly three-quarters of the St. Mary's County elite and two-thirds of the Virginia elite owned plate, jewelry or both. Like the rich in England, wealthy Chesapeake planters bought

plate both as a sound investment and as a sign of high social status. "I esteem it as well politic as reputable," William Fitzhugh of Westmoreland County, Virginia, commented, "to furnish my self with a handsom cupboard of plate which gives my self the present use and credit, is a sure friend at a dead lift, with out much loss, or is a certain portion for a child after my decease" (Walsh 1979:12). Few gentry in the Vale of Berkeley would have disagreed.

Some members of the Chesapeake's elite enjoyed much more elaborate housing than the five to six rooms common at this level (Main 1982:152). Benjamin Solley, a leading merchant of St. Mary's County died in 1675, inhabited a dwelling with four or five ground floor rooms, three chambers and a loft (SMCC Inventories, 281). The largest dwellings probably had about a dozen rooms. It is difficult to visualize the appearance of these houses. Most were likely to have been rambling wooden structures; there were very few brick or stone dwellings built in the 17th century (Carson *et al* 1981). The point to stress, however, is that for every example of a wealthy householder living in a "multi-room Great house," one can cite other examples of the rich living in typically small Chesapeake cottages (Walsh 1977:258-59). Apart from the exceptionally wealthy, the homes of Chesapeake planters tended "to be small, inconspicuous, and inconsequential" (Main 1982:153). In Maryland and Virginia, the vast majority of the homes of leading merchants and planters "might be mistaken for modest farm cottages in England" (Walsh 1979:7-8).

Table 3 tends to obscure important qualitative differences between furnishings in the two societies, since the data merely indicate the proportion of wealth holders owning certain items, not their value or quality. Hence, there might be a world of difference between an old wooden chair belonging to a Chesapeake planter and a great 'turkey work' chair owned by one of the Vale of Berkeley's wealthiest gentlemen. In the great parlor of John Smyth's house in North Nibley, Gloucestershire, there stood "one ovill table board [with a] Turkie Karpett, a dozen and a halfe of Turkie Chairs, one Turkie worke Couch, ..." worth, with a few

Table 3

STANDARDS OF LIVING OF HOUSEHOLDERS WORTH £250 AND OVER, VALE OF BERKELEY GLOUCESTERSHIRE, ST. MARY'S COUNTY, MARYLAND, LANCASTER AND NORTHUMBERLAND COUNTIES, VIRGINIA, 1650–1700

Household Item	Vale of Berkeley (N = 74) %	St. Mary's County (N = 58) %	Lancaster and Northumberland (N = 12) %
Boiling Equip.	59.5	94.8	100.0
Frying Equip.	13.5	72.4	83.3
Roasting Equip.	81.1	77.6	91.7
Other Cooking Equip.	9.5	34.5	–
Brass	98.6	94.8	91.7
Pewter	98.6	94.8	100.0
Ironware	95.9	94.8	100.0
Earthen/Stoneware	14.9	75.9	50.0
Fine Ceramics	–	5.2	8.3
Glassware	8.1	29.3	25.0
Knives	2.7	22.4	33.0
Forks	–	5.2	–
Spoons	4.1	44.8	50.0
Table/Tableboard	95.9	89.7	100.0
Tableframe	62.2	–	8.3
Chair	98.6	94.8	91.7
Bench/Form	71.6	34.5	50.0
Stool	85.1	31.0	25.0
Settle	43.2	1.7	–
Couch	5.4	34.5	41.7
Other	5.4	–	–
No Seats	–	1.7	–
Table Linen	73.0	94.8	100.0
General Linen	95.9	96.6	100.0
Beds	100.0	98.3	100.0
Bedsteads	100.0	77.6	91.7
Sheets	54.1	93.1	83.3
Curtains/Valances	40.5	72.4	66.7
Warming Pan	44.6	62.1	50.0
Cupboard	39.2	37.9	50.0
Clothespress	47.3	12.1	–
Sideboard	51.4	5.2	–
Chest of Drawers	24.3	36.2	25.0
Desk	6.2	15.5	16.7
Chest/Trunk/Coffer	100.0	96.6	100.0
Lighting	47.3	75.9	83.3
Chamberpot/Closestool	24.3	36.2	25.0
Pictures	4.1	17.2	8.3
Books	37.8	51.7	91.7
Plate/Jewels	55.4	74.1	66.7
Clocks/Watches	28.4	22.4	8.3

Sources: See Table 1

other furnishings, £17 (GRO Inventories, 1692/159). Among the wealthy in the Vale, beds worth £5 or more were commonplace. Elaborate case furniture was usually valued at between £1 and £2, while tables and chairs might be three or four times more expensive than the normal value (GRO, Inventories, 1660-1699; PRO.PCC, PROB 4 and 5).

Expensive furniture is also to be found in the inventories of wealthy planters such as Colonel John Carter of Lancaster, James Bowling and Captain Joshua Doyne of St. Mary's (Lancaster County Records, Wills 8, 22-29, 32-34; SMCC Inventories, 1067, 1315). But old, broken or worn out goods are also commonly mentioned among the possessions of leading planters. Captain William Brocas of Lancaster County, a justice of the peace and former member of Virginia's Council, owned at his death in 1655, "a parcel of old hangings, very thin and much worn," "a parcel of old Chairs, being 7, most of them unusefull," "an old broken Cort Cupboard," "1 old rotten couch bedsteads," "1 old broken trunk, 7 guns most unfixt," and so on (Lancaster County Records, Deeds, 202-04; Deeds 2, 40). Similarly, many of the household possessions of John Godsell, a merchant who died in 1676 worth over £300, were described in his inventory as "old," "damnified," "motheaten," and "rotten" (Lancaster County Records, Wills 5, 19-22). Virtually all the furniture owned by Mr. Thomas Wilks, who died ten years later worth about £1000, is described as "old" (Lancaster County Records, Wills, 5 104-08).

Comparing the data presented in Tables 2 and 3, it is perhaps surprising that there were not greater differences between the living standards of the rich and other wealth groups. Like most householders, the Vale's rich ate their meals from pewter plates and drank from pewter flagons. Inventories show no evidence that wealthy persons owned fine ceramics, and less than a tenth of the £250 plus group possessed glassware. (It is, of course, possible that appraisers missed or failed to individually list these items.) Although the wealthy tended to have a greater range of furniture, articles such as couches, chests of drawers, and desks were far from common. Even case furniture, such as cupboards,

presses, and sideboards were to be found in barely half the inventories. These considerations apply also to the Vale's gentry. Of seven gentlemen worth over £250, none apparently possessed any special cooking equipment—fish plates, pastry dishes, pudding pots, apple or bread toasters—and there was no evidence of fine ceramics. Only two men owned glassware and only four had elaborate case furniture. The gentry had more expensive tastes in clothing and they tended to invest a larger proportion of their money in plate, but generally their domestic furnishings differed little from wealthy non-gentry. An altogether different *style* of living only becomes apparent among the top rank of gentlemen (country gentry), who built, or rebuilt, large country houses and furnished them with the most expensive and luxurious items (Atkyns 1712). What seems to be missing in the second half of the 17th century are upper class rituals such as tea, coffee, or chocolate-drinking, eating from tables set with fine porcelain, knives and forks. These developments awaited the 18th century.

Differences in the standards of living between the rich and the middling wealth groups were therefore a matter of degree rather than kind. Mildred Campbell's comments concerning the English yeomanry are just as applicable to the majority of middle and upper class householders in the Vale: "the inventories show . . . that the standard of living, in so far as the quality and variety of household furnishings reveal it, was remarkably similar among the yeomen of greater and less wealth. The difference lay in the numbers of rooms to be furnished rather than the style, variety and quality of the furnishings" (Campbell 1967: 238-39). Neither the economic elite in general, nor the gentry in particular, comprised a "Venetian oligarchy" in the 17th century. Class divisions were fluid and distinctions between middle and upper classes remained ill-defined (Wrightson 1977: 33-47).

Despite important differences in living standards between rich and poor, historians of the 17th century Chesapeake have tended to stress the essential similarity of the domestic environment. "All in all," the Carsons conclude, "there was a decided sameness about material life in southern Maryland throughout the 17th century. Partly it was a result of a limited choice of available consumer goods and partly a reflection of a community that was still more homogeneous, still less attenuated by extremes of wealth, than it became fifty years later." "Being rich," they suggest, "meant having more, not being different" (Carson and Carson 1976:17, 21). Research by Walsh supports this view and she notes that "while families in higher wealth levels enjoyed a greater degree of comfort than did poorer households, until the end of the period (1720), most did not use personal possessions to create a markedly different way of living from their poorer neighbors." The Chesapeake was "a place where social elites did not develop distinct identities based on patterns of consumption very different from those of groups somewhat below them" (Walsh 1979: 7-8).

This view should be qualified, however. The elite in Maryland and Virginia were no more monolithic than in England. Even at a relatively early stage of Chesapeake social development there were some individuals who, by virtue of their office, inherited status, or wealth, stood head and shoulders above the rest of the gentry. These men, such as the Carters, Lees, Wormeleys and Byrds of Virginia, ranked with country magnates in English society (Bailyn 1959) and clearly *did* develop a different style, as well as standard of living appropriate to their high status. As in England, therefore, a comparison of middle and upper class material possessions suggests a gradual rather than dramatic improvement in living standards, with a sharp break occurring only at the very pinnacle of the social order. In both societies, the distinction between top gentry and the rest of the squirarchy became clearer in the 18th century with the growth of magnate power (Plumb 1967; Speck 1977; Bailyn 1959; Morgan 1975).

Conclusion

The most important conclusion to be drawn from a comparison of material possessions in the two societies is the great poverty experienced by most Chesapeake planters during the 17th century. Even the lowest economic group in England had living standards comparable in many respects to those of householders of middling wealth in Maryland and Virginia. To put it another way, only householders belonging to the two upper wealth groups in the Chesapeake had living standards that would be accounted quite ordinary in England. Not only were essential items of furniture such as tables, seats, beds, and bedsteads often missing from the households of most planters, but there was also an important qualitative difference in furnishings. In general, the value of furniture in both societies was similar. Beds and bedding were commonly valued at between £1 and £5, tables between two and five shillings, chairs and stools a shilling, bedsteads five shillings, and more elaborate case furniture from a few shillings to over £1. Yet there was a much greater range of values in Maryland and Virginia than in the Vale of Berkeley; a consequence of a great number of very low valuations found in Chesapeake inventories.

A qualitative difference between furniture in the two societies is also suggested by descriptions used by appraisers. In English inventories, it is very rare for items to be described as "new" or "old," but in Chesapeake inventories the term "old" is extremely common. Old, broken, and worn goods still retained a certain value in the Chesapeake because it was cheaper to mend them, or use them for something else, than to buy new goods. Planters had to rely on English merchants to import manufactured goods, especially metalwares, which always seemed to be in short supply, hence the value of second hand items. Poverty was therefore reflected not only by an absence of essential furniture, but also in the often poor condition of the limited items that were owned. Housing was greatly inferior in Maryland and Virginia compared to England. While impermanent structures—squatters' shacks or pauper dwellings—existed in England, they were increasingly rare in the second half of the 17th century and did not house the majority of poor. Single or two-room farm cottages were also becoming less common in southern and central England as a consequence of the substantial rebuilding which occurred throughout the late Tudor and Stuart periods (Barley 1967; Smith 1985). Thus, in the

Vale of Berkeley, the poor and lower middling groups lived in houses of three to five rooms, built by local craftsmen of durable materials. Whereas in England, the trend during the previous two centuries had been towards more specialized room use and permanent structures, in the early Chesapeake, these developments were reversed: dwellings were not expected to last more than 20 to 25 years and a single or two rooms served a multiplicity of functions (Carson et al, 1981). Consequently, in most dwellings, there simply was not enough space for much furniture. The most useful item for the small planter was the versatile chest, which could serve as a table or seat as well as for storing goods.

The social and psychological implications of this transformation in living standards have yet to be fully considered by social historians or archaeologists. Obviously, important changes in domestic lifestyle must have resulted from the cramped living conditions experienced by the vast majority of planters along the tobacco coast. A division of domestic space according to gender and status could not be enforced in humble Chesapeake structures where men and women, masters and servants, parents and children all lived in close proximity. Were family tensions exacerbated by lack of privacy? To what extent did the "decided sameness" of material life in the 17th century Chesapeake erode traditional English social distinctions and alter perceptions of status? Did low standards of living contribute not only to an "architecture of transcience" but also to a *mentalite* of transience; an easy-come, easy-go attitude whereby people packed up their goods and moved on when debts became too great or the going too hard (Horn 1987)?

For the majority of English people who emigrated to the Chesapeake in the 17th century, one of the most important differences they would encounter in their new environment was a substantially lower standard of living. This was a consequence not of their own humble origins and lack of aspiration to create a better way of life, or of the relatively short life-span that most of them experienced but rather of the peculiar demands of tobacco culture, the increasingly unfavorable eco-

nomic climate, particularly after 1680, and the general difficulty of acquiring manufactured goods from England. Only the top 30% of planters, who managed to acquire over £100 in personalty at death, approached living conditions commonplace in England. Whatever advantages moving to the New World may have brought, for most settlers it did not bring domestic comfort. During the second half of the century, most planters endured a standard of living little different from that of the lowest levels of society in England.

ACKNOWLEDGEMENTS

This research could not have been completed without the generous assistance of the St. Mary's City Commission, and I would like to thank, in particular, Lorena S. Walsh and Lois Green Carr. The work on Lancaster and Northumberland Counties, Virginia, was supported by a grant-in-aid from the Colonial Williamsburg Foundation in 1978 and an ACLS—Fulbright Fellowship in 1985-1986. I am grateful to Barbara and Cary Carson, Lois Carr, Russell R. Menard and Lorena Walsh for permission to use unpublished material. I would also like to thank commentators of an earlier draft of this paper for their criticisms, especially Julie King, Henry Miller and Dennis Pogue. A version of this article was delivered to the Society for Historical Archaeology meeting in Savannah, Georgia, January 1987.

REFERENCES

ATKYNS, ROBERT
   1712 *The Ancient and Present State of Glostershire*. London

BAILYN, BERNARD
   1959 Politics and Social Structure in Virginia. In *17th-Century America: Essays in Colonial History*, edited by James M. Smith, pp. 90–115. University of North Carolina Press, Chapel Hill

BARLEY, M.W.
   1967 Rural Housing in England. In *The Agrarian History of England and Wales, 1500-1640*, edited by Joan Thirsk, Cambridge University Press, Cambridge, pp. 696–766.

BETTEY, J.H.
   1983 Seventeenth Century Squatters' Dwellings: Some Documentary Evidence. *Vernacular Architecture* 13: 28–30

CAMPBELL, MILDRED
1967 *The English yeoman in the Tudor and Early Stuart Ages.* Merlin, London.

CARR, LOIS GREEN AND LORENA S. WALSH
1978 Changing Life Styles in Colonial St. Mary's County. *Regional Economic History Research Center, Working Papers 1,* No. 3: 73–118.
1985 Changing Life Styles and Consumer Behavior in the Colonial Chesapeake. Paper presented at a conference on the Social World of Britain and America, 1600-1820, Williamsburg, Virginia.

CARSON, CARY
1974 The 'Virginia House' in Maryland. *Maryland Historical Magazine* 69: 185–96.

CARSON, CARY AND BARBARA CARSON
1976 Styles and Standards of Living in Southern Maryland. Paper presented to the Southern Historical Association, Atlanta, Georgia.

CARSON, CARY, NORMAN F. BARKA, WILLIAM M. KELSO, GARRY WHEELER STONE AND DELL UPTON
1981 Impermanent Architecture in the Southern American Colonies. *Winterthur Portfolio* 16(2/3): 135–96.

DEFOE, DANIEL
1971 *A Tour Through the Whole Island of Britain.* Penguin, London.

DE LACEY MANN, JULIA
1971 *The Cloth Industry in the West of England from 1640 to 1880.* Clarendon, Oxford.

GLOUCESTERSHIRE RECORD OFFICE
n.d. Probate Inventories, 1660–1699.

HALL, LINDA J.
1983 The Rural Houses of North Avon and South Gloucestershire. *City of Bristol Museum and Art Gallery Monograph* No. 6, Bristol.

HARRIS, P.M.G.
1978 Integrating Interpretations of Local and Regionwide Change in the Study of Economic Development and Demographic Growth in the Colonial Chesapeake, 1630–1775. *Regional Economic History Research Center, Working Papers,* 1(3): 35–72.

HARRISON, WILLIAM
1968 *A Description of England,* edited by George Edelen. Cornell University Press, New York.

HEY, DAVID
1974 *An English Rural Community: Myddle Under the Tudors and Stuarts.* Leicester University Press.

HORN, JAMES P.P.
1979 Servant Emigration to the Chesapeake in the 17th Century. In *The Chesapeake in the 17th Century: Essays on Anglo-American Society,* edited by Thad W. Tate and David L. Ammerman, pp. 51–95. University of North Carolina Press, Chapel Hill.

1981 The Distribution of Wealth in the Vale of Berkeley, Gloucestershire, 1660–1700. *Southern History* 3: 81–109.
1987 Moving on in the New World: Migration and Outmigration in the 17th Century Chesapeake. In *Migration in Early Modern England,* edited by Peter Clark and David Souden. Hutchinson, London.
In Adapting to a New World: A Comparative Study of
Press Local Society in England and Maryland, 1650–1700. In *Colonial Chesapeake Society,* edited by Lois Green Carr, Philip D. Morgan, and Jean B. Russo. University of North Carolina Press, Chapel Hill.

LANCASTER COUNTY, VIRGINIA
n.d. Lancaster County Records, Deeds and Wills, c. 1650–1699.

MAIN, GLORIA L.
1975 Probate Records as a Source for Early American History. *William and Mary Quarterly* 3(33): 89–99.
1982 *Tobacco Colony: Life in Early Maryland, 1650 to 1720.* Princeton University Press, Princeton.

MENARD, RUSSELL R.
1975 *Economy and Society in Early Colonial Maryland.* Unpublished Ph.D. dissertation, University of Iowa.
1976 The Comprehensiveness of Probate Inventories in St. Mary's County, Maryland, 1658 to 1777: A Preliminary Report. Unpublished ms. on file, Maryland State Archives, Annapolis.

MILLER, HENRY M.
1983 A Search for the "Citty of Saint Maries". Report on the 1981 Excavations in St. Mary's City, Maryland. *St. Mary's City Archaeology Series* No. 1, St. Mary's City.

MOORE, JOHN S.
1976 *The Goods and Chattels of our Forefathers: Frampton Cotterell and District Probate Inventories, 1539 1804.* Phillimore, Chichester.

MORGAN, EDMUND S.
1975 *American Slavery, American Freedom: The Ordeal of Colonial Virginia.* Norton, New York.

NORTHUMBERLAND COUNTY, VIRGINIA
n.d. Northumberland County Records, 1652-58, 1658-1666, 1666–1672.

PERRY, R.
1945 The Gloucestershire Woolen Industry, 1100-1690. *Bristol and Gloucestershire Archaeological Society* 64: 49–137.

PLUMB, J.H.
1967 *The Growth of Political Stability in England, 1675-1725.* Penguin, London.

PUBLIC RECORD OFFICE, LONDON
n.d. Probate Inventories, Prob 4 and 5.

RIDEN, PHILLIP, ED.
1985 *Probate Records and the Local Community.* Alan Sutton, Gloucestershire.

RUTMAN, DARRETT B. AND ANITA H. RUTMAN
1979 'Now Wives and Son-in-Law': Parental Death in a 17th Century Virginia County. In *The Chesapeake in the 17th Century*, edited by Thad W. Tate and David L. Ammerman. University of North Carolina Press, Chapel Hill.

ST. MARY'S CITY COMMISSION
n.d. Social Stratification in Maryland. National Science Foundation Grant GS-32272.

SALERNO, ANTONY
1979 The Social Background of 17th Century Emigration to America. *Journal of British Studies* 19: 31–52.

SHAMMAS, CAROLE
1980 The Domestic Environment in Early Modern England and America. *Journal of Social History* 14: 3–24.
1982 Consumer Behavior in Early America. *Social Science History* 6: 67–86.

SMITH, DANIEL BLAKE
1978 Mortality and Family in the Colonial Chesapeake. *Journal of Interdisciplinary History* 8: 403–427.

SMITH, PETER
1985 Rural Housing in Wales. In *The Agrarian History of England and Wales, 1640-1750*, edited by Joan Thirsk. Cambridge University Press, Cambridge.

SMYTH, JOHN
1889 *Berkeley Manuscripts. Volume 3*, edited by Sir John Maclean. Bellows, Gloucestershire.
1902 *Men and Armour for Gloucestershire in 1608*, edited by Sir John Maclean. Sutton, Gloucestershire.

SPECK, W. A.
1977 *Stability and Strife: England 1714-1760*. Arnold. London.

THIRSK, JOAN, ED.
1967 *The Agrarian History of England and Wales, 1500-1640*. Cambridge University Press, Cambridge.

WALSH, LORENA S. AND RUSSELL R. MENARD
1974 Death in the Chesapeake: Two Life Tables for Men in Early Colonial Maryland. *Maryland Historical Magazine* 69: 211–27.

WALSH, LORENA S.
1977 *Charles County, Maryland, 1658-1705: A Study of Chesapeake Social and Political Structure*. Unpublished Ph.D. dissertation, Michigan State University, East Lansing.
1979 'A Culture of Rude Sufficiency': Life Styles on Maryland's Lower Western Shore between 1658 and 1720. Paper presented to the Society for Historical Archaeology annual meeting. Nashville.

WRIGHTSON, KEITH
1977 Aspects of Social Differentiation in Rural England, c. 1580-1660. *Journal of Peasant Studies* 5: 33–47.

JAMES P. P. HORN
HUMANITIES DEPARTMENT
BRIGHTON POLYTECHNIC
BRIGHTON, EAST SUSSEX
ENGLAND

DAVID V. BURLEY

Function, Meaning and Context: Ambiguities in Ceramic Use by the *Hivernant* Metis of the Northwestern Plains

ABSTRACT

The 19th century *hivernant* Metis of the northwestern Canadian plains and parklands followed a way of life centered on communal bison hunting and frequent mobility. Contrary to what might be expected, excavations at five *hivernant* wintering sites consistently have recovered a variety of fragile, transfer printed, earthenware ceramics. In this context, ceramics, as a form of material culture, are seen to incorporate an ambiguity in function and meaning. In exploring this ambiguity, it is suggested that Metis ceramic use originates with an initial concern for female status and etiquette in Red River fur trade society. Ultimately, ceramics are argued to have assumed a much greater symbolic role. This role was integral in *hivernant* Metis social interaction and integration.

Introduction

Caught up in a materialist approach to culture, most archaeologists view artifacts solely as mediators between people and their environment. Only when function is not apparent, or where symbolic context is obvious, do many archaeologists move into the nonmaterial dimension of culture to interpret social context and "recover mind" (see Leone 1982). In the following paper, a study is presented where the divergence of function and meaning in one form of material culture necessitates understanding. This study centers on the use of transfer printed earthenware ceramics by 19th century communal bison hunting Metis of western Canada.

In western Canada, transfer printed ceramics are a principal constituent of artifact assemblages from all Metis wintering camps excavated to date. Both fragile in nature and conspicious in appearance, these materials seem out of context in the world of bison hunters. Why would a frequently mobile, semisedentary, hunting and gathering people maintain such a nonfunctional form of material culture in the face of more durable alternatives? A resolution of this question is found intricately tied to social symbolism and the use of material culture as a mechanism for ethnic integration and interaction. To the Metis ceramics have meaning far greater than function. They are part of the social world and they structure social action. They are an important component of Metis archaeology that can be understood only through a symbolic interpretation of material culture.

The Metis, Ceramics and Archaeological Context

The western Canadian Metis, as a distinctive ethnic group, emerged from the fur trade as the progeny of European and Euro-American traders and native wives (Foster 1976, Van Kirk 1980). Neither white nor Indian, the Metis found themselves between two worlds with widely disparate cultural systems (Peterson 1981). By 1800, a Metis population nucleus had become centered in the vicinity of the Red and Assiniboine rivers of what is today southeastern Manitoba. The Metis became further concentrated around the Red River settlement through the early 1800's (Figure 1).

The Metis participated in the western Canadian fur trade in many capacities including those of provisioner, voyageur, carter, tripman and, in several instances, independent trader. By 1821 and the consolidation of the northwestern trade by the Hudson's Bay Company, many of these services no longer were needed. One major exception was that of provisioner. With its network of trading posts stretched throughout the northwest, Hudson's Bay Company logistical structures required massive quantities of food; the Metis were quick to contribute to these needs. Provisioning was accomplished through bison hunting and the production of pemmican. Bison hunting also provided furs for the robe trade.

Through provisioning and the robe trade, many Metis became economically reliant upon bison.

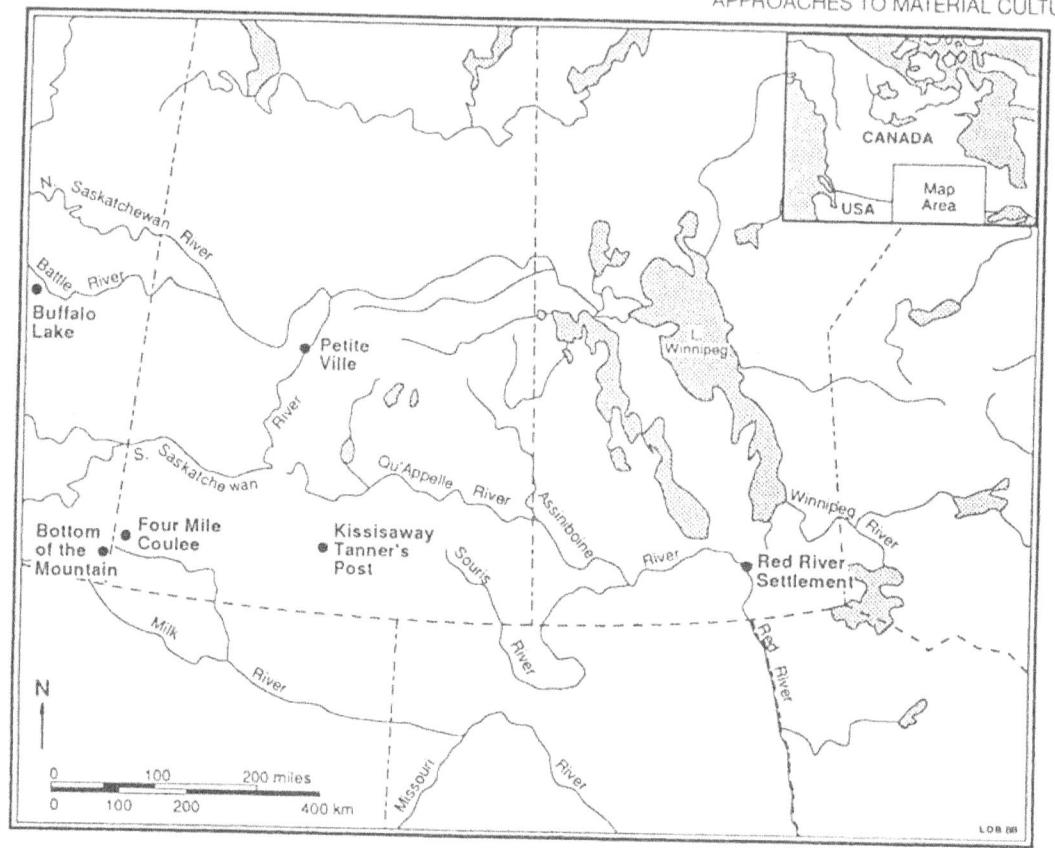

FIGURE 1. *Hivernant* Metis wintering site locations discussed in text.

Originating from Metis settlements at Red River and Pembina, semiannual communal hunts were carried out. Hunting brigades incorporated not only adult male hunters, but the full family group. Travelling considerable distances in any one hunt, these families transported their worldly possessions in the back of a two-wheeled Red River cart. Red River carts also were used to transport pemmican and robes back to the Hudson's Bay Company traders. The growing importance of communal hunting to the Metis economy is evident in the increasing size of the brigades over time. As described by Ray (1974:206), "in 1820, 540 carts were dispatched from the colony (Red River); ten years later the number had risen to 820 and by 1840 to 1210."

By the 1860s and 1870s, the effects of sustained hunting pressures on bison required the Metis to travel further in search of their livelihood (see Roe 1934). Many Metis found it necessary to abandon the annual return to the Red River colony and the practice of "wintering over" on the western Canadian plains and parklands became established. The wintering Metis, known as the *hivernant*, in all characteristics became full communal bison hunters (Anick 1976; Giraud 1986 among others). As communal hunters, the *hivernant* differed little from the mid 19th century Plains Indian. This pattern of hunting, mobility, and wintering over abruptly ended by 1880 with the virtual extinction of the bison.

A 1986 research project was implemented to examine the form and nature of late 19th century Metis culture change as affected by the near extinction of the bison (Burley, Horsfall and Brandon 1988). In transcribing the established research problems into a field strategy, one component of study focused upon an archaeological investigation of known *hivernant* wintering village locations. Three sites in southern and central Saskatchewan dating between the late 1860s and 1878 were selected for test excavation (Figure 1). These sites include Petite Ville (1870–1874) on the South Saskatchewan River, Four Mile Coulee (1874–1878) in the Cypress Hills and Kissisaway Tanner's wintering post (1868–1873) in the Dirt Hills. Comparable data on *hivernant* wintering sites had been collected by Elliott (1971) from Bottom of the Mountain in the Cypress Hills (late 1860's) and by Doll (1983; Doll and Kidd 1976) from Buffalo Lake in south central Alberta (1868–1872). Historical/archival research for each of these sites also has been carried out (Burley, Horsfall and Brandon 1988).

A *hivernant* wintering village generally can be described as a series of rapidly constructed cabins, varying numbers of Indian lodges and a wide range of activities with the whole ". . . intermingled in a confusion worthy of an Irish fair . . ." (Robinson 1879:254). *Hivernant* villages were seasonal, they were temporary, and they were constructed without a concern for long term settlement. Those sites examined in 1986, as well as in earlier studies, have a number of discrete clusters of visible surface features including chimney mounds, cellar depressions, refuse pits and pits created by the excavation of silts for chinking and fireplace construction. Each cluster is interpreted as an occupation locus for a multifamily residential group (Burley, Horsfall and Brandon 1988; also Elliott 1971).

The 1986 excavations at Petite Ville, Kississaway Tanner's Post and Four Mile Coulee were exploratory in nature and very limited in scope. However, from each site an assemblage of artifacts has been recovered that can be compared with those from Bottom of the Mountain (Elliott 1971) and Buffalo Lake (Doll and Kidd 1976, Doll 1983). Despite restricted sample sizes, these comparisons reveal a consistent and reasonably homogeneous pattern (see Table 1). For example, there is a relative paucity of architecturally associated specimens when compared with other post 1860 historic sites in western Canada. As well, with the exception to be discussed, there are few household items beyond those of immediate necessity. As a group, these assemblages characteristically lack cached or abandoned materials indicative of planned return on a seasonal basis; there also is a high degree of curation (Burley, Horsfall and Brandon 1988). Each of these qualities can be anticipated given the economic and settlement pattern structures of the *hivernant*. Not anticipated is the consistent presence of fragile earthenwares. Each of the sites has a transfer printed ceramic assemblage that is conspicious in its appearance and abundant relative to other components of Metis material culture.

As a consequence of Metis activity in the fur trade, a majority of their ceramics had been acquired through the Hudson's Bay Company. The principal supplier to the Hudson's Bay Company for the period dating between 1836 and the early 20th century was the Spode/Copeland Company of Staffordshire, England. Sussman's (1979) seminal study of Spode/Copeland transfer printed patterns found in western Canadian Hudson's Bay Company sites allows for the identification of individual design patterns for even small fragmented pieces. The patterns represented at four of the five *hivernant* sites are found in Table 2 and partially illustrated in Figure 2. The original analysis of the fifth site, Bottom of the Mountain, did not identify individual patterns. However, the Copeland manufacturer's mark has been recorded on several specimens and it is anticipated that Spode/Copeland ceramics are the dominant type (Elliott 1971:191, 223–24).

The Spode/Copeland ceramic patterns incorporate an ornate series of designs with little apparent meaning to the world of the *hivernant*. Images of strange places, odd customs and unrecognizable scenery seem out of context in the tool kit and personal effects of communal bison hunters. This deviation is emphasized further in consideration of the frequent mobility needed for bison hunting and the use of a two-wheeled Red River cart for transport. The remainder of the Metis assemblage reflects these problems of mobility and transport.

TABLE 1
HIVERNANT SITE ASSEMBLAGES BY FUNCTIONAL CATEGORY AND CLASS[†]

	Petite Ville	Four Mile	Kissisaway Tanners	Bottom Of The Mountain	Buffalo Lake
ARCHITECTURAL					
Nails	19(19)	47(43)	12(24)	82(11)	145(18)
Misc. Hardware	3(3)	1(1)	0(0)	4(1)	10(1)
KITCHEN					
Ceramics	18(18)	24(22)	12(24)	261(35)	206(25)
Bottle Glass	3(3)	22(20)	2(4)	169(22)	94(12)
Table Ware	0(0)	1(1)	0(0)	7(1)	2*
Misc. Kitchen	0(0)	1(1)	0(0)	30(4)	1*
HOUSEHOLD/ACTIVITIES					
Furniture Parts	1(1)	0(0)	0(0)	14(2)	0(0)
Stable/Transport	1(1)	1(1)	1(2)	6(1)	9(1)
Tools	0(0)	0(0)	0(0)	7(1)	9(1)
Trap./Hunt/Fish	0(0)	0(0)	0(0)	7(1)	4(1)
Misc. Other	4(4)	0(0)	0(0)	8(1)	2*
PERSONAL				0(0)	0(0)
Beads	79**	5**	7**	247**	4639**
Jewelry/Trinkets	2(2)	1(1)	1(2)	3*	3*
Button/Buckle	8(8)	3(3)	6(12)	32(4)	74(9)
Smoking	0(0)	0(0)	0(0)	12(2)	2*
Misc. Other	0(0)	0(0)	0(0)	20(3)	21(3)
ARMS					
Shot/Sprue	30(30)	4(4)	6(12)	8(1)	52(6)
Bullet/Case	2(2)	0(0)	0(0)	16(2)	18(2)
Flint/Parts	1(1)	1(1)	1(2)	1*	4(1)
MISCELLANEOUS	9(9)	3(3)	9(18)	75(10)	164(20)
ASSEMBLAGE TOTALS	180	114	57	1002	5450
PERCENTILE TOTAL	101	101	100	101	99

†Bracketed figures are percentages rounded to nearest whole number
*percentile is less than 0.5%
**bead frequencies are omitted from calculation of assemblage percentiles because of skew in the Buffalo Lake sample

(Sources: Burley, Horsfall and Brandon 1988, Doll 1983, Doll and Kidd 1976, Elliott 1971)

This ambiguity of context for fragile ceramics, what must be interpreted as a divergence of function and meaning, is made even more apparent through its recognition in historical observation. In 1840 Alexander Ross described a Metis hunting brigade in the following manner:

> Provisions were scarce, scarcely a child I met but was crying with hunger, scarcely a family but complained they had no food. How deceiving outward appearances are.... The state of the families in the camp revealed to me the true state of things: the one half of them were literally starving! Some I did see with a little tea, *and cups saucers too—rather fragile ware for such a mode of life*—but with a few exceptions of this kind, the rest disclosed nothing but scenes of misery and want.... (Ross 1957:253 emphasis added).

Failing to understand the significance of fragile ceramics to this hunting brigade, Ross was unable to decode the incorporated social message. The question remains as to what this message(s) may have been.

Metis Women, Status and the Symbolic Use of Ceramics

To understand the meaning of ceramics to the 1870's *hivernant* hunter, it is necessary to examine the origins of ceramic use for the Metis. From the observation of Alexander Ross, it is obvious that

TABLE 2

SPODE/COPELAND TRANSFER PRINT PATTERNS FOUND IN ARCHAEOLOGICAL CONTEXT AT *HIVERNANT* METIS SITES IN WESTERN CANADA

Design Pattern	Petite Ville	Kississaway Tanners	Four Mile	Buffalo Lake
Flower Vase	✓			✓
Pekin				✓
Pagoda	✓		✓	✓
Chinese Plants			✓	
Honeysuckle		✓		
Ivy	✓	✓		✓
"B-772"	✓			
"B-700"				✓
Seasons Variation		✓		
Continental Views				✓
Louis Quatorze				✓

(Sources: Burley, Horsfall and Brandon 1988; Doll 1983; Doll and Kidd 1976)

FIGURE 2 Some Spode/Copeland transfer print patterns found in *hivernant* Metis wintering sites (patterns adapted with permission from Sussman 1979)

transfer printed earthenwares had become integrated into *hivernant* material culture in those years prior to 1840. Between the turn of the century and 1840, the Metis were emerging as a distinctive ethnic group in the Red River settlement. In analyzing historical factors affecting Metis ethnicity, implicit symbolism in *hivernant* ceramics can begin to be recognized.

The origins of the Metis as an ethnic group are difficult to discern. Through the 18th century, a "breed" of people distinct from the "true natives" was beginning to be recognized in the vicinity of the Great Lakes (see Sprague and Fry 1983:12; also Peterson 1981). By 1800 the Metis began moving west and northward as a result of the eastern expansion of white settlers. From that time through to the early 1870's, the principal nucle-ation of Metis was found centered below the confluence of the Red and Assiniboine rivers in what has become known as the Red River settle-ment.

The nature of Red River society from the turn of the 19th century through to the 1860's was domi-nated by fur trade concerns (Van Kirk 1980 among others). An agricultural colony of Scottish settlers had failed to take hold and the power elite of the settlement became the officers and clerks of the Hudson's Bay Company. The bureaucratic struc-ture of the company had become the social struc-ture of the colony as a whole. This structure incorporated a series of closed ranks in which one's ethnic status dictated social position (see Pyszczyk 1985). The Metis, while dominant in population, were relegated to the lower ranks superior only to Indian peoples.

From the beginning of the western fur trade in the 17th century, liasons between Indian women and fur traders had been common. Both the North West Company and the Hudson's Bay company actively encouraged these unions for, among other things, the trading benefits they might bring through family alliances (Brown 1980, Van Kirk 1980). These unions frequently led to long term relationships that were solidified by the marriage rite *"a la façon du pays"*. Literally translated, this refers to "after the custom of the country" (Van Kirk 1980:37). The result of these unions was the growing population of Metis.

By 1820, the officers and clerks of the Hudson's Bay Company no longer considered it appropriate to take native wives (ibid. 171). In Red River, the mixed blood Metis had become the group to which the white fur traders looked for marriage partners. This led to a core of Metis women being integrated into the upper echelons of fur trade society. In their integration into this social hierarchy, each woman was expected to become, in Sylvia Van Kirk's terms, "quite English in her manner" (ibid. 145). Those who were most white, and those who were most "civilized," were those who were most highly sought. Ornate ceramics would form an integral component of the visual cues distinguish-ing "civilized behavior" in Metis women.

For Metis women, it is important to emphasize that it is not just the acquisition of ceramics that would be important. Rather, it equally involves the display and use of ceramics with appropriate social protocols. The formal tea service, the full table setting and the china cabinet became necessities. The degree to which mixed blood females were being moved to these "civilized behaviors" is aptly described by Van Kirk. She states:

> The officers were not interested in having their daughters learn menial domestic skills; they wanted them to *acquire the accomplishments of ladies* as befitted their status as daughters of the fur-trade gentry. Ever concerned to main-tain the distinction in rank between themselves and Com-pany servants, the officers had been painfully aware that in the past their native wives had not possessed the attributes which they considered appropriate to women of their station. Their *desire to raise their daughters in the English manner* was accentuated by the founding of Red River itself, in a colony which envisioned itself as being "a little Britain in the wilderness", class distinctions would become increasingly important. Company officers were anxious that their families be equipped to retain their social positions in Rupert's Land. Giving their daughters a refined English education, they hoped, would be sufficient to overcome the taint of their mixed blood (1980:147–48, emphasis added).

At the same time these Metis women were being integrated into the upper ranks of fur trade society at Red River, their brothers and their male off-spring were openly discriminated against and pre-vented from becoming company officers by Hud-son's Bay Company policy.

Were fur trade society to continue as described, this closed system would eventually have produced a distinct class separate from the Metis. In the 1820's, the *status quo* was abruptly challenged. Through the 18th century it had been the official policy of the Hudson's Bay Company to prohibit European women at their posts (Brown 1980). By the 1820's, this policy appears no longer to have been important nor enforced. In 1829, Governor George Simpson, the most powerful of Hudson's Bay Company officers in the northwest, took furlough to England to secure a wife of "breeding" in accordance with his status. With the arrival of Francis Simpson to the Red River settlement in 1830, the basis for an all-white social elite was put in place (Van Kirk 1980:204). This elite shunned even those Metis women who had been long established at the top of the social hierarchy.

The specific impact of this social conflict on the behavior of Metis women has been highlighted by Van Kirk (1980). As a result, it is suggested here that ceramic use intensified as a means to reinforce social position in a display of behaviorial etiquette. This would further solidify the symbolic role of ceramics within Metis lifeways.

Ceramics, Social Integration and the Hivernant Buffalo Hunter

It has been a straight forward matter to propose the origins of ceramic use among Metis with status and behavioral etiquettes of the fur trade. The question remains as to how the intensification of ceramic use among a small elite spread to the Metis as a whole. As well, one also must ask why earthenware ceramics became so integrated into Metis material culture that even the mobile hunting brigades carried along this seemingly inappropriate assemblage. Status display for egalitarian hunters and gatherers obviously is not the answer.

To address these questions, it is necessary to adopt a view of material culture that is foreign to the utility theory of most archaeological analyses. Individual artifacts are not simply adaptive materials tied directly to functional roles. Rather, they represent one component in a consumptive pattern and this consumptive pattern provides a structured and understandable universe. Together, artifacts form a social code with many imbedded meanings. In championing this approach to material goods, Douglas and Isherwood suggest:

> Instead of supposing that goods are primarily needed for subsistence plus competitive display, let us assume that they are needed for making visible and stable the categories of culture. It is standard ethnographic practice to assume that all material possessions carry social meanings and to concentrate a main part of cultural analysis upon their use as communicators (1979:59).

To Douglas and Isherwood, goods are a fabric of culture that define and initiate action. Consumptive activity becomes social activity since goods provide the means through which social sharing and integration occurs. In the context of the *hivernant*, ceramics have become more than something to eat or drink from or show one's position in the fur trade hierarchy. They are a commodity with imbued social meaning that is shared by all Metis. In this shared meaning, ceramics provide an intelligible social environment. This becomes the focal point for later discussion.

In arguing a theory of consumptive behavior, Douglas and Isherwood (ibid. 101-04) provide an interpretive framework for the selection and spread of material forms that can be used to explain the ceramic transition between a *cadre* of elite Metis females and the *hivernant* buffalo hunter. This framework, labelled the ''infectious disease'' or ''epidemiological'' model for the spread of innovation, is derived by Douglas and Isherwood from broad based comparative analyses of consumer behavior. Underlying this theory is a postulate that social groups emphasize and strive toward uniformity of context. Goods found within one household are likely to be acquired by another, provided a social meaning can be derived. As each new household acquires the material item, that household becomes immune while at the same time it becomes a source of ''infection''. Douglas and Isherwood state:

> Social contacts are not random. The likelihood of a[n] owner influencing anyone he never meets is low. Each member of the population who becomes an owner reduces the number of susceptible nonowners in a circle of friends. So the rate of spread is affected by any discontinuities, regional and social, in personal relationships (ibid.).

When the greatest majority of a social group acquires the goods in question, these goods become a necessary and mandatory component of material culture regardless of utility. In many instances, it might also be added, regardless of cost.

The Red River colony of the early 19th century was a focal point for the development of the Metis as an identifiable ethnic group. That there were recognized positions of status largely dictated by fur trade bureaucratic structures has been noted. Yet, until the establishment of Simpson's ''all-white'' social elite of the 1830s, social relations between the fur trade officers, the Canadian voyageur and the Metis were fluid. There is little to suggest the development of rigidly structured social relations and social isolates between the Metis woman of the upper class and other Metis. This openness for the Metis as a whole is clearly illustrated by the observations of Alexander Ross describing events at Red River:

> Such is the roving propensity of these people that they are never in their proper element, unless gossiping from house to house. Like a bird in the bush, they are always on the move; and as often in their neighbours' houses as in their own. It is not uncommon for a woman getting up in the morning, to throw her blanket about her and set off on a gossiping tour among her neighbours. . . . We hope the ladies alluded to will take a useful lesson from these remarks. And likewise reform their shopping propensity and love of fineries, which do not bespeak industrious habits. . . .
>
> The men are great tobacco-smokers, the women as great tea-drinkers . . . Debts may accumulate, creditors may press, the labourer may go without his hire, the children run naked, but the tea-kettle and tobacco-pipe are indispensable. We have already observed that they are passionately fond of roving about, visiting, card-playing, and making up gossiping parties. To render this possible, they must of course be equally hospitable in return; and, in fact, all comers and goers are welcome guests at their board (Ross 1957:192–93).

Ross (ibid.) further notes that the "Canadians and half-breeds are promiscuously settled together and live in the same way."

That hospitality and a *joie de vivre* is characteristic of the Metis as a people is amply recorded in historical description (for example Anonymous 1860; Robinson 1879; Giraud 1986). It is exactly these conditions in which we can expect a rapid spread of ceramic use to the Metis community as a whole. The Red River colony provides a bounded space within which social relations among intensive users (the elite) and others (the Metis as a whole) are open. As ceramic use spreads from one group to another, social meaning is transferred from visual displays of status to a shared form of material culture. By the 1840s, ceramics are so integrated into the Metis way of life, that they are found within the material culture of even the most "poor" and mobile of hunting brigades. They have become a necessary component of material culture. The question remains as to why.

The earlier observations of Alexander Ross

remark specifically on the significance of tea drinking and smoking in Metis social relations. In a still earlier quote, Ross queries the presence of tea cups and saucers at an otherwise destitute hunting brigade camp. Tea and tea cups, as well as tobacco, are components of Metis material culture tied to social action. Together they are requisites for activities in which information exchange and social sharing occurs. Ross scorns these activities as gossiping and idle behavior. The contrary position is argued here. Social action through tea drinking with its necessary requisite, cups and saucers, is integral to Metis ethnic integration; it provides a forum for structured interaction.

In returning to the excavated ceramic assemblages from the *hivernant* wintering camps tested in 1986, the nature of the ceramic assemblage does support the historical descriptions of tea drinking and ceramic use. Of those specimens identified, almost all are fragments of cups, saucers or small bowls. Cups, saucers and bowls also are the predominant vessel forms at Buffalo Lake (Doll 1983:31–32, 41–42; Doll and Kidd 1976: 17–18) and at Bottom of the Mountain (Elliott 1971:190–93, 223–25). At the latter two sites and at Four Mile Coulee a small number of plate fragments also occur. These statements must be cautioned with the note that shard size limits vessel form identification for many specimens.

While the social and integrative activities of *hivernant* women are emphasized through the earthenware ceramic assemblages, the archaeological record has no equivalent in European derived goods for male smoking behavior. In fact, within the five excavated *hivernant* assemblages, there are but two clay pipe fragments from Bottom of the Mountain (Elliott 1971:209, 237) and one other from Buffalo Lake (Doll 1983:35). These assemblage frequencies do not contradict Ross's assertions of male tobacco use. Rather, the *hivernant* were using a less fragile alternative. This alternative, a "Cree style" stone pipe, is fully documented and described by Elliott (1972) for the Bottom of the Mountain assemblage. The use of this more durable alternative for smoking, heightens the necessity for a symbolic interpretation of the fragile ceramic ware for tea drinking.

Conclusion

This paper began with the presentation of an ambiguous archaeological context that required understanding. This ambiguity is the presence of fragile and often times ornate earthenwares in the material culture assemblage of the *hivernant* Metis. All other aspects of the *hivernant* assemblage directly reflect a frequently mobile communal bison hunting lifeway. Throughout the paper attempts have been made to resolve and clarify this anomaly.

In addressing the position of ceramics in Metis lifeways, it has been necessary to move into a realm of explanation not easily dealt with by archaeologists. Simply put, the roles material goods play in the nonmaterial dimension of culture include social organization and social integration. The initial adoption of ceramics by the Metis has been linked to factors of status and social role. It has been subsequently argued that, through social contact and blending, ceramics became a requisite household ware for the Metis of the Red River. Finally, it is proposed that the importance of a ceramic assemblage in Metis lifeways ultimately is tied to a symbolic role in the behavioral realms of social sharing, information exchange and structured interaction. For a frequently mobile and everchanging population of communal hunters and gatherers, activities requiring ceramic use are the threads of ethnic integration. Ceramics are a requisite to social action and in this symbolic context meaning overrides function.

In carrying this paper through to its conclusions, one additional area that archaeologists all too frequently fail to explore has been touched upon. This is the issue of gender and its relationship to historical processes and ethnic group integration. From the preceding, it is clear that Metis women were instrumental in the maintenance of Metis social relations. As Foster, an historian, states:

> Among mixed-blood populations, the world of adult females was of some, if not equal or greater, importance in the sharing of experiences that became institutionalized as Metis ways. Unfortunately the male bias of the documents renders it most difficult to garner an appreciation of these experiences (1985:84).

Interpretive analysis of ceramics and ceramic use is one potential means by which it becomes possible to examine this role within the realm of archaeological study.

ACKNOWLEDGMENTS

The contents and readability of this paper were greatly enhanced by the comments of Lynne Sussman and two anonymous reviewers. The *hivernant* Metis archaeological and architectural study, upon which much of the paper is based, was funded through grants from the Social Sciences and Humanities Research Council of Canada and the Saskatchewan Heritage Assistance Program.

REFERENCES

ANICK, NORMAN
1976 *The Metis of the South Saskatchewan River.* Manuscript Report 364, 2 vol., Parks Canada, Ottawa.

ANONYMOUS
1860 To Red River and Beyond. *Harpers New Monthly Magazine* 1860(August):584–585.

BROWN, JENNIFER
1980 *Strangers in Blood, Fur Trade Company Families in Indian Country.* University of British Columbia Press, Vancouver.

BURLEY, DAVID, GAYLE HORSFALL AND JOHN BRANDON
1988 *Stability and Change in Western Canadian Metis Lifeways. An Archaeological and Architectural Study.* Ms. on file Archaeological Resource Management Section, Saskatchewan Department of Culture and Recreation, Regina.

DOLL, MAURICE F. V.
1983 *The Buffalo Lake Metis Site (FdPe 1). Report on Project 82-27 Field Season of 1982.* Ms. on file, Archaeological Survey of Alberta, Edmonton.

DOLL, MAURICE F. V., AND ROBERT KIDD
1976 *The Buffalo Lake Metis Site.* Ms. on file, Provincial Museum of Alberta, Edmonton.

DOUGLAS, MARY, AND BARON ISHERWOOD
1979 *The World of Goods. Towards an Anthropology of Consumption.* Allen Lane, London.

ELLIOTT, JACK
1971 *Hivernant Archaeology in the Cypress Hills.* Unpublished M.A. Thesis, University of Calgary, Calgary.

1972 Tobacco Pipes Among the Hivernant Hide Hunters: A.D. 1860–1870. *The Western Canadian Journal of Anthropology* 3(1):146–57.

FOSTER, JOHN E.
1976 The Origins of the Mixed Bloods in the Canadian West. In *Essays on Western History*, edited by L. H. Thomas, pp. 69–80. University of Alberta Press, Edmonton.
1985 Some Questions and Perspectives on the Origins of Metis Roots. In *The New Peoples: Being and Becoming Metis in North America*, edited by J. Peterson and J. Brown, pp. 73–91. The University of Manitoba Press, Winnipeg

GIRAUD, MARCEL
1986 *The Metis in the Canadian West*, translated by G. Woodcock, 2 vol. University of Alberta Press, Edmonton (original French edition published 1945).

LEONE, MARK P.
1982 Some Opinions About Recovering Mind. *American Antiquity* 47(4):742–60.

PETERSON, JACQUELINE
1981 *The People in Between: Indian-White Marriages and the Genesis of a Metis Society and Culture in the Great Lakes Region, 1680–1830*. Unpublished Ph.D. Dissertation, University of Illinois at Chicago Circle, Chicago.

PYSZCZYK, HEINZ W.
1985 The Role of Material Culture in the Structure of Fur Trade Society. In *Status, Structure and Stratification: Current Archaeological Reconstructions*, edited by M. Thompson, M. T. Garcia and F. Kense, pp. 399–406. The Archaeological Association of the University of Calgary, Calgary.

RAY, ARTHUR J.
1974 *Indians in the Fur Trade: Their Role as Hunters, Trappers and Middlemen in the Lands Southwest of Hudson Bay 1660–1870*. University of Toronto Press, Toronto.

ROBINSON, H. M.
1879 *The Great Fur Land or Sketches of Life in the Hudson's Bay Territory*. G. P. Putnam's Sons, Ltd., New York.

ROE, FRANK G.
1934 The Extermination of the Buffalo in Western Canada. *The Canadian Historical Review* 15(1):1–23.

ROSS, ALEXANDER
1957 *The Red River Settlement: Its Rise Progress and Present State*. Ross and Haines Inc., Minneapolis (original published 1856).

SPRAGUE, D. N., AND R. P. FRYE
1983 *The Genealogy of the First Metis Nation: The Development and Dispersal of the Red River Metis, 1820–1900*. Pemmican Publications, Winnipeg.

SUSSMAN, LYNNE
1979 *Spode/Copeland Transfer-Printed Patterns*. Parks Canada Occasional Papers in History and Archaeology, 23, Ottawa.

VAN KIRK, SYLVIA
1980 *Many Tender Ties: Women in Fur Trade Society, 1670–1870*. Watson and Dwyer, Winnipeg.

DAVID V. BURLEY
DEPARTMENT OF ARCHAEOLOGY
SIMON FRASER UNIVERSITY
BURNABY, BRITISH COLUMBIA
V5A 1S6

PARKER B. POTTER, JR.

What Is the Use of Plantation Archaeology?

ABSTRACT

This essay is a commentary on plantation archaeology inspired by a recent article by William H. Adams and Sarah Jane Boling (1989). By asking what is the use of plantation archaeology, this author does not mean to reject this increasingly popular archaeological enterprise. Rather, the purpose is to provoke serious reflection on two issues: (1) the reasons for doing plantation archaeology and (2) the audiences for such studies. The essay has three main parts: a general discussion of the status of self-reflection in plantation archaeology; a specific critique of Adams and Boling's piece; and a set of four suggestions for improving on Adams and Boling's work, *not* by changing their analysis but by paying greater attention to the contexts in which slave-owned ceramics existed in the past and the contexts in which these same objects exist today, as archaeological finds. This commentary is based on critical theory, and on the proposition that, whether it is explicitly interpreted for the public or not, any archaeological project is a public performance. Whenever archaeologists go about their archaeological work, they perform, at the very least, their own training and biases, their sources of funding and support, *and* the history of their research subjects, a history to which they may have only the most tenuous connections.

Introduction

It would be an overstatement to say that there is a revolution afoot in American archaeology, but there is enough of an honest difference of opinion within the field for Robert Preucel to have organized a Southern Illinois University/Center for Archaeological Investigations Visiting Scholar's Conference on what he terms the "processual/postprocessual debate" (Preucel 1991). Given this way of characterizing the current debate(s), it is important to note that postprocessual archaeology is less a coherent movement than it is a collection of kindred perspectives. Among the various postprocessual archaeologies, there is critical archaeology (Wylie 1985; Leone 1986; Leone et al.

1987; Washburn 1987; Potter 1989; Pinsky and Wylie 1990) which is based on the critical theory of the Frankfurt School (Held 1980; Geuss 1981; Arato and Gebhardt 1982). This commentary uses two elements of critical archaeology to form a critique of the recent article by Adams and Boling (1989) entitled "Status and Ceramics for Planters and Slaves in Three Coastal Georgia Plantations." Specifically, it is argued: (1) that Adams and Boling's article is not adequately self-reflective and (2) that this lack of self-reflection significantly impedes the authors' ability to understand the implications of their work and to anticipate the possible uses to which their conclusions could be put.

Adams and Boling's Conclusion

This critique begins with the last two sentences of Adams and Boling's article:

> Indeed, on such plantations slaves may be better understood within the context of being peasants or serfs, regarding their economic status. Their legal status was still as chattel slave, of course, but their economic freedoms were much greater than most people realize (Adams and Boling 1989:94).

The question here is a simple one. To whom is this statement directed? Or, stated another way, who is the audience for Adams and Boling's analysis and the conclusions they draw? Or, more aggressively, who would gain and who would lose as a result of social action based on a conclusion like this? This last question is a vital one, given the Frankfurt School understanding of the inseparability of knowledge and human interests.

These questions are asked because it is not evident from their article that Adams and Boling have asked them, either of themselves or of contemporary African Americans, the audience most likely to be affected by their work. These questions matter because it would be relatively easy for someone advocating a racist position to use a statement like Adams and Boling's conclusion as a starting point from which to claim that slavery was not such a bad deal for enslaved African Americans. This claim, in turn, could be used to argue that if slave life was not so bad, then contemporary

African Americans do not have as much to complain about as they think they do. This hypothetical argument may sound far-fetched, but one lesson in David Duke's recent political success in Louisiana is that there are plenty of people out there who would be more than happy to buy into an argument like the one just outlined. Moving from today's front pages to the academic literature, one can find many examples of the political use (and/or misuse) of archaeology and history. Clark (1957:259–260) on Nazi Germany, Silverberg (1968, 1974) on the Moundbuilder myth, Trigger (1980) on Native Americans, and Hall (1984, 1988) on South Africa are just several of the growing number of archaeologists who have turned their attention to the social use of archaeological knowledge in the societies that sponsor or support archaeological research. In addition, this issue seems to be a central theme in several volumes of the recently published "One World Archaeology" series (Layton 1988, 1989; Gathercole and Lowenthal 1990; Stone and MacKenzie 1990).

The only point here is that Adams and Boling's article would have been a more socially responsible piece of scholarship if they had considered and acknowledged the potential usefulness of their conclusions, particularly to those who would try to minimize the enormity of slavery in order to deny the legitimacy of current claims of racial discrimination against African Americans and to thwart the efforts of African Americans to achieve and preserve full civil rights. At this point, the term "social responsibility" needs to be defined.

This writer's intention is *not* to equate social responsibility with one particular theoretical or political viewpoint. Rather, in this situation, social responsibility means having a full awareness of the contexts and the consequences of the work one does, the conclusions one reaches, and the modes of expression one chooses. The entire academic enterprise and archaeologists' own professional lives are based on the idea that words are powerful things, and meaning resides at several levels in the texts researchers produce. Thus, as defined here, social responsibility means nothing more than using the most sophisticated methods available to mean what is said and to say what is meant, to an acknowledged audience. In early drafts of this article, the use of the term "social responsibility" troubled some readers. During the course of revision, this writer has discovered a good clear statement on this issue. Writing in the *Winterthur Portfolio* Forum, Edward Chappell (1989:287) says, "My argument, simply put, is that museums have a responsibility for the broad social implications of what they present, as well as for the accuracy and clarity of the subject with which they are dealing." He also notes that "most of us are too involved in a headlong pursuit of the past to glance over our shoulders at the effects that we and our predecessors have had on the world around us" (Chappell 1989:248–249)."

Finally, near the end of his article, Chappell argues the point on which this commentary is based:

> Clearly it is the responsibility of museum planners to anticipate . . . misreadings as well as to ensure the accuracy of the presentation and the physical setting. We must consider how exhibitions may be misinterpreted, as well as how we intend them to be understood (Chappell 1989:263).

Chappell's comments are directed toward the museum profession, but as already argued, it is reasonable to consider any instance of archaeological activity—and the products that result—as a public performance, as an exhibition in Chappell's sense.

As Sinclair emphasizes in a discussion of archaeology in Mozambique, controlling the uses of archaeological work is by no means a sure thing: "We are faced with a situation (which seems to occur widely) where the producer of even relevant scientific knowledge does not control the ambits within which such information is to be used" (Sinclair 1990:157). While researchers may sometimes (or frequently) lose control of the knowledge produced, they are *always* free to anticipate its potential impacts, and failure to do so is, in Chappell's terms, socially irresponsible.

To return to Adams and Boling, the irony in their article is that they have provided a potential weapon for a social and political position they no doubt find repugnant. The key to this irony is their apparent lack of self-reflection. The qualifer "apparent" is used because Adams has indeed presented these conclusions to African-American audiences (Adams 1989, pers. comm.). That fact needs to be *in the article itself*, as a part of an internal mechanism designed to protect the article's powerful conclusion from blatant misuse by those with an agenda that runs counter to the intentions of the authors. What Adams and Boling fail to provide is precisely what Epperson *does* provide when he characterizes his work in plantation archaeology as "addressing the construction of race within what remains a largely racist society" (Epperson 1990:35). Archaeologists may argue with Epperson's assessment of contemporary American society (this writer does not), but at least it is there to be examined; Adams and Boling give no clue as to their view of the world into which they are sending their research and its conclusions. Furthermore, Epperson is not shy about articulating his agenda, which is to help inform "the fundamental critique of oppression and domination, both historically and in the present" (Epperson 1990:35). This critique constitutes a "social and political commitment . . . to help create a more humane social order" (Epperson 1990:35). In contrast, Adams and Boling provide neither a reflexive commentary on their intentions nor a consideration of any of the various social agendas for which their work could be a tool.

Plantation Archaeology as Unreflective

A lack of self reflection is hardly unique to Adams and Boling. To the contrary, an unreflective viewpoint is exactly the perspective adopted in much of the plantation archaeology that has been carried out over the last 15 years (Leone and Potter 1988:307–312) and in fact, much of American archaeology (Potter 1989:21–45, 1991). For example, there is virtually no acknowledgment of contemporary social context in any of the articles in Singleton's (1985) edited volume, *The Archaeology of Slavery and Plantation Life*. Two particularly telling instances of this lack of reflection are William Kelso's (1984) book on Kingsmill Plantation and the large body of work inspired by John

Otto's (1984) book on Cannon's Point Plantation, based on his dissertation (Otto 1975).

The second chapter of Kelso's book, called "Above Ground," contains three sections: "Context," "Things," and "People." What is interesting is that most of Kelso's discussion of slaves and slave life appears in the section called "Things." The section on "People" is mostly reserved for slave-owning *white* people. This understanding of slaves as things certainly characterizes the time period about which Kelso is writing, but the way Kelso uses this 18th-century understanding, unreflectively, to form his own narrative strategy serves to perpetuate those categories today. That is, Kelso acknowledges neither the source of the categories he uses nor the historical justification for calling slaves "things." Thus, the idea that slaves were things is expressed in Kelso's own, living authorial voice. As a result, the reader is left with no logical alternative other than to conclude that Kelso himself, as an active member of 20th-century society, considers African Americans to have been things. Of course this is absurd, but Kelso invites this inappropriate interpretation by failing to understand that how one says something is a part of what one says. This point is far from esoteric, and has been made in discussions of archaeological education in Venezuela (Vargas Arenas and Sanoja Obediente 1990:51–52) and the United States (Kehoe 1990:213) as well as in discussions of museum exhibits on Native American topics (Lester 1987; Blancke and Slow Turtle 1990:125). In the case of Kingsmill Plantations, this writer would argue that no matter how sympathetically or humanistically slave life is presented in a section called "Things," there is no avoiding the implication that African Americans were things, that it was appropriate to think of them as such, and that it *still is* appropriate to think of African-American people as things.

This writer's solution to this problem is not to ignore or deny the 18th-century viewpoint, but instead to clearly label it both culturally and temporally and then to separate it carefully from the contemporary perspective that informs a particular piece of work on 18th-century slavery. In this case, since his section headings say otherwise,

Kelso should have told his readers explicitly that *he* does not think that African Americans are not people, that his section headings are intended to represent *only* a particular 18th-century viewpoint and not his own. Instead of assuming this category, Kelso could have explored its origins and history, working as Epperson does to "denaturalize" the category of race by demonstrating "that it is not a universal, natural, or inevitable aspect of the human condition" (Epperson 1990: 35). The starting point for all of this is self-reflection. If Kelso had considered the implications of his section headings, it is doubtful that he would have used them the way he did. The self-reflective question he could have asked himself is: "are my feelings on the humanity of African Americans accurately represented by these section headings?" Thus, this writer is not telling Kelso what to think or say, but only asking whether or not he *meant* to say what it seems that he *did* say, subtextually.

With regard to Otto's Cannon's Point work, this writer's criticism is somewhat different but also rooted in an unreflective viewpoint. Furthermore, the argument lies more with those who have followed Otto's example than with Otto himself, but because the issue to be dealt with was introduced to historical archaeology through Otto's work, that will be the focus of this discussion. Otto's goal in analyzing the archaeological record at Cannon's Point has been to investigate and describe the living conditions on an ante-bellum plantation, as a way of augmenting discussions of "the legal or social aspects of slave treatment" (Otto 1975:2) based on written records. The three principal realms of material culture Otto uses are houses, artifacts (such as ceramic and glass tableware), and food remains. The problem is that Otto's basic question and his analytical framework, used unreflectively, constitute a dangerous trap for plantation studies.

The spring in this trap is the idea of quality of life. While Otto is very careful to limit himself to *describing* the conditions of slave life, others have taken the logical step to *judging* the quality of slave life. Otto (1975:2), Singleton (1985:7), and Reitz et al. (1985:185) have all characterized the nutritional analyses of Fogel and Engerman (1974)

as controversial if not problematic. But the real problem with *Time on the Cross* is not the accuracy of the answers it provides, which is where the debate is currently being carried out. Rather, the problems with studies like *Time on the Cross* lie with the questions they ask and in their inattention to the sources of these questions. Put simply, is it really reasonable to pose *any* research question that could be answered with a statement that slave life was not all that bad? Is it reasonable to reach a conclusion along the lines of "everyone knows that these people were slaves, *but* they had nutritious food, adequate housing, and/or stylish tableware" as if food, living space, or ceramics could ever, under any circumstances, obviate the condition of involuntary servitude? Otto's questions and answers are not of this sort, but intentionally or not, Otto has set an agenda for plantation archaeology, and his work has encouraged others, including Adams and Boling, to think in this way.

As suggested above, the ability to ask questions that logically entail these seemingly unreasonable answers is based on a failure of reflection, and this failure is composed of several parts. First, the quality of slave life is invariably judged in western scientific terms that may or may not be appropriate to the lives being judged. Without demonstrating that these measures of quality of life are meaningful in terms of an 18th-century African-American worldview, their use constitutes a continuation—albeit an intellectual one—of the domination of master over slave. Lilla Watson, an indigenous Australian (or Murri) who is also a western trained academic, pinpoints this issue when she says:

> It is still a case of white academics and writers describing us and our culture, generally using Western concepts, categories, and definitions—i.e., white terms of reference. The areas of study undertaken represent white preoccupations, perspectives, and priorities. . . . We have had enough of being defined and described by whites, of having others determine what is relevant and important in Aboriginality. We will say who and what we are. It has taken a long time for white Australia to reach the point of being ready to hear what we say, rather than what others say about us (Watson 1990:92).

In discussing various western perspectives on Australian aboriginal culture, Barlow (1990:76–

78) goes well beyond the neutral term "etic," referring instead to "colonial knowledge," which he sees as a specific body of information used as a tool for cultural oppression. Watson and Barlow both identify *two* problems with Western categories. They are inappropriate to the people whose cultures are being studied *and* they are potentially injurious to the literal and cultural descendants of those research subjects. That is, the use of such categories is both bad science and bad politics.

Returning to plantation studies in the American South, there is the additional problem of false comparability. Many archaeological analysts of plantation slavery have followed Otto and Stanley South (1977, 1978, 1979, 1988) in adopting a radically functionalist approach. Orser (1989) provides a commentary on this trend. Archaeological plantation studies are so tied to a functionalist approach that it is probably a good idea to wonder about the degree to which the current popularity of plantation studies is driven by the fact that plantations lend themselves so readily to functionalism; it may well be the case that current archaeological studies of plantation slavery have far more to say to functionalist social scientists than they have to say to African-American descendants of plantation slaves. A principal by-product of all this is a systems-based mode of analysis that compares planters, overseers, and slaves on the basis of differential deposits of various classes of artifactual material. In such analyses, things stand for the people who used them—a plate for a planter and so on, and it is this identity between people and things that gives rise to the problem of false comparability.

Because they were made out of the same materials, or were the same objects, plantation houses, meals, and dishes are analytically interchangeable today in a way that the people who used those objects were absolutely *not* socially interchangeable 200 years ago. Furthermore, on most plantations, ceramic types circulated much more freely from table to table than did the people who ate at those tables. The probability of *any* kind of plate turning up on the table of a planter, overseer, or slave was far greater than the probability of a slave eating at a planter's table or a planter eating at a slave's table. To take this problem one step further, the ability to "translate" from slave life to overseer life to planter life through the use of scales based on ceramics, architecture, or food remains is dangerous because such translation is, in fact, the basis for judging the quality of life rather than simply describing the conditions of life. Slave-owned ceramics can be compared with planter-owned ceramics by means of Miller's (1980) price indices, but such an analysis, with ceramics in the foreground, ignores the fact that ceramics were not the glue that held a plantation together, slavery was. For both of these reasons, artifacts do not stand for the people who used them, or do so in a very limited way, *unless* they are examined in the context of a theory that gives precedence to the economic and social relations of slavery and which explicitly contradicts the social mobility implied by functionalist material culture analyses. This fallacy of letting things stand for people is the same issue Marx identifies as the fetishism of commodities when he says, "There it is, a definite social relation between men, that assumes, in their eyes, the fantastic form of a relation between things" (Marx 1977:246).

The key issue here is not quality of life, but rather *who controlled* the quality of life, the very issue that is obscured in analyses like Adams and Boling's. In effect, Adams and Boling argue that the ability of both planters and slaves to buy similar tableware is a more powerful social fact than the ability of planters to buy and sell slaves. Rather than studying the workings of slavery, analyses like these *assume* slavery and jump past it into one or another material culture subsystem. However, it is likely that on most plantations, most of the realms of material culture measured to determine the quality of life were controlled by white owners and overseers, indirectly if not directly. If slaves hunted their own game or bought their own ceramics, it is probably because their owners allowed them to do these things, and owners *certainly* had the power to prohibit these activities. This applies as well to the Africanisms that plantation archaeologists have worked so hard to identify. It is also likely that these limited "social freedoms," "cultural freedoms," and "economic freedoms" were carefully monitored, calculated, balanced, and traded off *by plantation owners* against other, more powerful unfreedoms. It was within the power of *any* plantation owner to grant (or restrict) a range of "economic freedoms," but it was most definitely *not* within the power of any slave to achieve the "freedoms" available to some slaves. Thus, slavery is a more significant social fact here than the possession of pearlware or porcelain. Slavery structured ceramic acquisition in a way that ceramic possession could not structure or affect the social relations of slavery; no amount of porcelain on his or her table could transform a slave into a planter. Discussions of quality of life, which *assume* slavery and therefore ignore its workings, can serve to mask the more profound material culture issue which is how material culture, some of it representing certain limited "economic freedoms," was used both overtly and covertly to control slaves and to enforce the dominance of their masters.

Having asserted the dominance of slave owners over slaves, and the pre-eminence of slavery among the various social facts of plantation life, one crucial distinction needs to be made. Specifically, acknowledging the ultimate power of slave owners over slaves is not the same thing as ignoring the fact that slaves were often able to improve their circumstances and shape many aspects of their daily lives. This writer clearly intends the former and rejects the latter. Without question, some slaves went to great lengths to preserve their own cultural traditions and to create new ones, but they usually did so within the larger context of a social and economic institution over which they had relatively little control. In this matter this archaeologist follows Orser (1989:35) who says, "Although plantation slaves helped create their world within the plantations of their bondage . . . it would be oversimplistic to state that they did so in isolation of the prevailing plantation social fields, or relations of production." On this point, Epperson (1990:36) states that "archaeologists must . . . struggle to recognize and celebrate the unique African-American heritage without glossing the context of oppression within which this oppositional culture was, and continues to be,

forged." Epperson borrows a solution to this conundrum, or at least a name for the solution, from feminist scholarship. This solution is the "double strategy" of "learning to fight inequality and injustice while preserving and fostering diversity" (Epperson 1990:35). In Epperson's approach to plantation archaeology, this double strategy consists of two goals, "valorization of the African-American culture of resistance and the denaturalization of essentialist racial categories" (Epperson 1990:36). This writer's intention here is to oppose the position, held in some quarters, that it is somehow paternalistic to acknowledge the dominance of slave owners over slaves.

As already argued with respect to Kelso, this writer does not believe Otto to be an apologist for slavery or for contemporary racism and is only suggesting that by failing to be adequately self-reflective, Otto and, more importantly, those who have followed his lead have chosen a set of questions and an analytical framework that perpetuates the worldview of the masters at the expense of representing the worldview of the enslaved. And they have done so without adequately considering the interests of the people most likely to be affected by their conclusions. While a working plantation is a perfect example of a social or economic system, it is a system that worked far better for some participants than for others. One solution to this classic dilemma of functionalism would have been to identify clearly the source of these questions and frameworks in 20th-century scholarship rather than in some continuity with or sympathy for antebellum slaveowners who justified slaveowning through paternalistic demonstrations of the "good" living conditions in their quarters. Otto could have used self-reflection to identify the highly problematic nature of his research orientation by asking himself: "how would a group of African Americans in former plantation country respond to a talk based upon my inquiry into the quality of life enjoyed/endured by their slave ancestors?" Or more pointedly, "of what use is it to contemporary African Americans to know the quality of the dishes used by their enslaved ancestors?" Relatively few plantation archaeologists have asked themselves questions like these, nor—

more importantly—have they asked such questions directly of the descendants of the people they are studying.

Furthermore, the point of this article is not to provide answers to these questions; this writer does not have any. The best that can be offered is a method (critical archaeology) that contains procedures for identifying constituencies, generating socially relevant research questions, and presenting results. Whatever answers may seem to be implied flow from the use of a social theory (Marxism) that assumes economic exploitation, as identified by class analysis. The hypothetical audience of African Americans invoked from time to time throughout this discussion is constituted by a use of critical theory. While it is clearly inappropriate for this writer to speak for African-American interests, this article has been written because it is even more inappropriate for Adams and Boling not to have considered contemporary African-American interests, a failure this writer attributes to a lack of reflection. To state this point another way, it is absolutely not appropriate to assert that Adams and Boling's potential African-American audience thinks about its cultural heritage in the same way that Lilla Watson thinks about Murri history, but it should have been Adams and Boling's place to *ask* whether this is the case or not. At this point, it is important to recognize that while this writer speaks of African Americans as if they all feel the same way and share the same interests, they clearly do not. For this reason, any effort to understand African-American interests in the archaeology of African-American heritage must be local, ongoing, and directed to specific communities.

Having touched on one of the ways in which Adams and Boling's article is of a piece with previous attempts at plantation archaeology, this writer would like to return to the article itself and will begin by describing the article's major flaw, its failure of reflection. This will be followed with four suggestions for solving this problem.

A Failure of Reflection

The principal criticism of Adams and Boling's article is its failure of reflection. There is simply no evidence in this article that Adams and Boling have made any effort to understand the needs and interests of an audience made up of the descendants of their research subjects. At the same time, however, Adams has given at least three talks based on his attempt "to provide blacks with a heritage they would otherwise not have known about" (Adams 1989, pers. comm.). Specifically, Adams has

> addressed several African-American audiences and made the same conclusion to them that the slaves on Georgia plantations had the ability to exercise a greater amount of freedom than is generally recognized; these audiences liked to hear that slaves could buy and sell many items and did not have to rely on massa for it (Adams 1989, pers. comm.).

There are two problems here. First, it is important to distinguish between the appreciation Adams' audiences have shown him for his scholarly interest in their past, which is no doubt quite real, and the more important goal of providing these audiences with interpretations they can use, in their own interests. These are two very different things, and Adams has demonstrated only the first. Adams and Boling's failure to fulfill this second responsibility may be rooted in the idea of their "giving" a heritage to African Americans rather than working with African Americans to create a place for them in the process of heritage production. The simplest way to achieve this would be to involve African Americans in the development of research questions rather than just presenting them with research conclusions based on questions that may or may not be relevant to their interests.

In such an endeavor, the point of reflection is not simply to anticipate how African Americans will react to a set of research results, but rather, it is to consider as broadly as possible the issue of what a particular community of African Americans can do with such results to advance their own interests. Stated another way, the pivotal question is not, "Did the audience applaud?" but instead, "Was the audience able to do anything with what they heard, after they left the auditorium?" As already noted, this line of reasoning is based on the Frankfurt School idea that knowledge is inseparable from human interests and social action.

Given this concern, it is reasonable to ask what is the use of analyses that downplay the institution of slavery while focusing on the ways that slaves were able to work around the dominance of their masters. Again it is important to remember that neither the ownership of porcelain nor the retention of Africanisms could *ever* deliver a slave from bondage. If the value of historical knowledge is its usefulness as a basis for future action, archaeologists have two choices in doing the historical archaeology of slavery. They can either present a version of the past that teaches people to outwit their oppressors while leaving the basis for oppression intact—which is what some plantation archaeology does—or present a version of the past that focusses directly on the structures of oppression. The hope is that this second approach will help people *of all races* to recognize contemporary vestiges of past domination and therefore to challenge and change the institutions that support domination rather than accepting domination and simply circumventing it. Placing too much emphasis on the limited freedoms available to some slaves and the ability of slaves to create certain aspects of their own world could do a disservice to contemporary African Americans engaged in the attempt to identify and challenge the racial discrimination that still exists in contemporary American society. From the standpoint of critical theory, studies like Adams and Boling's do little to foster the empowerment of contemporary African Americans.

Furthermore, if knowledge like the conclusion drawn by Adams and Boling is not especially useful to contemporary African Americans or is irrelevant to them, then this knowledge has the potential to be quite useful to opponents of equal rights for African Americans. If one accepts the Frankfurt School position that knowledge is never neutral, then knowledge is either for or against. And in this writer's opinion, it is nothing short of unethical to dig up the artifacts of a people's past if the resulting representation of that past is likely to be used against them. Wilcomb Washburn (1988) has recently, and publicly, scoffed at the idea that, "if, in excavating a site, the evidence seemed to suggest that the slaves, for example, were not so badly off, that line of work should be broken off for fear of

hurting the interests of blacks." While one would argue, in such a case, for reanalysis based on the premise that *by definition* slaves could never be well off, the position that Washburn ridicules really amounts to little more than an adaptation of the most basic standard of anthropological ethics: the injunction against ethnographers doing harm to their informants.

To sum up this argument, this writer finds fault with Adams and Boling for failing to reflect on the circumstances in which their archaeological work has been conducted. Specifically, they are conducting plantation research in the midst of a social, economic, and political environment in which the reverberations of plantation slavery are still echoing. By failing to listen to these echoes, Adams and Boling have chimed in without knowing what tune they are playing. In the criticisms already made above and in the four suggestions that follow, this writer is disputing neither the analytical competence Adams and Boling bring to their task *nor* their right to draw the conclusions they draw but is only suggesting avenues they might have wished to explore had they carefully considered the implications of those conclusions.

Four Approaches to Reflection

Interestingly, one way of improving Adams and Boling's article may be found in the article that follows theirs in *Historical Archaeology* 23(1). In his cogent and persuasive discussion of ceramic use by the métis in the Northwestern Plains of Canada, David Burley (1989) goes a step beyond determining who had what by paying careful attention to the various audiences for the cultural messages conveyed by ceramic use. Through the use of historical and ethnohistorical data, he is able to make considerable progress toward understanding ceramic artifacts in terms of their native meanings rather than simply in terms of the Spode/Copeland pattern books or Miller's (1980) CC index. By searching out a native point of view through a consideration of the audience for slave quarter ceramic use, Adams and Boling could have made a more compelling case for why African

Americans today should care about the monetary values of their ancestors' ceramic holdings. Furthermore, had they been looking in an appropriate way, Adams and Boling may have been able to find ways of seeing resistance to slavery, even in the use of Euroamerican objects by slaves. In fact, Otto (1975, 1984) has already had some success with this general kind of research in plantation archaeology. One of his principal conclusions from Cannon's Point is that different classes of material culture (architecture and ceramics) served different functions in representing and enacting the complex web of relationships that enmeshed planters, overseers, and slaves; similarities in architecture linked planters and overseers while similarities in ceramic holdings linked overseers and slaves.

Ironically, a second way of improving upon Adams and Boling's article may be found in the article that comes just *before* their piece. In his discussion of plantation archaeology in the Low Country of Georgia and South Carolina, J.W. Joseph pays some attention to the broader historical context of plantation slavery. Specifically, he sees a connection between the 1808 ban on the importation of slaves and the improvement of living conditions of plantation slaves (Joseph 1989:64–65). He realizes that after 1808 slaves were required not only to produce agricultural products, they were also required to reproduce the labor force of which they were a part. It is very likely that an improved "quality of life" contributed to the efficiency of this unique reproduction of the means of production. That is, the allegedly high quality of slaves' lives served the interests of their owners. Given this, Adams and Boling could have strengthened their analysis by considering more fully the broader context in which they found evidence for the economic freedom of some slaves. To their credit, Adams and Boling do consider the differences between gang-based labor and task-based labor but there are still important questions they leave unasked. How did slaves come to attain their economic freedoms? What was in it for their masters? The point here is the same one that Joseph recognizes: economic freedom for slaves, such as it was, or good living conditions, did not exist in a vacuum on the plantation. They were connected to other social and historical factors which need to be considered before a collection of porcelain shards can have any real meaning.

With respect to both of these criticisms, self-reflection would have shown Adams and Boling the narrow, acontextual data base with which they chose to work and the lack of weight this lack of context imposes on their conclusions. By ignoring the context of ceramic use and display as well as the social and historical context of slave life, Adams and Boling allow themselves to use a slender data base to arrive at conclusions that would be amusing if they were not potentially dangerous. In the final two suggestions, this writer goes beyond *Historical Archaeology* 23(1) and discusses two deeper issues which have been discussed in the work of Charles Orser and Theresa Singleton.

The logic that underlies Adams and Boling's conclusion is "sure they were slaves, *but.* . . ." It is precisely this readiness to separate the fact of slavery from various aspects of slave life that prevents Adams and Boling from framing an analysis that is useful to any African-American audience imaginable. As noted above, once one chooses to peel slavery off from diet or ceramic holdings or architecture, it becomes possible to ignore slavery completely and thus fail to see, or even to ask about, its role in these various aspects of life. Again, Vargas Arenas and Sanoja Obediente (1990) discuss the political power of the categories and compartments used to "hold" and discuss the past. An alternative approach, and the one taken by Orser (1987, 1988a, 1988b), is Marxian analysis that sees slavery as the key organizing factor behind *all* aspects of slave life. That is, Orser does not ghettoize slavery as just another independent variable in the lives of slaves. Thus, for Orser, the main material culture research question becomes: "how did this or that element of material culture contribute to the maintenance of a slave-based economy?" It is highly unlikely that the economic freedoms Adams and Boling identified came at no cost to the slaves who enjoyed them. Adams and Boling's analysis would have been more powerful if they had explored the question of how porcelain-buying slaves paid for the privilege of buying their own dishes. What was the trade-off? What did the slave owner get, or think that he or she got, by allowing this small measure of economic freedom? This line of inquiry is very likely one that Adams and Boling would have explored had they made a commitment to providing information that was potentially useful to an audience composed of African-American descendants of slaves instead of an audience composed of historical archaeologists whose primary agenda is refining and applying George Miller's ceramic indices.

The fourth suggestion for improving upon Adams and Boling comes from the work of Singleton and her key insight that African Americans today have relatively little interest in archaeology (Singleton 1988:364). In the same vein, Charles Fairbanks has said,

> I would like to admit to a personal lapse in the results of my work in slave and plantation archaeology. While it is certainly important to let other archaeologists and historians know what we have done, we have a larger and more imperative duty. That is to inform the people we are studying of those results. Throughout the country there is a large body of Black persons who should know what we have found out about their past. That they have not shown a great deal of interest until now is surely our fault (Fairbanks 1984:12).

Singleton's response to this problem is her argument, by example, that it is important for archaeologists to study carefully the popular environments in which their work is displayed, discussed, and used. In particular, Singleton discusses the place of plantation archaeology in the museum world and in the lives of contemporary African Americans.

Archaeologists would all do well to follow her lead by understanding that data are likely to have use-lives that extend beyond the immediate utilizations of them in site reports and scholarly articles. If an archaeologist does not take control over how her data are presented to the public at large, it is certain that control over the meaning of those data will fall to others with interests that may or may not be those of the archaeologist. This idea that knowledge is usually knowledge for a purpose gets back to the idea of social responsibility that was introduced earlier. Keeping track of the public representations of data, in the loci identified by Singleton, is simply a way of making sure that data always say what researchers mean and, in the case

of plantation archaeology, are never used to prolong the victimization of those who are already acknowledged to be history's victims. Historical archaeology should not contribute to making the descendants of victims *in* history victims *of* history and historical scholarship.

To follow up on Singleton's insight that historical scholars should attend to the public performance of the data they create, she also notes that slavery is being seen less and less as a taboo subject in museums. There are at least two parts to this phenomenon. First, history museum educators generally are starting to come to grips with a wide variety of controversial or painful aspects of the American past (Baker and Leon 1986; Patterson 1986; Crosson 1988; Sellars 1988; Brown 1989). In addition to this, and more specifically, museum educators are beginning to learn that there are ways of teaching about domination in the past without endorsing, encouraging, inviting, or inspiring more of the same, in the future. First among these techniques is the straightforward step of anticipating, openly acknowledging, and clearly rejecting any readily apparent yet inappropriate conclusion that could be drawn from a body of archaeological data. That is, archaeologists can try to predict the most egregious potential misuses of their work and then tell people what they mean, in part, by telling them what is *not* meant. This may sound simplistic or unnecessary, but perhaps Adams and Boling should have told readers explicitly not to use their analysis to conclude that slavery was not such a bad life. Dennis Pogue (1990:4) takes this very step when, after presenting archaeological evidence for a higher-than-expected degree of "material comfort," he clearly states that "the bottom line of all this is that they were still slaves, and this [finding] does not imply that their daily life was any less onerous." Without this kind of statement, it is difficult to distinguish between propositions Adams and Boling intend to test and beliefs they assume they hold in common with their readers.

Conclusion

This commentary concludes by taking the step that this writer has criticized Adams and Boling for not taking. Namely, this writer wants to be absolutely explicit about what this article is, and what it is not. First and foremost, and despite what the subtext may *seem* to say, this writer is not accusing Adams and Boling of racism, nor implying that they are apologists for slavery. Rather, it is suggested that they have framed a conclusion that could easily be used to advance a racist argument and that they have not done enough to anticipate and guard against such a misuse of their conclusion.

To restate the main point, this all flows from a failure of reflection. It is this failure of reflection that allows Adams and Boling to speak of the ability of slaves to purchase ceramics as "economic freedom" while ignoring the fact that the same set of equivalencies used to attach a monetary value to a teapot was also used to attach values to slaves. One must question the "economic freedom" of a $500 slave buying a $2.50 teapot from a shopkeeper who could not even conceive of calculating his or her own value as a purchase price in dollars and cents.

While Adams and Boling's conclusion might pass muster at a meeting of the Society for Historical Archaeology, it simply does not make a case for its usefulness to an audience made up of descendants of slaves. They would likely reject the notion that a few shards of porcelain equal economic freedom. And so too would the Daughters of the American Revolution. Archaeological collections from the homes of the Signers of the Declaration of Independence are full of shards of porcelain. The so-called "Fathers of Our Country" were free to make considerable fortunes before the Revolution, but they risked these fortunes in order to attain a greater freedom. If one accepts, at the level of popular historical discourse, that the freedom to make a great deal of money was not enough for this nation's greatest cultural heroes, one certainly should not accept an archaeological analysis that allows the ability of slaves to spend a little bit of money on a few pieces of porcelain to overshadow the fact of their bondage. Is so partial a freedom any kind of freedom at all?

Finally, if this essay was purely a rhetorical exercise, the previous sentence would have been its conclusion, but it is not. So far this writer has made a case for making plantation archaeology good politics. However, these same steps can make plantation archaeology good archaeology. As Epperson (1990:35) notes, "a social and political commitment will not only improve the quality of current archaeological research and interpretations, but also help to bridge the gap between academic disciplines and the communities archaeologists purportedly study and serve." At every point, the kind of self-reflection advocated herein will lead in two parallel directions. It will clearly lead to a plantation archaeology that is more useful to the hypothetical audience of African Americans that has been repeatedly invoked. And, importantly, this version of plantation archaeology will be better received *not just* because it is good politics. Self reflection, as discussed here, always involves a push for greater contextuality. To make Adams and Boling's ceramics really meaningful, this writer would have tried to analyze them in terms of a set of multiple contexts including: (1) aspects of ceramic use and display beyond simple possession, as indicated solely by discard; (2) the use of other classes of material culture; (3) the broad flow of the history of slavery; (4) the nature of localized attempts to preserve the institution of slavery; and (5) the enactment of serious attempts at resistance. All of this contextuality makes for good politics but also for good scholarship.

ACKNOWLEDGMENTS

I would like to thank Mark Leone for introducing me to many of the ideas that form the theoretical basis for this paper. I would also like to thank Gary Hume and Richard Boisvert of the New Hampshire Division of Historical Resources for their thoughtful readings of early drafts. Thanks are also due to Don Hardesty and the anonymous reviewers, whose work has made this a better paper. Finally, I would like to thank Nancy Jo Chabot, who is right about things more frequently than I take her good advice. For all the results of good advice not taken, I take full responsibility.

REFERENCES

ADAMS, WILLIAM H., AND SARAH JANE BOLING
  1989 Status and Ceramics for Planters and Slaves on Three Georgia Coastal Plantations. *Historical Archaeology* 23(1):69–96.

ARATO, ANDREW, AND EIKE GEBHARDT (EDITORS)
1982 *The Essential Frankfurt School Reader.* Continuum, New York.

BAKER, ANDREW, AND WARREN LEON
1986 Old Sturbridge Villiage Introduces Social Conflict into Its Interpretive Story. *History News* 41(2):6–11.

BARLOW, ALEX
1990 Still Civilizing? Aborigines in Australian Education. In *The Excluded Past,* edited by Peter Stone and Robert MacKenzie, pp. 68–87. Unwin Hyman, London.

BLANCKE, SHIRLEY, AND CJIGKITOONUPPA JOHN PETERS SLOW TURTLE
1990 The Teaching of the Past of the Native Peoples of North America in U.S. Schools. In *The Excluded Past,* edited by Peter Stone and Robert MacKenzie, pp. 109–133. Unwin Hyman, London.

BROWN, PATRICIA LEIGH
1989 Away from the Big House: Interpreting the Uncomfortable Parts of History. *History News* 44(2):8–11.

BURLEY, DAVID
1989 Function, Meaning, and Context: Ambiguities in Ceramic Use by the *Hivernant* Metis of the Northwestern Plains. *Historical Archaeology* 23(1):97–106.

CHAPPELL, EDWARD A.
1989 Social Responsibility and the American History Museum. *Winterthur Portfolio* 24(4):247–265.

CLARK, GRAHAME
1957 *Archaeology and Society. Third Edition.* Methuen, London.

CROSSON, DAVID L.
1988 Museums and Social Responsibility: A Cautionary Tale. *History News* 43(4):6–10.

EPPERSON, TERRENCE W.
1990 Race and the Disciplines of the Plantation. *Historical Archaeology* 24(4):29–36.

FAIRBANKS, CHARLES H.
1984 The Plantation Archaeology of the Southeastern Coast. *Historical Archaeology* 18(1):1–14.

FOGEL, ROBERT W., AND STANLEY L. ENGERMAN
1974 *Time on the Cross: The Economics of American Negro Slavery.* Little, Brown, Boston.

GATHERCOLE, PETER, AND DAVID LOWENTHAL (EDITORS)
1990 *The Politics of the Past.* Unwin Hyman, London

GEUSS, RAYMOND
1981 *The Idea of a Critical Theory: Habermas and the Frankfurt School.* Cambridge University Press, Cambridge.

HALL, MARTIN
1984 The Burden of Tribalism: The Social Context of Southern African Iron Age Studies. *American Antiquity* 49(3):455–467.

1988 Archaeology under Apartheid. *Archaeology* 41(6):62–64.

HELD, DAVID
1980 *Introduction to Critical Theory: Horkheimer to Habermas.* University of California Press, Berkeley.

JOSEPH, J.W.
1989 Pattern and Process in the Plantation Archaeology of the Low Country of Georgia and South Carolina. *Historical Archaeology* 23(1):55–68.

KEHOE, ALICE B.
1990 "In Fourteen Hundred and Ninety-two, Columbus Sailed . . .": The Primacy of the National Myth in U.S. Schools. In *The Excluded Past,* edited by Peter Stone and Robert MacKenzie, pp. 201–216. Unwin Hyman, London.

KELSO, WILLIAM M.
1984 *Kingsmill Plantations, 1619–1800: Archaeology of Country Life in Colonial Virginia.* Academic Press, New York

LAYTON, R. (EDITOR)
1988 *Who Needs the Past?* Unwin Hyman, London.
1989 *Conflict in the Archaeology of Living Traditions.* Unwin Hyman, London.

LEONE, MARK P.
1986 Symbolic, Structural, and Critical Archaeology. In *American Archaeology Past and Future: A Celebration of the Society for American Archaeology, 1935–1985,* edited by David J. Meltzer, Don D. Fowler, and Jeremy A. Sabloff, pp. 415–438. Smithsonian Institution Press, Washington, D.C.

LEONE, MARK P., AND PARKER B. POTTER, JR. (EDITORS)
1988 *The Recovery of Meaning: Historical Archaeology in the Eastern United States.* Smithsonian Institution Press, Washington, D.C.

LEONE, MARK P., PARKER B. POTTER, JR., AND PAUL A. SHACKEL
1987 Toward a Critical Archaeology. *Current Anthropology* 28(3):283–302.

LESTER, J.A.
1987 Lowering Curatorial Blinders. Paper Presented at the Annual Meeting of the American Association of Museums, San Francisco. Tape cassette, Vanguard Systems, Inc., Shawnee Mission, Kansas.

MARX, KARL
1977 The Fetishism of Commodities and the Secret Thereof. In *Symbolic Anthropology: A Reader in the Study of Symbols and Meanings,* edited by Janet L. Dolgin, David S. Kemnitzer, and David M. Schneider, pp. 245–254. Columbia University Press, New York.

MILLER, GEORGE L.
1980 Classification and Economic Scaling of 19th-Century Ceramics. *Historical Archaeology* 14:1–40.

ORSER, CHARLES E., JR.
1987 Plantation Status and Consumer Choice: A Materialist Framework for Historical Archaeology. In *Consumer Choice in Historical Archaeology*, edited by Suzanne M. Spencer-Wood, pp. 121–137. Plenum Press, New York.
1988a The Archaeological Analysis of Plantation Society: Replacing Status and Caste with Economics and Power. *American Antiquity* 53(4):735–751.
1988b Toward a Theory of Power for Historical Archaeology: Plantations and Space. In *The Recovery of Meaning: Historical Archaeology in the Eastern United States*, edited by Mark P. Leone and Parker B. Potter, Jr., pp. 313–343. Smithsonian Institution Press, Washington, D.C.
1989 On Plantations and Patterns. *Historical Archaeology* 23(2):28–40.

OTTO, JOHN SOLOMON
1975 *Status Differences and the Archaeological Record: A Comparison of Planter, Overseer, and Slave Sites from Cannon's Point Plantation (1794–1861), St. Simon's Island, Georgia*. Ph.D. dissertation, Department of Anthropology, University of Florida, Gainesville. University Microfilms, Ann Arbor.
1984 *Cannon's Point Plantation, 1794–1860: Living Conditions and Status Patterns in the Old South*. Academic Press, New York.

PATTERSON, JOHN
1986 Conner Prairie Refocuses Its Interpretive Message to Include Controversial Subjects. *History News* 41(2):12–15.

PINSKY, VALERIE, AND ALISON WYLIE (EDITORS)
1990 *Critical Traditions in Contemporary Archaeology*. Cambridge University Press, Cambridge, England.

POGUE, DENNIS
1990 News from Across Virginia. *Virginia Preservation* [The Newsletter of the Preservation Alliance of Virginia] (June):4.

POTTER, PARKER B., JR.
1989 *Archaeology in Public in Annapolis: An Experiment in the Application of Critical Theory to Historical Archaeology*. Ph.D. dissertation, Department of Anthropology, Brown University, Providence, Rhode Island. University Microfilms, Ann Arbor.
1991 Self-Reflection in Archaeology. In *Processual and Postprocessual Archaeologies: Multiple Ways of Knowing the Past*, edited by Robert W. Preucel. Center for Archaeological Investigations, Carbondale, Illinois, in press.

PREUCEL, ROBERT W. (EDITOR)
1991 *Processual and Postprocessual Archaeologies: Multiple Ways of Knowing the Past*. Center for Archaeological Investigations, Carbondale, Illinois, in press.

REITZ, ELIZABETH J., TYSON GIBBS, AND TED A. RATHBUN
1985 Archaeological Evidence for Subsistence on Coastal Plantations. In *The Archaeology of Slavery and Plantation Life*, edited by Theresa A. Singleton, pp. 163–191. Academic Press, New York.

SELLARS, RICHARD WEST
1988 The Texas School Book Depository Building: Preserving the Dark Side of History. *History News* 43(6):24–26.

SILVERBERG, ROBERT
1968 *Moundbuilders of Ancient America: The Archaeology of a Myth*. New York Graphic Society. Greenwich, Connecticut.
1974 *The Moundbuilders*. Ballantine, New York.

SINCLAIR, PAUL
1990 The Earth Is Our History Book. In *The Excluded Past*, edited by Peter Stone and Robert MacKenzie, pp. 152–159. Unwin Hyman, London.

SINGLETON, THERESA A.
1988 An Archaeological Framework for Slavery and Emancipation, 1740–1880. In *The Recovery of Meaning: Historical Archaeology in the Eastern United States*, edited by Mark P. Leone and Parker B. Potter, Jr., pp. 345–370. Smithsonian Intitution Press, Washington, D.C.

SINGLETON, THERESA A. (EDITOR)
1985 *The Archaeology of Slavery and Plantation Life*. Academic Press, New York.

SOUTH, STANLEY
1977 *Method and Theory in Historical Archaeology*. Academic Press, New York.
1978 Pattern Recognition in Historical Archaeology. *American Antiquity* 43:223–230.
1979 Historic Site Content, Structure, and Function. *American Antiquity* 44:213–237.
1988 Whither Pattern? *Historical Archaeology* 22(1):25–28.

STONE, PETER, AND ROBERT MACKENZIE
1990 *The Excluded Past*. Unwin Hyman, London.

TRIGGER, BRUCE G.
1980 Archaeology and the Image of the American Indian. *American Antiquity* 45(4):662–676.

VARGAS ARENAS, IRAIDA, AND MARIO SANOJA OBEDIENTE
1990 Education and the Political Manipulation of History in

Venezuela. In *The Excluded Past*, edited by Peter Stone and Robert MacKenzie, pp. 50–60. Unwin Hyman, London.

WASHBURN, WILCOMB E.
1987 A Critical View of Critical Archaeology. *Current Anthropology* 28(4):544–545.
1988 Announcing the "Guerrilla Archaeologist." Ms. on file, New Hampshire Division of Historical Resources, Concord, New Hampshire.

WATSON, LILLA
1990 The Affirmation of Indigenous Values in a Colonial Education System. In *The Excluded Past*, edited by Peter Stone and Robert Mackenzie, pp. 88–97. Unwin Hyman, London.

WYLIE, ALISON
1985 Putting Shakertown Back Together: Critical Theory in Archaeology. *Journal of Anthropological Archaeology* 4:133–147.

PARKER B. POTTER, JR.
NEW HAMPSHIRE DIVISION OF HISTORICAL RESOURCES
P.O. BOX 2043
CONCORD, NEW HAMPSHIRE 03302-2043

AARON E. RUSSELL

Material Culture and African-American Spirituality at the Hermitage

ABSTRACT

In this article, artifacts excavated from 19th-century African-American contexts at the Hermitage plantation near Nashville, Tennessee, are examined in light of their possible use in religious ritual, traditional healing, and other behaviors related to spirituality. While specific spiritual behaviors cannot be determined from the Hermitage archaeological and documentary record, the presence of a distinct African-American belief system at the Hermitage is suggested through comparison of selected artifacts from the Hermitage assemblage with various historical, folkloric, and archaeological sources. This belief system and its associated behaviors may have aided African Americans in achieving limited social and economic autonomy within the system of plantation slavery.

Introduction

In recent years, many historical archaeologists involved with the study of plantation slavery have attempted to address questions of African-American ideology in their analyses. Within this area of inquiry, a central focus of archaeologists has been the reconstruction of African-American religious ritual, along with other behaviors related to spirituality (Orser 1994:33). Several scholars have attempted to identify syncretisms between the African-American archaeological record and traditional West African religious practice (Brown and Cooper 1990; Cabak 1990; Ferguson 1992:109–120; Patten 1992; Adams 1994; Brown 1994; Orser 1994; Young 1994; Jones 1995; Wilkie 1995). The ideological motivation for these studies, following such scholars as Melville Herskovitz (1958[1941]) and Robert Farris Thompson (1983), has largely been to demonstrate the African descent of African-American culture, in opposition to the idea that traditional African cultures and worldviews were completely destroyed by the rigors of the middle passage and subsequent generations of slavery (Frazier 1957:3–21).

While these culture-historical questions are a necessary starting point for any study of African-American religion, scholars must begin to ask questions of their data that are more pointedly concerned with process and function in African-American culture: Why were particular ideas and behaviors retained from traditional West African cultures? What functions, if any, did they serve in enslaved African-American communities? How were these traditional beliefs transformed by processes of innovation, oppression, and creolization? These are some of the questions that must be addressed if the study of the religious and spiritual practices of enslaved African Americans is to have much relevance to students of African-American culture and anthropology.

The archaeological study of African-American spiritual behaviors has proceeded on several distinct levels of understanding. Initially, certain types of artifacts found in African-American contexts were thought of as possibly being associated with ritual behaviors. Leland Ferguson's (1992:1–32, 109–116) study of traditional African-American folk pots (colonoware), which presents evidence of religious and medicinal uses for these pots, is a classic example of this type of study. Other archaeologists have concerned themselves with the roles played by beads, metal charms, and Christian religious paraphernalia in African-American spiritual life (Smith 1987; Cabak 1990; Singleton 1991; Orser 1994; McKee 1995; Wilkie 1995; Stine et al. 1996). In addition, some attention has been paid to possible ritual uses of such "ephemera" as prehistoric lithic artifacts, modified potsherds, quartz crystals, smooth stones, and seashells (Klingelhofer 1987; Jones 1995; Wilkie 1995) which had previously been ignored by archaeologists whose main concerns lay in the reconstruction of diet and other physical conditions of enslaved life.

In addition, some researchers have attempted to identify archaeological contexts and assemblages that represent religious behavior on the part of enslaved African Americans. The best-known example of this approach is Brown and Cooper's (1990; Brown 1994) research at the

Historical Archaeology, 1997, 31(2), 63–80.
Permission to reprint required.

Levi Jordan plantation in east Texas. In this study, the authors attempted to define "activity areas" within the slave (later tenant) quarter that represented the primary occupations of the individual inhabitants. Among the occupations of the Jordan slaves and tenants so identified were those of African craftsman, political leader, and healer/magician. The healer/magician's cabin was distinguished by the presence of a "tool kit," recovered from a restricted area of the dwelling, consisting of:

> Several cast iron kettle bases; cubes of white chalk; bird skulls; an animal's paw; two sealed tubes made of bullet casings; ocean shells; small dolls; an extraordinary (for this site) number of nails, spikes, knife blades, and "fake" knife blades; small water rolled pebbles; two chipped stone scraping tools; several patent medicine bottles; and a thermometer (Brown 1994:109).

In the context in which they were discovered, this group of somewhat mundane artifacts was thought to be analogous to traditional "tool kits" employed by West African, Afro-Caribbean, and creole healer/magicians in curing rituals (Brown 1994:109–110). A similar discovery was made by archaeologists excavating an early 19th-century deposit beneath the Charles Carroll house in Annapolis, Maryland. Here, archaeologists discovered a group of 12 quartz crystals, along with a smooth black stone and a faceted glass bead. These objects appear to have been placed intentionally together, and were covered with an inverted pearlware bowl which had an asterisk-like design on its interior base (Logan 1992; Jones 1995). Lynn Diekman Jones (1995) states that this group of artifacts is similar to several *minkisi* (charms) employed by the Bakongo, a cultural group originating in the Congo-Angolan region of Africa. In addition, George Logan (1992) cites this group of artifacts as producing the "breakthrough" to the interpretation that African Americans lived and worked in the area of the Carroll house in which the objects were found.

The archaeological assemblages at the Levi Jordan plantation and at the Carroll house are particularly important to the study of African-American religion, as they are highly suggestive of the survival of African worldviews and religious knowledge during slavery. *Minkisi*, for example, are conceived of by the Bakongo as alive, each *nkisi* containing medicines which both embody and direct the spirit which dwells within it (Thompson 1983:117–118). The creation and use of *minkisi*, in addition to achieving particular ends, reflects a general conception of life, death, and the structure of the cosmos. This knowledge is codified in the Bakongo cosmogram, *Yowa* (Figure 1), in which

> God is imagined at the top, the dead at the bottom, and water in between. The four disks at the points of the cross stand for the four movements of the sun, and the circumference of the cross the certainty of reincarnation: the especially righteous Kongo person will never be destroyed but will come back in the name or body of progeny, or in the form of an everlasting pool, waterfall, stone, or mountain (Thompson 1983:109).

The amply documented presence of symbols similar in appearance, meaning, and function to this cosmogram, as well as objects similar to *minkisi*, in the New World (Thompson 1983:108–131) lends further weight to published interpretations of the archaeological record at the Levi Jordan plantation and Carroll house. In addition, this evidence strongly supports the idea that the belief systems reflected in the archaeological record of plantation slavery were not simply random amalgamations of Euroamerican "mental heirlooms," as suggested by Puckett (1968[1926]:2–3), but rather were coherent bod-

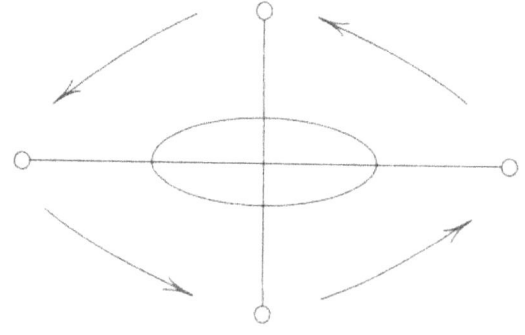

FIGURE 1. Bakongo Cosmogram *Yowa* (from Thompson [1983]).

ies of knowledge with clearly recognizable African roots.

At the same time, however, African-American culture must be viewed as the result of an intense process of creolization between Africans of varying cultural backgrounds, their African-American descendants, Native Americans, and Euroamericans (Mintz and Price 1992; Ferguson 1992). This process, combined with the relative isolation imposed upon communities of enslaved African Americans resulted in considerable local cultural variation. This variation, together with a paucity of documentary evidence, presents difficulties in determining the precise nature of the beliefs and practices reflected by the archaeological record in all but the clearest of archaeological contexts.

Another major stumbling block in studying artifacts with apparent spiritual and religious associations is that many objects documented as having served a role in African-American and West African spiritual behaviors are quite commonplace, becoming spiritually charged by specific ritual (MacGaffey 1991; Wilkie 1994:142). Many potential ritual objects can also be interpreted as having had utilitarian and/or domestic functions. For this reason, the findings at the Carroll house and at the Levi Jordan plantation, while spectacularly relevant to the study of African-American religion, cannot be considered a "Rosetta stone" for interpreting similar artifacts recovered from other African-American contexts, as has been suggested by art historian Robert Farris Thompson (Adams 1994).

The Hermitage

The remainder of this article consists of a discussion of various artifacts which are possibly connected to spiritual behaviors on the part of enslaved African Americans. The artifacts selected for inclusion in this study were excavated from contexts associated with the African-American antebellum occupation at the Hermitage, the 19th-century plantation home of Andrew Jackson, near Nashville, Tennessee. The material comes from five former African-American households at the Hermitage (Figure 2), selected both for their

intact antebellum deposits as well as for their varied locations on the plantation landscape. Two of the dwellings, known as the Triplex Middle (the central unit of a three-unit brick structure) (McKee et al. 1994) and the Yard Cabin (probably a log dwelling), are adjacent to the Hermitage mansion and were probably occupied by enslaved African Americans who worked in and around the mansion. A third structure, the South Cabin, was located approximately 165 m northeast of the mansion (Smith 1976:93–112). Cabin 3, one of a group of brick duplex dwellings about half a kilometer north of the mansion, likely housed enslaved African Americans occupied with agricultural tasks (McKee

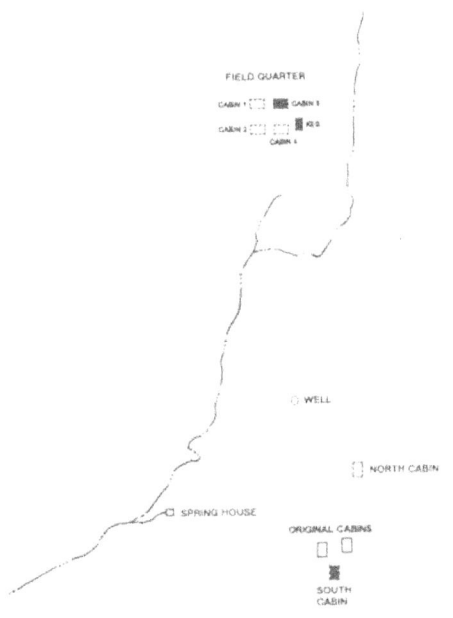

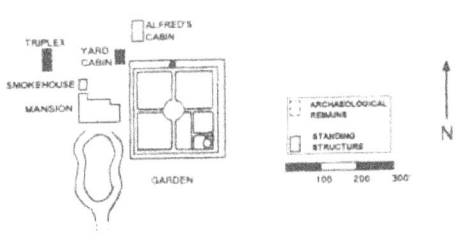

FIGURE 2 Map of the Hermitage property

1993; Thomas et al. 1995). The main period of occupation for the dwellings mentioned above falls between 1821, when the Jackson family moved from their initial log dwellings to the present Hermitage mansion, and 1857–1858, when the Jacksons moved off the property. In addition to these dwellings, this study discusses the remains of a log structure known as KES, located near Cabin 3 in the Hermitage field quarter. This cabin was probably occupied by enslaved African Americans during the first decades of the 19th century, prior to the construction of the Hermitage mansion and brick field quarter (McKee 1993).

While all of the contexts examined are quite rich in artifacts, the generally mixed and disturbed nature of the deposits makes it difficult to define specific activity areas within the dwellings. The entire assemblage from each dwelling, consisting of artifacts recovered from 19th-century midden deposits and from features such as root cellars within the dwellings, will therefore constitute the basic unit of analysis for comparing the various sites at the Hermitage. Due to these archaeological limitations, concrete interpretations of "spiritual" behaviors on the part of African Americans at the Hermitage cannot be made at the present time. In addition, the lack of historical documentation concerning the spiritual beliefs and practices of enslaved African Americans, along with difficulties in constructing analogies with African-American folklore and African ethnographic material (Mintz and Price 1992:52–60; Thomas 1995a), may make such assertions generally unwarranted. Certain artifacts from the Hermitage, however, such as three small brass fist-shaped charms, a pierced coinlike medallion, and a distinctive assemblage of glass beads seem to indicate the presence of an active system of beliefs among African Americans at the Hermitage (McKee 1995). The data available will also be used to point out similarities between the material cultures of enslaved African Americans living and working on various areas of the Hermitage property, as well as the apparent selectivity shown by these people in acquiring various types of material objects. Finally,

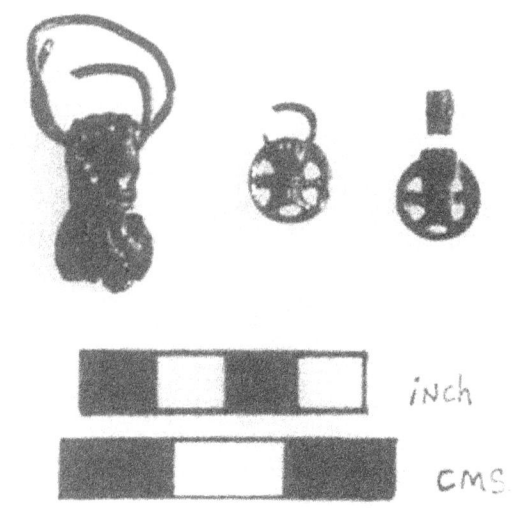

FIGURE 3. Hand-shaped copper alloy charms from the Hermitage.

some interpretation will be made of the apparent persistence of certain aspects of culture related to the spiritual realm throughout slavery, and the functions that these beliefs and behaviors may have served for the enslaved African-American community.

Material Culture

Categories of material culture may shed light on the lives of enslaved African Americans at the Hermitage. Hand charms, lucky bones, pierced coins, glass beads, "x" marbles, prehistoric stone tools, odd smooth stones, and modified ceramic sherds are treated further below.

Hand Charms

Three tiny copper alloy charms, each in the shape of a human fist (Figure 3), were recovered from African-American contexts at the Hermitage (Smith 1976; Singleton 1991:161; McKee 1993; Orser 1994:39–40). Two of these were recovered from Cabin 3, at the site's field quarter, while one was recovered from the South Cabin. Among other small objects probably used for personal adornment by African Americans at the

Hermitage, these are particularly evocative of meanings beyond the purely decorative. The word *hand* occurs frequently in African-American folklore as a generic term for any small—not necessarily hand-shaped—good-luck or protection charm (Puckett 1968[1926]), and this usage may relate to the significance that these objects had for enslaved African Americans at the Hermitage. Samuel Smith (1987:9) has pointed out the similarity between these charms and the Islamic "Hand of Fatima," used to ward off the evil eye. In addition, Larry McKee (1995) has noted a similarity with Latin American *figas* (hand-shaped charms) and *milagros* (votive items), which are thought to confer luck, fertility, and protection from supernatural forces. This physical similarity with *figas* and *milagros* suggests the possibility that these artifacts were brought to the Hermitage by African Americans acquired by Andrew Jackson in Florida (McKee 1993). References dating to the 1930s exist documenting African-American use of hand-shaped charms, including a reference to one stamped from metal (Hyatt 1970[1935]:583–585). Charms of this sort appear to have been used to ensure personal luck and protection from harm. Interestingly, Anne Yentsch (1994:32–33) has recovered an almost identical amulet from an enslaved African-American context in Annapolis, Maryland. This amulet and those recovered from the Hermitage are the only artifacts of this type reported in the archaeological literature. Larry McKee, director of archaeology at the Hermitage, is currently preparing an article describing the specific archaeological contexts and metallurgical composition of the Hermitage artifacts.

In the summer of 1995, the author brought photographs of the Hermitage "fist charms" along on a vacation to New Orleans, with the hopes that similar objects might be found for sale, and that information could be gathered concerning current and past uses of such objects. Although attempts to identify the Hermitage hand charm were unsuccessful, two different types of hand-shaped charms were encountered and purchased during a tour of the various voodoo and *botanica* shops in the city: a wooden

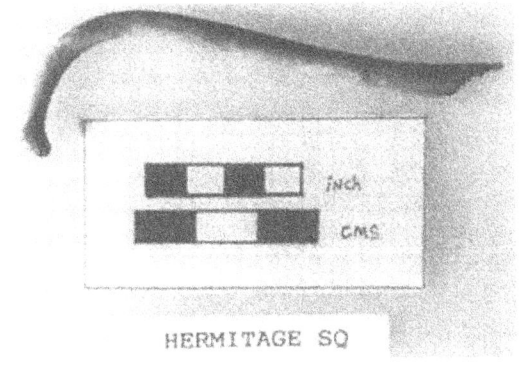

FIGURE 4. Raccoon penis bone from Cabin 3 root cellar.

"mojo hand" in the form of a human fist; and a "lucky hand root," a tiny plant resembling a human hand. Instructions for the use of these charms echoed Frederick Douglass's (1986[1845, 1982]:111) description of his, admittedly skeptical, use of a "certain root" as a protection charm. The specific meanings that the Hermitage hand charms held for their owners, along with the belief systems that they were a part of, are, of course, not made completely clear by these examples. These examples may, however, represent the continuity of a significant symbol in African-American culture, although questions concerning its specific origin remain unanswered.

Lucky Bones

Although folkloric anecdotes concerning the use of animal bones as charms by African Americans are quite common (Puckett 1968[1926]:256–259; Hyatt 1970:74–76), culturally modified bones—apart from such commercial items as buttons, combs, and knife handles—do not appear with any frequency in the archaeological record at the Hermitage. One possible exception is a raccoon penis bone recovered from a root cellar in the Cabin 3 West dwelling (Figure 4). A similar bone was recovered from an African-American context at Mount Vernon (Pogue and White 1991:44–46). The Mount Vernon bone has an incised line encircling its distal end, and was possibly used as a pendant. The Hermitage example is broken off in the area where the Mount Vernon bone is incised. Baskets of drilled raccoon penis bones, strung on leather thongs, are seen for sale in New Orleans "voodoo" shops for use as personal charms. Although these commercial examples exist in radically different contexts from the archaeological examples mentioned above, they suggest a continuing folk tradition concerning the use of these bones.

Highly problematic in terms of archaeology is the possibility that animal bones used as charms may not have been visibly modified in any way. Hyatt's (1970[1935]:74–76) documentation of the traditional "black cat bone" charm repeatedly highlights the circumstances of the bone's collection, rather than subsequent modification. The specially collected bone may be used without further alteration as an ingredient in a charm bag, or simply carried in a pocket.

Pierced Coins

Another example of an item of material culture repeatedly connected through folklore and archaeology with African Americans is the pierced silver coin. These coins have been widely documented by folklorists as having been

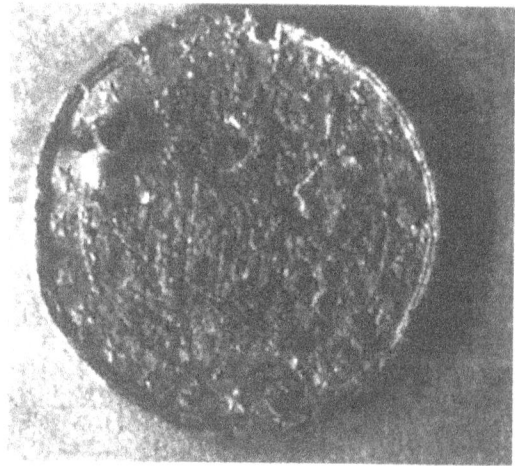

FIGURE 5. Pierced (white metal?) medallion (45.89 mm diameter), recovered from the middle unit of the Triplex.

used for good luck, protection from "conjuration" and as a general "cure-all" (Puckett 1968[1926]:314–315, 391). Pierced silver coins are often recovered from archaeological contexts associated with enslaved African Americans. These archaeological finds have been correlated with folklore, and with historical accounts of their use as adornments and charms by African Americans (Patten 1992:6; Orser 1994:41; Singleton 1995:131). Two items of this type have been recovered archaeologically at the Hermitage. One is a pierced (white metal?) medallion, recovered from the middle unit of the Triplex, in the mansion backyard (Figure 5). Another, a drilled dime dating between 1828 and 1836 (the hole is drilled through the date), was recovered from a 20th-century utility trench crossing the Yard Cabin site during excavations in the summer of 1996 (Larry McKee 1997, pers. comm.). The hole is drilled so that, when suspended, an image of an eagle on one side of the coin hangs right-side up. Unfortunately, this coin's uncertain context makes it impossible to associate it definitely with the 19th-century occupants of the Yard Cabin, although its date suggests that it was likely part of the 19th-century midden deposit at the site before the utility trench was dug.

Similarly to bones, coins have been used as charms without any modification, such as particular "lucky" coins carried in the shoe or in a pocket. Although usage of this type is practically impossible to determine archaeologically, particularly archaic or unusual coins such as a cut silver Spanish coin, dating to 1726, recovered from the yard of an enslaved African-American dwelling near the Hermitage mansion, as well as a cut coin dating to 1789 from Cabin 3, suggest that some African Americans at the Hermitage may have valued coins as keepsakes (McKee 1993:22).

Glass Beads

Glass beads, items commonly recovered from plantation excavations, have come under scrutiny from historical archaeologists as possibly having had meanings beyond the purely decorative for enslaved African Americans. A variety of researchers have argued that African Americans' uses of beads represent continuity between West African and African-American culture (Cabak 1990; Singleton 1991:164; Stine et al. 1996), indicate the presence of African-American women on sites (Smith 1977:159–161; Otto 1984:175), and indicate status differences within communities of enslaved African Americans (Otto 1984:72–74). European traders, in fact, exploited the pre-existing African preferences for certain types of beads in order to gain economic access to West Africa (Cabak 1990). It is likely, then, that enslaved African-Americans' uses of glass beads represent some degree of cultural continuity with West Africa, even if only through the continued preference for a specific category of material culture.

The assemblages of glass beads recovered from the various Hermitage dwellings selected for this study are illustrated by Table 1. Overall, the glass bead assemblage at the Hermitage is dominated by beads of hexagonal, drawn construction, making up 59 percent of all glass beads examined for this study, or 38 of a total of 64 beads. These beads are divided in color between blue, colorless, and black, with blue predominating (20 out of 37 beads, or 54% of this category). Blue beads of this type were recovered from all of the contexts examined here, except from the dwelling site near the mansion known as the Yard Cabin. Here, the entire collection of beads consists of just two green, globular, mandrel-wound beads. In addition to the glass beads, two bone beads were recovered from these dwellings, along with several naturally and artificially perforated sections of fossil crinoid stems that may have served as beads.

Although sample sizes are small, the residents of all of the slave dwellings examined, except for those at the Yard Cabin, appear to have had equal access to glass beads. This supports Brian Thomas's (1995b) thesis of a high degree of cooperation and reciprocity among enslaved African Americans at the Hermitage. The assemblages of beads recovered at these households—again, with one exception—are also quite similar to one another, which may indicate consensus among enslaved African Americans at the Hermitage as to which sorts of beads were desirable. The assemblage suggests that African Americans at the Hermitage had fairly open access to beads. No archaeological or documentary evidence reveals the exact method of acquisition, i.e., whether it was through direct purchase, barter within African-American trade net-

TABLE 1
GLASS BEADS FROM HERMITAGE SITES

Types	Triplex Middle	Cabin 3 East	Cabin 3 West	South Cabin	KES	Yard Cabin	Total
Blue hexagonal	3	10	3	3	2	0	21
Black hexagonal	1	0	2	4	0	0	7
Colorless hexagonal	3	0	0	5	1	0	9
Brown hexagonal	0	0	0	1	0	0	1
Colorless tube	0	0	0	1	0	0	1
Dark globular/spheroid	2	2	0	0	0	0	4
Blue globular/spheroid	0	0	2	0	1	0	3
Colorless globular/spheroid	0	0	5	0	1	0	6
Green globular/spheroid	0	0	0	0	0	2	2
Amber globular/spheroid	0	0	0	1	5	0	6
Turquoise toroid	0	0	1	0	0	0	1
Colorless faceted	0	0	2	0	0	0	2
Dark faceted spheroid	0	0	0	1	0	0	1
Total	9	12	15	16	10	2	64

works, direct or indirect distribution from the mansion household, or through other means.

Thomas (1995b:117–118) suggests that the notable lack of beads recovered from the Hermitage Yard Cabin may indicate accommodation on the part of house enslaved African Americans to white modes of dress. While this may have been true for the residents of the Yard Cabin, the bead assemblage at the Triplex middle, equally near the mansion, was more substantial. This suggests that both house and field enslaved African Americans at the Hermitage had access to and used beads. The notable lack of beads from the Yard Cabin may also indicate a lack of women and children, more often associated with African-American bead use than men, at this dwelling.

A cursory examination of beads excavated from historical Cherokee sites and Euroamerican trading sites in eastern Tennessee suggests that glass beads traded to Native American populations slightly before and during the initial occupation of the Hermitage were predominantly of different types than those acquired by enslaved African Americans at the Hermitage. At the Tellico Blockhouse site, a trading fort, spherical red beads with green cores make up 60.7 percent of the total bead assemblage (65 of 107 beads), while blue beads make up 2.8 percent of the assemblage (3 of 107 beads) (Polhemus 1977:212–213). In addition, no blue beads were recorded among the trade goods shipped from Philadelphia to the Tellico Blockhouse between 1797 and 1807, or listed in a 1798 inventory (Polhemus 1977:323). Of the 72,772 beads recovered in six field seasons from the historical Overhill Cherokee site of Chota-Tenase, lamp black and white are the predominant colors, and 80.4 percent of the total sample are seed beads (Schroedl 1986:427–436). In addition, "preliminary analysis of beads from Tomotley and Mialoquo suggests that black and white are the predominant colors at these Cherokee sites" (Schroedl 1986:427–436). Although the mechanisms of bead acquisition by enslaved African Americans are unclear, the distinction between the bead assemblage at the Hermitage and those in demand by nearly contemporaneous Native

American populations in the Upper South may indicate that enslaved African Americans were able to exercise some degree of personal choice in bead selection. In addition, Stine, Cabak, and Groover (1996:50–52, 55–57) note that, while blue beads are consistently predominant in archaeological African-American bead assemblages throughout the southern United States, Native American bead assemblages are quite variable and suggest that consumer choice played a role in the composition of each.

There are several possible African antecedents for the use of beads by African Americans at the Hermitage. Beads of all kinds are currently used throughout West Africa for decorative, medicinal, religious, and economic purposes (Thompson 1983:43, 93–95; Fisher 1984:90–103; Blier 1995; Stine et al. 1996:53–54). Melanie Cabak (1990) and Theresa Singleton (1991:164) state that blue beads are sewn on clothing by Muslims to ward off the "evil eye." Caesar Apentiik (1995, pers. comm.), a Ghanaian archaeologist working on the Hermitage excavation crew during the 1995 field season, reports that small beads similar to the blue and colorless hexagonal beads recovered at the Hermitage are currently used throughout Ghana by children, who wear them as a form of preventative medicine, a usage also described by Stine, Cabak, and Groover (1996:54) as widespread in West Africa. At the African Burial Ground in New York City, two child burials dating to the colonial era, one with waistbeads and another with a beaded necklace, were found, suggesting that this usage of beads persisted in the New World (La Roche 1994a:131–132, 1994b:14).

In addition, Apentiik stated that strings of beads are currently worn on the waists of some married Ghanaian women in order to ensure fertility. The use of waistbeads has considerable historical depth in Africa, and the beads themselves "have ontological, spiritual, metaphysical, and historical meaning" (La Roche 1994b:14). Native folklore suggests that enslaved African Americans on St. Eustatius, in the Dutch West Indies, used blue faceted beads in this manner, indicating the possibility that this practice was accepted by some Africans brought to the New

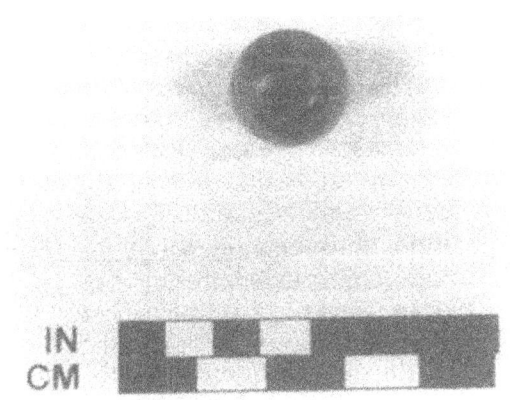

FIGURE 6   Stone marble with incised "x" from the South Cabin

World (Smith 1987:7–8). A more direct indicator of the survival of this practice in the New World is burial 340 at the African Burial Ground, that of a woman aged between 28 and 35, with "a strand of primarily blue waist beads found *in situ*" (La Roche 1994a:4). In addition, burial 340 exhibited dental modification, suggesting to researchers that she was born in Africa (La Roche 1994a:3; Stine et al. 1996:62).

Although it is difficult to assign specific meanings to the beads recovered at the Hermitage, the very presence and distinctiveness of the bead assemblage may indicate some degree of cultural autonomy on the part of enslaved African Americans at the Hermitage. The beads themselves appear to be more similar to beads traded to African markets by Europeans (Karklins 1985:7–39), and to those recovered from other African-American sites in the Southeast (Stine et al. 1996:50–52) than to those traded to nearby Native American groups in the Southeast. Even if bead choice and distribution at the Hermitage was entirely in the hands of the Jacksons, the particular beads selected may represent the continuation of a previous trade "negotiation" between Europeans and Africans. If the beads were acquired independently in local markets or from traders, their presence indicates the participation of enslaved African Americans in the local economy, as well as their choice to expend limited economic resources on beads. Although the specific function of the beads re-

covered at the Hermitage is unknown, their presence is an important piece of evidence of the limited, negotiated cultural and economic autonomy of enslaved African Americans at the Hermitage.

"X" Marbles

Among the large variety of stone, glass, and ceramic marbles recovered from African-American contexts at the Hermitage are three small limestone marbles that have "x" marks incised on their surfaces (Figure 6). These might simply be marks of ownership. On the other hand, the "cross in a circle" motif is evocative of the Kongo cosmogram (Figure 1). This motif has been noted on items of African-American manufacture, such as colonoware bowls (Ferguson 1992:110–116), and inscribed on objects of Euroamerican manufacture found in African-American contexts, such as spoons (Klingelhofer 1987:114–115; Young 1994). Two of the copper hand charms recovered at the Hermitage (Figure 3) can also be seen as an example of this motif (Thomas 1995b:121). Newbell Puckett (1968[1926]:319), in his collection of African-American folk beliefs, describes the use of the cross symbol in "conjuration," giving a game of marbles as an example of this use. In this example, the "x" is inscribed on the ground in order to give one's opponent bad luck in the game. Significantly, an almost identical "x"-incised marble was recovered from the Gowen farmstead, located about 5 mi. from the Hermitage (Weaver et al. 1993:280), possibly indicating shared beliefs and significant contact between enslaved African Americans living at the Hermitage and the African-American community at this nearby farm. Similar marbles have also been unearthed at a Kentucky plantation by Amy Young (1994). Further investigation of gaming practices in the rural South would perhaps be useful concerning questions raised here. These marbles may provide an example of how beliefs are spread through the informal education that children receive during play with one another and through instruction from adult caregivers.

Prehistoric Stone Tools

Prehistoric Native American stone artifacts were found in all African-American contexts at the Hermitage. These objects include a number of whole and fragmentary chert projectile points (Figure 7), a large amount of debitage, several ground stone tools, and a very small amount of prehistoric ceramic. The recovery of prehistoric artifacts in African-American contexts at the Hermitage raises the possibility that enslaved African Americans were actively collecting and using them for some purpose. An alternative explanation for this lies in the fact that the Hermitage property has been the site of human activity for thousands of years. The occurrence of prehistoric artifacts in African-American contexts cannot, for this reason, be solely attributed to the actions of historic period residents. Conversely, the abundance of prehistoric artifacts present in the fields and gardens at the Hermitage provided ample opportunity for their active collection and possible use by these people.

As a partial test of the idea that African Americans at the Hermitage actively collected and curated prehistoric stone tools, the ratios of chert flakes to stone tools were calculated for the cabin interior and feature fill for each of the dwellings examined (Figure 8). These ratios were then compared with the flake/tool ratio from excavation in the mansion garden, which is extraordinarily rich in prehistoric flakes and tools, and may have been the site of a considerable amount of prehistoric lithic production. It was predicted that if historic site occupants actively collected stone tools (and did not collect flakes), the ratio of flakes to tools would be lower in historic deposits. Unfortunately, the

FIGURE 7. Prehistoric artifacts from the West unit of Cabin 3

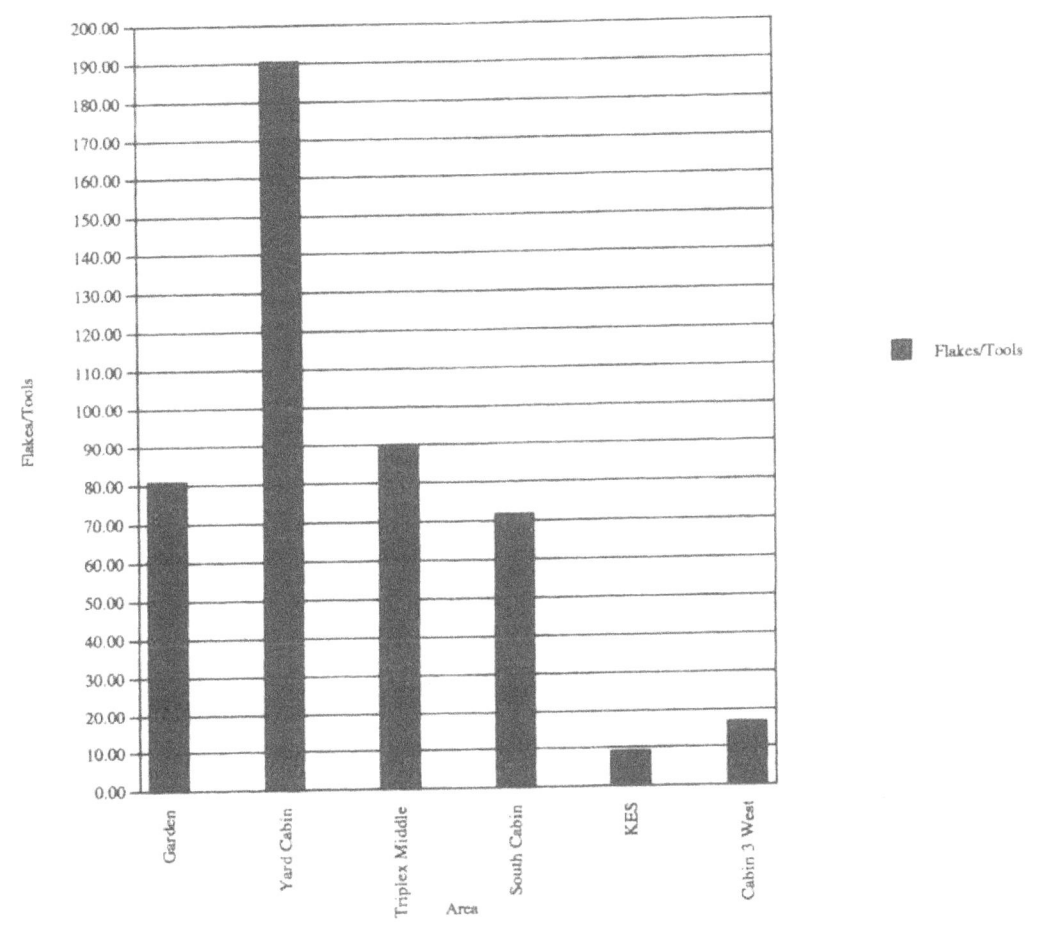

FIGURE 8. Graph showing ratios of chert flakes to flaked tools from the Hermitage Garden, and from historic midden deposits and feature fill at the Yard Cabin, Triplex Middle, South Cabin, KES, and Cabin 3 West sites.

results of this experiment were somewhat inconclusive. The flake/tool ratio decreases relative to the distance from the Yard Cabin (adjacent to the mansion garden), and may reflect prehistoric site use patterns rather than historic activity.

No distinct prehistoric middens or features have been encountered at the Hermitage, and it is probable that such prehistoric remains have been thoroughly mixed with later historic deposits through bioturbation—extensive rodent disturbance is evident at most Hermitage slave dwelling sites, or through cultural activities such as plowing. Although more research into the

Hermitage's prehistoric occupation must be done in order to properly address these questions, this does not preclude the possibility that some African Americans at the Hermitage collected stone tools.

Prehistoric artifacts are commonly recovered from African-American contexts throughout the Southeast, and several theories have been advanced to explain their presence. Puckett (1968[1926]:315) suggests that these objects were instrumental in the production of charms, either by virtue of their own intrinsic talismanic value, or in the ritual production of sparks with a steel strike-a-light. In my survey of New Orleans voodoo shops, I saw chert projectile points being sold in one shop as being "essential for your mojo bag."

A more direct explanation may be that the primary use of these objects was as utilitarian fire-starters, ready-made from high quality chert and easily collected by African Americans working in the fields at the Hermitage. Several of the points recovered do, in fact, show evidence of reuse as spark-strikers (Figure 9). These points show evidence of bashing along their edges, and a sample will be subjected to microwear analysis to look for more specific evidence of association with steel. Even if, however, it can be shown that these artifacts were used with strike-a-lights, we cannot determine the specific intentions of the striker beyond the creation of sparks. In addition, it is possible

that these artifacts simply represent the collections of children and other curiosity seekers.

Odd Smooth Stones

At each of the sites examined here, small chert nodules were recovered (Figure 10). Most of these artifacts are likely prehistoric hammerstones and small grinders, although some may have been collected and used by African Americans. Examples can be cited of African Americans using stones in conjuration, and similar worn, smooth stones were excavated at the Garrison plantation in Maryland (Klingelhofer 1987:116) and at Poplar Forest in Virginia, as well as at other African-American sites (Patten 1992). The function of these stones at the Hermitage, however, cannot readily be ascertained. In addition, a number of small, smooth pebbles

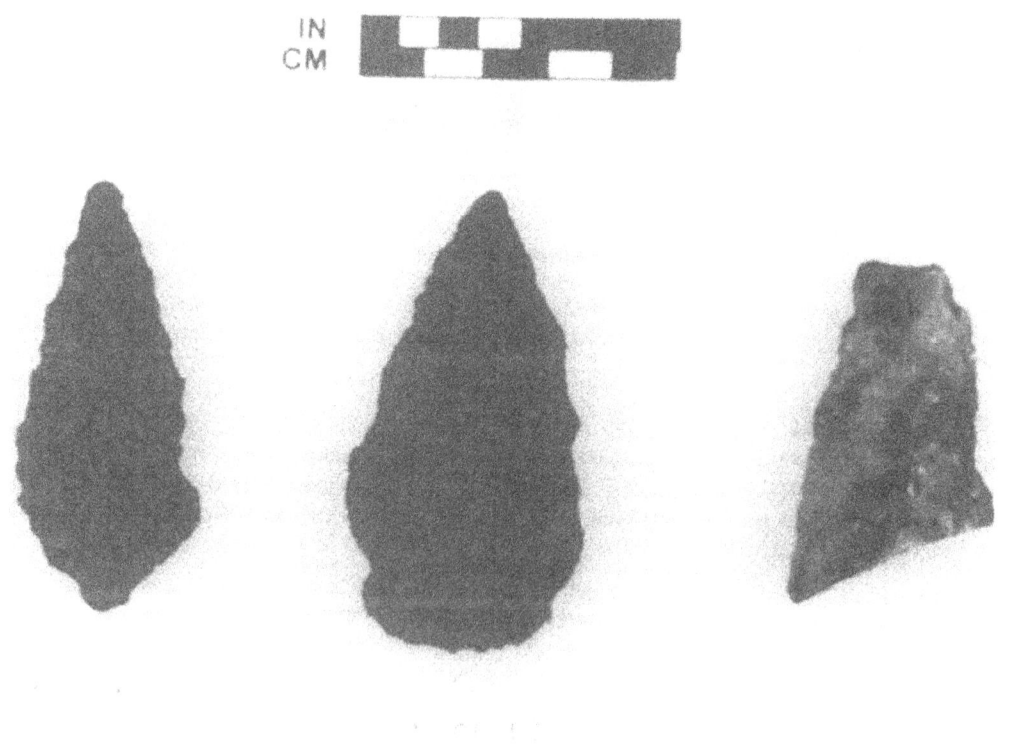

FIGURE 9 Prehistoric projectile points from Hermitage sites, with edge-wear possibly indicating reuse as spark strikers

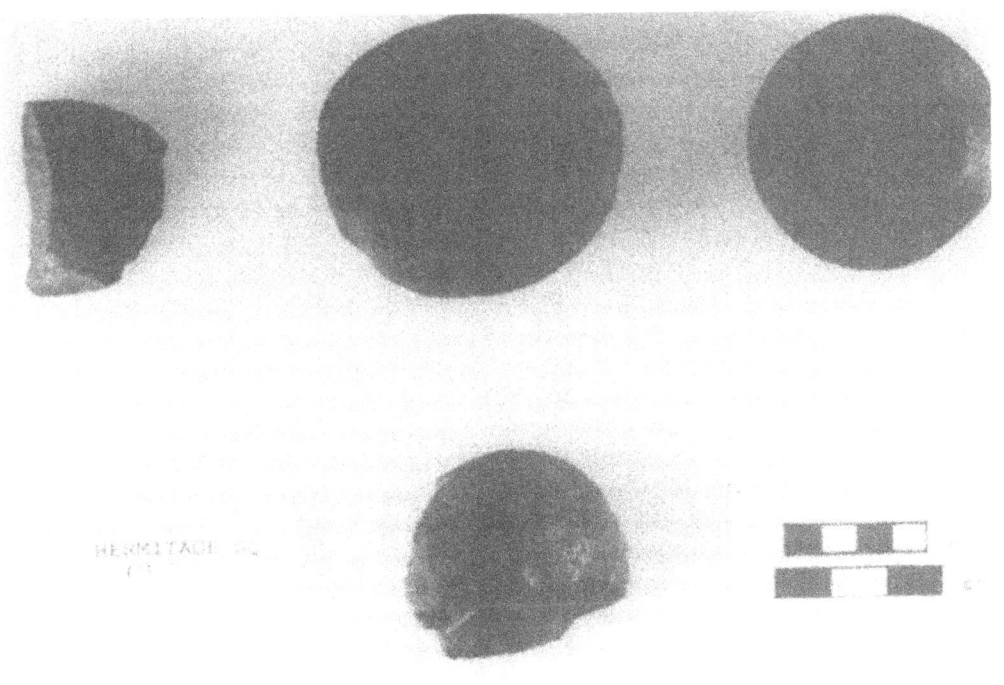

FIGURE 10. Round, smooth stones from the West unit of Cabin 3.

were recovered from the South Cabin area. While these pebbles appear to be of an ideal size to be used as gaming pieces, they may have been used for some other purpose, such as graveling a pathway.

Modified Ceramic Sherds

Several small ceramic sherds that appear to have been worked into "gaming pieces" were recovered at the Hermitage (Figure 11). Objects similar to these have also been recovered from African-American contexts in other regions, including Jamaica and Maryland (Klingelhofer 1987:115–117; Armstrong 1990:137–138). While these sherds are definitely worked, the functions that they served cannot easily be established. They do, however, look like checkers and may have been used as gaming pieces or counters.

In addition to these "gaming pieces," a number of much smaller, smoothly worn ceramic sherds were also recovered at the Hermitage. These artifacts, while relatively few in number, were recovered from all contexts examined for this paper. They are all approximately 5–10 mm in diameter and roughly triangular in shape. Artifacts of this type have been found at a number of sites throughout the Southeast and Middle Atlantic states (Wilkie 1994:271–273; Daniel Allen 1995, pers. comm.). These objects have been variously described as possible chicken or turkey gizzard stones (Smith 1976) and as "intentionally water worn" for possible use in charm bags, in divination rituals, or as gaming pieces (Wilkie 1994:271–273).

A sample of these sherds was shown to Emmanuel Breitberg, a faunal expert at the Tennessee Division of Archaeology. Breitberg (1995, pers. comm.) stated that the sherds appeared to have been worn by tumbling, possibly in a stream or in the gizzard of a bird, and that the sherds were of a size suitable for ingestion by domestic fowl. The types of ceramics that have been found to be worn in this manner are those that are relatively hard-bodied yet tend to break into large numbers of small sherds. Coarse earthenwares would be ground to dust in a very short time by gizzard action, while thick, hard-bodied stonewares tend to break into pieces too large to be ingested.

The use of potsherds as gizzard stones by domestic fowl helps to explain the rarity of these artifacts as well as their presence on a number of sites. As gravel consumed by domestic fowl is generally ground to dust and excreted within a day or so, the consumption and destruction of inedible grit by these birds occurs daily (Schorger 1966:94).

The only stones to survive this process would be either those excreted by the bird before being ground to dust, or those recovered from dead animals. Interestingly, I have received reports of an intentional turkey burial containing small whiteware sherds in the gizzard area (Leslie Stewart-Abernathy 1995, pers. comm.), as well as of "old blue dishes" being broken up and fed to hens (Camehl 1946[1916]:xvii). Gravel is not generally found in the gizzards of slaughtered domestic fowl, as the birds are not fed for 24 hours before slaughtering (Emmanuel Breitberg 1995, pers. comm.). It is, however, not known

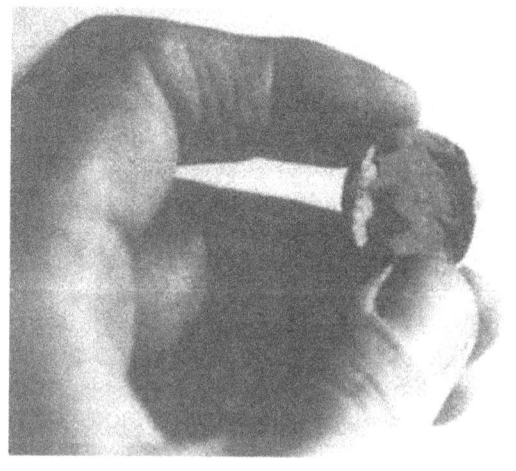

FIGURE 11. Reworked transfer-printed ceramic sherd from Cabin 2 in the Hermitage Field Quarter.

whether this practice was common at 19th-century farming operations such as the Hermitage.

The two best hypotheses to account for the presence of these sherds are intentional selection and alteration by enslaved African Americans, or the use of potsherds as gizzard stones by domestic fowl. The available information seems to favor the latter of these explanations. In addition, no reference to the use of potsherds or gizzard stones in African-American gaming or ritual has come to light during research.

Conclusion

Archaeological research at the Hermitage has not as yet provided the data necessary to delineate specific ritual behaviors on the part of the Hermitage's enslaved African-American population. However, the presence of items such as the brass "fist charms" and the distinctive bead assemblage are suggestive of both an active system of beliefs associated with specific items of material culture and the success of strategies employed by enslaved African Americans to acquire these items. Although the documentary record at the Hermitage is completely silent with regard to these objects, it is highly probable that the Jacksons were not actively engaged in providing beads and charms to their slaves. The presence of these objects, therefore, is an important piece of evidence of the limited economic autonomy that enslaved African Americans were able to negotiate with a planter-dominated society that was at turns indifferent to or directly opposed to slave participation in the marketplace economy. Several historical essays detailing the market-related activities of enslaved African Americans in the United States and Caribbean can be found in *Cultivation and Culture* (Berlin and Morgan 1993), and together provide a good overview of this complex subject.

As the archaeological study of questions related to African-American religion and ideology moves beyond the simple documentation of African "survivals," it is important to assess the significance that these beliefs and behaviors held in the African-American community. Wilkie (1995) notes the predominance of charms related to marriage, love, and family life. She suggests that the persistence of these beliefs reflected African-American attempts to maintain stable families and communities in the face of the strongly disruptive influence of slavery. Wilkie argues that the spiritual realm provided an autonomous sphere, compatible with African-American worldview, which allowed enslaved African Americans to exercise control over their own communities (Wilkie 1995). This, in turn, argues against the widespread perception that status in enslaved African-American communities was conferred mainly through relationships with the Euroamerican plantation household. Rather, it can be argued, following Mintz and Price, that "the institutions created by the slaves to deal with what are at once the most ordinary and most important aspects of life took on their characteristic shape *within* the parameters of the masters' monopoly of power, but *separate from* the masters' institutions" (Mintz and Price 1992:39).

Maria Franklin, in her assessment of Colonial Williamsburg's reconstruction of the Carter's Grove slave quarter, takes a similar standpoint when she argues that "of primary importance to enslaved blacks would have been their community in the quarters. It was a place where they could be themselves and where the creolized African-American culture was created" (Franklin 1995:149).

It has also been argued by Kenneth Brown (1994) that African-American practitioners of traditional medicine and ritual held an important place in the internal plantation economy. Status was ascribed to these individuals by traditionally-minded African Americans, and these healers played an important role in the African-American community from which they stood to benefit economically. This takes the argument for the autonomy of enslaved African-American communities one step further, by indicating the persistence and economic importance of a profession which was wholly unrelated to plantation production, and which was generally discouraged and even repressed by the white planter class.

In addition to their influence within the enslaved African-American community, respect for traditional African-American healer/magicians may have extended beyond the immediate plantation community, and even into the surrounding Euroamerican community. Although plantation owners generally decried the presence of "superstition" and "ignorance" among their enslaved, these wealthy, generally well-educated individuals were probably not representative of the bulk of the poorer white population who owned few if any slaves and formed the majority of the Euroamerican population in the antebellum upper South. These poorer whites, who generally shared with enslaved African Americans a broad sympathy with the spiritual realm, may have generally acknowledged the power of traditional African-American healers and "conjurers." In addition, the position of some enslaved African Americans as primary caregivers to members of the Euroamerican plantation elite, along with local reputations earned by successful traditional healers, may have convinced some slaveholders of the efficacy of these methods.

The hypothesis that whites, in addition to African Americans, sought treatment from traditional African-American healers is given further weight by an 1831 Tennessee law forbidding slaveholders from allowing their enslaved "to go about the country under the pretext of practicing medicine or healing the sick" (Public Acts of Tennessee 1831:122–123). The presence of this law would seem to indicate that such a problem was perceived by the state legislature. It is perhaps significant that slaveholders themselves are mentioned by this law as possibly permitting enslaved African Americans to practice medicine.

Traditional medicine, practiced by both whites and African Americans, may have been viewed as a healthier alternative to established "scientific" medical treatment, which often involved the administration of strong toxins to sick persons. Leaky bottles of a 19th-century cure-all known as "calomel" (mercurous chloride) excavated at the Hermitage South Cabin in 1974 prompted archaeologist Samuel Smith (1977:156–158) to advise caution when excavating 19th-century medicine bottles.

In conclusion, although archaeology at the Hermitage has not uncovered contexts that can be linked to specific ritual behaviors, the over-all artifact assemblage suggests that African Americans at the Hermitage actively participated in a shared pattern of beliefs that was distinct in many ways from the dominant planter ideology. In making this assertion, this study has tried to avoid the promulgation of archaeological "folklore." Although some of the analogies presented in this paper may be poorly founded, they are offered merely as suggestions to promote further research into this area of African-American history. There is really very little doubt that certain broad classes of African-American spiritual artifacts, such as charm bags prepared by skilled practitioners, have antecedents in a number of West African cultures (MacGaffey 1991; Jones 1995). It is important, however, to move beyond constructing genealogies of African-American belief systems and begin to question the functions that these beliefs and practices served in enslaved African-American communities. In addition, future research should be aimed at achieving a better understanding of the religions and cosmologies which underlay these practices.

Archaeological study of these questions will require particularly close attention to archaeological context, along with a willingness on the part of scholars to move artifact analysis beyond simple functional categories. It is important to recognize that enslaved African Americans participated in a shared system of beliefs that served important functions within their communities, and that successful strategies were employed by these men and women to practice and maintain these traditions in defiance of slaveholders. Ironically, the very ephemerality which characterizes these expressions of a functioning African-American belief system makes them quite difficult to observe archaeologically.

ACKNOWLEDGMENTS

My thanks to Larry McKee, director of archaeology at the Hermitage, and to Brian Thomas, research archaeologist at the Hermitage, for reading and commenting on an earlier draft of this article, as well as an initial version presented at The Society for Historical Archaeology Conference on Historical and Underwater Archaeology in 1996. Larry and Brian also generously provided access to the Hermitage artifact collection and photographic library during the preparation of this article, and gave a large amount of their own time in helping me see this project to completion. In addition, I acknowledge the support of the Ladies' Hermitage Association for my work, as well as the ongoing study of the Hermitage slave community of which it is a part.

REFERENCES

ADAMS, ERIC
  1994 Religion and Freedom: Artifacts Indicate that African Culture Persisted Even in Slavery. *African-American Archaeology* (11):1–2.

ARMSTRONG, DOUGLAS
  1990 The Old Village and the Great House: An Archaeological and Historical Examination of Drax Hall Plantation, St. Anne's Bay, Jamaica. University of Illinois Press, Urbana and Chicago.

BERLIN, IRA, AND PHILIP D. MORGAN (EDITORS)
  1993 *Cultivation and Culture: Labor and the Shaping of Slave Life in the Americas.* University Press of Virginia, Charlottesville.

BLIER, SUZANNE PRESTON
  1995 *African Vodun: Art, Psychology and Power.* University of Chicago Press, Chicago.

BROWN, KENNETH L.
  1994 Material Culture and Community Structure: The Slave and Tenant Community at Levi Jordan's Plantation. In *Working Toward Freedom: Slave Society and Domestic Economy in the American South,* edited by L. E. Hudson, pp. 95–118. University of Rochester Press, Rochester, NY.

BROWN, KENNETH L., AND DOREEN C. COOPER
  1990 Structural Continuity in an African-American Slave and Tenant Community. *Historical Archaeology* 24(4):95–118.

CABAK, MELANIE A.
  1990 Searching for the Meaning of Blue Beads to Afro-American Slaves. Manuscript on file, The Ladies' Hermitage Association, Hermitage, TN.

CAMEHL, ADA WALKER
  1946 *The Blue China Book: Early American Scenes and History Pictured in the Pottery of the Time.* Reprint of 1916 edition. Tudor Publishing, NY.

DOUGLASS, FREDERICK
  1986 *Narrative of the Life of Frederick Douglass, an American Slave.* Reprint of 1982, 1845 editions. Penguin, NY.

FERGUSON, LELAND
1992 *Uncommon Ground: Archaeology and Early African America, 1650–1800.* Smithsonian Institution Press, Washington, DC.

FISHER, ANGELA
1984 *Africa Adorned.* Harry N. Abrams, NY.

FRANKLIN, MARIA
1995 Rethinking the Carter's Grove Slave Quarter Reconstruction: A Proposal. *Kroeber Anthropological Society Papers* 79:147–162.

FRAZIER, E. FRANKLIN
1957 *The Negro in the United States.* Revised edition. Macmillan, NY.

HERSKOVITZ, MELVILLE J.
1958 *The Myth of the Negro Past.* Reprint of 1941 edition. Beacon Press, Boston, MA.

HYATT, HARRY MIDDLETON
1970 *Hoodoo—Conjuration—Witchcraft—Rootwork,* Vol. 1. Reprint of 1935 edition. Western Publishing, Hannibal, MO.

JONES, LYNN DIEKMAN
1995 The Material Culture of Slavery from an Annapolis Household. Paper presented at the Annual Meeting of The Society for Historical Archaeology Conference on Historical and Underwater Archaeology, Washington, DC.

KARKLINS, KARLIS
1985 *Glass Beads.* Parks Canada, Ottawa, ON.

KLINGELHOFER, ERIC
1987 Aspects of Early Afro-American Material Culture: Artifacts from the Slave Quarters at Garrison Plantation, Maryland. *Historical Archaeology* 21(2):112–119.

LA ROCHE, CHERYL J.
1994a Glass Beads Excavated from the African Burial Ground, New York City: Conservation, Analysis, and Interpretation. Unpublished M.A. thesis, Department of Museum Studies, State University of New York—F.I.T., New York, NY.
1994b Beads from the African Burial Ground, New York City: A Preliminary Assessment. *Beads: Journal of the Society of Bead Researchers* 6:3–20.

LOGAN, GEORGE C.
1992 *Archaeology at Charles Carroll's House and Garden and of His African-American Slaves.* Charles Carroll House of Annapolis, Baltimore, MD.

MACGAFFEY, WYATT
1991 *Art and Healing of the Bakongo Commented by Themselves: Minkisi from the Laman Collection.* Folkens Museum-Etnografiska, Stockholm.

MCKEE, LARRY
1993 Summary Report of the 1991 Field Quarter Excavation. *Tennessee Anthropological Association Newsletter* 18(1).
1995 The Earth Is Their Witness. *The Sciences* (March/April):36–41.

MCKEE, LARRY, BRIAN THOMAS, AND JENNIFER BARTLETT
1994 Summary Report on the Hermitage Mansion Yard Area. Manuscript on file, The Ladies' Hermitage Association, Hermitage, TN.

MINTZ, SIDNEY W., AND RICHARD PRICE
1992 *The Birth of African-American Culture: An Anthropological Perspective.* Originally published in 1976 as *An Anthropological Approach to the Afro-American Past.* Beacon Press, Boston, MA.

ORSER, CHARLES E.
1994 The Archaeology of African-American Slave Religion in the Antebellum South. *Cambridge Archaeological Journal* 4(1):33–45.

OTTO, JOHN SOLOMON
1984 *Cannon's Point Plantation, 1794–1860: Living Conditions and Status Patterns in the Old South.* Academic Press, Orlando, FL.

PATTEN, DRAKE
1992 *Mankala* and *Minkisi:* Possible Evidence of African-American Folk Beliefs and Practices. *African-American Archaeology* (6):5–7.

POGUE, DENNIS J., AND ESTHER C. WHITE
1991 *Summary Report on the "House for Families" Slave Quarter Site (44 Fx 762/40–47), Mount Vernon Plantation, Mount Vernon, Virginia.* Mount Vernon Ladies' Association, Archaeology Department, Mount Vernon, VA.

POLHEMUS, RICHARD
1977 *Tellico Blockhouse Site.* Tennessee Valley Authority, Chattanooga, TN.

PUBLIC ACTS OF TENNESSEE
1831 *Public Acts of the State of Tennessee passed by the General Assembly.* Jean and Alexander Heard Library, Law Library, Vanderbilt University Law School, Nashville, TN.

PUCKETT, NEWBELL NILES
1968 *Folk Beliefs of the Southern Negro*. Reprint of 1926 edition. Patterson Smith, Montclair, NJ.

SCHORGER, A. W.
1966 *The Wild Turkey: Its History and Domestication*. University of Oklahoma Press, Norman.

SCHROEDL, GERALD F.
1986 *Overhill Cherokee Archaeology at Chota-Tenasee*. Tennessee Valley Authority, Chattanooga.

SINGLETON, THERESA A.
1991 The Archaeology of Slave Life. In *Before Freedom Came: African-American Life in the Antebellum South*, edited by J. D. C. Campbell and K. S. Rice. University Press of Virginia, Charlottesville.
1995 The Archaeology of Slavery in North America. *Annual Review of Anthropology* (24):119–140.

SMITH, SAMUEL D.
1977 Plantation Archaeology at the Hermitage: Some Suggested Patterns. *Tennessee Anthropologist* 2(2):152–163.
1976 *An Archaeological and Historical Assessment of the First Hermitage*. Division of Archaeology, Tennessee Department of Conservation, Nashville.
1987 Archaeology of Slavery: Some Tennessee Examples. Paper presented at the Afro-American Local History Sixth Annual Conference, Nashville, TN.

STINE, LINDA FRANCE, MELANIE A. CABAK, AND MARK D. GROOVER
1996 Blue Beads as African-American Cultural Symbols. *Historical Archaeology* 30(3):49–75.

THOMAS, BRIAN WILLIAM
1995a Source Criticism and the Interpretation of African-American Sites. *Southeastern Archaeology* 14(2).
1995b *Community Among Enslaved African-Americans on the Hermitage Plantation*. Ph.D. dissertation, Department of Anthropology, State University of New York at Binghamton, Binghamton. University Microfilms International, Ann Arbor, MI.

THOMAS, BRIAN WILLIAM, LARRY MCKEE, AND JENNIFER BARTLETT
1995 Summary Report on the 1995 Hermitage Field Quarter Excavation. Manuscript on file, The Ladies' Hermitage Association, Hermitage, TN.

THOMPSON, ROBERT FARRIS
1983 *Flash of the Spirit: African and Afro-American Art and Philosophy*. Random House, NY.

WEAVER, GUY G., JEFFREY L. HOLLAND, PATRICK H. GARROW, AND MARTIN B. REINBOLD
1993 *The Gowen Farmstead: Archaeological Data Recovery at Site 40DV401 (Area D), Davidson County, Tennessee*. Garrow and Associates, Memphis TN.

WILKIE, LAURIE
1994 *"Never Leave Me Alone": An Archaeological Study of African-American Ethnicity, Race Relations and Community at Oakley Plantation*. Ph.D. Dissertation, Department of Anthropology, University of California at Los Angeles, Los Angeles. University Microfilms International, Ann Arbor, MI.
1995 Magic and Empowerment on the Plantation: An Archaeological Consideration of African-American World View. *Southeastern Archaeology* 14(2):136–148.

YENTSCH, ANNE ELIZABETH
1994 *A Chesapeake Family and Their Slaves: A Study in Historical Archaeology*. Cambridge University Press, Cambridge, England.

YOUNG, AMY L.
1994 Change and Continuity in African-Derived Religious Practices on an Upland South Plantation. Paper presented at the Southeastern Archaeology Conference, Lexington, KY.

AARON E. RUSSELL
DEPARTMENT OF ANTHROPOLOGY
WAKE FOREST UNIVERSITY
BOX 7807
WINSTON-SALEM, NC 27109